The Construction of
Homosexuality

The

Construction

of

Homosexuality

David F. Greenberg

The University of Chicago Press/Chicago & London

DAVID F. GREENBERG is professor of sociology at New York University. He is the author of *Mathematical Criminology*, coauthor of *University of Chicago Graduate Problems in Physics, with Solutions*, and *Struggle for Justice: A Report on Crime and Punishment in America*, and editor of *Corrections and Punishment* and *Crime and Capitalism: Essays in Marxist Criminology.* Greenberg holds a Ph.D. in physics.

The University of Chicago Press, Chicago 60637
The University of Chicago Press, Ltd., London

© 1988 by The University of Chicago
All rights reserved. Published 1988
Printed in the United States of America

97 96 95 94 93 92 91 90 89 88   54321

Library of Congress Cataloging-in-Publication Data

Greenberg, David F.
    The construction of homosexuality.

    Bibliography: p.
    Includes index.
    1. Homosexuality—History—Cross-cultural studies.
I. Title.
HQ76.25.G74   1988   306.7'66   88-10711
ISBN 0-226-30627-5

What land is this? What race of men? Who is it

I see here tortured in this rocky bondage?

What is the sin he's paying for? Oh tell me

to what part of the world my wanderings have brought me.

Aeschylus, *Prometheus Bound* (Grene, trans.)

Sunt lacrimae rerum.

Virgil, *Aeneid*

Was gleisst dort hell im Glimmerschein?

Richard Wagner, *Die Walküre*

Contents

Acknowledgments

I thank the many friends and colleagues who generously criticized my ideas and draft chapters, asked probing questions, informed me of their research, alerted me to useful sources, and translated passages from exotic languages. They include Howard Abadinsky, Robert S. Bianchi, Robert D. Biggs, Renee Billet, John Boswell, Glen W. Bowersock, Gene Brucker, Marcia H. Bystryn, Nancy Chodorow, John Clark, Peter T. Daniels, Mervin Dilts, Charles Donahue, Jr., Kent Gerard, Ogden Goelet, Jr., Michael Goodich, Cyrus H. Gordon, A. Kirk Grayson, J. Gwyn Griffiths, Barbara Hanawalt, R. H. Helmholtz, Harry A. Hoffner, Jr., Jennifer Hunt, George Kennedy, Judith Koffler, Jessica Lefevre, Sally Falk Moore, Kije Nemovicher, Vivian Nutton, Robert Padgug, Ilene Philipson, Wardell Pomeroy, Geoffrey Puterbaugh, Edward L. Schieffelin, Laurence Senelik, Antony E. Simpson, Christine Stansell, Connie Sutton, Samuel Thorne, Daniel Tompkins, C. A. Tripp, Colin Turnbull, Suzanne F. Wemple, Harriet Whitehead, and Walter L. Williams. I am particularly indebted to Vern Bullough, Wayne Dynes, Gilbert Herdt, Stephen O. Murray, Jeffrey Weeks, and an anonymous reviewer for taking on the heroic task of reading and commenting on an entire earlier draft. They undoubtedly saved me from many errors. I did not always agree with their comments, but collectively they helped me to produce what I hope is a better book. I am grateful to Mary Jane Ballou, Cynthia Beals, and Cynthia Pendergast for assistance in typing. Janice Feldstein managed to copyedit the manuscript without destroying the sense of what I wanted to say. It is a pleasure to acknowledge the hospitality of the London School of Economics, where part of my research was carried out.

This study would have been impossible without access to the collections of the New York Public Library, British Library, British Library of Political and Economic Science, and the libraries of the Warburg Institute, Wellcome Institute, Senate House, University of Chicago, New York University, Jewish Theological Seminary, Union Theological Seminary, UCLA, Harvard University, University of Michigan, ONE Institute, and the International Gay and Lesbian Archives. May the gods bless libraries!

Parts of several chapters have been adopted from journal articles with permission of the publishers, as follows:

"Christian Intolerance of Homosexuality," *American Journal of Sociology* 88 (1982):515–49 (with Marcia H. Bystryn), by permission of *American Journal of Sociology*.

"Capitalism, Bureaucracy and Male Homosexuality," *Contemporary Crises: Crime, Law and Social Policy* 8 (1984):33–56 (with Marcia H. Bystryn), © 1985 by Martinus Nijhoff Publishers, reprinted by permission of Kluwer Academic Publishers.

"Why Was the Berdache Ridiculed?," *Journal of Homosexuality* 11 (1985): 179–90, © 1985 by Haworth Press, Inc., Binghamton, N.Y.

Book Review of *Muelos: A Stone Age Superstition about Sexuality* by Weston La Barre, *Journal of Homosexuality* 13 (1987):124–28, © 1987 by Haworth Press, Inc., Binghamton, N.Y.

1   *Theorizing the Prohibition against Homosexuality*

If you are one who has been caught up in the homosexual syndrome—
won't you acknowledge the practice as an abomination in the eyes
of God, confess your sin, and come to Jesus in penitence and faith? May
God help you to do it today.

Harold S. Smith (n.d.)

Homosexuality . . . is a symptom of a disturbed personality.

Dr. Robert Kronemayer (1980)

Two, four, six, eight,
Gay is twice as good as straight.

Picketers chanting outside a church
where Anita Bryant was speaking.[1]

THE EYE OF THE BEHOLDER

Is homosexuality a sin, a manifestation of psychological pathology, or is it
healthier than the alternatives? The debate continues. And these are not
the only possibilities. For William Blackstone, a leading jurist of eighteenth-
century England, homosexuality was a "crime against nature."[2] To some
physicians of the late nineteenth century, it was a manifestation of inherited physiological degeneration. In the ancient Near East, male prostitutes
were believed to have special supernatural powers.

Each of these conceptions implies an appropriate response—religious
penitence, psychoanalysis, imprisonment, sterilization, sacramental intercourse, picketing Anita Bryant. Our goal is to understand these conceptions
and responses. Why have some societies invested homosexuality with ritual significance, while others have thought it to be one of the wickedest of
crimes? Why did a medical conception of homosexuality emerge? Why is
there resistance to gay liberation today?

[1]Quoted in Bryant and Green (1978).
[2]Blackstone (1811:205), book 4.

1

Our questions originate in developments within sociology, as well as in the larger society. For decades, sociologists have studied activities such as crime and drunkenness which the larger society has deemed deviant or undesirable. Researchers, leaving the harmfulness of these activities unquestioned, focused on their social and psychological causes. For example, sociologists who studied delinquency examined its roots in material deprivation and family pathology. As it happens, very little sociological work on the causes of homosexuality was undertaken, probably because the subject was considered more suitable for biologists and psychologists. Some researchers may have feared that if they studied homosexuality, they would be suspected of it themselves.

Labeling theory, a perspective that became influential in sociology in the 1960s, brought a different emphasis to deviance research.[3] Instead of studying the reasons why someone engages in behavior of which people disapprove, labeling theorists shifted attention to the reasons for the disapproval. Howard Becker summarized the essence of the perspective neatly:

> Social groups create deviance by making the rules whose infraction constitutes deviance, and by applying those rules to particular people and labeling them as outsiders. From this point of view, deviance is not a quality of the act the person commits, but rather a consequence of the application by others of rules and sanctions to an "offender." The deviant is one to whom that label has successfully been applied; deviant behavior is behavior that people so label.[4]

It is thus the existence of social prohibitions and the responses that back up the prohibitions, that make a behavior deviant. In a world where no one thought homicide wrong, it would not be deviant, no matter how frequently or infrequently people killed one another, and no matter how immoral or objectively harmful killing is. Deviance, then, is in the eye of the beholder. It is beliefs that homosexuality is evil, sick, or undesirable—and the corresponding efforts to punish, cure, or prevent it—that make homosexuality deviant. Whether or not these beliefs are true is beside the point.

Were social responses to behavior governed entirely by its objective features, this way of looking at deviance would gain us little. Whether we defined deviance as behavior that was intrinsically pathological, or as behavior that happened to be regarded as undesirable, we would still be studying the same behavior. Yet, as the quotations at the head of the chapter demonstrate, behavior does not completely govern responses to it. People can and do disagree violently about which behaviors should be

---

[3] Schur (1971).
[4] H. Becker (1963).

treated as deviant. These disagreements can have practical consequences for social policy. It is critical, then, to know how beliefs about deviance arise and gain acceptance.

In studying social definitions of homosexuality, we extend the concerns of labeling theory into the relatively neglected realm of human sexuality. We will want to know why some societies are comparatively hostile to homosexuality, while others tolerate or even fully accept and institutionalize it. But we will also be concerned with the ways in which homosexuality is conceptualized. It is not merely that some societies are more accepting than others; it is that the kinds of sexual acts it is thought possible to perform, and the social identities that come to be attached to those who perform them, vary from one society to another. There are societies, including some where homosexual acts are frequent, that lack any concept of a homosexual person. As we will see in a subsequent chapter, medieval inquisitors were not concerned with homosexuals, but with sodomites. It was not merely that people of the Middle Ages uttered a different word, but also that their system for classifying sexual actors was not the same as ours. For one thing, the medieval sodomite's partners did not have to be of the same sex.

Even the same word can change its meaning with time. When first coined in the late nineteenth century, the word "homosexual" had biological connotations that it later lost. A psychoanalyst today might refer to someone who has never been aware of sexual interest in someone of his own sex as a "latent homosexual," but lay people would probably not. Changing sexual typologies and images of persons who engage in acts that we classify as homosexual will be central to our concerns. Equally central will be theories that explain homosexuality and actual responses to it.

According to one school in the philosophy of science that is currently in vogue, the objective features of a phenomenon so little constrain the ways it is classified and theorized that these features can be disregarded in trying to understand why a particular classification system or scientific theory has been adopted.[5] By extension this would also be true for nonscientific theories and explanatory schemes. However, this claim is implausible. If it were true, the objective features of a phenomenon could change without any necessity for a corresponding revision in what is said about that phenomenon. Yet surely a chemist who is asked to tell us the composition of an apple will answer differently if a pear or peach is substituted for the apple. An underlying objective reality may not entirely *determine* perceptions of that reality, but this does not mean that it has no effect at all on perceptions. For this reason, when reconstructing a phenomenology of homo-

[5]Collins (1981).

sexuality for different cultures, it is relevant to reconstruct, to the limited degree possible, the patterns of actual sexual behavior associated with perceptions of it.

GAY HISTORY AND THE GAY MOVEMENT

In more ways than one, the gay-liberation movement has made a study of this sort intellectually possible. People rarely study the origins of rules they support, or ask questions about the categories that give structure to those rules. The partial success of the gay-liberation movement's efforts to refute popular beliefs that homosexuality is harmful has done much to stimulate the study of its prohibition.

Like other groups that have suffered discrimination and repression, gays have begun to recover their past,[6] documenting the history of repression and of struggles against it. The very first historical and comparative studies of homosexuality were the products of the earliest wave of the homosexual emancipation movement. As early as 1883, John Addington Symonds compiled materials on ancient Greece in an attempt to show that homosexuality could be noble and dignified when valued by society rather than repressed.[7] Edward Carpenter, who collected reports by travelers and anthropologists about homosexuality among primitive people, claimed that homosexuals tended to have exceptional mental and spiritual abilities that made them superior.[8] Both were lovers of men.

With the destruction of the homosexual-liberation movement at the hands of the Nazis, historical research on homosexuality virtually ceased. By default, most scholarly discussions of homosexuality were medical or psychiatric. The physicians and psychiatrists who wrote of it were primarily interested in its causes, prevention, and treatment and saw little reason to turn to history or the social sciences. Their training led them to view sexuality as presocial and individual, so that the ways it was expressed and the responses it received could not be illuminated by knowledge of their social context. Historians, anthropologists, and sociologists, who might have approached the subject with other questions and interests, rarely did so.

From time to time, historical treatments of homosexuality did appear,

---

[6]The extent to which this past is "theirs" is, in fact, very much open to question. Some writers casually assert continuity; thus Fone (1980:xvii) writes, "gay people have always been here . . . we have a history as ancient, rich, and honorable as the heterosexual history which rarely if ever mentioned us." Boswell (1980) subtitled his study of early Christian responses to homosexuality, *Gay People in Western Europe from the Beginning of the Christian Era to the Fourteenth Century.* J. N. Katz (1976) entitled his anthology, *Gay American History.* The continuity of etiology and social identity implied by this terminology requires careful examination, which it has not heretofore received.

[7]Symonds (1975).

[8]Carpenter (1914).

but their concerns rarely went beyond the identification of famous figures of the past as homosexual. Apologetic in tone, they sought to persuade readers that if Socrates, Shakespeare, Michelangelo, and Whitman were homosexual, then popular prejudices against homosexuality must be unjustified.[9] Possibly these works had limited value as propaganda. Perhaps they helped homosexuals maintain their self-esteem at a time when stereotypes of homosexuality were overwhelmingly negative. But they did little to illuminate such issues as the influence of social factors on sexual preference, the social organization of sexuality, and the ways people thought about sex and tried to regulate it.

The gay-liberation movement of the past fifteen years has vastly broadened the scope of scholarly writing on homosexuality. It has weakened prejudice enough to permit scholars to publish without committing professional suicide, and it has expanded the demand for this research. The result has been a number of histories of the liberation movement,[10] and more general surveys of homosexuality in different historical periods and in different parts of the world.[11] These broad treatments have been followed by specialized studies of homosexuality in particular places and periods.

The conceptual framework of many of the newer studies differs radically from that of the older ones. Mary MacIntosh pointed the way in a pathbreaking article published in 1968 that proposed to consider homosexuality as a social role whose origin and changing content could be studied historically. This approach leads to the reconstruction of subcultures, identities, discourses, communities, repression, and resistance.

To understand why perceptions of homosexuality and social responses to it vary, we must examine evidence from a wide range of societies. No scholar working exclusively with primary sources could hope to amass the necessary evidence in a single lifetime. Fortunately, the studies historians have already done make this unnecessary. While these studies could be used to compose a synthetic history, that is not the purpose of this work. Though I will allude to episodes of persecution, I will not recount them in detail; others have already done this. My goal will be to explain why these episodes occurred—and why, at certain points in history they stopped occurring. The specialized histories, which tend to be more descriptive than analytical, furnish the materials needed for our sociological purposes. Ten years ago this sort of analysis would have been impossible, for too little of the primary research had been done. It is the renaissance in homosexuality studies that has made the present investigation possible.

---

[9]Gide (1950), Garde (1964).

[10]Teal (1971), Humphreys (1972), Lauritsen and Thorstad (1974), Steakley 1975), Faderman and Eriksson (1980), Marotta (1981), D'Emilio (1983a), B. D. Adam (1987a), S. O. Murray (1987b).

[11]Karlen (1971a), Bullough (1976, 1979), J. N. Katz (1976, 1983), Tripp (1975), Carrier (1980).

Entrepreneurship and Social Conflict

The premise of almost all recent sociological attempts to understand the origins of deviance-defining rules has been the observation that rules do not make themselves. In the words of Howard Becker,

> before an act can be viewed as deviant, and before any class of people can be labeled and treated as outsiders for committing the act, someone must have made the rule which defines the act as deviant.[12]

To gain approval for a new deviance-defining rule, those who have strong convictions about its desirability will seek to persuade others of their views. Typically, they will lobby and put pressure on decision makers. Because they take the initiative in trying to change public morality, Becker has dubbed them "moral entrepreneurs."[13] Despite their own certainty that humanity will profit from their efforts, critics often see them as self-righteous and authoritarian, seeking to impose their own moral standards on others.

Moral entrepreneurs are a familiar feature of the political landscape: Ralph Nader, Anita Bryant, and in England, Mary Whitehouse, are contemporary examples. That crusaders such as these can sway and mobilize public sentiment is surely true. Yet in modern societies a multitude of entrepreneurs crusade on behalf of a host of causes. Some gain a following but fail to make a lasting impact, others are ignored, and still others succeed beyond all expectations. What explains these different outcomes? Why do entrepreneurs choose one cause instead of another? Why do they appear at particular moments in history? The concept of "moral crusader" does not answer these questions.

Nor does it tell us whether some people are more likely to become moral entrepreneurs than others. Deviance theorists have attempted to do this by conceiving of society as divided into distinct groups: classes, races, religions, ethnic groups, occupations, sexes. These groups may have clashing interests and diverging moral values. In pursuit of its interests, one group may seek to define the activities of another group as deviant. For example, physicians of the late nineteenth century sought to enhance their incomes through legislation barring midwives from delivering babies.[14]

Clashes among groups can occur over moral values as well as over conflicting interests. As long as a group thinks that its moral code applies only to itself, it will make no effort to impose it on others. Orthodox Jews, believing that the dietary laws of *kashrut* are binding only on Jews, have never

---

[12]H. Becker (1963:162).
[13]H. Becker (1963:147).
[14]Ehrenreich (1973), Arney (1982).

tried to prevent gentiles from eating pork and shellfish. On the other hand, when a group thinks its morals should serve as a standard for others, it may try to persuade or coerce nonmembers to conform.

Conceivably, those whose behavior is the target of a deviance-defining effort could be won over, so that they voluntarily abandon the activities they, too, have come to define as deviant. Often, though, the target group defends its own moral standards or upholds its interests and resists being defined as deviant. It insists that the activities in question are not deviant, but innocuous or beneficial. In resisting the effort to make their activities seem deviant, the target group may criticize the reasoning or attack the motives of those who are doing so. It may engage in a campaign of its own, seeking to influence opinion and gain support. What ensues, then, is a "deviance contest" whose outcome depends on the relative power of the two (or more) groups engaged in the contest.[15]

This general perspective has informed numerous studies of deviance-defining or normalizing legislative acts. The studies have differed in the groups found to be responsible for the legislation and the motives ascribed to them. Chambliss attributed fourteenth-century English vagrancy legislation to landlords who wanted to control agricultural wage-laborers in the aftermath of the Black Death. In this instance the relevant group was a class, and its motive was economic self-interest. Dickson's study of the 1937 Marijuana Tax Act, and Embree's analysis of the Harrison Act of 1910, which criminalized opium derivatives, also interpreted legislation in terms of material interest, but the relevant groups were government bureaucracies, not classes. Gusfield characterized the Prohibition movement as a "symbolic crusade" by a declining small-town Anglo-Saxon middle class seeking not material advantage, but the preservation of a social status threatened by the growing social and political importance of urban-based immigrants from countries where alcohol consumption was an accepted part of daily life. Humphries found the professionals (doctors, lawyers) who participated in the movement to repeal abortion legislation to be advancing their own occupational interests, while the concerns of feminist participants were partly material and partly symbolic.[16]

Though research of this kind has traced many deviance-defining rules to the interests, moral values, and political power of particular groups, the origins of rules prohibiting homosexuality cannot be so easily uncovered. Since homosexuality is found in all social classes, it is unlikely that a dominant class would seek to repress it to gain an advantage over a subordinate class. Because it is found in all races, nationalities, and ethnic groups, it also seems unlikely that a prohibition could have arisen because one race,

---

[15] Schur (1980).
[16] Chambliss (1964), D. T. Dickson (1968), Embree (1977), Gusfield (1963), Humphries (1977).

nationality, or ethnic group sought material benefits or higher social status by prohibiting the sexual practices of others. In so doing, it would also be prohibiting its own practices.

One could conjecture that at some time in the past, heterosexuals sought some sort of advantage by repressing homosexuality. It can be a convenient charge with which to smear a political opponent and has been used in just that way on more than one occasion.[17] But it is farfetched to suppose that the prohibition was invented for that purpose. Surely there are other ways of tarnishing a reputation. Perhaps heterosexuals wanted to raise their status relative to that of homosexuals by prohibiting the latter's sexual practices. But why would they have been so concerned about status? Gusfield's study showed that the small-town middle class of late-nineteenth- and early-twentieth-century America had good reasons for feeling its status threatened. Until recently, though, there was no comparable threat to heterosexuals. Unless we imagine everyone to be constantly preoccupied with gaining status at the expense of everyone else, this explanation falls flat. Moreover, it is doubtful that homosexuals were a distinct social group with a definite status before homosexuality became deviant.

Apart from its seeming inability to explain the existence of social rules prohibiting homosexuality, the group-conflict perspective seems incapable of telling us why homosexuality is conceived of in different ways at different times, for example as a sin in the Middle Ages, but as a psychological condition in the early twentieth century.

CONSENSUS AND FUNCTIONALISM

A number of sociologists have commented that group-conflict explanations of laws seem inapplicable to those behaviors that never become the focus of group conflict because virtually every social group in society agrees as to their harmfulness. They argue that some kinds of behavior are so destructive that, if they were not checked, they would jeopardize the very existence of organized society. Were murder, assault, and theft to be tolerated, life would quickly become "nasty, brutish, and short." Functionalists contend that laws prohibiting these behaviors were not adopted to benefit some particular group at the expense of others. On the contrary, they say, everyone benefits from the stability and order that these laws insure, and everyone supports them.

[17]The Roman emperor Justinian and his empress Theodora had political opponents arrested and tortured on charges of homosexuality (Boswell, 1980:172–73). Most historians believe that charges of sodomy were brought against the medieval Knights Templar as a pretext for the suppression of the order and the seizure of its enormous wealth. The furor over an alleged man-boy sex ring in Boise, Idaho, in 1955 was instigated by politically powerful figures to destroy a reform-minded city administration (Gerassi, 1966). Insinuations of homosexuality figured in several of the 1984 congressional campaigns.

This line of reasoning can be questioned at many points. Michalowski and Bohlander point out that politically powerful groups can manufacture a consensus.[18] The very adoption and enforcement of a law can sway public opinion. Rules against interpersonal violence go back so far in history that we cannot always know whether a law came before or after a consensus. In concrete instances, the consensus sometimes evaporates. For example, most Americans say that forcible rape is one of the most serious of crimes. Yet, in 1984, when four young men were convicted of rape in New Bedford, Massachusetts, after a trial that left little room for doubt as to their guilt, a crowd numbering thousands of men and women gathered to protest the conviction. Some argued that the victim should have been convicted, too.[19] Even if people from all classes had been in favor of these rules, it does not follow that the views of the lower classes were taken into account in the adoption process; they could have been completely ignored. Then, too, even a consensus that is spontaneous and takes everyone's views into account could be mistaken. Everyone may think that something is harmful and may be certain that prohibiting it could be wise; but they could all be wrong.

The functionalist argument that social rules benefit the entire society can be considered independently of the question of consensus, for if opinions about these rules can be based on false premises, opponents of a rule might conceivably benefit from its adoption without knowing it. All that is necessary for the functionalist argument to be valid is that those who make the rules be correct. But people are not omnisicient; no one can know for sure just what social arrangements are optimal, or how to bring these arrangements about. It is not even clear just what it means to say that a social arrangement is optimal.

Even if the position that rules are *invariably* beneficial to all must be rejected, we cannot disregard the possibility that sometimes they are. The advantages to be gained from following some rules may be so obvious that they will occur to almost anyone who thinks about them. Under these circumstances, the harmful consequences of a prohibited behavior may suffice to explain why it is considered deviant.

Darwinian biology suggests another basis for a functionalist argument. Although plants and animals do not try to evolve or adapt to their environment, the principle of survival of the fittest guarantees that species will do so or face extinction. When human societies compete for limited resources, this principle also holds for them. Those that adopt innovative social practices favorable to survival will gradually displace those that do not. Maladapted societies will tend to disappear.

[18] Michalowski and Bohlander (1976).
[19] Chancer (1985).

Could a process like natural selection explain a prohibition against homosexuality? It is tempting to answer in the affirmative, on the grounds that heterosexual intercourse has until recently been a prerequisite to biological reproduction. In the absence of a taboo against homosexuality, one might reason, the human species would have died out. The taboo was thus an evolutionary necessity. Those societies that adopted it—for whatever reason—early in history, survived. Those that did not, disappeared.

This explanation implicitly assumes that everyone has homosexual drives so strong as to require powerful repression to keep them under control, yet not so strong as to make social controls ineffective. That would be odd. The existence of these drives has not been demonstrated, and if the evolutionary argument is correct, they would seem to be an evolutionary disadvantage. One might expect them to have disappeared over the centuries, eliminating the need for repression. Yet this has not happened.[20]

Although a society composed of people whose sexual preferences are exclusively homosexual would quickly die out, sexual preferences need not be exclusive. Even if sexual partners were chosen entirely at random at each mating, without regard to sex, birthrates would remain high enough to sustain population growth.[21] Homosexuality is currently tolerated in the Philippines, which has a high birthrate,[22] but not in the People's Republic of China, where the government is making strenuous efforts to reduce it. Pederasty was institutionalized among the Big Namba of the New Hebrides, yet they had an exceptionally high fertility rate.[23] So it is doubtful that prohibitive norms now in effect can be explained by demographic considerations.

Another problem with the functionalist argument is its assumption that all societies must encourage population growth. Because food supplies can be precarious, excessive population growth is at least as serious a problem for many peoples as insufficient growth. In these societies, abortion, infanticide, and extended postpartum-sex taboos help to adjust the population to the carrying capacity of the land. Under these circumstances, homosexuality might have adaptive value so long as it is not exclusive or too common. In fact, the anthropologist Marvin Harris has reasoned, on just this basis, that tolerance of homosexuality develops in response to concern over an exploding population.[24]

---

[20]Sociobiologist Edward Wilson (1978:150–55) has turned this argument around, suggesting that the persistence of homosexuality must mean that it confers an evolutionary advantage. This, too, remains undemonstrated (G. E. Hutchinson, 1959; Ruse, 1981; Futuyma and Risch, 1984; G. D. Wilson, 1987).

[21]There are species of bugs that do just that (Wickler, 1972:48–49).

[22]Whitam (1987).

[23]Harrisson (1937:410).

[24]M. Harris (1981).

If Harris is correct, attitudes toward homosexuality should be permissive in societies where population pressures are especially severe. Werner has tested this prediction by examining data from the Human Relations Area Files (HRAF), an archive of anthropological studies of many different peoples, set up to facilitate comparative research. Werner found thirty-nine societies for which information was available regarding efforts to encourage or curb the birthrate, and attitudes toward homosexuality.[25] As predicted, pronatalist societies (those that discouraged abortion and infanticide) tended to discourage homosexuality, while antinatalist societies tended to encourage it. There were exceptions, but the relationship was reasonably strong. However, when I attempted to confirm the coding of societies as favorable or unfavorable to homosexuality by examining the ethnographic sources, I frequently found myself in disagreement with Werner's codings. Some seemed questionable, others totally wrong.[26] I also disagreed with the way in which the natalist policies of some societies were coded. When I used my codings instead of Werner's, the evidence no longer supported the functionalist explanation.

There are some cultures—Western Christianity is one of them—in which attitudes toward homosexuality are linked to those concerning procreation. What seems questionable, however, is that this linkage is common throughout the world, or necessary. In contemporary Western societies, the numbers of people involved in homosexual relations on a long-term basis are probably not great enough to have a major impact on the birthrate, even with the relaxation in attitudes that has occurred in recent years.

An alternative functionalist argument, expressed by Kingsley Davis, focuses not on the biological requirements of reproduction but on its social aspects:

> sexual intercourse is necessary for procreation and is thus linked in the normative system with the institutional mechanisms that guarantee the bearing and rearing of children. The sexual and reproduction norms become intertwined. . . . In evolving an

[25] Because D. Werner (1979) does not list the thirty-nine societies, it is difficult for readers to check his conclusions; however, he supplied me with the list. The societies coded as pronatalist but not accepting homosexuality are the Aymara, Yahgan, Bahia, Cagaba, eastern Apache, southeastern Salish, northern Saulteaux, Buka-Kurtachi, Mbuti Pygmies, Ila, Kurd, Yugoslavia, Lepcha, western Tibet, and Ashanti. Those with antinatalist policies that did not accept homosexuality are the Chiriguano, Creek, Tikopia, and Kung Bushmen. Societies where homosexuality was acceptable for at least some people, but whose policies are pronatalist, are Navaho, Aleuts, Azande, Mossi, Hottentot, and Koryak, while those with antinatalist policies that accept homosexuality are the Yanoama, Trumai, Nambicuara, Bororo, Tupinamba, Papago, Crow, Samoa, Malekula, Aranda, Mongo, Tanala, Chukchee, and Siwans.

[26] My disagreements with Werner's codings are spelled out explicitly in the appendix to chapter 2.

orderly system of sexual rights and obligations, societies have linked this system with the rest of the social structure, particularly with the family. They have also tended to economize by having only one such system, which has the advantage of giving each person only one role to worry about in his sex life— namely a male or female role. . . . In sum, one can explain the generally negative attitude toward homosexuality by the fact that every viable society evolved an institutional system fostering durable sexual unions between men and women and a complementary division of functions between the two sexes. To do this, it cannot at the same time equally foster homosexual relations.[27]

That some societies have developed norms regarding sex, reproduction, and gender that devalue homosexuality is undeniable. However, Davis's assertion that "every viable society" *must* organize sex, gender, and reproduction in ways that do so is far from true. A large volume of anthropological evidence, to be considered in the next chapter, demonstrates the contrary. Davis simply never considers that alternative ways of organizing reproduction and gender might be possible. His description of the gender system as a "complementary division of function" between the two sexes is one that contemporary feminist writings have thoroughly discredited, for it implies that this division is mutually beneficial, rather than exploitative. Even if a certain division of functions between men and women once had adaptive value, it is not necessarily true that it does now.

Cultural Transmission

A number of scholars have maintained that Western societies have been far more repressive toward homosexuality than the indigenous cultures of Asia, Africa, and the Americas. They explain this unique repressiveness by referring to the "Judeo-Christian tradition," which has supposedly been transmitted virtually unchanged from one generation to the next since the time of Moses or Jesus. As a result of religious indoctrination, contemporary Western attitudes and laws reflect the needs of the biblical period, not those of today.[28]

As it happens, Judaism and Christianity are not the only religions hostile to homosexuality: Zoroastrian scripture is as harshly denunciatory as any Jewish or Christian writings. More important, a "cultural-transmission" theory leaves many questions unanswered. Why did Judaism develop such antagonistic attitudes toward homosexuality? If the early Christian church

[27] Kingsley Davis (1961:325, 339, 341).
[28] Lauritsen (1974), Crompton (1978a).

broke with some Jewish practices, such as dietary restrictions, circumcision, and observance of Saturday as the Sabbath, why did it preserve others? If, in the course of centuries, Christians were to modify or abandon some early doctrines (such as the prohibition of usury and, for Protestants, priestly celibacy), why not all? In some parts of the world, religious prohibitions against homosexuality are virtually ignored.[29] Why has this not been true in the West?

A further difficulty for an explanation that relies only on religious tradition is its failure to explain why the stigma attached to homosexuality has begun to weaken only in recent years, even though secularization has steadily eroded the impact of religious beliefs over the course of centuries. Psychoanalytic theory, which in some versions has betrayed a deep anti-homosexual bias, is a *secular* belief system. Thus, even if we concede that religious teachings play some role in shaping contemporary attitudes,[30] additional factors must be involved.

PSYCHOANALYTIC THEORY

It has become a commonplace to ascribe repressed homosexuality to those who display extreme animosity toward homosexuals. Freud suggested something along these lines:

> It seems to me that the sexual perversions have come under a very special ban, which insinuates itself into theory, and interferes with scientific judgement on the subject. It seems as if no one could forget, not merely that they are detestable, but that they are something monstrous and terrifying; as if they exerted a seductive influence; as if at bottom a secret envy of those who enjoy them had to be strangled.[31]

This type of response is called a "reaction formation": there is a desire, but the superego forbids its expression. Even to acknowledge its existence can be threatening. The reaction formation fends off the anxiety provoked by the forbidden impulse by assuring the subject that he or she does not feel the impulse after all. What better testimony to one's heterosexuality could there be than dread or anger toward homosexuality? Because it is fueled by a

[29] The Koran condemns homosexuality in a number of passages, though without mentioning a specific punishment; yet homosexual relations have been practiced openly and without censure in many parts of the Islamic world (R. Levy, 1962:234; Patai, 1973:99; M. Daniel, 1975/76; Bullough, 1976:205–44; Wormhoudt, 1980; Southgate, 1984).

[30] Survey research shows that religious affiliation influences attitudes toward homosexuality, but accounts for a very small part of the variability in attitudes in a national sample (Spitze and Huber, 1983). Insofar as Jewish and Christian denominations share a common religious prohibition against homosexuality, this is not terribly surprising.

[31] Freud (1964:330). See also Wittels (1944).

suppressed impulse, the reaction is stronger and more irrational than would be expected from a simple belief, not implicated in psychological conflict, that homosexuality is undesirable. The defense is raised unconsciously: the subject is not aware of the prohibited desire, for it is never allowed to come into consciousness. Nor is the subject aware of the reasons for the powerful reaction to it—unless these are disclosed through psychoanalysis.

There is some evidence for the existence of a reaction formation driving some people's hostility to homosexuality. However, the psychoanalytic explanation is incomplete. It assumes the existence of an internalized prohibition that stands in the way of experiencing or acting on homosexual impulses. Ordinarily, the superego learns such internalized prohibitions from parents or parent substitutes. Before a reaction formation can develop, then, there must already be negative views of homosexuality in the culture. The existence of these views is what needs to be explained. Psychoanalytic theory might conceivably explain the transmission of an existing prohibition from one generation to another, and the reasons for its resistance to rational criticism, but it does not explain how this prohibition came into being. At some point in time, however far back, something other than a reaction formation must have created the prohibition.[32]

SOCIAL STRUCTURE

Several scholars have suggested that perceptions of homosexuality and responses to it are determined by a society's social structure. Particular attention has been given to the question of when homosexual subcultures and identities first appeared. It is generally agreed that neither are present in primitive societies. Although homosexual roles may be recognized, mere involvement in a sexual relationship with someone of the same sex does not become the basis for classifying someone as a distinct type of person. This remains true in all the early civilizations, as well as in feudal social systems.

Several historians have suggested that male-homosexual subcultures appeared for the first time in history in the late seventeenth, eighteenth, or early nineteenth century in the context of capitalist urbanization, and that a specifically medical discourse, attributing homoerotic attraction to an underlying physiological condition, arose in the late nineteenth century when doctors first encountered the subculture. Lesbian subcultures arose, it is said, only in the early twentieth century, when it became possible for women to live independently of men.[33]

[32]Freud (1964:359) implies as much when he notes that internal impediments to libidinal expression "arose originally, in primitive phases of human development, out of real external obstacles."

[33]J. Weeks (1977a), Foucault (1980), J. N. Katz (1983:137–74), D'Emilio (1983b), B. Adam (1985b, 1987a), Hansen (1985), Kinsman (1987).

A full and careful examination of all available evidence, particularly from continental Europe, confirms this model only in part. Urbanization was critical to the formation of homosexual subcultures, but large cities were present in Europe before the end of the seventeenth century. Social networks with subcultural characteristics, organized on the basis of male homosexuality, can be documented earlier than this. There is also fragmentary evidence for the existence of publicly visible social networks of tribades, or lesbian women, as early as the eighteenth century. Naturalistic, quasi-medical explanations of homosexuality were being proposed before the late nineteenth century, and those to whom the explanations applied played an active role in formulating them.

Fernbach has tried to link the repression of male homosexuality in late-nineteenth-century England with the development of industrial capitalism. At that time, entrepreneurs attempting to accumulate capital for investment often delayed marriage to avoid the costs of supporting a wife and children.[34] These costs were especially high because women were excluded from the paid, middle-class sector of the labor market. Fernbach argues that the repression of male heterosexuality imposed by late marriage created a strain toward homosexuality which had to be suppressed in order to preserve the family. This was essential because it was the family that carried out the task of socializing the next generation. According to Fernbach, the Labouchère Amendment was passed in 1885 to fulfill this function. The amendment extended the scope of legislation against male homosexuality considerably beyond the prohibition against anal intercourse in earlier English law.

Fernbach's reasoning is problematic for a number of reasons. First, it leaves earlier measures against homosexuality unexplained, and makes the questionable assumption that the trend of nineteenth-century English attitudes toward homosexuality was clearly one of greater repressiveness. There are reasons for skepticism. Between 1533, when the first act punishing buggery was issued, until 1861, convicted sodomists could be, and often were, hanged. In that year, the maximum penalty for sodomy was reduced to life in prison.[35] Under the Labouchère Amendment, the maximum penalty was cut to two years' imprisonment. Thus the pattern was one of declining severity, not increasing repression. This pattern is difficult to reconcile with a theory based on the need for harsher sanctions.

Second, the Labouchère Amendment was tacked on at the last minute to the Criminal Law Amendment Act, which attempted to stop child prostitution by raising the age of consent for girls from thirteen to sixteen. During

---

[34]Fernbach (1976). He furnishes no statistics, but Gillis (1974) indicates that the average age at marriage for English professional men in the period 1840–70 was 29.9 years, which was quite late.

[35]24 & 25 Victoria c. 100 (H. M. Hyde, 1970:92).

two years of debate over the bill, homosexuality was never mentioned—
not in Parliament, and not in the pamphlets issued by the extraparlia-
mentary purity organizations that campaigned for the act. Debate on the
amendment was cursory, and a number of scholars have suggested that the
members of Parliament who voted for it may not have understood that it
applied to relations among adults, not just to those between adults and children. Labouchère himself probably intended the amendment as a joke,
which, contrary to his expectations, backfired when the act was adopted.[36]
As there were only a handful of prosecutions during the first decade of the
act—some of them undertaken only reluctantly, and in the case of Oscar
Wilde, under provocation from the defendant, the initial enforcement can
hardly be described as vigorous.[37]

Fernbach forgets that large numbers of female prostitutes provided sexual
outlets to middle-class men in Victorian England.[38] His explanation cannot
account for the neglect of lesbianism in English law (which criminalized only
male homosexual acts). If the male sexual drive could not be contained
without the help of the criminal law, why was similar reinforcement not
needed to control female sexuality? France managed well enough without
laws against homosexuality among consenting adults; one wonders, then,
why England needed such legislation. The most plausible answer is that
she didn't.

A very different argument has been advanced by John Boswell, who
points out that rural communities are culturally more homogeneous than
cities. Lacking exposure to different life-styles, rural residents tend to be
intolerant of diversity. As homosexuals are a minority, they will be treated
with greater intolerance in rural society. This reasoning leads Boswell to
argue that the waxing and waning of repression in Europe from the Roman
Empire to the high Middle Ages can be explained by the rise and decline of
city life.[39]

Boswell's thesis receives support from contemporary survey research
showing that intolerance of homosexuality is inversely related to the size of

---

[36] H. M. Hyde (1970:135–36), Plummer (1975:117). F. B. Smith (1976) notes that Labouchère
was a libertarian and friend of Oscar Wilde's who editorialized against the act in a newspaper
he published. When it appeared that the campaign would fail, he introduced his amendment
as a joke, to discredit the act, in the same way that southern congresspersons in the United
States added discrimination on the basis of sex to the Civil Rights Act of 1964, which had been
introduced to deal with racial discrimination.

[37] H. M. Hyde (1956, 1970:137–52), Simpson, Chester, and Leitch (1976).

[38] Accurate estimates of the number of prostitutes working in nineteenth-century England
are not available, but Tannahill (1980:356) considers 50,000 to be a reasonable guess for
Greater London in 1840. Even if this figure is exaggerated, contemporary sources make clear
that there were plenty available for men who wished to patronize them. Large numbers of
prostitutes also worked the larger European and North American cities.

[39] Boswell (1980).

the place of current residence, and even more strongly to the size of the place of residence at age sixteen.[40] Yet there are difficulties with Boswell's argument. He assumes that homosexuality is found in only a minority of the population, that people can be divided more or less neatly into homosexuals and heterosexuals, and that this distinction is meaningful in earlier periods of history. As subsequent chapters demonstrate, however, there are some societies in which homosexuality is not restricted to a minority, but is rather extremely common, approaching universality. In Greek or Roman antiquity, homosexuality was not—as far as we can tell—rare, and was not assumed to reflect something intrinsically distinctive about those who engaged in it. It was not confined to the cities, and positive attitudes toward it can be found in writers who lived in the countryside. Thus it is unlikely that homosexuality came to be rejected in late antiquity because of growing intolerance for minorities. As those who engaged in homosexual relations were not seen as a distinct type of person, they would not have been viewed as a minority.

Patterns of variability in response to homosexuality are also difficult to reconcile with Boswell's explanation. Some of the societies in which homosexuality is extremely common are entirely rural. He himself notes that the increased repression of the thirteenth century is difficult to reconcile with his logic, for then towns were growing in size. Gays remain vulnerable to street assaults and murders in the largest of contemporary American cities, probably more so than in small towns. The anonymity of large cities reduces the effectiveness of informal social control, and the gay communities of large cities are more likely to be visible to straights. This very visibility seems to enrage some viewers. While the contemporary survey findings cannot be ignored, they do not appear to be helpful in understanding historical or cross-cultural variations in social responses to homosexuality.[41]

AN ALTERNATIVE APPROACH

The manifest inadequacies of the above explanations indicate the need for renewed efforts. Conventional strategies for identifying the sources of deviance-defining rules do not offer us much. They are oriented largely to the explanation of specific legislative acts, while ignoring the backdrop of sentiment against which legislation takes place and which must be taken into account if informal methods of social control, such as ridicule and social ostracism, are to be understood. Periods of explicit conflict may be overemphasized in relation to slower, less spectacular shifts in beliefs and attitudes.

In the chapters that follow, I try to go beyond the conventional state-

---

[40] Stephan and McMullin (1982), T. C. Wilson (1985).
[41] Additional difficulties in Boswell's analysis will be highlighted in subsequent chapters.

focused strategy by attempting to root beliefs about sexuality in the structures of everyday life. As people live in society, they grapple with and try to come to terms with it. In so doing, they develop ideologies that explain, justify, or challenge it.[42] Possibly they act on the basis of their ideologies. Their actions generate exposure to new experiences, which in turn may induce them to modify their previously held beliefs. Of course, the ideas so developed need not be a direct, unmediated reflection of a social reality. In general, people interpret experience in the light of previous ideas and conceptual schemes, not with a mental tabula rasa.

Experiencing the world and developing ideas about it are not activities carried out in isolation. People communicate their ideas to others, who often adopt them, though passive acceptance cannot be taken for granted. People will not accept a new ideology unless it makes sense to them. It needn't be correct, but it must seem to be. Ideologies that fail to integrate and make sense of experience will be rejected—though they may be revived at a later date.

Social differentiation complicates things. Not everyone engages in the same social practices or is exposed to the same experiences. Many of the differences are patterned: they differ for males and females; they vary with class and occupation. The resulting differences in ideology create the possibility of group conflict, though whether conflict will actually take place will depend on such factors as costs, perceptions of benefits, opportunities, resources, and ease or difficulty in mobilizing members of the group.

All these processes—experiencing the world, conceptualizing it, communicating, mobilizing, engaging in conflict—take place in history. Over time, the social arrangements that give structure to our lives evolve. With new social relations developing out of conflict or consent, with the introduction of new technologies of production, distribution, and communication, with new socialization practices producing new types of human beings, new types of experience result and lead to the creation of new ideologies or the resurrection of old ones.

Evolving social structures and ideologies also change sexual socialization and create or close off sexual opportunities, thus transforming sexual practices. Though potentially homoerotic response appears to be possible for

---

[42] For a long time, Marxists used the term "ideology" to refer to false ideas about social and political existence that mask the oppressive, exploitative aspects of reality. These ideas were supposedly invented by an unscrupulous ruling class to secure its superior position and passively accepted by the rest of the population. Newer Marxist writings on ideology avoid the crudities of the orthodox approach. For example, Sumner (1979:20) defines ideology as "the basic or simple elements (the ideas, images, impressions, notions, etc.) of any form of social consciousness." It is an "outcome and element of social practice which reflects the world of that practice within the consciousness of human beings." He does not assume that ideology is false or deceptive; it may or may not be. My approach is similar to Sumner's.

all human beings, the extent to which this possibility is realized varies widely among individuals and societies. As we have been stressing, the cultural meanings attached to homosexuality when it occurs are equally variable. Just as these meanings shape sexual practices, changes in these practices also have consequences for sexual meanings.

Theoretical application of this conceptual framework to any concrete problem, such as beliefs and attitudes about homosexuality, requires the specification of just what aspects of social life are relevant. This is the task of social theory. Because several theories may prove helpful, it seems best not to settle on one alone at the start, especially in a field where so little is securely known. A number of possibilities will be explored in subsequent chapters.

PROBLEMS OF EVIDENCE

Problems of evidence and interpretation arise often in social-science research, but in our kind of study more than in most. Earlier generations tended to be reticent about sexual matters. Homer does not tell us whether the relationship between Achilles and Patrocles was sexual. The author of 1 Samuel is equally silent about David and Jonathan. The Middle Ages had no Kinsey to cårry out survey research on sexual practices or attitudes.

The destruction of major archives has made our task even harder. Napoleon struck a blow against religious repression by destroying the records of the Inquisition, thereby depriving us of records documenting the persecution of sodomites in early modern Europe. The Arab destruction of the library at Alexandria in the seventh century, and the torching of the Mayan library by Jesuits in the sixteenth, wiped out important sources of information.

For much of human history, only a tiny proportion of the population was literate. Written sources typically reflect the concerns of that tiny elite: priests, officeholders, members of the upper classes. The sexual beliefs and practices of the illiterate masses remain much less known to us than do those of the literate minority.

The gaps in our knowledge of women are especially great. Most historical sources were written by men and reflect their concerns, not those of women. Only fragments of Sappho's poetry survived destruction at the hands of Pope Gregory VII in 1073.[43] In some societies, men's and women's activities were so separate that men had very little knowledge of women's lives. For these reasons we know far less about lesbianism than about male homosexuality, and much less about women's views of homosexuality than about men's.

Ambiguity in the texts that survive is a further problem. For instance,

---

[43]J. N. Katz (1983:422).

some of the collections of customary laws from thirteenth-century France prohibit *bouggerie*. As this is the term from which the modern word "buggery" is derived, some writers have concluded that these measures were directed against homosexuality. However, in the thirteenth century *bouggerie* did not have a sexual connotation. It referred to the Albigensian heresy, which was introduced into France by Bulgarians.[44] Some medieval authors used the term "sodomy" quite broadly; it did not always refer to homosexuality. Dante went so far as to refer to poets who refused to write in the vernacular as committing "spiritual sodomy."[45] It is not always clear from the context just what the word meant.

These evidentiary problems should be kept in mind at all times. Frequently, they are so severe as to make a definitive test of theoretical ideas impossible. To enable readers to assess the strength of evidence, I present it as fully as is feasible. Where assertions are not backed up by evidence, the reader may assume that the claim is made on theoretical rather than on empirical grounds. It would be tiresome to reiterate at every turn that theoretical claims are not invariably correct, but I trust that readers will not forget. The attentive reader will, in fact, note many issues that merit further research. I hope that some will be stirred to undertake it.

LARGER IMPLICATIONS

Apart from helping us to understand societal responses to homosexuality, our investigation may be able to clarify larger issues in the sociology of deviance. The literature on the social creation of deviance categories is currently far from satisfactory. Many of the difficulties highlighted in this chapter plague not only the literature on homosexuality, but other deviance categories as well. While the present study hardly resolves all unsettled questions, it may be able to point to new directions for the field. Consequently, the study of responses to homosexuality is more than just another case study of a taboo.

But the potential value of our investigation is not restricted to the clarification of theoretical issues. The questions we will be examining are of immediate political relevance. The victories won by the gay movement are now threatened by major resistance. Some of the states that decriminalized consensual homosexual relations among adults have restored the repealed legislation, or revised ambiguously worded statutes to make clear that homosexual acts are forbidden. In a recent decision, the United States Supreme

---

[44] Wakefield (1974), Bullough (1976:390–92). This is clear from the customary of Beauvaisis written by Philippe de Remi (1842:1.157, 2.85), which deals with the procedures to be followed in cases involving heretics, Jews, and *Bougres*.

[45] Pézard (1950:294–311).

Court has upheld Georgia's antisodomy statute.[46] The Family Protection Act, introduced in Congress during the first Reagan administration, denies Legal Aid Societies the right to "promote, defend or protect homosexuality." An Arkansas statute permits schoolteachers to be fired for "advocating, soliciting, imposing, encouraging or promoting public or private homosexual activity in a manner that creates a substantial risk that such conduct will come to the attention of school children or school employees."[47] An understanding of this resistance may strengthen efforts to overcome it.

[46] Bowers v. Hardwick, 106 S.Ct. 2841 (1986).
[47] Gold (1982).

I   Before Homosexuality

2 *Homosexual Relations in Kinship-Structured Societies*

In making known to us societies whose sexual practices are radically different from our own, travelers and anthropologists have taught us that our sexual culture is not universal to the human species. In some band and tribal societies, homosexual relations occupy a very different place than in ours. This difference is of particular interest in that the human species has lived in band and tribal social structures for most of its existence.

Bands and tribes organize social life primarily on the basis of kinship. Their economies are largely based on some combination of hunting and gathering, horticulture, and animal husbandry. They have no state—that is, no distinct, sovereign political body with authority to command. Some anthropologists call band and tribal societies "simple," to contrast them with the more highly differentiated and socially complex industrial societies; others refer to them as "primitive," to emphasize their technological limitations. But in the study of sexual practices and ideology it is the centrality of kinship to social life that is most relevant.

It is useful in discussing homosexuality to distinguish several different forms on the basis of the relative social statuses of the participants. Three forms are considered in this chapter: *transgenerational* (in which the partners are of disparate ages), *transgenderal* (the partners are of different genders), and *egalitarian* (the partners are socially similar). A fourth pattern, in which partners belong to different social classes, will be taken up in the next chapter.[1]

Several investigators have tried to determine the prevalence of homosexuality, the degree of its acceptance, and its relationship to other features of a society by coding a large sample of cultures for this information, and then examining the patterns statistically.[2] In principle, this approach can be

[1] The first three types were first distinguished by Gorer (1966:184–92); Trumbach (1977), B. Adam (1979a), and S. O. Murray (1987b) also make use of them. My fourfold typology is also employed by B. Adam (1985), whose terminology I have adopted only in part. The categories are, of course, crude; and in some instances the distinctions are blurred.

[2] Ford and Beach (1951:129–38), Carroll (1978), D. Werner (1979), Reiss (1986).

used to study the relationship between homosexuality and type of kinship system, residence rule, or any other variable for which information can be extracted from the ethnographic sources. The publication of codes for homosexuality-related variables for a standard sample of societies greatly facilitates this sort of research.[3] However, when it comes to homosexuality, the ethnographic reports are not always reliable or easy to interpret.[4] Statistical analysis is further complicated by problems of missing data: for many societies, information about homosexuality is totally lacking.[5] Consequently, we will only consider the ethnographic materials qualitatively, drawing primarily on sources dealing with homosexuality in Africa, Asia, the Pacific islands (Oceania), and among native Americans.[6] Material on homosexuality in Europe and the ancient Near East will be considered in later chapters, to facilitate comparison with subsequent developments in those regions.

TRANSGENERATIONAL HOMOSEXUALITY

In many societies, male homosexual relations are structured by age or generation: the older partner takes a role defined as active or masculine; the younger, a role defined as passive or female.[7] Often the relationship is believed to transfer a special charisma to the younger partner. Among the Coerunas Indians of Brazil, an apprentice healer was taught by going into the woods for an extended time with an older healer, who communicated his special powers to his pupil sexually, while also teaching him methods of curing illness.[8] In Morocco, a saintly person could transmit his holiness or

---

[3] Broude and Greene (1976), Minturn, Grosse, and Haider (1969).

[4] See the appendix to this chapter.

[5] Standard statistical procedures can be invalid when there are missing data.

[6] Space limitations preclude a full listing of the enormous number of sources. An old but still useful survey can be found in Karsch-Haack (1911). More recent cross-cultural overviews, such as those of Ford and Beach (1951), Opler (1965), Karlen (1971a:464–510), Klein (1974), Tripp (1975), Davenport (1977), Trumbach (1977), and Carrier (1980), are also useful, but draw on a very limited range of sources. S. O. Murray (1987b, d) documents the diversity of patterns. Valuable bibliographies have recently appeared for sub-Saharan Africa (Dynes, 1983) and Latin American Indians (Foster, 1985).

[7] Humphreys (1970) has criticized this terminology, pointing out that the boy who fellates an older man may be more active than his partner. For this reason Humphreys proposes the substitution of the technically more precise "insertor" and "insertee" for "active" and "passive." That terminology is also not linked to gender. But Humphreys' terminology has not caught on, and the older vocabulary seems to correspond more to the perspective of the participants, at least as it is reported in anthropological sources. As used here, the term "transgenerational" does not necessarily imply that the partners belong to distinct generations, only that their ages are socially recognized as being different.

[8] Martius (1844:111–31), I. Bloch (1933:105). This was also true of the Bororo of Brazil (Trevisan, 1986:22).

virtue to his sexual partner of the same or opposite sex. Skills could be conveyed in the same way:

> It is common belief among the Arabic-speaking mountaineers of Northern Morocco that a boy cannot learn the Koran well unless a scribe commits pederasty with him. So also an apprentice is supposed to learn his trade by having intercourse with his master.[9]

In early-twentieth-century Morocco the personal qualities that made men admirable were so closely identified with their sex that they could be acquired by incorporating a man's sex organ into one's body. Though these qualities were connected with masculinity, they were not believed to be inherited along with biological sex, or easily cultivated. A contribution from someone who had them could be helpful, and was considered socially acceptable (status achievement did not have to reflect one's own unaided efforts). Apart from sexual gratification, the contributor had the satisfaction of having his special virtues recognized.

Transgenerational homosexual relations have been studied most thoroughly in New Guinea and parts of island Melanesia, where, in a number of cultures, they are a part of boys' initiation rites, and are thus fully institutionalized.[10] Most New Guinea cultures do not have these practices, but they have been found with only slight variations in perhaps 10 to 20 percent.[11] After leaving his mother's hut at age twelve to thirteen to take up residence in the men's house, a Marind-Anim boy enters into a homosexual relationship with his mother's brother, who belongs to a different lineage from his own. The relationship endures for roughly seven years,

---

[9] Westermarck (1926:148).

[10] In some New Guinea groups, such as the Kaluli, homosexuality is not ritualized at all, but appears to be entirely secular (Schieffelin, 1982). In many others it is only partly ritualized.

[11] The New Guinea groups in which transgenerational male homosexuality has been found include the Bugilai and Kiwai Islanders of the Fly River basin (Chalmers, 1903a, 1903b; Landtmann, 1927; F. E. Williams, 1936), Etoro and Onabasulu (R. Kelly, 1974, 1976), Baruya (Godelier, 1976, 1982:90–94), Gebusi (Knauft, 1985–86:32–33, 264–66), Kaluli (Schieffelin, 1976, 1982), Keraki (F. E. Williams, 1936; Rubel and Rosman, 1978:20), Marind-Anim (Wirz, 1922; Van Baal, 1966, 1984), Bedamini (Sørum, 1980, 1984), Sambia (Herdt, 1981, 1987a), Ai'i (Schwimmer, 1984), Jacaq (Boelaars, 1981:84), and Kimam of Irian Jaya (Serpenti, 1965, 1984; J. P. Gray, 1985). The *naven* ritual of the Iatmul, who live in the Sepik River region, contains symbolic expressions of male homosexuality (Bateson, 1958:81–82), and pederastic practices may have been present earlier—the cult was in disarray by the time Bateson did his fieldwork (compare Mead, 1955:79, with Herdt, 1984). Transgenerational male homosexuality is or was found elsewhere in Melanesia, among the Big Namba of Malekula in the New Hebrides—now Vanuatu (Deacon, 1934:261; Harrisson, 1937:410; Layard, 1942; Guiart, 1952, 1953), the Tolai of the Gazelle Peninsula (Van Gennep, 1960:171; A. L. Epstein, 1979; Herdt, 1984), and on East Bay of Santa Cruz (Davenport, 1965). Citations to additional older sources can be found in Karsch-Haack (1911:91–95) and Bleibtreu-Ehrenberg (1980). Knauft (1987) provides a useful review.

until the boy marries.[12] An Etoro boy's career in homosexuality starts around age ten, when he acquires an older partner, ideally his sister's husband or fiancé (so that brother and sister receive semen from the same man). The relationship continues until the boy develops a full beard in his early to mid-twenties. At this point, the now-mature young man becomes the older partner of another prepubescent boy, ordinarily his wife's or fiancée's younger brother. This relationship continues for roughly fifteen years, until the older partner is about forty. His involvement then ends, except for initiation ceremonies, which include collective homosexual intercourse between the initiates and all the older men or, if he takes a second wife, with her younger brother. Because taboos on heterosexual intercourse are extensive, while there are none on homosexual relations, male sexual outlets are predominantly homosexual between the ages of ten and forty.[13]

Practices are similar for the other groups. Starting at age seven to ten, Sambia boys engage in homosexual relations for ten to fifteen years, first as fellator, then as fellated. Homosexual activity can continue after marriage (though it often ends then), but only until men become fathers. As with the Etoro, the ideal partner is the sister's husband, but this is not always possible.[14] Among the Kaluli, the relationship, which begins at age eleven or twelve, lasts only a few months. However, homosexual involvement may occur on an optional basis in the men's hunting lodges during periods of protracted male seclusion from women before marriage.

Involvement in these practices is not restricted to a minority of the population, nor is it sought by the youths. All males are obliged to participate. Provided partners are chosen in conformity with exogamy rules (extended incest taboos), participation is not stigmatized but approved. Involvement is restricted to a limited part of the life cycle, and for adults, does not preclude heterosexual relations. Although some few men never marry, most do, and eventually become exclusively heterosexual.[15]

The mode of intercourse varies from tribe to tribe. It is oral among the Kuks, Tchetchai, Sambia, Etoro, and Baruya; anal among the Kaluli, in the Auya region, and among the men of East Bay. Among the Onabasulu it involves masturbation and smearing of semen over the body of the younger partner. Kimam novices are inseminated anally by slightly older initiates, but the semen of older men is rubbed on bodily incisions after being collected in ritualized collective intercourse with women.[16]

The prescribed relationship between older and younger partner is invari-

---

[12]Van Baal (1966:845).

[13]Kelly (1974, 1976).

[14]Herdt (1981:238).

[15]Schieffelin (1976:124, 126; 1984), Herdt (1987b).

[16]Davenport (1965), Gajdusek (1968:115, 165–66, 196, 212), R. Kelly (1974, 1976), Herdt (1981, 1984), Godelier (1982), Schieffelin (1984), Serpenti (1984).

ably asymmetric: the older inseminates the younger, never the reverse. During the course of a life cycle, each male serves in both capacities, the youthful recipient becoming a donor when he reaches the appropriate age. Both partners retain a masculine gender.[17]

The homosexual practices are justified by the belief that a boy will not mature physically unless semen is implanted in his body by an adult. Valued male qualities, such as courage, proficiency in hunting, and the ability to dominate women, are transmitted in the same way. Repeated intercourse builds up a supply of the vital substance in the boy's body. By contrast, heterosexual intercourse is considered physically debilitating to men: it depletes their vitality. Were a man to give all his semen to a woman, she would grow too strong and dominate him. The entire cluster of homosexual beliefs and practices is kept secret from women, lest they learn that their subordination is a precarious accomplishment, rather than part of the order of nature.[18]

We have very few accounts of transgenerational lesbianism. Middle-aged women of Easter Island reportedly seduce young women, but the relationships are not described as ritualized or institutionalized.[19] The sixteenth-century explorer Leo Africanus was shocked to learn that women diviners of Morocco sometimes seduced young women who consulted them, but since they also engaged in "unlawful venerie" with one another,[20] age difference may not have been a significant element of the relationship.

There are hints of ritualized lesbianism for a few Melanesian cultures,[21] but little detail except for the Baruya. Just as older Baruya men help boys grow by feeding them semen, lactating mothers nourish prepubescent girls who are not their own daughters by offering them their breasts. The Baruya believe that a mother's milk derives from the semen her husband feeds her orally, to strengthen her; she in turns transmits it to a younger girl. The interaction does *not* involve vulvic stimulation; that would not transmit the life-force.[21]

Explanations

Strictly speaking, the explanation of patterned homosexual practices lies outside the scope of our project, which is to understand perceptions of

[17]This is generally true in transgenerational homosexuality, but not without qualification. Married Marquesan men sometimes have casual sexual involvements with young boys, whose bodies, they say, are soft, like young girls (Suggs, 1966:121). New Guinea men sometimes refer to their young male lovers as "wives." But this probably denotes a social role, not a gender role.

[18]R. Kelly (1976), Schieffelin (1976:124–26), Herdt (1981:286–87), Creed (1984).

[19]Metraux (1971).

[20]Carpenter (1914:38).

[21]Harrisson (1937:410), R. Kelly (1976), Godelier (1982:97–98), Keesing (1982), Schwimmer (1984).

homosexuality, not homosexuality itself. Nevertheless, information about homosexual practices permits us to test theories that try to explain the prevalence and types of homosexuality present in a society. As these theories may have bearing on our concerns, we will use our material for such tests where it is possible to do so, keeping in mind that the absence of homosexuality in a society calls for just as much explanation as its presence.

Because information about lesbianism is so scarce, efforts to explain transgenerational homosexuality have focused on the male pattern.[22] The variation in mode of intercourse among the different New Guinea tribes argues against a Freudian explanation based on fixation at an oral or anal stage of childhood sexuality, for there would be little reason to expect differences in the stage of fixation among groups so similar in way of life.

Another psychoanalytic explanation of male homosexuality sees it as a response to castration anxiety induced by the Oedipus conflict. According to the theory, a boy who fears that his father will punish his incestuous desire for his mother may try to placate his father by assuming a feminine identity, thus denying his heterosexuality—and by implication, his love for his mother. He thus becomes a passive, effeminate homosexual.[23] Although evidence for castration anxiety does appear in Marind-Anim mythology,[24] fathers in the New Guinea cultures that institutionalize homosexuality are not particularly threatening or punitive. Moreover, the alternation in sexual roles appears inconsistent with this explanation. It is particularly significant that Melanesian male homosexuality does not entail the adoption of a female gender identity, as would be expected if castration anxiety were the critical factor.

Westermarck attributed the pederasty he observed in the northern regions of Morocco to the scarcity of sexually available women, who were kept secluded.[25] Among the Arabs of the plain, he noted, women were less restricted, and boy love was not found. The Sambia of New Guinea make a similar claim about their homosexuality. They note their fear that heterosexual intercourse will deplete their vital forces, and their distaste for masturbation, but also point to the scarcity of women. There are, in fact, 120

[22] Were the Baruya pattern of transgenerational lesbianism more common and more widely dispersed throughout the world, one might be tempted to postulate its historical priority in remote antiquity and hypothesize that the male pattern is derived from it, as the New Guinea equations penis = breast, semen = milk might suggest. Speculation along these lines would inevitably turn to band or tribal initiation rites for girls, or some other sort of women's religious ceremonies. This possibility cannot be ruled out altogether—there is evidence for it in ancient Greece—but as far as we know the Baruya pattern is so rare that it makes more sense to suppose that it derives from the male pattern and is found only under very special circumstances.

[23] Freud (1970:145).

[24] Van Baal (1966:951).

[25] Westermarck (1917:466–67); see also Tomasic (1945).

men for every 100 women.[26] The ratio is similarly skewed in some of the other New Guinea groups.[27] Consistent with this explanation, Layard notes that male homosexuality is universal in the interior of North Malekula, where powerful chiefs monopolize the women, but virtually absent in the Small Islands, where there are no chiefs.

Isolated cases from other parts of the world seem to conform to this explanation; e.g., on Friday nights, when their religion forbids heterosexual intercourse, African Mossi chiefs indulge in pederasty.[28] Polygamy among the Dahomeyans leads to a severe shortage of women, resulting, according to Gorer, in "serious sexual perversions."[29]

Yet this explanation can hardly be the whole story, for there are too many exceptions. The Mamlukes who ruled medieval Egypt indulged in pederasty with boys from the Central Asian steppes. Yet the Mamlukes had wives.[30] Lower-class women and female prostitutes are readily available to the men of the Swat Pukhtun of Northwest Pakistan, but they consider the most satisfying form of sexual gratification to be anal intercourse with a *bedagh* (passive male partner). Although pederasty has declined among Western-educated Swat men in recent decades (prominent men used to have several *bedaghs* in their retinues for convenient access, but don't anymore), most young men's first sexual experiences are still with *bedaghs* or with receptive peers, and many adult men have youthful male lovers.[31] Big Namba chiefs retain their boy lovers even after marriage, some preferring them to the extent that they rarely resort to their wives.[32] Married men of East Bay consider heterosexual relations pleasurable, and average two copulations a day, yet most also have affairs with boys.[33]

On the other side of the coin, the Bena Bena, a people of the New Guinea highlands, have a comparable shortage of women, but no institutionalized male homosexuality.[34] Young men of the Akwe-Shavante, a Gê people of the Brazilian interior, yearn for heterosexual experience which they cannot easily obtain because girls of their own age are already married; yet there appears to be little male homosexuality.[35] The Dani of New Guinea abstain from heterosexual sex for years at a time (there is a five-year postpartum

---

[26] Herdt (1981:281).

[27] Rappaport (1967:15–16), R. Kelly (1974:172), Gell (1975:48). The mortality rate in warfare being higher for men than for women, these figures presumably reflect infanticide and deaths during childbirth. Polygyny further reduces the availability of women.

[28] Tauxier (1912:569–70).

[29] Gorer (1935:141–42).

[30] S. O. Murray (1987g).

[31] Lindholm (1982:148–49, 224–25).

[32] Deacon (1934:261), Harrisson (1937:410).

[33] Davenport (1965).

[34] Langness (1967).

[35] Maybury-Lewis (1967:82).

sex taboo) without turning to homosexuality.[36] Obvious homosexuality is not the only possible response to a shortage of women. Celibacy, polyandry, masturbation, and illicit heterosexual affairs, such as are found in the Upper Tor region of New Guinea,[37] are also possible responses. An explanation of homosexuality that rests on the unavailability of women must explain why these alternatives are foreclosed. In addition, scarcity of women does not explain the asymmetry of transgenerational homosexuality. Why is the partner always younger or older, rather than the same age?

Anthropologists have offered explanations along a variety of lines. Hage has suggested that ritualized pederasty has much in common with male penile subincision, practiced by the Murngin and Arunta in Australia, as well as by the Wogeo in New Guinea.[38] Penile subincision attempts to simulate female genitalia and make men menstruate. Hage argues that the practice reflects the symmetry of social organization of these two tribes, whose clans compose two mutually exclusive, exogamous moieties. These rituals, Hage argues, display parallels of form and content with the male initiation rites of New Guinea. Both are intended to stimulate growth. Both, he suggests, have their origin in dual organization, which is common in New Guinea and Australia. The cultural emphasis on growth, he speculates, arises with "big man"-type politics,[39] in which social status is not conferred by birth but is achieved by individual effort. Sodomy, like ritual bleeding, is thus a magical act performed to foster status attainment.

The details of this argument do not stand up. Neither the Sambia nor the Big Namba have "big men." The Big Namba have hereditary chiefs,[40] while the Sambia have no formal political leaders of any kind.[41] Although an empirical analysis of marriage patterns shows that the six Etoro patrilines constitute two moieties, the Etoro themselves do not know this.[42] The Kaluli do not have moieties. Unlike subincision, New Guinea homosexual acts are not restricted to special rituals, but are repeated frequently over a period of years (ideally every day for the Sambia). While Westermarck's Morocco materials confirm that pederasty can be linked to individual aspirations for status and achievement, there is little homosexual competitiveness in New Guinea "homosexual" cultures. No one claims that his semen is superior to other men's. Sambia boys are encouraged to obtain semen from a number of different men. In some groups (the Kimam, Marind-Anim), semen from

---

[36] Heider (1976, 1979:78–79).

[37] Oosterval (1959).

[38] Hage (1981).

[39] A "big man" is a leader whose influence depends on his being able to attract and retain followers by giving them gifts or loans, rather than on inheritance of office (Sahlins, 1963).

[40] Harrisson (1937).

[41] Herdt (1981).

a number of men is pooled before being ritually administered to the boys. The rituals strengthen the males collectively, and therefore do not figure in the competition among men. The Nduindui, who live on the northwest coast of the island of Aobo *do* have a big-man political system, but not ritualized homosexuality.[43]

Keesing, Herdt, and other earlier anthropologists have noted that institutionalized Melanesian homosexuality is found primarily in the West Papuan Gulf region, the Fly River basin, Southeastern Irian Jaya, and the coastal fringe of Northeastern Irian Jaya, as well as on nearby islands to the east. The few known New Guinea exceptions are located in territories that border on these regions, or have received immigrants from them. Cultural and linguistic evidence suggests that these peoples stem from a common immigration of non-Austronesians, possibly as long ago as 10,000 years, making their pederastic practices quite old. A second, later immigration of Austronesians may have settled the Eastern Melanesian islands without eradicating the ancient ritual complex.[44] Subsequent migration up the Fly and Sepik Rivers carried the pattern inland, bypassing the highlands. A further infusion may have come from northern Australia (see p. 36).

Weston La Barre has argued that ritual pederasty is an extraordinarily old practice; he traces it, along with cannibalism and head-hunting, to the Paleolithic (Old Stone Age), contending that all three practices stemmed from the belief that semen, which carries the life-force, is produced in the brain, stored in the brain marrow, and transmitted along the spinal column to the testes.[45] La Barre thinks the belief developed several hundred-thousand years ago, following the discovery of the male role in paternity.

To primitive people who knew little of anatomy or physiology, it would have seemed quite logical that the élan vital, the force that keeps us alive and creates the next generation, should be produced in the head, the seat of consciousness. In La Barre's view, cannibalism and head-hunting were pursued not to obtain protein, as several anthropologists have proposed,[46] but to obtain the highly valued male qualities of courage, virility, and prowess in hunting and warfare. Though produced in the head, these qualities

[42] R. Kelly (1974).

[43] However, they can generate personal power through ritualized exhibition of *mock* homosexuality (M. R. Allen, 1984).

[44] The Austronesian language family is also called Malayo-Polynesian. Most New Guinea languages are classified as non-Austronesian or Papuan, but they are not all members of a single family (R. Clark, 1979). It is possible, however, that many of the non-Austronesian languages are descended from Austronesian languages, but have diverged to the point where the common origin has been obscured (Groube, 1971; Terrell, 1986).

[45] La Barre (1984). Related suggestions can be found in Onians (1951:105–22, 205–7) and Rawson (1973:48).

[46] Harner (1977a, 1977b), M. Harris (1977), Ortiz de Montellano (1978).

were in their essence sexual and could be acquired through intromission of semen as well as by eating. Pederasty, which transmitted these qualities to the next generation, was, then, a logical consequence of primitive sexual ideology.

Our knowledge of Paleolithic life is scant, but some of it supports La Barre. Excavations in sites as scattered as Europe, Asia, Africa, and the American Southwest have found evidence that early men ritually killed and extracted the brains of their fellows [47]—though we cannot be sure that the brains were eaten, or, if they were, who ate them and for what purpose. However, doubts have been raised that the male role in paternity had been discovered so early; [48] if not, early cannibalism would probably not have had anything to do with the acquisition of virility. Phallic preoccupations appear in cave paintings, rock carvings, and sculpture starting in the late Paleolithic (from roughly 17,000 B.C.), and persist into later periods. [49] Of the few Stone Age depictions of sexual intercourse, several seem to portray male homosexual connections. [50] Headhunting and pederasty are associated in some contemporary New Guinea cultures, so it is not entirely implausible that they were also associated in the Stone Age. But we don't know this, and almost certainly never will.

Clues to the survival of archaic homosexual practices in Melanesia can be gleaned by comparing those New Guinea societies that institutionalize homosexuality with those that do not. Lindenbaum and Schwimmer have made such comparisons and find that though relations between men and women tend to be somewhat antagonistic in both, they are much more so in the "nonhomosexual" societies. One reason is that in the "homosexual" societies, men's and women's productive activities tend to be complementary and benefit both spouses. By contrast, men in the nonhomosexual soceities exploit women by appropriating the products of their labor for use in ceremonies that enhance male, but not female, prestige. [51] Women in the

[47] H. Schutz (1983:30–31), La Barre (1984:13–15), J. Robbins (1985).

[48] G. Rubin (1977) suggests, quite plausibly, that paternity would not have been discovered until herding began, probably in the late Paleolithic. Before that, individual animals would not have been observed over a long enough time period for the connection between copulation and conception to be made. For humans, the length of time between conception and visible pregnancy may have been too long for the connection to be made readily. The large number of obese female figurines from late Paleolithic Europe, together with the paucity of male figures (Gimbutas, 1981, 1982; Schutz, 1983:46–51), readily lends itself to conjecture that they were used in fertility rites prior to the discovery of paternity. Their disappearance and the introduction of phallic symbolism in the late Magdalenian are thus readily explained by the discovery of the male role.

[49] G. Clark (1967:82), Leroi-Gourhan (1968), Frischauer (1969:45), Cucchiari (1981), Gimbutas (1982:216–34).

[50] Vanggaard (1972:82–84), A. Ross (1973:90).

[51] Lindenbaum (1984), Schwimmer (1984).

homosexual societies are not nearly as subordinated. The proximity of their natal villages enables them to call on their relatives for support in the event of a dispute with their husbands. If necessary, they can go home. Homosexual relations are found, then, where they are most needed to solidify male power against challenges from women. They function to reproduce male-dominated gender relations where they are shaky.[52]

Lindenbaum has called attention to another difference.[53] In almost all the homosexual societies, marriage occurs through the exchange of women, usually sisters, without payment of bridewealth. The small size of the groups and the shortage of women can make these exchanges difficult, especially when the lack of an available woman of marriageable age in one of the groups delays the completion of the exchange. A homosexual relationship between the two brothers-in-law enlists libidinal gratification and ties of affection to maintain the exchange obligation. In this way, hierarchical sex between individual males preserves equality between patrilineages. In the larger and more prosperous societies of the New Guinea highlands, on the other hand, marriage is accomplished through the payment of bridewealth, and institutionalized homosexuality is absent.

Pederastic practices among Australian aborigines confirm a connection between delayed sister-exchange marriage and male homosexuality.[54] Tribal elders control access to wives, who are valued as collectors of food. A fa-

---

[52] This conclusion casts doubt on Carleton Coon's (1931) attribution of men's interest in boys in the Jebala region of Morocco to their low esteem for women. Although individual instances that fit Coon's explanation can be found (classical Athens), exceptions come readily to mind, e.g., Sparta, and the Mamlukes, whose wives, according to S. O. Murray (1987g), enjoyed *high* social status. However, there are seeming exceptions to the Schwimmer-Lindenbaum hypothesis within Melanesia that cast doubt on their hypothesis. The Big Nambas practice ritualized pederasty, yet they are one of the most male-supremacist of Melanesians (Layard, 1942:489), and the forms their pederasty takes reflect their phallocracy. The creation of solidarity among male agnates (members of a patrilineal descent group) is a major goal of initiation rites among the Small Islanders, but these rites do not entail pederasty (though they do involve mock anal penetration by ancestral spirits). The rights and status of women among the Nduindui of west Aoba are exceptionally high, but again, homosexuality is not institutionalized. Aspiring big men, however, can gain special powers through mock-homosexual or heterosexual incest at special ceremonies (M. R. Allen, 1984). Allen takes this as an indication that homosexuality is considered abhorrent, but it seems more likely that it is the incest and age-role inversion (the novices are invited to take the active role) that is considered shocking and dangerous.

[53] Lindenbaum (1987).

[54] Sources referring to homosexuality among the Australian aborigines include Hardman (1889), Ravenscroft (1892), Purcell (1893), Mathews (1900a, 1900b, 1901, 1902a, 1902b), W. E. Roth (1908), Strehlow (1913:98–122), Westermarck (1917:460), Roheim (1926:70, 1933, 1945:72, 122, 1950:118–19, 1958, 1974:242), Spencer and Gillin (1927:2.470, 486; 1938:554–670), Kaberry (1939:257), Berndt and Berndt (1951:67). Additional sources can be found in Karsch-Haack (1911:65–90).

ther who has marriageable daughters may elect to exchange them for additional wives for himself, rather than for his sons, who may then be unable
to marry. For lack of a spouse, a son may become engaged to a girl when
she is born and then have to wait years until she is old enough to marry. In
the interim, he may take the girl's older brother as a substitute wife, greas-
ing his body, and having sexual relations with him through frottage, or
rubbing, without penetration.

Most of the sources are old, and do not indicate whether insemination
was believed to be necessary for a boy to mature, but scattered references to
sodomy in connection with native dances and initiation ceremonies suggest that some groups might have considered it necessary. Purcell, for example, mentions that in the bora ceremony—the third male-initiation rite
in the Kimberley District of Western Australia—youths drink semen from
the young men in the camp. So did elderly dying men (a practice not reported from New Guinea),[55] on the theory that as a carrier of life semen
should help preserve it. On the other hand, Pilling found no evidence of a
ritual component to homosexuality among the Tiwi, whom he studied in
1953–54.[56] Sexual relations among future brothers-in-law occurred regularly soon after puberty, but without the large age-differentials reported at
the turn of the century.[57]

The existence of a land connection between Australia and New Guinea
across the Torres Straits until about 900 B.C. makes it quite plausible that
the New Guinea pattern, which is concentrated on the southern coast and
in sites accessible from the south by river, had a common origin with the
Australian. It could have been imported any time after New Guinea was
first settled, about 50,000 years ago, but its restricted dispersion in New
Guinea may argue for a later date.

It is likely that human bands were small and widely scattered throughout
most of the Old Stone Age. We do not know for sure what marriage practices
prevailed then, but it is quite possible that they were band-exogamous. Exogamous marriages create alliances, which facilitate trade and can promote
peaceful relations. Under these circumstances marriages could have involved sister exchange. But, as in New Guinea, sister-exchange marriages
would have been difficult when the exchanging groups were numerically
small. A skewed sex ratio would have increased the difficulty. Skeletal evi-

[55] Purcell (1893).

[56] Pilling (1983).

[57] As no one has studied the matter, it is unknown whether the age-differentiated homosexuality found to be essentially universal among young boys and bachelors of the Batak of Lake
Toba in northern Sumatra is related to the Australian and New Guinea practices. As elsewhere, the participants all eventually marry heterosexually (Money and Ehrhardt, 1972:
130–31).

dence suggests that in early human populations, the ratio of adult men to adult women was approximately 5 to 4, comparable to that of contemporary New Guinea societies.[58] The acceptability of a male substitute when no sister was available for exchange would have facilitated marriages. It is quite possible, then, that this type of homosexuality dates back to the origins of exogamy, and was invented independently in different groups.

Schwimmer and Lindenbaum explain transgenerational male homosexuality by the functions it serves for men—in helping them dominate women, or secure wives. What these explanations lack is any account of erotic attraction. They simply assume that if male homosexuality is needed to strengthen male solidarity or to make marriage obligations more secure, it will spontaneously appear and be institutionalized. Questions of how homosexuality is produced, and why it is not resisted, are not raised.

Following Layard's lead, Herdt has addressed these issues in a provocative analysis that links social structure with the social psychology of gender identity.[59] It is a commonplace of anthropology that male-initiation rites detach boys from their mothers and are thus instrumental in establishing a masculine identification.[60] The need for such a process would seem to be high in many New Guinea tribes.[61] Commonly, husbands and wives do not sleep together. Etoro and Kaluli families live in a longhouse, with separate sleeping quarters for men and women.[62] The men and women of a Marind village live in separate dormitory-style houses which members of the opposite sex are forbidden from entering; consequently spouses never spend the night together.[63]

These sleeping arrangements are a response to the threat of raids from neighboring villages. Marriage is clan-exogamous, and this often means that wives come from other villages. In mountainous terrain, where travel is difficult, these villages will be located nearby. Yet these are precisely the villages with which chronic warfare over territorial boundaries or theft of pigs is carried on. In other regions, wives are not drawn from "true enemy" villages, but since alliances are unstable, all villages are potentially hostile. As a result, men fear that in event of a nighttime raid their wives will betray them by supporting their own relatives.[64]

[58] Vellois (1961), Levi-Strauss (1969:479).

[59] Layard (1955, 1959), Herdt (1981).

[60] Whiting, Kluckhohn, and Anthony (1958), R. F. Murphy (1959), Van Gennep (1960), M. R. Allen (1967:18–27).

[61] Dundes (1976), M. R. Allen (1984).

[62] R. Kelly (1976), Schieffelin (1976).

[63] Van Baal (1966:46, 48).

[64] The Sambia, who are unusual in that husbands live in the same household with their wives and children, are also exceptional in taking a high proportion of their wives from other

As women take care of small children, these arrangements alone would reduce contact between fathers and their offspring. Postpartum-sex taboos reduce this contact even further. Sambia fathers cannot see their babies for the first six months after birth, and may see them only infrequently during the next six months. Husbands and wives do not resume sexual relations until about twenty months after a birth, and to avoid becoming aroused husbands are expected to avoid their wives during this period. For all practical purposes wife avoidance implies child avoidance, and as a result, fathers have very little contact with their children during the first two years of life—and not much more after that.[65]

Because fathers interact so minimally with their small children, the children tend to identify with their mothers.[66] This identification provides the basis for gender identity later in life. Myths that show uncertainty of male identification, or anxiety about boys becoming women, indicate that this identification is problematic for Sambian boys.[67] Because the sexual division of labor is sharp, and men's participation in warfare, which is largely a male activity, is especially valued, boys' tendency to identify with their mothers poses a threat to the gender system.

This threat is enhanced by marriage and residence patterns. For military reasons, men almost always live patrilocally; this arrangement strengthens the solidarity of the fighting force by keeping together boys who have grown up together. As already mentioned, women usually come from neighboring, potentially hostile villages. A boy's identification with his mother is thus an identification with a potential enemy. It could weaken the village's defense. It is thus of critical importance that boys be separated from their mothers, and made to identify with their fathers.

Homosexual practices help to accomplish this by establishing a lengthy, intense association with an older man, and by investing the relationship with erotic energies. The sexual ideology lends support to this separation. As boys are taught that women are dangerously polluting, and that heterosexual intercourse is harmful to men, they avoid women and minimize

---

clans living *in the same village*. Even so, husbands and wives never sleep together; the men sleep in a men's house (Herdt, 1981:208–14).

[65] Herdt (1981:208–12).

[66] Many studies confirm that when fathers are absent from the household, or when they are present but mothers are the dominant parent, sons tend to be more feminine, exhibit cross-sex identification, and display a greater degree of gender nonconformity as adults (Bach, 1946; Burton and Whiting, 1961; Bieber, 1962; Schofield, 1965; Hetherington, 1966; Barclay and Gusmano, 1967; Biller and Borstelman, 1967; Drake and McDougall, 1967; Greenson, 1967; Stoller, 1968; Biller, 1972; Manosewitz, 1972; Longabaugh, 1973; Stephan, 1973; Green, 1974; Gilmore and Gilmore, 1979; Bell, Weinberg, and Hammersmith, 1981). Some of the studies are methodologically weak, but the consistency of findings is impressive.

[67] Herdt (1981:263–94).

their sexual involvement with them. The belief that implanted semen secures their masculinity reassures them that they are in no danger of relaps-
ing toward femininity when they finally marry.[68]

Herdt's data suggest that this process is not entirely successful. Boys do
acquire a male identity, and take up male-identified tasks. Transvestism is
unknown, as is effeminacy among adult men. However, sexual-identity
conflicts persist, and manifest themselves in the homosexual relationship.
In addition to helping the younger partner acquire a male identity, the relationship also permits the older partner to express his residual identification
with his mother by "mothering" his prepubescent partner. The Sambians
make this identification explicit by comparing the penis to a breast, and semen to mother's milk. At the same time, the older inseminator narcissistically identifies himself with his younger partner, and thus re-creates in
fantasy the lost world of mother-son love.[69] For this to work, the partner
must be younger; and since mother and son are from different clans, the
partner must be, too. Normally, he is from his mother's.[70]

The situation for girls is quite different. Their identification with their
mothers poses no threat to the gender system, and so there is no need for
rituals designed to change their gender identity. Baruya lesbianism quite
likely reflects maternal identification, and may well entail a narcissistic
identification with the younger partner as well, just as for males. The infrequency of such relationships in New Guinea may reflect the opportunities
for realizing this identification in conventional mothering.

Where homosexuality is institutionalized, and participation universal,
the belief system that supports it coincides with the ideology that dictates
responses to it. In societies that are so small in scale and so undifferentiated

---

[68]Some few men seem unable to overcome the fear that heterosexual intercourse will harm
them, and never marry. Such cases are deviant within Sambian culture (Herdt, 1987).

[69]Freud (1953). Because the father is too remote a figure in the young son's life to constitute
a rival, and because he does not discipline the child, the oedipal complex plays no role in this
dynamic. The Marind, however, do show evidence of castration anxiety. It can be traced to the
son's sexual attraction to his mother. She is physically close, and because her relationship with
her husband is strained and emotionally unsatisfying, she can be expected to focus her emotional energies on her children. The son responds to his mother, but cannot do so sexually
because of incest prohibitions.

[70]No comparable dynamic is at work for the younger partners. They are quite happy with
their mothers. When separated from them, they report a sense of loss, and anxiety over the
initial homosexual experience. Only gradually do they learn to like homosexual contacts
(Herdt, 1981:279). The effectiveness of this learning is attested to by Gajdusek (1968:115), who
found that wherever his medical research took him, boys tried to seduce him. In the Upper
Ruffaer Valley, friends greeted one another with such phrases as "I will eat your genital
organs," or "I will take your penis to my mouth" (Gajdusek, 1963). However, Herdt has informed me that a minority of the Sambian youth never learn to like homosexuality; they participate because they must, but give it up as soon as it is permissible to do so.

socially, divergent sexual ideologies do not arise.[71] There is, then, no social conflict over homosexuality, and no stigma attached to it. Indeed, it does not become the basis for imputing a distinct social identity.

However, even where homosexuality is not institutionalized, it is not necessarily considered deviant. It may still occur, but less frequently. On the Small Islands

> it is rare, and such relationships as exist almost always consist in a Small Island boy being the passive partner in a temporary union with an adult native from the Malekulan mainland. . . . The Small Islanders' attitude towards such relationships are a comic look and the remark "What a waste of time when there are so many women."[72]

Minority status alone, then, does not lead to prejudice, discrimination, or repression. Repression arises only when there is a special reason for it.

TRANSGENDERAL HOMOSEXUALITY

In transgenderal homosexuality, one of the partners relinquishes the gender (sexual identity) ordinarily associated with his or her anatomical sex and lays claim to the gender associated with the opposite sex.[73] The homosexual relationship is thus modeled on a heterosexual pattern. One of the best-studied examples of transgenderal homosexuality is found among the Indians of North America.

The North American Berdache

The Spanish and French explorers and missionaries who visited the New World quickly became aware of Indian men who dressed as women and engaged in homosexual relations. Father Charlevoix found the Iroquois to have

> an excess of effeminacy and lewdness. There are men unashamed to wear women's clothing and to practice all the occupations of women, from which follows corruption that I cannot express. They pretend that this usage comes from their religion. These

---

[71]Sexual antagonism and separation do create the possibility that men and women will hold discrepant views. Virtually nothing is known of what Melanesian women think about male homosexuality; in theory they know nothing about it. Whatever they think, they do nothing to stop it.

[72]M. R. Allen (1984). The Gahuku-Gama of New Guinea appear to take a similar view: "homosexuality . . . is foolish rather than immoral. People denied any knowledge of it, but they were not morally affronted by the idea, taking the more practical view that it would be silly, as well as undignified, to indulge in it" (Read, 1955).

[73]In the abstract, one could imagine homosexual relations in which both partners changed gender, but this pattern is never reported in the anthropological literature.

effeminates never marry and abandon themselves to the most infamous passions.[74]

Another Jesuit priest, Father Pedro Font, noted that among the California Indians he visited in 1775–76,

> some men dressed like women, with whom they go about regularly, never joining the men. . . . I asked who these men were, and they replied that they were not men like the rest, and for this reason they went around covered this way. From this I inferred that they must be hermaphrodites, but from what I learned later I understood that they were sodomites dedicated to nefarious practices.[75]

The French named these men *berdaches*. The Persian root, *bardag*, refers to a young slave. Imported into the Romance languages, it came to denote males who played a receptive role in homosexual intercourse.[76] In the American Indian context, the term came to refer to men or women who dressed like persons of the opposite gender and who often, but not invariably, had sexual relations with persons of the same biological sex and conventional gender. A few berdaches may have been hermaphrodites, but most were anatomically normal. Anthropologists have sometimes implied that they were largely confined to the Plains Indians, but they have been documented for most of the other cultural areas. It is likely that most Indian bands and tribes had them.[77]

[74] Charlevoix (1744:303).

[75] Font (1930–31:105), Heizer and Whipple (1970:204), J. N. Katz (1976:291).

[76] The evolution of the word is traced in Courouve (1982) and Dynes (1985a:19–20). Katz (1976) has published an exceptionally useful collection of original documents on berdaches, along with an extensive bibliography. A series of review essays summarizes the sources in greater detail than is possible here, and explore a variety of theoretical issues (Karsch-Haack, 1911:284–362, 505–8; Angelino and Shedd, 1955; Stewart, 1960; Tüllman, 1961; S.-E. Jacobs, 1968; Forgey, 1975; Whitehead, 1981; Callender and Kochems, 1983a, b; Blackwood, 1984; W. L. Williams, 1986). I refer to berdaches in the past tense, because the role has disappeared in most groups (Parsons, 1939; Stoller, 1976). Where it survives, it does so under conditions radically different from those of the past (Liberty, 1983; Powers, 1983; W. L. Williams, 1986).

[77] Callender and Kochems (1983a) question the existence of an Iroquois berdache on the grounds that Lafitau, who also visited the Iroquois, did not report one. However, Loskiel (1794:1.14) and Charbonneau (Wied, 1839:133) corroborate Charlevoix. Assertions that an Indian group lacked berdaches can often be refuted by a sufficiently extensive search for sources. Thus Callender and Kochems find little evidence for berdaches along the Atlantic seaboard, but Karsch-Haack (1911) summarizes much literature that refers to them. Whitehead claims that Eskimos had none, but again, Karsch-Haack (1911:284–86) cites many sources to the contrary. Several authorities suggest that the Comanches did not have an institutionalized berdache role (Kardiner, 1945:56–57, 88; Minturn, Grosse, and Haider, 1969), but Bancroft (1874:1.515 n. 127) quotes an early source that suggests the opposite. For the Cherokees see W. L. Williams (1986:4).

Where the transformation of gender was complete, berdaches adopted the clothing, occupational specializations, mannerisms, and speech patterns of the opposite gender. Male berdaches associated with women rather than men, danced women's dances, participated in women's rituals, and observed taboos appropriate to women. They abstained from hunting and warfare and instead wove baskets, pounded acorns, dressed and tanned hides, quilled, and worked in the fields.

In parallel fashion, female berdaches adopted male social roles. Thus, after an early-nineteenth-century Kutenai woman separated from a Canadian trader, she became a berdache, wore male apparel, carried gun, bow, and arrow, joined the men of the tribe in hunting and going to war, and lived with a number of wives in succession.[78] As girls, Cocopa female berdaches played with boys, made bows and arrows, and hunted birds and rabbits. They adopted a male hairstyle, had their noses pierced as men did, and went to war, fighting as men. They had sexual relations with women and married them.[79]

On occasion, the transformation of gender was only partial. In some groups, male berdaches hunted and fought, though they wore men's clothing when they did so.[80] Male berdaches of the Pima and Navaho were not required to cross-dress.[81] In a number of groups, they did both men's and women's work.[82] A Klamath woman married another woman but continued to wear women's clothing. Yet, after her spouse died, she referred to herself as a man and tried to talk like one.[83] A mid-nineteenth-century Gros Ventre woman raised by the Crows took up male occupations, achieved renown for her exploits in combat against the Blackfeet, was a highly successful hunter, and became one of the highest chiefs. She eventually married four wives, but "during her whole life no change took place in her dress, being clad like the rest of the females with the exception of hunting arms and accoutrements."[84]

These partial transformations, along with data on social responses to berdaches, have led some anthropologists to argue that Indian conceptions of gender have too casually been assumed to be dichotomous. In some groups they may have been, for the sources indicate that in those groups, berdaches were treated just like someone of the opposite sex.[85] In others they were treated as intermediate between men and women, or in other

---

[78] Schaeffer (1965).
[79] Gifford (1934). For the Surprise Valley Paiute, see I. T. Kelly (1934).
[80] Callender and Kochems (1983a), Powers (1983).
[81] W. W. Hill (1935, 1938).
[82] W. W. Hill (1935), Mirsky (1937), Mead (1961).
[83] Spier (1930).
[84] Denig (1953).
[85] Osgood (1958), E. Blackwood (1984).

ways that distinguished them from both their biological sex and the sex they claimed to be. For this reason, some anthropologists have argued that berdaches represented a mixing of genders, or that Indian cultures had more than two genders and assigned berdaches to a gender of their own. In still another perspective, Indian genders were not discrete but fluid, just as gender roles were. Thus Piegan and Blackfeet women could take on many aspects of the conventional male social role without becoming a berdache.[86] Possibly Indians were not as concerned as American anthropologists with analytical precision in this area.[87]

Gender transformations could be initiated in several ways. Most often a female spirit or goddess appeared to a young man some time before his male puberty rite and ordered him to become a woman.[88] But the dream could come later in life. After a nineteenth-century Snake woman who was married dreamed that she was a man, she began to wear her husband's clothing, participated in hunts, and went on the warpath with the men. Her exploits earned her the title of "brave," and she was admitted to the council of chiefs.[89]

In other instances, parents interpreted a small male child's preferences for objects associated with women rather than men (e.g., baskets instead of bow and arrow) as a sign that the boy was destined to become a berdache and proceeded to raise him as a girl.[90] Sometimes male captives and cowardly warriors were forced to assume a female identity;[91] they, however, were not considered to be berdaches, though they could be subjected to homosexual relations.

The berdache status was not necessarily permanent. Although most berdaches seem to have maintained the role for life, Spier tells of a Klamath adolescent who wore women's garb and performed women's tasks, but later abandoned the female role and became a chief who married seven wives.[92] A Mohave woman berdache became heterosexual after having married several women in succession.[93]

---

[86] O. Lewis (1941), W. L. Williams (1986).

[87] Mandelbaum (1940), Martin and Voorhies (1975), Whitehead (1981), J. Miller (1982), Callender and Kochems (1983a, 1985). S. O. Murray (1983) points out that, generally speaking, most peoples of the world are unconcerned with developing and applying rigidly defined categories to phenomena, but are rather content with a considerable degree of conceptual ambiguity.

[88] Bourke (1892), Bowers (1950, 1965). Dreams were an established basis for making important life choices in many Indian groups.

[89] Smet (1905:1017–18), J. N. Katz (1976:302–3); see also Spier (1933) and Devereux (1937).

[90] Simms (1903), Kroeber (1925:46), Spier (1933), Gifford (1934:294), Devereux (1937), Hill (1938), Liette (1962:112–13), J. N. Katz (1976:614 n. 30).

[91] Park (1938:21), Tixier (1940:182), Reichard (1950:140–41), Lurie (1953), L. H. Morgan (1966:14, 329), Landes (1968:27, 206).

[92] Spier (1930:52).

[93] Devereux (1937).

Most male berdaches were exclusively homosexual. As unmarried men, they could have sexual relations with any other men who were not forbidden by kinship restrictions, and some married other men. They never took other berdaches as partners, only men whose gender was masculine. Nothing is known about the proportion of the male population that had sexual relations with berdaches, though there are hints that it may have been high.[94] The sexual orientation of same-sex partners was, in most instances, almost surely not exclusively homosexual. In like manner, female berdaches often courted and married feminine wives. The age of partners does not appear to have been a significant element structuring relationships between berdaches of either sex and their partners.

Though it was a common correlate of the berdache role, homosexuality was not a necessary component of it. In some groups berdaches remained celibate, had heterosexual relations, or took both male and female partners.[95] Where the role was assumed in adulthood, it was commonly preceded by heterosexual experience; and if it was abandoned, heterosexual activity might be initiated or resumed.[96]

The variability in berdaches' sexual preferences, along with the existence of homosexuality that did not entail gender-crossing or mixing, implies that the essence of the role was not homosexuality but gender anomaly. Homosexuality seems to have been less a cause of the transformation than one of its frequent consequences. It was a favored option, not a requirement.[97]

Its wide dispersion, and its resemblance to Old World institutionalized roles, suggests that the berdache role is extremely old (see below). However, most efforts to explain its existence have focused on more recent conditions. Many anthropologists have seen the male berdache as responding to the emphasis Indian culture gave to military combat. Though young men were eager to establish reputations as great fighters, they were also afraid of being killed.[98] Becoming a berdache, it has been argued, was a way of avoiding this risk.[99]

Once a social role is institutionalized, and when recruitment to it is voluntary, individuals can adopt that role for any number of reasons. Fear may

[94] Loeb (1934), Hassrick (1964:121–22), Landes (1968:112), Catlin (1973:214–15), W. L. Williams (1986).

[95] Stevenson (1904:37–38), Fletcher and La Flesche (1911:133), Lowie (1912), Teit (1930:384), Forde (1931), Gifford (1934:294), Loeb (1934), W. W. Hill (1935), Olson (1936), Mandelbaum (1940), Devereux (1948), Angelino and Shedd (1955), Opler (1965), Landes (1970:196–97).

[96] Devereux (1937), Schaeffer (1965), Callender and Kochems (1983a).

[97] Callender and Kochems (1983a).

[98] Landes (1968:206–7).

[99] Devereux (1937), Mirsky (1937), Hoebel (1949:459, 1978:102), Mead (1961), Hassrick (1974:121–22), Hudson (1976).

[100] Landes (1968:206–7).

have led some Indian men to become berdaches. Yet that was hardly necessary, for in some groups that had berdaches, it was possible for young men
to avoid combat without becoming one.[100] In a number of groups, berdaches fought along with male-identified men, or accompanied them to
battle, carrying food and retrieving the dead.[101] And the infants selected for
feminization by their parents could hardly have been chosen for their cowardice. Moreover, there appears to have been no correlation between the
presence of berdaches in a given group and the importance of fighting to
that group.[102]

With gender transformation at the core of the berdache role, it may be
more fruitful to look at the berdache phenomenon in the larger context of
gender.[103] Because rights and privileges in one activity sphere do not necessarily correlate with those in other spheres, discussions of "the status of
women" (or men) are necessarily imprecise.[104] Variability within groups
can complicate generalizations. Still, by comparison with New Guinea,
precontact American Indian women were on the whole relatively advantaged. Though not formal equals of men, they had a great deal of autonomy in carrying out socially necessary tasks and, as a few examples will
show, could achieve power, prestige, and recognition.

Iroquois women held major political posts; they participated in decisions
about war and peace, had charge of the public treasury, and arranged marriages. Though they could not serve on the Council of Elders (the highest
ruling body of the League), they elected its members and could initiate im-
peachment proceedings. Half the religious leaders were women. The land
and its harvest all belonged to women, and it was they who distributed
even the food that men brought in from the hunt.[105] Algonkian women also
held public office and played a major role in the domestic economy and
in trade.[106]

Schlegel notes that Hopi women of the late-nineteenth and early-twenti-
eth century did not play a formal role in public life. Nevertheless, their
influence

> as the mothers, sisters and wives of men who make community
> decisions cannot be overestimated. These women, after all, con-
> trol the houses the men live in; and the man's position in the

[101] Henry and Thompson (1897:163–65), Thwaites (1900:129), Swanton (1922:373), Trowbridge (1938), J. N. Katz (1976:285), Callender and Kochems (1983a), W. L. Williams (1986).
[102] Hoebel (1949:459), Callender and Kochems (1983a).
[103] Whitehead (1981) develops much the same argument, and also compares the American
Indians with New Guinea peoples.
[104] Whyte (1978).
[105] J. K. Brown (1970), Wallace (1971).
[106] Grumet (1980).

home is to a large extent dependent upon his relationship to the female head. Women do not hesitate to speak their minds, whether in the privacy of the home to male kin and their visitors or in public meetings. One example illustrates what is in effect the veto power of women: in one village the chief and his sister were divided over a political issue concerning the village, and she refused to play her role in the Soyal ceremony, led by the chief, until he capitulated. As Hopi men readily admit, women usually get their way.[107]

Among the Wyandots (Hurons), "the women were supreme in political matters. They elected chieftains of both sexes, with a marked preponderance of women, for every tribal council consisted of forty-four females and eleven males."[108]

Following their release in 1868 from the reservation to which they had been forcibly relocated, the Navaho remained matrilineal and matrilocal.[109] Land, houses, and livestock were under the traditional ownership or control of women. In adulthood, women were surrounded by their kin, who could provide social and economic support; men were not. Since husbands retained obligations to their families of origin, who resided in other villages, they were absent from their wives a good deal. Wives inevitably exercised as much or more power in family matters as their husbands. In addition, blood payment for killing a woman was higher than that for killing a man—another indicator of women's high status.[110]

Contact with whites often proved detrimental to Indian women. For example, among the Plains Indians, women's autonomy declined as the fur trade made it profitable for men to exploit women's labor. Yet even here their subordination was far from complete.[111]

New Guinea men dominated their women to a much greater degree. The difference can be seen in the gender ideologies of the two regions. The Hopi regard men's and women's roles to be distinct but complementary. Both are necessary; neither is devalued or feared.[112] By contrast, New Guinea men consider women to be inferior. Though resentful of men, they largely accept the male view:

[107] Schlegel (1977).

[108] Vaerting and Vaerting (1923:192).

[109] In matrilineal kinship systems, descent is traced through the female line. Children belong to their mother's descent group, not to their father's. Matrilocality refers to residence rules in which a married couple resides near the wife's family of origin.

[110] Hill (1935), Hamamsy (1957).

[111] Weltfish (1971), A. Klein (1983), Medicine (1983), E. Blackwood (1984). See, however, C. B. Richards (1957).

[112] Schlegel (1977:264).

> They agree that men are superior to women and know more.
> They attribute male superiority largely to the fact that men do
> not menstruate or bear children. They are ashamed of menstrua-
> tion and wish to be men.[113]

On the other hand, the men view women as highly threatening.[114]

The reasons for these differences cannot be explored here, but they have
major implications for gender transformation.[115] An Indian man who abandoned the male gender did not undergo a profound loss of status, privilege, or power. By contrast, a New Guinea man who switched gender
would become someone that his culture told him was profoundly inferior.
No wonder, then, that Indian men sometimes chose to become women, or
that their parents chose to feminize them; and that New Guinea men never
make that choice—notwithstanding their ambivalent gender identities.

I do not mean to imply that becoming a berdache was nothing more than
a matter of status-seeking. No doubt other factors helped to determine who
became a berdache and who did not. It is only to suggest that status considerations influenced the way Indians responded to these factors. A cross-
cultural study of male transvestism carried out by Munroe, Whiting, and
Hally lends support to this argument. They cross-classified a sample of societies on the basis of whether transvestism was present, and whether sex
distinctions in seven different spheres of activity were above or below the
media. Societies with low sex differentiation were significantly more likely
to have transvestism than those with high sex differentiation.[116]

What of the female berdache? Parental decisions to masculinize their
daughters were sometimes undertaken for practical reasons. If a Kaska
family had several daughters but no sons, they might raise one of the girls
as a boy so they would have someone who could hunt meat for them in
their old age. Such daughters dressed as men, hunted, and resisted male

---

[113] Langness (1967).

[114] Strathern (1972).

[115] That Indian wives were not taken from hostile clans must surely have been one of the
factors. In addition, many Indian tribes were, like the Navaho, matrilineal and matrilocal; the
New Guinea villages described earlier were patrilineal and patrilocal. As mentioned above,
matrilocality is generally associated with a relatively advantaged position for women because
wives are surrounded by their own kin, who can support them in the event of conflict with
their own husbands. Matrilineality implies that wealth and office are distributed on the basis
of relationship to women, and this, too, works to their advantage (Martin and Voorhies,
1975:224–29; Whyte, 1978; Sanday 1981:176–79). To be sure, not all American Indian groups
were matrilocal. However, some had become patrilocal only in recent times (Eggan, 1964:
45–77; Hudson, 1976:185), and the favorable status of women may have represented a cultural
survival reflecting earlier residential and descent rules.

[116] Munroe, Whiting, and Hally (1969).

sexual advances, preferring to take women as lovers.[117] In this instance, the berdache was a solution to a problem created by the malintegration of a gender-based division of labor and a distribution system based on immediate kinship ties. An elderly couple could not expect distant clan members to supply them with meat on a regular basis, and so couples who had no sons had to go without unless they adopted a son or transformed a daughter into one.

Economic considerations were also at work in the story of the Crow berdache who became a chief. At first she gave away the hides she brought in from the hunt, and cured and dried the meat herself. Eventually she decided to trade the hides, but this required dressing and preparing them—a traditionally female task. Having achieved great prestige in male terms, she was unwilling to spend her time on tasks that were conventionally carried out by women. Instead she found a wife, and in a few years married three more.[118]

Just as men will be more likely to abandon their gender when women's social standing is comparatively high, so women should have less incentive to do so under these conditions. Consistent with this observation, female berdaches were rare by comparison with their male counterparts.

Responses to Berdaches

The anthropological literature describes the social responses berdaches evoked within their own groups in seemingly contradictory terms. Many reports say they were accepted or even revered. On his first voyage down the Mississippi in 1673–77, Father Marquette found that among the Illinois and Nadowessi,

> They are summoned to the Councils, and nothing can be decided without their advice . . . through their profession of leading an Extraordinary life, they pass for Manitous. That is to say, for Spirits, or persons of Consequence.[119]

The Chippewas "looked upon them as Manitous, or at least as for great and incomparable geniuses."[120] Davydov, a Russian explorer who visited Kodiak Island off the coast of Alaska in 1812, reported that among the Koniag Indians, male children raised from birth or early childhood to be female "are not looked down upon, but instead they are obeyed in a settlement and are

---

[117] Honigmann (1964:129–30). Something analogous may have been responsible for the West Indian custom by which the sixth son of a woman who had no daughters was raised as a female (Waitz, 1864:376).

[118] Denig (1953).

[119] Thwaites (1900:129).

[120] W. J. Hoffman (1891:153).

not seldom wizards."[121] Among the Oglala, berdaches gave new names to tribal members who were undergoing a life crisis.[122] The Crow berdache chopped down the first tree for the Sun Dance.[123] At the conclusion of a successful military campaign, Cheyenne berdaches organized and conducted the Scalp Dance. Navaho, Creek, and Yokut berdaches performed special functions at funerals.[124] The Sioux, Fox, and Sack Indians feasted their berdaches and granted them "extraordinary privileges."[125] A Zuñi berdache

> was called upon by her own clan and also by the clans of her foster mother and father when a long prayer had to be repeated or a grace was to be offered over a feast. In fact she was the chief personage on many occasions.[126]

A seventeenth-century report indicates that the Yuma *had to* have four berdaches, suggesting that they performed essential ritual functions.[127]

As Davydov suggests, the attribution of unusual spiritual powers to berdaches in certain Indian groups enabled some to become shamans, thereby gaining the respect and high income of healers. However, even when no distinctive occupational role for berdaches is noted, sources commonly refer to the great respect in which they were held.[128] An Ojibwa male berdache's housekeeping skills made him a valued addition to a household.[129] Handicrafts fashioned by Oglala male berdaches were valued as masterpieces and commanded a good price.[130] Cheyenne berdaches often served as matchmakers, making them popular with young people.[131]

Other sources speak of berdaches as being accepted by their people without necessarily being held in unusually high esteem.[132] As individuals, they

[121] Quoted in Hrdlička (1944); see also Dall (1870:402).
[122] Powers (1977:38).
[123] Lowie (1935:48).
[124] Kroeber (1925:497–501), S.-E. Jacobs (1968).
[125] Catlin (1973:214–15).
[126] Stevenson (1904). The reservation of distinctive ritual roles for berdaches demonstrates that in at least *some* respects they were not treated just like any other member of the opposite sex.
[127] Signorini (1983). Stephen Murray informs me that Indians of the American southwest did *everything* in fours. That this extended to the berdache role only confirms its full integration into tribal culture.
[128] Smet (1905), Hill (1935), Denig (1953), Lurie (1953), Fages (1970), Landes (1970:195), Lafitau (1976).
[129] Tanner (1956:89–91).
[130] Powers (1977:23).
[131] Grinnell (1923:41–42).
[132] James (1822), Dorsey (1894), Kroeber (1925), Beals (1933), Olson (1936), Stewart (1942), Tanner (1956).

were not barred from high honors. Stories tell of a Snake woman who "by some fearless actions . . . has obtained the title of 'brave' and the privilege of admittance to the council of the chiefs,"[133] and of a Gros Ventre woman who was made one of the leading Crow chiefs in recognition of her daring military exploits.[134]

Alongside the sources that refer to berdaches as honored or accepted, there are others that describe negative responses. The Papago "scorned" berdaches;[135] the Cocopa "apparently disliked" them.[136] The Choctaws held them "in great contempt,"[137] the Seven Nations "in the most sovereign contempt."[138] The Klamath subjected berdaches to "scorn and taunting;"[139] the Sioux "derided" them.[140] Pima berdaches were ridiculed, though not otherwise sanctioned,[141] as were Mohave berdaches who claimed to possess the genitals of the opposite sex.[142] The Apache treated berdaches respectfully when they were present, but ridiculed them behind their backs.[143] Although the Zuñi accepted their berdache, "there was some joking and laughing about his ability to attract the young men to his home."[144] In some groups, berdaches' partners were also ridiculed or despised.[145]

While some reports of hostility seem to express the authors' feelings rather than those of the Indians, many—particularly those that describe berdaches as being ridiculed—have the ring of authenticity. The range of reported responses to the berdaches—from reverence to derision—has never been explained in the abundant anthropological literature. For the most part, anthropologists have merely described the berdache phenomenon or speculated about the reasons individuals became berdaches.

Some of the variability in responses can be traced to differential acculturation to white attitudes. At times Indians were influenced by exposure to white people's repugnance to transvestism and homosexuality. Elderly Lakotans considered berdaches to be holy, but young people ridiculed them, evidence that Navaho views have become less tolerant. One of Powers's Oglala informants was told that *winktas* (berdaches) were good sha-

[133] Smet (1905).
[134] Denig (1953).
[135] Drucker (1941).
[136] Gifford (1934).
[137] Bossu (1962:169).
[138] Charlevoix (1974).
[139] Spier (1930).
[140] Hassrick (1964).
[141] W. W. Hill (1938).
[142] Devereux (1937).
[143] Opler (1941, 1969).
[144] Stewart (1960).
[145] Linton (1936), Mirsky (1937), Drucker (1941), Devereux (1947).

mans, but that those who took them as sexual partners would be tortured after death, a story that has all the earmarks of Christian influence.[146]

Yet it is doubtful that all the reports of negative responses can be dismissed as reflecting white influence; those that describe ridicule may reflect an indigenous response. After all, the prevalent white attitude toward homosexuality and transvestism has until recently not been mild amusement, but rather horror and disgust.

Data on Indian responses to berdaches are too sparse to permit a rigorous comparative analysis. The majority of ethnographic reports are brief and superficial, often devoting no more than a sentence or two to the topic. Some Indian groups felt that the berdaches should be kept secret from whites, and berdaches themselves learned that it was best to keep their identities to themselves.[147] Consequently, our approach must be tentative and exploratory. We suggest that berdaches were both honored *and* ridiculed, and seek to explain this seemingly incongruous response.

One possible explanation can be derived from the berdache's relationship to warfare. We have already cast doubt on the contention that men assumed the berdache role primarily to escape fighting. Yet, even if this explanation is false, it is possible that the Indians themselves believed it. Men who routinely risked injury and death in combat might have envied and resented men whose gender role allowed them to avoid this risk. Ridicule could have been a way of coping with this ambivalence.

This explanation implies that berdaches were ridiculed not because of their homosexuality, but because of their gender. Such a distinction is meaningful because, as we already noted, not all berdaches were homosexual, and not all individuals who engaged in homosexual acts were berdaches. Yet this explanation is questionable. Among the Mohave, ridicule focused on the male berdache's claims to have a female anatomy rather than on his supposed cowardice. Mohave berdaches themselves teased other men for being cowardly,[148] something they would not have done had they themselves been vulnerable to this accusation. Sometimes a berdache's partners were ridiculed, even though they did engage in combat.[149] Had psychological ambivalence connected with fighting been responsible for the ridicule, we would expect the ridiculers to have been exclusively male. In some groups, however, men accepted the berdaches but women scorned them.[150]

Landes' study of the Santee Dakota, a Sioux-speaking group, suggests

[146] Powers (1977:122, 1983).
[147] Kroeber (1940), W. L. Williams (1986).
[148] Devereux (1937).
[149] Linton (1936), Devereux (1937), Mirsky (1937), Drucker (1941).
[150] Spier (1930). Callender and Kochems (1983b) conclude that the few statements describing

an alternative explanation. She describes the process by which, over a period of years, a young Santee man became a *winkta*. As a boy, he had preferred beadwork and housework to boys' sports. With approval for his
transformation coming through his dreams, he adopted female attire and
forms of speech.[151]

The *winkta's* transvestism elicited no special response until he began to
flirt with and attempt to seduce many of the men in his village. At this
point the villagers held a formal ceremony exiling the *winkta* for life. This
was a very severe penalty, greater than that imposed for homicide. Following his exile, the *winkta* took up residence in a neighboring village. There
he was welcomed by the women, who were grateful for his contribution to
women's work (male berdaches often excelled in performing traditionally
female tasks), and by the men, who were happy to partake of his "hospitality" (not described further, but presumably the reference is to sexual
hospitality). Despite this seemingly positive reception, the *winkta* was per-
sistently subjected to flirtatious teasing.

Why would two Santee villages have responded so differently to the
same behavior? Almost all the men in a Santee village were members of a
single patrilineal clan. Kinship was classificatory, with remote ties counting
almost as strongly as immediate ones. Marriage was exogamous, with residence preferentially patrilocal. Thus the men of the *winkta's* natal village
were members of his own patriclan and consequently forbidden to him by
rules of exogamy. The *wintka*, then, was exiled not because of his homosexual proclivities or his adoption of a female gender, but because of his disregard for incest taboos. Had he attempted to seduce his classificatory
sisters, he would also have been exiled, for this was the standard penalty in
cases of heterosexual incest.

The men of the second village were classificatory cross-cousins. As such,
they were acceptable marriage or sexual partners for the *winkta*: "Sexual
liberties were allowed between a berdache and men of the strange village,
who were all unrelated to him."[152] Yet, if sexual liberties were allowed, why
was the *winkta* ridiculed for taking advantage of them? The explanation lies
in joking relationships. Landes notes that

> joking relatives—cross-cousins and siblings-in-law—were prop-
> erly maligned in public. . . . Cross-cousins of both sexes and
> siblings-in-law of both sexes were supposed to joke publicly. As
> among the Ojibwa, this included flirting that was officially "in-

---

women as hostile toward berdaches were "brief, unconvincing, and sometimes derivative,"
so too much should not be made of this datum.

[151] Landes (1968).

[152] Landes (1968:128).

nocent" but that actually ran often to sexual intercourse, and it
included public taunting which also might ignore limits,[153]

The institutionalization of teasing and ridicule was far from unique to the
Santee; on the contrary, such joking relationships were an indigenous cul-
ture-trait that was present throughout North America.[154] These relationships did not always involve cross-cousins, as they did among the Santee,
the Ojibwa, and the Cree; sometimes they involved aunts and uncles or
siblings-in-law, or even persons who did not stand in a special kinship relationship to one another.[155] The joking often involved sexual themes.

The single example of the Santee makes a weak basis from which to gen-
eralize to all Indian groups. Unfortunately, the published ethnographic reports do not provide much information about the contexts for the social
responses in other groups. Where ridicule is reported, we are told little
about the social identities of the ridiculers and their kinship ties, if any, to
the berdache. From this single example, then, I suggest that in the very few
instances where a strongly negative response is reported, it was not to the
status of the berdaches or to their sexual preferences, but to their violations
or attempted violations of traditional rules of sexual exogamy. The more
frequently reported ridicule may have amounted to nothing more than the
treatment persons in joking relationships—ordinarily relatives, but sometimes others—meted out to one another. Indeed, in many instances it may
have been a way to signal sexual interest.[156]

What makes this generalization more than speculative is that the Santee
were not alone in subjecting homosexual relationships to the same rules of
incest and exogamy that governed heterosexual relationships. Hill mentions that this was the case for the Navaho *nadle*, or berdache.[157] A number
of South American and Melanesian cultures also tolerated or even institu-

---

[153] Landes (1968:37–38).

[154] Landes (1937), Drucker (1941:132), Stewart (1942), D. Eggan (1943), Spindler and Spindler
(1957), Aberle (1961), Driver (1969:383–84), Hoebel (1978:34–35).

[155] Personal communications from Walter L. Williams, and from Charles Callender and Lee
Kochems. Joking relationships are also found on other continents (Radcliffe-Brown, 1940).
Thus it is a convention for paternal cousins of the same age, sex, and generation of the Nuer to
trade obscenities covering "every possible kind of sexual act, the sodomy motif being the most
prominent" (Evans-Pritchard, 1951:159–60).

[156] D. F. Greenberg (1985). This interest may have been fairly widespread. Powers (1977:123)
indicates that Oglala Sioux men—how many is not stated, but one senses that it was not just a
few—flirted with berdaches. The Zuñis who kidded berdaches about their ability to attract
young men (Powers, 1960) sound envious. Broch (1977) reports the simultaneous teasing and
flirtatious expression of sexual interest in a young Hare Indian whose behavior was not unlike
that of a berdache.

[157] W. W. Hill (1935).

tionalized homosexuality while restricting it to the same rules of exogamy that applied to heterosexual relationships.[158]

As for descriptions of the ridiculing of berdaches, none of the sources suggests that berdaches were subject to ridicule more than other joking partners. Devereux, who reports several episodes in which Mohave berdaches were teased,[159] also notes that the Mohave attitude toward sex was "completely humoristic," so much so that it was difficult to obtain serious answers to interview questions.[160]

The teasing male berdaches received, then, might have centered on their homosexual preferences without having been caused by them. Plausibly, berdaches would have been teased just as much had their sexual partners been of the opposite sex. Where berdaches' partners were ridiculed, this too could have been in the context of a joking relationship, without signifying anything deeper about attitudes toward homosexuality. In American Indian cultures, persons of respect and prestige, including chiefs, were not spared ridicule. It was a mild form of social control used to take pretentious people down a peg or two.[161] Consequently, there would have been no inconsistency between ridiculing berdaches (especially when they made false claims about their anatomy) and holding them in respect, or even regarding them as holy.

Two factors may account for the Indian acceptance of berdaches, and their homosexual involvements with other men. First, by comparison with New Guinea "homosexual" cultures, Indian male identities do not appear to have been so insecure. Though fathers were sometimes away from home hunting or raiding, they were sufficiently present to serve as a secure source of identification for most male children. Thus a man who identified himself as female was not psychologically threatening to other men. By contrast, the emphasis placed on the elimination of residual female identity in New Guinea male rituals suggests that New Guinea men would find a berdache too anxiety-provoking to tolerate. He would remind them of those layers of identity that they strive to repress.

Whitehead notes a second likely factor: by comparison with the New Guinea societies that institutionalize homosexuality, American Indian groups were more individualistic.[162] All males of postinitiation age participate in the male cult of a New Guinea village. By contrast, many North American Indian tribes had religiously focused men's sodalities (private as-

---

[158] Roheim (1933), Deacon (1934), F. E. Williams (1936), Lévi-Strauss (1943, 1969), Van Baal (1966), Godelier (1976), R. A. Kelly (1976), Schieffelin (1976), Hugh-Jones (1979), Herdt (1981).

[159] Devereux (1937).

[160] Devereux (1950).

[161] Burland (1973), Hoebel (1978).

[162] Whitehead (1981).

sociations) whose membership was voluntary and did not include all clans or village members. The contents of religious bundles (medicine bundles) were individualized. The greater size of many tribes (which often numbered in the thousands, while New Guinea village populations are often less than a thousand) and their higher level of technology supported a degree of occupational specialization unknown in New Guinea. Important career decisions were often decided by dreams, a method that lies outside direct social control and therefore implies a certain degree of individualism. It is consistent with this broad pattern of individual choice that individuals should be able to select their own gender. As the choice did not threaten any value that was critical to the well-being of the group as a whole, there was no reason to suppress it.

The situation may have been a little more complicated for female berdaches. The highly successful Crow and Snake berdaches achieved positions of great influence and prestige. As noted, a woman berdache was given a prominent part in Zuñi clan ritual. No stigma was attached to the role among the Quinault Indians of the Pacific Northwest.[163] No doubt aided by her success at hunting, farming, and treating illness, a Mohave *hwame* had no trouble finding wives, though she and her wives were subjected to ridicule.[164] All this is consistent with the responses to male berdaches.

That some Indian groups had difficulty conceiving of women adopting male identities is suggested by the response of Papago informants to a question about woman berdaches: they laughed at the very idea.[165] Their mirth may well have reflected the high social status of Papago women, who told Underhill that while men performed rituals to gain power from the spirits, women did not need to do so because they already had powers without ceremonies or spirits.[166] Why, then, would a woman want to become like a man?

Schlegel points out that female berdaches might have been rare because in matrilineal societies they imply a loss of reproductive potential to the lineage, something members might want to discourage.[167] The existence of female berdaches among the Crow, Kaska, Navaho, and Western Apache—all of them matrilineal—does not entirely discredit this argument, for those groups lacked a strong clan or lineage organization capable of enforcing its interests.[168] Nevertheless, an undercurrent of uneasiness about the loss of reproductive potential implied by lesbianism shows up in legends from

[163] Olson (1936:99).
[164] Devereux (1937).
[165] Underhill (1939:186–87).
[166] Underhill (1939:91–92).
[167] Schlegel (1983).
[168] In a world sample of societies, Paige and Paige (1981:72–78) find fraternal interest groups

several groups about women who gave birth to monstrous babies after having sexual relations with women.[169] A similar legend appears in one of the Hindu Puranas.[170]

More broadly speaking, we might expect some attempt to discourage or punish transgenderal lesbianism whenever this threatens an important interest of the group or the interests of a powerful segment of the group, provided the group is organized so that it can uphold its interests collectively. In a patrilineal society such an interest might be the loss of a daughter or sister to give to a prospective ally or provider of a bride in another lineage.

Transgenderal Homosexuality Outside North America

Social roles strikingly similar to the berdache have been reported for many of the stateless Central and South American Indian groups, including foragers, horticulturists, and herders. A late-eighteenth-century Jesuit missionary to Argentina found wizards of both sexes among the Moluches and Puelches in the valley of the Rio Negro and the territory north of it:

> The male wizards are obliged (as it were) to leave their sex, and to dress themselves in female apparel, and are not permitted to marry, though the female ones or witches may. They are generally chosen for this office when they are children, and a preference is always shown to those who at that early time of life discover an effeminate disposition. They are clothed very early in female attire, and presented with the drum and rattle belonging to the profession they are to follow.[171]

Since the sixteenth century, transvestite shamans have also been reported among the Araucanians, a large tribe living in southern Chile and parts of Argentina. In earlier times the shamans communicated with the spirits before any major group decision, such as war and peace, could be made; today they are respected, though also feared for their supernatural powers. Nevertheless, in recent years the shaman role has increasingly been filled by women.[172] Male-transvestite shamans have also been re-

---

to occur less often in matrilocal societies; since matrilocality and matrilineality tend to go together (Martin and Voorhies, 1975:185), that is probably true in matrilineal societies as well.

[169] W. Jones (1907:151), Lowie (1910:223).

[170] O'Flaherty (1980:40–41). These legends seem to reflect the belief, identified by La Barre (1984) as Paleolithic in origin, that an infant's bones derive from its father. In the absence of one, the child will be misshapen. It should be noted that none of these legends describes gender transformation. It is not clear that the fear they imply would carry over to a relationship between two women, one of whom has changed her gender. Some versions of the story are less fearful of lesbianism (Elwin, 1949:96).

[171] Falkner (1935:117).

[172] E. R. Smith (1855), Titiev (1951:115–17), Hilger (1957:68, 128), Steward (1963), Faron

ported for the Guajire, a cattle-herding people of northwest Venezuela and north Colombia,[173] and the Tehuelche, hunter-gatherers of Argentina.[174]

As among North American Indians, not all the reported instances of transgenderal homosexuality or transvestism involve shamanism.[175] Social responses to male-to-female gender transformation in these groups are similar to those of North American Indians. Berdaches were accepted, encouraged, condoned, respected, used sexually, but were also the subject of frequent joking. There are very few reports of lesbianism, suggesting that it may not have been as common as in North America. Wilbert reports that it occurred among Yanomamo women, but was considered "repulsive,"[176] without mentioning who considered it so, or what if anything was done about it.

A role analogous to that of the berdache is reported for parts of the East Indies. The *manang bali* of the Iban (Sea Dyak) of turn-of-the-century Sarawak (in northwestern Borneo) adopted female costume in obedience to supernatural instructions conveyed in dreams and seduced young men. Toward the end of the nineteenth century they were popular as curers—in fact, they were the most highly regarded of shamans. They excelled at arbitrating disputes, and were generous in using their wealth to aid followers in need. Many became village chiefs.[177] They were also present among the Ngadju Dyak of Southern Borneo,[178] the Bugis of South Celebes, the Pelew Islanders, and in Malaya.[179] Once common, the *manang bali* has been slowly disappearing. Some were still alive in 1951 when Derek Freeman did fieldwork in what is now Malaysia, but the role is now virtually unknown.[180]

(1964), Metraux (1967:181–83, 206, 234). W. L. Williams (1986:141) attributes the shift to the Spanish suppression of homosexuality.

[173] Watson-Franke (1974).

[174] Cooper (1963).

[175] Karsch-Haack (1911:363–446) summarizes the earlier sources for male homosexuality among Latin American Indians. More recent sources include Beals (1932:122, 205), Freyre (1946:117, 223–24), Steward and Faron (1959:223), G. and A. Reichel-Dolmatoff (1961:49–50), Cooper (1963), Hernandez de Alba (1963), Kirchhoff (1963), Métraux (1963), Murra (1963), Steward (1963), Salmoral (1966), Guerra (1971:55–56, 76, 85–86, 124, 154), Wilbert (1972:101), Gregor (1977:254), Wagley (1977:160), Clastres (1977:90–92), Hemming (1978:386), Kracke (1978). S. W. Foster (1985) has compiled a useful bibliography of literature dealing with homosexuality among Central and South American Indians, but not all entries involve transgenderal homosexuality (e.g., Spix and Martius, 1824:246, and Reichel-Dolmatoff, 1971:19–20).

[176] Wilbert (1972:55).

[177] Perelaer (1870:ch. 1), H. L. Roth (1968:270–71), Sandin (1957), Sutlive (1976).

[178] Kraef (1954), Wales (1957:80–81), Sandin (1957), Eliade (1964:352), Wulff (1960), Schärer (1963:53–59).

[179] Kubary (1888:35), Main (1913:196), Frazer (1962:2.204–6, 253, 256), H. L. Roth (1968:270–71, 282).

[180] Jensen (1974:143–45).

Among the Paleo-Siberians (Chukchee, Koryak, Kamchadal, Asiatic Eskimo), male shamans were ordered by a female spirit to dress as women. As the spirit often became a supernatural spouse who was jealous of earthly women, many of the shamans acquired male sexual partners who had intercourse with them anally, and most of them married other men. However, some continued to live with their wives and fathered children, even while dressing as women. In contrast with the American Indian practice, entry into shamanism may not have occurred mainly in adolescence. Some elderly men with wives and children became transvestite shamans.[181]

Tranvestism also used to be practiced by shamans in the Vietnamese countryside,[182] Burma,[183] in India among the Pardhi, a hunting people,[184] and in the southeast, by the Lhoosais,[185] as well as in Korea.[186] It may also have been present in the Nepal Himalayas.[187]

Late-eighteenth-century explorers and missionaries who visited Tahiti invariably noticed men who dressed as women and who engaged in homosexual relations. Captain Bligh, one of the first to write of them, believed that nowhere in the world were they so common and observed that they were as highly respected and esteemed as women.[188] According to the English missionary James Wilson, *mahūs*

> chose this vile way of life when young; putting on the dress of a woman they follow the same employments, are under the same prohibitions with respect to food, etc., and seek the courtship of men as women do, nay are more jealous of the men who cohabit with them, and always refuse to sleep with women.[189]

The principal chiefs took them as wives. Homosexuality that did not entail gender transformation for either of the partners was also common and accepted.[190]

There are still *mahūs* in Tahiti, but not many; rarely is there more than

---

[181] Rechberg und Rothenlöwen (1813), W. G. Sumner (1901), Bogoras (1904:449 ff.), Jochelson (1905:52–53), Czaplicka (1914), Sternberg (1925), Ohlmarks (1939:293–301), Ducey (1956), Eliade (1964:257–58), Bleibtreu-Ehrenberg (1984).

[182] Heiman and Lê (1975).

[183] Webster (1948:192), Orr (1951), Spiro (1977:229–30).

[184] Kosanbi (1967).

[185] Lewin (1870:255).

[186] Hagenauer (1929), Osgood (1951), C. A. Clark (1961), Rutt (1961), Henthorn (1971:45), S. O. Murray (1987h).

[187] R. L. Jones (1976), Sagent (1976).

[188] Bligh (1792:2.16–17).

[189] J. Wilson (1799:200).

[190] Turnbull (1813:382), Lisiansky (1814:199), Dulaure (1825:419–34), Karsch-Haack (1911:235–42), Williamson (1924:392–93), Bouge (1955), Danielsson (1956:147–50), Robert Levy (1971, 1973:130–32), Oliver (1974:369–74).

one to a village. They are somewhat effeminate, associate with women, do women's work, and dress as women. They say they wish they had women's bodies. Their sexual partners, whom they fellate, say that they resort to them only occasionally, when women are not available, or because they provide greater pleasure than women. Young women regard *mahūs* with a bit of contempt, thinking of them as sissies who lack the courage and prowess they admire in conventionally gendered men.[191] Though some men consider *mahūs* disgusting, most regard them as "natural" and are not judgmental. Their partners are considered perfectly normal.[192] There are also *mahus* on the Marquesan Islands.[193] They

> adopted the life of a woman, dressed in women's garb, allowing their hair to grow long. They devoted themselves to all the activities and relationships of women rather than to those of men. Native informants told me that these men were not deformed physically, but that they merely preferred a woman's life and desired men.[194]

Today the *mahū*'s distinguishing feature is his gender, not his sexual orientation, which may or may not be homosexual.[195] Sources dating back to the late eighteenth century indicate that homosexuality was not restricted to the *mahūs*, but was quite common among other men as well.[196]

Both male and female homosexuality were present and accepted on the Austral Islands, and among the New Zealand Maori.[197] On Tonga (one of the Friendly Islands) the transgenderal homosexual role was recognized; it was called *fakaleiti*; in Pukapuka, it was *wakawawine*.[198] Until recently, Mangaia, one of the Cook Islands, had several transvestites, but according to Marshall, they did not choose male sexual partners.[199] Nor did the transvestites of Rapa, south of the Society Islands. Indeed, one extremely effeminate man had a wife and several children.[200] Perhaps their equivalents in earlier times did engage in homosexual relations, but it is also possible that *mahūs* were always defined by gender transformation, not by sexual orientation.

[191] Oliver (1981:293).

[192] Gilbert Herdt tells me that some of the Tahitian *mahūs* have recently taken jobs as female impersonators in nightclubs for tourists, a striking case of cultural adaptation to Westernization.

[193] Suggs (1966:83).

[194] Handy (1923:103).

[195] Biddle (1968), Kirkpatrick (1983:177–78).

[196] Danielsson (1956:149).

[197] Karsch-Haack (1911:235), Danielsson (1956:149), Laurie (1985).

[198] Karsch-Haack (1911:244–48); Ritchie and Ritchie (1979:100).

[199] D. S. Marshall (1972).

[200] Hanson (1970:112).

Some sources assert that homosexuality was rare in Samoa, Hawaii, and the Marshall Islands, and the subject of scorn when it occurred.[201] However, Mead documented extensive casual involvement in homosexual relations on the part of Samoan boys and girls,[202] and Munroe found institutionalized male transvestism to be long-standing; the role incumbents were called *fa'afafine*.[203] The Hawaiian reports stem from visits made long after missionaries had been active, and traditional culture all but destroyed. Earlier sources confirm the presence of homosexuality for the Marshall Islands,[204] and indicate that it was common in Hawaii before contact, at least among the aristocracy.[205] The translation of *mahū* as "gentle" or "feminine" in early missionary dictionaries for Samoa and Hawaii suggests that the role was institutionalized in both places.[206] It has not completely disappeared in Hawaii, where beauty contests for *mahūs* are well attended.

Scholars have given much less attention to homosexuality in sub-Saharan Africa than in the Americas or Pacific Islands. Still, religious transgenderal homosexuality is reported for a number of tribes across Africa.[207] The *mugawe*, a powerful religious leader of the Kenyan Meru, is considered a complement to the male political leaders and consequently must exemplify feminine qualities: he wears women's clothing and adopts women's hairstyles; he is often homosexual, and sometimes marries a man.[208] Among the Kwayama, a tribe of Angolan Bantu cultivators and herders, many diviners, augurers, and diagnosers of illness wear women's clothing, do women's work, and become secondary spouses of men whose other wives are female.[209] South African Zulu diviners are usually women, but roughly 10 percent are male transvestites;[210] their sexual tastes are hinted at in S. G. Lee's remark that "in Zululand the marriage of a male diviner is greeted

[201] Kramer and Nevermann (1938:186 ff., Wedgewood (1943), Handy (1951/52).

[202] Mead (1928:70, 136, 147–48).

[203] Munroe (1980), Ritchie and Ritchie (1979:100).

[204] Hernsheim (1880), Ploss (1917:521–26).

[205] Malo (1903:93, 103), Kamekau (1961:234), Beaglehole (1961:1226), W. L. Williams (1985).

[206] Danielsson (1956:450).

[207] Older sources for African homosexuality, not all of it transgenderal, are summarized in Karsch-Haack (1911:131–84, 471–87); Dynes (1983) lists more recent sources. In addition, see Browne (1799:293), Delafosse (1912:92), Tauxier (1912:569–70), Butt-Thompson (1929:175), Lhote (1956:28), Krige (1965:276–77), and the references cited in this and the next chapter. Some sources refer to cultic homosexuality without specifically mentioning gender transformation (e.g., Talbot, 1926:766, 1927:34–36), though it may have been present. In some cultures, transvestism may not imply homosexuality. Thus some Bala (Basonge) men avoid work and wear women's clothing, but deny any homosexuality (Merriam, 1972). Of course, this denial need not be taken at face value.

[208] Needham (1973).

[209] Estermann (1976:197).

with Rabelaisian incredulity."[211] A hundred years ago, many eunuchs lived in Ba-kongo villages of the lower Congo and participated in a cult associated with the moon.[212] Some Hausa male prostitutes in Katsina, a city in the north of Nigeria, adopt female garb and mannerisms and participate in a spirit-possession cult,[213] but the cult and its association with male homosexuality almost surely antedate urbanization and Islam.[214] Brazilian and Haitian cults derived from West African religions also feature cross-dressing and male homosexuality.[215]

Homosexuality associated with male-to-female gender change, but seemingly lacking a special religious significance, appears in a number of other groups, including the pastoral Nandi of Kenya,[216] the Dinka[217] and Nuer of the Sudan,[218] the agricultural Konso and Amhara of Ethiopia,[219] the Ottoro of Nubia, [220] the Fanti of Ghana,[221] the Ovimbundu, a herding and slave-trading people of Angola,[222] the Thonga, farmers of Rhodesia,[223] the Tanala and Bara of Madagascar,[224] the Wolof of Senegal,[225] and the Lango, Iteso, Gisu, and Sebei of Uganda.[226]

For some of these peoples the transvestite role was institutionalized; in others probably not. But even where it was not, the transformation of gender seems to have been pretty much taken at face value. The Amhara have difficulty understanding why a man would give up male privileges, but tolerate those who do so.[227] Though immediate kin are ashamed of male transvestites (presumably seeing them as failing to live up to an ideal of

---

[210] Ngubane (1977:142).

[211] S. G. Lee (1958).

[212] Johnston (1884:402–9).

[213] Pittin (1983); see also M. F. Smith (1954:64), P. Hill (1967:233), and Besmer (1983:18–19).

[214] J. Greenberg (1941, 1946), Besmer (1983).

[215] Landes (1940, 1947), Leacock and Leacock (1972:104–6), Fry (1985), Trevisan (1986: 171–74), S. O. Murray (1987 f.).

[216] Karsch-Haack, 1911:178–79), Bryk (1933:227–30).

[217] Karsch-Haack (1911:174).

[218] MacDermot (1972:119).

[219] Hallpike (1972:150–51), Messing (1957:550).

[220] Nadel (1955).

[221] Christensen (1954:92–93, 143).

[222] Falk (1920), Hambly (1934a:181, 1934b), Weyer (1961).

[223] Karsch-Haack (1911:178–80), Colson (1958:139–40). These early sources cast doubt on Junod's (1962:98) contention that masturbation and homosexuality were unknown to the Thonga before European contact. He himself concedes that there are linguistic grounds for thinking homosexuality indigenous.

[224] Leguevel de Lacombe (1840:97–98), Linton (1933:298–99), Kardiner (1939:265–66, 296).

[225] Gorer (1935:11), Crowder (1959:68).

[226] Driberg (1923:110), Laurance (1957:107), La Fontaine (1959:34), Goldschmidt (1967: 133–39).

[227] Female-to-male transvestism is also known to the Amhara; it, too, is accepted as an "act

masculinity), no one else is; women accept them as if they were siblings.[228] Though Senegalese Moslems deny "men-women" burial, they are not otherwise subject to discrimination. In fact, they are socially sought after as the best conversationalists and dancers.[229]

Origins of the Pattern

The Toradjus of the Celebes explain transgenderal homosexuality in much the same way anthropologists explain American Indian berdaches: cowardice. Prior to pacification, they say, men were warriors. Those who feared fighting became *bajasas* (deceivers), a socially accepted role, and wore women's clothing. Once fighting was suppressed (and missionaries began propagandizing), fewer *bajasas* were seen.[230]

However, because many of the non-American societies in which analogous roles are found are not exceptionally bellicose, anthropological speculation about the origins of the pattern has rarely focused on cowardice. It has centered instead on the association between religious function and transvestism.[231] Some scholars have seen the transvestite priest or shaman as a corporeal representation of a hermaphroditic or androgynous god who symbolizes the unity that overcomes sex differences.[232] Yet transvestite shamans are more often devotees of a goddess than of a double-sexed deity.[233] In some American Indian groups, berdaches did not seem to have any special religious function; nor did the Polynesian *mahūs.*

On the other hand, linguistic evidence from Polynesia suggests that *mahūs* may at one time have been shamans. In Maori, *mahu* means "to heal." In Mangaian, *mau* means "to be healed." In Samoan, *mafu* can be "to heal a wound" or "a male homosexual."[234] Evidently, the transsexual role

---

of God," but men suspect that it is motivated by a desire to gain male privileges (Messing, 1957:550).

[228] Messing (1957).

[229] Gorer (1935:11), Crowder (1959:68).

[230] Kraef (1954).

[231] But see Sauer (1802:176). Another explanatory strategy stems from psychiatry. La Barre (1970:182) postulates that transvestite shamanism is a manifestation of preoedipal paranoia. Ducey (1956) concludes that the shamans have oedipal desires and castration anxiety as well as a preoedipal fantasy of identification with the mother and her imagined phallus. Whatever the worth of these suggestions, they do not explain why the transvestites become shamans, or why some cultures institutionalize the role and others do not.

[232] Baumann (1955:354), Eliade (1964).

[233] For the Pelew Islanders, see Kubary (1888:35); for the Limbu of Nepal, see R. L. Jones (1976) and Sagent (1976); for Algonquin Indians see Keating (1824:221–22). Hermaphroditic deities seem to have been primarily a European phenomenon.

[234] Andrews and Andrews (1944:76), Milner (1966:119), Tregear (1969:194).

was once joined to that of the shamanizing healer, but the roles then become separated.

Alternatively, male-to-female transvestite religious leaders have been interpreted as bridges between "primitive matriarchy" and a later patriarchy. On this theory, the first shamans were women, but as their power diminished they were replaced by men who at first had to impersonate women.[235] This thesis is said to be supported by the absence of female-to-male priestly transvestism.

The paucity of historical data on gender relations for most kinship-structured societies and the absence of contemporary societies in which women literally rule men have led anthropologists to treat theories that invoke primitive matriarchy with great skepticism. In historical times, transitions between matricentered and patricentered descent and residence rules have occurred in both directions.[236] What's more, there is little in the sources to suggest that institutionalized gender transformation was transitional. In many societies it seems to have been quite stable until destroyed by contact with Europeans. Moreover, though female-to-male transvestism occurs less often than male-to-female, it is not unknown.

The archaeological record suggests that shamanism dates back at least to the Upper Paleolithic period, but it does not provide any evidence about transvestism. Men wearing animal skins appear in cave paintings in Spain and France beginning about 35,000 years ago, and later in Scandinavian and North African rock carvings. These figures are usually interpreted as shamans engaged in sympathetic hunting or increase magic,[237] though it is also possible that they represent the "spirit of the animals." Rock carvings of men with erections (or conceivably wearing penis sheaths) suggest that Stone Age dances or rituals may have had a sexual component.[238] As far as we can tell, though, these representations do not show cross-dressing. This doesn't mean it didn't occur, only that we have no pictorial record of it.[239]

Around 25,000 to 22,000 years ago, Europeans began carving "Venus" figurines from stone and ivory. They are found as far east as Siberia, and in Central Europe they persist into the Neolithic. Similar statuettes, of an Asiatic appearance, are found in the lowest levels of excavation in Mexico and

[235] Czaplicka (1914), Kraef (1954), Wales (1957:80–81), Eliade (1964:157–58), A. Evans (1978:17).

[236] Ember and Ember (1971), Divale (1975:1984).

[237] Campbell (1969:299–312).

[238] Davidson (1967:23–25), Lommel (1967), Campbell (1969:282–312), A. Ross (1973).

[239] A few pieces of mobiliary art from the Aurignacian and Magdalenian eras may be double-sexed, and it is possible that they represent hermaphroditic deities or transvestite shamans. But there is too little to make much of (Giedion, 1964:180–81).

Peru, but disappear with the first signs of warfare.[240] They are usually regarded as Mother Goddess idols, responsible for fertility, but may have had more complex connotations.[241]

The remains of a temple found in the Ukraine and dating from 5000 to 3500 B.C. contain large numbers of clay women, but only a few men, suggesting that early goddess worship may have been maintained primarily by women,[242] but this is late evidence and from a single location only. In many contemporary primitive cultures, men worship goddesses, and this could certainly have been true in Stone Age cultures as well. In any event, the sculptures are not detailed enough to tell us whether some of the seemingly female figures are actually male transvestites.

The very simplest contemporary bands of food collectors, such as those of the African pygmies, do not have shamans; they appear only at the point when bands undergo a transition to numerically larger and socially more complex tribal structures.[243] It is not known for sure just when in European prehistory this transition first occurred. Most scholars have assumed that Paleolithic Europeans lived in thinly dispersed nomadic hunting bands of very small size, with the transition to more complex, sedentary, tribal structures taking place only when food sources were domesticated in the third millennium B.C. (several thousand years earlier in the Middle East). However, the archaeological record does not exclude the possibility that there were tribes in the Upper Paleolithic. There is evidence for permanent occupation in at least some regions of Europe during interglacial and interstadial periods, when food resources were abundant.[244] It is thus likely that some Paleolithic bands evolved into complex clan structures and had shamans. The extremely wide dispersion of the transvestite shaman role, among peoples whose later ways of life have been very diverse, suggests that the role does date back to the late Paleolithic (if not earlier). Migrations subsequently carried it long distances, for example, from Siberia into the Americas. The Polynesians who settled in Madagascar may have brought institutionalized male transvestism with them. There is no reason to think that men replaced women as shamans (though it is possible they did); it is

[240]Spinden (1928: ch 1, 51, 53), G. R. Levy (1963:54–55, 79–80, 1979), Gimbutas (1981, 1982:9, 152), H. Schutz (1983:25).

[241]Hawkes (1958), Marschack (1972:281–340).

[242]Gimbutas (1982:72–73).

[243]O'Keefe (1982:35–54).

[244]R. G. Klein (1980), Voss (1980), Gamble (1983), Jochim (1983). When wild food is sufficiently abundant, sedentary tribes can form on the basis of a food-collecting economy. Thus the aboriginal California Indians supported a tribal structure and high population densities by hunting, fishing, and gathering (Baumhof, 1963; Testart, 1982). Proximity to salmon fishing may have lent itself to tribal formation in Paleolithic Europe (Wobst, 1976; Rowley-Conwy, 1983; Jochim, 1983).

equally possible that men and women both shamanized throughout the Old Stone Age and have continued to do so up to the present in many groups, the men evoking awe by bridging or transcending gender categories.

Although our sources are too sketchy to permit a full analysis for most of the world regions that have had transgenderal homosexuality in fairly recent times, our earlier suggestion that the acceptance of the berdache reflects the generally high social status of women may have had validity in other culture regions as well. The Paleo-Siberians appear to have been matrilocal,[245] a marital arrangement favorable to female power. Among the Kamchadal, wives had the sole right to dispose to family property. Women are considered to have been "dominant" among the Dyaks.[246] Robert Levy has documented the low degree of gender differentiation in Tahitian culture: body postures and movements strike Westerners as androgynous, and traits like aggressiveness and gentleness are not sex-linked.[247] Most personal names can be held by males or females, and the Tahitian language has no grammatical categories based on gender. Although some activities are carried out mainly by one sex or the other, most are done by both. Apparently gender distinctions were larger before European contact, but even then

> The early observers took note of women chiefs with effective political power, of women participating in sports (sometimes wrestling with men), of upper-class women dominating and sometimes beating their husbands, and of many women who were curious, active, independent, and seemingly very little under submission to their men. For purposes of political power, descent was reckoned in both the maternal and paternal lines, and, as indicated by the mention of female chiefs, a woman could sometimes find herself, because of her geneological superiority and abilities, in a position of power.[248]

Similarly, Peacock notes with regard to traditional Indonesian culture that "'Pure' Javanese tradition does not condemn homosexuality and regards a very wide range of behavior, from he-man to rather (in our terms) 'effeminate,' as properly masculine."[249] With gender differentiation so low, the social distance a man had to travel to take on a female social identity was not great, and the sex of someone's sexual partner was simply not very important.

[245] Czaplicka (1914).
[246] Vaerting and Vaerting (1923:74, 204).
[247] Robert Levy (1973:232–39).
[248] Robert Levy (1973:234).
[249] Peacock (1968:204).

EGALITARIAN HOMOSEXUALITY

In both transgenerational and transgenderal homosexuality, partners are differentiated on the basis of their social characteristics and the roles they play in sexual encounters. The younger member of the male transgenerational pair is ideal-typically the insertee, or receptive partner. While at a later stage of life he may become an "insertor," or "active" partner for someone younger, he does not reverse roles to become active with an older partner or receptive with a younger; to do so would be highly deviant. In transgenderal homosexuality the partners are distinguished by their gender, which in turn governs the sexual roles they play.

Egalitarian homosexuality is distinguished from these patterns in that roles don't exist, are unstable, or have no relationship to the partners' social traits. A partner who is active on one occasion may be passive the next. Or mutual masturbation may be practiced. Partners are likely to have the same gender and be about the same age; but when they are not, the differences do not determine sexual roles. Within the relationship, the partners treat each other as social equals.

Egalitarian homosexual relations can begin in adulthood. For example, Nandi women of Kenya have lesbian affairs for the first time as adults.[250] Lesbian affairs were virtually universal among unmarried Akan women of the Gold Coast (now Ghana), sometimes continuing after marriage. Whenever possible, the women purchased extralarge beds to accommodate group sex sessions involving perhaps half-a-dozen women.[251] Hottentot men who enter into a compact of mutual assistance often become lovers.[252] Frequently, though, relationships of this kind develop among children and adolescents. Observers usually describe them as casual or as involving "exploration," "experimentation," or play, though the participants may take them seriously. Participation does not necessarily imply an exclusive homosexual orientation later in life. Thus in the East Bay community of a Melanesian island, young single men who are good friends or even brothers may take turns in accommodating each other sexually, but are not considered lovers. Later they marry women, but often take boy lovers as well.[253] Shepherd boys of the Qemant (pagan-Jewish peasants of Ethiopia) and Amhara of Gondar Province in Ethiopia engage in anal and intercrural in-

[250] Bryk (1933:226). In turn-of-the-century Zanzibar, women engaged in mutual cunnilingus and stimulation with ebony or ivory dildoes (Baumann, 1899; I. Bloch, 1933).
[251] Personal communication, Eva Meyerowitz, based on her fieldwork in the Gold Coast during the 1940s.
[252] Schapera (1930:242–43).
[253] Davenport (1965).

tercourse beginning at about age eight, with only mild teasing from adults who watch them in action; but then desist when they marry.[254]

Similar practices are found in other regions of the world. Adolescent boys of the Kwoma, a New Guinea tribe of the Sepik River District, "play" at copulation with one another, but a cultural prejudice against the receptive role discourages adult involvement.[255] Boys and girls of the Argentinean Pilaga engage in homosexual masturbation up to age five, but then their interests turn to the opposite sex.[256] Parents scold Alorese boys for engaging in homosexual "play," but consider the episodes too trivial to warrant sterner action. They react more strongly, though, to girls who masturbate one another, the difference in response no doubt reflecting the sharper repression of female sexuality in Indian life. Homosexuality appears to be absent among adults, except for soldiers and prisoners.[257] Adults consider Samoan boys who sleep together and engage in homosexual relations to be playing, so they do nothing to discourage them. In Samoa, sex acquires social significance through marriage and children, and these are not at stake in a homosexual relationship.[258]

Ostensibly casual homosexual relationships among youngsters have also been reported for the Manus of the Admiralty Islands north of New Guinea[259] and the Tikopia.[260] Notwithstanding a great deal of same-sex physical contact (embraces, hand-holding), male homosexuality is reputedly uncommon on Bali.[261] Yet when it does occur it evokes little interest; practitioners eventually develop an interest in women and marry them.[262]

One of the factors governing the persistence of adolescent homosexual relations into adulthood is the availability of opposite-sex partners. In Dahomey, male and female homosexuality are both common and considered normal in adolescence, when the sexes are segregated; but at later ages they are much less common, and because they are considered un-

---

[254] Gamst (1967, 1969:106, personal communication, 1985).

[255] Whiting (1941:50–51).

[256] Money and Erhardt (1972:140).

[257] Du Bois (1944:70).

[258] Mead (1928).

[259] Mead (1930:166).

[260] Firth (1936:494–95).

[261] This was not true in the past; early Dutch sources state that male and female homosexuality was practiced openly on Bali (J. Jacobs, 1883:14–15, 134–37; Ploss and Bartels, 1899:1.453; Westermarck, 1917:459; B. Werner, n.d.:74–79; Mead, 1955:62). Transgenderal homosexuality has by no means disappeared (Geertz, 1960:291–92). Mead (1961) reports that male and female itinerant dancers were courted by village men, though under Western influence the attraction was coming to be disapproved. See also Rhodius and Darling (1980:45).

[262] Covarrubias (1965:144–45, Belo, 1970).

desirable, concealed.[263] Most male Yanomamo teenagers have sexual relationships with one another, but desist at marriage.[264] The same is true for
young Araucanian men in Chile and Argentina.[265] Until they reach seventeen, Akuna boys of New Guinea place their penes in other boys' anuses,
with some disapproval from adults, who consider the activity dangerous;
the practice ends with the end of sexual segregation.[266] Adolescent homosexual relationships may persist for young Marquesan Islanders of marriageable age who have not found a fiancée or spouse, as well as for Cubeo
men in the Northwest Amazon in the same situation.[267] Where villages are
small, and where female infanticide or polygyny is practiced, women are
especially likely to be in short supply. In the absence of restraint, temporary homosexual outlets may be sought as a substitute. Thus, among the
Kanaka Popinee of New Caledonia in Melanesia, "youths console each
other" between puberty and marriage, because the chief monopolizes the
young women.[268]

Age-grading—the formal classification of individuals whose ages are
close together into distinct social groups, often having ritual or military
functions—can lead to temporary homosexuality when it entails the sexual
segregation of a particular age-grade. Youths of the Bororo of central Brazil
have sexual relations with one another in the men's house, which they are
permitted to enter after passing several initiation tests. When visited by
Karl von den Steinen in 1894, "couples in love could be seen amusing themselves under a communal red blanket." [269] Among the Nyakyusa, a pastoral
people of Tanzania, boys leave their parents' homes at about age ten and
found a new village on the outskirts of the old one. The new village continues to accept additional age-mates for five to six years and then closes.
The boys remain in the village, without female companionship, until they
marry. The arrangement is related to the strong taboo on mother-son incest. Since the father may have young wives whom the son may inherit at
his father's death, incest might tempt a boy who remained in his father's
house. The boy's departure helps to preserve the father's monopoly on
marriageable women, and reduces conflict among fathers and sons.

As the older men who own the cattle needed for bridewealth may use
their herds to acquire additional wives for themselves rather than to purchase wives for their sons, young men may have to wait a long time before

[263] Gorer (1935:141–42), Herskovits (1967:288–89).
[264] Grilier (1957:80), Chagnon (1966:61–63, 1977:76).
[265] Hilger (1957:68, 128, 249).
[266] Du Toit (1975:219–20).
[267] Goldman (1963:181), Suggs (1966:83).
[268] Jacobus X (1896); see also Foley (1879).
[269] Quoted in Trevisan (1986:21–22).

marrying. Homosexual relationships with their age-mates in the boys' village help them adapt. These relations continue until marriage but not after, and are tolerated as a substitute for heterosexual affairs. The residents of a boys' village are drawn from various lineages, so these relationships do not violate incest taboos.[270] By providing a substitute for the young women that the young men might prefer, homosexuality among the Nyakyusa protects the gerontocracy. Were homosexual outlets not available, the junior men might insist on being given a share of their fathers' cattle so that they could marry sooner. Their homosexuality thus perpetuates the system of domination that gives rise to it: it is simultaneously a response to heterosexual deprivation and a means of mitigating it.

The situation among the polygamous Tiwi of the Australian Torres Straits is in some ways similar: fathers betroth their daughters at birth to men they want as allies, creating a serious shortage of women for young men. Boys initiate homosexual relations at a fairly young age (often seven), and indulge freely in the "bachelor's camp" (ages eleven to fourteen), where they live in the bush, isolated from women. Eventually, they choose someone who might become a future brother-in-law as a regular partner.[271] Male homosexuality among the Onge of the Little Andaman Island off Burma has also been explained by the monopoly on younger women held by the older men.[272]

Hunting, fishing, and trapping can also deprive men of heterosexual outlets for a time, as women are often barred from these trips. On an expedition lasting only a few days the deprivation is too short to be consequential, but trapping, fishing, and big-game hunting can lead to longer absences. When these activities are carried out by pairs of men or small groups, emotional and sexual attachments can easily develop. Or the men may anticipate the deprivation and provide for it; when the Tapirape Indians of Central Brazil used to go on hunting trips, they took along adult men who served as receptive partners in anal intercourse. One of these had changed his gender and married a man, but the others had not; some were married to women, yet also made themselves available to men.[273]

The development of homosexual relations under comparable circum-

---

[270] M. Wilson (1951:87–88, 1959:197), Eisenstadt (1956:253–55). Homosexuality ascribed to deprivation is also common among young Tutsi and Hutu men in Ruanda (Maquet, 1961: 77–78), and was so among young Nkundo men and women of the Congo—less so now that marriage has become easier (Hutstaert, 1938:86–87).

[271] Pilling (1983). Egalitarian homosexuality is reported for boys and girls of other Australian tribes as well (Roheim, 1933, 1958:223; Berndt and Berndt, 1951), but full details are lacking.

[272] Cipriani (1961, 1966:22–23).

[273] Wagley (1977:160), Trevisan (1986:65). In some North American Indian groups, berdaches accompanied hunting expeditions for the same purpose (J. N. Katz, 1976:612–13).

stances in other groups cannot always be determined from the sources. Thoreau, for example, tells of the deep friendship of an Indian and a white man who shared a cabin for a winter, hunting and trapping together, but he does not say whether they were lovers.[274] Lafitau, a French Jesuit missionary in early-eighteenth-century Canada, describes intense and socially recognized "special friendships" among Indians from coast to coast:

> they become Companions in hunting, in war, and in fortune; they have a right to food and lodging in each other's cabin. The most affectionate compliment that the friend can make to his friend is to give him the name of Friend.[275]

Lafitau remarks that these friendships "admit no suspicion of apparent vice, albeit there is, or may be, much real vice." He suspects, but doesn't seem to know. The missionaries, he says, "suppressed attachments of this kind on account of the abuses which they feared would result from them," but their fears may have been based on little more than their own experiences in monasteries. Or may not have been.

John Weeks was able to learn more of the practices of the African Bangala. Though a man who sodomized a woman could be executed, sodomy between men was very common and regarded without shame. It generally took place when men visited strange towns or were away at fishing camps, without their wives.[276] Weeks did not comment on the availability of local partners, but Sorenson's observations of Indians of the central northwest Amazon are suggestive. When young unmarried men of another village came to visit, host youths tried to seduce them to keep them away from the local women.[277]

The penetration of a wage economy into precapitalist societies can also lead to sexual segregation. To earn money, the young men of New Guinea and the Solomon Islands now commonly work away from home on plantations for several years, while native women remain in their home villages. The workers, housed in crowded, all-male labor compounds away from women, often turn to each other for sex.[278] Homosexuality is simi-

---

[274] Thoreau (1961:291 ff); see also W. L. Williams (1986:90–91).

[275] Quoted in J. N. Katz (1976:288–89).

[276] John Weeks (1909).

[277] Sorenson (1984).

[278] Mead (1930:198), Oliver (1955:202), Hogbin (1970). If taken at face value, Oliver's comments about the relationships among Siuian workers would be puzzling. His informants described homosexual intercourse as "bizarre" while also affirming it to be more enjoyable than heterosexual intercourse (on the basis of what all of them said was secondhand information). These responses suggest that informants were telling the interviewer what they believed he wanted to hear. As missionaries had been active on the island, natives would have been exposed to Western views of homosexuality at their most rejecting.

larly reported to develop among the South African Tswana and Thonga in the mining compounds, where boys and men are lodged in an all-male environment.[279]

Though deprivation of heterosexual outlets may be conducive to egalitarian homosexuality, it is neither necessary nor sufficient. There was a certain amount of homosexually oriented horseplay among sexually deprived male youths of the Shavante, a seminomadic hunting and gathering people of the Brazilian interior, but nothing more.[280] Conversely, married men of East Bay are active boy-lovers.[281] A strong homosexual component pervades close friendships of young married Mayan men as well as bachelors in southern Mexico[282] and among Guatemalan Indians.[283] In the central northwest Amazon region of Colombia and Brazil, mutual masturbation and genital fondling are an expected part of friendly male interaction among both bachelors and young married men.[284] Among the Barasana of Colombia, a young man's relationship with his "brothers-in-law" (that is, his male affines at the same genealogical level) "become increasingly close and familiar. A young man will often be in a hammock with his 'brother-in-law,' nuzzling him, fondling his penis and talking quietly, often about sexual exploits with women."[285] Lévi-Strauss had noted similar fondlings among the Nambicuara, continuing after marriage as they did among the Barasana.[286]

In general, indulgence of homosexual play among prepubescent youths is found when adults accept rather than repress children's heterosexual interests. Tolerance towards the expression of sexuality in childhood tends not to discriminate against homosexuality. Indeed, since homosexual relations do not jeopardize marriage alliances or risk pregnancy, they are sometimes tolerated more readily than youthful heterosexual affairs.

As we have seen, egalitarian homosexual relationships are sometimes found among adults, but they are not usually institutionalized. Where they exist, they are usually not recognized publicly, but are carried on on an individual and often temporary, sometimes covert basis, and commonly do not exclude heterosexual relationships or marriage. They have no implications for gender identity or for a social identity based on sexual orientation.

In many cultures, the institutionalized gender system poses an obstacle to egalitarian same-sex relationships among adults. For example, the tradi-

---

[279] Schapera (1938), Gunther (1955:523), Junod (1962:98).
[280] Maybury-Lewis (1967:82).
[281] Davenport (1965).
[282] Gossen (1984).
[283] Reina (1966:279–86).
[284] Sorenson (1984).
[285] Hugh-Jones (1979:109).
[286] Lévi-Strauss (1943), S. O. Murray (1987e).

tional North American Indian household rested on a gender-based division of labor, with husband and wife performing complementary tasks, all of them critical to the survival of the family. A household composed of two biological men performing only tasks defined as male (e.g., hunting, military combat) would have lacked someone to perform the "female" tasks (gardening, gathering food, quilling, weaving). An all-female couple would have been equally deficient.[287] In societies with generalized commodity exchange, these services can be purchased, but that is not possible in the money-free kinship-structured societies we are considering. Labor is not generally available for hire.

As many women's tasks were performed collectively, the man who did them had to work with other women—making him a potential rival to the other men of the tribe. His participation in women's tasks therefore required his adopting a female social identity, signaling his unavailability as a sexual partner of the other women. That was the berdache's solution. Even in the absence of a gender change, the sharing that underlies egalitarian relationships is threatened when one of the partners takes up work defined by custom as appropriate to the opposite sex, while the other does not.

More complex household arrangements would still have been possible. For example, a married man could have taken a female wife to meet his household needs, and a male spouse as well. But competition between the men for the favors of the wife would have led to instability unless one of the men abandoned heterosexuality by taking on a female identity. Since men who married berdaches often took them as second wives, this was a common Indian solution.

Male competitiveness poses a further obstacle to an egalitarian relationship. The twelfth-century Danish historian Saxo Grammaticus makes this point when telling of two pirates who

> were so careful to preserve temperance that they are supposed never to have resorted to intoxicating liquor, afraid that continence, a great bond between courageous men, might be forcibly shattered if they over-indulged.[288]

If men are accustomed to compete with one another for status, and conceive of sex in terms of domination, then egalitarian relations must be asexual if they are to continue. Thus, among the highly patriarchal Swat Pukhtun of Pakistan, sex always involves domination, and as a result, male lovers cannot be friends, or friends lovers.[289] It is this principle that explains

---

[287] Some berdaches did perform both men's and women's tasks, but this is a solution in which all efficiency gains from specialization are lost. The fact that two berdaches never established households together suggests that Indian gender ideology was not totally flexible.

[288] Saxo Grammaticus (1979:172).

[289] Lindholm (1982:226).

why male homosexuality *among* the highly assertive Iatmul of the Sepik River region of New Guinea is forbidden, while *outside* boys who visit Iatmul villages run the risk of being anally raped.[290]

Where male culture is not competitive and sex does not entail domination, an egalitarian sexual relationship between males can be more stable, as it can be when differences of age, status, and gender exclude competition. One has the impression that where lesbian relationships are not repressed in kinship-structured societies, and do not entail gender transformation, they tend more often than male homosexual relationships to be egalitarian, possibly because women are not socialized to compete for status with other women, or to dominate.[291]

Rejecting Societies

The preceding survey can leave little doubt that many cultures, scattered widely around the world, accept some form of homosexuality. It should be equally clear that simple involvement with another person of the same sex never becomes the basis for ascribing a distinctive social identity based on that involvement. However, gender transformation, such as occurs for the berdache or *mahū*, generally does become the basis for a distinctive social identity. Whereas no particular explanation for homosexual desire is thought necessary, gender transformation is explained, e.g., in terms of someone's innate character (in the case of berdaches).[292]

This widespread acceptance does not necessarily imply an across-the-board tolerance or indifference, for the acceptance of one form does not necessarily guarantee the acceptability of other forms. Though Alorese boys "play" at homosexuality, adult men abstain.[293] The Ila of Northern Rhodesia fine men for engaging in pederasty (much less than they fine men for performing cunnilingus on a woman), fearing that it might impregnate a boy; but a male transvestite, perhaps homosexual, was called a "prophet" and not penalized in any way.[294] Transgenderal homosexuality appears to be altogether absent in the New Guinea societies that institutionalize male-homosexual pederasty, while the American Indian groups that accepted

[290] Mead (1955:79).
[291] See, however, J. Gay (1985) on "mummy-baby" relationships in Lesotho. Mazur (1985) suggests that all primates, including humans, have a built-in, hormonally based tendency to maintain or enhance their status by dominating partners in face-to-face interaction. This domination can take many forms, including sexual. Whether that is so, or whether status-seeking behavior is entitely social in origin, it is clear that it can take many forms other than sexual. Egalitarian sexual relationships seemingly free from status competition do occur. Though Mazur postulates his assumptions to apply to women as well as men, he concedes that most of his evidence concerns men.
[292] W. L. Williams (1986:49–52).
[293] Du Bois (1944:101–2).
[294] Smith and Dale (1920:74, 436).

transgenderal homosexuality do not seem to have institutionalized, or had much of, the transgenerational form. Lesbianism seems less common, and may be less tolerated, than male homosexuality.

There are quite a few societies in which all forms of homosexuality are reported to be extremely rare. It is said to be infrequent among the Muria, a tribal society of India,[295] and has never been recorded for the Fan of Gabon.[296] It is unknown in Aitutaki, [297] and Heider saw no signs of it among the Dani of New Guinea.[298] "Unnatural vice" was unknown to the Ba-Mbala, a Bantu people of Africa.[299] The inhabitants of Truk, in the Pacific all denied it took place,[300] as did the Gilyak, the Paleo-Siberians of Sakhalin Island,[301] and the Sebei of eastern Uganda.[302] Marsden found "the different species of horrid and disgustful crimes . . . against nature" to be unknown in Sumatra when he lived there in the late-eighteenth century.[303] Kenyatta claims the Kikuyu of Kenya are free from homosexuality.[304] Lovedu women are "innocent of Lesbian practices."[305]

Gray and Ellington identify a number of other groups in which male homosexuality is rare or absent: the Comanche, Ifugao, Jivaro, Lepcha, Lesu, Nambicuara, and Timbira.[306] They note that in a world sample of thirty-eight societies there is a strong negative correlation between observation of couvade on the one hand, and frequency of transvestism and homosexuality on the other. In couvade, husbands observe certain restrictions during

[295] Elwin (1947:447).

[296] Trezenem (1936).

[297] Beaglehole (1957:191).

[298] Heider (1979).

[299] Torday and Joyce (1905).

[300] Gladwin and Sarason (1953).

[301] Sternberg (1961).

[302] Goldschmidt (1967:133–39). Homosexual relations were regarded, according to Gold-schmidt, as something considered wrong, but informants indicated that such activity would be met by ridicule or insults, not formal action. In one episode, a man had intercourse with another man while he slept. On awakening, the victim retaliated by subjecting his assailant to the same treatment—a response suggesting the lack of an internalized repugnance to homosexuality, but associations of homosexuality with dominance and aggression. Male transvestites were present and accepted.

[303] Marsden (1966:261).

[304] Kenyatta (1953). Leakey (1977:3.1029–30) indicates that a man who "attempted to commit an unnatural act on a boy or another man" would be reported to the council and, if convicted, had to pay a fine. The Kikuyu seem to have been generally restrictive in sexual matters. Heterosexual intercourse in an unconventional position or during the daytime was considered polluting. It might be preferable to think of the Kikuyu as antisexual rather than antihomosexual; the fine for bestiality was considerably larger than that for homosexuality.

[305] Krige and Krige (1943:290).

[306] Gray and Ellington (1984). The Nambicuara do not belong on this list; see Lévi-Strauss (1943).

and after their wives' confinement in childbirth. Following the lead of Robert Munroe and his collaborators,[307] Gray and Ellington suggest that couvade originates in male gender-identity conflict. This conflict, they argue, would make male transvestism too threatening. Since male transvestism is associated with homosexuality in their sample, they conclude that strong conflict over gender identity will lead to the suppression of homosexuality. In their sample, no societies have both couvade and frequent homosexuality, which is consistent with their argument. However, Paige and Paige challenge the alleged connection betwen couvade and gender-identity conflict.[308] They find virtually no correlation between couvade observance and exclusive mother-child sleeping arrangements in a much larger sample. Such sleeping arrangements are ordinarily thought conducive to gender-identity confusion in male children. Yet it can be argued that it is the proximity and salience of the father or other adult males that is of greater relevance to the formation of a son's male gender identity.[309] Ultimately, the lack of any measure of sexual-identity conflict in Gray and Ellington's study leaves the interpretation of their correlation uncertain; couvade-observing and "frequent homosexuality" societies may differ in other ways that account for the correlation. To complicate matters further, the relationship between gender identity and homosexuality is undoubtedly not simple.

The absence of homosexuality need not necessarily imply that it is viewed negatively: Holmberg observed no homosexuality among the Siriono Indians of Eastern Bolivia despite the seeming absence of any social sanctions.[310] There are, however, a number of societies whose reactions are reported as being decidedly negative. The Bantu of North Kavirondo in Kenya used to consider homosexual acts a source of ritual impurity, requiring purification.[311] Though the claim should be regarded with skepticism, La Fontaine contends that at one time the Gisu of Uganda killed those who engaged in homosexuality; now, however, they merely scorn it, without revulsion.[312]

[307] Munroe (1980), Munroe, Munroe, and Whiting (1973).

[308] Paige and Paige (1981:167–208).

[309] Carroll (1978).

[310] Holmberg (1950). This is also true of the Dogon of Mali. Though ignorant of male homosexuality, they thought it was a wonderful idea when it was explained to them. They noted that it would enable young men to obtain sexual satisfaction from one another at work, instead of wasting time pursuing women (Parin, Morgenthaler, and Parin-Matthey, 1963; Endleman, 1986).

[311] Wagner (1949:106–9).

[312] La Fontaine (1959:34). Male-to-female and female-to-male transvestism were both present. Both practices were considered ridiculous, perhaps caused by an evil spirit or witchcraft. De Rachewiltz (1963:280) mentions no hostile reaction to Gisu homosexuality, only its pres-

Among the Kwoma of the Sepik River District of New Guinea,

> Sodomy is believed to be unnatural and revolting, and infor-
> mants were unanimous in saying that anyone who would submit
> to it must be a "ghost" and not a man. Although this sanction
> theoretically applied only to the person who played the passive
> role, it seemed to be effective in restricting the practice.[313]

When asked about homosexuality, the natives of Lesu, a Melanesian island, said they had never heard of it; when it was described to them, they
were horrified.[314]

Berdaches of the Sinalwa of the northwest Mexican coast were viewed
with horror and called an insulting name.[315] The Dogon of what was the
French Sudan think someone would have to be mad to engage in a homosexual act,[316] though they respond to rare occurrences only with humor,
not with punishment.[317] Among the Santal of India, someone who engages
in a homosexual act is fined but, after an act of ritual penance and purification, is accepted back into normal tribal life.[318]

Reasons are given in an appendix to this chapter for thinking that at least
some of these reports can be discounted as inaccurate or as representing
Western influence. Yet some cannot be so readily dismissed. There are
probably indigenous peoples who abhor homosexuality. Being unsure of
the phenomenon itself, and especially dubious about particular purported
instances of it, we would be on shaky ground in trying to develop an elaborate explanation for it. In a general way we can suggest that in these societies, the age and gender systems in which influential members have a
stake may be incompatible with the particular kind of same-sex sexual relationships that tend to arise in those societies. We have already commented
on the way competitiveness makes it difficult for men to accept a sexual
role defined as subordinate or inferior. Male supremacy may rule out
effeminacy, along with the transgenderal homosexuality that often accom-
panies it. If children are regarded as asexual, pederasty will be forbidden.

Though the total rejection of homosexuality seemingly does occur, our

---

ence. A slightly different association with witchcraft is found among the Mandari of East Africa: witches are believed to have a strong interest in bestiality, homosexuality, or intercourse
with an immature girl. Homosexuality itself is considered ludicrous and by itself does not necessarily lead to suspicions of witchcraft (Buxton, 1963).

[313] Whiting (1941:51).

[314] Powdermaker (1933:226).

[315] Beals (1932:205).

[316] Paulme (1940:386). The discrepancy between this report and that cited in footnote 310
merits investigation.

[317] Delafosse (1912:92).

[318] Mukherjea (1962:438).

survey suggests that it is uncommon. Where it occurs, the negative social response tends to be mild; often it entails nothing more than ridicule or scorn. What is true of the Brazilian Mehinaku—that "girls who experiment in lesbian affairs or men who participate in homosexual encounters are regarded as extremely foolish, but no one would directly interfere"[319]—holds true for almost all societies that lack centralized political authority.

APPENDIX: METHODOLOGICAL PROBLEMS IN ANTHROPOLOGICAL RESEARCH ON HOMOSEXUALITY

The older anthropological literature on homosexuality leaves almost everything to be desired. Most ethnographies ignore the subject. Although Pilling collected considerable data on male homosexuality among the Australian Tiwi, Hart and Pilling do not mention it in their book on the Tiwi.[320] Evans-Pritchard published his article on sexual inversion among the Azande only in 1970, decades after his fieldwork had been completed.[321] Broude and Greene suggest that many anthropologists do not report on sexual practices because it is not customary to do so. Fear of being suspected a participant or of not being permitted to return to a research site may well add to this reticence.[322]

Often, however, nothing is reported because no information was collected. Read recalls that it never occurred to him to ask about homosexuality in one New Guinea village he studied, despite persistent published reports of ritualized sodomy in New Guinea dating back to the late-nineteenth century. Even though he saw a good deal of same-sex physical contact, he simply assumed that homosexuality could not be a part of the culture.[323] Firth "collected few data" on mutual masturbation and pederasty—but was nevertheless confident enough to assert that homosexuality "plays no great part in native sexual life."[324] Herdt's *Guardians of the Flutes*, the first book-length study of homosexuality in a kinship-structured society, was published only in 1981.[325] The situation is even worse for lesbianism than for male homosexuality. Most anthropologists have been male, and men are often prevented by indigenous norms of propriety from questioning native women about sexual matters.

So deficient are the sources that of the 186 societies in the Human Relations Area File's Standard Sample used in much quantitative anthropologi-

[319] Gregor (1977:254).
[320] Hart and Pilling (1960).
[321] Evans-Pritchard (1970).
[322] Broude and Greene (1976).
[323] Read (1980).
[324] Firth (1936:494–95).
[325] Herdt (1981).

cal research, information on the frequency of homosexuality is available for only 70, and on attitudes toward it, for only 42.[326] When so much information is missing, the representativeness of the societies for which data are available must be considered suspect. And when the effective sample size is small, multivariate statistical analysis becomes impossible.

When homosexuality *is* discussed, it frequently receives no more than a passing reference. We may be told that it is "common" or "infrequent" (vague terms indeed), but nothing about who engages in it or under what circumstances. Social responses are described with equally frustrating superficiality. Typically, nothing is said about how the information was obtained. Was a report that the natives loathe homosexuality based on the testimony of a single informant, or many? Was the testimony confirmed by observing someone do something when an incident occurred? Usually, the reader has no way of knowing. To complicate matters further, some authors fail to distinguish among transvestism, homosexuality, and hermaphroditism.

Even where more information is provided, its reliability is not always high. In most societies, sexual activity normally takes place in private. This means that anthropologists cannot learn about it through observation, but must depend on what others tell them. Truthfulness cannot always be expected. Native prudishness can be a problem. Fortune found that the Dobuans did not talk freely about sex, and gave evasive or dishonest answers to direct questions.[327] However, reticence in discussing sex is not always indigenous. Most peoples have had extensive contact with Western missionaries, explorers, tourists, and anthropologists. Inevitably, they have learned of Western attitudes, in some cases through direct suppression of indigenous sexual practices.

Secrecy and denial of activities known to be offensive to whites are understandable responses. Thus the Trobriander who told Malinowski that homosexuality was a "bad custom" may have been telling him what he had learned white men wanted to hear.[328]

Where sex is an element of religious ritual there can be further reasons for secrecy. Lurie reports that among the Winnebago Indians knowledge of the berdache was supposed to be kept hidden from whites.[329] At first Herdt's Sambian informants unanimously denied homosexual practices; only after six months' time did they trust him enough to confess that ritualized sod-

---

[326] Broude and Greene (1976).

[327] Fortune (1932:243–48).

[328] Malinowski (1967:83). His use of the word "custom" suggests that homosexuality was not unfamiliar to the Trobrianders. Malinowski's (1929:448, 468–70) more extended remarks suggest that it was not common except in jail, and in plantation barracks and mission stations. It was considered a poor substitute for heterosexual relations. When it did occur it was the subject of ribald joking, but did not provoke any other penalty.

[329] Lurie (1953).

omy was part of their initiation rituals.[330] A researcher who spent only a
short time in the field would probably not have learned this.

Even when informants make no attempt to mislead an interviewer, serious misunderstandings can ensue when a researcher's questions unwit-
tingly embody Western stereotypes and categories. When Davenport began
interviewing Melanesian informants, he asked if they knew anyone who
had no sexual desire for women, but only enjoyed sex with men. No one
did, and so he concluded that there was no homosexuality. Later he learned
that "at some time during his life, very nearly every male engages in extensive homosexual activities," but not to the exclusion of heterosexual outlets.[331] MacDermot was told by his Nuer informants that anyone who
engaged in homosexual relations would be killed. Later he learned of a
man who began to dress as a woman. When a religious leader conferred
with the spirits, they endorsed the gender change. The transvestite eventually married a man, and nothing was done. Once the man took on the
social identity of a woman, the Nuer did not consider the marriage to be
homosexual.[332] Given the culturally discrepant meanings revealed by these
episodes, we must wonder just what Powdermaker told her Lesu informants to elicit their reactions of horror.[333]

For many cultures, sexual mores have been deeply affected by prolonged
and extensive exposure to the sermons of missionaries, the lectures of
school teachers, and the offhand comments of traders, tourists, and government agents. Lurie found that among the Winnebago, "the berdache
was at one time a highly honored and respected person, but . . . the Winnebago had become ashamed of the custom because the white people
thought it was amusing or evil."[334] When Hallpike tells us that male homosexuality is currently unknown to the Tauade of southeast New Guinea,[335]
we must wonder whether this does not reflect the influence of Christian
missionaries, who have been active among the Tauade since the early years
of this century.

Apart from exposure to restrictive moral standards, Western contact has
led almost everywhere to profound changes in the character of indigenous
social life. American Indians of both continents—to take only one example—were decimated by disease, starvation, and war. The fur trade and
the buffalo hunt, which was transformed by the introduction of horses, led

---

[330] Herdt (1981).

[331] Davenport (1965).

[332] MacDermot (1972:99, 119). The situation was similar among the Lango of Uganda. According to tribal law, homosexual relations, like incest and witchcraft, were punishable by
death. However, if one of the partners changed gender he could live with his partner un-
disturbed (Driberg, 1923:209–10).

[333] Powdermaker (1933:226).

[334] Lurie (1953). For the Hopi see Aberle (1977).

[335] Hallpike (1977).

to mass migrations and dramatic changes in North American Indian economic life and kinship arrangements. Forced relocation to reservations had
catastrophic consequences for tribal life. In many parts of the world, conquest and the establishment of a centralized political authority have ended
intergroup warfare. The differential impact of contact on men and women
has often altered gender relations. If sexual customs spring from a particular
way of life—and this assumption is at the core of virtually all anthropological or sociological thinking about human sexuality—then such profound
upheavals inevitably bring about major changes in sexual expression and
attitudes. In some groups, outright sexual repression at the hands of Western (or Western-educated) government officials has further altered traditional patterns of sexual expression.[336]

These changes can be discerned by comparing earlier and more recent
reports of American Indian berdaches. Ralph Beals's Nisenan informant saw
three or four in his childhood, but, Beals reports, only one was now alive.[337]
Prince Maximilian found many Crow berdaches in 1840, but by the early
twentieth century only one was living.[338] According to Landes, the Poto-
watami berdache tradition was passing by 1870–80, though a few were still
left when she did her field work in the mid–1930s.[339] Nineteenth-century explorers noted the presence of transvestism among the Koniag Indians of Kodiak Island in 1802, 1812, and 1814, but by 1851 it had almost disappeared.[340]

In like manner, homosexuality was once universal among youthful Tukuna males of the Peruvian northeast,[341] but Nimuendaju saw none.[342] Mid-
nineteenth-century reports describe the *manang bali* ("man transformed as
woman") of Borneo as being common, but another source, written in 1911,
found them rare. Now they are unknown.[343] Tahitian *mahūs*, too, are far
less common than in the late eighteenth century.[344]

Over the past few centuries, much of the world has undergone a massive
shift in the frequency and social acceptability of same-sex sexual relations.
Information about these topics acquired after decades or centuries of contact with whites, and after the destruction of an indigenous way of life,
cannot be casually assumed to hold for the pre-contact period. Yet researchers typically treat each of the "cultures" of the Standard Sample as

---

[336] Van Baal (1966) documents the repressive activities of Dutch missionaries to New Guinea.
For repression of berdaches at the hands of Spanish and American governments, see J. N.
Katz (1976:318), Duberman (1979), and W. L. Williams (1986:131–51, 175–200).

[337] Beals (1934).

[338] Lowie (1912:226).

[339] Landes (1970).

[340] Hrdlička (1944:78). Callender and Kochems (1983) provide additional examples.

[341] Tessman (1930).

[342] Nimuendaju (1952).

[343] Jensen (1974:143).

[344] R. Levy (1973).

pristine, independent of every other culture in the sample—even though many have been heavily exposed to western influence for long periods.[345]

To see how these difficulties render quantitative research on homosexuality problematic, we consider the codings Werner adopted in his study of the acceptance of homosexuality.[346] Werner found thirty-nine societies in the Human Relations Area File (HRAF) that provided information on attitudes toward homosexuality, and also on pro- or antinatalist practices such as abortion and infanticide. He was concerned with both variables because he wanted to study the relationship between them. On the basis of the documentation in the files, Werner coded the following nineteen societies in the sample as "not accepting" homosexuality: Aymara, Yahgan, Bahia-Brazil, Cagaba, East Apache, South East Salish, Northern Saulteaux, Buka-Kurtachi, Mbuti Pygmies, Ila, Kurd, Yugoslavia, Lepcha, West Tibet, Ashanti, Chiriguano, Creek, Tikopia, and !Kung Bushmen.

To assess the reliability of Werner's ratings, I returned to the files and compared my reading of the sources with his codings. In many instances I found reasons for classifying the societies differently from the way Werner did. Here are the codings I consider questionable:

1 *Aymara.* The HRAF sources for Aymara attitudes toward homosexuality say that "sex perversions" are now uncommon, but that male and female homosexuality existed in the early nineteenth century, along with male transvestism, which was common.[347] Tschopik attributes their disappearance to vigorous suppression "on the part of the Church and the local Mestizos." Werner is not coding indigenous Aymara beliefs and practices when he reports them as not accepting homosexuality; he is reporting Roman Catholicism. Drawing on the same sources, Ford and Beach classified the Aymara as accepting some forms of homosexuality.[348]

2 *Yahgan.* Two sources in the file refer to homosexuality. Cooper indicates that the Yahgan "joke about unnatural vice, but do not practice it,"[349] while acknowledging that another source, whose reliability he finds difficult to assess, reports homosexuality to be common. Gusinde (1937) mentions that the Yahgan believe in the existence of male and female spirits hostile to men, who try to seduce them. Anyone who succumbs is lost. At best the first source tells us that homosexual acts were infrequent. The second does not indicate that the Yahgan rejected homosexuality. Rather, the

---

[345] Even apart from Western influence, the assumption that the societies in the sample are independent is frequently a dubious one. Groups that have a common origin, or that interact, are not independent. Conventional methods of dealing with this problem in the Standard Sample are far from adequate. Most researchers (e.g., Reiss, 1986) simply ignore the problem.

[346] D. Werner (1979).

[347] Tschopik (1946:514), La Barre (1948:133). See also Murray (1987c).

[348] Ford and Beach (1951:130).

[349] Cooper (1917:170).

myth warns about the dangers of sex with seductive strangers. Both sources suggest that homosexual desire was common among the Yahgans.

3 *Bahia-Brazil.* Hutchinson mentions that several homosexuals in the community are well known.[350] The children of one who is married left him when they found out he was a homosexual prostitute. He had "quite a trade" of men, most of them unmarried, some married. Although people knew who his customers were, his clients were not ostracized in any way. It was common for adolescent boys to experiment with homosexuality. A married man had to leave town when he was caught molesting a small boy. Two women living together, one of them bearded, were "considered hilarious by the neighbors." In short, no action was taken against any form of male homosexuality except for child molesting,[351] and two women living together were thought funny. We are not told explicitly that the women were lesbians. If they were, lesbianism might or might not have been responsible for their mirth; it could as easily have been their broader violation of gender expectations, or even the unusual appearance of one of them. The negative reaction of children to the realization that their father was a homosexual prostitute can no more be taken as an indication of hostility toward homosexuality than a comparable reaction to a mother's heterosexual prostitution could be taken as revealing antipathy to heterosexuality.

4 *Cagaba.* Here there are several sources. Reichel-Dolmatoff states that male and female homosexuality are known in all the towns, but homosexual relations involving adults and children are punished severely.[352] This suggests a prohibition against pedophilia, not homosexuality. Bolinder mentions that homosexuality was common at the time the Indians were discovered, a claim also supported by Brettes, who reports having caught Indians in the act. He has much reason, he adds, for thinking that homosexual acts formed part of their secret ceremonies, but had not been able to obtain proof. He quotes a Spanish author as saying that homosexuality was common, and that "they filled their temples with a thousand abominations and obscene figures" to arouse themselves for it.[353] It is hard to read nonacceptance into any of this.

5 *Eastern Apache.* Opler quotes several late-nineteenth-century sources who assert that berdaches are "not mistreated, but . . . privately ridi-

[350] Hutchinson (1957:140–41).

[351] To take an episode involving child molesting as evidence for attitudes toward homosexuality involves considerable stretching. It can be tempting to do that when information is sparse, and missing data a problem. Other investigators have succumbed to the same temptation: thus Broude and Greene (1976) code the Rwala Bedouins as strongly disapproving or punishing homosexuality. The source they cite, Musil (1928:473), states that the penalty is death, but the only example he reports involves a slave who raped a small boy. No evidence for social responses to a consensual relationship is available.

[352] Reichel-Dolmatoff (1951:90).

[353] Bolinder (1925:113–14), Brettes (1903:33–37).

culed." [354] A more recent informant told him that a homosexual would be killed as a witch. However, this testimony must be treated with great suspicion. There is no evidence that the Apaches or any other North American Indian group ever killed anyone for homosexuality or transvestism. The possibility of Christian influence must be taken seriously. In a more recent study of a Mescalero Apache living on a reservation in New Mexico, Opler concluded that

> transvestites and hermaphrodites were permitted to live reasonably unhampered lives among these Apache. There was some ridicule of them behind their backs, but they were treated respectfully to their faces. [355]

Since Werner codes societies where homosexuality is ridiculed but receives no more serious sanctions as "not accepting," he can legitimately code the East Apache as not accepting homosexuality even if he discounts the witchcraft story as misinformed or as an expression of outside influence. Yet our discussion of the ridicule response to berdaches in this chapter raises questions about whether the joking behavior that Opler mentions should indeed be interpreted as evidence for nonacceptance.

6 *South-East Salish.* Again there are several sources. Ray reports that though there were words for male and female homosexuality, no adult examples were known. The punishment for them was whipping. [356] Cline did find berdaches. They "were not frowned upon. . . . People much given to joking might make such an one his butt." They were regarded not as "religious worthies" but rather as "good-for-nothings." [357] This does suggest a mildly negative attitude. However, Teit, who found a few men dressing and acting like women, states that they usually became shamans, did women's work, and cured people. Young men visited and joked with them, but did not have sexual relations with them. [358] These sources are sufficiently contradictory to raise questions about their reliability, or to suggest historical change. Under this circumstance any coding is risky, but the bulk of the evidence is consistent with the same joking acceptance of berdaches found in other Indian groups.

7 *Northern Saulteaux.* Werner's coding rests on Hallowell's remark that "persons of the same sex do not use the term that defines permissible sex relations, so homosexuality is ruled out" by rules of exogamy. [359] But this simply means that incest taboos were applicable to homosexuality, not that it was ruled out altogether. He adds without explanation that he had learned

---

[354] Opler (1941:79–80, 425–26).
[355] Opler (1969:101–2).
[356] Ray (1933:143).
[357] Cline (1938:119, 137).
[358] Teit (1930:384).
[359] Hallowell (1955:293–95).

of cases involving male and female homosexuality among the unmarried. The Saulteaux had no organized penal sanctions of any kind; no one had the authority to impose a penalty on anyone else. It was even considered culturally unacceptable to express moral disapproval of someone else openly. Thus no one could have been actively punished or ostracized for a homosexual act. Hallowell goes on to narrative a myth telling of a woman killed by her husband after she deserted him for another woman, and a real-life episode involving an aunt who had an affair with her niece. Both women were married. One husband beat his wife, the other left his. Neither episode provides unambiguous evidence of attitudes toward lesbianism, as both involve adultery and desertion. Northern Saulteaux men could legitimately use violence to defend their sexual rights over women.[360] An earlier source found berdaches to be rare but well known; some took husbands and lived with them as their wives.[361]

At the end of the eighteenth century, the related Southern Saulteaux had several berdaches who "[were] never ridiculed or despised . . . , but [were], on the contrary, respected as saints, or beings in some degree inspired by the Manitou . . ."[362] This makes it all the more unlikely that the Northern Saulteaux were indigenously hostile to homosexuality.

8 Ila. Werner's coding is based on Smith and Dale's observation that pederasty, "which is not so rare," is held in "abomination" because someone who submitted to it might become pregnant; a fine of three or four cows was imposed on the adult.[363] However, it is not clear that the response was the same when both parties were adults. Need it be added that the men who engaged in the not-so-rare practice probably did not hold it in abomination? Smith and Dale also report a man, probably homosexual, who dressed as a woman, did women's work, and lived with women. He was called a "prophet,"[364] a term that suggests special religious powers. It is doubtful that the Ila rejected transgenderal homosexuality. Drawing on the same evidence, Ford and Beach classified the Ila as accepting some forms of homosexuality.[365]

9 Kurds. Masters describes an entertainment spot reputed to be a hangout for homosexuals because soldiers from the army congregated there.[366] No action was taken against the establishment, and it does not appear that the soldiers were discouraged from patronizing it by its reputation. Masters reports that homosexuality was sometimes a temporary feature of adolescence and usually ended at about eighteen by marriage. Civil and religious law prohibited anal intercourse, which was rare; and the term "homo-

---

[360] Hallowell (1955:299–300).
[361] Skinner (1911).
[362] P. Grant (1890:357).
[363] Smith and Dale (1920:436).
[364] Smith and Dale (1920:74).
[365] Ford and Beach (1951:130).
[366] Masters (1953:80, 264).

sexual" was used as an insult. Given the patriarchal character of Kurdish culture, one suspects that the insults referred only to the receptive role, not to homosexuality in general. Whatever the law prohibited, it appears not to have mirrored popular feelings, at least not on the basis of Masters's evidence.

10 *Yugoslavia.* Tomasic describes a form of sworn brotherhood and sisterhood which "take on some homosexual aspects."[367] The pacts among men are celebrated in church, despite the disapproval of the orthodox priests in Montenegro, who considered the relationships vice-ridden and contrary to nature. This source clearly shows full acceptance of homosexual relations in the villages. Only priests in the capitol disapproved. By arbitrarily coding Yugoslavia as not accepting homosexuality on the basis of this disapproval, Werner is simply recording another instance of official Christian opposition to homosexuality. He ignores the popular attitude in the villages, which was evidently quite different. As this example makes clear, when attitudes within a society vary, no single coding will suffice. Werner's approach breaks down in the face of disagreement.

11 *Western Tibet.* In a lecture on Tibetan marriage practices, Prince Peter reported that, as far as he could determine, "homosexuality [was] condemned even in the monasteries, and certainly despised if practiced."[368] He could find no proof of it. Fifteen years later, however, he had received testimony from three independent sources confirming that it was a well-established practice in all the large Buddhist monasteries. Informants were divded about the situation in Ladakh (which shares the culture of Western Tibet), some indicating that homosexuality was a punishable offense under Kashmiri law (which is heavily influenced by Islam, and cannot be taken as reflecting Tibetan Buddhist thinking) and therefore did not exist anywhere in the country (!), while others were of the opinion that it was widespread, in and outside the monasteries. In addition, the Tibetan language included terms for all the varieties of "sexual perversion" known in the West.[369] This is hardly evidence that Tibetans reject homosexuality.

12 *Chiriguano.* Nordenskiold reports that "it is not regarded as a disgrace among these Indians to be the active one in a homosexual relationship, but the passive one is deeply despised. He is regarded as a woman."[370] Several drunk Chiriguano men raped a visiting Chave Indian, who later committed suicide, so great was the shame. Werner's coding, "not accepting," fails to recognize role distinctions of great importance to the Chiriguano.

13 *Creek.* Werner rates the Creeks as "not accepting" homosexuality on the basis of a beating given in 1766 to a young man for "being more effeminate than became a warrior; and with acting contrary to their old religious rites and customs, particularly because he lived nearer than any of the rest

[367] Tomasic (1948:79).
[368] Prince Peter (1948).
[369] Prince Peter (1963:385–86).
[370] Nordenskiold (1912:221–27).

to an opulent and helpless German, by whom they supposed he might have been corrupted."[371] However, the existence of berdaches who performed well-defined social tasks is established for the Creeks as early as 1564.[372] An eighteenth-century source found sodomy to be frequent among the Creeks.[373] This makes it very unlikely that homosexuality was not accepted. The young man was probably beaten because of his involvement with a white man, not because of his gender or sexual conduct. Ford and Beach classified the Creeks as accepting some forms of homosexuality on the basis of the same evidence.[374]

14 *Tikopia.* Firth indicates that mutual masturbation and pederasty are practiced.[375] "Such a person is called 'filthy hand'—he grasps with his hand to set up his member, then removes his hand, and rubs on the fundament of another man." Tikopian men also claimed—hypocritically in Firth's opinion—to find masturbation disgusting because they disliked touching their genitals. The term "dirty hand" may reflect this dislike; it does not necessarily indicate a special opprobrium for homosexuality. Firth mentions no sanctions taken against those who engaged in it. In a personal communication to the author, Firth indicated that while he was sure that homosexuality was uncommon on Tikopia, it entailed no moral stigma; it was simply thought silly. This attitude, he was confident, did not derive from Western contacts.

The absence of more favorable views of homosexuality on Tikopia is of interest in relation to claims that demographic factors govern attitudes to homosexuality. In 1928 when Firth did his fieldwork, the population density on Tikopia was high, close to the carrying capacity of the land. The Tikopia were well aware of the relationship between the population size and the standard of living, and utilized celibacy, coitus interruptus, abortion, and infanticide to curb the population growth.[376] Yet the population did not turn to institutionalized homosexuality.

Of the nineteen societies Werner classified as "not accepting" homosexuality, fourteen were clearly, or at least arguably, misclassified. Five were probably classified accurately on the basis of Werner's coding rules. To see exactly what "not accepting" homosexuality implied in those societies, we review the HRAF sources for them as well.

1 *Buka-Kurtachi.* According to B. Blackwood, homosexuality is rare on the plantations, where indentured men labor for three years isolated from women; older men dislike young people signing up for this reason.[377] In some legends, homosexuality has harmful consequences. Blackwood's informants denied having homosexual relations with older men when they

[371] Swanton (1928:364).
[372] Le Moyne (1875:7–8, Swanton (1922:373), J. N. Katz (1976:285–86).
[373] Roman (1961:56), J. N. Katz (1976:613 n. 14).
[374] Ford and Beach (1951:130).
[375] Firth (1936:494–95).
[376] Firth (1936:39), Kirch (1984:116–17).
[377] B. Blackwood (1935:128–29).

lived together in the bush. Possibly they were telling the truth; possibly they would not have spoken candidly about such a topic to a white woman. She does not mention any sanctions for engaging in homosexuality.

2 *Mbuti Pygmies.* Turnbull reports that in Mbuti hunting bands, male homosexuality is rare and lesbianism unknown.[378] "Mbuti who practice such behavior are regarded by men with derision; women have a particular horror of homosexuals." Though unrelated members of the same sex often sleep with legs wrapped around one another for warmth, it is considered undesirable to hold someone too tightly while doing so. Homosexual intercourse is considered horrible, a great insult. In a letter to the author clarifying these passages, Turnbull states that when men sleep huddled together, sometimes one ejaculates, but he then ridicules himself for this "accident." Small children engage in "imitative sexual play" of all kinds, and are commonly laughed at by adults when the pairings are homosexual; but they are not otherwise punished or criticized. The thrust of the humor is that conception, which is extremely important to the Mbuti, cannot result from homosexual intercourse. Neither Turnbull nor earlier students of the Mbuti detected any instances of homosexual penetration. Turnbull speculates that it may occur, but rarely, as a manifestation of affection. He adds that he does not see the Mbuti as rejecting homosexuality so much as favoring procreation very strongly. Their response appears rather milder in his letter than in his book.

3 *Lepcha.* The Himalayan Lepcha consider sodomy to be a highly antisocial act, likely to produce a year of disaster. It results from eating the flesh of pigs that have not been castrated. Those who engage in it are not blamed, as no one would eat an uncastrated pig knowingly. Several episodes indicate that nothing was done to men who engage in it. For example, one man, while drunk, sodomized several people who were sleeping. After that, people avoided sleeping near him, but did nothing else. Boys engage in mutual masturbation; this is considered funny.[379]

4 *Ashanti.* According to Christensen, the Ashanti say that cowards, sexual deviants, and the mentally retarded, all of whom tend to stay home in the company of women, have a "light" *sunsum,* or personality, while extroverted women or lesbians have a "heavy" *sunsum.*[380] No sanction is mentioned. In an interview with the author in January 1987, anthropologist Eva Meyerowitz, who did fieldwork among the Akan (the Ashanti are one of the main Akan peoples) in the 1940s, indicated that at that time men who dressed as women and engaged in sexual relations with other men were not stigmatized at all, but accepted. There were good reasons for Akan men to become women, she commented—the status of women among the matrilineal Akan was exceptionally high. The situation may have changed later, she thought, as a result of missionary activity.

[378] Turnbull (1965:122).
[379] Gorer (1938:102–3, 110).
[380] Christensen (1954:92–93).

5 *!Kung.* Among these bushmen, "homosexuality is not permitted."[381] Whether any cases were observed, and if so, what was done about them, is not stated.

In short, homosexuality is somewhat disvalued in these societies but, so far as we are told, is not actively punished. When the relationship between antinatalist policy and rejection of homosexuality is recomputed with the recordings adopted here, the relationship falls from .49 to .19, and is no longer statistically significant at the conventional .05 level. In fact, it is smaller than some other relationships that Werner finds, e.g., between frequency of homosexuality and patrilocality (=.23) and between frequency of homosexuality and extended family households (=.23).[382] Were one to code as rejecting homosexuality only those societies that actively did something beyond expressing verbal disapproval to prevent or punish it, the relationships would disappear entirely.

[381] E. M. Thomas (1959:89).

[382] A coefficient of ± 1 implies that one variable can be predicted perfectly from knowledge of the other. A coefficient of zero implies that knowledge of one variable does not improve predictions of the other. A statistically significant relationship is one that is unlikely to have arisen by chance.

3　Inequality and the State: Homosexual Innovations in Archaic Civilizations

All but a handful of the kinship-structured societies discussed in the preceding chapter are (or were) stateless. As such, they lack specialized political bodies with jurisdiction over an extended territory and population. They may restrict political participation on the basis of age and sex, so that important decisions are left to male elders or heads of families; yet the function of government is not monopolized by full-time leaders or employees. Where there are chiefs or wise men, their role is to a large extent advisory: they influence primarily by persuasion, not by giving orders or punishing disobedience.

By contrast, the political leadership of a state is formalized, and concentrated in personnel who are distinct from the rest of the population: kings, dictators, and elected representatives have authority to make rules, allocate collective resources, and decide disputes by imposing settlements, coercively if necessary. A full-time staff carries out policies and enforces decisions. Even though the Shilluk of the Sudan had a king, they did not have a state, because his powers were so limited:

> He did not nominate, and had no veto power over the election of, clan chiefs and chiefs of settlements or lineages, but merely confirmed them in office. The king had only sacerdotal status; he reigned but did not rule. . . . He had no governmental machinery nor administrative structure beyond the royal court, and they had no delegative powers.[1]

Over time, the growth of the state tends to weaken the clan and lineage ties that structure social life in stateless societies. This can be a slow process: in some civilizations, extended kinship ties remained important for centuries.[2]

---

[1]Krader (1968:38–39).

[2]Because the process of state formation is not completed instantly, some early states differ from chiefdoms only to a degree (Krader, 1968:86–88; Classen and Skalnick, 1978:21; Bargatzky, 1985). That is why it was not inappropriate to include some African kingdoms among the stateless societies discussed in the previous chapter.

Inequality in the distribution of wealth is typically low in kinship-structured societies. Limitations in the technical capacity to produce wealth make it difficult for anyone to accumulate much of it. Among hunter-gatherers, everyone is likely to own or be able to manufacture the primitive tools used to obtain food and make clothing, so that no one can be deprived of the necessities of life. Among cultivators and herders, one family may acquire more land (or more fertile land) or livestock than another, but these differences are quantitative, not qualitative, and are often temporary. In some kinship-structured societies, ritualized gift-giving and institutionalized redistribution keep inequalities within bounds.

In other societies, disparities of fortune are more pronounced and more stable. When one stratum gains control of the means of production, it can become a distinct class, extracting surplus from the direct producers of wealth. For example, slaveowners appropriate what their slaves produce, and landowners grant access to their lands only in return for rent. Thus quantitative differences in wealth become qualitatively significant social categories.

As a rule, societies that have states tend to be economically stratified.[3] Compared to stateless societies, they have greater occupational differentiation, more elaborate systems of exchange and redistribution, and technologies that are more advanced. They encompass wider territory and larger numbers of people.

The first states in human history came into being in several parts of the world between five and six thousand years ago in societies whose economies combined agriculture with animal husbandry, handicraft, and commerce. Production was carried out by slaves or serfs, wage laborers, or self-sufficient households. Sometimes the state organized large-scale construction projects (the building of pyramids, temples, canals, and roads) using war captives or corvée labor. These are the societies we call archaic civilizations.

Most archaic states were monarchies, but in some, power was more widely shared: the original Athenian polis was ruled by a king, but eventually became a restricted democracy. The archaic state was always linked closely to an organized religion. Economic inequality and political rule require legitimation, and in the archaic states this was achieved with the help of a priesthood whose loyalty was secured by kinship ties to the ruler, or by uniting the head of the church and the head of state in a single figure. Many rulers claimed divinity, divine descent, or divine inspiration. The

---

[3]Why this should be so has been the subject of much discussion (Service, 1975; Cohen and Service, 1978; Friedman, 1979; Haas, 1982), but the question cannot be taken up here.

early state religions were invariably polytheistic, with deities created in the image of animals or humans, male and female.

The early states fought wars to capture trade routes or slaves, secure natural resources, put down rebellions, and repulse invasions. Warfare is also endemic to many stateless societies, but archaic states were able to wage war on a larger scale because they could more easily field armies without suffering disastrous declines in food production.

The rise of many archaic civilzations entailed the replacement of matrilineal kinship systems with patrilineality.[4] To attract well-to-do sons-in-law, parents tried to provide ample dowries for their daughters, reducing the wealth available for payment of brideprices. As a result, only wealthy men could afford more than one wife. They, however, sometimes had many: rulers' harems could number in the hundreds.

When wealth is inherited patrilineally, knowledge of paternity becomes critically important, for it provides the basis of claims to property. This is the reason premarital virginity came to be highly valued in women, and wives were punished severely for adultery. Male sexuality was usually less restricted, except when it infringed on the rights of other men over women. Thus Sumerian-Babylonian society was monogamous in the sense that a man could have only one wife, but men also had sexual access to concubines, slaves, and prostitutes.[5]

To protect their sexual rights, men allowed women less freedom than in band or tribal societies. Sometimes women had to be veiled, or could not

---

[4] The universality of the transition from matriarchy to patriarchy seems more dubious now than when postulated by Briffault (1927). Still, the first four Egyptian dynasties traced descent through the mother; the rest, through the father (Petrie, 1914:182; 1923:110–11; Krader, 1968:55). At least in theory, the Elamite throne was inherited through the mother (explaining the existence of brother-sister marriage among the royalty), but in practice, not always. For commoners, inheritance was at first uterine, but eventually became agnatic (through the father) (Hinz, 1972:89–90). Mythological evidence strongly points to an early matrilineality for the Greeks (Thomson, 1965) which had disappeared by the Homeric Age. The Etruscans observed mother-right, and there is evidence that other peoples of the ancient Mediterranean also did so (Thomson, 1965:149–203; Hood, 1971:117). However, Pembroke (1965, 1967) has raised questions about the evidence for matrilineality among some of these people. The Chinese ideogram for a man's family name is constructed from the radical for women (Needham, 1956:108), suggesting that marriage once involved exhange of men between matrilineal clans (Granet, 1930:154; 1975:39). The transition appears to have taken place in Shang times (second millennium B.C.) (Chêng, 1960:216; Levenson and Schurmann, 1969:18–32; Ho, 1975:274–81). In Japan, matrilineality may have survived as late as the fourth century, when endemic warfare favored transmission of land to the oldest son, who would normally have been better able to defend it (Munro, 1971:591; Sansom, 1962:362). The evidence from pre-Islamic Arabia is mixed (Wilken, 1884; W. R. Smith, 1903:29–39; Ryckmans, 1986).

[5] Saggs (1962:185).

appear in public without a chaperone. Though often excluded from public affairs, they could sometimes exercise influence indirectly through male relatives, especially sons.

SEXUALITY IN ARCHAIC CIVILIZATION

The basic unit of production and consumption in archaic civilization was the household, not the band or clan.[6] It was organized on the basis of complementary role differentiation, and though this can be accomplished homosexually, as in berdache marriages, the need for children made this choice unrealistic for peasants and craftsmen. Consequently, heterosexuality had a privileged status for most of the population. The wealthy were an exception: they could adopt children, and use slaves or servants as laborers. Their economic status made homosexual marriages possible. Such marriages are recorded in China for both men and women—in the latter case only when the introduction of wage labor permitted women a degree of financial independence from men.[7]

The importance of propagation to human life is reflected in the prominence of heterosexuality in religion and myth. In ancient Chinese thought, the interpenetration of *yang* and *yin* (the male and female principles) animates the whole universe.[8] The Hindu god Krishna was renowned for his pursuit of the cowgirl Radha, and had many wives. The Babylonian goddess Ishtar propositioned the human hero Gilgamesh. The Egyptian god Horus was conceived in the postmortem union of Osiris and his sister Isis. The Canaanite Asherah was the consort of El, king of the pantheon. Other ancient deities symbolized the interdependence of male and female in a single hermaphroditic body.[9]

A heterosexual emphasis is also seen in ritual. The *hieros gamos*, or sacred marriage to promote fertility, was celebrated annually in ancient Egypt,

[6] This includes the extended households of the aristocracy, which included slaves and dependents as well as family members.

[7] McGough (1981), Sankar (1985). Boswell (1980:69, 82) contends that marriages of all-male couples took place in the Roman Empire, but this claim is controversial; see, for example, Colin (1955–56). I know of no evidence suggesting that Roman law recognized such marriages; that of the Emperor Heliogabalus can obviously not be taken as typical. For the purpose of the present argument, though, that is irrelevant; there may have been men living together in quasimarriages in the absence of legal sanction.

[8] Bullough (1976:281–83).

[9] Römer (1903), Dupouy (1906:33, 44), Baumann (1955), Danielou (1960), Delcourt (1966), Bullough (1976:266–67), Westendorff (1977c), Ochshorn (1981:32–33), Hornung (1982:170–71). Admittedly, divine hermaphroditism is not the same thing as divine heterosexuality, but it does represent an endorsement of the gendering of the universe and accords equal status to both sexes.

Mesopotamia, and Canaan: it took the form of ceremonial intercourse between the king and a priestess.[10] In Athens, the Archon Basileus participated in a sacred marriage.[11] Certain Hindu cults require intercourse between monks and nuns.[12] According to Herodotus, Babylonian women had to undergo ritual defloration at the hands of a stranger before they could marry.[13]

Women prostitutes who had intercourse with male worshipers were attached to the sanctuaries and temples of ancient Mesopotamia, Phoenicia, Cyprus, Corinth, Carthage, Sicily, Israel, Egypt, Libya, and West Africa, as well as ancient and modern India.[14]

Divine heterosexuality was no more incompatible with other options than it is among humans. The Hindu god Sāmba, son of Kṛishṇa, seduced mortal women, and was also known for his homosexuality.[15] In addition to marrying Hera and chasing nymphs and women, the Greek Zeus abducted Ganymede. Apollo impregnated nymphs and women, but also fell in love with the male Hyacinth. Poseidon, who married Amphitrite and pursued Demeter, also raped Tantalus.[16] Roman gods, too, often showed a lively interest in both sexes.[17]

Despite the importance of heterosexuality in the cultures of the early civilizations, then, homosexuality was far from unknown. Some of the forms

[10]Frankfort (1948:296–99, 330–31), E. O. James, 1958:114–22, 130–31), Kramer (1969), J. Conrad (1973:84).

[11]Pollard (1965:79–86).

[12]Walker (1968:390–92).

[13]Herodotus (1954:92), 1.199. Herodotus's account is confirmed by Strabo 17.1.6 and the Apocryphal Epistle of Jeremiah 6:43, and for fourth- and fifth-century Syria and Phoenicia by Ephrem Syrus, as well as by Augustine in the *City of God* 4.10 (Yamauchi, 1973). Some tribal societies practice ritual defloration, so that the practice is not as strange as it may seem at first.

[14]Baudin (1885:14), A. B. Ellis (1890:142–44), Dubois (1906:584–86), Dupouy (1906:33), Hartland (1907), Bertholon (1909), G. A. Barton (1914), Hogarth (1914), R. V. Russell (1916: 373–84), Westermarck (1921:222), Brooks (1941), Henriques (1961:1.177), Astour (1966), Delaporte (1970:87), Yamauchi (1973), Desai (1975:107, 148, 155). The evidence for ancient Israel consists of Biblical passages, 1 Sam. 2:22, Amos 2:7–8, Isa. 8:3, 57:3–9, Hos. 4:12–14. The existence of cult prostitution in Egypt has been considered much less certain (Yamauchi, 1973; Carlton, 1977:109). To my mind, the clearest evidence for its existence in early Egyptian history comes from the pyramid texts, which date from the Fifth and Sixth dynasties. Utterance 235 states, ". . . you [referring to the deceased pharaoh] have copulated with the two female guardians of the threshold of the door" (Faulkner, 1969:56). This is exactly what the sons of Eli did in 1 Sam. 2:22! Although Herodotus 1.182 suggests that the Egyptians had abolished cult prostitution, Strabo 17.1.6 indicates otherwise. By the fifth century B.C., the Vedic Mahāviata rite, involving coitus with a female prostitute on an altar, had already become anachronistic (Desai, 1975:14).

[15]Walker (1968:2.343), Bullough (1976:267).

[16]Borneman (1977), Sergent (1985).

[17]Lilja (1978:222).

in which it appeared resemble those found in kinship-structured stateless societies, but there were also new features. This chapter describes some of the innovations; the next discusses social responses.

MALE CULT PROSTITUTION

Male homosexual prostitution having religious significance was an institutionalized feature of the archaic civilizations of the Mediterranean. Most authorities think it was practiced in the Temple of Solomon in Jerusalem, as well as in the worship of neighboring peoples.[18] Yet a few scholars have expressed skepticism.[19] A close examination of the sources is thus in order. There are three: the Hebrew Bible, writings by other peoples of the ancient Near East, and Greek and Roman texts that discuss the religious practices of neighboring civilizations.

The biblical passages, which I quote in a slightly revised version of the Jewish Publication Society's translation, are as follows:

> There shall be no harlot [*qdeshah*] among the daughters of Israel. And there shall be no sodomite [*qdesh*] of the sons of Israel. Thou shalt not bring the hire of a harlot [*zonah*] or the price of a dog [*kelev*] into the house of Yahweh thy god for any vow; for both of these are an abomination [*toavat*] unto Yahweh thy god.[20]

> For they also built them high places and pillars and Asherim on every high hill, and under every leafy tree; and there were also sodomites [*qadesh*] in the land; they did according to all the abominations of the nations which Yahweh drove out before the children of Israel.[21]

> And he [Asa, king of Judaea] put away the sodomites [*qdeshim*] out of the land, and removed all the idols that his fathers had made. And he also deposed Macaah his mother from being queen because she had made an abominable image for an Asherah.[22]

> And he [Josiah] put down the idolatrous priests, whom the kings of Judaea had ordained to offer in the high places in the cities of Judaea, and in the places round about Jerusalem; them also that offered unto Baal, to the sun, and to the moon, and to the constellations, and to all the host of heaven. . . . and he broke down the houses of the sodomites [*qdeshim*] that were in

[18]G. R. Taylor (1965), Terrien (1970), Tripp (1975:5), A. Evans (1978:24–25).
[19]Patai (1967:296), Boswell (1980:99), Ide (1985:76).
[20]Deut. 23:18–19.
[21]1 Kings 13:23–24.
[22]1 Kings 15:12–13.

the house of the Lord, where the women wove coverings for the Asherah.[23]

Literally, *qdesh* (m.) and *qdeshah* (f.) denote someone who is sacred or consecrated. *Qdesh* is usually rendered as "sodomite," with homosexuality implied, even though the term has nothing to do with the city of Sodom; *qdeshah* is customarily translated as "harlot" or "temple prostitute." The biblical passages clearly link the *qdeshim* and *qdeshot* with the worship of gods detested by the followers of Yahweh, but say nothing of their sexual activities. The joining of *zonah* (prostitute) to *kelev* (dog) suggests that the latter is not merely a term of scorn, but a sexual reference, perhaps to someone who has intercourse in a doglike position. The words *zonah* and *qdeshah* were sometimes used interchangeably, as in the story of Judah and Tamar.[24] The parallel construction in Deuteronomy identifies *qdesh* and *kelev* as a male counterpart.

Support for this identification comes from other cultures of the ancient Near East. In Akkadian, *qadishtum* was a holy priestess (who may or may not have been a prostitute). Ugaritic temple personnel included *qdshm*. At Memphis, a monument to Qudshu, a Syrian goddess associated with love and fertility, refers to her as "the prostitute."[25] A Phoenician inscription on Cyprus dating from the fourth century B.C., referring to a category of temple personnel who played a role in the sacred service of Astarte, identifies the *kelev* as a religious functionary of some kind.[26] The Sumerogram for *assinu*, a male-homosexual cult prostitute (see below), joins the symbols for "dog" and "woman."[27] Revelation 22:15 excludes dogs along with sorcerers, whoremongers, and idolaters from the holy city; surely it is referring not to canines, but to men who played a sexual-sacramental role in religion. Deuteronomy prohibits cult prostitution because the Hebrews were adopting the practice from their neighbors.

It does not follow from the identification of *qdeshim* as male cult prostitutes that their partners were men: Patai points out that they could have served barren women who hoped to conceive by having intercourse with a holy man.[28] In some Hindu cults, wives have intercourse with priests who represent the god.[29] There is no direct evidence for this custom from the

[23] 2 Kings 23:5–7.
[24] Gen. 38:15, 24.
[25] Yamauchi (1973), G. Lerner (1986).
[26] Barton (1893–94), Cooke (1903:65), Astour (1966).
[27] Plessis (1921:228–29), Bottéro and Petschow (1975).
[28] Patai (1967:296).
[29] Jennings (1891:67).

ancient Near East, though it has been reported in the recent past for Morocco, Egypt, and Syria.[30] It does seem incompatible with the restrictions Hebrew men placed on female sexuality,[31] but the story of Elisha and the barren widow[32] could be a garbled version of it.

Some of the evidence for homosexual cult practices in surrounding cultures is ambiguous, but clearly rules out male *heterosexual* prostitution. For example, Hittite texts document the existence of male transvestite eunuch temple priests but do not state clearly that they had sexual relations with worshipers.[33] Babylonian and Assyrian texts refer to *assinu* and *kurgarru*, religious functionaries particularly associated with the goddess Ishtar, who danced, played musical instruments, wore masks, and were considered effeminate. They were often depicted carrying a spindle for weaving—a symbol of women's work.[34] The Akkadian myth, "The Descent of Ishtar to the Netherworld," refers to one whose radiant beauty gives unbounding joy to all who behold him. A text prophesying that "if a man touches the head of an *assinu*, he will conquer his enemy"[35] indicates that such functionaries were believed to have magical powers. To ward off the dangers posed by an eclipse of the moon, the king ritually touched the head of an *assinu*—or the *assinu* the head of the king (the text is unclear). They could also heal illnesses.[36] Prayers and treaty curses attributed the power to turn men into women to the goddess Ishtar, and explained that she had turned the *assinu* and *kurgarru* into women to demonstrate her awesome powers. They were clearly transvestites. References to them as "neither male nor female," "incomplete," "half-men," and as "lacking something," point to castration.[37] Surely, their responsibilities did not include fertilizing women.

Most specialists have concluded that the *assinu* and *kurgarru* were homosexual prostitutes,[38] but some consider this uncertain.[39] The ambiguity of most textual references leaves room for doubt, but a few are explicit. One, an omen, promises that "if a man has intercourse with an *assinu*, trouble will leave him."[40]

[30] Westermarck (1926:148), Briffault (1927:3.228).

[31] Deut. 22:20–29.

[32] 2 Kings 4.

[33] Garstang (1910:361), Hoffner (1973b).

[34] One is unavoidably reminded of 2 Kings 23:7, in which women, very likely joined by gender-changed men, weave cloth for the Asherah, the Canaanite Ishtar.

[35] *Assyrian Dictionary* (1968:341).

[36] Plessis (1921:228–29). Why the head? In Freudian theory it symbolizes the penis.

[37] *Assyrian Dictionary* (1971:557–58), Hillers (1973), Bottéro and Petschow (1975).

[38] Plessis (1921:228), D. W. Thomas (1960), Saggs (1962:fig. 51c), Kramer (1963:141–42), John Gray (1964:135–36), Hillers (1973).

[39] *Assyrian Dictionary* (1958:341, 1971:557–58), Frazer (1962), Nock (1972), Oden (1972:39).

[40] Grayson and Redford (1974:148–49).

The noun *assinu* has the same root as *assinutu*, "to practice sodomy." One of the omens in a series uses this expression, predicting that "the owner of the sacrificial lamb [being killed so that the diviner can inspect its liver] will practice sodomy [submit to anal intercourse] if the lamb's right cheek is dark." The term denoted homosexual sodomy alone, and did not necessarily imply a ritual context.[41] The conclusion that one of the *assinu*'s functions was to serve as the receptive sexual partner of male worshipers in anal intercourse,[42] perhaps particularly with those who wanted trouble to leave them, seems inescapable.

The situation was undoubtedly the same for the Sumerian chanter-priests, whose titles, translated literally, mean "womb," "penis-anus," and "anus-womb."[43] Ritual *heterosexual* intercourse was at least sometimes anal as well. Sumerian priestesses were called *assinutum*, the feminine form of *assinu*, because, though sexually active as hierodules, they were supposed to avoid pregnancy. They thus limited themselves to a method that avoided the risk of conception.[44] Babylonian and Assyrian cuneiform texts assert that "the high priestess will permit intercourse per anum in order to avoid pregnancy,"[45] and stamp seals found at the Ishtar temple in Babylon, now in the British Museum (but not on display), show sexual intercourse, in many instances anal.[46] There being no recognizable references in Meso-potamian sources to oral sex (fellatio or cunnilingus), it seems quite certain that the male prostitutes submitted to anal intercourse.[47]

[41] *Assyrian Dictionary* (1958:204, 341).

[42] We do not know the identity of the *assinu*'s partners. The general public was not admitted to Babylonian temple services (Lambert, 1973), but there could have been separate facilities, perhaps in the courtyard or in nearby sacred groves. Toorn (1985:25) implies any male could be a client.

[43] Allegro (1970:76, 222 n. 31).

[44] Astour (1966), G. Lerner (1986). If Isa. 8:3 and 57:3–9 refer to cult prostitution, as they seem to, the Israelite prostitutes did not restrict themselves to this method, for they did have children. The Mesopotamian method may have lasted long. According to Maimonides, the lost *Book Concerning Nabean Agriculture* by ibn-Washya describes rituals for the grafting of fruit trees in Egypt, Persia, and Mesopotamia that involve a man having "shameful and unnatural intercourse" with a maiden; it is to protect Jews from such practices, he says, that they are forbidden from eating fruit from grafted trees (Eliade, 1962:35).

[45] *Assyrian Dictionary* (1958:325).

[46] Leemans (1952:22).

[47] Biggs (1969). Kinsey et al. (1949) state that the intercourse was oragenital, but present no evidence to support their claim. Kinsey's collaborator, Wardell Pomeroy, has informed me that Kinsey was often careless about historical and anthropological questions. Tripp (1965:5) re-peats Kinsey's claim, suggesting that the contemporary Jewish practice of *metsitsah bapeh* de-rives from the ancient ritual. In this practice, the *mohel*, or circumciser, sucks the blood from the wound of a newly circumcised boy to prevent infection. The practice is known from Tal-mudic sources and is still in use in some Orthodox communities today, though most have

Related cult practices flourished in connection with the worship of the West Asian mother goddesses—Cybele, Dea Syria, Aphrodite, Hecate, Artemis, Magna Mater, Anaitis, Ma, Astarte. All had a castrated and/or dying effeminate lover. Some had beards. All were attended by castrated or transvestite priests. Although the goddesses represented abundance, good fortune, and fertility, they also brought destruction, particularly to men who scorned their sexual overtures.[48]

Roman writers tell us of the Cybele cult practices.[49] Every March, Cybele's followers mourned the death of her androgynous lover Attis (her son in some versions of the myth) by holding ecstatic dances and striking themselves with swords and whips. At the height of frenzy, initiates severed their genitals with a sharp stone or shard of broken pottery (metal instruments were forbidden) and assumed women's clothing.[50]

When the veneration of Cybele was first introduced to Rome during the Second Punic War, the Romans disdained her emasculated priests, and forbade citizens from undergoing initiation. But the cult spread as the orientalization of the Empire progressed. Bands of *galli* roamed the countryside dressed as women, scourging themselves, dancing, and begging. In the *Metamorphoses*, also known as *The Golden Ass*, Apuleius portrays the *galli* as passive homosexuals who seek out virile young peasant lads to satisfy their cravings; Lucian paints a similar picture in *Lucius, or the Ass*.[51] However, none of the Hellenistic sources mentions *ritual* homosexuality. Perhaps the cult practices had become desacralized by then. In *The Life of Constantine*, the church historian Eusebius Pamphili, bishop of Caesarea (260?–340), implies, without being too explicit, that the effeminate priests of the goddess worshiped on Mount Lebanon still engaged in homosexual cult practices in his own time;[52] however, as a Christian, Eusebius could have been trying to smear goddess worshipers by imputing to them practices long since abandoned. Without corroboration from contemporaneous pagan sources it is hard to be sure.

Nock has questioned the homosexuality of the eunuch priests, suggesting that they castrated themselves to insure their sexual continence, not to

---

abandoned it as unsanitary. It is unlikely to have had anything to do with cult prostitution, especially since the Babylonians and Assyrians, who had cult prostitutes, did not circumcise.

[48] Farnell (1909:481), Augustine [*City of God* 7.26] (1950:379–81), Harding (1971:142), Nock (1972:7–15), Hillers (1973), Vermaseren (1977), Barnes (1981:247).

[49] The main Roman sources are Ovid, *Festi* 4.183; Martial, *Epigrams* 2.81, 5.41.3, 9.84.4; Lucian (1919), *De Syria Dea* and *Lucius, or the Ass*; and Pliny, *Historia Naturalis* 3.48.165.

[50] Weigert-Vowinkel (1938), E. O. James (1958:76–77), Sanders (1972), Riencourt (1974:128–32), M. Stone (1976), Vermaseren (1977), Balsdon (1979:228–29), Tannahill (1980:251).

[51] Kiefer (1934:123–27), Lucian (1967), Karlen (1971a:61), Bullough (1976:131).

[52] Eusebius (1890:534–35), Dupouy (1906:37).

effeminize themselves or make themselves attractive to male partners.[53] Many peoples believed that celibacy was necessary for the successful performance of certain religious functions, and this could have been true of the priests of the Mother Goddess. The archaic belief that semen is the essence of life, whose retention in the body guarantees immortality,[54] would have supported the practice. Donning female garb could have been a way of showing that conventional male social roles were being abandoned. Nock dismisses the sources that impute homosexuality to the priests on the grounds that in antiquity charges of homosexuality were made lightly. However, he ignores the earlier Mesopotamian and Phoenician evidence. Taking all the sources together—a procedure justified by the prolonged and extensive contacts among the various civilizations of the Mediterranean—it can be safely concluded that anal intercourse formed a part of goddess worship from very early times throughout the Near East, with the possible exception of pharaonic Egypt. If Eusebius is to be believed, it was still going on on Mount Lebanon until Constantine had the shrine of the moon goddess destroyed in the early fourth century.

The Hebrews were part of this world. They interacted extensively with Canaanites, Phoenicians, and Mesopotamians, and adopted some of their religious practices. The evidence presented here points to homosexual intercourse with *qdeshim*, who "did according to all the abominations of the nations, which Yahweh drove out before the children of Israel,"[55] as one of the practices they adopted. There is no evidence for analogous lesbian cult prostitution, though female transvestism appears in Canaanite mythology,[56] and the Roman writer Juvenal—not a particularly trustworthy source—contended that women participating in an annual ceremony in honor of the Bona Dea engaged in lesbian acts.[57]

Scholars have noted the resemblance of Śakti (goddess) worship on the Indian subcontinent to the West Asian cults.[58] Until the practice became illegal in 1948, when India achieved independence, some of the Hindu temples in many parts of the country had women and boy prostitutes.[59] Communities of *hijras*, pre- and postoperative transsexual devotees of the Mother Goddess (Parvati, Bahuchara Mata), who dress as women, sing and dance, and beg for alms, can still be found in a number of cities, especially in the north. They perform when male children are born, and reputedly

[53] Nock (1972:7–15).
[54] La Barre (1985).
[55] 1 Kings 14:24.
[56] Hillers (1973).
[57] Juvenal, *Satire* 6.306–45; Bullough (1976:147–48).
[58] Main (1913:198–99), Ehrenfels (1941:191), Kumar (1974:8–9).
[59] Farquhar (1929:408–9), Mayo (1927:32).

kidnap and castrate young boys. Many engage in homosexual prostitution, though not in a cultic context.[60]

Goddess cults of South India and Sri Lanka also involve male transvestism (but not prostitution at present), ritualized gashing of the head (symbolic castration), impotence anxiety, and fear of heterosexual intercourse. The consort of the virginal Sri Lankan goddess Pattini is killed and castrated or disemboweled (symbolically castrated). Some of these cults may have been brought to Southern India by Syrian traders in the first few centuries A.D. and adopted by indigenous Buddhist and Jainist merchants who married foreigners.[61]

Receptivity to the new cults can be explained by psychological predisposition (discussed below) and already existing goddess worship in Dravidian folk religion, which involved berdachelike male transvestism.[62] This worship was almost certainly quite archaic. Archaeological and linguistic evidence points to goddess worship and the veneration of the generative organs as prominent features of the Indus Valley civilization that flourished in Western India c. 2700–1700 B.C. The figure of a naked dancing girl, possibly a temple prostitute, has been found in the ruins. Cultural dissemination of these institutions from Sumeria, which traded extensively with the Harrapan civilization, is quite likely.[63] The indigenous tribes of Southern India are thought to be descendants of the pre-Aryan Harrapan civilization.

Hindu religious and legal texts frown on homosexual cult practices.[64] Male prostitution was probably not a part of early Indo-European religion. Hence later cult transvestism and homosexuality are unlikely to have originated with the Aryan invasions; most likely they were indigenous, and survived because the invaders often co-opted local cults rather than destroy them.

---

[60] R. V. Russell (1916:3.206), Carstairs (1956), M. E. Opler (1960), Shah (1961), Mark (1981), Nanda (1984, 1985, 1987).

[61] Obeyesekere (1984). In some of the cults, male worshipers cut hair from their heads and offered it to the goddess (Desai, 1975:140–41).

[62] T. H. Levin (1870), Obeyesekere (1984).

[63] The Indian Śakti and the Sumerian mother goddess both ride on lions and have husbands who ride on bulls. The Sumerian mother goddess was called Nana; in Gujrat (now Pakistan), she was called Nana Devi (Sarup, 1958; Basham, 1959:19–25; Kumar, 1974:8–9; Fairservis, 1983).

[64] Homosexuality is considered an offense in the *Arthāshāstra* (*Treatise on Material Gain*) 3.17, 4.13, a text dated to the fourth century B.C., and the *Yājñavalkya* (2.293), a lawbook from the fourth to fifth centuries A.D. According to the *Baudhāyana Dharmasutra* (3.7.2), placed by some scholars at 300–100 B.C., a homosexual act is as heinous as killing a Brahmin. The highly influential *Manusmrti* (*Laws of Manu*) 11.175, c. 185–149 B.C., makes homosexuality a source of ritual pollution to Brahmins and mandates purification through ritual immersion. The *Vishnusmrti* 37.5 (a work derived in part from the *Manusmrti*), says that a man could lose his caste for engaging in it (J. J. Meyer, 1952: 242 n. 1; Bullough, 1976:247; Banerji, 1980:139–42). Discussion of these texts is deferred to chapter 5.

The Meaning of Homosexual Cult Prostitution

The male cult prostitutes of the ancient Near East bear more than a casual resemblance to the American Indian berdaches described in the previous chapter. Just as the Near East cults linked gender transformation to the service of a goddess, some berdaches took up cross-dressing at the command of a female spirit or goddess.[65] The explorer W. H. Keating reported that the Winnebago considered the moon

> to be inhabited by an adverse female deity, whose delight it is to cross men in all his pursuits. If during their sleep this deity should present herself to them in their dreams, the Indians consider it enjoined on them by duty to become *Cinaedi* [receptive homosexuals]; and they ever after assume female garb.[66]

On the other hand, there are differences. Although dreams were sometimes taken as omens in the ancient Near East,[67] there is no evidence that they figured in decisions to undergo castration in the service of the goddess.[68] Intercourse with berdaches does not seem to have had religious significance, and the healing rituals of those who became shamans did not involve sex. Berdaches were not eunuchs; and they were not attached to temples, or part of a religious hierarchy.

As I've already argued in the preceding chapter, the geographical distribution of the transvestite shaman role is too great to be due to cultural diffusion in historical times. More plausibly, the *assinu* and *galli* evolved from an indigenous berdachelike shamanism in the prehistoric Near East. Their special features (affiliation with a temple, castration) developed in the transition from a kinship order to a class-differentiated city-state.

Clinical work with male-to-female transsexuals—anatomically normal males who consider themselves female—some of them seeking sex-reassignment surgery, may shed light on the origins of these special features. Transsexuals seem to show diverse developmental patterns.[69] In one, however, exceptional physical and psychological proximity to the mother

---

[65] There is also a striking parallel to the eunuch priests of the Ba-kongo, a Bantu people of the lower Congo, who participated in phallic worship in small temples. Although H. H. Johnston (1884:409) does not explicitly connect them with goddess worship, he indicates that they performed a special dance for the new moon at which a white male fowl was sacrificed. He says nothing about homosexuality.

[66] Keating (1824:210–11).

[67] Moran (1969).

[68] In contemporary Sri Lanka, recruitment to the priesthood of the goddess Pattini often occurs through visions in adolescence (Obeyesekere, 1984), and this could have been true in antiquity.

[69] Stoller (1971), Green (1974), Person and Ovesey (1974a, 1974b), Newman and Stoller (1974), Steiner (1985).

in the first year of a son's life—entailing closeness so extreme that he hardly knows where he begins and she leaves off—leads to a sense of the self as female.[70] Individuation proceeds normally except in the area of attachment to the mother's femaleness and femininity. The father is either absent or so aloof and indifferent that he cannot serve as a source of male identification. Incestuous heterosexual desire for the mother is absent from the relationship because the son does not consider himself male. Oedipal conflict is absent because the father is not sufficiently present in the family to constitute a meaningful rival. Consequently, the son has no castration anxiety. He derives no pleasure from his penis (he rarely masturbates), which he wants removed, to bring his anatomy into congruence with his psychosexual identity.[71]

A slightly different psychoanalytic explanation focuses on preoedipal anxiety stemming from separation from the mother in early childhood.[72] In this model, a small male child wants to become autonomous by detaching himself from his mother. Yet he also fears the loss of his mother's nurturance, and therefore introjects his mother, making her part of his own ego.

As the son secures himself against the threat of maternal loss by introjecting his mother, he also incorporates her punitive attitudes toward his own sexuality, so that they become part of his own superego. Sexual arousal later in life will awaken these attitudes. Heterosexual intercourse will be experienced as threatening because union with someone of the opposite sex (symbolically, with the mother) jeopardizes a precarious individuation established through separation from the mother.

Self-castration and the donning of women's clothing, it is argued, are responses to these anxieties. To be sure, they are not the only conceivable responses, but they are plausible responses.[73] They assure the introjected mother that she will never be abandoned for someone else, but in a manner that precludes the frightening possibility of incest.

Anxieties concerning separation and maternal loss should be most acute when a woman's social roles are most restricted, and her relationship with her husband intensely frustrating. Under these conditions, a mother's emotional energies will tend to focus on her son, whose future independence

[70]Stoller (1976b:54) suggests that this identification occurs at first through passive conditioning and imprinting, rather than through the more active process of introjection, on the uncertain ground that a very young infant may not be capable of fantasy. But he adds that by the end of its first year, the pretranssexual son actively pursues femininity.

[71]Stoller (1976b). Extreme though this desire may be, it is not psychotic. Transsexuals are not delusional. They understand that their anatomy is male; they simply want to change it. By contrast, Daniel Paul Schreber, the German magistrate analyzed by Freud (1911), actually believed that his body was becoming female.

[72]The explanation has been applied specifically to priestly castration in the service of the Mother Goddess by Weigert-Wovinkel (1938), Bettelheim (1962:90–93), and Slater (1968).

[73]Homosexuality without gender change would be another possible outcome.

she both envies and resents. While she may be able to take vicarious satisfaction in her son's later accomplishments, she may also try to preserve his
dependence on her as long as possible. Though her interaction with him
may be erotically tinged, she may respond with hostility to his maturity—
especially his sexual maturity—since she will have to abandon him to his
wife when he marries. It follows that men brought up by mothers who are
intensely involved with them, and who discourage their sexuality, will find
adult women sexually dangerous; they arouse but, like the mother, cannot
be touched.[74]

We do not know the family histories of the *galli* or other transvestite
priests, but what we know of the goddess cults favors the second of these
two models. The goddess's destructive rage at mortal men who reject her
overtures is readily interpreted as a reflection of the child's fear of incest
and the threat of his ego boundaries that it represents. The castrated, effeminate, dying son-consort represents the male child who identifies with
his mother, loves her, and is punished for it. Flagellation and castration not
only administer this punishment to the mother-fixated son, but also induce
bleeding, a simulation of menstruation. Whereas Stone Age goddesses are
visibly pregnant, those of the archaic civilizations are virginal—a denial of
the mother's threatening sexuality.[75] It is consistent with the dynamics proposed that men of ancient Mesopotamia were troubled by impotence, and
sought magical cures for it.[76]

Spratt considers the family process postulated in the second model to be
typical of traditional Indian families, and links this process with the prevalence of male transvestism in village rituals for the goddess.[77] Obeyesekere
notes that a number of Indian family practices, some of them dating back at
least 1500 years, would tend to produce mother fixation in male children.[78]
Fathers indulge their little girls, but then marry them at a young age to men
they may not know. Overnight they become subservient strangers in households dominated by in-laws. Husbands are often emotionally distant, sexually inhibited by Brahmanic traditions holding intercourse to be polluting
and dangerous. Failing to find emotional gratification from their husbands,
mothers become strongly attached to their infant sons, kiss their penises,
and act seductively toward them. In Sri Lanka, sons sleep next to their
mothers until age four or five, sometimes almost until puberty. The father
sleeps elsewhere, but comes in to have intercourse, in the child's presence,
with his wife.[79]

[74]Bibring (1953), Slater (1968:39), Dinnerstein (1976), Obeyesekere (1984).
[75]Obeyesekere (1984).
[76]Hoffner (1966), Biggs (1967), Hillers (1973).
[77]Spratt (1966:181–98).
[78]Obeyesekere (1984).
[79]It is hardly surprising to learn from Mayo (1927:34–35) of the widespread prevalence of

Slater thought that subordinated mothers were especially characteristic of classical Greece, and found much evidence in Greek mythology for the themes expected on the basis of the family dynamics postulated in our second model.[80] Yet Greeks of the classical age were repelled by ritual castration.[81] The practice was found primarily in Asia Minor.

The difference can be laid to the role of the father. If he is a salient figure in the family, he can provide a basis for male identification despite the child's intense attachment to his mother. His presence should instigate oedipal conflict and fear of castration by others—themes one finds in Greek, Indian, and Sri Lankan mythology[82]—but not self-castration, which will be greeted with horror. Where the father is absent, on the other hand, identification with the mother is potentially stronger and may lead to transvestism without castration anxiety, and self-castration to deny one's masculinity.

Greek fathers were not ordinarily absent from home for long periods, nor are contemporary Indian fathers; hence the rarity of institutionalized transvestism and self-castration.[83] However, merchants of West Asia engaged in long-distance commerce were probably away from home for months at a time, as were professional soldiers in the standing armies of the monarchies. By contrast, the citizen-soldiers of the Greek city-states were not professionals and lived at home. Terms of service in the Roman army, on the other hand, grew to great length: the general and political leader Marius (d. 86 B.C.) permitted plebes to enlist for as long as twenty years, just about the time that self-castration began to make inroads.[84]

---

impotence among Indian men. O'Flaherty (1980:51) and Obeyesekere (1984:454) comment on the prevalence of impotence anxiety in Indian culture.

[80] Slater (1968).

[81] This repulsion may be even older. Some fragmentary texts from seventh-century B.C. Ionia cast scorn on a male effeminate who may have been an adept of a goddess (Sergent, 1984:295).

[82] For Greek mythology see Slater (1968). Obeyesekere (1984) discusses Indian and Sria Lankan myths.

[83] Self-castration themes do appear in Greek myths associated with Crete. Clement of Alexandria, a Greek theologian of the second century A.D. who had been initiated into the Phrygian rites before his conversion to Christianity, tells of a myth in which Zeus castrates a sheep and throws the severed genitals at Rhea, his mother, pretending to punish himself for having raped her (Weigert-Vowinkel, 1938). The story hints at the substitution of animal for human castration in an earlier era. The source is quite late, but could have been based on much earlier sources. It is intriguing that Minoan kinship is thought to have been matrilineal. In some tribal societies, matrilineal kinship leads to long periods of father absence because the father must fulfill family obligations in his natal village. Butterworth (1966:135–74) suggests that traces of shamanistic sex-change practices in Greek mythology (seen in the stories of Tiresius and Kaineus) may be Asiatic in origin, brought by the invasion of Europe by horsemen from the eastern steppes at the turn of the second millennium B.C. A Minoan origin is equally possible. Many culture traits entered Greece by way of Crete.

[84] Nisbet (1964:257–71).

Of course we have no direct proof that eunuch priests were children of absent soldiers or merchants. Moreover, it is probable that most male children raised in such families did not castrate themselves. Men of the matrilineal Nayars of the Malabar coast of South India did not traditionally live with their wives; often they were away from home for long periods serving in the armies of the rajahs.[85] Yet most became neither transvestite nor transsexual. In most families, other males would have been present, and mothers were not so seductive and hostile to their sons' heterosexuality as to produce an outcome so extreme as self-mutilation.[86] However, if the family configuration described here was common in antiquity, gender ambivalence would have been common enough to create awe and fascination with eunuchs on the part of the populace.

This awe and fascination made it possible for individual acts of castration to evolve into an institutionalized part of priestly initiation. Perhaps an individual eunuch attracted veneration, founded a local cult and established a sanctuary or temple, or took up residence in a preexisting temple. Such an individual could certainly have been a berdache or a transvestite shaman. Alternately, castration could have evolved from tribal rituals involving mild cutting. 1 Kings 18:26–28 describes the prophets of Baal cutting themselves with swords and lances while dancing in a leaping manner around the altar on Mount Carmel. Lucian of Antioch, a Christian theologian of the third century, reports that gashing with knives was part of the Syrian ceremony of mourning for Adonis.[87] The prophets of the goddess Kali also cut themselves with swords when performing an annual rite in Kerala, India.[88] Paleolithic cave art showing dancers in animal skins leaping testifies to the antiquity of such rites.[89]

Worshipers of the goddess who castrated themselves would undoubtedly have invented myths to explain their actions. These myths would inevitably embody residues of the psychological processes that gave rise to the castration, while disguising them from the initiates themselves by attributing responsibility to the goddess. Being composed from the raw materials made available by the surrounding culture, these myths would necessarily incorporate prominent themes of that culture, such as the annual vegetation cycle.[90] Provided there were enough young men who responded to their anxieties by amputating their genitals, it would not have

[85] Gough (1959, 1961).
[86] In fact, mothers were prohibited by norms of restraint from conversing with adult sons about sexual matters (Gough, 1961).
[87] Gaster (1950).
[88] Obeyesekere (1984:602).
[89] Allegro (1977:171–73).
[90] In Near Eastern myth and ritual the yearly death and resurrection of the son-god was equated with the annual vegetation cycle.

taken long for self-castration to become established in the annual rituals. Evidently there were enough. Once established, the prestige of the role might have made it attractive even to young men not especially plagued by maternal separation anxiety.

The attractiveness of intercourse with a eunuch priest remains to be explained. By castrating himself and putting on female garb, the priest was not becoming just any woman. Unconsciously, he may have been identifying with his mother, but in the terms of his own culture, he identified himself with a goddess, and presumably acquired some of her powers. Anal intercourse was her method. Although Ishtar was the goddess of love and had many lovers, she was childless. The female hierodules who consecrated themselves to her were called *naditu*, barren,[91] because their sexual practices could not result in pregnancy. It was in imitation of the goddess and her divine partners that they and their male counterparts in the priesthood submitted to anal sex. The male worshipers who had intercourse with the priests and priestesses were uniting with the goddess herself. As the cuneiform text quoted earlier indicates, this union was propitious: the goddess must have looked favorably on a gift of precious semen. It brought good fortune to the worshiper and his household, just as the sacred marriage of the king to the high priestess each spring did for the entire kingdom.[92]

SODOMY IN MALE INITIATION RITES

One would hardly expect to see institutionalized male transgenerational homosexuality of the Melanesian variety (described in chapter 2) in the archaic civilizations. The conditions that seem to give rise to it in Melanesia do not exist in the early civilizations. With the pacification of an extended territory, wives are no longer taken from enemy villages, and marriage is not arranged through sister exchange between cross-cousins.

Yet ritualized, transgenerational male homosexuality was a part of early Greek culture. Dominated from the time of the Dorian invasion (c. 1200 B.C.) by powerful, culturally conservative noble families, the eastern part of Crete

---

[91] Astour (1966).

[92] It was not always or only the king who participated in the *hieros gamos*. An Old Babylonian liver model says that the high priest has regular sexual intercourse with the ēntu-priestess (Toorn, 1985:167 n. 206). A related logic seems to be at work among the West African Fang, who consider anal homosexual intercourse to convey healing powers from the passive to the active partner (Tessman, 1959); and among the Zulu, whose warriors, after killing someone, must cleanse themselves of the pollution by having intercourse with a woman or boy of another village (Krige, 1965:276–77). In some Hindu Tantric cults, a worshipper could absorb special powers by inserting a finger into the anus of a man who fellated a third party (Bullough, 1976:263). In some of the Indian Śakti cults, neophytes try to acquire occult power by having anal intercourse with a dead man (or genital intercourse with a dead woman) (Allegro, 1977).

kept up ancient customs well into historical times.[93] One of these customs was an initiation rite for aristocratic youths that bears remarkable resemblance to tribal rituals. Boys were taken from their mothers by *kouretes* (armed male dancers). Under the auspices of the pre-Olympian Mother Goddess cult of Rhea and Zeus, the boys were cleansed of maternal contamination and reborn as men. A men's house figured in the ceremonies, and bull roarers (devices widely used in tribal rituals to simulate the sound of bulls or thunder) were used to terrify the initiates.[94]

As described by Ephoros, a historian of the fourth century B.C., and repeated almost verbatim by Strabo,[95] the initiation had a homosexual component. The boy, chosen for his character and manliness, was abducted in a prearranged mock kidnapping and taken to the country for several months of hunting, feasting, and homosexual sex. When released he was given a military outfit, an ox for sacrifice to Zeus, and a drinking cup.[96] It was considered shameful not to be chosen. Those who participated were honored throughout their lives.[97]

Sparta, too, institutionalized homosexual relations between mature men and adolescent boys, as well as between adult women and girls, and gave them a pedagogical focus.[98] The few accounts we have, all written by foreigners, do not claim that the relationships were part of initiation rites, but the Spartans were secretive about their institutions, and strangers would not necessarily have learned the details. However, many aspects of Spartan homosexuality and marriage customs point to tribal origins. Participation was mandatory for all youths of good character. There were ordeals—a common feature of tribal initiation. At their conclusion, all boys in the same-age grade had to marry—as in many tribes. Even after marriage, men lived in men's houses, not with their wives. Wives and male lovers were shared with age-mates.[99] Like Crete, from whom the Greeks believed Spartan institutions were borrowed, Sparta preserved ancient customs that had disappeared in other city-states.[100]

[93] Marrou (1956:27), Willets (1962:297).

[94] Harrison (1927:17 nn. 3, 4, 61–66).

[95] Ephoros 70; Strabo (1928:155), 10.4.21; Dover (1978:189–90).

[96] The cup may have had sacramental significance, or it may have denoted admission to the ranks of men; women and children were not permitted to drink wine.

[97] Bremmer (1980), Sergent (1984:24–53).

[98] Buffière (1980:68–71), Golden (1981:163–76). The ancient writers were divided about the sexual aspects of the relationship. Several contended that while the "inspirer" and his "listener" could sleep together, penetration was forbidden. Plato, however, believed otherwise.

[99] Age grading is most often found in noncentralized political systems, and commonly features the sexual sharing of wives; the practice reduces jealousy among age-mates (Baxter and Almagor, 1978).

[100] Müller (1839:2.300–6), Pogey-Castries (1930), Michel (1952), Marrou (1956:27), A.H.M.

The notion that Greek homosexuality had its origin in Dorian tribal initiations goes back to Müller,[101] who suggested—without knowing anything
of Melanesian life—that its purpose was the mechanical implantation of
character via the semen. Bethe and other scholars find support for this thesis in the graffiti with homosexual themes found near a temple of Apollo on
the island of Thera, a Spartan colony; they interpret the inscriptions as a
record of an initiation.[102] Others, though, consider the graffiti to be nothing
more than frivolous obscene scribbling.[103]

The early history of Greek tribal cults remains obscure,[104] but mythology
points to the existence of male initiation rites with a homosexual component. In many myths, including the foundation myths of a number of the
city-states, a young man performs heroic feats of hunting under the supervision of an older initiation master with whom he sometimes has a homosexual relationship. On completion of the ordeal he is recognized as an
adult and marries, sometimes to a wife provided by his master. Even though
our sources for the myths are late, cultural details of the stories place them
in the Dark Ages or earlier, when hunting was still important to the economy—not only as a source of food, but to protect crops and domestic animals from lions and wild boars. The names of some of the heroes and gods
in the stories appear in Mycenean Linear B tablets, suggesting that the
myths and associated rituals could date back to c. 1500 B.C., if not earlier.[105]
They were probably not Minoan, but rather Indo-European.[106] Other west-

---

Jones (1967:7), Pacion (1970), Gentile (1976), Calame (1977:1.392, 427–44), Buffière (1980:65–
76), Dover (1978:186, 192–94), Giacomelli (1980), J. T. Hooker (1980:135–37), Cartledge (1981).

[101] C. O. Müller (1839).

[102] Bethe (1907), Jeanmaire (1939), Vanggaard (1972:23–49), Patzer (1982).

[103] Semonov (1911), Marrou (1956:367), Buffière (1980:58), Dover (1978):122–23).

[104] Dietrich (1974).

[105] Jeanmaire (1939:450–55), Eliade (1965:108–9), Brelich (1969:198 f.), Rubin and Sale (1983),
Sergent (1984), Sartre (1985), Graf (1986). The Dorian invasion was a couple of hundred years
later. However, protracted interaction over a period of centuries in the second millennium
B.C., when the Dorians were still nomadic, on the fringes of the Mycenean world, gave the
Dorians and Mycenians a common religious culture. The Dorians may have disrupted Greek
life c. 1200–1000 B.C., but they probably did not change its religious cults very much (Dietrich,
1974:263). Male homosexual relations were as characteristic of those parts of Greece not conquered by the Dorians (e.g., Elis and Boeotia) as they were in the Dorian regions—evidence
that pederasty was not brought in by the Dorians. The absence of references to homosexuality
in Homer is sometimes taken as evidence that institutionalized pederasty must be post-
Homeric (i.e., later than the eighth century B.C.). But male homosexuality is implied in several
passages. When Telemachus visits Nestor, the host supplies his guest with his only unmarried son as a bed companion (*Odyssey*, bk. 3). The relationship between Achilles and Patrocles
will be discussed below.

[106] This line of reasoning must be treated with caution. Even if the names of gods that figure
in later stories of homosexuality date back to the second millennium B.C., it does not follow

Indo-European peoples also appear to have had homosexual initiation rites for young men.[107]

Our discussion of homosexual initiation in New Guinea directs us to look for two explanatory features—sexual antagonism, possibly linked with the taking of wives from hostile villages, and marriage by means of sister exchange.[108] Unfortunately, there is little evidence for either. Warfare between cities may have been common in the Dark Ages, but unity of males against potentially hostile and powerful wives is not a significant theme. The heroes of the legends do not marry their cousins, even when—as in the stories of Meleager and Odysseus—the initiation master is a mother's brother.[109] And though the claim has been made that Indo-European kinship terminology makes sense only on the basis of cross-cousin marriage,[110] most specialists think otherwise. They conclude that Proto-Indo-European marriage was exogamous to the patrilineage, but ordinarily to a stranger, not a cousin.[111]

Even in the absence of cross-cousin marriage, relationships between a mother's brother and his sister's son were exceptionally affectionate—unlike father-son relationships, which tended to be cold and formal. Foster parentage was a common institution among the Indo-European peoples, and in many instances the foster father was a mother's brother. In ancient Iran, the mother's brother was called "upbringer" or "foster father." Vedic texts suggest that this was also true for the Indo-Aryans. Scattered evidence suggests that among the ancient Hittites, Greeks, Romans, Celts, and Germans, mother's brothers were often foster parents.[112] Under these circumstances, it would be natural for the foster parent to supervise initiation, and perhaps to ritually sodomize his ward, without supplying his own daughter as a wife.

With the qualification that male homosexual practices were not uniquely Dorian, Bethe's suggestion that they were implicated in tribal initiation practices seems sound. Participation was limited to the noble youths, and may have been important in solidifying the cohesiveness of the ruling-class

---

that institutionalized homosexuality does. Myths can change over time, so that homosexual stories about Zeus or other gods could have appeared later (Figuiera, 1986). Though hunting did not disappear with the rise of agriculture (Detienne, 1979:79), its importance in the culture of Greek male homosexuality (Schnapp, 1984) suggests the antiquity of institutionalized pederasty. In the early vases, homosexual relations develop outside the city, on the hunt.

[107] Bremmer (1980). Chapters 4 and 6 discuss these rituals.
[108] See chapter 2.
[109] Rubin and Sale (1983).
[110] Benveniste (1973:181–92).
[111] Friedrich (1966), Szemerényi (1977), Trautmann (1981:349–56).
[112] Bremmer (1976, 1983, 1987), Graf (1986).

male aristocracy against the centrifugal tendencies of a culture that stressed individual military prowess and provided no overarching state to stave off the war of all against all. The belief that special attributes could be communicated sexually may have helped to legitimate noble rule.

There are hints in the ethnographic literature suggesting that in the transition from an egalitarian to a stratified social order, pederastic relations come to be restricted to an elite. In the Hawaiian and Caroline Islands of Polynesia, male homosexual relations (probably transgenerational, definitely not transgenderal) were institutionalized among the aristocrats of the Areoi Society, but not among the population at large.[113] This restriction often has an economic as well as normative dimension. Mossi chiefs have their young male *soronés*, while the less affluent commoners do not.[114] Big Namba chiefs of New Guinea have many boy lovers, commoners only one.[115]

THE LOVE OF WARRIORS

Male homosexual relations in the archaic civilizations also occurred in military settings. The early civilizations were often at war, and for much longer stretches than in the materially impoverished primitive societies. Wars were fought almost exclusively by men,[116] and boys' education stressed the martial arts and virtues.

As in many kinship-structured societies, soldiers were often barred from any contact with women, lest they lose their masculine strengths, or be polluted. According to Gilbert Murray, the Achaeans who fought at Troy were votaries who had sworn an oath to abstain from intercourse with women until they had captured the city.[117] Extended periods of separation from women would have been conducive to homosexuality, especially under conditions of warfare, whose participants share the intense emotions associated with the risks of combat.[118]

Many of the early civilizations passed through a stage in which political leadership was monopolized by a military aristocracy. Warfare took the form of armed champions fighting at close quarters as individuals or in small clusters, accompanied by squires. Centralized coordination was virtually nonexistent,[119] and warriors were highly competitive. While a cultural

[113] W. Ellis (1969:243). For Hawaii, see also Kamakau (1961:234) and Sagan (1985:206); for Tahiti, Lisiansky (1814:199) and Williamson (1924:393).
[114] Tauxier (1912:570).
[115] Deacon (1934:170).
[116] Briffault (1927:1.451–58) shows that in many primitive societies women do fight. Even some of the early states maintained special corps of women warriors. The increasing restrictions on women that typically accompanied the growth of the early states brought an end to such "Amazon" corps.
[117] G. Murray (1934:132–33).
[118] Symonds (1975).
[119] G. Murray (1934:152), Saggs (1965:121), Dupuy and Dupuy (1970:7), Greenhalgh (1973),

emphasis on personal valor and bravery would have made a champion erotically attractive to other men, rivalry would also have stood in the way of an egalitarian relationship.[120] Though some sexual relationships could have developed some aristocratic warriors who fought together as equals, most would have had to involve partners who could not be considered competitors.

The aristocratic warrior societies do seem to have had extensive male homosexuality, which was completely accepted. Archaeological evidence shows that c. 500 B.C., when they were founding the La Tene culture in France and the northern part of Switzerland, large numbers of Celts were armed for military raids of looting.[121] Their political organization took the form of decentralized chiefdoms, with patron-client relationships linking aristocrats and commoners.[122] According to Aristotle,[123] the Celts esteemed homosexuality. Writing in the first century B.C., Diodorus Siculus found Celtic women charming, and every indicator of their social status suggests that it was quite high.[124] Nevertheless, he added,

> the men are much keener on their own sex; they lie around on animal skins and enjoy themselves, with a lover on each side. The extraordinary thing is they haven't the smallest regard for their personal dignity or self-respect; they offer themselves to other men without the least compunction. Furthermore, this isn't looked down on, or regarded as in any way disgraceful: on the contrary, if one of them is rejected by another to whom he has offered himself, he takes offence.[125]

Evidence that the Celtic love of warriors may have extended to the British Isles (which the Celts invaded c. 200 B.C.) can be found in the Irish saga *Tain Bo Cuailnge*. The hero Cuchulain explains that he does not want to fight his foster-brother and former comrade-in-arms Ferdia:

Garlan (1975:121–23). Thus in the *Iliad* 2.362–63, Nestor calls on Agamemnon to "Set your men in order by tribes, by clans . . . and let clan go in support of clan, let tribe support tribe" (Homer, 1951:85). This mode of deployment was not conducive to a unified command system, but as long as the clans claimed men's allegiances, there could be no other form of warfare. The more bureaucratized states made greater use of disciplined phalanxes (Yadin, 1963: 49, 112).

[120] Ungaretti (1978). The Norse saga of the two blood-brother warriors Thorgeir and Thormod nicely illustrates this point; their friendship ended when one speculated aloud as to which of them would best the other were they to fight (Vanggaard, 1972:120).

[121] Filip (1982).

[122] Crumley (1974).

[123] *Politics* 2.9.7.

[124] Dillon and Chadwick (1967:194–95).

[125] Diodorus Siculus, *Bibliotheke Historike*, bk. 5, quoted in Herm (1977:58). His source was the Greek Stoic historian and traveler Posidonius, whose works are not extant. Strabo (*Geography* 4.4, 6) and Atheneus 603A present a similar picture.

> Fast friends, forest companions
> We made one bed and slept one sleep
> In foreign lands after the fray.[126]

The epic is of course late, but Ireland's isolation allowed aboriginal Celtic folkways to survive into the early Middle Ages.

The Babylonian *Epic of Gilgamesh* describes an intimate relationship between Gilgamesh, king of the city-state of Uruk, and Enkidu, a totally uncivilized, virile wild man sent by the gods in response to complaints from the nobles that Gilgamesh was sexually exploiting their sons and daughters.[127] After a belligerent confrontation in which Gilgamesh emerged victorious, the two became close friends and embarked on a series of dangerous adventures together.

Explicit homosexual references are lacking, but there are hints that the relationship between Gilgamesh and Enkidu was sexual. When Gilgamesh dreams of a meteorite, the mother-goddess (or his mother?) interprets the dream:

> Forsooth, Gilgamesh, one like thee
> Was born on the steppe,
> And the hills have reared him.
> When thou seest him, [as (over) a woman]
> thou wilt rejoice.
> The nobles will kiss his feet;
> Thou wilt embrace him and [. . .] him;
> Thou wilt lead him to me.

This interpretation is followed immediately by a second dream:

> In the street
> [Of] broad-marted Uruk
> There lay an axe, strange was its shape.
> As soon as I saw it, I rejoiced.
> I loved it, and as though to a woman,
> I was drawn to it.
> I took it and placed it
> At my side.[128]

[126] Kinsella (1969:186).

[127] The Sumerian King List places Gilgamesh as fifth ruler in the First Dynasty of Uruk c. 2700–2500 B.C. A tablet found at Ebla has a tale about him, making a date of 2500 B.C. reasonable for the first written version of the legend. The earliest extant texts date from 2100–2000 B.C. The story underwent further elaboration in subsequent centuries. Gilgamesh may have been a foreigner, possibly a vassal of Kish (Tigar, 1982:13, 184–85, 242–43). Jacobsen (1930) clarifies the nature of the exploitation.

[128] Tablet 2 of the Old Babylonian version of the legend; the translation by E. A. Speiser appears in Pritchard (1958:1.46–47). In Jacobsen's (1930) translation, Gilgamesh "cohabits" with

The mother-goddess explains: "Because I made it vie with thee." Enkidu then appears and fights with Gilgamesh. The meteorite and axe must symbolize him. Both meteorite and axe are female symbols;[129] thus it is indirectly suggested that Gilgamesh was attracted to Enkidu as a woman. Later, when Enkidu dies, Gilgamesh "veiled his friend like a bride" and moaned "bitterly like a wailing woman."[130]

Despite these ample hints, most scholars have concluded that the relationship was not sexual. The case for a homosexual relationship is strengthened, however, by the existence of sexual puns in the dream episodes. The Akkadian word for meteorite is *kisru*, while the word *kezru* denotes a "male with curled (i.e., dressed) hair," the male counterpart of *kezertu*, a female prostitute. The word for axe in the second dream is *hassinu*, an apparent word-play on *assinu*, a male-homosexual cult prostitute.[131] Though Enkidu was certainly not effeminate, he is analogized to a female prostitute by virtue of the subordinate sexual role he played after being defeated by Gilgamesh.[132]

Parallels to the Gilgamesh-Enkidu relationship have often been seen in the biblical story of David and Jonathan, and in the devotion of Achilles and Patrocles for one another in the *Iliad*. After David slew Goliath,

---

the axe; his mother's interpretation, "The axe which you saw is a man; you cohabited with him as with a woman because he will be a match to you," brings out the sexual implications more clearly.

[129] The meteorite at Pessinus in Phrygia was worshiped as an image of the mother goddess Cybele; in pre-Islamic times, the Ka'aba in Mecca was venerated as a goddess (Eliade, 1962: 20). In modern Ghana, the Akan—a people whose culture was heavily influenced by that of ancient Libya—continue to regard meteorites as symbols of the Great Mother (E. Meyerowitz, 1955:71–72). The strange shape of the axe suggests that it could have been the double-headed axe found in Asia Minor and Minoan ruins. The weapon is never depicted in the hands of a male god, only in the possession of goddesses, women, or male votaries of goddesses (Willets, 1962:20; Nilsson, 1971:220–27; Friedrich, 1978:24). Allegro (1977:127) suggests that it was a fertility symbol: "The lower edges of the blade represent the woman's opened thighs, the central shaft-hole her vagina, and the shaft itself the inserted penis. The expressive graphic symbolism finds philological support in the words for the implement in ancient Sumerian, Indo-European, and Semitic." I suspect that it could have been the axe used to geld the eunuch priests of the goddess. In a Phoenician myth, Eshmun cuts off his sexual organ with an axe to foil the amorous mother of the gods, Astronoe (Hillers, 1973). The juxtaposition of the meteorite and the axe in the story bring to mind the Scythian myth, told by Herodotus 4.5, of gold objects, including an axe, falling from the sky. It is remarkable that the double-headed axe was still used in fairly recent times in West and Central African fertility cults which involved ritual bestiality and homosexuality (Talbot, 1927:8).

[130] Pritchard (1958:1.61).

[131] Kilmer (1982).

[132] This characterization seems at odds with their great friendship. However, the Gilgamesh Epic as it has come down to us is a composite of stories written down at different times. In the Sumerian tale *Gilgamesh, Enkidu, and the Netherworld* (the source for tablet 12 of the Akkadian),

> The soul of Jonathan was knit with the soul of David, and Jonathan loved him as his own soul. And Saul took him that day, and would let him go no more to his father's house. Then Jonathan made a covenant with David, because he loved him as his own soul.[133]

Later, when told that Saul and Jonathan had fallen in battle, David lamented both deaths, recalling that Jonathan's love had been "wonderful . . . surpassing the love of women."[134]

The relationship between Achilles and Patrocles was no less intense. Patrocles was Achilles' "beloved companion . . . whom I loved beyond all other companions, as well as my own life. . . . My heart goes starved for meat and drink, though they are here beside me, by reason of longing for you. There is nothing worse than this I could suffer, not even if I were to hear of the death of my father."[135] Achilles' grief at the death of Patrocles was so extreme that even Zeus and Athena took pity.[136]

In neither case does the text mention a sexual aspect to the relationship, but this need not be decisive. The Hebrew Bible underwent extensive editing before being put into final form, and an explicit homosexual relationship between David and Jonathan could easily have been deleted by priestly editors. Nevertheless, homophilic innuendos permeate the story. Saul loved the young David "greatly" and made him his armor bearer.[137] Learning that David and Jonathan had become intimates, Saul flew into a rage, tried to kill David, and cursed Jonathan: "Thou son of perverse rebellion, do not I know that thou hast chosen the son of Jesse to thine own shame, and unto the shame of thy mother's nakedness?"[138] No doubt Saul's fear of David's growing popularity contributed to his explosive outbursts, but sexual jealousy runs through the narration like a red thread.

Gilbert Murray suggests that Homer is not more explicit about Achilles and Patrocles because the text was censored.[139] Greek acceptance of homosexuality[140] makes censorship unlikely, but if homosexuality was still ritualized in Homer's day, his silence might have been an effort to protect a cult secret. Homer says little about religion in the epics, though it is unlikely he

---

Enkidu is Gilgamesh's servant and never becomes his friend, as he does in the Old Babylonian fragments (Tigar, 1982:26–46).

[133] 1 Sam. 18:1–2.
[134] 2 Sam. 1:26.
[135] *Iliad* 9.205, 18.82, 19.319–22. The quotations are from Homer (1951:203, 377, 400–401).
[136] *Iliad* 19:338–41.
[137] 1 Sam. 16:21.
[138] 1 Sam. 20:30.
[139] G. Murray (1934:125).
[140] See chapter 4.

considered it unimportant. Later epics, written in periods when we know homosexuality flourished, say little about it,[141] suggesting that arguments based on silence can mislead. Nor can we accept Barrett's argument that Achilles' and Patrocles' lively interest in women counts against their having been lovers;[142] the one interest need not have precluded the other.[143]

Consideration must be given to the possibility that Achilles and Patrocles had once been lovers but were so no longer at the time Troy was besieged. Xenophon tells us that Greeks who served as mercenaries for Cyrus the Younger took along or captured young boys, not yet of fighting age, to use as sexual outlets.[144] Too young to fight, they were not rivals of their older partners, and consequently posed no threat to their wards' competitive but fragile egos. The relationships sometimes became intense, occasionally leading to lifelong ties.[145]

The city of Thebes maintained an elite Sacred Band of three hundred homosexual lovers—older *heniochoi* (charioteers) and their young *paraibatai* (companions), who were given a complete set of military equipment on reaching maturity. Arrangements of this kind may have originated in early days of chariot warfare in the Near East. The Code of Hammurabi (c. 1725 B.C.) refers to *girsequ*[m], chamber servants in the palace, who were receptive male homosexuals. In astronomy a *girsequ* was a charioteer.[146]

Charioteers were always accompanied by propugnators, who protected their vulnerable spots. The latter held an important position, but subordinate to that of charioteer. Tacitus tells us that the drivers of the British Celtic chariots were always noblemen, while their propugnators were their clients.[147] This is likely to have been true everywhere, for only the wealthy could afford a horse and chariot. The inequality of age in the Theban Band, and the differences in social status between driver and companion in Baby-

[141] Sergent (1983:240).

[142] Barrett (1981); see *Iliad* 9:663–68.

[143] Many post-Homeric Greek authors assumed the relationship was sexual (Licht, 1963: 451), but they could have been projecting the mores of their own time onto an era they no longer knew well.

[144] *Anabasis* 2.6, 4.6, 8, 5.3. A similar practice was found among the Azande. Bachelors between the ages of twenty and thirty-five who served in military units at the court of a prince or king before the colonial government was established brought boys with them, to perform the traditional wifely functions. Though in most instances the relationships were seen as temporary substitutes for heterosexual marriages, some married men also took boy-wives. Upon adulthood, the boys took younger male lovers (Seligman and Seligman, 1932:506–7; Evans-Pritchard, 1970, 1974:36–37).

[145] Ungaretti (1978).

[146] Driver and Miles (1955:245). The evidence about chariot warfare bears directly on Achilles and Patrocles because the *Iliad* is set in a poorly remembered Mycenean past when wars were fought with chariots.

[147] *Agricola* 12.1 (Greenhalgh, 1973:15).

Ionia and Celtic Britain—and no doubt everywhere else—insured that the champion and his escort were not competitors. They were free to entertain a homosexual relationship. In Thebes such relationships existed and were explicitly recognized.

These relationships need not have been permanent. As the younger partner matured and became an adult, the sexual aspect of the relationship probably ended in most cases, leaving a legacy of emotional attachment. This could easily have been the case of Achilles and Patrocles.

The conditions of warfare, we may conclude, seem to have encouraged homosexual bonding between male warriors in some of the early civilizations. This was especially true when weak military organization left military leadership to individual heroes and their followers. The relationships that ensued typically involved males of discrepant ages or social statuses. Where armies were organized more bureaucratically, relationships of this kind would have been less common.

THE LOVE OF WOMEN FOR WOMEN

Lesbian relationships were rare among adult women in most kinship-structured societies. The extent to which that was also true in the archaic civilizations probably varied somewhat. Early Greek civilization may have had ritualized lesbian initiations for young women—in the case of Sparta, continuing into the classical age [148]—but if comparable rites were performed in other early civilizations, evidence of them has been lost. The restriction of women's religious and political roles that accompanied the rise of early civilizations may have entailed the suppression of female initiations and inattention to myths with lesbian themes. [149]

These restrictions encouraged lesbian relations by depriving women of male companionship, and by fostering close relationships with other women. Princes and wealthy men of the Azande in southern Sudan have large numbers of wives, all of whom must necessarily do without their husband most of the time. The risk of death for adultery discourages extramarital heterosexual affairs. Instead, women turn to other women. The ease of disguising a lesbian affair as a simple friendship makes it difficult for husbands to interfere, even though most dislike lesbianism and fear that it could magically injure them. [150]

Most Athenian women of the classical age were confined to the home much of the time, and had little opportunity to meet women of their own

---

[148] Calame (1977:1.427–44), Giacomelli (1980).

[149] Borgeaud (1979:53–54).

[150] Evans-Pritchard (1970). Some of the relations that develop between Kuwaiti Arab and Negro women may also stem from heterosexual deprivation (H.R.P. Dickson, 1949:202–4).

social status. However, if they were at all affluent, they spent that time in the women's section of the house, where men did not enter, alone with female slaves. What they did with one another is anyone's guess; Greek men did not write about that sort of thing. In the case of Egypt, paintings show women being dressed or coiffed by female servants. The scenes are sensuous, but not sexual. Whether lesbian relationships commonly developed between mistresses and their servants is unknown.

Wherever harems existed, as in India and the Near East, they became known for lesbianism.[151] Harem women were deprived of men (except for eunuch guards) and spent most of their time with one another. Inevitably, their emotional and sexual involvements centered on co-wives. Jealous husbands might threaten severe punishments, but the seclusion of women must have made detection very difficult.

CLASS-STRUCTURED HOMOSEXUALITY

Class-structured homosexuality appears with the dawn of economic stratification. Here the two partners are drawn from different economic strata or classes, the wealthier partner purchasing or commanding the sexual services of the poorer. The partners may differ in age, gender, or preference for particular types of contact, but these differences do not define the relationship. What does is the preference of the wealthier partner. Thus Captain Bligh, visiting Tahiti in the late eighteenth century, observed a chief sucking the penis of his attendant.[152] By the usual conventions linking rank and sex role, this transaction should not have occurred. The attendant should have been sucking the chief. However, the chief occupied a social position that enabled him to gratify his personal preference irrespective of conventions about homosexual roles. In societies where social relations are commercialized, wealth bestows sexual power.

Two forms of class-structured homosexuality were particularly common in antiquity: prostitution and intercourse with slaves. After examining each we will turn to the related topic of castration in nonreligious contexts.

Prostitution and Master-Slave Relations

The demand for prostitutes in antiquity came from merchants and sailors far from home, and from men who had difficulty gaining sexual access to partners who did not have to be paid (because patriarchal restrictions made

---

[151]Surrieu (1967:135–45), Karlen (1971:232–33). The *Kāma Sūtra* (*Aphorisms on Love*) of Vatsyayana (c. A.D. 400) refers to harem lesbianism (Desai, 1975:172), and it is depicted luminously in the *Sundarakanda* section (ch. 7) of the epic *Rāmāyaṇa*, attributed to Valmiki (1978: 323–24), who may have lived in the third century B.C.

[152]Oliver (1974:371). In another episode, a Tahitian nobleman who boarded Captain Cook's ship offered six hogs for the use of one of the sailors (Beaglehole, 1961:1226).

it difficult to obtain respectable women and boys). The supply developed in response to the growth of economic inequality. With the disintegration of the redistributive channels of clan society and the privatization of the means of production, the dispossessed sometimes turned to prostitution to support themselves. But not all prostitutes were poor. Tahitian and Rwandan chiefs used their wealth to attract men who were not impoverished to their court, and made them available to guests.[153] In the absence of taboos or legal restrictions against homosexuality (see chapter 4), male homosexual prostitution developed alongside female heterosexual prostitution.[154]

Even when the kinship order is intact, economic inequality can lead to homosexual prostitution. Transgenerational male homosexuality was universal in the Big Namba chiefdoms of Malekula Island in the New Hebrides, the boys' lover being his sister's true or possibly classificatory sisters' husband. Though he had exclusive sexual rights, he could sell these rights to other men. Since the boy worked in his partner's garden, an element of economic exploitation entered the relationship.[155] Similarly, in the Libyan oases of Siwah and El Garah fifty years ago, parents prostituted their sons to the wealthier men.[156] No comparable pecuniary elements are mentioned in the ethnographies of the more egalitarian New Guinea cultures.

With the emergence of well-defined classes, prostitution became ubiquitous, and freed from its cultic trappings. It was a feature of everyday life in ancient Mesopotamia; there was even a guild for practitioners. A hint of exploitation appears in an Assyrian tablet dated at 716 B.C. that refers to them:

> When a male prostitute (*sinnisanu* = effeminate man) entered the brothel, as he raised his hands in prayer, he said, "My hire goes to the promoter. You [Ishtar] are wealth, I am half.[157]

Athens and other Greek harbor towns had male brothels from an early date, but it was considered shameful for a free citizen to prostitute himself for money. A law attributed to Solon, himself a pederast, provided that an Athenian citizen who did so was barred from certain religious functions and public affairs, and could not speak before the Assembly or Council on pain of death.[158] If a father or guardian prostituted his minor ward for

---

[153] Maquet (1961:78), Oliver (1974).

[154] I know of no evidence for lesbian prostitution in antiquity. Leaving aside the question of demand, few women of the archaic civilizations were socially and financially independent enough to become clients of lesbian prostitutes.

[155] Deacon (1934), Creed (1984).

[156] Cline (1936).

[157] Lambert (1960:219).

[158] Zimmerman (1947:306), Bullough (1976:112), Buffière (1980:202–3), Dover (1978:19–34). The text of the law has not survived, and we cannot even be certain that it was actually promulgated by Solon. It is even possible that no such law ever existed (Dover, 1978:33; Buffière,

money, the ward was absolved of traditional responsibilities toward elderly parents or guardians.[159] It was contrary to the egalitarian ethos of citizenship for a free man to place himself at the service of someone else for money. Someone who would sell his body, it was said, might as readily sell the interests of the state. The use of legislation to enforce this ethos reflects the recognition that economic pressures associated with the commercialization of the Greek economy were eroding the social basis of citizenship to a potentially explosive degree. It was Solon who prohibited indebted Athenian citizens from being sold abroad into slavery.

Foreigners were not covered by Solon's legislation, and for this reason it is thought that many of Athens's male prostitutes were aliens. While some may have become prostitutes from economic necessity, others were prisoners of war who had been sold into brothel slavery. Plato's *Phaedrus* is named for a citizen of Elis who had been captured by the Spartans and sold to an Athenian house of prostitution.[160]

Although the Athenians stigmatized prostitutes, they did not deprive them of all legal rights; according to Aiskhines, prostitutes could go to court to collect from nonpaying customers. Patronizing prostitutes was considered perfectly acceptable, not shameful or illegal. Each year, the Athenian Council confirmed a special tax on male prostitutes, suggesting that they were numerous enough to warrant attention as a source of revenue.[161]

By all acounts, prostitution flourished in Rome after the Second Punic War (218–201 B.C.), when wealth poured into the city, and the large-scale displacement of free farm laborers by slaves created massive unemployment. Brothels opened not only in Rome, but also in large and medium-sized towns throughout Italy.[162] A reference in a public speech of the elder Cato to the high price of male prostitutes makes clear that only the affluent could indulge.

Most male prostitutes were slaves owned by a procurer;[163] however, some prostitutes were freedmen or even free. Under Augustus the government began taxing male prostitutes, and also granted them a legal holiday,

---

1980; 198–99). Athenian legal records in the classical age were in such disarray that it would have been virtually impossible for the Athenians to verify that such a law truly dated back to Solon.

[159] Buffière (1980:200).

[160] Licht (1963:439).

[161] Dollinger (1862:242), Dover (1978:30, 40), Buffière (1980:205).

[162] Verstraete (1980).

[163] One of the reasons early Christian writers deplored the common practice of selling unwanted children into slavery was that they were so often prostituted until they reached maturity (young prostitutes were more desirable).

April 24. By the early empire, distinct active (*exoleti*) and passive (*cinaedi*) homosexual prostitutes were serving specialized client tastes.[164]

Wealthy men had another homosexual outlet as well: their slaves. Although Athenian law barred slaves from entering gymnasia (where many pederastic affairs were initiated), or from having affairs with free men, they were at the disposal of their owners. While owners were prohibited from raping their slaves, in practice slaves who had been raped had few remedies.[165] Roman slave owners could also use them for sexual purposes with impunity, and some kept sizable male harems. Commerce in male slaves to be used sexually persisted for centuries.

In modern times, colonialism and tourism have added new dimensions to class-structured homosexuality. It is the soldier or administrator of the conquering power, or the affluent tourist, who is able to purchase the sexual services of native males. The French, for example, found boys readily available in Indo-China, where oral homosexual practices were indigenous, and in North Africa, where pederasty was already common. In today's world, visitors from other nations are equally able to take advantage of the opportunities provided by third-world poverty.[166]

Castration

The archaic civilizations castrated men for secular reasons, as well as for the cultic purposes already described. Sometimes they crushed or surgically removed only the testicles; sometimes they amputated both penis and testicles. These practices are rarely, if ever, performed in kinship-structured societies, where sanctions generally involve payment of restitution to an injured party and do not lead to permanent change of social status, or in the early democratic city-states like Athens and Republican Rome.[167] The appearance of mutilation almost invariably marks the appearance of pronounced social stratification and the weakening of kinship structures relative to centralized political power. Under these conditions, offenders and their kin may be incapable of compensating the offending party. In addition, individual offenders become expendable and can be sanctioned in

[164]Roberts and Donaldson (1926), Kiefer (1934:114), Kroll (1962:177–80), Earl (1967:18), Bullough (1976:141–42), Balsdon (1979:225–26), Boswell (1980:68, 70, 79, 144), Verstraete (1980), Veyne (1982), Lilja (1983:29–31). In the early Roman empire, the term *cinaedus* was also used for men who served as gigolos for women (Dynes, 1985a:31).

[165]Buffière (1980:201–5).

[166]Jacobus X (1896:1.91–114), Corre (1894), Veze (1921), Thieuloy (1971), Rossman (1976:112–31).

[167]Paige and Paige (1981:144) explain this on practical grounds: if fathers castrated their sons, the sons would have no wives and children to protect, and consequently would have no motivation to enter into a military alliance with their fathers. But this is too narrow a view, for such considerations would not preclude the castration of other men's sons.

ways that demonstrate to all that the ruler possesses awesome power, so great that it can destroy anyone who challenges it. Sanctions like castration thus serve to discourage political opposition.

According to Herodotus, the Assyrians were the first to introduce castration for nonreligious reasons into the Near East.[168] While their claim to priority is not well established,[169] confirmation that the Assyrians did practice castration comes from Isaiah, where the prophet warns King Hezekiah:

> And of thy sons that shall issue from thee, whom thou shalt beget, shall they take away; and they shall be eunuchs in the palace of the king of Babylon.[170]

Babylon was then (late eighth century B.C.) ruled by the Assyrians.

The Assyrians imposed castration as a punishment for some crimes as early as the second millennium B.C., but found eunuchs so useful that they turned to other sources as well. Many were captured in war or kidnapped in slave raids.[171] Others were emasculated in childhood by their families to gain financial security and upward social mobility.

Eunuchs' sexual disabilities made them especially useful as household servants. Fearful that virile men would seduce their sons, Greek aristocrats purchased eunuchs from the Phoenicians to tutor their children.[172] Because

---

[168] Herodotus 1.135.

[169] A Moslem source, obviously late and untrustworthy, but perhaps based on knowledge of Egyptian custom, explains Joseph's remarkable political career in the court of Pharoah to his being a eunuch who provided sexual services, at first to Potiphar, then to the king (Edwardes, 1967:103–5). An inventory of trophies taken from the Libyans c. 1300 B.C. lists 13,230 penises of captives, evidence that the Egyptians practiced castration at an early date (Tompkins, 1962:14).

[170] Isa. 39:7.

[171] The extent of this practice may be gauged from Isaiah's prophecy:

> For thus saith the Lord concerning the eunuchs that keep my sabbaths, and choose the things that please Me, and hold fast by My covenant: Even unto them will I give in My house and within My walls a monument and a memorial better than sons and daughters; I will give them an everlasting memorial that shall not be cut off (56:4–5).

Had there been few Hebrew eunuchs it is unlikely that Isaiah would have taken the trouble to abolish the exclusion from the religious community mandated by Deut. 23:2, "He that is crushed or maimed in his privy parts shall not enter into the assembly of the Lord."

[172] Tompkins (1962:17). Phoenician trafficking in boys dates back to Homeric times; the *Odyssey* refers to Phoenician shipmasters purchasing or kidnapping boys to be sold to wealthy purchasers (14.297, 15.449). Although there is no explicit reference to homosexuality, it is unlikely that such drastic means were needed to acquire household servants. More likely, the victims were intended for the beds of the purchasers. Because the Greeks considered castration so reprehensible, they never performed it on other Greeks, even those from hostile city-states. A biblical reference to the sale of boys into slavery, probably sexual, appears in Joel 4:3.

they could not impregnate, eunuchs were used in the Eastern kingdoms as harem guards.

The potentates of the East found eunuchs politically invaluable. According to Xenophon, Cyrus the Great, who ruled Persia in the sixth century B.C., preferred eunuchs as his officers because men without wives would be loyal only to him. Unable to establish a new dynasty by fathering children, they were unlikely to stage a palace coup.[173] Under Cyrus's successor, Darius, eunuchs

> acquired a vast political authority and appeared then to have filled all the chief offices of state. They were the king's advisors in the palace, and his generals in the field. They superintended the education of the young princes, and found it easy to make them their tools.[174]

Babylon had to send Darius five hundred castrated boys as tribute, along with a thousand talents of silver.[175] Later, Bagoas, an emasculated general of Artaxerxes III, led the Persian conquest of Egypt.[176] Some of the eunuchs were able to amass enormous wealth.

Eunuchs were often given preference for bureaucratic office because they could not jeopardize the imperial succession or transmit their offices to heirs. Many were foreigners, cut off from their families. Those of indigenous origin were generally from modest family backgrounds—the local peasantry or gentry—and therefore personally dependent on the ruler for the preservation of their exalted social status and incomes. They were thus useful in the never-ending royal efforts to curb the aristocracy, whose power, based on land, remained strong. By staffing the centralized bureaucracies with eunuchs who were utterly dependent on them, the emperors were in theory also able to prevent officeholders from becoming too independent, thereby limiting their personal power. In practice, eunuchs often gained enormous power over emperors by controlling access to them.[177]

Diocletian introduced eunuch officeholders to the Roman Empire at the end of the third century A.D. at a time when the cultural influence of the East was growing. To regularize the collection of taxes he built up an exten-

---

[173] Xenophon (1870:229), *The Cryopaedia;* Tannahill (1980:247).

[174] George Rawlinson, quoted in Coser (1964).

[175] In like manner, when Periander, tyrant of Corinth from 625 to 585 B.C., paid tribute to the king of Sardis, he sent three hundred boys to be castrated for palace service (Licht, 1963: 496–97).

[176] Tompkins (1962:14–15). Josephus held that Daniel had been castrated and sodomized by Nebuchadnezzar (Edwardes, 1967:105), but the source is untrustworthy except as evidence that the emasculation of high officials was so common in the despotic empires that it could be taken for granted.

[177] Wittfogel (1957:354–62), Coser (1964), Hopkins (1978:172–96), Paige and Paige (1981:144).

sive centralized bureaucracy that grew over the next two hundred years in response to the barbarian invasions. Eventually, most of the high-ranking civil-service positions in the Eastern Empire came to be held by eunuchs.[178]

Not every eunuch was used homosexually, but many were. The harem of King Darius III of Persia included both concubines and eunuchs, as did that of Artaxerxes. After Alexander the Great defeated Darius he began to copy Persian ways, adding to his harem a number of eunuchs whom he took as sexual partners. Nero and his castrated lover Spores lived together as husband and wife until Nero's death. When performed early in life, castration prolonged the boyish beauty the ancients considered desirable; consequently eunuchs were in great demand as homosexual partners.[179]

Although many Romans found castration repugnant, the practice was not easily suppressed. Domitian is thought to have outlawed emasculation in the first century A.D., but he apparently had little success, for Hadrian campaigned against it in the latter part of the second century, and Constantine made it a capital offense in the early fourth. Further prohibitions came in the fifth century under Leo I, and in the sixth, from Justinian. Nevertheless, the demand for castrated boys was so great that the trade persisted; they were a familiar sight in the late Eastern Empire. As it was forbidden to castrate Roman citizens, boys were purchased or kidnapped from peoples living outside the empire. Religious prohibitions notwithstanding, the use of eunuchs to staff government offices grew under the Christian emperors and remained a prominent feature of Byzantine political life. Until the early nineteenth century, the boy sopranos who sang in the Sistine Chapel were castrates.[180]

[178] Bullough (1976:326–28).

[179] Wittfogel (1957:356), Fürstauer (1965:256), Seibert (1974:51), Hopkins (1978:194), Boswell (1980:82).

[180] Heriot (1956), Edwardes (1967:182), Karlen (1971:50), Bullough (1976:326–30), Boswell (1980:67 n. 25), Buffière (1980:30).

4   *Early Civilizations:*
Variations on
Homosexual Themes

With the possible exception of the Egyptians and the Hebrews, none of the archaic civilizations prohibited homosexuality per se. Some forms or some roles were considered acceptable; others not. Social responses to the unacceptable forms varied greatly.

We learn of these responses from several sources. Law codes tell us the formal rules enforced by the state, but not about popular attitudes and informal sanctions applied interpersonally in everyday life. For these we look to myths, legends, folktales, literature, and figurative art, recognizing that even these stem largely from a literate male elite and may not adequately reflect the thinking of the illiterate masses, or of women.

To assess the range of variability of responses to homosexuality in the different archaic civilizations, we examine homosexual practices and responses to these practices in ancient Mesopotamia, Egypt, Israel, Greece, Rome, China, among the Mayans, the Aztecs, and Incas, the Hindus, and in a civilization that was not archaic, but was influenced by several that were—Islam.

MESOPOTAMIA

None of the early legal codes of Mesopotamia—the Laws of Urukagina (2375 B.C.), the Laws of Ur-Nammu (2100 B.C.), the Laws of Eshnunna (1750 B.C.), and the Laws of Hammurabi (1726 B.C.) prohibits homosexual acts. The only possible reference to homosexuality is a provision in the Hammurabi Code concerning sons adopted by palace eunuchs,[1] and it is not certain that all of the latter engaged in homosexuality.

The Hittite laws, dating from the second millennium B.C., make father-son incest a capital offense along with father-daughter and mother-son incest, but do not mention mother-daughter incest. In addition, they classify

---

124   [1] Para. 187.

intercourse with a male or female ghost as a sin or abomination, without specifying a penalty.[2] Nonincestuous homosexuality is not mentioned.[3]

The Middle Assyrian laws, which originated in the middle of the second millennium B.C., contain two provisions dealing with homosexuality. The first, paragraph 18, concerns unproved slanderous accusations:

> If a seignior started a rumor against his neighbor in private, saying "People have lain repeatedly with him," or he said to him in a brawl in the presence of (other) people, "People have lain repeatedly with you; I will prosecute you," since he is not able to prosecute (him) (and) did not prosecute (him), they shall flog that seignior fifty (times) with staves (and) he shall do the work of the king for one full month; they shall castrate him and he shall also pay one talent of lead.[4]

The preceding paragraph provides a similar penalty (forty stripes instead of fifty) for a man who makes an unproved accusation that a neighbor's wife is behaving like a common prostitute by taking many lovers. In both cases it is a punishable offense to spread a libelous rumor without being able to prove it. Evidently, it was a little worse to accuse a man of allowing himself to be used homosexually on a regular basis than to accuse someone's wife of adulterous promiscuity. In both instances, it would seem, the habitual receptive role could be grounds for prosecution. Perhaps the offense was practicing prostitution outside the guild; in essence, without a license. Alternately, the paragraph may refer to cases where the rumormonger was unable to substantiate his allegations when challenged in a

---

[2]Pritchard (1955:196), M. Daniel (1963), Friedrich (1971:83, 113–14), Hoffner (1973a). Some commentators think that the passage refers to dreams about ghosts (Friedrich, 1971:83), but this seems doubtful. Dreams were not the subject of legislation in any other early civilization. Bullough (1971, 1976:54) erroneously identifies the Hittite law against incest as Assyrian.

[3]Some scholars have claimed that Hittite law provided for male homosexual marriages (Zimmern, 1922; Goetze, 1955; Riemenschneider, 1955), but most Hittitologists now reject this contention (Hrozny, 1922; Neufeld, 1951; Hoffner, 1963:37, 392–93; Imparata, 1964:55; Friedrich, 1971; Schuler, 1982:103; personal communication, Harry A. Hoffner, Jr.). It survives largely in the writings of nonspecialists (e.g., Boswell, 1980:21; Ide, 1985:67).

[4]Pritchard (1955:181). This paragraph requires extensive commentary. A "seignior" is someone of high social rank, an aristocrat. The Assyrian word *tap-pa-u*, here rendered as "neighbor," has been the subject of some discussion (Driver and Miles, 1935:65–68; Cardascia, 1969:132; Bottéro and Petschow, 1975). It is the Assyrian equivalent of the Hebrew *re'a*, and in the present context it is best understood as someone who resides in one's vicinity, without necessarily being a relative. The provision that the slanderer be castrated is not entirely unambiguous. Driver and Miles translate the passage as "he shall be cut off" and suggest that this may imply social ostracism (1935:70, 391). Cardascia (1969:133) understands the passage as specifying some sort of marking or branding of the offender.

private suit. No records of prosecution that would clarify the provision have come to light.

Paragraph 20 concerns homosexual rape: a man convicted of forcing or coercing someone to submit to anal intercourse is to be subjected to forcible penetration and then castrated. The active role is not criminalized as long as it is consensual.[5] Though some of these codes were based in part on case law, they were not necessarily intended to be applied in court. Still, they record the ideal standards of behavior of the time.[6]

Extralegal sources provide us with a fuller picture of sexual attitudes and practices. Anal intercourse was part of the sexual repertoire: it is depicted in figurative art from Uruk, Assur, Babylon, and Susa as early as the beginning of the third millennium B.C.[7] There is no evidence that fellatio or cunnilingus was practiced, either heterosexually or homosexually. Neither seems to have been forbidden; there are simply no references to them.[8]

Zimri-lin, king of Mari, and Hammurabi, king of Babylon, both had male lovers; Zimri-lin's queen refers to them matter-of-factly in a letter.[9] That there was no religious prohibition against homosexuality is clear not only from the existence of cult prostitution,[10] but also from the text of an *Almanac of Incantations,* which contains prayers favoring, on an equal basis, the love of a man for a woman, a woman for a man, and a man for a man.[11]

The Babylonians were greatly concerned with divining the future. One section of the *Šumma alu,* a manual for that purpose, prognosticates the future on the basis of sexual acts. Most are heterosexual, but five involve male homosexuality:

> If a man has intercourse with the hindquarters of his equal (male), that man will be foremost among his brothers and colleagues.
>
> If a man yearns to express his manhood while in prison and

---

[5]Published translations (Driver and Miles, 1935:71, 391; Cardascia, 1969; 133–35) are misleading on this point; they wrongly suggest that the prohibition applied to all acts of anal homosexual intercourse. However, the voice of the verb *na-ku* in this passage implies the use of force (Bottéro and Petschow, 1975; personal communication, Robert D. Biggs; see also the entry for *nakû* in Soden, 1967). Were the passage to refer to consensual homosexuality, the penalty would make no sense; referring to coercion, it follows the pattern of analogic penalties common to ancient law: "an eye for an eye," "a rape for a rape." Implicitly, the state was willing to sponsor active, aggressive homosexual behavior under special circumstances.

[6]Driver and Miles (1952:1.53), R. Harris (1961), Yoffee (n.d.).

[7]Bottéro and Petschow (1975).

[8]Biggs (1969).

[9]Moran (1969).

[10]See chapter 3.

[11]Bottéro and Petschow (1975). The love of a woman for a woman is not mentioned. Nor is it mentioned in an astrological text of the neo-Babylonian period (Biggs, 1967).

thus, like a male cult-prostitute, mating with men becomes his desire, he will experience evil.

If a man has intercourse with a (male) cult prostitute, care [in the sense of "trouble"] will leave him.

If a man has intercourse with a [male] courtier, for one whole year the worry which plagued him will vanish.

If a man has intercourse with a [male] slave, care will seize him.[12]

None of the acts elicits moral condemnation, but some are auspicious whereas others are not. Homosexuality itself carries no implications; neither here nor anywhere else does the concept of a homosexual person even appear. What matters are the roles and statuses of the parties. To penetrate someone of high social status (an equal, a cult prostitute, a courtier) anally is favorable; to be involved with one's slave, unfavorable. The Babylonians may have felt that a sexual connection would erode a master's authority over his slaves. To prefer the receptive role, perhaps exclusively, appears to have been negatively regarded except in a cultic context. An apodictic curse warns that "one will make him the object of repeated coitus."[13]

EGYPT

Most of the ancient Egyptian papyri and inscriptions that have survived deal with funerary and religious themes and contain only a few references to homosexuality. In the absence of the royal archives that have given us the Mesopotamian law codes, we do not have even a single legal text. In addition to the obvious difficulty this creates in discovering what the Egyptians thought about homosexuality, it makes the very translation of texts problematic. When words that we think might designate homosexuality appear in only a few sources that may have been written a thousand years apart, it is not easy to determine just what they mean.[14]

Hermaphroditic deities were present in the Egyptian pantheon, as in the Mesopotamian.[15] The West Asian mother-goddesses had their counterparts in Isis, goddess of the moon and fertility. Yet there were differences in the myths of the two regions. Rather than bringing destruction to a son-spouse, Isis resurrected her brother-husband Osiris (who was not her son).[16] Sacred prostitution was probably not well established in Egypt, and in long

---

[12] Grayson and Redford (1973:149). Lesbianism is also mentioned in a divinatory apodosis, in a context that suggests it may not have been unusual (Bottéro and Petschow, 1975).

[13] Bottéro and Petschow (1975).

[14] Lefébure (1912:192), Goedicke (1967), Te Velde (1967:30–31), Westendorf (1977a), Borghouts (1981).

[15] Baumann (1955), Leclant (1960), Sauneron (1961), Westendorf (1977b), Hornung (1982: 170–72), J. Baines (1985).

[16] Budge (1972:202), Ochshorn (1981:45–46).

stretches of Egyptian history may not have existed at all.[17] There is no evidence that men castrated themselves in the service of a goddess or that homosexual intercourse was performed for cult purposes.

Cult prostitution may have failed to take root in Egypt because of the way the kingdom was unified. Some scholars think unification was achieved when nomadic, sun-worshiping desert tribes from Upper Egypt (in the south) conquered the sedentary cultivators of the delta (Lower Egypt).[18] The defeated farmers may have engaged in ritual sex to promote fertility, but the victorious nomads almost certainly did not. Though the goddesses of the indigenous farming culture survived, their cults were presumably abolished or transformed by the conquerors. One suspects that once irrigation was established, ceremonial interest would have shifted from the promotion of crop growth to the control of the flooding of the Nile, for which sexual rites would not have provided a magical analogue.[19] The absence of maternal destructiveness toward men in myth suggests that Egyptian family arrangements did not give rise to the psychodynamics associated with religious self-castration, as they seem to have done in Asia Minor.

The coronation ceremony for a new king looks very much like it evolved from an earlier tribal ritual that transferred charismatic powers homosexually, but in the historical period the transmission was symbolic, not sexual.[20] Unlike kinship-structured societies that ritually sodomize all male

---

[17] Even if my surmise that Utterance 235 of the pyramid texts refers to cult prostitution (see note 14 to chapter 3) is correct, the absence of unambiguous references in later dynasties is suggestive. The Douleq Papyrus (c. 1400 B.C.) suggests that female temple prostitutes may have served the cat goddess (Carlton, 1977:109), and Breasted (1906:4.74–75, 5.132) concludes from para. 128 of the Papyrus Harris (twelfth century B.C.) that women captured in war were made to serve as temple prostitutes, but the papyrus does not actually state the nature of their services. That is true of many of the references to female temple slaves or personnel mentioned by Hogarth (1914). The Egyptians seem to have regarded sexual intercourse as ritually defiling and prohibited it inside their temples (Quibell, 1907:12–14; Manniche, 1977). By the Ptolemaic period the situation may have changed. The Greek geographer Strabo, who visited Egypt just after it had been conquered by Rome, reports that one of the most beautiful girls of an illustrious family was dedicated to Amun, became a prostitute, and had intercourse with men until she menstruated; then she was married (17.1, 46). This practice may have been borrowed from Babylonia, where a similar custom was noticed by Herodotus some hundreds of years earlier (1.199).

[18] Mendelsson (1974), Griffiths (1980).

[19] The pyramid text cited in note 14 to chapter 3 suggests that this hypothesized shift of interest did not occur overnight. Indigenous religious practices often persist for a time even in high circles, after being suppressed.

[20] The Egyptians believed that a god could transfer vital power to a human by means of "magnetic passes" of the hand over the neck and down the spine, or by an embrace. In the time of Ramses II and III (thirteenth and twelfth centuries B.C.), a personification of the god Ptah embraced the king during the coronation, saying, "I have embraced your flesh, in giving it life and vitality, the fluid of life behind you, that is to say, quietude and health." In other

youths, or the aristocratic societies that do it only to young nobles, the Egyptian ceremony was performed for the king alone. His was a charisma not shared by ordinary mortals, even aristocrats.

Even in the absence of ritual performance, Egyptian culture retained the belief that homosexual intercourse with a god was auspicious. In one coffin text, the deceased vows, "I will swallow for myself the phallus of Rēᶜ . . . ;" another, referring to the earth god Geb, says, "his phallus is between the buttocks of his son and heir." [21]

Two fragmentary manuscripts attest to the existence of homosexuality outside a cult context toward the end of the Sixth Dynasty [22] (c. 2272–2178 B.C.). The texts begin by describing a conspiracy to obstruct a judicial hearing, but the outcome of the conspiracy is unknown because part of the manuscript is missing. The narration resumes by telling of a commoner who discovers that King Neferkare (Pepi II) was making regular secret nocturnal visits to the home of General Sisene, a top royal administrator, who was unmarried or living without a wife. A homosexual relationship between Neferkare and his general is clearly implied. Because of a gap in the manuscript, the connection (if any) between the conspiracy and the affair is unclear.

The published translation of the manuscript is neutral in tone and nonjudgmental in its treatment of the affair, but in a letter to me, the Egyptologist J. Gwyn Griffiths insists that "the whole piece conveys an atmosphere of royal corruption." Posener, the translator, points out that Neferkare's ninety-year reign was a period of political decline in which the monarchy came under the sway of the nobility. Both episodes, he suggests, can be seen as manifestations of decay. Yet this interpretation is speculative. Even if it is valid, it does not necessarily follow that Egyptians of the time viewed homosexuality negatively. Someone who had no prejudice against heterosexuality might nevertheless raise an eyebrow upon learning that the president of the United States was paying secret nocturnal visits to the home of a female cabinet officer. The Egyptians might have considered it undignified for the king, who was considered the incarnation of divinity, to have

---

rites it was Amun who transferred "magnetic fluid" this way (Moret, 1902a:22–24, 99–101; 1902b:45–48, 100–108; 1911:25–26; Budge, 1909:73; Nibley, 1976:241–86). These ceremonies recall the simulated anal homosexuality in the rituals of the Iatmul of the Sepik River region of New Guinea, recorded by Bateson (1958). It is certainly reasonable to think that in an earlier age the Egyptians enacted the transfer of fluids bodily rather than by means of magnetic passes of the hand. I have been unable to find any textual basis for Edwardes's (1967:11) claim that new pharaohs were ritually masturbated and sodomized by the high priest; he cites none.

[21] Faulkner (1973:2.162, 264). For homosexual intercourse with Osiris in the coffin texts see Faulkner (1973:1.93–94).

[22] Posener (1957), Manniche (1987:73–74).

an affair with a mere mortal. Pharaoh was considered so sacred that most people were not even permitted to touch him.[23]

The existence of a tomb for two manicurists and hairdressers of King Niuserre of the Fifth Dynasty (c. 2600 B.C.) suggests that in this early period homosexuality may not have been stigmatized. Bas-reliefs on the walls of the tomb depict the two men in intimate poses, holding hands, embracing, noses touching. Egyptian art rarely depicts men and women embracing; scenes of two men doing so are virtually unknown. None of the drawings is sexually explicit, but Egyptian art rarely was. If the men were lovers, it would be reasonable to conclude that male homosexuality was fully accepted. Both men were wealthy, and their position at court prestigious. Their tomb was a gift from the king (as indeed all tombs theoretically were).[24]

An unusual degree of intimacy is also shown in depictions of King Ikhnaton (1379–1362 B.C.) and his son-in-law and probable co-regent Smenkhare. They are shown together nude—a convention quite rare in Egyptian representations of royalty. On a stele, Ikhnaton strokes Smenkhare under the chin. Smenkhare is given titles of endearment that had been used previously for Ikhnaton's concubines and queen. Ikhnaton is depicted with a swollen belly, a generally feminine physique, and without genitals.[25]

Several texts indicate that the Egyptians stigmatized the receptive role in anal intercourse between men just as the Mesopotamians did. In a coffin text of the Heracleopolitan Period (Ninth and Tenth Dynasties), consisting of magical passages to be recited after death to gain immortality, the deceased boasts, "Atum [a god] has no power over me, for I copulate between his buttocks."[26] The formula equates interpersonal power with sexual role performances: he who can force a god to submit to him sexually has nothing to fear from him.[27]

A connection between homosexual role differentiation and gender stereo-

---

[23] Goedicke (1960) argues that it was the office of the pharaoh and not the person who held it that was divine. For our purposes it may make little difference. See also Posener (1960).

[24] Moussa and Altenmuller (1977), Reeder (1983). Riefstahl (1972) suggests that an ithyphallic statute found in a tomb from the Eleventh or Twelfth Dynasty (Middle Kingdom) could have been a representation of a catamite companion to serve him in the next world. The interpretation is controversial.

[25] Newberry (1928), Deakin (1966), Gazeau (1981). Giles (1972:95) suggests that Ikhnaton's physique is intended to signify homosexuality; Aldred (1968), however, suggests that Ikhnaton had Fröhlich's syndrome, a disorder of the pituitary gland. Both may have been true.

[26] Deakin (1966), Griffiths (1969:44), Bullough (1973a, 1976:65).

[27] A similar notion may be present in a text from the pyramid of King Teta of the Sixth Dynasty. One translation reads:

Osiris Teta! Wake up! Horus causes Thoth to bring to thee thine enemy, he sits thee on his back, he shall not defile thee. Make thy seat upon him. Come forth!

typing is evident in the mythological conflict between two gods, Horus and Seth. The story of their enmity is very old, probably dating back to the pre-dynastic conflict between Upper and Lower Egypt, which it represents metaphorically. In a version of the myth dating from the reign of Rameses V in the Twentieth Dynasty, c. 1160 B.C., the gods held a trial to adjudicate the conflicting claims of Horus and his older brother to succeed Osiris as ruler of Egypt. When the trial recessed for the night,

> Seth made his penis erect, and put it between Horus' buttocks, and Horus put his hand between his buttocks, and received Seth's semen. Then Horus went to tell his mother Isis: "Help me, Isis my mother! Come, see what Seth has done to me." And he opened his hand and let her see Seth's semen. With a scream she took her weapon and cut off his hand, and threw it in the water, and conjured for him a hand to make up for it.

When the trial resumed, Seth pleaded:

> "Give me the office of Ruler, L.P.H., because as for Horus here, I have played the male role with him." Then the Ennead [the nine gods judging the trial] screamed aloud, and belched and spat in Horus' face.[28]

Isis's reaction to the episode—cutting off Horus's hand—suggests that Seth's semen was so contaminating that it could not be washed or wiped off: it had to be cut off, along with the hand it had polluted. Westendorf points out that the Egyptians believed semen had the effect of poison when introduced into the body—presumably in the "wrong" spot.[29] Given this ideological manifestation of antipathy to most forms of nonprocreative sex, Seth's aggression was a particularly grave transgression.

Since gender roles are defined only by contrast, Seth's announcement that he played the "male role" implies that Horus's role was "female." Although both Seth and Horus are morphologically male, the myth defines their gender not by their anatomy but by the roles they played. To penetrate is to be male; to be penetrated, female.[30]

Sit thou upon him, he shall not commit an act of paederasty upon thee (Maspero, 1884:40; Budge, 1973:26–27).

However, an alternate translation by Griffiths (1969:41–42) denies any homosexual element. Maspero and Budge are no longer considered trustworthy translators, and it may be that their version is in error here.

[28] W. K. Simpson (1972:120), Grayson and Redford (1973:76).

[29] Westendorf (1977a).

[30] Judging from the Old Kingdom texts already cited, this stereotyping may have been absent very early in Egyptian history. A text from the pyramid of Pepi I, who ruled almost immediately after King Teta (see note 27), has Horus and Seth about the same age (in the later

Seth shows no embarrassment at having played the male role; he brags of it, confident that his claim to the throne will be enhanced, not weakened, by the revelation. On the other hand, for Horus to have acted as a "female" by being sexually receptive, even against his will, was so radically incompatible with kingship that the gods openly display their contempt for him. Social roles must be consistent. Men dominate women; kings dominate their subjects. He who rules the kingdom must have the personal traits needed to dominate rival claimants to the throne and cannot, therefore, be someone his brother successfully rapes. Once the claim is made that the king possesses unique charismatic qualities, his biography must be able to sustain the claim.

Temple inscriptions at Edfu from the Ptolemaic (Greco-Roman) period show how long this logic persisted. They imagine the god Min, identified with Horus, eating lettuce (whose milk-sap is identified with semen) so that he can anally penetrate and impregnate his male enemy (presumably Seth), humiliating him by turning him into a female.[31] All these texts show the active role in anal sex between men to be one of aggression against an enemy, in which a man can take pride. The passive role, considered feminine, was regarded as shameful.

Another set of texts seems to show negative attitudes toward any type of involvement in homosexuality. Chapter 125 of the *Book of the Dead,* a set of mortuary and religious spells inscribed on mortuary papyri, which first appeared in the Eighteenth Dynasty (but incorporating earlier material), contains "negative confessions," in which the deceased proclaims his innocence of a long list of sins. As translated by John Wilson, two confessions pertain to homosexuality:

> (A20) I have not had sexual relations with a boy.
> (B27) O His-Face-Behind Him, who comes forth from Tep-het-djat, I have not been perverted; I have not had sexual relations with a boy.[32]

Many variant texts survive. In some versions, line A20 omits the "boy" and is better translated as "I have not had debauched sexual relations." Despite

version, Horus seems much younger than Seth), and the advances are mutual (Leclant, 1977; Griffiths, 1980:6–8). In accounting for the shift, it may be significant that in the feudal period which brought the Sixth Dynasty to a close, women lost rights, and a fairly egalitarian monogamy was replaced by a more clearly male-dominant polygamy (Pirenne, 1965:48–49).

[31]Griffiths (1969:45–46). The equation of milk-sap from lettuce with semen is also found in Greek myth: Hera gave birth to Hebe, or Youth, as a result of eating lettuce (Detienne, 1979:105 n. 168).

[32]Pritchard (1955:34–35). Tep-het-djat was a sanctuary of the Memphis region (Montet, 1950).

the use of the word "boy" in the translation of B27, the age of the partner is actually indeterminate. A more precise translation would be, "I have not had sexual relations with a male lover."[33]

The significance to be attached to these disavowals is not entirely clear. Goedicke suggests that they are sophistical: the deceased selected for denial acts he had not done, so as to avoid having to confess to those he had.[34] Even if this was so, the inclusion of homosexual relations makes sense only if they had been viewed somewhat negatively. That they were, at least in some strata, is confirmed by the temple inscriptions at Edfu, in Memphis. They list, among forbidden acts, "to couple with a *nkk* or *ḥmw*. The later terms, though probably not exact synonyms, have been taken to refer to someone who acts as a receptive male homosexual.[35] Elsewhere, the word *ḥmw* means coward; since it is derived from the word for "woman," it might better be translated as an "effeminate poltroon."[36] It would be difficult to say whether this was a term of opprobrium applied stereotypically to anyone who preferred a receptive role in homosexual anal intercourse, or only to a distinct, socially recognized homosexual role. As in the *Book of the Dead*, the *active* role is prohibited. The inscriptions are quite late (Ptolemaic), but possibly derive from older sources.

Beyerlin suggests that the negative confessions could have been based on formulas priests had to utter when entering temples.[37] Though priests could be married, they had to remain chaste while in service (for a period of a month, three times a year) and were held to special standards of purity, including restrictions on diet and clothing.[38] It was they who were responsible for the inscriptions in the Edfu temples.

It is helpful to recall that the negative confessions first appeared as a distinct funerary collection at a time when burial practices were becoming Osirianized and extended to the middle and official classes. The deceased in the *Book of the Dead* tried to identify himself with Osiris,[39] and thus claimed a life of exemplary moral purity that would not necessarily have

[33]Budge (1895:198–203, 348–49; 1901:368–70), Maystre (1937:40–41), Barguet (1967:161), Goedicke (1967), Thausig and Kerszt-Kratschman (1969), Beyerlin (1978:64–66), private communication from J. Gwyn Griffiths. This phrasing is found even in a copy of the *Book of the Dead* prepared for a woman, suggesting that the text was copied in a routinized, mechanical manner with little attention to the contents. Manniche (1967) points out that the possibility of lesbianism was recognized, as evidenced in a passage in a dream book, "If a woman has intercourse with her, she will experience a bad fate."

[34]Goedicke (1967).
[35]Lefebure (1912:192), Montet (1950).
[36]Personal communication, Ogden Goelet, Jr.
[37]Beyerlin (1978:64).
[38]Kees (1961:91–92), Casson (1975:89–90), Brier (1980:37–38).
[39]Breasted (1912:272–76).

been expected in everyday life.[40] Since the negative confessions required nothing more than a verbal denial, they do not necessarily suggest that male homosexuality was more than a minor peccadillo. The infractions included in chapter 125 range from blasphemy and killing to gossiping.

Goedicke suggests that the *Book of the Dead* signaled a shift in attitudes. The *Instructions of Vizier Ptahhotep,* dating from the Fifth Dynasty, warns against forcing a boy to submit after he protests; the negative confessions and temple inscriptions from Edfu are later and seem more general.[41] Possibly the aggressive connotations of the active role were so profound as to taint all homosexual activity. Alternately, disdain for homosexuality may have been restricted largely to the priesthood. Priests and moralists might well have regarded the flagrant commercialized sex of port cities like Memphis and Thebes, whose brothels were renowned in the ancient world,[42] as unsavory and best avoided.

Their attitudes were not necessarily shared by other Egyptians. Egyptian wisdom literature warns men against female prostitutes and adulterous affairs, but those red-light districts flourished. Though many Egyptians seem to have been sexually inhibited and modest,[43] there were also those who used aphrodisiacs, collected erotica, and displayed a strong interest in sexual adventure.[44]

We cannot take for granted that these libertines had homosexual interests. Some of the factors that contributed to the eroticization of male relationships among Greek men were absent in Egypt. Its natural borders kept it relatively secure from foreign foes for long periods of time. Internal pacification was achieved at an early date, so that in historic times Egypt never went through a "heroic age" comparable to that of Greece. Under these cir-

---

[40]Thus, out of respect for Horus, the pig, an animal sacred to Seth, was forbidden to the king, royal officials, and priests. But archaeological findings from the Ramesside Period show that pigs were eaten by state workmen in Thebes (Kees, 1961:91–92). However, a text from the late Heracleopolitan Period—earlier than the *Book of the Dead*—suggests that at one time male homosexuality could have been a prosecutable offense (Goedicke, 1967).

[41]Goedicke (1967) also suggests that passages in *The Instructions of 'Onchsheshonqy* refer to homosexuality. The demotic text, written for the guidance of a small-town resident or peasant farmer, is probably late Ptolemaic; its presumed earlier source is thought to be no later than the fifth or fourth century B.C. Glanville (1955:33) translates one sentence as "Do not take a youth for your companion," and supposes that it advises against pederasty, but Ogden Goelet, Jr., informs me that the word translated here as "youth" can also mean a servant or slave. The passage may be warning against fraternizing across class lines, and need have nothing to do with sex. Glanville (1955:54–55) translates another passage, "bend down (?) to every one (?)," but the text is so fragmentary that little confidence can be placed in any reconstruction. The "advice" offered in this translation is implausible.

[42]White (1953:122).

[43]Personal communication, Robert Bianchi.

[44]White (1953:122), Omlin (1973), Manniche (1987:106–15).

cumstances, the "love of warriors" would not become an important element of male culture. The absence of visual representations of homosexual acts in Egyptian erotica suggests that it was not common or a strong interest. Still, within these libertine circles, it may not have been considered evil.

As far as we can tell, homosexuality per se was not a category in Egyptian thought. There was no distinctive word for a homosexual person, only composite terms suggesting that gender was the critical category. Involvement in homosexuality was not assumed to be exclusive (though it may have been for some Egyptians); the god Seth, for example, was sexually aggressive toward the goddess Anat, as well as toward his brother Horus.[45] Ikhnaton, lover of Smenkhare, was married and sired offspring. The negative confessions and temple inscriptions refer to acts, not inclinations or states of being.

THE HEBREWS

Jewish Scripture is our primary source for Hebrew views of homosexuality in antiquity, but uncertainty over the dating and interpretation of critical passages complicates analysis. The interpretative difficulties can be seen in the story of Sodom and Gomorrah, as recounted in Genesis 19. When Lot offered hospitality to the angels visiting Sodom, the men of the town surrounded his house, calling out, "Where are the men that came in to thee this night? Bring them out to us that we might know them." Lot refused: "I pray you, my brethren, do not so wickedly," and offered his two virgin daughters as a substitute.

In an episode recounted in Judges 19, with many parallels to the story of Sodom, an old man of Gibeah offered overnight lodging to a Levite traveler and his Benjamite concubine. Some of the townsmen surrounded the house, calling, "Bring forth the man that came into thy house, that we may know him." The Levite offered his concubine as a substitute; the men "knew her, and abused her all night until the morning," when she was found dead.[46]

Several ambiguities cloud the interpretation of these stories. One stems from the double meaning of the Hebrew verb "to know." Usually it refers to cognition, but it can also be a euphemism for sexual intercourse. Some scholars have argued that in this context the verb is unlikely to have had a sexual connotation.[47] The Sodomites, they suggest, may only have wanted

---

[45] W. Dawson (1936).

[46] Most commentators have held that the episode in Judges is derived from the story of Sodom, but Niditch thinks the Genesis story is derivative from Judges. Linguistic considerations suggest a late, probably postexilic date for Judges 19, but the story is set in the period before the monarchy and may well be much older (G. F. Moore, 1895:402–4; Eissfeldt, 1965: 267; Boling, 1975:278; Coleman, 1980:29–39; Niditch, 1982).

[47] Bailey (1955:2–3), J. J. McNeill (1971:42–50), Boswell (1980:94–96), Ide (1985:21).

to learn the identity of Lot's guests. Perhaps they were supposed to register with the authorities, but didn't. Yet this argument is undercut by Lot's interpretation of the request as wicked, and by the angels' blinding the men of the mob. Surely they would not have done so had the mob only wanted to engage in a friendly chat. In addition, Lot describes his daughters as never having "known" men, a clear reference to their virginity. In the episode in Judges, sexual interest is implied not only in the rape of the concubine, but also in the use of the word "know" to describe the rape. This usage makes it especially difficult to argue that the episode does not concern homosexuality. Most scholars continue to find homosexual themes in the two stories.[48]

For centuries, biblical commentators have interpreted the destruction of Sodom and Gomorrah as a demonstration of God's wrath toward homosexuality. Yet later biblical references to Sodom do not even mention homosexuality; they suggest that the city was destroyed because of its inhospitality to guests.[49] Since the angels were sent to Sodom and Gomorrah because of the inhabitants' great (and unspecified) wickedness,[50] it is not clear that inhospitality was the sole complaint. Yet even if—as I have argued—homosexuality was involved, it was not consensual homosexuality but homosexual rape. Sexual aggression against strangers was not necessarily forbidden, but to threaten a *guest* with rape was a particularly outrageous violation of hospitality norms. In a world without Hilton chains, hospitality to travelers was enjoined by all ancient moral codes.

It is noteworthy that Genesis describes the men of Sodom and Gibeah as being interested in performing homosexual rape. The texts treat this interest matter-of-factly, as evidence for their general immorality. There is nothing in the narration to suggest that their sexual interests were unusual for their time. The attempted substitution of female victims in both episodes also suggests that homosexuality was usually not an exclusive taste. This is just what we found in Mesopotamia and Egypt.

A second set of passages concerns cult practices. We have already discussed the passage in Deuteronomy 23:18–19:

> There shall be no harlot [*qdeshah*] among the daughters of Israel. And there shall be no sodomite [*qdesh*] of the sons of Israel. Thou shalt not bring the hire of a harlot, or the price of a dog, into the house of Yahweh thy God for any vow; for even both of these are an abomination unto Yahweh thy God.

[48]Spijker (1968:67–74), Niditch (1982), Scroggs (1983:73), Edwards (1984:35–41).
[49]The references in the Hebrew Bible are Deut. 29:23, 32:32; Isa. 1:9–10, 3:9, 13:19; Jer. 23:14, 49:18, 50:40; Lam. 4:6; Ezek. 16:46–56; Amos 4:11; Zeph. 2:9.
[50]Gen. 18:20.

The reasons for thinking this passage deals with cult prostitution have already been reviewed in chapter 3.[51] The prohibition of this practice in a milieu where it was prevalent, reflects religious-political conflict between Yahweh cultists and adherents of the polytheistic religions associated with the surrounding civilizations.[52] Waves of Semitic immigrants had infiltrated Canaan and conquered its city-states around the thirteenth century B.C.[53] Some of the immigrants may not have been Hebrews, but Hebrews worshiping their tribal god Yahweh were among them. With the Hebrews' military successes during the conquest, the mixed nomads began to identify with the Hebrews and their religion. It seems likely that they were joined by Canaanite peasants liberated by the conquest from the tax burden of a highly stratified society.[54] These Canaanites, though, are unlikely to have abandoned their own religious beliefs and rituals altogether.

Following the conquest, the Israelites settled in Canaan and took up farming. They intermarried with the Canaanites, offering sacrifices to local deities (Baalim, Asheroth), and celebrating their planting and harvest festivals.[55] They left "nothing undone of their practices." [56] Called back to the faith of their fathers, centered on Yahweh, a god of war, storms, and thunder (but not of crops) who resided on Mount Sinai, they nevertheless returned to the gods of their neighbors time and again. Syncretism was evidently extensive.[57]

[51] The prohibition of cross-sex dressing in Deut. 22:5 is frequently taken as dealing with cult prostitution as well, but this is unclear. The passage is usually translated as "A woman shall not wear that which pertaineth to a man, neither shall a man put on a woman's garment" (Jewish Publication Society of America translation), but a more literal translation would read, "A woman shall not bear a man's implement (or weapon) and a man shall not wear that which symbolizes a woman." Male cult prostitution did involve transvestism, but we have no knowledge of women dressing as men in connection with cult ritual or prostitution. Of course they may have done so. Hoffner (1966) suggests that the passage may deal with magic rituals concerned with the restoration of male sexual potency or the destruction of an enemy's. However, it is also possible that the prohibition was merely intended to uphold gender distinctions and does not concern cult matters.

[52] Allegro (1970:215 n. 1) speculates that the name "Yahweh" derives from the Sumerian *IA-U, spermatozoa, and signifies male sexuality. Edwardes (1967:59–64) points to phallic elements in the early Yahweh cult; however, these do not appear to have been related to agriculture.

[53] Noss (1963:509–10), Malamat (1982), Yadin (1982).

[54] Mendenhall (1962), Gottwald (1979).

[55] Noss (1963:512–14).

[56] Judges 2:19.

[57] Wellhausen (1885:17f.). The extent and significance of this syncretism are controversial. Zeitlin (1984) and other Bible critics note that parts of the text bear the earmarks of late authorship and, read carefully, do not suggest extensive apostasy. Thus, the Israelites are described as having gone astray after *baalim*, and making Baal-Berith their god (Judges 8:33). But Baal-Berith, Lord of the Covenant, could only have been an epithet of Yahweh, whose worship in

It is often suggested that religious borrowing continued under the first monarchs, possibly to win the loyalty of the indigenous population; but the evidence for syncretism under Saul and David is not great.[58] However, Solomon employed Phoenician architects in the construction of his temple, and they borrowed their design from that of the Syrian, Shechemite, and Hazorite temples. To accommodate his many foreign wives, Solomon built temples to their gods and offered them sacrifices.[59]

Even in premonarchical times, devout Yahwists may have been offended by the fertility cults' use of "magical" techniques to control the gods.[60] The Jewish view that humans cannot force God to do anything may have been present even at this early date. Later, sharpening gender stereotypes and restrictions on women would have intensified hostility to cult prostitution; under the monarchy, the prophets railed against female promiscuity and prostitution. However, there is no evidence of conflict between the worshipers of Yahweh and the followers of other gods during the early monarchy.[61]

Open resistance to the fertility cults first appeared under Ahab, ruler of the northern kingdom of Israel (874–853 B.C.). Under the influence of Jezebel, a Phoenician princess, he sponsored the public worship of Baal, built him an altar, and also built an Asherah.[62] This marriage, like many of Solomon's, was a device for cementing an alliance with a foreign power. Zeitlin argues that the cult had little popular support and aroused determined opposition from faithful Yahwists.[63] However, Elijah complained to Yahweh that "the children of Israel have forsaken thy covenant, thrown down thine altars, and slain thy prophets with the sword . . ."[64] When he asked the assembled Israelites to choose between Baal and Yahweh, they

---

local shrines and *bamoth* (high places) became anathema after the centralization of the Yahweh cult in Jerusalem under Josiah (620 B.C.). Other passages, though, cannot so easily be dismissed as stemming from a centralizing mentality. Yahweh, for example, commanded Gideon to "throw down the altar of Baal that thy father hath, and cut down the Asherah that is by it, and build an altar unto Yahweh thy God . . ." (Judges 6:25–26). Here a local altar is acceptable. Archaeological findings from a number of sites testify to the existence of religious syncretism before and during the monarchy (J. N. Schofield, 1967; Eakin, 1971:216–17; P. D. Miller, 1985). Further excavation may be necessary to disclose its full extent.

[58] The case for syncretism under Saul and David rests in part on Saul having named one of his sons Eshbaal (a man of Baal), and David having named one of his *Beeliada* (Baal knows) (1 Chron. 8:33, 14:7). But these theophoric names are ambiguous, for as Zeitlin (1984:175) argues, Baal could have been a title of Yahweh. His position gains support from 2 Sam. 5:20, where the site of one of David's victories against the Philistines is named Baal-perazim.

[59] 1 Kings 11:4–8.

[60] Rad (1962:1.34–35), Hoffner (1966).

[61] Eakin (1977:194–200, 212–13), Soggin (1977).

[62] 1 Kings 16:31–33.

[63] I. M. Zeitlin (1984:290–95).

[64] 1 Kings 19:10, 14.

remained silent.[65] To the extent that popular opposition did exist, it probably centered on the execution of Yahwist priests and the destruction of Yahweh's altars.

The later kings of Judaea continued to follow the political winds in their patronage of foreign religious cults. When Ahaz (died c. 720 B.C.) was besieged by the Aramean and Israelite armies, he asked the Assyrians for aid. When they responded favorably, he paid them tribute and also set up a copy of the Assyrian altar in the Temple of Yahweh.[66] Later, when the Edomites and Philistines attacked, Ahaz shut the Temple and sacrificed to the Aramean gods, who had shown their greater power by defeating him some time before.[67] A century later, Manasseh erected altars for Baal and Ashtoreth in the Temple courtyards and introduced an image of Asherah into the Temple itself.[68] Assyrian annals portray Manasseh as a vassal-king of Assyria.[69] Undoubtedly, he was trying to accommodate the religious practices of his sponsors.

A policy of accommodating foreign cults or synthesizing them with the worship of Yahweh was presumably favored by the priests of the various cults, as well as by foreign residents, court circles favorable to the neighboring powers, and farmers, for whom the fertility cults would have had great significance. Women were especially devoted to the polytheistic cults,[70] possibly because of their greater concern with fertility, possibly because they could identify more readily with a religion that featured goddesses and priestesses than with one that had neither. Yahweh was depicted largely in male terms and was served exclusively by male priests. Opposition would have come from the priests of Yahweh, whose jealousy they projected onto their god, and his adherents among the laity. This might have included herders, who had little reason to be interested in rites connected with agricultural fertility, and most certainly the prophets, who associated foreign worship with class inequalities and royal grandiosity that violated ideals of egalitarianism associated with the tribal period.

Those Judaean kings who sponsored campaigns against the foreign cults did so in a spirit of nationalistic self-assertion. Asa destroyed the idols after winning a decisive military victory against an Ethiopian army.[71] His successor, Jehosephat, who continued Asa's religious reforms, allied with Israel and won major military victories, preserving Judaea's political inde-

---

[65] 1 Kings 18:21–22.
[66] 1 Kings 16:5–18; 2 Chron. 28:1–8.
[67] 2 Chron. 28:16–26.
[68] 2 Kings 21:1–18; 2 Chron. 33:3–9.
[69] Cogan (1974), Oded (1977).
[70] Jer. 44:15.
[71] 1 Kings 15:22, 2 Chron. 14–15.

pendence.[72] Hezekiah, who destroyed the Asherim, purified the Temple, and restored the worship of Yahweh in its earlier form, did so in the context of his successful defiance of Assyrian rule. His attempt to centralize the observance of Passover in Jerusalem[73] can be seen as a tactic to strengthen royal power and prepare for the political recovery of Israel. Josiah's reforms, which involved burning the Asherah that had been placed in the Temple, destroying places of worship, and killing priests throughout the land,[74] were undertaken at a time when Assyrian power had been seriously weakened by an Egyptian revolt. Indeed, the Assyrian Empire was overthrown by the Medes and Persians during Josiah's reign.

In each case, the repression of foreign cults entailed the suppression of the homosexual prostitution that went with them. Asa "put away the *qdeshim* out of the land."[75] Jehosephat "put away out of the land . . . the remnant of the *qdeshim* that remained in the days of his father Asa."[76] Josiah "broke down the houses of the *qdeshim*, that were in the house of Yahweh, where the women were weaving coverings for the Asherah."[77] It was during his reign that a book of the Law, thought by most scholars to have been Deuteronomy, was conveniently discovered in the Temple. Although some of the manuscript may have been written earlier, many scholars think it was forged during Josiah's reign in order to legitimate his reforms.[78] It is in Deuteronomy that the prohibition of cult prostitution appears.

The extent of popular support for these efforts is hard to gauge, but may not have been great. The worshipers whose religious sanctuaries and paraphernalia were destroyed could only have been antagonized. When Jeremiah prophesied to the Judaeans in exile in Egypt,[79] a "great assembly" of men and women gathered to complain:

> But since we let off to offer to the Queen of Heaven, and to pour out drink-offerings unto her, we have wanted all things, and have been consumed by the sword and by the famine.[80]

[72] 1 Kings 22:41–50, 2 Kings 3; 2 Chron. 17–20.

[73] 2 Kings 18–20, 2 Chron. 29–31.

[74] 2 Kings 23; 2 Chron. 34:1–7.

[75] 1 Kings 15:12.

[76] 1 Kings 22:47.

[77] 2 Kings 23:7.

[78] Oded (1977) points out that the manuscript could have been written during an earlier period of reform, and then hidden in the Temple during the "corrupt" reign of Manassah and Amon; I. M. Zeitlin (1984) speculates that it might have been written by Yahweh loyalists during the reign of Manasseh. These possibilities pose no problem for our argument.

[79] Jeremiah himself came from Anathoth, a town named for the Canaanite Anat, who had evidently not been forgotten some centuries after the Hebrew conquest. Could her worship have remained alive as well?

[80] Jer. 44:15–18.

Others may have reasoned that political and military contests showed how strong a nation's gods were. If Judaea defied Assyria with impunity, if Yahweh worshipers were able to destroy their opponents' temples and altars, it could only mean that Yahweh was stronger than Baal or Ashtoreth, and that his rituals, rather than theirs, should be performed.

It cannot be stressed too strongly that none of the campaigns against cult prostitution was directed at homosexuality in the population at large. The targets were religious cults associated with foreign powers. Nationalistic rulers suppressed these cults when they strove for independence from rival powers. In so doing, they tried to abolish the ritual practices associated with these cults, including homosexual prostitution.

None of the biblical passages we have examined thus far suggests that the Hebrews viewed homosexuality any differently from the way other peoples of the ancient Near East viewed it. There are passages in Leviticus that might suggest a very different conclusion, but we defer a discussion of them to the next chapter, where it will be argued that they represent a fairly late development. Provisionally, we conclude that at least until the Babylonian exile in 586 B.C., the Hebrews had no prohibition against homosexuality. Some of them engaged in it as part of their polytheistic religious practices on and off from the time of the conquest of Canaan to the exile.

CLASSICAL GREECE

Contacts with the East beginning in the late Neolithic (end of the fourth millennium B.C. to 2800 B.C.) gave Crete its goddess worship.[81] Minoan depictions of men wearing women's clothing in cult scenes suggest that that worship included homosexual cult prostitution, as it did in West Asian goddess worship.[82] Later Greek myths of gods changing men into women (e.g., Tiresias, Kaineus) may derive from garbled recollections of transvestism in the pre-Olympian cults.[83] By the time the Greeks emerged from the Dark Age and produced the writings that tell us of life in the classical age, they considered these cult practices to be alien.[84]

By that time, the homosexual component of tribal initiation rites had also disappeared in most of Greece. The desexualization of Greek initiations did

[81] Swindler (1913), Vercoutter (1954), Dietrich (1974:9).

[82] Paribeni (1908), Briffault (1927:2.531).

[83] Butterworth (1966:135–74), Dietrich (1974).

[84] Fragments 180–83 of Archilochus, a poet of the seventh century B.C., are especially intriguing in this connection. As reconstructed by Lasserre, they satirically identify a certain horn-player associated with the worship of Cotytto (a pre-Olympian Thracian Mother Goddess and patron of lewdness and homosexuality) and Sabazios (a Thraco-Phrygian god associated with the Mother Goddess and later identified with Dionysius) as *muklos*, a term usually used to refer to a lascivious women. Diodorus Siculus 4.4, writing in the first century B.C.,

not, however, lead to the disappearance of homosexuality: vase paintings, drama, poetry, oratory, and philosophical treatises show that from the sixth century on, secularized male homosexuality flourished in many of the Greek city-states. Nowhere was it prohibited by law. Public opinion was complex and undoubtedly not uniform, but did not generally stigmatize sexual contacts between males.[85] Relations between women were also known. Few written records of it survive, but vase paintings show lesbian activities among female prostitutes.[86]

The extent of homosexual participation is difficult to judge. In Sparta it seems to have been universal among male citizens. In Athens, only the wealthy would have had the leisure to loiter near the gymnasia, or the wealth to purchase gifts for the adolescents they were trying to seduce. Many of the male couples depicted in Attic vase-paintings clearly belong to the urban patriciate that flourished in Athens during the roughly half-century of Peisistratid rule that began in 561 B.C.[87]

This was a period of decline for the old Athenian aristocracy. Prevented by the tyranny and the rise of the hoplite army from participating in politics and warfare on the same basis as in the past, aristocrats competed for youthful male flesh. The symposium or banquet, originally the common meal of a tribal age-grade's warrior club, lost its educative function and became more hedonistic. Originally associated with the forest and the hunt, pederasty moved within the city walls and became domesticated, a theme of poetry and visual art.[88]

---

refers to Sabazian rites "celebrated by night and in secret on account of shameless ceremonies attending them." These rites were obviously sexual, and in light of what we know about the practices associated with Mother Goddess worship in Asia Minor, it is a reasonable inference that Archilochus is calling the target of his satire a cult prostitute. Sabazius was worshiped by private associations in Athens in the fifth century B.C., but was then regarded as a foreign god (Nilsson, 1940:93; Lewis and Short, 1955:477, 1609; Hammond and Scullard, 1970:294, 941; Burkert, 1985:179).

[85] Pogey-Castries (1930), Flaceliere (1962:49–85), Licht (1963), Eglinton (1964), Bullough (1976:92–126), Verstraete (1977, 1982), Boardman and La Rocca (1978), Dover (1978), Ungaretti (1978), Buffière (1980), T. Lewis (1982/1983), Foucault (1984a), J. M. Lewis (1985), Sartre (1985), Saslow (1985). D. Cohen (1987) sees greater ambivalence and thinks that pederasty could have been illegal in classical Athens.

[86] Pomeroy (1975:88), Dover (1978:173), Saslow (1985). One of the few surviving sources is the poetry of Sappho, but most of her poems are known only in fragments, and their interpretation as expressions of lesbian sentiments has been challenged (Hallett, 1979). Though derived from the Greek island Lesbos, the word "lesbian" did not have the same connotations in antiquity as it does now. Then it signified "shameless and uninhibited sexuality" of all kinds (Dover, 1978:183). My usage is anachronistic.

[87] H. A. Shapiro (1981).

[88] Schnapp (1984), Bremmer (1988).

Of course, youthful partners did not have to be rich; perhaps that is why they often asked for gifts. Some were prostitutes and/or slaves.[89] Nor were participants always city-dwellers. Solon's lover, Pisistratus, came from the rural town of Brauron; and Xenophon feared that the foreman on his farm would find a male lover and neglect his chores.[90]

The institutionalization of male homosexuality in ancient Greece has sometimes been attributed to the inferior position of women.[91] Athenian girls were unschooled, and the women were denied the opportunity to familiarize themselves with politics and civic affairs. Husbands tended to find them boring. Foreign-born women (mistresses and prostitutes) were available for cash and did provide extramarital heterosexual outlets, but paid partners do not necessarily provide the same emotional satisfactions as lovers. For lack of anything better, it is argued, men turned to other males (though with an enthusiasm that suggests many men found them more than just a second-best alternative). Yet the extreme subordination of Athenian women was fairly recent in the classical age, and as the evidence considered in chapter 3 indicates, male homosexuality was much older. Women of the Homeric age were not nearly as subordinate as in the classical age. According to Plato, homosexuality did not become institutionalized in Ionia, where women were especially secluded; whereas it did in Aeolia, where they were not.[92]

Slater has argued that Greek male homosexuality arose from the fear of women implanted by emotionally frustrated mothers, and had a strong narcissistic component.[93] However, small boys were not raised primarily by their mothers, but by male slaves who served as pedagogues.[94] Freud points out in *Three Essays on the Theory of Sexuality* that a male child raised by men may more readily accept homosexuality in adulthood; the early attachment to the father or father-surrogate is simply transferred to another male later on.[95] Conceivably this—along with the absence of repression—was a contributing factor.

What is of greater interest to us is how and what the Greeks thought about homosexuality, and what they did about it. Greeks of the classical age had no word for a homosexual (or heterosexual) person. With few exceptions, the Greeks assumed that ordinarily sexual choices were not mutu-

---

[89] Döllinger (1862:242), Licht (1963:436), Krenkel (1978), Wilkenson (1978); Keuls (1985:153, 296–97).

[90] R. J. Hoffman (1980).

[91] Fisher (1965), Symonds (1975:24–41), Dover (1978:201–3), Buffière (1980:553).

[92] Wilkenson (1978).

[93] Slater (1968).

[94] Buffière (1980:557).

[95] Freud (1953).

ally exclusive, but rather that people were generally capable of responding erotically to beauty in both sexes. Often they could and did.[96]

An ambisexual capability is implied in the comments made by the Greek historian Alexis about Polycrates, the wealthy ruler of Samos in the sixth century B.C. Alexis expresses his astonishment that even though Polycrates had imported many expensive goods,

> the tyrant is not mentioned as having sent for women or boys
> from anywhere, despite his passion for liaisons with males.[97]

In the same century, Aristogeiton, who, with his young male lover Harmodius, won renown by assassinating Hipparchus, the tyrant of Athens, also had a mistress.[98] It was said of Alcibiades, Athenian general and politician of the last half of the fifth century B.C., "that in his adolescence he drew away the husbands from their wives, and as a young man the wives from their husbands."[99] His older contemporary, Socrates, whose attraction to young men is immortalized in the dialogues of Plato,[100] also, according to Xenophon, patronized female prostitutes.[101] Before he speaks at the symposium, the other guests all praise sexual love, irrespective of its object, with the only qualification being that of Pausanias—that it should be noble, not base.[102] Timarkhos, who confessed to his homosexual experiences when put on trial in 346 B.C., also partied with flute girls and *hetaerai* (paid mistresses or high-class prostitutes).[103]

The assumption of bisexuality persists in later sources. In the writings of Theocritos, a pastoral poet of the third century B.C., a young woman abandoned by her lover prays,

> Whether it be woman that lies by him now, or whether man,
> may he as clean forget them as once, men say, Theseus forgot
> . . . the fair-tressed Ariadne."[104]

The poet Meleager, whose *Garland* was completed around 100 B.C., writes:

---

[96] Dover (1978:1), Foucault (1984a). One of the few exceptions is Plato's *Symposium* (1975: 192–93), in which Aristophanes refers to certain men as "born to be a lover of boys or the willing mate of a man." Even such men, under social pressure, marry and beget children, indicating that their sexual responses were not exclusively homosexual.

[97] Jacoby (1950:523), Padgug (1979).

[98] Keuls (1985:194).

[99] Diogenes (1891:172), Foucault (1984a:208).

[100] *Charmides* 154c, 155c–e, *Phaedrus* 241d.

[101] Xenophon (1897:121–22), *Memorabilia* 3.11.

[102] D. Levy (1979). In Xenophon's version of the event, Kritoboulos, who praises his *eromenos* Kleinas, is described as a newlywed (*Symposium* 2.3, 4.12–16).

[103] Keuls (1985:298).

[104] Theocritus (1950:19), *Idyll* 2.44. Likewise in the *Idyll* 5, Cometose, who asserts his current interest in women, boasts of having buggered Lacon in the past.

Aphrodite, female (sc. deity), ignites the fire that makes one mad for a woman, but Eros himself holds the reins of male desire. Which way am I to incline? To the boy or to his mother? I declare that even Aphrodite herself will say: "The bold lad is the winner!" [105]

Still later, Lucian, a satirist of the second century A.D., expresses this catholicity of taste in the short story "The Ship or the Wishes." One of the characters, Timolaus, wishes he owned a set of magic rings that would fulfill his desires. The ring he wants most will

make the pretty boys and women and whole peoples fall in love with me—no one will fail to love me and think me desirable: I shall be on every tongue. Many women will hang themselves in despair, boys will be made for me and think themselves blessed if I but glance at one of them, and pine away for grief if I ignore them. [106]

This interchangeability of boys and women was widely taken for granted. Thus Xenophon remarks that when prisoners of war were ordered released, "the soldiers yielded obedience, except where some smuggler, prompted by desire of a good-looking boy or woman, managed to make off with his prize." [107] Similarly, when Plato argues in the *Laws* that it was possible for people to exercise sexual restraint, he recalls that the renowned athlete Ikkos of Taras "never had any connexion with a woman or a youth during the whole time of his training." [108]

To be sure, it was recognized that some men preferred women, and others, male partners. Atheneus, for example, remarked that Alexander the Great was indifferent to women but passionate for males. [109] In Euripides' play *The Cyclops*, Cyclops proclaims, "I prefer boys to girls." [110] Plato never married. The philosopher Bion (third century B.C.) advised against marriage and restricted his attention to his (male) pupils. [111] The Stoic philosopher Zeno (late fourth and early third centuries B.C.) was also known for his exclusive interest in boys.

Aristophanes' speech in Plato's *Symposium* explains these preferences by fantasizing that the ancestors of the human race had two pairs of arms and legs, two heads, and two sets of sexual organs. [112] Some were double males,

[105] Dover (1978:63).
[106] Lucian (1959).
[107] Xenophon (1890:177), *Anabasis* 4.1.14.
[108] Plato (1968:407), *Laws* 840A.
[109] Symonds (1975:190).
[110] 582–84. Euripides (1959:5.208).
[111] Diogenes (1891).
[112] 189D–193D.

some double females, and some half male and half female. After the gods split the twins, their descendants sought, and continue to seek, reunion with the "missing half," whether of the same or opposite sex. Since humans who preferred same-sex partners would still have had to reproduce heterosexually for the myth to explain same-sex preferences in the next generation, it is not so clear that Aristophanes' explanation implies exclusive sexual choices. Still, it does presume specialized preferences.

Hellenistic writers even imagined debates about the relative merits of male and female partners. Some argued that it made little difference. One of the characters in Plutarch's *Erotikos,* or *Dialogue on Love,* argues that "the noble lover of beauty engages in love wherever he sees excellence and splendid natural endowment without regard for any difference in physiological detail." He will be "fairly and equably disposed toward both sexes, instead of supposing that males and females are as different in the matter of love as they are in their clothes."[113] His interlocutors, however, have more definite tastes. So do the protagonists in *Love,* a sophistical treatise attributed to Lucian. Even here, though, the arguments in favor of boys or women largely concern the practical advantages of each. Moral considerations are never raised, and boy lovers win the debates as often as those who prefer women.

In this sense, homosexuality and heterosexuality are treated as having equal status.[114] Thus Athanaeus remarked that "Sophocles liked his young lads in the same way that Euripides liked his women."[115] As long as they were exercised in moderation, sexual preferences for boys or women did not become the basis for imputations of moral character or competence in other spheres of life.[116]

Note that in most of these passages it is boys, not men, who are placed on an equal footing with women. This preference for youths stemmed from the intensely competitive individualism of Greek male culture.[117] Male competitiveness developed as clan structures broke down and property became privatized. It dominated aristocratic life everywhere except Sparta, where the kingship was hereditary, the senate of elders elected for life (minimizing rivalry for political office), and wealth distributed equally. Greek men were sensitive to status distinctions, and since status among the freeborn was not fixed, men vied for position.

[113] Plutarch (1969:415), *Moralia* 767.

[114] Halperin (1986a,b) points out that the speech of Aristophanes in Plato's *Symposium* postulates the same psychological·process for erotic desire of males for males, females for females, and males and females for one another: in each case, attraction is the desire for a substitute for the other half of the original twin.

[115] Quoted in Ungaretti (1982).

[116] Buffière (1980:481–550). See, however, D. Cohen (1987).

[117] Ungaretti (1978). Age disparities are especially evident in Theognis, *Elegies* book 2.

Preoccupation with status pervaded sexual culture to the point where the Greeks could not easily conceive of a relationship based on equality. Sex always involved superiority. Though *The Interpretation of Dreams* by Artemidorus Daldianus dates from the second century A.D., it reflects earlier attitudes on this score quite accurately. The section on sexual dreams indicates that

> having sexual intercourse with one's servant, whether male or female, is good; for slaves are possessions of the dreamer, so that they signify, quite naturally, that the dreamer will derive pleasure from his possessions. . . . If a man is possessed by a richer, older man, it is good. For it is usual to receive things from such people. But to be possessed by someone who is either younger than oneself or destitute is unlucky. For it is usual to give things to such people. The same also holds true if the possessor is older but a beggar. . . . Possessing a brother, whether he is older or younger, is auspicious for the dreamer. For he will be on top of his brother and disdainful of him. And whoever possesses his friend will become his enemy, since he will have injured his friend without provocation.[118]

Submission was evidently not dishonorable when it was to someone whose social status was clearly superior, e.g., a rich older man. But when the partners were of similar social status (brother, friends), possession implied status derogation, and this was an insult. The Persian soldier who, on a red-figure vase painting, presents his behind to a sexually aroused Greek man is being humiliated by his captor.[119]

Most men accommodated these status considerations by choosing a status inferior (a slave or prostitute), or a free younger partner, whose youth made him ineligible for military service or political office—hence someone who was not a rival. The idealized homosexual relationship thus involved an adult lover, usually between the ages of twenty and thirty (the *erastes*), and an *eromenos* or *paidika*, a prepubescent adolescent whose beard had not begun to grow. The relationship was ordinarily temporary, ending or becoming a nonsexual friendship when the youth reached maturity.[120]

Affairs between two adult men were less common, and were somewhat stigmatized, though not severely. Plato thought highly of those who

> love boys only when they begin to acquire some mind—a growth associated with that of down on their chins. For . . . those who begin to love them at this age are prepared to be always with them and share all with them as long as life shall last.[121]

[118] Artemidorus (1975:59–60).
[119] Keuls (1985:292–93).
[120] Dover (1978:16), Ungaretti (1978), Buffière (1980:21), Lewis (1982/83), Foucault (1985).
[121] Plato (1975:111), *Symposium* 181D.

The relationships between Agathon and Euripides, Parmenides and Zeno, and Crates and Polemo all continued into adulthood, apparently without creating any serious problems for them.[122]

Ideally, the older partner in a pederastic relationship strove to win the admiration and love of the younger through exemplary conduct, while the younger sought to emulate the older. Sex thus served to prepare young men for adulthood. In Sparta this pedagogic function was heavily militarized, while in Athens it involved preparation for the more varied life of an Athenian adult. Its importance in the Hellenistic era may be inferred from Plutarch's remark about boys' upbringing:

> the nurse rules the infant, the teacher the schoolboy, the gymna-
> siarch, the athlete, his lover (*erastes*) the youth, who, in the course
> of age is then ruled by law and his commanding general.[123]

He does not even mention the boys' parents!

Plato makes clear in the *Symposium* that it was perfectly acceptable to court a lad, and admirable to win him.[124] The youth, on the other hand, was not to appear too eager to be seduced, nor was he to initiate a courtship. On the contrary, he was supposed to be coy, to resist, to test the sincerity and worthiness of his lover. Their reputations hanging in the balance, youths had to be careful not to cross the line between honorable and discriminatory acquiescence and shameful overeagerness or manipulability. Aristophanes' defense of homosexually active youths in the *Symposium*:

> Some say they are shameless creatures, but falsely: for their be-
> havior is due not to shamelessness but to daring, manliness, and
> virility, since they are quick to welcome their like. Sure evidence
> of this is the fact that on reaching maturity these alone prove in a
> public career to be men.[125]

shows how thin and ambiguously placed that line was. It had significance for a young man's later career, for to be able to say no to an enticing but inappropriate liaison was to demonstrate self-mastery and invulnerability to manipulation. These were important character traits in a political leader.[126] With so much at stake, fathers tried to shield their sons from importunate suitors much the way Victorian fathers who themselves sought out young girls tried to safeguard their daughters' virginity.[127]

[122] Diogenes (1891:161), Buffière (1980:613), Ungaretti (1982).

[123] Quoted in R. Lambert (1984:79).

[124] Plato (1975:112–23), *Symposium* 182–85.

[125] Plato (1975:143), *Symposium* 192A.

[126] Foucault (1984a).

[127] Dover (1978:82–83, 92, 103), Foucault (1984a), D. Cohen (1987). At one time, for example, there had been a law in Athens barring men from the gymnasium. But by Socrates' day it had fallen into desuetude.

Although adults who succeeded with youths were applauded, those who took a receptive role after normal age were considered suspect, if not despised. According to Plutarch, writing under the Romans,

> we class those who enjoy the passive part as belonging to the lowest depth of vice and allow them not the least degree of confidence or respect or friendship.[128]

The comedies of Aristophanes, considered to reflect the views of ordinary citizens (in contrast to the more affluent aristocrats who surrounded Socrates), almost never lampoon men who love boys or boys who reciprocate their love. There are, however, numerous barbs against adult men who assume the passive role, especially when their partners are younger.[129] Middle Comedy drama makes the same distinctions: in a play by Alexis, who wrote in the fourth and third centuries B.C., a man is ridiculed for depilating himself to do things "fit only for beardless boys."[130]

Gender considerations had much to do with this contempt for passivity. The upper-class Athenian family in the classical age was highly patriarchal. Though women managed the household, they were also restricted to it. They lacked all legal personality, were subjected to forced marriage, and were vulnerable to male violence. The relationship between husbands and wives was one of unambiguous domination.[131] In Greek thinking, the family served as a model for all sexual relationships. If in heterosexual couples the male was active and the wife responsive, then in homosexual couples, the active, insertive partner was male, the passive, receptive partner, female. And to be female was to be inferior to men. For a male to submit to another man sexually was thus to declare himself unworthy of manhood. Aristophanes' complaint about adult men who engage in passive homosexuality is that they act like women, something real men should not do.[132]

Whereas the insertive homosexual role seemed so natural to most Greeks as to require no special explanation, a preference for a passive, female role—a preference that seemingly implied an abdication of privilege and concession of inferiority—seemed sufficiently incongruous to call for an explanation. Aristotle attributed this taste to habituation resulting from

---

[128] Plutarch (1969:425), *Moralia* 768E.

[129] Cody (1976), Dover (1978:137), Buffière (1980:179, 185–90).

[130] Lilja (1983:36). As Ungaretti (1982) points out, one must not make too much of the gibes in the comedies. A role or behavioral pattern made the butt of laughter on the stage did not necessarily evoke the same response in real life. To take an almost contemporary example, the comedian Jack Benny elicited countless laughs by depicting himself as a tightwad—from which it may be inferred that wealthy people are ideally expected to be generous. But it would be a considerable exaggeration to assert that in real life, misers are ridiculed or stigmatized.

[131] Keuls (1985).

[132] Buffière (1980:185–92).

"gross indignities since childhood."[133] In the pseudo-Aristotelian *Problemata Physica* 4.26, the passive role is explained physiologically, as a result of the deflection of semen to the rectum.[134]

Because the subordination of the young is a seemingly natural, and for any individual, temporary feature of a patriarchal social order (to some extent, of any social order), it was possible for an adolescent to allow himself to be seduced by an older man without opprobrium. His behavior reflected only temporary, not permanent submission and was therefore not stigmatizing. Despite this dispensation for youth, and even though most men preferred handsome, muscular youths as partners,[135] youths could not entirely escape suspicion of effeminacy. Plato wonders in the *Laws*, "who will not blame the effeminacy of him who yields to pleasures and is unable to hold out against them? Will not all men censure as womanly him who imitates the woman?"[136] Treating a lad like a woman could hardly be expected to masculinize him.[137]

To avoid the threatening gender implications of anal penetration, intercourse was often face-to-face and intercrural—though inevitably there were exceptions.[138] Ideally, the *eromenos* was not supposed to derive sexual pleasure from the experience; he was supposed to consent to sex out of gratitude or admiration, not lust.[139] Again, we know that there were exceptions, possibly many.[140] Nevertheless, suspicions that a boy enjoyed his ex-

---

[133] Aristotle (1959:206), *Nicomathean Ethics* 7.57.

[134] Aristotle (1927), *Problemata Physica* 4.26. The nucleus of the work may be Aristotelian, but some parts of it are thought to date from the fifth or sixth century A.D. (Forster, 1928; Siraisi, 1970). Aristotle's physiological explanation of sexual preferences—without known parallel in antiquity— is less remarkable when it is recalled that he was a biologist. Though the wording of Fragment 19 of Parmenides' *On Nature* is obscure, it may offer a rival, genetic theory of pathic homosexuality. That, at least, was how the passage was interpreted in the fifth century A.D. by Caelius Aurelianus (1950:903), following Soranus, an early second-century physician of the methodist school. In his *On Chronic Diseases* 4.9, Caelius Aurelianus compares pathics to tribades, and suggests that their bizarre preferences cannot be treated somatically, but only mentally.

[135] Vase paintings suggest that during the fourth century a shift in taste toward more androgynous partners may have developed (Dover, 1978:69–73).

[136] Plato (1968:403), *Laws* 837c.

[137] Foucault (1984a).

[138] Dover (1978:100–109), Ungaretti (1982). The issue obviously did not arise with prostitutes. The demand for anal intercourse from female prostitutes was high; there, too, gender considerations did not arise, and clients got what they wanted if they were willing to pay (Aristophanes, *Plutus* 149ff.; Henriques, 1962:27–28, 68).

[139] Thus in the *Symposium* 8.21, Xenophon declares, ". . . the boy does not share in the man's pleasure in intercourse, as a woman does; cold sober, he looks upon the other drunk with desire" (quoted in Dover, 1978:52). See also Golden (1981:128–29, 312–15; 1984), Keuls (1985:277–85), Halperin (1986b).

[140] Ungaretti (1982).

perience or had played a female role were often raised and not easily allayed, particularly if the relationship continued after the boy reached maturity.

Attitudes toward prostitution also figured in the ambivalent response to the *eromenos*. Though it was not illegal, it was considered shameful for a citizen to become a prostitute.[141] In a relationship between an *erastes* and an *eromenos*, both parties were ideally supposed to act from the loftiest of motives. But if an *eromenos* asked his lover for an expensive gift, was he implicitly prostituting himself? As with gender boundaries, distinctions between prostitution and romantic love proved to be difficult to draw in practice. As a result, boys' motives were often suspect.[142]

It would be a gross error to suppose that the Athenians thought less of homosexuality because they belittled male effeminacy or sometimes suspected teenage lovers of unbecoming motives. Pederasty did not lurk in the shadows of Greek life; it was out in the open. The gods practiced it, and it had its own patron god—Eros. In legend, it exemplified the noblest qualities of devotion and sacrifice. Lyric poets celebrated their youthful flames. In Plato's *Phaedrus*, homosexual love inspired by male beauty had the potential to develop into the most exalted love for ideal beauty and truth. By comparison, the object of heterosexual love lacked the special qualities that could inspire a spiritual or philosophical quest. In Thebes and Sparta, military organization was based on homosexuality. Even those who deplored some of its ramifications[143] never questioned that all men were capable of powerful homosexual attraction.

Nevertheless, as Foucault rightly suggests, homosexuality was problematic to the Athenians.[144] Their extreme democratic individualism and competitive status-seeking, channeled largely into political affairs, placed an enormous burden on personal character. Sexual comportment was a field on which character was revealed. It was not the only one—behavior in battle counted for much[145]—but it was an important one; important because male supremacy was such an integral element of Athenian life. So integral that the culture of male supremacy colored all social relations.

[141]Scroggs (1983:38–42). How shameful prostitution was in the official, or public morality may be gauged from the fact that someone who engaged in it was forever barred from addressing the assembly, holding public office, or entering the cult shrines. Fathers or guardians could be punished for forcing a boy into prostitution. Procuring for a woman or boy of free status was a punishable offense, as was rape, even of a slave (Dover, 1978:19–31; Parker, 1983:94). In practice, Winkler (1988) points out, these norms were invoked only when one of the small elite was trying to discredit a political opponent.

[142]Dover (1978:146).

[143]See chapter 5.

[144]Foucault (1985); see also D. Cohen (1987).

[145]Ungaretti (1982).

PRE-CHRISTIAN ROME

The Etruscans were a people who lived in what is now Italy during the first millennium B.C. The precise extent to which Etruscan culture was influenced by contributions from Lydia in Asia Minor (where Herodotus said the Etruscans originated), Greek and Phoenician settlers (whose presence in Sicily and Sardinia is attested as early as the eighth century B.C.), and the indigenous Villanovans remains controversial; there is evidence for all three.[146] From the Phoenicians they took their Astarte-worship; whether cult prostitution came with it is unknown but not unlikely.

Leaving aside the question of sacral homosexuality, the Etruscans' sybaritic way of life, and the liberties their women enjoyed, shocked their less affluent neighbors and earned them a reputation for loose morals. According to Theopompus, a Greek historian of the mid-fourth century B.C., after a gathering of family or friends,

> the servants bring in sometimes courtesans, sometimes handsome boys, sometimes their own wives. When they have taken their pleasure of the women or the men, they make strapping young fellows lie with the latter. . . . They certainly have commerce with women, but they always enjoy themselves much better with boys and young men. The latter are in this country quite beautiful to behold, for they live lives of ease and their bodies are hairless.[147]

Parallel observations, all derived from Theopompus, can be found in the writings of Aristotle and other Greeks. Unfortunately, Theopompus is not considered a wholly reliable source. Still, there is no reason for thinking him wrong about the prevalence of pederasty among the Etruscans.

The extent to which the less affluent Roman peasants shared Etruscan sexual mores is not known. Late Roman writers depicted their ancestors as devout, sober, and monogamous, but the Romans often idealized their past and consciously rewrote history to serve patriotic ends.[148] While one would not expect Etruscan-style orgies from a community of poor farmers, male homosexuality is far from unknown in peasant societies.[149] The

---

[146] R. Bloch (1960:28, 34; 1969:65–68), Scullard (1967:34–57).

[147] Quoted in Athenaeus, *Learned Banquet* 12.517d (Heurgon, 1964:34–35). Confirmation that the Etruscans knew of male homosexuality comes from the pederastic scenes in the frieze of the "Stackelberg" tomb at Cornelo (see Beilage 2 in F. H. Walter, 1921).

[148] Karlen (1971:44).

[149] For example, Swiss, Albanian, German, and Russian male peasants are all reported

Romans took much from the Etruscans, including religion, art, and architecture.[150]

There are the barest of hints that the Romans, who shared with the Greeks a common Indo-European heritage, also shared their tribal homosexual initiation rites. Mars, the principal Roman god in ancient times, was associated with the Indo-European expansion. His sons, Romulus and Remus, nursed by a she-wolf, founded Rome. Wolves were sacred to Mars. Seemingly there is nothing here to suggest homosexuality. However, drawings on a box discovered at the ancient Latin city of Palestrina-Praeneste depict a naked Mars with several youths. This could have been an initiation scene.[151] According to Livy, Romulus led bachelors or *iuvenes* in hunting, brigandage, warfare, and abduction of women.[152] Some of these activities were associated with male initiation classes among other Indo-European peoples, including the Spartans. The she-wolf of the legend may actually have been a male initiator wearing a wolf skin. Norse and Teutonic warriors wore wolf and bear skins to absorb the ferocity of the carnivore, and the wolf and bear had special significance for initiates in Greece.[153] When we recall that the Sambia of New Guinea, who prepare male youths for adulthood by sodomizing them, equate the penis with a breast, and semen with mother's milk,[154] it does not seem farfetched to suppose that the legend of Romulus and Remus derives from an almost-forgotten homosexual initiation ceremony.

Those ceremonies could have been part of the Bacchic mysteries. We do not know just when the mysteries first entered Italy, but they may have done so at an early time. The worship of Dionysos-Bacchus was probably imported to Greece from West Asia, perhaps in Minoan or Mycenean times;[155] it could have come to Italy directly from Asia Minor, or indirectly, via the Greeks. By the sixth century B.C., Bacchus was associated with the chthonian goddesses at Tarentum. The Greeks in Campania had a Bacchus cult of their own in the first half of the fifth century B.C.[156] The wide extent

---

to have been willing to participate in homosexual relations without hesitation or inhibition (Näcke, 1908; I. Bloch, 1933:31; H. Ellis, 1936:11; Karlinsky, 1976).

[150] Alföldi (1963:201).

[151] Dumézil (1966:1.208–13, 243–44).

[152] Livy, 1.4–16.

[153] Sergent (1984:118).

[154] Herdt (1981:233).

[155] Swindler (1913:9), Astour (1967:176–85). Dionysos's parentage—he was the son of Zeus and (in different versions of the myth) Demeter, Persephone, Dione, or Semele—links him with pre-Olympian religion. Inscriptions found at Pylos show that he was already a god in the thirteenth century B.C. (Graves, 1955:1.109).

[156] Dumézil (1966:2.516).

of Bacchic worship in the second century B.C., when a scandal broke out in connection with its orgiastic worship, suggests that the cult had never died out, despite its exclusion from the state religion. Perhaps it had survived in the Italian countryside all along, unknown to city-dwellers. In Greek myth, Dionysius was the *eromenes* of Polumnos (and the *erastes* of Adonis), and the Dionysian mysteries were connected with male-homosexual initiation rites at Megara and Argos.[157]

Though he is considered an unreliable source,[158] Valerius Maximus, a Roman historian of the first century A.D., reported an incident involving male homosexuality as early as the fourth century B.C., suggesting that it was known in very early times,[159] but there is little to indicate that it was common. Romans of the early Republic seem to have been more prudish than the Greeks. They never felt comfortable with public nudity (statues of men, for example, are clothed, unlike those of the Greeks) and did not value sensuality or male beauty as highly. Roman institutions such as the family and educational system were not as favorable to an institutionalized male erotic interest in other males,[160] and this seems to have been the Roman view of the matter as well. Cicero and Plutarch both traced the origin of Greek pederasty to the gymnasium.[161] In fact, much of the Roman vocabulary of homosexuality consisted of Greek loan words.[162]

Though it may have been less institutionalized a feature of Roman life than of Greek, homosexuality was by no means uncommon. Polybius, a Greek historian who visited Rome in the second century B.C., reported that *most* young men had male lovers.[163] Many of the leading figures in Roman literary life in the late Republic—Catullus, Tibullus, Vergil, and Horace—wrote homophile poetry.[164] From at least 160 B.C., *eromenoi* were a conspicuous feature of Roman life—as were *hetaerai*.[165] Sextus Propertius, a poet of the first century B.C., prayed that his enemies would fall in love with women, and his friends with boys.[166] Juvenal, a satirist of the first and second centuries A.D., wrote of young Armenian lads being corrupted when they came to Rome.[167] Roman homosexual tastes were so taken for granted that

[157] Sergent (1984:220, 225).
[158] Lilja (1983:106).
[159] Boswell (1980:64–65), Bremmer (1980).
[160] Lambert (1984:81–82).
[161] Cicero (1927:406–13), *Tusculan Disputations* 4.33; Plutarch, *The Dialogue on Love* 751.
[162] Adams (1982:123, 228), MacMullen (1982).
[163] 31.25.5; Boswell (1980:72), Rudd (1986:217).
[164] Kiefer (1934:186–202), Bullough (1976:144–46), Boswell (1980:72–73).
[165] Griffin (1976).
[166] Veyne (1982, 1985).
[167] *Second Satire* 44–50, quoted in Balsdon (1979:225). In isolation, this passage might suggest that male homosexuality was primarily an urban phenomenon, but in *Casina*, a comedy

when Antony asked Herod to send his young brother-in-law Aristobulus to the Roman court, Herod refused, because

> he did not think it safe for him to send one so handsome as was Aristobulus, in the prime of life, for he was sixteen years of age, and of so noble a family; and particularly not to Antony, the principal man of the Romans, and that would abuse him in his amours, and besides, one that freely indulged himself in such pleasures as his power allowed him without control.[168]

Even after making allowances for malicious gossip, we can conclude that many of the Roman emperors had homosexual tastes, often not exclusive.[169] Male prostitution flourished throughout Italy.[170]

As in Greece, sexual preferences were frequently not exclusive. The poet Martial, writing in the first century A.D., took ambisexuality for granted in one of his *Satires:*

> And when your lust is hot, surely
> if a maid or pageboy's handy, to attack
> instanter, you won't choose to grin and bear it?
> *I* won't! I like a cheap and easy love![171]

Indifference to the sex of a sexual partner is equally manifest in other literary sources, including Catullus, Philostratus, Horace, Plautus, and Tibullus.[172] The poet Meleager wrote love verses to women and men alike.[173] The "rake's progress" traced by Dio Chrysostom took him from women to male partners:

> Bored with harlots, he seduces well-bred girls and married women and when this becomes too tedious, because it is easy, he turn in his last state of degeneracy to seducing boys.[174]

---

of Plautus (254–184 B.C.), homosexual horseplay between Lysidamus and Olympio is supposed to reveal their rustic manners (R. L. Hunter, 1983:70). Note also the homoerotic banter between a shepherd and goatherd in Theocritus, *Idyll* 5.

[168] Josephus (1880), *Antiquities of the Jews* 15.2.6. Antony was at the time the lover of Cleopatra.

[169] One of our major sources for the sexual habits of the emperors is Suetonius, *Lives of the Caesars.* Though he is not considered the most trustworthy source, his employment as imperial secretary to Trajan and Hadrian gave him access to the imperial archives. Pike (1965:246) points out that as far as the later emperors are concerned, his statements were vulnerable to challenge from those who had personal knowledge of the emperors' biographies and therefore are unlikely to have been wildly off base.

[170] Bullough (1976:141–42), Verstraete (1980).

[171] *Satires* 1.2.116, quoted in Kiefer (1934:5).

[172] Boswell (1980:72–74), Lilja (1983:21, 75–77).

[173] Meleager (1975), 94.12.41.

[174] *Oration* 7, 133–52, quoted in Balsdon (1979:226).

According to Cato, Julius Caesar was "every woman's husband and every man's wife."[175] In speeches denouncing his opponents Verres and Gabinius, Cicero characterized both of them as bisexual.[176] Pathic males were often accused of adulterous affairs with women.[177]

Lesbianism was also known to the Romans, but it is difficult from the few references to it in literature to get a sense of its prevalence, the customs surrounding it, or the meanings it had and the responses it evoked.[178]

Historians have often asserted that the Romans must have had a negative view of male homosexuality because it was illegal under the *Lex Scantina*, promulgated in the second or third century B.C. However, the text of the law has not survived, and little is known about its provisions. Men were prosecuted under the *Lex Scantina* in later centuries, often for political reasons, but it is uncertain that the charges had anything to do with homosexuality, and the penalties do not appear to have been serious. Even when Cicero mentions homosexuality in denouncing his opponents, he never suggests that it was illegal.[179] Moreover, a trial is reported in which a man found in the bedroom of a married woman gained acquittal on adultery charges after testifying that he was there for an assignment with a male slave.[180] This casts grave doubt on the illegality of homosexuality.

To many Romans of the late Republic, oral sex and anal intercourse were highly aggressive acts. One of Catullus's poems threatens his critics:

[175] Quoted in Richlin (1983:88); see also Boswell (1980:75).

[176] Lilja (1983:89–90, 92).

[177] Boswell (1982/1983) argues that Roman writers did recognize predominant or exclusive sexual interests, but some of his examples are ill-chosen. Sextus Propertius, whose lines were quoted above, had a mistress, making him an implausible candidate for exclusive homosexuality, as Boswell considers him on the basis of a misleading translation. Nevertheless, it can hardly be doubted that some Romans, perhaps many, had exclusive sexual tastes and that these tastes were taken into account when relevant. The parasite Gnathon is clearly distinguished from the other characters in Longus's *Daphnis and Chloe*, a pastoral romance of the second or third century A.D., on the basis of his attraction to Daphnis (never stated explicitly to be an exclusive attraction). But this interest has little significance for the way he is treated in the novel. He is not considered a special type of person because of it. Likewise in *Clitophon and Leucipe*, a novel of the late third century A.D. by Achilles Tatius (1977), Charicles, Clinias, and Menelaus are depicted as exclusively homosexual, Clitophon as exclusively heterosexual. But these tastes, though recognized, have no particular social consequences. Another character is described as being attracted to both males and females (B3.10).

[178] Seneca (1974:86–87), *Controversiae* 1.2.2.23; Martial 1.90.7, 7.67.1, 7.70.1; Juvenal 6.311. Juvenal thought sexual relations between women impossible; Lucian's (1961:379–85) *Dialogues of the Courtesans* mentions them, but discloses little.

[179] G. Williams (1968:551), Bailey (1975:64–66), Wilkenson (1978), Baldson (1979:227), Boswell (1980:65–68), Lilja (1983:92, 112–21), Richlin (1983), Gray-Fow (1986).

[180] Valerius Maximus 8.1. *Absol.* 12, cited in Boswell (1980:65), Lilja (1983:110 n. 96), Richlin (1983:217).

> I will bugger you and I will fuck your mouths
> Aurelius, you pathic, and you queer, Furius,
> who have thought me, from my little verses,
> because they are a little delicate, to be not quite straight.[181]

Statues of the god Priapus stood erect in Roman gardens to threaten intruders with sexual assault, and according to Valerius Maximus, convicted adulterers were sometimes handed over to the servants or slaves of cuckolded husbands to be raped (or killed, fined, flogged, or mutilated).[182]

The perception of homosexual acts as aggressive led to strenuous efforts to protect freeborn youths from seduction. Quintilian's *Institutes of Oratory* advises parents to have their children educated at home rather than at school, and then to make sure a trustworthy chaperone is present.[183] To rape, seduce, or proposition a freeborn youth (or maiden), or for an official to pressure his subordinates to submit to him, was beyond the pale. The shame such acts incurred can be inferred from the suicide of Laetorius Mergus, a tribune of the early third century B.C., when summoned by the comitia on charges of trying to seduce an underling during the Third Samnite War. In later centuries, a charge of seducing a free youth could discredit the testimony of a witness in a court case.[184]

To some Romans, even sex with slaves or prostitutes was dishonorable,[185] but that was not the prevalent view. For most Romans, it was the social status of the partner that made a homosexual act unacceptable. Male prostitution was lawful; it was taxed, and the prostitutes had a legal holiday of their own.[186] Many a young man had a *concubinus*—a male slave to use sexually before marriage.[187] As possessions, slaves were expected to be passive and subordinate; they had no honor that could be compromised by their compliance. To Plautus, they were perfectly acceptable as sexual partners: "as long as you hold off from a bride, a single woman, a virgin, young men and free boys, love anybody you please."[188] In the *Satyricon* of Petronius, the slave Trimalchio confesses, "For fourteen years I pleasured him; it is no disgrace to do what a master commands. I also gave my mistress satisfac-

---

[181] Catullus 16, quoted in Richlin (1983:146). Winter (1973) discusses the poem.

[182] Kiefer (1934:31–32), Richlin (1983:66, 215).

[183] Quintilian (1887:18–21), *Institutes of Oratory* 1.2.

[184] Balsdon (1979:225), Boswell (1980:63, 70), MacMullen (1982), Lilja (1983:106–12), Richlin (1983:224–25).

[185] MacMullen (1982).

[186] Kiefer (1934:114), Boswell (1980:70, 72).

[187] Kiefer (1934:321), Richlin (1983:221).

[188] Plautus, *Curculio* 35–38, quoted in Richlin (1983:222).

tion." [189] Much of the homophile verse written in Latin may have been dedicated to slaves. [190]

In a political system that relied heavily on patronage, the hierarchy of subordination included freedmen who remained dependent on their former masters. According to a lawyer quoted in Seneca the Elder, "sexual service is an offense for the free born, a necessity for the slave, and a duty for the freedman." [191]

Even when it was considered socially inappropriate, homosexual desire was not considered abnormal as long as it took the active form. Lucretius thought erotic interest in "a lad with womanish limbs" to be entirely normal. [192] Quintilian, who advised parents to guard their sons, added that much of the problem in raising children to a high moral standard is that "they see our mistresses, our male objects of affection." [193] The Pompeiian graffiti referring to homosexuality, mostly written after the city was destroyed by a volcano in A.D. 62, treat it with good humor. [194] As in Greece, the Romans tended to consider the passive or receptive role incompatible with the honor and dignity of a free citizen, especially when it continued into adulthood. Sexual submission to a powerful patron was, seemingly, a familiar way of building a career, [195] but it left the client vulnerable to potentially ruinous denunciations. [196] A man's failure to live up to the standard of masculinity expected of someone in his rank was especially disturbing in a society that was attempting the systematic subjugation of the entire known world.

The growth of empire and long periods of peace intensified Roman concerns about effeminacy. As wealth from the conquered territories flowed into Rome, a life of conspicuous luxury became possible for a minority. Under Greek influence, the rich filled their days and nights with banquets, drinking, gambling, and theatergoing, wore perfumes and jewelry, and

[189] 75.11, quoted in Finley (1983:96).

[190] Richlin (1983:23). Horace said that he preferred slaves as sexual partners, regardless of whether they were male or female: "I like my sex easy and ready to hand" (*Satires* 1.2.116–19, quoted in Finley, 1983:96). Distinctions were sometimes made between someone else's slaves and one's own. The quaestor Gaius Gracchus reassured parents, in a speech delivered in 124 B.C., that "your sons were treated with more decorum than in a general's tent. . . . If any prostitute entered my home or anyone else's slave-boy was sought on my behalf, consider me the lowest and vilest of mankind" (quoted in MacMullen, 1982), discreetly saying nothing about his own slaves.

[191] *Controversiae* 4, quoted in Boswell (1980:78), Lilja (1983:30 n. 69).

[192] *De rerum natura* 4.1053, cited in Gray-Fow (1986). Lucretius, it may be noted, was a married man.

[193] Quintilian (1887:20), *Institutes of Oratory* 1.2.

[194] Lilja (1983:97).

[195] Lambert (1984:81–82).

[196] Julius Caesar in Suetonius, *Div. Iulius* 2.49; Augustus in Suetonius, *Augustus* 68, 71, Cicero *Pro Caelio* 3.6.

carried on extramarital affairs, both heterosexual and homosexual. Effeminacy was not as stigmatized in this circle as it had been among the yeoman farmers or soldiers.[197] The homoerotic poetry of the late Republic reflects this devotion to the pursuit of carefree, self-indulgent pleasure.[198]

Some considered this new life-style dissolute and debauched and feared that it would weaken the empire militarily. Flagrant effeminate homosexuality within this leisure class was seen as part of this life-style and was sometimes condemned in the name of rustic simplicity. Cassius Dio's history of Rome imagines Queen Boudicca of Britain deprecating the Romans for bathing in warm water, eating dainties, and sleeping on soft couches with boys.[199]

The extramarital heterosexual affairs of this circle were no less a subject for complaint. Sallust, lamenting the moral decline that began with the plunder of foreign wealth and culminated in the Catiline conspiracy, deplored

> the passion which arose for lewdness, gluttony, and the other attendants of luxury . . . men played the women, women offered their chastity for sale; and to gratify their palates they scoured land and sea; they slept before they needed sleep; they did not await the coming of hunger or thirst, of cold or of weariness, but all these things their self-indulgence anticipated. Such were the vices that incited the young men to crime, as soon as they had run through their property.[200]

Horace, too, linked the civil war with vice and immorality.[201]

It was in this atmosphere that the Emperor Augustus issued the *Lex Julia*

---

[197] Boswell (1980:82) notes that prejudices against effeminacy declined in the early Empire, and that then homosexual marriages between men or between women were recognized. This change in life-style explains why. In less affluent circles, where gender differences in the division of labor persisted, so did the old prejudices. Juvenal, living in poverty, wrote bitter satires of avarice, corruption, and perverted gender roles among Romans of the upper class. That prejudice against effeminacy did not necessarily entail rejection of all homosexuality is evident in the epigrams of Martial, a Spanish provincial of the first century A.D., who lampooned young men who depilated their bodies, but openly expressed homoerotic desires in his writings (Kiefer, 1934:165).

[198] Kiefer (1934:41), Earl (1967:18), Griffin (1976), MacMullen (1982), Balsdon (1979:224). Critics have sometimes argued that Roman homoerotic poetry had no relation to real life because it was copied from Greek literary models (G. Williams, 1968:551), but Griffin (1976) points out that by the late Republic, Hellenistic life-styles and cultures had penetrated Rome to a considerable extent. It wasn't just poetry that was copied: the life described in the poems was imitated as well. It spread to the Eastern provinces, too. In *On the Special Laws* (3.7.37–42), Philo, writing in first-century B.C. Alexandria, grumbles that "in former days the very mention of it was a disgrace, but now it is a matter of boasting not only to the active but to the passive partners" (quoted in Bullough, 1976:169). He saw them everywhere.

[199] Cassius Dio (1927:93), book 62.

[200] Sallust (1960:23) 13.3–13.5.

[201] Wallace-Hadrill (1982).

de adulteriis coercendis sometime between 18 and 16 B.C. Like so many later revolutionaries, Augustus worried that the new generation, which had not known the devastation of the war that brought him to the throne, took peace and prosperity for granted and lacked firm moral character. He wanted to ensure that enough boys were born to meet future military needs, but men were declining to marry to have children, so as not to tie themselves down with responsibilities that would interfere with having a good time.

The *Lex Julia* was Augustus's response to these concerns. The punishment of adultery, formerly a totally private matter, became a state function. Incentives were provided for marriage and childbearing. Because very little of the text has survived, its details are not known. Jurists of the early third century held that it prohibited the statutory rape of a male minor, but it is not clear whether this was part of the original statute or whether they were extending its scope by interpretation.[202] In any event, since resources were not allocated to enforcement, the legislation, which was bitterly resented,[203] had little impact, and homosexual relations continued to be carried on in public without interference during the first two centuries of the Empire, often by the emperors themselves. When accused of plotting against the Emperor Domitian toward the end of the first century A.D., Julius Calvaster claimed that he and his co-conspirator had met for homosexual purposes,[204] suggesting that it was then neither illegal nor seriously stigmatized. Writing in the second half of the second century, Aulus Gellius, a judge, observed that the Augustinian laws on having children were "ancient history" and hermaphrodites, "instruments of pleasure."[205]

CHINA

Like the Roman Empire and the kingdoms of the Near East, the ancient Chinese Empire was predominantly agricultural. Wars among the feudal states in the first millennium B.C. destroyed much of the old feudal aristocracy, leaving China ruled by a divine emperor who headed a centralized bureaucracy and court-based aristocracy. Extended family ties were socially important, considerably more so than in the Western civilizations. Commerce flourished in some periods of Chinese history, but without alto-

---

[202] Keesel (1972:2.859–63), Bailey (1975:68–69), Boswell (1980:71 n. 47, 1979), Raditsa (1980). Keesel suggests that the *Lex Julia* might have dealt only with a youth who responded to a seduction attempt, while the *Lex Scantina* dealt only with his seducer. But this is sheer speculation. The Romans themselves debated whether a married woman's lesbian affairs constituted adultery under the *Lex Julia* (Boswell, 1980:82–83).

[203] Griffin (1976), Wallace-Hadrill (1982).

[204] Dio 67, 11.4, cited in Lambert (1984:83).

[205] *Noctes Atticae* (*Attic Nights*) 2.15, 16.110, 3.5, 4.1, 9.4, 16.7, cited in Zimmerman (1947:411).

gether eroding traditional status differences based on birth. Given these similarities, sexual patterns should resemble those seen in the other ancient empires. In many ways they did.

The earliest Chinese references to male homosexuality appear during the Han dynasty.[206] Van Gulik concludes that male homosexuality was quite fashionable in this period,[207] and it may have been—the first three emperors of the dynasty all kept "powdered and rouged boys" as well as wives. So did the later Han emperors. Han sources also mention that some princes kept young boys as catamites. These relationships appear to have been entirely secular; if there had ever been cult prostitution or ritualized homosexual initiation rites, no evidence of them has survived.[208]

Homosexuality is attested outside court circles only at later dates. The poet Li-Po (d. A.D. 762) wrote love poetry to his young male lover,[209] and in the Five Dynasties Period (A.D. 907–960), transgenerational male-homosexual relationships were generally accepted. When the older *ch'i hsung* called at the home of the younger *ch'i ti*, he was welcomed by the entire family as if he had been a prospective bridegroom. If the *ch'i ti* later married, it was customary for the *ch'i hsung* to pay the expenses.[210]

Patriarchal power was too strong for a lesbian equivalent to emerge in ancient China; only when foreign trade and investment made it possible for women to subsist independently of fathers or husbands did lesbian marriages—not necessarily transgenerational—formalized by contracts and gifts, emerge.[211]

Transgenderal homosexual relationships also seem to have flourished at this time, especially between actors. Women were barred from the stage,

[206] The Western Han ran from 202 B.C. to A.D. 9, the Eastern Han from A.D. 25 to 220.

[207] Gulik (1961:28, 62). He also states (p. 48) that lesbianism was very common during the Chou dynasty (1122 B.C. to 255 or 221 B.C.), but this claim should be treated with caution; the sources are hardly adequate to sustain conclusions about the prevalence of sexual orientations or practices in different periods of Chinese history.

[208] Ritualized heterosexual intercourse did play a role in ancient Chinese folk religion (Granet, 1975:44–46). Although the Chinese developed an elaborate sexual philosophy (Bullough, 1976:281–314), cultic intercourse did not become part of the official state religion. As a result, the Chinese were shocked and indignant at the homoerotic Tibetan rites practiced at the court of Shun-Ti, the last Mongol emperor in the fourteenth century (Heissig, 1966:52–53; Francke, 1981). Ritualized transgenderal male homosexuality associated with shamanism may also have been present in the Silla kingdom (early Korean civilization) (Rutt, 1961).

[209] Matignon (1899).

[210] Mitamura (1970:64). In Korea, such relationships were typically initiated by widowers and had no stigma; the youth would later marry heterosexually (Rutt, 1961). Scott (1954) found that pederasty was extremely common, virtually universal, in seventeenth-century Siam, but does not provide details of the relationships. In French Indo-China adult men commonly had boy lovers, even if they were married (Corre, 1894:13).

[211] Hirschfeld (1935a:81), McGough (1981), Sankar (1985).

and the men who played female roles also seem to have played receptive roles offstage in sexual relationships with actors who played male roles.[212]

Though a law against male prostitution called for heavy penalties during the brief Cheng-ho period (A.D. 1111–17), it thrived during the Northern Sung and Southern Sung dynasties (1127–1279). The prostitutes had a guild of their own and appeared in public rouged and adorned as women.[213] At some point, they acquired their own god, Tcheou-Wang.[214] This was a period of economic expansion, the spread of a cash economy, and growing inequality. The larger cities brought together poor males who had to rent their bodies to support themselves and middle- and upper-income men with the money to pay for them. This conjunction persisted, and so did prostitution. When the Jesuit Matteo Ricci visited Peking in 1583 and again in 1609–10, he found male prostitution to be altogether lawful, and practiced openly:

> there are public streets full of boys got up like prostitutes. And there are people who buy these boys and teach them to play music, sing and dance. And then, gallantly dressed and made up with rouge like women these miserable men are initiated into this terrible vice.[215]

To his dismay, no one thought there was anything wrong with it. Several hundred years later, European travelers still reported that no one was ashamed of homosexuality. Government officers appeared in public with their fourteen-to-eighteen-year-old pipe-bearers, and male brothels operated in Canton and other cities.[216]

References to eunuchs appear in oracle bones of the Shang dynasty, c. 1300 B.C. Evidently the Shang castrated captured soldiers of the Chiang, a Tibetan people they conquered, presumably to prevent them from procreating, but it is not known what they did with them. Probably they were enslaved. The castration of *Chinese* men began early in the Chou dynasty as a punishment for crime. Some men were sentenced to castration; others had the option of choosing it to avoid execution.[217] As in other ancient civilizations that castrated criminals, the Chou period was one of great social differences between lords and serfs.

Like the Assyrians, the Chinese found ways to put the men they cas-

[212] Cheng (1963), Bullough (1976:304–7).

[213] Gernet (1959:109–10), Gulik (1961:163).

[214] Doré (1916:1021).

[215] Spence (1984:220).

[216] Jacobus X (1896:1.97–102), Karsch-Haack (1906:1–62), Henriques (1961:250–51), Van Straten (1983:98–99, 137).

[217] Tompkins (1962:31–33), Mitamura (1970:45, 55).

trated to good use. During the Chou dynasty, the imperial palace began to use eunuchs to guard the royal wives and concubines, and as domestic servants. The number allocated each member of the royal family came to be fixed by law; for the emperor it was 3,000.

Because they could not succeed to the throne, and were personally dependent on the emperor, eunuchs were eventually entrusted with important state functions. During the second half of the Chou dynasty they served as political advisers and heads of armies and figured prominently in government in the Han and later dynasties.[218] When the demand for palace eunuchs exceeded the supply of men castrated involuntarily, volunteers were sought. As officials were often in a position to extort bribes, some eunuchs became quite wealthy. To obtain these positions, men castrated themselves or were castrated by parents who hoped to achieve upward social mobility for the entire family.

Although it is unlikely that all eunuchs were implicated in homosexual relationships, a number of them did become sexual partners and/or lovers of the emperors they served.[219]

MAYANS, INCAS AND AZTECS

At the time of the Spanish Conquest in the early sixteenth century, berdaches were present in many of the kinship-based Indian groups of Central and South America.[220] There were also hereditary chieftainships, characterized by marked inequalities of wealth,[221] in which chiefs kept transvestite men for their own sexual purposes.

The more complex civilizations of the Yucatan, the Pacific Coast, and the valley of Mexico were all based on agriculture, arts and crafts, and state-sponsored polytheistic religions administered by full-time priests. Still, there were important differences among them. When the Spanish arrived, Mayan civilization consisted of independent city-states ruled by hereditary nobles; it had been declining culturally and militarily for some centuries. The Aztecs had been a migratory band of hunters and warriors that settled and built Tenochtitlan (now Mexico City) around A.D. 1345. A hundred years later they began to expand, building an empire by conquest and alliance, rigorously subordinating every other social consideration to militarism. The Incans were indigenous to the Pacific Coast, where they had been preceded by earlier civilizations. They had begun to build their em-

---

[218] The Korea kings of Korea used palace eunuchs similarly in the period before the Yi dynasty, which began in A.D. 1392 (Osgood, 1951:146; Rutt, 1961; Mitamura, 1970:17).

[219] Matignon (1936), Wittfogel (1957:356), Cheng (1963:157–58), Bullough (1976:302–9), Hopkins (1978:186).

[220] See chapter 2.

[221] Helms (1979), Creamer and Haas (1985).

pire less than a century before the Spanish arrived. Unlike the Aztecs, they attempted to foster linguistic, cultural, and legal unity throughout the vast territory they acquired.

The artifacts that archaeologists have discovered provide a little information about homosexuality in the Mochica and Chimu civilizations that preceded the Incas in Peru. Many pieces of pottery have survived, and they frequently depicted sexual interactions, some of them homosexual.[222] It is a reasonable inference that the practices so profusely were considered acceptable. Unfortunately, there are no written sources to tell us more.

Apart from the Peruvian erotic pottery, our main sources are Spanish soldiers and missionaries, and Indian chronicles written under Spanish influence. One of the Spanish sources, Bartolome de las Casas, writing in 1542, reported that Mayan parents supplied their adolescent sons with boys to use as sexual outlets before marriage, but that if someone else sodomized them, the penalty was equal to that for rape.[223] Since de las Casas denied the existence of homosexuality in some other Indian groups, his attribution of homosexuality to the Mayans cannot be attributed to a blanket prejudice against Indians. Other missionaries also reported widespread male homosexuality among the Mayans.[224] Young Mayan men lived in men's houses until they married at about age twenty.[225] Transgenerational or egalitarian homosexual relations could have been carried on there, but this is not known. In some Mayan regions—though probably not all—phallic religious cults, possibly involving homosexuality—were being maintained in the pre-Spanish period.[226] Nevertheless, men defeated in battle were insulted with an epithet that the translator renders "homosexual," but that probably referred to male effeminacy or the receptive role in anal intercourse.[227]

Father Pierre de Gand, also known as de Mura, found sodomy to be virtually universal among the Aztecs, involving even children as young as six.[228] Cortez also found sodomy to be widespread among the Aztecs, and admonished them to give it up—along with human sacrifices and cannibalism. Bernal Diaz del Castillo, who accompanied the Cortez expedition of 1519, and who is considered the most truthworthy of the historians who

---

[222] J.E.S. Thompson (1972:20–21), Kauffman-Doig (1978), Arboleda (1981). In one collection, 3 per cent of the specimens showed two men engaging in anal intercourse, and 1 percent showed lesbian scenes. Since much of the pottery was destroyed by missionaries, little significance can be attached to these percentages (Guerra, 1971:255–58).

[223] Guerra (1971:76).

[224] J.E.S. Thompson (1972).

[225] Anton (1973:28).

[226] J.E.S. Thompson (1972:20–21, 46, 169), Helfrich (1972).

[227] Scholes and Roys (1948:91), C. Taylor (1987).

[228] Bancroft (1875:467).

wrote about the conquest of the Aztecs, reported the existence of boys dressed as girls who made a living through homosexual prostitution, religious leaders who did not marry but engaged in sodomy, and temple idols who imitated them. One of the Aztec gods, Xochipili, was the patron of male homosexuality and male prostitution; he may have been taken over from the earlier Toltec civilization, which had a reputation for sodomy among both the Mayans (whom the Toltecs conquered), and the Aztecs (who conquered the Toltecs).[230]

Some of the peoples who made up the Inca empire also had institutionalized homosexuality. This includes the Yauyos, who had "public houses filled with men who dressed as women and painted their faces," the Liysacas of Lake Chucuito, and Indians in the vicinity of Puerto Viejo in the north (now Ecuador) and on the island of Puna. In some parts of the empire, boys were dedicated to the temple, where they were raised as girls; chiefs and headmen had ritual intercourse with them on special holidays. The Inca princes themselves, however, did not engage in these practices.[231]

These reports clearly point to widespread practice and acceptance of secular and religious transgenderal male homosexuality, very much as in the archaic civilizations of the ancient Near East. Other reports, however, contradict this picture. De las Casas and de Herrera contend that reports of widespread sodomy were greatly exaggerated.[232] The Inca laws, providing for death by burning, suggest no great acceptance of homosexuality.[233] The laws of the Chichemecs, who migrated into central Mexico before the Aztecs, have been recorded by Fernando de Alva Ixlilxochitl, a descendant of the kings of Texcoco, whom the Aztecs conquered. In cases of male homosexuality,

> To the one acting as a female, they removed his entrails from the bottom, he was tied down to a log and the boys from the town covered him with ash, until he was buried; and then they put a lot of wood and burnt him. The one acting as a male was covered with ash, tied down to a log until he died.[234]

Aztec law was equally stern in providing the death penalty for male and female homosexuality and transvestism.

Enforcement of the Aztec sodomy legislation in the conquered provinces

---

[229] Idell (1956:21, 87), Guerra (1971:52, 123–24); Mendelssohn (1974:180), C. Taylor (1987).

[230] J.E.S. Thompson (1966:113–27), C. Taylor (1987).

[231] Flornoy (1956:128–29), Scott (1966:57), Brundage (1967:187), Guerra (1971:91–93), Murra (1980:154).

[232] Bancroft (1875:467 n. 98), Guerra (1971:67–73, 153–54).

[233] S. F. Moore (1958:170).

[234] F. Katz (1958).

was placed in the hands of officials appointed from time to time to search out cases and appears to have been sporadic. In the more remote provinces, enforcement was probably nonexistent.[235] The lax enforcement of laws providing the death penalty for adultery suggests that the Aztecs lacked the administrative capability of enforcing morals legislation throughout the empire, or were not sufficiently concerned to do so. It is one thing to proclaim an ideal standard of behavior, another to alienate a population by executing those who do not live up to it.

Although the Inca empire is generally depicted as having been more centralized administratively, Moore and Metraux argue that the Incas never developed a smoothly functioning bureaucracy.[236] Of necessity, most governmental administration remained in the hands of self-supporting, preconquest local rulers. Moreover, while Inca laws were theoretically applicable throughout the empire, the Incas made no attempt to suppress local custom or religious practice. Reports of homosexuality coming from so many different regions of the Inca empire despite sanguinary legislation against it point to the absence of any serious effort at enforcement.

Even if they were not vigorously enforced, Aztec and Inca laws betray attitudes that differ radically from those of other archaic civilizations. One possible explanation for the difference has to do with the relationship between cult homosexuality and state formation. We suggested in chapter 3 that in the ancient Near East, homosexual cult prostitution probably originated in a Siberian-type shamanism that became incorporated into a state religion. However, the Aztecs had no shamans. Conquering peoples who did, they may have wanted to suppress indigenous shamans to eliminate potential sources of resistance to their rule. When the Aztecs and Incas legislated against homosexuality, they may have been trying to substitute the political state and its official religion for the shamans of tribal society.[237] Recall that in many Central and South American Indian cultures, shamans were frequently male-to-female transvestites who engaged in sexual relations with other men.

It might be argued that, if the Spanish Conquest had not occurred, the Aztecs would eventually have brought cult prostitution into the state religion as an expression of concern over fertility. On the other hand, the exceptional yield of maize as a food crop may have reduced Aztec anxiety over fertility. It is equally plausible that palace eunuchism would have developed as a tool of despotic rule, and that this would in turn have led to homosexuality within royal circles.

[235] Bancroft (1875:467–68).
[236] S. F. Moore (1958:13–15, 90, 98, 131), Métraux (1970:110).
[237] Farb (1968:182), Brundage (1975).

That the harshness of Inca and Aztec legislation toward homosexuality involved more than a reaction to indigenous berdaches is suggested by the equally severe penalties imposed on other violations of morals legislation. The Incas punished pimps and prostitutes severely, by death if the offense was repeated. Incest and adultery were capital offenses in both empires. Drunkenness was illegal under the Incas and a capital offense under the Aztecs.[238] Abortion was also a capital offense under the Aztecs.[239] Aztec youths lost their rights to land if they did not marry by a certain age.[240] Inca men were also forced to marry.[241]

These provisions suggest that the laws were devised to channel all energies into conquest and to encourage the breeding of soldiers. Anything that might weaken the military strength of the empire by encouraging licentiousness was to be suppressed. Aztec religious codices depicted sex as a serpent,[242] and fathers advised sons against premature entanglements with women.[243] Women were downgraded in myth and religion, and descent changed from matrilineal to patrilineal.[244] Male effeminacy became intolerable. The objection, then, was not to homosexuality per se, but to extramarital sex, intoxication, and gender ambiguity.

The possibility that Aztec and Incan legislation was not as harsh as the reports suggest must also be considered. The Inca laws of the chronicles are "brief to the point of inadequacy" and "must generally be looked upon with considerable reservations."[245] They were not written down, and thus have come to us through Spanish-influenced sources dating from a generation after the Conquest.[246] Because the Spanish bishops destroyed the Aztec and Mayan libraries, none of our sources for Aztec or Mayan law predates the Conquest.

There is particular reason to be concerned about the reliability of sources about homosexuality: it figured in the polemics and debates about Spanish colonial policy. To justify their exploitation of the natives, conquistadors portrayed them as subhuman beasts whose devotion to sodomy, incest, cannibalism, and human sacrifice demonstrated that they lacked normal moral sensibilities.[247] The clergy, on the other hand, sought converts and

---

[238] S. F. Moore (1958:170), Guerra (1971:23–25, 35, 162–63), Anton (1973:24–25, 37).
[239] Bancroft (1874:469).
[240] Kurtz (1978).
[241] Tannahill (1980:302).
[242] Berland (1973).
[243] Bullough (1976:44–45).
[244] Leacock and Nash (1977), Nash (1978).
[245] S. F. Moore (1958:170).
[246] X.X.X. (1962).
[247] While the secular sources may have exaggerated the prevalence of homosexuality for

thus tried to protect the Indians from exploitation by portraying them in a more favorable light. They are thus likely to have underestimated the incidence of homosexuality and to have exaggerated opposition to it.[248]

The Spanish clergy could even have produced a distorted picture of Indian morality without intending to deceive. Interviewers can easily elicit untruthful or misleading responses to questions, particularly when they are in a position of power. An early-seventeenth-century Peruvian historian, Garcilaso de la Vega, complained that the Indians tried "to soothe the Spaniards and flatter them, answering questions as think the questioner wants them answered and not with the truth."[249] The conquistadors came from a country that killed men for homosexuality, and they carried the habit with them to the New World. The Spanish burned "sodomites" in the Puerto Viejo region. Once the Inquisition was established, it did the same in Mexico. When Balboa came to Panama, he killed forty transvestites by feeding them to his dogs.[250] In an atmosphere of terror, there is little reason to expect informants to tell the truth.

HINDU CIVILIZATION

There is no definite evidence that the Aryans who invaded India initiated their youths sexually, but it is possible that they did so while they were still migrants, as part of their Indo-European heritage. Weber notes that traces of warrior heroism and chiefdoms, of the sort familiar in Homeric Greece, are evident in the *Ramayana* and the *Mahabharata*.[251] This literature, a product of the Indo-Aryan invasions, provides evidence that there were once associations of young men, stages of probation for youths, and bachelors living in longhouses before marriage. These institutions were associated

---

these reasons, it is unlikely that they manufactured their accounts out of whole cloth, for their descriptions correspond too closely to those of the North American berdaches.

[248] Guerra (1971:75), Tannahill (1980:289–91). One of the obvious examples of a Spanish chronicler coloring native accounts with his own prejudices is a myth attributed to Peruvian Indians in which a shining angel descends from heaven with a sword and kills giants who engaged in sodomy (Guerra, 1971:90; Tannahill, 1980:295).

[249] Tannahill (1980:290–91). Alfred Russell Wallace encountered the same difficulty on his trip to Amazonia in 1848 to 1852 (Shoumatoff, 1986).

[250] Greenleaf (1961:33–34), Guerra (1971:48–49, 149), Bullough (1976:32). According to Peter Martyr, who wrote the first chronicle of the expedition, after the forty were killed the population dragged out others and pleaded that they, too, be executed. He claimed that the commoners blamed the transvestites for many of the natural disasters from which they had recently suffered, including storms, floods, famine, and diseases (Guerra, 1971:48–49; Bullough, 1976:32). There is a question, though, of whether he was reporting the Indians' views or his own. The notion that homosexuality could cause natural disasters figured prominently in early modern Christian literature.

[251] Weber (1968:63).

with pederasty in ancient Sparta. Some scholars see in the Maruts of the *Vedas*—the oldest Hindu religious literature—groups of young men who formed an initiation class.[252] O'Flaherty notes that the Hindi word for milk is often used to refer to semen and that medical texts recommend drinking semen to cure impotence.[253] If these are clues to the presence of rituals involving homosexual fellatio, they were presumably discontinued once kingdoms were established. The Vedas do not refer to them.[254]

The Aryans entered India as pastoral warrior-nomads, contemptuous of the sedentary cultivators they conquered.[255] Female deities played a relatively modest role in their religion.[256] Religious leaders were conventionally gendered priests (Brahmins), not transvestites or transsexuals. They married women. Their authority, which rested on knowledge of written sculpture, formulaic prayer, and performance of the sacrifices, was incompatible with orgiastic worship.[257] Like the Aztec, Hebrew, and Egyptian priests, they recoiled from indigenous fertility-cult practices associated with planting and prohibited them in the law books they prepared.[258]

Sustained by a very ancient tradition that sexual abstinence magically bestows power and immortality,[259] the Brahmins defined a wide range of sexual practices as polluting. Homosexual acts were forbidden[260] along with some heterosexual practices and solo performances.[261]

This rejection of homosexuality did not result in much repression. The *Laws of Manu* imposes only a mild penance for homosexual contact—ritual immersion with clothes on. The law codes themselves, addressed primarily

[252] Wikander (1938), Renou (1968:15).

[253] O'Flaherty (1976:340).

[254] Fišer (1966:62–63).

[255] The *Laws of Manu* 10.84 forbid Brahmins and kshatriyas from engaging in farming. Even in modern times they have not been attracted to it (Briffault, 1927:3.59).

[256] Proto-Indo-European religion had only a few minor, unelaborated nature goddesses. The Indo-Aryans acquired more powerful female deities from the sedentary populations of the territories through which they traveled. Typically, these goddesses lost powers and functions as they became spouses of male gods (Robbins, 1980). See, however, Kumar (1974:9).

[257] Weber (1958:137). Orgiastic worship tends to be indiscriminate and requires little specialized training. It thus tends to subvert caste distinctions as well as authority based on a command of esoteric knowledge acquired through formal training. Cult prostitution also equalizes worshipers (anyone's semen is as good a contribution as anyone else's), and crosses caste lines. In contrast to Mesopotamian cult prostitution, which united worshipers with transsexual priests, the Brahmin alone drank the hallucinogenic *soma* in Hindu ritual.

[258] None of the Vedic literature involves the worship of erotic forces or deities. The Rig Veda, reduced to writing in about the eighth century B.C., refers to phallus worshipers disparagingly (7.21.5, 10.99.4) (De, 1959:86).

[259] Babb (1975:230–33), La Barre (1984).

[260] See chapter 3, note 64.

[261] J. J. Meyer (1952:242 n. 1), Bullough (1976:245–80), Banerji (1980:139, 142).

to Brahmins, state ideals and were not necessarily applied rigidly. Local custom was to be accommodated.[262] Decentralized administration of justice in local princely courts, and the absence of any formal ecclesiastical organization, virtually ensured that it would be.

Custom was often far from ascetic or antihomosexual. Pre-Aryan sex worship was accommodated rather than suppressed. Though Śiva was not a full-fledged god in the Vedic literature, he later became the focus of a phallus cult. Some eroticism appears in the *Brāhmaṇas*, written down c. 300 B.C. or later.[263] In an atmosphere of extreme tolerance, Śakti worship and heterodox tantric cults based on sacramental intercourse persisted—unmolested by practitioners of extreme asceticism and self-denial. Notwithstanding the statement in the *Mahabarata* that oral sex is a crime, it is depicted in the erotic temple sculptures, as are lesbian scenes and bestiality.[264]

Nor does eroticism appear to have been confined to religious settings. The *Silippadhikaram*, a Tamil epic of the second century A.D., states that the city of Puhar reserved a separate quarter for prostitutes.[265] Eunuchs, some of them dressed as women, were part of court life and enriched its sexual opportunities as early as 400 B.C.; they remained a part of the royal households until Independence. The Kama Sutra and subsequent sex manuals published over the centuries provided detailed instruction in many nominally prohibited practices. Some parts of India were renowned for oragenital techniques that the codes prohibited.[266] Pederasty and male prostitution flourished in Hindu cities, even more in Moslem regions.[267] Lesbianism is reported, as well as sexual relations between masters and servants, and between male equals.[268] Even some of the gods occasionally engaged in homosexual activity, perhaps the best evidence that tendencies toward asceticism did not lead to a general repugnance toward homosexuality. Asceticism was admired, but it was only one component of a complex culture with many variant, contradictory strands. Kama, the god of love and desire, was worshiped, and the *Vishnupurana* reminded members of all castes that they were to find sexual satisfaction with their spouses.

It can be safely assumed that the deterioration in the status of Indian women which occurred in historical times[269] led to a devaluation of male

---

[262] Derrett (1973:2–3), Trautmann (1981:294–95, 303).

[263] De (1959:86, 89), Walker (1968:390–92).

[264] *Mahabharata* 7.73.43; A. V. Ross (1968:103), Desai (1975:142).

[265] Reddy (1973).

[266] J. J. Meyer (1952:242 n. 1), Saletore (1974:195).

[267] The extent of tolerance in civilian life may be gauged by the experience of the French abbé Jean Antoine Dubois (1924:312), who visited India at the beginning of the nineteenth century. A Brahmin he asked about the male transvestite prostitutes seen in the streets of all the larger Indian towns replied, "there was no accounting for tastes."

[268] Farquhar (1929:408), Bullough (1976:245–80).

[269] Briffault (1927:345–49), Altekar (1956), Boulding (1976:189–90).

effeminacy, but not to the point where temple prostitution or eunuchism was prohibited.[270] They became illegal only after India gained Independence. The status considerations that entered into male homosexual relations are revealed in an episode reported by Burton, in which a high-caste Brahmin had been playing the active role in an affair with a low-caste partner. On one occasion they voluntarily reversed positions. Afterward the Brahmin was "stung by remorse and revenge, loaded his musket and deliberately shot his paramour," a crime for which he was later hung.[271]

Jainism and Buddhism broke from Hinduism in the middle of the first millennium B.C. in northeast India at a time when Aryan control was still new and the caste system not firmly established. Mahavira (599–527 B.C.), the founder of Jainism, and Gautama Buddha (560–640 B.C.) were both noble *kshatriyas* (members of the aristocratic warrior caste) who rejected brahminical claims to supremacy. Both rejected the Hindu pantheon, prayers, and rituals and held that anyone, regardless of caste, could attain enlightenment. To varying degrees, both embraced asceticism. It was a logical choice, both because self-denial was already valued in the Vedas and because asceticism was already "democratic"—anyone could pursue it. It was thus a challenge to caste systems and to priestly claims to special sacerdotal status.

In Jainism, liberation from material existence is achieved through extreme bodily mortifications. Monks forswear all sexual contact; the laity may marry, but must remain faithful to their spouses.[272] This doctrine could hardly have favored homosexuality, but it was so unsympathetic to all kinds of sexual expression that it did not especially single out homosexuality for special repression. The severity of its demands has limited its appeal; there are only a couple million Jains in the entire world.

Buddhism, founded a generation later, eschewed extremes of asceticism in favor of a "Middle Way" in which liberation is achieved by suppressing all desire. As in Jainism, this entailed chastity for monks and nuns, Buddhism, too, could hardly favor homosexuality. As it evolved, though, it developed heterodox tantric cults that permitted intercourse, primarily heterosexual.[273] In practice, homosexuality didn't do too badly in Buddhist lands.[274]

[270] The families of most contemporary hijras try to discourage them from cross-dressing, and peers ridicule them, though at the same time encouraging them by taking them as sexual partners (sometimes paying them as well). In the Southern Indian languages of Telugu and Tamil, the term used to refer to the hijras carries a derogatory connotation lacking in the North (Nanda, 1985).

[271] Richard Burton (1886:237–38).

[272] *Sutrakritangu* 1.9.10, 10.13. In addition, a wise man is advised to refrain from urinating, vomiting, and having bowel movements (1.9.12)! (Jacobi, 1968:302, 308).

[273] Bullough (1976:270–76).

[274] For China see above; for Japan see chapter 6. Topley (1954) and Leach (1958) discuss les-

The House of Islam

Climactic and ecological factors greatly delayed state formation among the tribes of the Arabian peninsula. Except for Yemen in the south, where more hospitable conditions gave rise to agriculture, irrigation, a monarchy, and temple priesthood as early as 1000 B.C., Arab society at the end of the sixth century A.D. consisted largely of stateless pastoral warrior-nomads of the desert and town-based merchants and craftsmen. Religion centered on the worship of astral and fertility deities derived at least in part from neighboring agrarian civilizations. Through contact with Jewish, Christian, Manichaean, and Zoroastrian traders and missionaries, the tenets of ethical monotheism were becoming known. Political and military dealings with the Byzantine and Sassanid (Persian) Empires, and pilgrimages to Mecca, helped generate a sense of national identity and fueled territorial ambitions.[275]

The worship of three goddesses, Allat, al-'Uzza', and Manat, at the Ka'aba in Mecca in pre-Islamic times raises the question of homosexual cult prostitution. However, there is no evidence of this. It was only after Mohammed's death that pashas began donating eunuchs to the service of the temple, and the service was not sexual.[276] Apart from cult expressions, homosexuality was known to the Arabs, but probably not surrounded with much romantic sentiment. Pre-Islamic erotic poetry does not mention it.[277] If more recent reports of bedouin life can be extrapolated into the past, homosexuality was probably rare among desert nomads, but more common in towns.[278]

As in Egypt and Mesopotamia, effeminacy was considered contemptible; it figured in proverbial intertribal taunts:

> I swear, the seas and the deserts are smaller than the asses of the Benou Lakit (a Bedouin tribe)! They are the most infamous of all horsemen, the vilest of those who walk on foot.[279]

---

bian marriages in Chinese Buddhist convents in Singapore. It is tempting to speculate on the possibility that the sexual prohibitions of the Hindu law codes were borrowed from Buddhism. The *Arthashastra*, which prohibits homosexuality, dates to around 325 B.C., by which time Buddhism had become widely known in India. The Hindu priests could have been trying to win back apostates by displaying an equally strong commitment to a sexually restrictive morality.

[275] Brockelmann (1960:1–12, Grunebaum (1970:13–26), Hodgson (1974:1.71–145), Engineer (1980:12–40), Lapidus (1982).

[276] Burckhardt (1829:158–59).

[277] Lyall (1930), M. Daniel (1977), Wormhoudt (1980).

[278] Thesiger (1959:125).

[279] M. Daniel (1977).

Mohammed drew on this traditional contempt, as well as on the biblical story of Sodom and Gomorrah he had learned from Jews and Christians, in condemning homosexuality as a violation of Allah's will, though without prescribing a specific penalty.[280] This condemnation must be placed in the broader context of a generally restrictive, though not ascetic, sexual morality in the Koran. The wine-drinking and pursuit of women of which the bedouins were enamored were frowned on by the town merchants of Mecca, who included Mohammed's own tribe, the Quraysh.[281] Still, his placing eternally youthful male and female virgins in Paradise to serve believers[282] suggests that this repudiation of hedonism was not unambivalent.

Over time, Moslem religious writings became more punitive toward homosexuality. A number of *hadith* (sayings attributed to Mohammed and collected or forged after his death) call for the death penalty.[283] Converts from Judaism and Christianity may have been responsible for this punitiveness. During its first two centuries, Islam grew primarily through conversion. Most converts were members of the upper classes who had had a classical Hellenistic education that exposed them to Roman, Jewish, and Sassanian law, as well as to the ecclesiastical law of the Eastern churches.[284]

These influences are quite apparent. Most of the *hadith* favor stoning sodomites to death. In one exception, Ali, Mohammed's son-in-law and the fourth caliph, wanted to burn them in imitation of the destruction of Sodom. Abu-Bakr, Mohammed's father-in-law and the first caliph, is reported to have had a man burned for passive anal homosexuality. Stoning was the traditional Jewish penalty; and though the matter is not certain, Byzantine law may have provided for burning since the end of the fourth century A.D., as we discuss in chapter 5. Descriptions of the horrible tortures awaiting sodomites in hell also bear the earmarks of Christian influence.[285] Islam's claims to be the true successor to the religion of Abraham left it open to the importation of moral standards and penal sanctions not native to Arabia.[286]

[280] Koran 7.80–81, 11.79–84, 12.77–78, 21.74, 22.43, 24.27–33, 26.165–68, 27.56–59, 29.27–34.

[281] B. Turner (1974:34–35), Engineer (1980:60).

[282] The Koran does not state the service to be sexual, but later Moslem literature does (Bouhdiba, 1985:75).

[283] S. Talbot (1963), J. A. Bellamy (1979), Farah (1984:38).

[284] Bellamy (1979), Schacht (1970).

[285] M. Daniel (1977), Bellamy (1979), Farah (1984:38), Bullough (1976:205) neglects these writings when he characterizes Islam as a "sex-positive religion." Views of sexuality have not been uniform within Islamic civilization.

[286] Other elements of Islamic practice can also be traced to Jewish sources, e.g., the prohibition against eating pork and possibly the prescription of prayer five times a day (the Koran calls for twice or thrice a day) (Grunebaum, 1970:46). The establishment of criminal penalties for "offenses" in which both participants are consenting was itself novel, a manifestation of state formation. Under tribal law, penalties were inflicted by the clan of an injured party, and

The impact of these writings on broader opinion may not have been great. In the early days of the Umayyad caliphate, judges were dependent on local governors, and did not always follow the letter of the written law.[287] Also, the evidentiary standard required for conviction in Islamic courts was difficult to meet. In an eighth-century literary "duel" in which the poets Jarir and al Farazdiq exchanged extravagant sexual insults, the great majority are heterosexual, but some are homosexual. None suggests that homosexuality is sinful or evil.[288] Women's sexual conduct, which could potentially besmirch family honor, was given far more attention than male homosexuality.

Within decades of Mohammed's death, Arab armies conquered Palestine and Syria, then Mesopotamia, Iran, Egypt, and North Africa. Soon after, Moslem armies captured Sicily and India. Male homosexuality was already common and accepted in some of these regions. Christianity and Zoroastrianism had probably not altogether eradicated this acceptance by the time of the Arab conquest. Nevertheless, literary conservatism stood in the way of any poetic treatment of homosexuality for a century. Only with the advent of the Abbasid caliphate in the middle of the eighth century do we find poets writing homoerotic verse to beautiful youths.[289]

As in Greece, relationships that persisted after the youth reached adulthood drew criticism. Abu-Nuwas (A.D. 810), a lyric poet who lived in Basra and Baghdad, defended his own involvement in such a relationship:

> Jealous people and slanderers overwhelm me with sarcasm
> because my lover has started to shave.
> I answer them: friends, how wrong you are!
> Since when has fuzz been a flaw?
> It enhances the splendor of his lips and his teeth,
> like silk cloth which is brightened by pearls.
> And I consider myself fortunate that his sprouting beard
> preserves his beauty from indiscreet glances:
> it gives his kisses a different flavor
> and makes a reflection glisten on the silver of his cheeks.[290]

---

then only for injuries. Mohammed's abolition of collective responsibility for crime reflects the weakening of clan ties in response to the growth of commerce, but individualism had not proceeded to the point where each individual would be left to go his or her own way. Political leaders were vested with responsibility for the moral standards of the community. The idea that both parties to a male homosexual encounter should be punished came, of course, from Judaism or Christianity.

[287] Sourdel (1979:59).

[288] Ibn Atiyah (1974), Wormhoudt (1980).

[289] M. Daniel (1977), Wormhoudt (1980).

[290] Quoted in M. Daniel (1977).

Arab authors were, of course, familiar with Greek literature,[291] but their love poetry has its own stylistic authenticity; it was not simply copied from Greek models.

Some authors identified themselves as attracted to both women and boys. When Beha Ed-Din Zoheir, a poet of thirteenth-century Cairo, couldn't have the woman he wanted, he turned to a boy:

> My mistress is proud,
> she expels me from her presence
> she refuses me her mouth
> and abandons me to insomnia,
> Then I went to find a
> young and obliging boy.
> Beautiful as the moon and the stars,
> he poured me a drink.
> "Drink," he said. But I answered him:
> "No! drink this cup yourself!
> I am already drunk with love,
> there's no need to add more intoxication." [292]

Samau'al ibn Yahya (d. 1180), a Jewish convert to Islam, wrote that many eminent men of his time had turned to male youths because their physicians had warned them that intercourse with women would cause gout, hemmorhoids, and premature aging.[293]

Others had more definite interests. Some poets found women repulsive.[294] To compete more effectively with boys, women began to emulate them, cutting their hair short and depilating their bodies.[295]

None of this ample literature suggests that male homosexuality was stigmatized or repressed. On the contrary, it was pervasive and highly visible:[296] "the sexual relations of a mature man with a subordinate youth were

[291] The Hellenistic debates over the relative merits of boys and women undoubtedly served as a model for the Jahiz dialogue, "Singing Slave Girls" (Pellat, 1969).

[292] Quoted in M. Daniel (1977).

[293] Jacquart and Thomasset (1985:171).

[294] M. Daniel (1977), Bürgel (1979).

[295] Bouhdiba (1985:142).

[296] Bianquis (1986). This enthusiasm for male love has often been attributed to the subordination and seclusion of women (purdah). Yet, as has already been noted, male homosexuality is uncommon among bedouins, even though they are sometimes deprived of women for months at a time. A survey of male students at the American University in Beirut found that 38 percent had had some homosexual experience and 69 percent had had some heterosexual experience, frequently with prostitutes (Melikian and Prothero, 1954). The comparable figures in a survey of U.S. college students were 27 percent and 45 percent (Finger, 1947). Clearly, the unavailability of women does not explain higher levels of Arab involvement in male homosexuality. Also see Hanry (1970:85–87).

so readily accepted in upper-class circles that there was often little or no effort to conceal their existence."[297] After returning from a trip to Egypt, the thirteenth-century Dominican friar William of Adam wrote, "These Saracens, forgetting human dignity, go so far that men live with each other in the same way that men and women live together in our own land."[298] Christian boys, he claimed, were sold into slavery in Egypt, where they were turned into prostitutes.[299] Jews living in Egypt and Arab Spain followed the example of their neighbors in turning to pederastic love.[300] Judging from the erotica of the time, lesbian relationships were also quite familiar.[301]

Pre-Moslem stereotypes regarding male homosexual roles persisted, even though Moslem religious writings prohibited both. Though there was neither word for, nor a concept of, a homosexual person, an adult man who took pleasure in the anal-receptive role was scorned and thought to require an explanation. Some thought the "condition" to be due to the smoking of hashish; others thought it to be of genetic origin or followed the pseudo-Aristotelian *Problemata Physica*. To play an active penetrating sexual role was, on the other hand, entirely normal, no matter who was being penetrated.[302]

Islamic legalism prevented the writings of theologians and legal scholars from fully reflecting the popular attitude. Though the mystic theologian al-Ghazali (d. A.D. 1111) wrote poems to boys he loved, he also expressed sharp disapproval of homosexuality.[303] Perhaps to protect himself, Ibn Hazm, a Spanish Berber of the eleventh century, appended to his *The Ring of the Dove*, a frank collection of romantic poetry, both heterosexual and pederastic, a condemnation of sinning and an apotheosis of continence.[304]

Social cleavages within Islam must have affected this divergence of views of male-male love. As the Arab empire expanded, its ruling stratum siphoned off wealth; wage levels fell and social inequality grew.[305] Pious scholars and theologians criticized these violations of traditional Arab norms of tribal egalitarianism and Koranic standards of social justice in the name of religion.[306] If, as is likely, pederasty was most visible in aristocratic circles, opposition to it may have reflected class antagonism, as well as tension be-

[297] Hodgson (1974:2.146).
[298] Quoted in M. Daniel (1977).
[299] N. Daniel (1979).
[300] Schirmann (1955), Goiteen (1979), N. Roth (1982), Leneman (1987).
[301] Nafzawi (1975), Bouhdiba (1985:142).
[302] F. Rosenthal (1971:81–83, 1978), Schmitt (1985).
[303] M. Daniel (1977), Bellamy (1979).
[304] Ibn Hazm (1978).
[305] Lombard (1975:146–47).
[306] B. Lewis (1968:21–22).

tween secular and religious elites. It is revealing that Ibn Khaldun, the great historian and sociologist of the fourteenth century, blamed the decay of civilization on fornication and homosexuality and thought those who committed a homosexual act should be stoned, while at the same time including homoerotic poetry in his magnum opus, *The Muqaddimah.*[307] He seems to have considered the homosexual impulse normal, but its social manifestations in the upper classes, where it was associated with sensuosity and softness, pernicious. Empires were built and maintained by force of arms, which required toughness and virility, not the emotional intoxication and pursuit of pleasure surrounding boy love.

Despite the social pressure to condemn male homosexual relations in print, the Koran's failure to specify a punishment left some room for maneuver. Al-Hakam (d. A.D. 822), an emir in Spain, held that sodomites should be beaten with fewer strokes than those guilty of other sexual infractions.[308] Some authorities authorized intercourse with males provided they were not Moslem—making relations with non-Moslem slaves captured or purchased from abroad acceptable. There was a brisk market for them.[309] Others concluded that the hadith reserving the legal shedding of Moslem blood for three offenses alone—adultery, homicide, and denial of faith—precluded any corporal punishment for homosexuality.[310] Sufi mystics found a way to interpret sexual congress with male youths as leading, in Platonic fashion, to union with the divine.[311]

Notwithstanding the opposition of Islamic religious law, a de facto acceptance of male homosexuality has prevailed in Arab lands down to the modern era,[312] though in some times and places discretion has been required.[313] It is represented in erotica, though with no great emphasis, from the thirteenth century down to the present.[314] In Morocco, boys were kidnapped, sold to adult men for sexual gratification, and released when too

---

[307] Ibn Khaldun (1967:2.295–96).

[308] Bellamy (1979).

[309] Lombard (2975:146). Some Malikite jurists reinterpreted Koran 9.120 as authorizing the sodomy of non-Moslems (Schmitt, 1985).

[310] M. Daniel (1977).

[311] Schimmel (1975:287–343, 1979), Bullough (1976:235–38), M. Daniel (1977), Boswell (1980:27 n. 49), Bouhdiba (1985:119), Bianquis (1986).

[312] Reuben Levy (1962:234). Crapanzano (1973), Patai (1973), and Schmitt (1985) explain the high level of male homosexuality as a consequence of child-rearing practices that are common to Arab populations of the Middle East. Unfortunately, there is little solid knowledge of these practices, and their effects on later sexual orientation are not firmly established.

[313] Contemporary Iran is a well-publicized example. With support from the lower classes and petty bourgeoisie hurt by Western-style modernization, the Iranian clergy have led a harshly enforced legalistic religious fundamentalism hostile to illicit sex.

[314] Nafzawi (1975), Bouhdiba (1985:142–45).

old to be of further interest.[315] The demand for youthful male flesh was not restricted to a tiny, clandestine underground. Louis de Chenier, the French consul-general in Morocco in the late eighteenth century, found the public baths to be

> receptacles of debauchery, into which men were introduced into the dress of women; and the youth of the city ranged the streets after sunset, in the same disguise, to prevail upon strangers to go with them to the inns, which were rather houses of prostitution than places for the convenience and repose of travellers.[316]

Pederasty was an "established custom,"[317] with boys readily available in the towns.[318] As late as 1952, when Marc Oraison visited Morocco, male students of the Islamic University engaged in homosexual relations openly and publicly.[319]

In nineteenth-century Algeria, "the streets and public places swarmed with boys of remarkable beauty, who more than shared with the women the favor of the wealthier natives."[320] Tunisia in the 1930s also had male prostitutes, but they were badly outnumbered by female practitioners of the trade.[321] In Siwah, an oasis town of Libya, pederasty was practiced very widely, with parents prostituting their own sons.[322] It would be of considerable interest to know whether the practice was more pervasive in Libya. A psychiatric survey of Iraq found male and female homosexuality to be common among men and women.[323] And Burkhardt, traveling in Syria in the early nineteenth century, found that "unnatural propensities are very common" among the Druse.[324]

Joseph Pitts, an Englishman who visited Cairo toward the end of the sev-

---

[315] Coon (1931:110–11).

[316] Chenier (1788:1.74). Public baths provided a convenient locus for male and female homosexual liaisons throughout North Africa and Turkey. They were the only places where it was considered socially acceptable to be nude in the presence of another person of the same sex. As bathing was required for ritual purity, every town had at least one; large towns, many (Grotzfeld, 1970:88–91), Bouhdiba (1985:167). In sixteenth-century Turkey, the women's baths had such a reputation for lesbian love affairs that some husbands did not allow their wives to go to them. While some husbands were willing to tolerate their wives' covert affairs, they treated openly scandalous behavior very harshly, e.g., by killing the wife (Busbecq, 1977:146).

[317] G. Maxwell (1966:175).

[318] Richard Burton (1886:222), Houel (1912:139–42), Rossman (1976:117–21), Hervé and Kerrest (1979).

[319] Oraison (1975:96).

[320] Henriques (1961:355); see also Duchesne (1853) and Richard Burton (1886:222).

[321] Bouhdiba (1985:191).

[322] Cline (1936), Khun de Prorok (1936:64), Maugham (1950:80).

[323] Al-Issa and al-Issa (1971).

[324] Burkhardt (1822:202).

enteenth century, wrote that while it was dangerous for women to walk in certain districts, it was

> more dangerous for boys, for they are extremely given to sodomy. . . . yet this horrible sin of sodomy is so far from being punished among them that it is part of their discourse to boast and brag of their detestable actions of that kind.[325]

When the French writer Flaubert visited Cairo in 1850, he discovered what he called "bardashes." Writing to a friend, he commented, "Here it is quite accepted. One admits one's sodomy, and it is spoken of at table in the hotel. . . . It's at the baths that such things take place."[326] A generation later, a German physician discovered male dancers dressed like dancing girls and sharing their "abandoned morals," performing at festivals in Upper Egypt.[327]

Sohar, a town of Oman, on the Gulf of Arabia, supports male transsexuals (sing. *xanith*) who engage in homosexual prostitution. They make up about 2 percent of the adult male population. The practice is not approved— parents firmly discourage their sons when they begin to cross-dress. But it is not illegal. Rather, these cross-dressing sons are tolerated, both because it is considered no one else's business and because they are thought to protect women by providing a sexual outlet for single men, of which there are many.[328] Patrons of the *xanith* are considered normal, and even the *xanith* can recover a respectable social status by consummating a heterosexual marriage.[329]

The situation has been little different in non-Arab Islam. Ever since the sixteenth century, Western visitors have commented on the pervasiveness of Turkish pederasty. Large numbers of boys were captured or purchased for personal use, placed in brothels, or resold; the demand for them struck all observers as remarkable.[330] A highly romanticized pederastic love was also deeply rooted in Albania under Ottoman rule, among Christians as well as Moslems.[331] The Mamlukes, a military aristocracy of freed slave-warriors, primarily of Turkish and Circassian extraction, were renowned

[325] Quoted in Freeth and Winstone (1978:48); see also Richard Burton (1886:225).

[326] Flaubert (1979:111). Flaubert's "bardashes" were not necessarily gender-crossers, as American Indian berdaches were. In this context, the term refers to males who engaged in receptive anal male homosexuality (Courouve, 1982; Dynes, 1985a:19–20).

[327] Klunzinger (1878:190–91); see also Lane (1963:388–89), Karlen (1971:235), Bullough (1976: 233–34). Bullough informs me that they were still present when he was in Egypt in the 1960s.

[328] Oman imports foreign laborers, who come without women.

[329] C. E. Russell (1935:342), Wikan (1977), Shepherd (1978).

[330] Näcke (1904, 1906), H. Ellis (1936:2.11), Drake (1966), Karlen (1971:228, 235), Blanch (1983:110), and chapter 10 below.

[331] Näcke (1908, 1966), H. Ellis (1936:2.10–11), Crompton (1985:105–57).

for pederasty with youths purchased from non-Moslem peoples of Central Asia.[332]

John Fryer, who traveled to Persia in the late seventeenth century, found that

> The Persians, when they let go their Modesty, put no bounds to their lascivious Desires, not being content with Natural Inclinations, outdo the Sensuality of the hottest Beasts, who never attempt on other than the Females of their own Species, but these, oh shame! covet Boys as much as Women.[333]

John Chardin, who visited Persia some decades earlier, found numerous houses of male prostitution, but none offering females. Some of the greatest Persian love poetry was written to boys;[334] and erotic art, though predominantly heterosexual, also represents pederastic relations.[335] Ibn Iskander, a fair-minded emir of the eleventh century, advised his son to divide his attentions equally between women and youths.[336] Pederasty was still very much in vogue in the late nineteenth century.[337]

Burton found the cities of Afghan to be "saturated with the Persian vice" at the end of the nineteenth century. Afghan merchants were invariably

> accompanied by a number of boys and lads almost in woman's attire with kohl'd eyes and rouged cheeks, long tresses and henna's fingers and toes, riding luxuriously in *Kajawas* or camel-panniers. They are called *Kuch-i safari,* or travelling wives, and the husbands trudge patiently by their sides.[338]

Male homosexuality remains common in Afghanistan, as does harem lesbianism.[339]

The Dutchman Johann Stavorinus found that among the Moghuls of Bengal,

> the sin of Sodom is not only in universal practice among them, but extends to a bestial communication with brutes, and in particular with sheep. Women even abandon themselves to the commission of unnatural crimes.[340]

[332] S. O. Murray (1987g).
[333] Fryer (1967:396).
[334] Moll (1891:42–43), M. Daniel (1979), Southgate (1984).
[335] Surieu (1967), Welch (1979).
[336] Surieu (1967:170), Bullough (1976:224).
[337] A. Wilson (1876:229), Richard Burton (1886:233–34), S. G. Wilson (1896:229).
[338] Richard Burton (1886:235–36).
[339] Dupree (1973:198), Coffin (1966:37).
[340] Stavorinus (1798:455–57).

The Moslem rulers of India often maintained youthful male lovers,[341] and male brothels flourished. Burton visited a number of them in 1845.[342]

At first glance, the early Mongols appear to have been an exception to the broad pattern. The *Great Yassa*, a law code issued by Ghenghiz Khan or at his death for the still-pagan Mongol tribes around A.D. 1219, to supplement Mongolian customary law, mandated the death penalty for both sodomites and adulterers.[343] This is not what one would expect in a tribe of nomadic pastoralists with a shamanistic religion.[344] It seems likely that this severe penalty reflects the influence of Christians, Jews, or Moslems, to whom Ghenghiz extended hospitality. Ghenghiz was himself illiterate, and might well have called on a literate foreigner to prepare a code of laws.[345] Soon thereafter, the Mongols converted to Islam. Despite their continuing attachment to the *Great Yassa*, as well as the negative view of homosexuality in Islamic law, "the descendents of those hordes who conquered central and northern Asia under Ghenghiz Khan and Timour, the Usbek Khans, had plunged so deep into it as to consider it a bad sign for one to keep himself free from this universal habit."[346] They did not repress it in China.[347] The Tatars, according to Samuel Purchase, "are addicted to Sodomy or Buggerie."[348]

As in many of the other early civilizations studied in this chapter, the gender and status associations of sexual roles in male homosexual relations made it possible to punish or humiliate someone by subjecting him to homosexual rape.[349] This was the practice in the Southern Sudan until the late nineteenth century.[350] According to Burton, men caught in Persian harems were turned over to slaves to be anally raped.[351] Just a few years ago, an Iranian student wearing Western-style clothes, who laughed during a demonstration, was raped by a group of teenage militia loyal to the Ayatollah Khomeini.[352]

[341] Babar (1926), Yasin (1958:107), Henriques (1961:174), Badayuni (1973:2.13–17), Saletore, 1974).

[342] Richard Burton (1886:205, 237), Dubois (1906:312), G. R. Scott (1954).

[343] Riasanovsky (1929:57), C. Dawson (1955:15, 17). Insofar as the only surviving fragments of the *Great Yassa* are in Moslem writings, the possibility of later interpellation should not be taken lightly.

[344] Krader (1968:69).

[345] Vernadsky (1938). Other, roughly contemporary travelers mention the Mongols' harsh punishment of adultery, but say nothing of homosexuality (Rockhill, 1900:79–80).

[346] Döllinger (1862:238).

[347] Homosexuality is not mentioned in the *Chih-yüan hsin-ko*, the law code of the Yüan (Mongol) dynasty, as far as it can be reconstructed (Ch'en, 1979).

[348] Richard Burton (1886).

[349] Dundes, Lead, and Özkök (1970), Vanggaard (1972:104–7).

[350] Budge (1973:27).

[351] Richard Burton (1886:235).

[352] Cowan (1985).

Where Islam has been forced to accommodate indigenous cultures, the gender implications of homosexuality may be weakened. The Swahili (mixed Arab-Africans) of Mombasa, Kenya, are a case in point. Though Islam endorses male supremacy, East African culture allows women a considerable degree of autonomy and independence. Though sex differences are important to the Swahili (who are Moslems), women are de facto less subordinate to men than in Arab Islam. Male youths who engage in sexual relations with older men are not analogized to women, though they are considered contemptible because of their poverty and subservience to older, wealthier clients in a culture that attaches great importance to wealth and status.[353]

Mombasa women may be unique in the Islamic world in having open social networks of lesbian couples modeled on the patron-client system of male homosexuality. These relations, involving older, wealthier women who are divorced or widowed and their younger, penurious lovers, are made possible by a property system that permits women to own and control wealth and to live independently of men. No gender connotations attach to these relationships either; the older woman may dominate her younger lover, but she is not considered masculine.

SUMMARY

That there should be some differences in the way homosexuality is organized and perceived in civilizations separated by long distances and great spans of time is hardly surprising. What is more striking in the comparisons made possible by the juxtapositions in this chapter are the similarities. For example, three of the four types of homosexual relations posited in the typology of chapters 2 and 3—the transgenderal, the transgenerational and the class-differentiated—were culturally recognized in the civilizations considered and helped to organize thinking about same-sex sexual relations.

With only a few exceptions, male homosexuality was not stigmatized or repressed so long as it conformed to norms regarding gender and the relative ages and statuses of the partners. In many of the early civilizations based on agriculture, male homosexual relations were invested with sacramental significance.

The major exceptions to this acceptance seem to have arisen in two circumstances. The first is when a nomadic people that lacked institutionalized cult homosexuality conquered another that had it. The conqueror may then have legislated against homosexuality for fear that cult leaders would provide a focus for resistance to the occupation. The second is when religion shifted from the veneration of deities who are immanent in the world,

---

[353]Shepherd (1987).

to the worship of transcendent gods. Immanent deities, imagined on human or animal models, are gendered and can be sexual; the latter are more abstract, and cannot express themselves sexually.[354] Though abstract deities are not intrinsically hostile to any particular form of sexuality, the social processes responsible for their rise often seem to lead to sexual repression.

Involvement in homosexuality was ordinarily considered to be nonexclusive. Exclusive object choices could also be recognized, but typically carried no broad implications for the life-chances as long as they did not entail unconventional gender identification or role adoption, or commercial motivation. Outside a cult context, adult male, effeminate homosexuality was generally scorned as incompatible with the comportment expected of male citizens, but was rarely subject to severe repression. It was, however, thought odd enough to call for an explanation, and in some of the early civilizations this explanation took a biological or physiological form. Some allowance was typically made for youth.

Sharp class inequalities could lead the middle and lower classes to deplore homosexuality as part of a dissipated life-style that threatened the vitality of the nation. The participation of boys and young men from the lower classes in homosexual relations across class lines, as prostitutes of dependents of rich men, may have added to class resentments and led to a general condemnation of homosexuality.

Far less can be said about lesbianism. In some cultures, women lacked sufficient independence to make lesbian relations possible very often. But extreme collective seclusion of women free from male supervision, as in Oriental harems, may facilitate lesbianism. In some civilizations men tended to be unhappy about it, seeing it as a threat to male domination of women. Where women have a public sphere of autonomy and independence, men may have been more willing to acknowledge and recognize lesbian relations. Sparta institutionalized them, Athens did not.

[354] R. J. Hoffman (1984).

5 Sexual Asceticism
in the Ancient World

The evidence considered in chapters 3 and 4 suggests that with the possible exception of pharaonic Egypt, male homosexuality was accepted in the context of a broader acceptance of human sexuality as a positive good. This acceptance came to an end in late antiquity with the spread of an asceticism that was hostile to all forms of sexual pleasure.

Sexual asceticism developed primarily within dualistic philosophies or religions that opposed good and evil, spirit and flesh, male and female. These oppositions were largely unknown to pagan polytheism, whose deities could be both benevolent and malevolent, or altogether amoral. Some shared the bodily characteristics of males and females.

The connection between sexual asceticism and dualism was not a logical one: asceticism does not follow inevitably from a dualistic world-view (though it may follow from particular dualistic world-views). Rather, both originated in the social processes that transformed the societies of the ancient Mediterranean. These processes differed in detail and timing in different parts of the world; however, much of the region shared in five developments of great significance.

First, as large cities grew and became important administrative and religious centers, the agricultural and fertility themes associated with the polytheistic religions lost much of their meaning. Peasants in the countryside may have been little affected by this development, but urban-dwellers were. Thus, when the pagan Roman emperor Julian, who ruled from A.D. 361 to 363, tried to revive the traditional temple sacrifices, he found little interest. It wasn't that everyone had converted to Christianity, only that they had become indifferent to the official state religion. The immediate consequences of this development were greatest in the Near East and in parts of North Africa, the regions in which male homosexual intercourse had religious significance.[1]

Second, the growth of long-distance trade and imperial expansion

---

[1] Transgenderal male cult prostitution is confirmed for the Carthaginians by Julius Firmicus Maternus (1970:ch. 4), a Latin writer of the early fourth century A.D. Saint Augustine, too, refers to the eunuch priests of the Mother Goddess in *City of God* 7, 26.

184

brought adherents of different religions into contact with one another. One consequence was the diffusion of religious practices involving homosexuality to regions where they were not indigenous, e.g., the introduction of the *galli* into Rome. However, the emergence of vast empires also helped prepare the way for syncretic transnational monotheistic religions.[2] This, too, tended to undermine the basis for cult practices involving homosexuality. It was not that polytheism is inherently more hospitable to homosexuality than monotheism,[3] but that sexual magic is more acceptable to the former.

Third, as the gap between a fabulously wealthy aristocratic class and the slaves, serfs, artisans, and small traders below them grew, the "have-nots" became increasingly critical of hedonistic pleasures only the rich could afford. Criticism of the gender-role violations implied when men devoted themselves to pleasure-seeking instead of hardening themselves in physical labor or combat figured in reactions to affluent life-styles. We have already seen in the Hellenistic context how criticism of male homosexuality was bound up with a critique of an entire way of life associated with great wealth.

Fourth, the larger scale of politics in the kingdoms and empires reduced popular participation in public affairs, giving rise to political estrangement from government, passivity, feelings of helplessness, and psychological withdrawal from the world. One consequence of this disengagement was a repudiation of bodily pleasures and desires.

Fifth, catastrophic wars and conquests shook the national existence of the various Mediterranean societies, shattering all sense of confidence and certainty in the world, and leading many to withdraw from mundane concerns into sexually abstinent lives of contemplation or spirituality.

The implications of these developments will be considered as we examine shifts in attitudes toward homosexuality in Iran, among the Hebrews, and in the Hellenistic world. This discussion will provide the background for understanding early Christian views of homosexuality.

IRAN

Iran—or as the Greeks called it, Persia—was settled by diverse Indo-European peoples who relinquished pastoral nomadism in favor of sedentary agriculture and animal husbandry. Culturally and linguistically they were close to the Aryans who conquered India; their deities were the same and they had the same tripartite social structure of priests, warriors, and peasants. It is altogether unlikely that these nomads worshiped a Mother

---

[2] Oost (1968:31), Teixidor (1977:13–17), Geffcken (1978:1–31), Freyne (1980:264–66). The argument is that the establishment of multinational empires ruled by a single figure provided the earthly example that made plausible the existence of a single god who ruled all the earth.

[3] This is suggested by R. Hoffman (1984).

Goddess or practiced cult prostitution,[4] though once settled in Iran some may have borrowed such practices from Assyria, which dominated the region for a considerable period.[5] Several scholars have concluded that the early Iranians had men's associations within which transgenerational homosexuality may have had a place as part of the transition to adulthood.[6] We have already seen evidence for the same custom in other Indo-European peoples.

Zoroastrianism, founded in Iran at an unknown date by the prophet Zoroaster (Zarathustra),[7] who reformed the old Aryan religion, took a far harsher view of homosexuality. The subject is not mentioned in the *Gathas* (the earliest Zoroastrian scriptures), which are attributed directly to Zoroaster. However, the later *Vendidad*, or *Code Against the Devas*, which contains much of the Zoroastrian moral teaching, places sodomites among the ranks of those who may be killed on the spot, along with brigands, burners of carrion in a fire, and criminals taken in the act.[8] Later texts, from the ninth century A.D., continue to regard homosexuality as heinous.[9]

Why this hostility? Insofar as we will be exploring the role of philosophical dualism in shaping sexual attitudes, it is worth noting that one of the most pronounced features of the Zoroastrian world-view is the dualistic opposition of good and evil. It has been argued that this opposition reflects the persistent raids on farming settlements by predatory nomad warriors faithful to the old Aryan religion. The enemies of social order—those who raided, robbed, and killed—could not be accommodated, only fought; and so they were identified with the principles of evil in the universe.[10]

This dualism did *not* extend to the opposition of sexes, or of mind to body. Zoroastrian scripture preached temperance and restraint, but never advocated celibacy or sexual abstinence. Marriage was expected. Male supremacy—a common feature of societies that practice animal husbandry[11]—was taken for granted, and there was some tendency to view women as temptresses, but this was a minor theme. For the most part, women do not figure in Zoroastrian mythical writings at all.[12] There is little here that would lead to the repression of homosexuality as part of a broader rejection of all kinds of sexuality.

[4] Zoroastrian religion has no goddesses.
[5] Huart (1972:xiii).
[6] Wikander (1938), Widengren (1969:52), Bleibtreu-Ehrenberg (1981:119).
[7] Zoroastrian sources place Zoroaster in the sixth or seventh century B.C., but some scholars have argued for substantially earlier dates (Zaehner, 1961:33; A.V.W. Jackson, 1965:17–18; Duchesne-Guillemin, 1969; Boyce, 1975:3, 190; Gnoli, 1980).
[8] *Vendidad* 8.73–74; Geiger (1882:341–42).
[9] Bullough (1976:69).
[10] Noss (1963), A. V. Jackson (1965:138).
[11] Sanday (1981:170–72).
[12] Zaehner (1961:232–35).

The early history of Zoroastrianism suggests other possibilities. It has been argued that Zoroaster's abandonment of the old Aryan cult associated with a nomadic way of life was a response to its unsuitability under conditions of permanent settlement. Sacrifices of oxen must have been onerous to farmers; and the drunken, orgiastic rites involving the drinking of *haoma* (the Hindu *soma*) in connection with the worship of a dying vegetation god would have been inconsistent with the sobriety and self-control demanded of peasants in a harsh mountainous environment.[13] Class antagonism may have been at work as well. Early Indo-Aryan society was ruled by a military aristocracy that supported priests and heavy sacrifices. Poor peasants like Zoroaster would have found the sacrifices burdensome; hence his opposition to ritual and sacrifice.[14]

Cyrus the Great united the Medes and Persians and established an empire under the rulership of the Achaemenid dynasty in the middle of the sixth century B.C. Faced with the practical task of ruling an empire composed of religiously diverse peoples, the kings promoted tolerance and even sponsored and subsidized non-Zoroastrian cults. Contact with Elamite and Mesopotamian civilization quickly led to religious syncretism. Artaxerxes II, who ruled from 404 to 359 B.C., set up the worship of the goddess Anahita in towns throughout the Empire. She was a Mother Goddess, and as elsewhere, her worship involved sacred prostitution.[15] Magis (priests of the old Aryan religion) in mountainous regions away from the court would have been less touched by Semitic influences, and less susceptible to royal pressure. They could have reacted against the importation of alien religions and their associated sexual rites. Wikander observes:

> the polemic directed against the whore in various passages of the Avesta, particularly in the yašt, to Anahita, was in fact directed against certain forms of her cult admitting this usage.[16]

It is quite plausible that the repression called for against male homosexuality had the same origin. The Zoroastrian prohibition against intercourse with courtesans points to a broader opposition to the milieu of the court.

That these repressive attitudes were not shared in ruling circles is suggested by Herodotus's observation that male homosexuality was quite the thing.[17] Palace eunuchism was established early in the Achaemenid dynasty and may have involved homosexual relations. The Latin writer Quin-

---

[13] Zaehner (1961:81), Noss (1962:464, 467).

[14] Gnoli (1980:186).

[15] Strabo xi, 532; xii, 559; xv, 733 (Rogers, 1929:237), Gnoli (1980:216), Duchesne-Guillemin (1983).

[16] Wikander (1946:89), quoted in Duchesne-Guillemin (1983).

[17] Herodotus 1.135 claims that the Persians had learned pederasty from the Greeks. As Plutarch points out in *De Heroditi milignitate* 13, this is not very likely.

tus Curtius Rufus mentions the large number of effeminate men who attended Darius III.[18] The emperor Artaxerxes was intimate with a lovely rouged youth.[19]

Early in the Achaemenid dynasty, Zoroastrianism probably had few adherents. Zoroaster's religious reforms won converts in the court of Vishtaspa, a chief or king in Eastern Iran, but encountered stiff opposition elsewhere. Zaehner concludes that "the bulk of the people of Western Iran at the time of Herodotus would not seem to have been greatly influenced by any recognizable form of Zoroastrianism."[20] Neither Herodotus nor Xenophon mentions Zoroaster's name, suggesting that neither he nor his religion was widely known.

The early rulers of the dynasty were almost surely not full-fledged Zoroastrians,[21] but they did worship Ahura Mazda, Zoroaster's god. To win the loyalty of subject peoples, they respected the religions of the lands they conquered. So did the later rulers—Artaxerxes I, II, and III, and Darius Codomannus—who can be identified more definitely as Zoroastrian.[22] Cult prostitution seems to have continued without governmental interference in the conquered territories, and perhaps in Iran itself.

The Persian defeat at the hands of Alexander the Great in 330 B.C. ended the brief state sponsorship of Zoroastrianism. The Parthian Arsacids, who ruled Iran from 250 B.C. to A.D. 226, seem to have had little interest in it. The royal court in this period was heavily Hellenized, with Greek sports being introduced into some cities. The cults of Anahita and Mithra also flourished.[23] None of these developments would have hindered homosexual expression. That they did not is confirmed by the remark of Sextus Empiricus, a Greek physician and philosopher writing around A.D. 200, that among the Persians "it is the habit to indulge in intercourse with males."[24]

The *Vendidad* was a product of the Parthian period,[25] the work of magis who synthesized the Zoroastrian cult with the older Aryan fire worship. Their hatred of Hellenistic culture[26] may have added to an earlier opposi-

[18] *History of Alexander the Great* 3.3, 14, and 21 (Cook, 1983:137).

[19] Fürstauer (1965:256). Unfortunately, Fürstauer fails to indicate which Artaxerxes this was, or to cite a source.

[20] Zaehner (1961:167).

[21] Though they considered Ahura Mazda the greatest god, the early Achaemenid rulers explicitly invoked other gods and sometimes claimed their support. Not only did they not mention the name of Zoroaster, but theophoric Zoroastrian names never appear in the tablets of the royal library at Persepolis (Gray and Cary, 1926; A. V. Jackson, 1965:154–56; Cook, 1983).

[22] Zaehner (1961:73–75; A. V. Jackson (1965:167–68).

[23] Rogers (1929:237), Huart (1972:111), Gnoli (1980:220).

[24] *Pyrrhoniae Hypotyposes* 1.152.

[25] Herzfeld (1947:738, 779), Boyce (1975:295).

[26] Herzfeld (1047:745).

tion to cult prostitution, producing an especially extreme hostility to homosexuality. The legalistic obsession with bodily purity and pollution, so pronounced in the *Vendidad*, may also have been a response to foreign conquest and domination.

How widely the views of the priests were shared is difficult to say. Zaehner suggests that the *Vendidad* had little practical significance, noting that it lists "impossible punishments for ludicrous crimes. . . . If it had ever been put into practice, [it] would have tired the patience of even the most credulous."[27] But that may be overly optimistic. In a spirit of nationalism, the Sassanian dynasty (A.D. 226–652), which succeeded the Parthians, revived Zoroastrianism, making it a state religion, in part as a counterfoil to Christianity. Though "the majority of the cultivators were not Mazdaeans [worshipers of Ahura Mazda] but clung to their natural cults and customs,"[28] the centralizing state made magis judges and teachers, giving them power and influence. Intermittently, they instigated persecutions of other religions and introduced cruel punishments for law violators.[29] That they may have introduced a major crackdown on homosexuality in line with their holy scriptures is suggested by some remarks of Ammianus Marcellinus, a Roman historian born in Antioch of Greek parents. Writing in the latter part of the fourth century, when Iran had been under Sassanian rule for some 150 years, he observed that though "most" Persians

> are extravagantly given to venery, and are hardly contented with a multitude of concubines; they are free from immoral relations with boys.[30]

The Arab invasion in the middle of the seventh century brought Zoroastrian influence to an end. Since that time, the dominant religion of Iran has been Islam, and despite official Islamic opposition to homosexuality, it has been widely practiced and accepted.[31] The current imposition of the death penalty in the Islamic Republic is a historical aberration. In the meantime, the Zoroastrians, a minority population in Persia and India, where they are known as Parsis, continue to hold homosexuality in abhorrence. The Parsi *Rivayat* attributes passive sodomy to Ahriman, the Zoroastrian devil, and regards it as a source of putrefaction and corruption.[32]

[27] Zaehner (1965:27, 171).

[28] Trimingham (1979:127).

[29] Huart (1972:122–58), Trimingham (1979:160).

[30] Ammianus Marcellinus (1937:392–93), *Rerum gestarum libri qui supersunt* 23.6, 76.

[31] Westermarck (1917:462–67), H. Ellis (1936:13–14), Karlen (1971:234–35); also see chapter 4 of this book.

[32] Dumézil (1974).

THE HEBREWS

Chapter 4 traced the biblical prohibition of male cult prostitution in Deuteronomy to the war waged by Yahweh worshipers against Canaanite-Pales-
tinian fertility cults during periods of nationalistic fervor. This prohibition
did not extend to homosexuality in other contexts. However, two passages
in Leviticus seem to prohibit *male* homosexuality more generally:

> Thou shalt not lie with mankind as with womankind; it is
> abomination.[33]

> And if a man lie with mankind, as with womankind, both of
> them have committed an abomination: they shall surely be put
> to death; their blood shall be upon them.[34]

Lesbianism is not mentioned.[35]

Boswell has suggested that these prohibitions could have been issued
with cult prostitution in mind.[36] At first glance this seems unlikely, for most
of the other sexual prohibitions of these chapters do not involve religious
rituals; they prohibit incest, adultery, and intercourse with menstruating
women—prohibitions that apply at all times, not just during rituals. However, Leviticus 18:21, "And you shall not give any of thy seed to set them
apart to Molech," does deal with a religious practice; consequently Boswell
cannot be ruled out of court. Nonetheless, I will proceed on the supposition that the prohibitions of Leviticus were intended to be general. That is
how they were understood in later generations.[37]

Insofar as the Zoroastrians prohibited male homosexuality, and the Egyptians may have done so, one might wonder whether they could have influenced Hebrew views. Egyptian influence on biblical Hebrew culture and

[33]*Lev.* 18:22. The translation given here is the conventional one, but in the Babylonian Talmud, *Seder Nezikin, Tractate Sanhedrin* 54a–b, Rabbi Akiva (c. A.D. 50–132), the greatest sage of
his generation, maintains that the passage should be read "thou shalt not be lain with by mankind as with womankind" (Epstein, 1935). The basis for this alternative reading is the absence
of vowels in the Hebrew text. This absence makes it possible to read the verb as *tishkhav* (lie
with) or *tishakhev* (be lain with). Since other early civilizations stigmatized only the receptive
role, Rabbi Akiva's suggestion is quite attractive; however, it is not consistent with Lev. 20:13,
which calls for the punishment of both parties, or with later understanding of the passage.

[34]Lev. 20:13.

[35]This may mean that lesbianism was not considered wrong, but more likely it meant that it
was handled by fathers and husbands, rather than by public authorities. In talmudic times,
rabbinic authorities considered lesbian sex obscene and debated whether it implied loss of
virginity, but did not regard it as a very serious matter. See *Tractate Shabbath* 65a–b and *Tractate
Yebamoth* 76a (I. Epstein, 1936a:512–13, 1938a:311; Scanzoni and Mollenkott, 1978:61).

[36]Boswell (1980:101 n. 34).

[37]Scroggs (1983:76).

law can be demonstrated,[38] but there is no clear evidence for it here. There is little reason to think that the Egyptians considered homosexuality to be a particularly serious matter, and none that they transmitted their views of it to the Hebrews. The warning of Leviticus 8:13, "After the doings of the land of Egypt wherein ye dwelt, shall ye not do," weighs against an Egyptian origin for the prohibition, even though the attribution to Egypt of the various practices prohibited in Leviticus must be treated with caution.

The plausibility of Zoroastrian influence hinges largely on uncertainties of chronology. Iranian influence on the Hebrews could hardly have been great before the Persian victory over Babylonia brought an end to the Babylonian exile. Textual considerations, however, make clear that Leviticus was not put into final form until after the exile. The work is not concerned with the monarchy, which had been crushed by the Babylonians, or indeed, with any type of civil authority. Chapter 26, which describes the horrors of defeat and exile in the prospective language of prophesy,[39] was clearly written after the event. On the other hand, authorship later than the generation of Ezra, c. 400 B.C., or possibly somewhat earlier, when the Samaritans were excluded from the newly reconstituted Jewish community, is excluded by the Samaritan acceptance of the entire Pentateuch, including Leviticus. Thus the final redaction of the work can be dated to the sixth or fifth century B.C.[40]

Even if the final editing of Leviticus was late, some of its material is probably much older. Incest prohibitions, for example, surely antedate the exile, though they may not have been written down until then.[41] Chapters 18 and 20, which both forbid homosexuality, appear to be parts of two distinct, earlier collections of prohibitions, but some of the individual commandments may have been inserted at the time of the final recension.[42]

[38] Parallels have been noted between Proverbs in the Bible and the Egyptian test, "The Instruction of Amen-em-Opet" (J. A. Wilson, 1958). Hebrew circumcision could have derived from the Egyptian practice, and the Egyptians may have prohibited the eating of meat and dairy products together (personal communications, Ogden Goelet, Jr.). When the Egyptians conquered the Delta, they introduced a prohibition against the consumption of swine, which had previously been sacrificed and eaten in religious ceremonies (Kees, 1961:91–92); this could have been the source of the Hebrew prohibition against eating pork products.

[39] "And you will I scatter among the nations" (Lev. 26:33).

[40] Eissfeldt (1965:207–8), Noth (1965:15), Ackroyd (1968:84–87), Phillips (1970:185–86), Talmon (1970), J. R. Porter (1976:1, 5, 136), Widengren (1977). Porter (1976:5) concludes that Leviticus seems "to presuppose ritual practices which only became normative with the building of the second temple," which was completed in 517 B.C. This reasoning leads to a date no earlier than the middle or late sixth century B.C. But see note 45 below.

[41] Lev. 18:6–17 and 20:11–21.

[42] Noth (1965:136) notes, for example, that the verses of Lev. 18:19–23, which involve human sacrifice, intercourse with a menstruating woman, male homosexuality, and bestiality, are not very unified and may have been added to the original set of incest prohibitions.

This chronology at least permits Persian influence, and indeed Vinck argues that Leviticus was compiled under Persian auspices.[43] To promote cultural and political unity within the area, he suggests, the Persians favored ecumenicism; and the editors of Leviticus responded by incorporating the religious teachings of Diaspora Jews, the Samaritan upper classes, and Persian authorities. However, as we have already seen, there is no evidence that the Achaemenid rulers of Iran were hostile to homosexuality.

Nevertheless, points of similarity between Zoroastrian purity doctrines and those in Leviticus do suggest Iranian influence. For example, both view corpses as ritually defiling. The period of ritual impurity after childbirth is exactly the same in both.[44] This could hardly be a coincidence. Since Hebrew influence on Iranian religion is unlikely to have been great, the parallels are best explained in terms of Iranian influence on Hebrew scripture—not necessarily with royal sponsorship. Thus the homosexuality prohibitions of Leviticus could have had a Zoroastrian source. But since we do not know for sure when the Zoroastrians became hostile to homosexuality, we cannot be certain of this. It is a possibility, but no more than that.[45]

Even though the Persians may have sponsored the compilation of Leviticus or influenced its contents, its concerns are Hebrew, not Iranian. It is especially important to understand these concerns because borrowings from Persia were quite selective. For example, the Persians favored consanguinous marriages, while Leviticus rejects them as incestuous. Presum-

---

Eichrodt (1961:1, 82) thinks Lev. 18:19–23 is transposed from an earlier location just after Exod. 22:17.

[43]Vink (1969).

[44]Neusner (1977:13).

[45]Neusner (1966:15, 1976:139–49) argues against extensive Persian influence by pointing out that talmudic writings from the Sassanid period, when Babylonian Jews had greater exposure to Persian culture, show little knowledge of Persian religion or evidence of direct influence. Most of the Jewish population lived in villages and small towns, and thus had little contact with the urban priesthood. Yet in earlier centuries, Persian policies of religious toleration left a very favorable impression on the Jews; some considered Cyrus to be the Messiah. As a cupbearer at the Persian court (and probably a palace eunuch), Nehemiah would have been well acquainted with Persian religious beliefs, and this is likely to have been true of many of the exiled aristocrats. Moreover, there are Persian loan-words in some of the Jewish apocalyptic literature (B. A. Pearson, 1975:1–19, 85–129). Scattered throughout the whole kingdom, as the Book of Esther 3:8 says they were, the Jews would have become familiar with the religion of the magis, who were not restricted to the larger cities. The rural priesthood, we have already suggested, may have been more extreme in its doctrines than the magis associated with the court. Some scholarship places the decisive rift between Samaritans and Judaea not in the generation of Ezra, but considerably later, just before the Macedonian Conquest in 333 B.C., or in Hasmonean times (Cross, 1966; Freyne, 1980:23–24, 274). On this view, Persian influence on Leviticus could have occurred during two centuries of Persian rule over Palestine and need not have occurred during the Exile.

ably, Iranian beliefs would have been most influential when they had some particular relevance to the situation of the Jews. It is this situation we must now examine. At the time of the Babylonian exile (586 B.C.), war had left Judaea devastated. Its cities were in ruins, and a large part of the upper classes had been deported. Those who remained were impoverished and demoralized. Some concluded that Yahweh had abandoned the land,[46] or that the disaster had been precipitated by the abandonment of sacrifices to other gods in the aftermath of Josiah's religious reforms.[47]

In the absence of the king and his officials, who had been taken to Babylonia, the priests were attempting to give leadership to what was left of the population. Leviticus, especially its Holiness Code (chapters 17–26), was an attempt to provide a basis for continuing priestly authority. It argued that the catastrophe did not mean Yahweh had been defeated by the Babylonian gods; the fault lay rather with the population itself, which had only to obey the priests to bring the nightmare to an end. Since Leviticus seems to incorporate traditions of the Jerusalem priesthood as well as other Hebrew cultic traditions, Porter suggests that the Holiness Code may have been the product of a collaboration between Jerusalem priests returning from exile and priests from other parts of Judaea, who had taken refuge in Jerusalem.[48]

The Holiness Code is concerned—to a point that strikes the modern reader as obsessive—with sacrifices, purity, and pollution. To avoid further catastrophe, Yahweh's wrath had to be placated. Even earlier, Hebrew religion had had some notions of sin, guilt, and expiation. In the aftermath of unprecedented calamity, the sense of threat and insecurity grew, and rules to stave off further disaster were multiplied.[49] Many concern sexuality; others, with differentiating the Hebrews from surrounding peoples.[50] The Jews were called upon to be holy as their god was holy. With the Jeru-

---

[46] Ezek. 8:12.
[47] Jer. 44:15–19.
[48] J. R. Porter (1976:5, 136).
[49] Eakin (1971:155).
[50] Davies (1982) has suggested that Hebrew sexual prohibitions were part of a strategy for maintaining exclusiveness. He argues that, if you want to stop a people from interacting with others and thereby assimilating, a sensible strategy is to forbid them from having sexual relations. Thus the prohibition of homosexuality could have been a way of discouraging assimilation. The argument is unpersuasive, though, for to prevent assimilation one need only forbid sexual relations with outsiders. When Ezra returned from Babylonia, he sent away all the foreign wives, but did not prohibit marriage. Hebrew law, however, forbids all homosexual relations, including those where both partners are Jews. Moreover, Davies does not explain why the Jews, and the Zoroastrians, whose prohibition of homosexuality he explains in similar terms, should have been more concerned than other peoples with preventing assimilation. Nor does he explain why fornication with foreigners was not prohibited.

salem Temple in ruins (before the Second Temple was completed), holiness was being extended from the priesthood and the Temple to the people of Israel and their land, from the world of ritual to the world of everyday life. Or rather, the world of ritual was being extended *into* the world of everyday life, so that the boundary between the two was being dissolved. Holiness itself consisted of abiding by rules attributed to Yahweh.

The logic of this new religious system bears more than a passing resemblance to that of the young boy who, in Freudian theory, resolves an oedipal complex. To stave off the jealous father's castration threat, the boy gives up his incestuous desire for his mother and internalizes the father's rules. By making them a part of his superego, he becomes like his father, behaves as expected, and avoids punishment. In Leviticus the priests call on the Hebrews to placate their jealous father-god by giving up the obnoxious practices of other nations (including worship of the Mother Goddess), and becoming holy like him.

The parallel can be extended to the outcome of internalization. The more effectively the standards of the father or the god are internalized, the more violations—or even thoughts about violations—will evoke feelings of blameworthiness. The feelings of guilt evident in Leviticus[51] suggest that, for its priestly authors, this process had already begun by the time of the exile. The catastrophe was taken as a sign of collective guilt and a demonstration that more rigorous repression was needed. The political and psychological needs of the priesthood coincided.[52]

It remains to be explained why conquest and devastation, events having no direct relationship to sex, should have led to such strong priestly preoccupation with it. Priests were not celibate, so there is no reason they should have been especially frustrated. One possibility is suggested by Freud: the sexual impulses we learn to repress do not disappear. The struggle between these impulses and the superego—often waged unconsciously—thus becomes a persistent source of anxiety and guilt. However, sexual socialization is typically not very precise, so that children, and often adults, are often uncertain about just what is and is not forbidden. Then, when a disaster strikes, someone who has residual feelings of guilt related to sexual conflicts may conclude that the disaster was occasioned by a sexual dereliction: "If I'm being punished I must be guilty of something, and it must have something to do with sex." A process of this sort could have produced demands for sexual renunciation, including the renunciation of homosexuality.[53] The reasoning is predicated on the assumption that gods harm

---

[51] It is in Lev. 16:29–34 and 23:27 that a Day of Atonement is mandated.

[52] The Jewish response to later crises displays the same pattern. 2 Macc. 5:18 attributes the religious persecution of Antiochus IV to the "many sinful acts" the Jews had committed. Other similar responses to disasters will be cited later in this chapter.

[53] Gilbert and Barkun (1981) suggest that in Western history, disasters have often been fol-

people only when they deserve it; in other words, that they are not capricious, and they do not destroy lives and kingdoms for mere sport. This is a notion that could probably not have developed until monarchs effectively pacified their territories, and established predictable, law-bound procedures for administering justice.

The treatment of sexual offenses in Leviticus suggests that the level of anxiety associated with sex was quite high. The offenses of the Holiness Code are an "abomination" to the Lord. Violators are to be "cut off from their people"[54] or put to death, lest the land "vomit out" those who defile it. With the collective existence of the people at stake, the harsh penalty becomes understandable.[55]

Boswell's Interpretation of the Abominations of Leviticus

John Boswell's interpretation of the homosexuality prohibitions of Leviticus differs radically from the one presented here. He argues that the Hebrew word *toevah* (abomination), applied to the offenses listed in the Holiness Code, does not designate acts that are "intrinsically evil, like rape or theft," but rather those that are "ritually unclean."[56] This is terribly misleading. Leviticus does recognize forms of ritual uncleanness that are not morally condemned, e.g., childbirth, seminal emission, heterosexual intercourse, and menstruation.[57] Purification from these pollutions is accomplished quite simply through bathing and sacrifice. The word *toevah* is not used to refer to these conditions, nor are they punished.

When the word *toevah* does appear in the Hebrew Bible, it is sometimes applied to idolatry, cult prostitution, magic, or divination, and is sometimes used more generally.[58] It always conveys great repugnance. Idolatry was not simply unclean; it was a grave offense. Boswell's distinction be-

---

lowed by episodes of repression against homosexuality. The argument developed here explains why this should be so. Unfortunately, Gilbert and Barkun neither explain their observation nor provide the historical examples that would make the claim plausible. The many historical disasters not followed by repression of homosexuality warn us against positing a universal law.

[54] Lev. 18:21, 20:13. There is some uncertainty about what the phrase "cut off from their people" means. Phillips (1970:28, 95) takes it to mean excommunication, but others have concluded that the death penalty is implied.

[55] It bears keeping in mind that sex was by no means the only aspect of life subjected to rules and restrictions in Leviticus. Criteria of cleanliness were also laid down with respect to food. Shortages following the devastation of war may well have resulted in anxiety about food. Another possible explanation for the twin emphases on sex and food, suggested by anthropologist Mary Douglas, will be considered later in this chapter.

[56] Boswell (1980:100–101).

[57] Lev. 12:2–5, 15:16, 15:18, 15:19–28.

[58] Gen. 46:34, Exod. 8:22, Deut. 7:25–26, 22:5, 23:18, 24:4, 25:16, 32:16, 2 Kings 23:13, Isa. 1:13, Jer. 7:10, Prov. 12:22, 15:8, 15:26, 16:5, 17:15, as well as the passages in Leviticus already cited.

tween acts that are truly evil and those that are mere ritual violations is completely extraneous to the authors of Leviticus, for whom everything prohibited by Yahweh is totally wrong. That intercourse with a menstruating woman is also classified as an abomination along with homosexuality is an indication not, as Boswell suggests, that the latter offense was considered trivial, but rather that the former was considered extremely grave. However silly they may seem to contemporary rationalists, menstrual taboos are taken very seriously in many primitive societies. Late biblical Palestine was one of them.[59]

Boswell goes on to suggest that the gravity of the offenses of Leviticus 18 and 20 cannot be inferred from the invocation of the death penalty, but proposes no alternative explanation for such a punishment. Trivial violations do not usually call for execution. The threat that the entire people of Israel could be vomited out of the land in retribution for the prohibited acts suggests that the offenses were considered serious indeed.

Boswell concludes with the observation that neither the Talmud nor Maimonides treated homosexuality as "uniquely reprehensible." His use of the Talmud, compiled in the postbiblical era, and of Maimonides, who lived in the twelfth century, to draw conclusions about biblical times is historically unsound. However, both sources treat homosexuality as Hebrew scripture does—as one of a number of offenses that merit a very severe penalty. Not uniquely severe (something no one has claimed), but quite severe. Neither source dissents from the appropriateness of the death penalty or moderates it, except to exempt minors below the age of thirteen (as in every other criminal case), and molesters of small children.[60] *Sanhedrin* 54a-b insists that even those who commit only the "first stage" are to be executed.[61]

Postbiblical Judaism

The centuries following the return from exile in Babylonia included long periods of peace and prosperity, economic growth and urbanization, religious and cultural autonomy under the Persians and Syrian (Seleucid) rulers; and under the Hasmoneans, the restoration of national sovereignty, and national expansion. These periods were punctuated by conquests, religious persecutions, revolts, civil wars, assassinations, massacres, deportations, desecrations of the Temple, and in A.D. 70, its destruction at the hands of the Romans, along with the razing of Jerusalem.

These mixed experiences evoked a wide range of responses; among them, asceticism—abstinence from sensual pleasure and withdrawal from

---

[59] See Ezek. 18:5–9. Christians of the Middle Ages also took menstrual taboos very seriously (C. Erickson, 1976:195).

[60] Moses ben Maimon (1965:13).

[61] I. Epstein (1935:367–72).

engagement with the world. Following the Macedonian victory in 333 B.C., groups of especially pious Hasidim began to take extreme precautions to avoid defilement, interpreting Jewish law with great rigor. To avoid desecrating the Sabbath through childbirth, they permitted sexual intercourse only on Wednesdays. Despite their scrupulous observance of the Law, they insisted on making sin-offerings to atone for sins they might have committed unknowingly.[62]

Much of the ascetic literature pinpointed sex as a particularly perilous enticement. The apocryphal *Jubilees*, written in the late second century B.C., calls for sexual abstinence on the Sabbath, insists on bodily modesty, and demands that women who fornicate be burned.[63] Numerous passages in the *Testament of the Twelve Patriarchs* name fornication as one of the worst sins, the source of evil, and blame women for getting men into trouble.[64] The *Testament of Judah* warns that immoderate consumption of wine leads to fornication, one of the worst possible evils.[65] The *Psalm of Solomon* and the *Wisdom of Jesus the Son of Sirach*[66] strike similar themes.

Some of the Essene groups of the time practiced celibacy; and the recently published text of the Temple Scroll of the Qumran community, probably composed in the second century B.C., calls for a reconstituted Jerusalem in which all residents were to remain sexually continent.[67] The destruction of the Second Temple reinforced these ascetic tendencies, and the defeat of Bar Kochba's revolt in A.D. 135 strengthened them further.[68]

Still, this was only one response; many others avoided extremes of asceticism. The *Testament of Naphtali* cautions, "there is a season for a man to embrace his wife, and a season to abstain therefrom for his prayer."[69] *Tractate Yebamoth* of the Babylonian Talmud condemns the celibate: "He who does not engage in propagation of the race is as though he had shed blood."[70] The Jerusalem Talmud compares the man who takes a vow of sexual abstinence to "a man who takes a sword and plunges it into his heart,"[71] and warns against adding additional restrictions to those required by the

---

[62] Bronner (1967:41–55).

[63] *Jubilees* 3.31, 20.4, 50.8. By contrast, mishnaic authorities held that the Sabbath was an especially appropriate time for sex, e.g., in *Nedar* 3.10, 8.6, and *Baba Kamma* 82a (Charles, 1913:2.81–82; Charlesworth, 1985:2.60, 93, 142).

[64] *Testament of Reuben* 2:8, 4:6, 5:1, *Testament of Simeon* 5:3, *Testament of Levi* 9:9, 14:6, *Testament of Benjamin* 9:1 (Charles, 1914:2.297–99, 302, 310, 358; Charlesworth, 1985:1.782–84, 786, 791, 827).

[65] Charles (1913:2.315–25), Charlesworth (1985:1.798–99).

[66] *Psalm of Solomon* 2:13–15, 8:10–13, 16:7–8, 13:4; *Wisdom of Jesus the Son of Sirach* (Charles, 1913:1.345–46).

[67] Milgrom (1978).

[68] *Jewish Encyclopedia* (1902:2.167–68), Bronner (1967:151–53), Oppenheimer (1977:145).

[69] *Testament of Naphtali* 8:8 (Charles, 1914:2.339).

[70] 63b (I. Epstein, 1936a:427).

[71] 9.1.

Torah.[72] The involvement with the world implied by party politics (Pharisees and Sadducees) and revolutionary militancy (Maccabees, Zealots) shows that extremes of withdrawal from the world remained limited to discrete segments of the population—though the emphasis given to warnings against asceticism shows that it must have had a substantial appeal.

Hellenistic culture made substantial inroads during the period of Syrian domination, and continued to do so under the Hasmoneans. In 174 B.C., Jason, the high priest, sponsored the construction of a Greek gymnasium adjacent to the Temple, where young men, including priests, exercised in the nude;[73] in the following century, gladiator contests were held in Jerusalem in a Roman-style circus.[74] These were hardly otherworldly or ascetic developments.

Hellenism had its greatest appeal for the aristocracy of large landowners who resided in Jerusalem and for priests who had become wealthy and powerful through their control of the Temple treasury.[75] To them, Hebrew law and culture were barriers to full participation in world commerce and world culture.[76]

The peasants and urban artisans, craftsmen, and merchants found Hellenism less appealing. True, many learned Greek in the course of business dealings with non-Jews. About a third of the inscriptions from Palestine in the first century B.C. are in Greek. Many Jews read the Bible in Greek and prayed in that language. Some scribes may even have studied Greek logic and styles of textual exegesis.[77] But only the wealthy could afford a Greek education, and the political reforms that accompanied the introduction of a gymnasium education—in essence, an attempt to turn Jerusalem into a Greek polis—excluded the poor from citizenship.[78] The extravagances of the rich and the military adventures of an expansionist government meant higher taxes. The masses, therefore, tended to support the Pharisaic opposition to Hellenization and its aristocratic sponsors.

Although the Pharisees favored the relaxation of some biblical laws, especially those that peasants could not easily observe, they also favored the

[72] Bronner (1967:153); see also *Encyclopedia Judaica* (1971:xii.906–7).
[73] Tcherikover (1959:159–64), Reicke (1964:52–53), McCullough (1975:113–14).
[74] Smallwood (1976:84).
[75] Tcherikover (1959:120, 142, 252), Hengel (1980:66, 75). In Maccabean times the Temple served as a deposit bank as well as a place of worship and sacrifice; as a result it held enormous assets (Tcherikover, 1959:120).
[76] For example, Antiochus III (242–187 B.C.) had ruled, presumably under orthodox pressure, that only sacrificial animals could be kept in Jerusalem. This restriction severely limited the role that Jerusalem could play in trade. Ritual prohibitions restricting economic dealings with the Gentile world remained in effect until the siege of Jerusalem in A.D. 66–70 (Hengel, 1980:43).
[77] Morton Smith (1956), Lieberman (1963), Rivkin (1966), Freyne (1980:138–45).
[78] Tcherikover (1959:162–64).

elaboration of purity laws and their extension to the population at large. These laws restricted contact not only with non-Jews, but also with Jews whose observance was less strict.[79] Directly and indirectly, they served to make those aspects of upper-class life-style that were for all practical purposes unreachable also seem undesirable. The laws—or at least their acceptance—can thus be seen as an adaptation to material deprivation.

With the sharpening of class antagonism, the preoccupation of the Pharisees with purity provided grounds for condemning the rich, who disregarded the restrictions[80]—an important source of emotional gratification for the lower classes. The Pharisaic doctrine of the immortality of the soul supplied an added dimension to this gratification. Unlike their rivals, the Sadduccees, the Pharisees believed that the soul survived the body, to be judged by God. If the wicked prospered in this world, they would nevertheless be punished in the next. The observant Pharisees, on the other hand, could look forward to rewards in the afterlife to compensate for their present deprivation.[81]

None of these developments favored a relaxation of the biblical prohibition against male homosexuality. In fact, all known references to it in Jewish literature from the Hellenistic era are negative. The *Sibylline Oracles* states that the righteous have neither "disgraceful desire for another's spouse or for hateful and repulsive abuse of a male" and admonishes those to desist who in the past "impiously catered for pederasty and set up in houses prostitutes who were pure before. . . . In you also kings defiled their ill-fated mouths."[82] The coming of the Messiah, the author prophesies, will bring an end to war, murder, adultery, and the "illicit love of boys." The *Testament of Jacob*, from the second or third century B.C., lists among those who will not inherit the Kingdom of God, those who "have sexual intercourse with males."[83] Pseudo-Phocylides, a Jew who wrote in Greek some time between the first century B.C. and the first century A.D., rewrote the Ten Commandments to prohibit homosexual arousal—as well as improper forms of intercourse with one's wife.[84] II Enoch, a work of the late first century A.D., foresees a time when people will repudiate God, embrace iniquity, and engage in wrongful forms of intercourse, "that is, friend with friend in the anus, and every other kind of wicked uncleanness which it is digusting to report."[85] The Mishnah bars the sale of sheep or slaves to

[79]Rivkin (1966), Oppenheimer (1977:17), Freyne (1980:306–7).
[80]Tcherikover (1959:258).
[81]S. Zeitlin (1962:175–87).
[82]4.34–35, 5.386–93.
[83]7.19, 20 (Charlesworth, 1985:1.917).
[84]Horst (1978:110), Charlesworth, 1985.2.574).
[85]34. Charlesworth (1985:1.158).

non-Jews, to protect them from bestiality and homosexuality.[86] *Tractate Shabbath* 149b of the Babylonian Talmud echoes the traditional Near Eastern view that it is degrading to be forcibly sodomized, but departs from that view in seeing the sodomizer as also degraded. Nebuchadnezzer, who, according to legend buggered the kings he conquered, was in turn humiliated in like fashion.[87]

Even if Leviticus had never been written, the ascetic temperament would have found homosexuality objectionable, just as it did heterosexuality, which the Bible did not prohibit. Popular hostility to Hellenistic culture and the gymnasium education of the upper classes easily extended to pederasty, with which it was closely associated in the popular mind.[88] Probably more important in the long run, the Pharisees' emphasis on strict obedience to the Law prevented a relaxation or abandonment of the Leviticus prohibition not only in the Hellenistic era, but in rabbinical Judaism in subsequent centuries down to the present.

Despite their repugnance, Jewish references to homosexuality from the Hellenistic period lack the hysterical tone of Leviticus. For example, R. Judah held that as a precaution against pederasty, a bachelor should not teach elementary school, and two men should not sleep under the same blanket. But other authorities ruled that this was an unnecessary precaution because Jews do not engage in the forbidden activities.[89] *Sukkah* 29a attributes solar eclipses to homosexuality, but also to the death of the vice-president of the Sanhedrin, the simultaneous death of two brothers, and the failure of anyone to come to the aid of a betrothed maiden who cries out in the city.[90] The cosmos may find these events shocking, but the commu-

[86] *Misheh Torah, Hilkhot Rotzeakh*, ch. 12, halakhah 12, based on Mishnah, *Avodah Zarah*, ch. 1, mishnah 7 (quoted in Tamari, 1987:47).

[87] I. Epstein (1938a:760–63), Ginzberg (1913–28:4.259, 336–37, 6.423 n. 100, 426 n. 107).

[88] 2 Macc. 4:9–16 (S. Zeitlin, 1954). Book 3 of the *Sibylline Oracles*, probably written between 163 and 45 B.C. in Egypt by a Jew, prophesies that the Macedonians will be destroyed by Romans, who will also be oppressive. They will "launch on a course of unjust haughtiness. Immediate compulsion to impiety will come upon these men. Male will have intercourse with male and they will set up boys in houses of ill-fame and in those days there will be a great affliction among men and it will throw everything into confusion" (ll. 183–87, Charlesworth, 1985:1.366). Lines 595–600 compare the Jews favorably to virtually all other known peoples: "they are mindful of holy wedlock, and they do not engage in impious intercourse with male children, as do Phoenicians, Egyptians, and Romans, specious Greece and many nations of others, Persians and Galatians and all Asia, transgressing the holy law of immortal god, which they transgressed." The Greeks are singled out for special advice: "Avoid adultery and indiscriminate intercourse with males . . ." (ll. 762–64, Charlesworth, 1985:1:375, 379).

[89] *Kiddushin 82a.* Nevertheless, the sages ruled, bachelors should not teach elementary school, because doing so would bring them into contact with their pupils' mothers, who might seduce them. Unmarried women were likewise forbidden from teaching young children, to prevent them from meeting their students' fathers (I. Epstein, 1936b).

[90] I. Epstein (1938b:130).

nity is not jeopardized by them as it is in Leviticus by the threat that the people will be vomited out of the land.[91]

This lessened sense of threat can be traced to the social changes that had taken place in Palestine after the period of Persian suzerainty. Like the rest of the Torah, Leviticus was written for a stable agricultural community whose religious life was dominated by the priesthood. In the centuries following the return from exile, economic growth and urbanization destroyed the stability and moral basis of the agricultural community. With the growth of commerce, the pursuit of wealth took precedence over bonds of kinship and neighborliness, and life became more individualistic. The earlier centralization of Yahweh worship in Jerusalem had already made religion more remote to the people in the countryside, and the Hellenization of the high priesthood under Antiochus IV (c. 170 B.C.), discredited the priesthood in the eyes of commoners.

In response to needs for emotional security that were not being met by the priesthood or its cult, Pharisaic Judaism arose, substituting the authority of the scribes for that of the priests. By multiplying purity rules that regulated every aspect of human life, far beyond what the Torah required, it provided assurance against the free-floating anxiety generated by the insecurity of the age, and the inability of the written law to provide guidance to an urban people faced with novel dilemmas.[92]

Whereas biblical law offered no personal reward for conformity (no heaven, no life after death), and divine sanctions that were by their nature collective (e.g., drought, famine, plague, captivity), Pharisaic belief in an afterlife where virtue would be rewarded and vice punished *individually* made obedience a matter of the highest personal importance.[93] Yet, because

---

[91] In view of the importance later attached to the story of the destruction of Sodom and Gomorrah in Genesis, it is significant that the talmudic references to homosexuality never refer to this story. The Jewish apocryphal literature associates those cities with prohibited forms of *heterosexuality*. The *Testament of Levi* 14:6, for example, prophesies:

> wedded women shall ye pollute, and the virgins of Jerusalem shall ye defile; and
> with harlots and adulteresses shall ye be joined, and the daughters of the Gen-
> tiles shall ye take to wife, purifying them with an unlawful purification; and
> your union shall be like unto Sodom and Gomorrah (Charles, 1913:2.313, Charles-
> worth, 1985:1:793).

Likewise, the *Testament of Benjamin* warns, "ye shall commit fornication with the fornication of Sodom, and shall perish, all save a few, and shall renew wanton deeds with women" (Charles, 1913:1.358). This passage suggests that the sin of Sodom was an illicit form of intercourse with women. The first writers to assert unambiguously that the sin of Sodom involved homosexuality were Philo (1935:6.69–71), *On Abraham* 26.133–36, and Josephus (1930:194–95, 200), *Jewish Antiquities* 1.11.1, 3. *Midrash Rabbah* on Genesis (sixth century A.D.) identifies homosexuality as the sin of Sodom, an identification perpetuated by Rashi in the eleventh century (Coleman, 1980:74).

[92] Rivkin (1970).

[93] Because salvation could be attained individually, without the mediation of priests or sacri-

reward and punishment were individual, not collective, other people's violations became less worrisome, at least at the level of conscious concern.

The Jewish response to homosexuality in this period was thus partly one of generalized rejection of sexual pleasure,[94] which only incidentally implied hostility to homosexuality, and partly one of legalistic adherence to an earlier prohibition simply because it appeared in writings that were considered divine and that threatened dire punishment for disobedience. Yet the individualization of religion made a policy of repression less pressing. Though homosexuality was treated quite seriously when it did occur—until conquest deprived Jews of the right to administer their own law—it appears to have been infrequent and not a constant source of panic. Far greater attention was given to the regulation of heterosexual intercourse and to other sources of impurity, such as food or menstrual blood.

This relative lack of concern persisted into the Middle Ages. Maimonides held that Jewish men were so unlikely to engage in homosexuality that they could be permitted to sleep together; however, Joseph Caro, the sixteenth-century author of the *Shulchan Aruch,* a codification of Jewish law, dissented on the grounds that "in our times, when lewdness is rampant, one should abstain from being alone with another male." Yet a hundred years later, R. Joel Sirkes lifted this restriction as unnecessary because "such lewdness is unheard of in Poland."[95]

GRECO-ROMAN THOUGHT

The first signs that Greek acceptance of male homosexuality was waning appear in the fourth century B.C., in Plato's dialogues. Plato fled Athens after Socrates' execution, abandoning politics for philosophy. He sought in the timeless realm of pure Ideas the certainty and security that could not be found in the ephemeral world of city-state politics.

This search had, in fact, deeper roots than the death of a beloved teacher. The Athenian defeat in the Peloponnesian War contributed to the sense that worldly affairs were precarious, if not treacherous. In the aftermath of the defeat, Athenians began to question whether the abandonment of tra-

---

fices, their role in Judaism was necessarily diminished. These developments helped Judaism to survive, albeit drastically transformed, after the Romans dispersed the population.

[94]For example, Philo's (1937:1.2.9) "On the Special Laws" heralds the reduction in sexual pleasure as one of the benefits of circumcision. In the same work (1937:498–501), 3.7.37–42, Philo expresses extreme hostility to pederasty and male effeminacy (also see Baer, 1970:46, 51; Dynes, 1985b). Though greatly influenced by Greek philosophy, the discussion to follow suggests that, while the philosophers may have supplied some of Philo's arguments, their work was not the source of his intense feelings. The source was almost certainly the Judaism of his day.

[95]*Encyclopedia Judaica* (1971:8, 962).

ditional values and customs had contributed to the loss. Suspicion fell particularly on the Sophists, whose teachings of cultural relativism seemed to encourage the adoption of new ways of thinking. Plato shared these suspicions, and remarked that his doctrine was an attempt to find a protected realm of standards beyond the differing customs of different peoples, unaffected by the perpetual flux postulated by Heraclitus.[96] A dualistic distinction between mind and matter had been introduced into Greek philosophy a generation earlier, by Anaxagorus. It is the sort of distinction one might expect to be made by a male leisure class in a society where slaves provide freedom from manual labor, women take responsibility for running the household, and politics, philosophy, and art—the realms of subjectivity and initiative—are exclusively male domains.[97] Plato made the distinction the basis for a derogation of the physical, which began to share the lower social status of those whose work entails the manipulation of the physical world. He saw the material world, which is transient, as insignificant by comparison with the Ideas, which never change.

For Plato, the ideal life was to be spent seeking and discussing Beauty, Truth, and the Good. Although bodily perfection could inspire this pursuit,[98] lust itself was evil because it leads to an undignified, slavish, animallike surrender to the passions.[99] It places temperance and reason in jeopardy,[100] and fails to judge the worthiness of its object properly.[101]

Although Plato recognized that lust could be heterosexual or homosex-

---

[96] *Laws* 889b–890b; Swain (1916:48–66).

[97] Philosophical dualism may have originated earlier, with the development of a distinct priestly caste or stratum. This occurred early in Indo-European society (Benveniste, 1932, 1938; Dumézil, 1958:7–33; Lincoln, 1981). If so, its oppositions became more important only later, with the expansion of slave ownership. Thomson (1955) concludes that the demand for slave labor in Athens increased greatly in the latter half of the fifth century B.C. By the fourth century, Athenians were supported primarily by their slaves; even poorer citizens typically had a few. He (pp. 258–62) and Losev (1985) have suggested that mind/body dualism itself sprang from the master/slave relationship. The slave's body is owned by the master, who dictates all the slave's actions. Only in the world of thought is the slave self-determining. Thus the slave experiences a radical separation between thought and behavior. Though they do not mention it, much the same can be said of the female experience under conditions of extreme patriarchal domination. According to Aristotle's *Metaphysics* 1.5, the male/female distinction was one of the fundamental oppositions of the Pythagorean school, along with odd/even, right/left, and good/evil, but it is not clear from his comments that the female category was considered inferior. Bullough (1976:162) assumes that it was, but the importance of women in Pythagorean communities (Boulding, 1976:261) raises questions. Pythagorus himself predated the Peloponnesian War, and his dualism is generally considered an Oriental importation.

[98] Plato, *Symposium* 211c–e, *Phaedrus* 145b, 250d, 265b; Dover (1978:160–62); Nussbaum (1986).

[99] Xenophon, *Symposium* 2.8–14, *Memorabilia* 1.2.29f.; Dover (1978:159–60).

[100] Plato, *Republic* 403b.

[101] Plato, *Symposium* 181.

ual, he took for granted that the strongest sexual impulse would be homosexual.[102] Though these impulses were potentially dangerous,[103] Plato did not condemn pederasty itself. He considered spiritual love to be noble and conceded that even physical love was commendable when undertaken for a worthy purpose, such as self-improvement.[104] By implication, homosexual relationships between teachers and students, or masters and apprentices, were legitimate if they enhanced the learning process.

In his final work, *Laws*, Plato abandoned faith in the possibility that homosexual desire could be channeled into salutary forms. To preserve moderation and to avoid "the frenzied madness of love," Plato insisted that sex must be potentially procreative and restricted to spouses.[105] These criteria excluded homosexual relations.

Before Plato, asceticism had occupied only a minor place in Greek culture; it was relevant mainly in religious contexts. Priests of certain cults had to remain celibate, and worshipers were expected to abstain from sex before certain rites.[106] Plato gave asceticism a much greater importance by arguing on secular grounds that *everyone* should abstain from bodily pleasure on *all* occasions.[107] Later Greek philosophers responded to the insecurity of the Hellenistic Age, which was marked by warfare and political instability until the Roman Conquest in the second century B.C., by following his lead.[108] Many remained celibate to avoid the distractions of sex and family.

In the generation following Aristotle, Epicurus (342–270 B.C.) founded a school in Athens where he taught renunciation of the world. Although he held that the pursuit of pleasure was the highest good in life—a belief seemingly more favorable to hedonism than to asceticism—this was to be achieved through the attainment of tranquillity or equanimity. Epicurus therefore advocated prudence and moderation, rather than satiety or hedonism. All excess was to be avoided, but no distinction was made between homosexual and heterosexual partners.[109] Within the framework of Epicurean philosophy, which was not dualistic, there was no reason to make such a distinction.

[102] Dover (1978:162, 164).

[103] Plato's views of the dangerousness of homosexuality may have been shaped by political considerations: "In the exclusive political clubs at Athens, 'friendship' was highly prized, and for many members, these bonds were reinforced by homosexual ties." Extremist clubs used men—who may have been recruited through aristocratic pederasty networks—as murder squads. Many rulers were assassinated by their *eromenes* (Africa, 1982).

[104] *Symposium* 184b–185b, *Euthydemus* 282b.

[105] *Laws* 838e, 839a–b, 841d–e.

[106] Frazee (1972).

[107] Swain (1916:8–66).

[108] There were periods of comparative tranquillity in this era. In the prosperous years following Alexander the Great, interest in asceticism reached its nadir (Swain, 1916:145).

[109] Buffière (1980:478–79).

Although Epicurus did not demand celibacy of his followers, members of the communities founded by his disciples sought deliverance from the burdens of everyday life by avoiding marriage and children,[110] and, one suspects, from the entanglements of homosexual relations as well. Lucretius, an Epicurean of the first century B.C., raged against sexual love of all kinds in *De rerum natura;*[111] it was an obstacle that stood in the way of quietude.

The Stoic school, founded by Zeno, a contemporary of Epicurus, was also based on a nondualistic view of the world. It preached indifference to all events outside one's own control, and therefore acceptance of one's lot in life. The wise man was indifferent to pain or pleasure, but lived in accord with nature, governed by his own reason. Irrational impulses and excessive emotions were to be eliminated. Sexual excitement, experienced as a "violent fluttering of the soul," a form of morbidity or disease, was one of the commonest of these rejected impulses.[112]

Although the Stoics considered physical satisfaction to be an unworthy goal, they did not call for celibacy. In a radical departure from earlier Greek sexual morality, they held the sexual function of the body to be morally indifferent, just like other bodily functions—from which it followed that love of men or women was to be viewed strictly from the point of view of expediency. Zeno and Chrysippus, a leading Stoic of the third century B.C., both held that homosexual and heterosexual love were permissible under the right circumstances.[113] Cynicism, another school of philosophy, was based on the repudiation of worldly comforts. Its founder, Antisthenes, a student of Socrates, considered homosexual affairs acceptable provided the partner was worthy, and so did his disciple Diogenes (412–323 B.C.).[114]

There are some obvious commonalities in the various schools of philosophical thought that flourished in Greece following Socrates' death. Whatever their differences on questions of epistemology or ethics, all considered a life devoted primarily to physical pleasure to be noxious. Some individuals may have lived celibate lives, yet none called for sexual abstinence for everyone, and none thought that homosexuality should be suppressed. It was the quality of the relationship that was important, not the sex of the partner. Moderation was called for, not repression. Plato's general attitudes toward sex were widely shared by Greek philosophers, but his conclusions about homosexuality in the *Laws* were highly idiosyncratic.

As Rome made itself the master of the Mediterranean, the distinction between Greek and Roman culture began to fade. Greek philosophy became an important part of Roman education, and youths preparing for careers in

[110]Randall (1970:24–31).
[111]Ch. 4.
[112]Rist (1963:25–49, 1978).
[113]Rist (1963:68), Arnold (1971:276–87), Buffière (1980:469–70), Dover (1978:130).
[114]Rist (1963:55–60), Buffière (1980:459–61).

government commonly studied in Athens. Cicero (106–43 B.C.) and Seneca (54 B.C.–A.D. 39) became Stoics, and helped to make Stoic doctrines known to the Romans.[115]

Several factors made Greek philosophy especially appealing to Romans. The traditional Roman state religion, weakened by the exposure to foreign cults that began during the Punic Wars (246–201 B.C.), had no solutions for the terrible sense of insecurity generated by the civil wars of the late Republic. After Augustus came to power, the Senate turned government over to the emperor. Some men of the upper classes turned to the entertaining diversions of the idle rich, but many found this life spiritually impoverished and meaningless. Stoicism helped to reconcile these anomic aristocrats to their inability to affect the political developments of their time.[116]

The influence of Stoicism can be seen in Cicero, who described homosexuality as shameful when practiced openly.[117] Even when kept within the bounds of modesty, homosexual love, he observed, causes unrestrained anxiety, passion, and longing. Cicero acknowledged, though, that this is equally true of heterosexual love. Since he considered love to be volitional, he recommended avoiding it.

The privatization of aristocratic social life that followed the atrophy of politics under the emperors led not only to introspection and philosophizing, but also to a new emphasis on the family. At the same time, the rising status of women may have made domestic life more attractive.[118] In Plutarch's *Dialogue on Love*, Daphnes looks forward to friendship developing between spouses "in due course" after marriage[119]—something probably not anticipated in upper-class households in Plato's day—though Plato hoped to foster marital friendship by suppressing extramarital sex.[120] Musonius Rufus, a Stoic philosopher of the first century A.D., argued that marriage was a help, not a hindrance to philosophers. Maintaining that heterosexual marriage based on "perfect companionship and mutual love of husband and wife" is the foundation of social life, necessary for the perpetuation of the species and a precondition of personal happiness, he condemned all adulterous relations—homosexual and heterosexual—singling out the former as an outrage against nature.[121] Homosexual love is present in the Hellenistic novels, but only incidentally. The plots typically center on a pair of young lovers, one male, one female, who remain faithful to one

[115] Wenley (1963:25, 37).
[116] Wenley (1963:38–45), Earle (1967:46).
[117] Cicero (1927:406–13), *Tusculan Disputations* 4.32–34.
[118] Seltman (1955:153–55), Pomeroy (1975:120–39), Boulding (1976:349).
[119] Plutarch (1969), *Dialogue on Love* 751c.
[120] *Laws* 839b.
[121] Lutz (1947), Buffière (1980:499–501).

another despite temptations and ordeals that separate them before marriage. The novels give marital fidelity an importance for men that it had not had before.[122]

In the short run, the philosophers had very little impact on public opinion or sexual behavior. Within some circles, homosexual relations were still conducted openly and without apology. The reputation of the emperor Trajan, who ruled from A.D. 98 to 117, was unsullied by his well-known involvement in a pederastic relationship.[123] His successor, Hadrian, put up sculptures of his drowned lover Antinous, whom he deified. Like other Roman voluptuaries, Commodus, who ruled in the late second century, kept a little boy, naked except for jewelry, and often slept with him.[124] Tatian, a Syrian Christian who lived in Rome in the second century, wrote that the Romans "try to collect herds of boys like grazing horses."[125] Poets continued to write romantic homophile verse. The proponent of pederastic love in Lucian's dialogue *On Love* defends it as an "ordinance enacted by divine laws," based on love and devotion, not in the least shameful.[126] But the intellectual groundwork for later repression was being laid, and social supports for male homosexual relations were beginning to weaken.

The Appeal to Nature

Musonius Rufus was by no means the first to introduce references to nature into discussions of sexuality. Plato classified as "natural" the pleasure derived from intercourse between men and women for procreation, and as contrary to nature the intercourse of men with men or women with women. He also considered it to be unnatural for a young man to play the part of a woman in intercourse, pointing to the example of animals; and praised the chastity of the birds and beasts as worthy of emulation.[127]

Boswell warns us that some care is needed in interpreting these passages to avoid introducing understandings of "nature" that belong to later ages.[128] He notes that the Greek word *phusis*, conventionally translated as "nature," carried multiple connotations, among them, "favoring procreation."

[122] Foucault (1984b:262–66).

[123] R. Lambert (1984:84).

[124] Herodian (1961:40–42).

[125] Tatian (1982), *Oratio ad Graecos* 33; quoted in MacMullen (1982).

[126] Buffière (1980:651), MacMullen (1982), Scroggs (1983:46), Lambert (1984:80). Whether Lucian wrote *On Love* is in dispute. Current critical opinion places it in the second century A.D., when Lucian lived, not in the fourth century as indicated by Boswell (1980:86 n. 126) and Lambert (1984:80). The Greek philosopher and rhetorician Longinus, who lived in the third century A.D., quotes it (personal communication, Mervin Dilts). Boswell refers to the work as *Affairs of the Heart*.

[127] *Laws* 636b–c, 836c, 840d–e.

[128] Boswell (1980:13–14 n. 22).

Thus, by referring to homosexuality as *para phusin*, contrary to nature, Plato could have been saying only the obvious—that it could not lead to progeny. However, as Boswell concedes, *phusis* carried other meanings as well. Originally, *phusis* meant innate attributes such as physical characteristics; later, by extension, personality and character traits not acquired by learning. To Antiphon, a pre-Socratic orator, it referred to requirements imposed by conditions not established by human convention, to violate which would be objectively harmful whether or not anyone else ever learned of the violation. The word also denoted what was appropriate to someone born into a particular social status, including his rights and privileges. Contemporaries of Socrates (Herodotus, Hippocrates) gave the word the additional connotation of normalcy.[129] Socrates probably intended to evoke all these meanings when he used the phrase. It seems clear that in *Laws* he is more concerned with curbing excess appetites than with maximizing the birthrate. After all, the elevated, noncarnal love that Plato favored was also nonprocreative, and Plato's opposition to heterosexual promiscuity would be difficult to explain if sterility had been the only issue.

Despite his appeal to the behavior of animals, Plato did not think that in general they provided a proper standard of human conduct; that was to come from reason. It is only because Plato thought sex irrational, and considered a restrictive sexual morality to be desirable on other grounds, that he pointed to the animals, who happened by instinct to conform to that morality (or so he mistakenly thought). For Plato, sex always had to be justified by something other than pleasure. In the earlier dialogues, the improvement of the partners was a sufficient justification; in *Laws* it was not.

By the early fifth century B.C., Sophists and medical writers were beginning to use *phusis* to refer to a patient's physical or psychological condition.[130] Yet there isn't even a hint that Plato had medical abnormality in mind when he spoke of homosexuality as contrary to nature. Nothing in Plato's writings suggests that he considered homosexual desire to be abnormal.[131] Though Greek physicians wrote of various sexual disorders, they did not consider homosexuality to be one.[132] It is altogether unlikely that other Greeks did.

Once introduced into philosophical discussions of homosexuality by Plato, references to "nature" appeared in many Greek writings on the sub-

---

[129] Ferguson (1959:56–57), Pellicer (1966:18–29), Adkins (1972:106–8).

[130] Adkins (1972:109).

[131] Dover (1978:165–70).

[132] Foucault (1984b:147). The fifth-century Roman physician Caelius Aurelianus (1950:413, 901–5; see also Boswell 1980:75–76 n. 67) attributed pathic male homosexuality, which he considered abnormal, to a genetic accident (claiming the authority of Parmenides) but considered the active form normal, present in many healthy men.

ject, including some that derogate it. In Plutarch's satirical dialogue, *Beasts Are Rational*, Gryllus observes that "to this very day the desires of beasts have encompassed no homosexual mating" to back up his argument that animals live better than humans because they live naturally.[133] Even great heroes like Agamemnon and Heracles fail to match the standard set by pigs. The point may have been made tongue in cheek, but it nevertheless appealed to a sense of disaffection from the mores, which were perceived as artificial departures from the good life. As knowledge of the variability of custom grew, it became necessary to invoke a standard superior to custom or state-made law to criticize prevailing social habits. Nature provided a standard that seemed to transcend personal preference or custom.

The Hebrew belief that Yahweh had established the order of the universe left Hellenized Jews particularly receptive to appeals to nature. Thus Pseudo-Phocylides wrote that "even animals are not pleased by intercourse of male with male."[134] The writings of Philo, a Jewish neo-Platonist of late-first-century Alexandria, were especially influential on early Christian thinking.[135] He described the men of Sodom as violating a "law of nature" by "deep drinking of strong liquor and dainty feeding and forbidden forms of intercourse. . . . men mounted men without respect for the sex nature which the active partners shared with the passive," leading eventually to sterility.[136] Those who transform their "male nature to the female . . . debase the sterling coin of nature," and those who love them "pursue an unnatural pleasure."[137]

There are also literary references. When Daphnis fends off Gnatho's clumsy seduction attempt in Longus's novel, *Daphnis and Chloe*, he lectures him on the mounting habits of farm animals:

> billy-goats mount nannies, that is very right indeed, but no one
> has ever seen a billy mount a billy; nor rams mount rams instead
> of ewes, nor cocks tread cocks instead of hens.[138]

In Lucian's *Love*, a fictionalized debate between defenders of boy love and partisans of women, one of the champions of heterosexual love argues that "nature" has created erotic attraction to perpetuate the species. To abandon the specialized sex roles implied by this purpose—in which the male gives semen and the female receives it—is degrading.[139]

[133] Plutarch (1968:xii).

[134] Horst (1978:238–39).

[135] Bullough (1976:168), Dynes (1985a).

[136] Philo (1935:71), *On Abraham* 135–37.

[137] Philo (1937:489–90), *The Special Laws* 37–39.

[138] Longus (1910:162–63), *Daphnis and Chloe* 4.10. I have modernized the mid-seventeenth-century translation into English.

[139] Buffière (1980:481ff.). The argument is also made that if everyone practiced homosexu-

These arguments did not go uncontested. One of the other speakers in the dialogue cites examples of animals that were "naturally" homosexual and comments that culture and civilization improve on nature; thus, even if homosexuality is unnatural, it does not follow that it is bad.[140]

The fairly evenhanded treatment of prohomosexual and antihomosexual arguments in the roughly contemporaneous *Dialogue on Love* by Plutarch shows that, as late as the second century A.D., homosexuality was not *generally* condemned, but it also shows that homosexuality had its critics. Presumably, they were numerous enough and vocal enough to warrant the serious attention they were given in these dialogues. Though not yet illegal, homosexuality was already being placed on the defensive.

This development cannot be attributed to Christianity, which was still a small sect, not well known or influential. Nor can it be attributed to the spread of Greek philosophy. The philosophers looked askance at sex, but for the most part did not condemn homosexuality. The new Roman attitudes can only be explained as the consequence of social developments: the changing character of politics and the transformation of the family, as women began to receive education and play a more active role in the economy and in public life, led to new conceptions of sexual morality.

EARLY CHRISTIANITY
The New Testament

Christianity arose within Judaism in Roman-occupied Palestine at a time of great religious ferment and political tension.[141] It soon evolved into a distinct religion and proselytized among Gentiles as well as Jews.

Any discussion of perceptions of homosexuality in early Christianity inevitably begins with the New Testament. Several passages have been understood as referring to homosexuality, but their precise interpretation remains controversial. There is a possible reference to male homosexuality in a puzzling passage in the Gospel of Matthew. The passage reads, in the King James Version, as follows:

> But I say unto you, that
> whosoever is angry with his brother [without a cause],
> shall be in danger of the Judgment:
> and whosoever shall say to his brother, *Raca,*

---

ality exclusively, the human race would become extinct, and this is presumably contrary to the natural goal of self-preservation. The fairly widespread recognition that the birthrate was then falling may have lain behind this argument.

[140]Strato, a Peripatetic philosopher who headed the Lyceum, had already made the same argument in the early third century B.C. (Buffière, 1980:518).

[141]Freyne (1980).

> shall be in danger of the council:
> but whosoever shall say, Thou Fool,
> shall be in danger of hell fire.[142]

The absence of the word *raca* in other Greek texts has made it difficult to know what to make of this passage. One intriguing possibility is that *raca* is actually the Hebrew *rakha* (soft), and carries connotations of effeminacy and weakness. By implication, the phrase refers to passive effeminate male homosexuals.[143] The case for this reading is strengthened when it is recalled that in Akkadian the syllable *raq* is used as a prefix to denote a woman's name or occupation. It appears in compounded form in the words for a woman, a particular kind of nun, and the female genitals.[144] The Akkadian symbol derives from the Sumerogram for a woman.[145] It has also been suggested that the Greek word *moros*, translated here as "fool," actually refers to a male homosexual agressor.[146] This reading makes the threatened punishment far more plausible.[147]

Assuming this reading to be correct, Matthew confirms the rabbinical sources that show Hellenistic Judaism condemning both active and receptive male homosexual roles; in this passage, the active role is more vigorously condemned than the passive. It is tempting to infer that Jesus' denunciation of those who speak abusively to others about their homosexual practices, unaccompanied by any condemnation of the practices themselves, implies a defense of those who engage in them. This would go considerably beyond the text; however, it is an issue to which we will return.

The remaining New Testament passages are all attributed to Paul. The First Epistle to the Corinthians states:

> Know ye not that the unrighteous shall not inherit the kingdom of God? Be not deceived: neither fornicators, nor idolators, nor adulterers, nor effeminate [*malakoi*], nor abusers of themselves with mankind [*arsenokoitai*], nor thieves, nor covetous, nor drunkards, nor revilers, nor extortioners, shall inherit the kingdom of God.[148]

[142] Matt. 5:22. All New Testament translations are taken from the King James Version.

[143] Schulthess (1922), Johansson (1984a).

[144] Borger (1971:91).

[145] Personal communication, Barry Kolb.

[146] Johansson (1984a).

[147] Johansson's surmise that "the council" refers to the *Beth Din ha-Gadol*, the highest tribunal in the land, seems less plausible. Would Jesus have brought charges against his followers in the courts? In 1 Cor. 6:1–6, Paul advises the faithful to resolve disputes internally. It seems more likely that Jesus is referring to an organ of the Christian movement established to discipline members and resolve conflicts without going to court.

[148] 1 Cor. 6:9–10.

The term *arsenokotai* appears again in the First Epistle to Timothy:

> Knowing this, that the law is not made for a righteous man, but
> for the lawless and disobedient, for the ungodly and for sinners,
> for unholy and profane, for murderers of fathers and murderers
> of mothers, for manslayers, for whoremongers, for them that
> defile themselves with mankind [*arsenokotai*], for menstealers,
> for liars, for perjured persons, and if there be any other thing
> that is contrary to sound doctrine.[149]

Literally, *malakoi* means "soft ones." Most translators render it as "effeminates" or "catamites," implying receptive anal homosexuality—or use a
less precise term, like sodomite or homosexual.[150] This usage is well attested. Plato observes in *Phaedrus* that an older lover "will plainly court a
beloved who is effeminate [*malthakos*]."[151] *Oi Malthakoi*, a comedy of Cra-
tinus, deals with effeminate men.[152] There exists an Egyptian letter dating
from roughly 145 B.C., in which *malakos* almost certainly refers to passive
male homosexuality.[153] However, Boswell (1980:106) notes that the word
could take on other meanings as well. Dio Chrysostom, a Greek scholar
(d. A.D. 115), observed that someone who loved learning might be called
malakoteran,[154] an epithet conveying lack of masculine vigor, but not necessarily homosexuality. In Plutarch's *Dialogue on Love*, *malthakos* refers to
decadent, enervated *heterosexual* love.[155] Sometimes the ancients could not
tell from the context what the word meant. Dionysius of Halicarnassus
(1950:150–51) expressed uncertainty over whether the tyrant of Cumae
was called *malakos* because he was effeminate, or simply because he was
gentle.[156]

Considering this multiplicity of connotations, Boswell's confidence that
homosexuality is not intended seems misplaced.[157] He might be right in

---

[149] 1 Tim. 1:9–10. Many scholars think that Timothy was not written by Paul, but was forged
in the second century, with only a few quotations from Paul thrown in (Kümmel, 1975:366ff.;
Coleman, 1980:99–100). That is a question that goes far beyond the scope of the present study.

[150] Bailey (1975:38–39), Horner (1978:97).

[151] *Phaedrus* 239C, quoted in Scroggs (1983:53).

[152] Johansson (1985).

[153] Deissman (1927:164), Horner (1978:97, 139 n. 21), Edwards (1984:83).

[154] Dio Chrysostom (1951:112–13), *66th Discourse*, l. 25. This connotation, however, does not
fit the context of 1 Cor. 6:9–10.

[155] Plutarch (1969:9.318–19), *Moralia* 751B.

[156] Dionysius of Halicarnassus (1950:150–51), *Roman Antiquities* 7.2.4.

[157] Boswell's (1980:107) observation that *malakos* "is never used in Greek to designate gay
people as a group or even in reference to homosexual acts generically" is true but misleading,
as the word *is* used to refer to those who take a particular role in a homosexual relationship.
To strengthen his argument, Boswell claims that in Matthew 11:8, *malakos* means "sick." That
is quite wrong; there the word describes cloth, and clearly means "soft." Neither meaning fits
the context of 1 Cor. 6.

suggesting that the passage may concern those who are "wanton" or "licentious," but the possibility of a narrower construction can hardly be denied. The positioning of the word next to "adulterers" might suggest that a sexual meaning is appropriate.[158] Scroggs's idea that *malakos* refers to an effeminate call-boy is simply speculative.[159] More plausibly, the term in this context referred to homosexual cult prostitutes. Corinth and Ephesus, where Timothy was stationed, were strongholds of the Mother Goddess and had long-established religious prostitution. It is also conceivable that Paul was not concerned with precision and deliberately chose a term that was derogatory but not precise. His First Epistle to the Corinthians is more concerned with making the general point that Christian liberty did not mean license to engage in depraved behavior[160] than to articulate a precise set of strictures.[161] He assumed that his readers had a pretty good idea of what sorts of behaviors were out of bounds.

The translation of *arsenokoitai* has also been debated. Most Bible translations assume it has to do with male homosexuality.[162] Bailey is more specific, asserting, but without saying why, that it has to do with male homosexuality.[163] Scroggs somewhat arbitrarily narrows the term even farther, to the clients or patrons of a *malakos*.[164] In this view, Paul is simply enunciating the condemnation of prostitution on the part of an upper-class citizen that was shared by the entire Greco-Roman world. However, Boswell suggests that *arsenokoitēs* may not refer to homosexuality at all.[165] In the myriad of instances homosexuality is mentioned in Greek literature, he notes, the word *arsenokoitēs* is never used. His linguistic analysis leads him to suggest that it refers to active male prostitutes who served men or women.

The details of Boswell's argument have been challenged by several scholars—to this nonspecialist, persuasively.[166] These challengers suggest that

---

[158] The juxtaposition of adultery and male homosexuality appears often in writings from late antiquity, both pagan (Lutz, 1947) and Jewish. Pseudo-Phocylides inserted homosexuality into the Ten Commandments next to adultery.

[159] Scroggs (1983:106).

[160] Abbott (1898:214).

[161] Scholars have given some attention to the structure and sources of the lists of sins in these passages. Paul may have drawn on preexisting vice lists or even games of chance (Deissman, 1927:315–17; W. D. Davies, 1948:116–17; Osborn, 1976:19; Scroggs, 1983:104–6). It seems clear that the lists are not logically ordered, and that the particular choice of items is less significant than the general tenor conveyed by the whole.

[162] Boswell (1980:338) offers a convenient survey of translations. For further discussion see Petersen (1986).

[163] Bailey (1955:38).

[164] Scroggs (1983:108).

[165] Boswell (1980:342–50).

[166] G. R. Edwards (1984:82), D. F. Wright (1984), Johansson (1985). The arguments are technical and cannot be summarized here.

arsenokoitēs was coined in an attempt to render the awkward phrasing of the Hebrew in Leviticus 18:22 and 20:13 into Greek,[167] or that it derives from an almost identical construction in the Septuagint translation of the Leviticus prohibitions.[168] A neologism was needed precisely because the Greeks did not have a word for homosexuality, only for specific homosexual relations (pederasty) and roles. Subsequent usage of the word in early Christian writings (e.g., in Eusebius, Aristides, and the second *Sibylline Oracle*) are consistent with a homosexual meaning.

The first chapter of Paul's Epistle to the Romans depicts the depravity of the gentile world, which rejected God and turned to idoltary:[169]

> For this cause God gave them up unto vile affections: for even their women did change the natural use into that which is against nature: And likewise also the men, leaving the natural use of the women, burned in their lust one toward another; men with men working that which is unseemly, and receiving in themselves that recompense of their error which was meet. And even as they did not like to retain God in their knowledge, God gave them over to a reprobate mind, to do those things that are not convenient; being filled with all unrighteousness, fornication, wickedness, covetousness, maliciousness; full of envy, murder, debate, deceit, malignity; whisperers, backbiters, haters of God, despiteful, proud, boasters, inventors of evil things, disobedient to parents, without understanding, covenant-breakers, without natural affection, implacable, unmerciful: who, knowing the judgment of God, that which they commit such things are worthy of death, not only do the same, but have pleasure in them that do them.[170]

This little outburst is conventionally taken to prohibit both lesbianism and male homosexuality. In itself this is remarkable; almost all condemnations of homosexuality in the ancient world were directed exclusively to the male form. Neither the Old Testament nor the other references to homosexuality in the Pauline epistles mention lesbianism. However, the reference to women is ambiguous: Paul did not say that they turned to other women, only that they changed the natural usage. Since Paul insisted in other writings that women subordinate themselves to men, he could be referring here to women who adopt the superior position in heterosexual

---

[167] Scroggs (1983:85–86).

[168] D. F. Wright (1984).

[169] Käsemann (1980:33). The passage quoted seems clearly derived in part from a Jewish work, *The Book of Wisdom*, (chs. 13, 14), written after 50 B.C., probably in Greek (Charles, 1913:556–59).

[170] *Rom.* 1:26–32.

intercourse.[171] Pseudo-Phocylides' roughly contemporaneous injunction, "And let not women imitate the sexual role of men,"[172] may suggest a broader concern with sexually assertive women in Hellenistic Judaism. The parallel drawn to men with the words "And likewise . . ." has led some commentators to reject this possibility,[173] but perhaps too casually. The idea that male homosexuality and female homosexuality form a conceptual unity was uncommon in antiquity. Paul might have seen the violation of gender role expectations as a common thread linking some heterosexual acts with those involving male homosexuality. On the other hand, lesbianism was known in Rome,[174] and Paul might have wanted to comment on it in a letter to believers living there. This being so, no definitive reading seems possible.

Several commentators have noted that by limiting his phillipic to men who abandon the "natural use" of women by turning to other men, Paul seems to be excluding those whose nature is exclusively or innately homosexual.[175] It is doubtful, though, that Paul had such a distinction in mind. More likely, he did not consider homosexual preferences to be innate or exclusive. That was the general assumption of his time.

Paul's references to "nature" betray Stoic influence.[176] He would have been exposed to it in Tarsus, where he was born; it was a major Stoic center.[177] Stoic ideas were also quite prominent in Hellenistic Jewish literature. Paul was addressing Romans, who would have been familiar with Greek philosophy. Still, as a Jew, Paul could not allow nature to be the ultimate arbiter of morality. That was God's role.

That Paul did not regard deviations from what is natural as *invariably* bad is shown by his use of the term elsewhere. In Romans 11:24, for example, Paul describes God as acting contrary to nature.[178] Nevertheless, it is clear that he did view *this* deviation negatively. He is describing a people who, in ignorance of God, plunged into many forms of vice and wickedness, homosexuality among them. The enormity of their crimes was so great that they deserved to die.[179]

---

[171]*Col.* 3:18–19, *Eph.* 5:22–25; for discussion see D. S. Bailey (1955:40), Bullough (1976:180).
[172]Horst (1978:239–40).
[173]Scroggs (1983:114).
[174]For example, Messalina (d. A.D. 48), the wife of the emperor Claudius, "compelled by torture the women of her court to join with her, not only in bacchanalian orgies, but in vice too shameless to be named" (Abbott, 1898:217). Brooten (1983) cites a number of references to lesbianism in the Greco-Roman world, all derogatory.
[175]J. J. McNeill (1976), Boswell (1980:107).
[176]Horner (1978:105–6), Käsemann (1980:34, 48).
[177]Arnold (1971:99).
[178]Boswell (1980:110–13).
[179]Boswell's (1980:112–13) contention that the passage does not imply moral condemnation,

It could be argued that, even if all this is true, Paul's manifest concern is not with homosexuality in general, but with lust.[180] Stoic thought, after all, condemned lust without rejecting homosexuality. Is it possible that Paul had a more favorable view of homosexuality informed by love and governed by respect, modesty, and dignity? Since he was not writing a systematic treatise we cannot know for sure, but his Jewish heritage makes that unlikely. Every reference to homosexuality in Hellenistic Jewish writings is condemnatory. Paul's own religious upbringing was strict, and he describes himself as zealous up to the time of his conversion.[181] Although Paul did not regard Jewish law as binding on Christian believers,[182] he may not have been able to overcome teachings inculcated in his earlier years. His views on women were traditionally Jewish in their patriarchy and went considerably beyond Roman opinion of the day.[183]

Paul's comments on heterosexual relations do not suggest that he would have found homosexuality acceptable under any circumstances. He advocated celibacy on the grounds that someone who is married is more concerned with pleasing his spouse than with pleasing God—an inappropriate priority when the end of the world is at hand.[184] A same-sex spouse would presumably pose the same problem. To prevent fornication, marriage was permitted to those who could not remain chaste.[185] Sexuality was not something Paul valued for itself, or for the contribution it could make to an interpersonal relationship. He saw sex as lust, therefore as something that was best suppressed or, if that was impossible, permitted only the most restricted outlet. This is asceticism accommodating itself to the masses by conceding as little as possible.[186] Someone who held these views of hetero-

---

and that the reference to "that which is unseemly" and "that recompense of their error which was meet" only concerns social disapproval, is untenable. Paul is describing idolators. He could not have regarded the worship of false gods as a trivial sin, and the vices to which the idolators were given could not have been so trivial as to merit only social disapproval. In fact, Boswell himself emphasizes that the Romans of Paul's day did not generally disapprove of homosexuality, and the peoples of the Near East did not either, for as we have shown in chapter 3, many engaged in it as part of their religious worship. So Boswell's interpretation is inconsistent. The concluding lines of the passage, which Boswell omits, make clear the strength and passion of Paul's condemnation.

[180] Boswell (1980:115–17).

[181] Acts 22:3.

[182] Rom. 6:14, Gal. 2:3.

[183] Ste. Croix (1981:106–60).

[184] 1 Cor. 7:29, 32–24.

[185] 1 Cor. 7:1–2, 9.

[186] Paul's reluctant concession to heterosexual marriage runs counter to what is now considered mainstream Jewish thought, which was much more positive toward heterosexual relations directed toward procreation. But our earlier discussion as well the sources cited in Ste. Croix (1981:555 n. 9) indicates that sexual asceticism was a significant tendency among Jews

sexuality is unlikely to have regarded homosexuality with favor even when its context was one of love, affection, and loyalty. There is little in Paul's writings to suggest that these personal sentiments counted for much with him. He himself was burdened with a sense of sin and guilt and struggled to overcome his sexual desires.[187] This is not a condition that encourages generosity toward the stray sexual impulses of others.

One may wonder whether Jesus and his other disciples shared Paul's views. The quotation from Jesus in Matthew 5:22, already discussed, does not reveal enough to permit even an opinion. Since they shared the same cultural heritage as Paul, one imagines they would have agreed. However, Morton Smith's analysis of the New Testament, other works of early Christian literature, and Roman sources points in a different direction.[188] Smith concludes that Jesus broke sharply with Jewish legal restrictions,[189] believing that his religious-magical powers gave him and his followers freedom to disobey the Law. He thinks Jesus conducted secret baptismal initiations at which mystical secrets were imparted, and at which ritual homosexual intercourse may have taken place; also, that the sect as a whole, or perhaps only certain tendencies within it, was fairly licentious. After Jesus' crucifixion, this tendency was fought by Paul, whose sense of sin transcended the Law,[190] and by Jesus' brother James, who assumed the leadership of the Christian community in Jerusalem. James's concerns were practical: he wanted Jewish converts to conform to Jewish law because nonconformity provoked persecutions from Jewish fanatics.[191]

Smith's reconstruction is, of course, speculative, and difficult to reconcile with Jesus' views of divorce[192] or with his commendation of those who have "made themselves eunuchs for the kingdom of heaven's sake,"[193] but it is not ungrounded in the sources. It may be objected that, if homosexual relations among the original Christians had become public knowledge, the rab-

---

under Roman domination, even though it never became the dominant ideology. It is worth noting that Paul does not adopt the Stoic position that sex within marriage was justifiable if its goal was procreation. Believing the end of the world to be near, that would have been pointless (Meeks, 1983:101). His goal in allowing the marriage debt was to forestall other forbidden sexual excesses. He expresses his concern about this again in 1 Thessalonians 4:3–5: "For this is the will of God, even your sanctification, that you should abstain from fornication: That every one of you should know how to possess his vessel in sanctification and honor; Not in the lust of concupiscence, even as the Gentiles which know not God."

[187] Rom. 7.
[188] M. Smith (1973a:113–14, 1978:254–65, 273).
[189] Galilean Jews of Jesus' era had a reputation for laxity with regard to the Law (Freyne, 1980:309–323); Jesus' own willingness to break it may have reflected this background.
[190] Rom. 6, Gal. 2.
[191] Acts 21:20–40.
[192] Matt. 19:3–9, Mark 10:11–12.
[193] Matt. 19:12.

bis would have used the information for propaganda purposes; yet they did not.[194] Still, the practices could have been confined to Jesus' inner circle and kept secret.

There is evidence that some of the Christian Gnostic sects rejected the position of Paul and James and engaged in orgiastic practices, including homosexual practices, in their ceremonies.[195] The tendency that later became recognized as the orthodox church suppressed these practices among its own members, so that by the second century the love feast, or *agapé*, had been transformed into the desexualized eucharist.[196]

The Early Church

Whatever the precise views of Jesus and the apostles, early Christian writings of the first and second centuries, such as the *Didache*, the *Epistle of Barnabas*, and the *Demonstratio Evangelii* of Justin Martyr, were unequivocally opposed to male prostitution and pederasty—probably the most visible forms of homosexuality in their time.[197] Clement of Alexandria denounced homosexuality as nonprocreative, therefore unnatural.[198] The *Apocalypse of Peter* imagined the terrifying chastisement in hell of those who engaged in homosexual relations.[199] In the early third century, Tertullian wrote that those who engaged in "all the other frenzies of passions [other than adultery and fornication] . . . beyond the laws of nature" should be banished "not only from the threshold, but from all shelter of the Church, because they are not sins, but monstrosities."[200]

Boswell has challenged the common supposition that this hostility originated in Judaism.[201] He points out that early Christian writers rarely cited the Old Testament as grounds for detesting homosexuality, and argues that the early church did not consider Jewish law to be binding on Christians. It

[194] Coleman (1980:106).

[195] Benko (1967, 1984:54–78), Vanggaard (1972:151–52), M. Smith (1973a:114, 1978:254–65, 273), Bullough (1976:187). The Gnostic sects tended toward philosophical dualism, but not all adopted ascetic doctrines. While dualism can lead to avoidance of a world perceived as evil, it can also accommodate the view that those who have achieved a higher spiritual level cannot be contaminated by the material world or by sin, and therefore can do anything. In the tantric sexuality of the late Purānas, "one may perform the *act* of sexual intercourse without losing one's purity, as long as the mind remains uninvolved" (O'Flaherty, 1969). Thus dualism can accommodate licentiousness as well as asceticism (Obolensky, 1948:50, 52, 186), Salisbury (1985b:203).

[196] Tarachow (1955), M. Smith (1973b:446–47), Bullough (1976:186–87), Dynes (1985b).

[197] Lake (1925:311), Roberts and Donaldson (1926), Bailey (1955:83–84), Bullough (1976:194), Boswell (1980:139–40 n. 9, 346).

[198] Boswell (1980:355–59).

[199] M. R. James (1945), Dodds (1965).

[200] J. Bingham (1844:232–33), Roberts and Donaldson (1926:77).

[201] Boswell (1980:102–5).

is true that, as the church grew, most converts were not Jewish, and would hardly have been swayed by a quotation from Leviticus. Many early Christian leaders had Gentile family backgrounds; their attitudes must have had some source other than Christianity. Still, Paul's Jewish upbringing was, in all likelihood, a factor shaping his views of homosexuality, even if not the only one. Moreover, some Christian leaders—including Tertullian, Origen, Clement of Alexandria, and Eusebius of Caesarea—did cite the Leviticus prohibitions and considered them valid for Christians.[202]

Though the New Testament was an independent source of authority for Christians,[203] Boswell points out that the early Christian polemics against homosexuality rarely refer to the passages now thought to refer to homosexuality, and the arguments they present are not scriptural. However, they do betray the influence of Greek philosophy. Greek culture influenced Judaism before the Roman Conquest, and became even more influential afterward, helping to shape Christian thought. Stoic ethics and neo-Platonist doctrines, which became popular in the third century A.D., both contributed to the Christian synthesis.[204]

Stoic morality was becoming stricter under the emperors. Seneca, Musonius Rufus, and Epictetus held out chastity as an ideal, with sexual intercourse allowed only within marriage, and then only for the purpose of having children.[205] In questions of ethics, neo-Platonist thought shared much with Stoicism.[206] Plotinus, an Alexandrian neo-Platonist of the third century, urged celibacy, as did his pupil Porphyry.[207] Diogenes Laertius, another scholar of the third century, praised those who refrained from marrying.[208] Other Greek and Roman writers, not necessarily Stoics, held that procreation was the sole legitimate reason for sexual intercourse.[209] This criterion excludes homosexuality.

Christian theologians often had a classical education and were familiar with these writings. Although the premises of these non-Christian writings were often incompatible with Christian theology, Christians nevertheless borrowed arguments from them. For example, Clement of Alexandria quoted from Plato's *Phaedrus* and *Laws*.[210] Yet their appeal owed less to the

---

[202] D. F. Wright (1984). Following Philo, Clement also mentions the destruction of Sodom as having to do with male homosexuality in his fantastic *Paedagogus* 2.10.

[203] Clement of Alexandria, for example, cites Rom. 1:26–37.

[204] Swain (1916:80), Wenley (1963:114–25), A.H.M. Jones (1966:24), Randall (1970:142–43).

[205] Lutz (1947), Arnold (1971:347–48).

[206] Zeller (1962:22–24).

[207] Bullough (1976:150).

[208] 6.2, 29 (Schwartz, 1979).

[209] Boswell (1980:129–30).

[210] Boswell (1980:357–59).

persuasiveness and authority of Greek rhetoric than to the social developments of the time, which favored sexual asceticism. Had this not been so,
Greek writings in favor of pederasty would have had greater influence.
John Chrysostom (A.D. 345–407), for example, knew Plato, but denounced
his support of pederasty.[211]

These developments were both political and economic. As governmental
administration became bureaucratic and impersonal, and imperial in scale,
city politics atrophied. From the first century A.D., the Roman Senate "had
never done more than register its assent to an imperial motion." After the
imperial capital was moved to Nicomedia, then Byzantium, it could not
even be consulted on a regular basis, for the emperor rarely visited Rome.[212]
Popular assemblies in the conquered provinces "generally sank into insig-
nificance or disappeared entirely under the principate."[213] As the financial
burdens of public office grew, the less affluent stratum of the propertied
class (the so-called decurions) began to avoid public service, so that compulsion had to be applied.[214] By the third century, private donations for
public buildings dropped dramatically, marking a decline in civic spirit
among the very wealthy.[215]

The third century brought unprecedented challenges to the Empire. Emperor after emperor was murdered by mutinous troops. As civil war raged,
rival armies destroyed towns and ravaged the countryside. Territory was
lost to the Sassanid Persians and the barbarian Germans. "Famine, plague,
chronic inflation, every imaginable evil, it seemed, sapped public confidence. . . . Even the gods were shaken."[216]

Economic problems gave asceticism a particularly wide appeal in the
eastern provinces of the Empire, especially in third-century Egypt and
Syria.[217] The heavy burden of taxation, and the sharpening of class divisions in peasant villages, played havoc with middle-class aspirations.
Ascetic doctrines that advocated sexual abstinence and withdrawal from
worldly affairs appealed especially to this class by offering a strategy for
coping with desires frustrated by uncontrollable external conditions.[218]

[211] E. A. Clark (1979).

[212] A.H.M. Jones (1966:121, 128).

[213] W. H. McNeill (1958:203).

[214] Ste. Croix (1981:465–74).

[215] P. Brown (1978:48).

[216] J. H. Smith (1976:21).

[217] Economic crisis did not begin in the third century. There was serious economic hardship
in Palestine in the first century A.D. Dickey (1928) concludes that the apocalyptic mood of the
time was a direct consequence of the dire economic straits of the laboring classes. A more
detailed study of the economic problems facing the Galilean peasantry can be found in Freyne
(1980:155–207).

[218] Dickey (1928), Vööbus (1960a:120), P. Brown (1978:31, 82–85). B. Russell (1959:118) comments about the detachment from reality in Plotinus's writings that

Inability to affect the course of events through political institutions generated a malaise among the Roman upper classes, paving the way for Greek philosophy, and so Stoic neo-Platonist doctrines spread among the educated.[219] The old Roman religion based on agricultural rites declined in Rome itself (though not in the countryside), despite politically motivated governmental efforts to revive it. Oriental mystery religions (Mithraism, Manichaeanism, the worship of Isis and of the Magna Mater, as well as Pauline Christianity and various brands of Gnosticism) filled the void, winning converts by promising immortality and union with God through initiation rituals and personal purity. Denial of the body and its sensual impulses was a major aspect of purity (as it was in the Greek philosophies), so that by A.D. 100 ascetic currents were visible, even if not predominant features of Roman religious life.[220]

The crises of the third century can only have strengthened tendencies to see life as meaningless or evil. Manichaeanism, a dualistic religion that taught the sinfulness of sex and the evil of procreation, spread rapidly.[221] Loosely organized groups of ascetic aristocrats leading lives of Christian chastity and prayer could be found in Rome before A.D. 300 and are known to have existed throughout the fourth century.[222] The renewed military threat posed by the ravaging of Gaul in A.D. 406 at the hands of the Franks, Sueves, Vandals, and Alans, and the Visigothic sack of Rome in 410, greatly enhanced the appeal of ascetic versions of Christianity and led to a flurry of conversions.[223]

Some of the most prominent themes in the Patristic literature of this period reflect these experiences. Essays in praise of virginity, written for male readers, expand on the cares and worries associated with the support of wives and children. Emphasis is placed on curbing anger and controlling the appetites for food and sex. Secular sources of happiness are described in tones of unrelieved pessimism as inevitably transitory, and the temporal world is portrayed as a vale of suffering and disappointed hopes.

In some parts of the Empire, response to these ideas appears to have been wide. According to a chronicler of asceticism in the Syrian Orient, in

---

> This is not surprising when one considers the state of the Empire. It would take a man of utter blindness or else supreme fortitude to maintain an even temper of straightforward cheerfulness in face of the disorders of the time. A theory of ideas which treats the world of sense and its miseries as unreal is well suited to reconcile men to their fate.

Obviously, the same could be said of Plotinus's contemporaries.

[219] Barker (1966:11), A.H.M. Jones (1966:24, 121, 128, 279).
[220] Angus (1925), Oost (1968:13), Randall (1970:100–106).
[221] Bullough (1976:189–92), J. H. Smith (1976:26).
[222] P. Rousseau (1978:80–81).
[223] P. Rousseau (1978:80–81, 90).

the latter part of the fourth century, "great masses turned to the monastic life, contributing to the depopulation of the communities in the villages and towns, a process that took on steadily growing dimensions." [224] It has been estimated that, in Egypt, as much as 5 percent of the Christian population, which was roughly half the total, belonged to ascetic monasteries. [225]

Although the bulk of the converts to Christianity were from the lower middle classes who were hit hardest by the economic catastrophe, [226] some of the most prominent came from well-to-do families. The contrast between the certainty of salvation and the uncertainties of secular political careers figured in the conversions of Ambrose, Jerome, and members of Augustine's circle, among others. [227]

Needless to say, the Christian ascetic antipathy to sex extended to homosexuality. We have already seen a number of texts from the first and second centuries that were extremely hostile. This hostility persisted in subsequent centuries. The apocryphal *Apocalypse of Paul*, found in Tarsus and possibly dating from the third century, envisions men and women in a pit of tar and brimstone in hell; they are identified as "those who have committed the iniquity of Sodom and Gomorrah, men with men." [228] In *Against the Opponents of the Monastic Life*, a work preoccupied with the unimaginably horrible chastisement that awaits sinners after death, John Chrysostom describes homosexuality as a foul, disgusting corruption responsible for the destruction of Sodom. Pederasty, he insists, is so dangerous, and yet so omnipresent, that to protect them from it, boys should be sent to live in monasteries for one or two dozen years starting in late childhood. His *Commentary on Romans, Homily 4*, maintains that "there is nothing, absolutely nothing more demented or noxious than this wickedness." [229]

This is extreme, but less so when measured against the Christian ascetic's repudiation of all forms of sexual expression. Some precedent for this rejection had already been set by the New Testament. Revelation 14:4 describes a procession of the redeemed as consisting of (male) virgins not defiled by women, and Luke 20:35 holds that "they which shall be accounted worthy to obtain that world, and the resurrection from the dead, neither marry, nor are given in marriage."

---

[224] Vööbus (1960a:112).

[225] Brady (1952:92).

[226] A.H.M. Jones (1966), Knowles (1969:14).

[227] P. Rousseau (1978:93).

[228] P. Coleman (1980:116).

[229] John Chrysostom (1865:217–19), Festugière (1959:206–7), Boswell (1980:361–63). The patristic literature gave less attention to relations between women, but also viewed them negatively, albeit with less passion than relations between men; see, for example, Tatian (1982:60, 62), *Oratio ad Graecos* 33; Tertullian (1954:2.745, 939), *De Pallio* 4.9, *De resurrectione mortuorum* 16.6; Brooten (1983).

Yet these passages were balanced by others much less extreme. Paul may have thought celibacy preferable to marriage, but still, it was "better to marry than to burn." [230] Marriage was no sin, and sex within marriage was not only acceptable, but a duty if desired by one's spouse. Jesus rejected fasting, comparing his followers to the guests at a wedding who cannot be denied food;[231] and when hungry he gathered food, even on the Sabbath.[232] It was said of him that he was "gluttonous, and a winebibber." [233]

Church leaders of the second through the fourth centuries gave sex much greater attention, and with few exceptions, rejected it far more vehemently and completely than did the authors of the New Testament.[234] The second-century apocryphal *Acts of the Apostles* maintained that married persons should refrain from sex,[235] and the *Acts of Paul and Thecla* proclaimed that only virgins would be resurrected.[236] In the early Syrian church, only the unmarried could be baptized,[237] and some Western bishops of the second century made continence compulsory for church members.[238] Some early Christians tried to live up to these standards by living in "spiritual" (celibate) marriages.[239]

Virtually all the fathers of the church—Gregory of Nazianzus, Gregory of Nyssa, John Chrysostom, Ambrose, Jerome—praised virginity and looked on sex with horror.[240] Tertullian regarded violations of chastity as worse than death.[241] Ambrose described those who preserve chastity as angels, those who lose it as devils.[242] A number of theologians, including Eustathius of Sebastia, a bishop of the fourth century who introduced monasticism into Armenia, held that married people could not be saved. Athanasius, fourth-century patriarch of Alexandria, held that "the appreciation of virginity and chastity was the supreme revelation and blessing brought into the world by Jesus." [243] The influential *Gospel of the Egyptians* taught that Jesus came to "destroy the works of the female," i.e., sexual

[230] I Cor. 7:12.
[231] Mark 2:19.
[232] Mark 2:23–25.
[233] Matt. 11:19.
[234] Clement of Alexandria (c. A.D. 150–220) was one of the exceptions; he urged all Christians to "hasten to accomplish marriage" (Clemens, 1870:86).
[235] These works also condemn the consumption of meat and wine, and the ownership of personal possessions (S. L. Davies, 1980:12, 32–33).
[236] Dodds (1965:4).
[237] Vööbus (1951).
[238] R. M. Grant (1970:271).
[239] Salisbury (1985b:125–26).
[240] Mendieta (1955), Dodds (1965), Tannahill (1980:138–43).
[241] Bullough (1973b:98).
[242] *Concerning Virgins* 1.9 (Schaff et al., 1895:371), Salisbury (1985a).
[243] Bullough (1973b:97).

reproduction.[244] To be like the angels was to be spiritual; to be carnal, un-spiritual. Sex was the essence of carnality, hence the antithesis of spiritual-ity. Heterosexual desire was natural, but only in man's fallen state. To attain spirituality required that one overcome sexual desire and, as Gregory of Nyssa made clear, every other kind of passion as well.[245] His *On Virginity*, written toward the end of the fourth century, argued that

> Corruption has its beginning in birth and those who refrain from procreation through virginity themselves bring about a cancellation of death by preventing it from advancing further because of them. . . . A safe protective wall is the complete es-trangement from everything involving passion.[246]

Only by developing the self-control needed to renounce the world with its temptations, and oneself, could deliverance be attained.[247]

A number of the Gnostic versions of Christianity held equally negative views of sex. The Marcionite communities in Iran and Mesopotamia were celibate, and the followers of Valentius—the best known of them being Origen—castrated themselves. This practice became common in Syria and Mesopotamia.[248]

In that the Christian church was not centrally administered prior to the conversion of the Emperor Constantine in A.D. 313 no single doctrine of sexual conduct prevailed. Instead, each bishop exercised authority in his own diocese, influenced only by the moral authority and persuasiveness of his fellow bishops. However, by the middle of the third century, some church leaders began to oppose excessively rigid sexual discipline, know-ing that it would hinder recruitment and lead to the loss of members.[249] Church councils of the fourth century acted to prevent the loss of members by prohibiting self-castration and, for a time, by refusing to require celibacy of priests. By the late fourth to early fifth centuries, perfectionism, includ-ing sexual abstinence as a requirement of church membership, had been definitely rejected, though Western synods were coming to insist on it for priests.[250]

Augustine was a key figure in this development. Possibly he found the prevalent view of sex difficult to reconcile with his own extensive sexual history—which included a mistress and wife, as well as homoerotic attrac-tion to a male friend—prior to his conversion.[251] Had he endorsed the doc-

[244] Dodds (1965:4), Boswell (1980:158).
[245] Salisbury (1985a).
[246] Saint Gregory of Nyssa (1967:48, 65).
[247] Mendietta (1955), Saint Gregory of Nyssa (1967), P. Brown (1978:86–88).
[248] Vööbus (1951:15–16), Bullough and Brundage (1982:16–17).
[249] R. M. Grant (1970:221).
[250] Bullough (1973b:100, 1976:319–20).
[251] *Confessions* 3.i refers to Augustine's homoerotic interest.

trine that only virgins could be saved, he would have had to accept the absolute impossibility of his own salvation—a tough nut to swallow. In any event, Augustine did not reject sex as totally as did the other church fathers. For Augustine, the critical opposition was not between flesh and spirit, but the Stoic one between the passions and reason. It followed that virginity was not necessarily the supreme good. Sex could be good, too, if governed by reason, not concupiscence. Such would be the case when it was engaged in, without lust, by a married couple, to produce children.[252]

As Bullough points out, the early church competed with rival sects, including the Gnostics, for members.[253] The success of what is now considered the orthodox church may have been due in part to the way it reconciled the demand for asceticism and personal purity with the necessities of organizational survival. The requirement of the Gnostic sects that all adherents practice celibacy might have discouraged potential conversions, and would have prevented organizational growth through procreation. In contrast, the orthodox requirement of sexual abstinence only for a clerical elite facilitated organizational growth. At the same time it provided an ideological basis for the legitimation of hierarchical authority within the Church.

This sexual liberalization may have made life psychologically easier for those who had little interest in homosexuality, but it offered little to those who did: Augustine's criterion for acceptable sex ruled out homosexual expression just as unequivocally as the more total rejection of sex in other patristic writings. He insisted that there are

> those foul offences which be against nature, to be everywhere and at all times detested and punished; just as were those of the men of Sodom: which should all nations commit, they should all stand guilty of the same crime, by the law of God, which hath not so made men that they should so abuse one another.[254]

It must be kept in mind that the views of bishops and theologians were not necessarily shared by the entire laity. Once Christianity became the official religion of the Empire, many converted for reasons other than spiritual

---

[252] Noonan (1966:107–39), Erickson (1976:191), Wood (1981), Salisbury (1985a). It is important to note that this criterion was not required by scriptural authority. As we already noted, the Pauline epistles were not concerned with procreation as a goal of sex.

[253] Bullough (1973b:111).

[254] Augustine (1957:39), *The Confessions* 3.viii. Boswell's (1980:150–51) contention that Augustine saw in homosexuality merely behavior that was "incongruous" and "contrary to human nature," "not characteristic of the human sexuality familiar to him" is badly misleading, as B. Williams (1982) also notes. Augustine was quite familiar with the eunuchs consecrated to the Great Mother, who walked the streets of Carthage (see *City of God* 7.xxvi), and had experienced homosexual desire himself (see n. 251 to this chapter). A hundred years later, Salvian (1930), a priest, reported that the Carthaginians gloried in pederasty. Boswell's suggestion that Augustine was simply confounded by an unfamiliar phenomenon is hard to credit.

conviction and were not attracted to the ascetic life. The new Christians of fourth-century Antioch still went to the theater and the hippodrome and marched in the processions of Bacchus and Demeter.[255] Antioch was prosperous, with much wealth and little poverty,[256] so the factors favorable to asceticism elsewhere were largely absent there. Indeed, John Chrysostom complained about the brazen display of homosexual interest within the Church leadership:

> Those very people who have been nourished by godly doctrine, who instruct others in what they ought and ought not to do, who have heard the Scriptures brought down from heaven, these do not consort with prostitutes as fearlessly as they do with young men. . . . None is ashamed. . . . Indeed . . . there is some danger that womankind will become unnecessary in the future, with young men instead fulfilling all the needs women used to.[257]

Chrysostom made many enemies by opposing these and other practices he found objectionable.[258] Confirmation of the standards that prevailed in Christian communities of that period comes from Lactantius, who taught rhetoric in Nicomedia in the early fourth century. After a vehement denunciation of pederasty, he complained that "these practices . . . are regarded as light and sort of honorable."[259]

Even though most pagans and Christians did not adopt an ascetic life themselves, their veneration of ascetics tells us that awe of sexual abstinence, and of asceticism more generally, went beyond a tiny elite. This veneration was not restricted to Christians. According to Inge,

> Galen and other Pagan writers show that the practice of lifelong continence by the Christians made a great impression on their neighbors; it was considered a proof of such self-control as could be expected only from philosophers.[260]

Had there been a gross disparity between Christian ideals and popular values, conversions to Christianity before it became the official religion of the

---

[255] Festugière (1959:404).

[256] Liebeschuetz (1972:356).

[257] *Against the Opponents of the Monastic Life* 3.8, quoted in Boswell (1980:131–32). It is tempting to dismiss the passage as hyperbole on the part of someone whose severe personal anxiety about his own suppressed homosexual impulses led him to project them on others. But his contemporary, Libanius, a pagan who by no means shared Chrysostom's extreme views (see below) also described the open pursuit of pederasty as being extremely common in Antioch (Festugière, 1959:200–204).

[258] Schaff (1886:5).

[259] Lactanteus (1964:457–58).

[260] Inge (1923:1670).

Empire would be puzzling. Thus, lay Christians are likely to have considered sexual abstinence an ideal way of life, even if it was not the way they chose for themselves.[261]

Care is thus needed when speaking of early Christian hostility to homosexuality. Though no Christian theologian spoke up in favor of homosexuality, some were more hostile to homosexuality than to other kinds of sex. Tertullian clearly thought that homosexuality contravened "the laws of nature" more than heterosexual adultery or fornication in any orifice.[262] John Chrysostom complained equally about the interests of churchgoers in looking over attractive women and boys,[263] but his hysterical tirades were reserved for pederasty. Yet for many other writers, hostility was directed to all sexual experiences not intended to lead to procreation within marriage—homosexual or heterosexual.

This evenhandedness can be seen in the *Didache*, which adds both sodomy and fornication to the Decalogue;[264] and in the *Apocalypse of Peter*, where fornicators and adulterers are tortured alongside males and females guilty of homosexual relations.[265] Saint Basil of Nyssa, the founder of Christian monasticism, wrote in A.D. 375 to another bishop, that "He who is guilty of unseemliness with males will be under discipline for the same time as adulterers." Saint Gregory of Nyssa explained the reason for this evenhandedness in a canonical letter written to the bishop of Melitene in 390: both heterosexual adultery and homosexual intercourse are unlawful pleasures.[266]

The canons adopted in 309 by the Council of Elvira (now Granada, in Spain) also treat homosexual and heterosexual violations of church law similarly. So far as is known, Elvira was the first church council to formulate rules for the regulation of sexuality, and it devoted considerable attention to the topic: 37 of the 82 canons adopted concern sex. The one dealing with homosexuality specifies that men who engage in sexual relations with boys should not be admitted to communion even at death.[267] Other canons

---

[261] One of the few indications of rank-and-file views comes from the *Didascalia Apostolorum*, which provides information on a Greek-speaking Arabic or Syrian church of the third century that adopted a policy of not taking gifts from male or female prostitutes. This may reflect a reading of Deuteronomy 23:18–19 similar to the one defended in chapter 4 of this book (Harnack, 1908:157–58). The document says nothing about noncommercial sexual transactions, and even the prostitutes are not denied church membership and attendance.

[262] Roberts and Donaldson (1926:77).

[263] Boswell (1980:160 n. 97).

[264] Lake (1925:303–4).

[265] M. R. James (1945:507–516).

[266] J. J. McNeill (1976:79), Gauthier (1977).

[267] Not too much should be made of the restriction of the prohibition to boys. Laeuchli (1972:101) points out that the council was not legislating a general code of sexual conduct; it

specify the same rigorous penalties for adulterous women, and women involved in pandering and prostitution.[268]

The church, then, responded to the social and economic crises of the Roman Empire with an intense suspicion of all forms of sexuality, along with other forms of worldly self-indulgence. During the first two centuries of Christianity, prominent bishops and theologians demanded celibacy of all Christians. Organizational considerations, however, forced the church to back away from such an extreme requirement. The church ultimately accepted heterosexuality within marriage, for the purpose of having children. Intercourse that was not potentially procreative was forbidden.

The Late Roman Empire

Recall our conclusion in chapter 4 about the legal status of homosexuality in the Roman Republic: it was almost certainly not illegal. This remained the case for the first two centuries of the Empire.[269] Jurists of the early third century, however, were extending earlier morals legislation to prohibit the seduction of a male minor.[270] One of the most eminent, Julius Paulus, praetorian prefect (chief judicial officer of the Empire) under Alexander Severus, wrote (certainly with little effect) that someone who forced a slave to submit to a homosexual act was to be considered guilty of corrupting him.[271] Perhaps it was these developments that led Sextus Empiricus, a Greek physician of the late second and early third centuries, to write that homosexuality was illegal.[272] Enforcement was another matter; given the chaotic conditions of the third century, it would hardly have been feasible in some parts of the Empire, and certainly not a high priority. The gap between law "on the books" and law "in action" could be large in antiquity.[273]

These rulings did not cover prostitution, which Philip the Arabian tried to ban in A.D. 249. But the effort was a failure, for male prostitution continued without interference well into the next century.[274] Further legislation was adopted in the fourth century, when Constans and Constantius, sons of Constantine, promulgated a law in 342 with the following text:

---

was taking up concrete cases that had been presented to the Spanish bishops. Moreover, pederasty was probably the form that homosexual relations then primarily took.

[268] Laeuchli (1972:126–35).

[269] Occasional assertions to the contrary, such as one finds in Aristides, *Apology* 13:7, are not necessarily to be taken literally. Musonius Rufus claimed that it was illegal to have intercourse with one's wife for pleasure alone (Lutz, 1947).

[270] Keesel (1969–72:1.335–39, 2.859–63), Bailey (1975:68–69), Boswell (1980:71 n. 47, 179).

[271] T. Wiedemann (1981).

[272] Sextus Empiricus (1933).

[273] According to Athenaeus (1854:904), a Greek scholar who lived in Egypt in the late second and early third centuries A.D., it was illegal to shave in Rhodes, but no one was prosecuted and everyone did it. He implied that shaving was effeminate (*The Deipnosophists*, 18).

[274] Syme (1968:107), D. S. Bailey (1975:66–67, 71), Boswell (1980:121–22).

> When a man "marries" in the manner of a woman, a "woman" about to renounce men, what does he wish, when sex has lost its significance; when the crime is one which it is not profitable to know; when Venus is changed into another form; when love is sought and not found? We order the statutes to arise, the laws to be armed with an avenging sword, that those infamous persons who are now, or who hereafter may be, guilty may be subjected to exquisite punishment.[275]

The precise scope of this statute remains a matter of debate. Bailey suggests that the law may have been "facetious" (but does not suggest a reason for the enactment of a law that had facetious intent), or perhaps dealt only with prostitution[276]—though there is no mention of prostitution in the text. Boswell thinks the law was serious, but argues that it outlaws homosexual marriages only.[277] Lauritsen, on the other hand, concludes that it deals with all male homosexual acts.[278] The question hangs on the appropriate translation of a Latin word that has more than one meaning, so it cannot be settled by appealing to a dictionary. The references to exquisite punishment and avenging swords, however, seem to favor Lauritsen's reading, in that the language seems too extreme to apply to marriage alone but not to other types of homosexual relations as well. It is hard to imagine someone becoming so incensed about homosexual marriages without having comparably strong feelings about sexual encounters not involving marriage.

That Constans should have sponsored such legislation is especially striking in view of his own reputation for scandalous behavior with "handsome barbarian hostages."[279] It may be that he was not expressing his own feelings when promulgating this legislation, but trying to placate public outrage at his own indecencies.

Similar controversy surrounds a statute of the emperors Theodosius, Valentinian, and Arcadius. Issued in 390, the law was incorporated into the Theodosian Code in 438 and accepted in both East and West. Boswell contends that it refers only to "forcing or selling males into prostitution," while Bullough and Lauritsen see it as a more general condemnation of passive male homosexuality. Bailey is not sure.[280]

Part of the problem is that two texts for the statute survive, but only one mentions brothels. After deploring the "pollution of effeminacy in males" and the loss of "rustic vigor," the text that does mention brothels reads:

[275] *Theodosian Code* 9.vii.3 (Pharr, 1952:231–32).
[276] D. S. Bailey (1975:70–71).
[277] Boswell (1980:123).
[278] Lauritsen (1985).
[279] J. H. Smith (1976:79).
[280] D. S. Bailey (1975:71), Bullough (1976:332), Boswell (1980:124), Lauritsen (1985).

O Orientius whom we love and cherish, praiseworthy therefore
is your practice of seizing all who have committed the crime of
treating their male bodies as though they were female, submit-
ting them to the use becoming the opposite sex, and being in no
wise distinguishable from women, and—as the monstrosity of
the crime demands—dragging them out of the brothels (it is
shameful to say) for males. . . . In the sight of the people shall
the offender expiate his crime in the avenging flames that each
and everyone may understand that the dwelling place of the
male soul shall be sacrosanct to all and that no one may without
incurring the ultimate penalty aspire to play the part of another
sex by shamefully renouncing his own.[281]

As the only coercion mentioned is that applied by Orientius, Boswell's interpretation finds little support. The primary concern is obviously effeminate male homosexuality; prostitution seems secondary. The rationale
given for the penalty clearly applies to more than just prostitution. If enforcement was directed at brothels, it was probably for practical reasons.
Then, as now, sexual transactions in private residences were not easily prevented. Practical limitations on enforcement may have spared even brothels. Chrysostom, who was virulently antihomosexual, never mentions the
legislation, and Evagrius's *Ecclesiastical History* says that a special tax on
homosexual prostitution was collected at least until the end of the fifth
century.[282]

This fourth-century legislation may have been the basis for the provision
in Justinian's Code that homosexual offenders were to be executed. The
code, issued in 529 and revised in 533, was prepared by a commission
headed by Tribonian, a pagan, on the basis of preexisting imperial legislation. That the incorporation of this provision was simply mechanical and
did not reflect current views can be excluded in the case of homosexuality,
for after the code was published, Justinian issued two *novellae* (imperial
edicts) reiterating the death penalty for repeat offenders—though permitting penitents who confessed and renounced the crime to escape with
their lives.[283]

---

[281] Hyamson (1913:82–83). If, as the law states, Orientius was already arresting people,
there must have been prior legislation enabling him to do so. This could have been the law of
Philip the Arabian prohibiting homosexual prostitution, or the law of Constans and Constantius (if the latter is interpreted as dealing with prostitution).

[282] D. S. Bailey, (1975:72), Boswell (1980:71 n. 48), Bullough and Brundage (1982:18–19). The
anonymous source for one of the texts, writing shortly after the statute was issued, regarded it
as the equivalent of the Leviticus prohibition, which was not restricted to coercion or prostitution (Hyamson, 1913:82–83).

[283] D. S. Bailey (1975:73–77).

Since all antihomosexual legislation from the fourth century on was introduced by Christian emperors, it has generally been assumed to have reflected specifically Christian attitudes—attitudes not shared by pagan Romans.[284] One episode often taken as evidence for a discrepancy between Christian-inspired law and the sentiments of a largely pagan population involves the arrest of a popular charioteer in Thessalonika in A.D. 390 on charges relating to homosexuality. The Thessalonikans rioted in outrage at the arrest and killed a Gothic officer of the Empire. The charges are usually assumed to have involved consensual sex, and the arrest is believed to have been made under the Theodosian constitution. But there is some reason to think that the charge was rape, and it is not known for sure whether the arrest was made before or after the legislation.[285] If the episode was in fact a rape, popular outrage may have reflected antagonism to the Goths, rather than acceptance of homosexuality. Nor can we be sure that the arrest of a less popular figure would have elicited the same reaction.

Had antihomosexual legislation been enacted from specifically religious concerns, it seems likely that Julian the Apostate would have repealed it. During his short reign (361–63) he attempted—though without too much success—to undo the Christianization of the Empire begun a generation earlier by Constantine. But Julian left the statute of Constans and Constantine intact.

Nor can it be argued that the use of the state to enforce morals rules having to do with consensual sex was specifically Christian; Augustus had already done so in his marriage legislation several centuries earlier, and the practice was continued by the harsh penalties for adultery imposed under the Antonine rulers, who were not Christian.[286]

Boswell argues that it was more or less a coincidence that antihomosexual legislation of the late Empire was enacted by Christians. In the West, the Christian church was the only organized entity to survive the German invasions. It thus became

> the conduit through which the narrower morality of the later
> Empire reached Europe. It was not, however, the author of this
> morality. The dissolution of the urban society of Rome and the
> ascendance of less tolerant political and ethical leadership occa-
> sioned a steady restriction of sexual freedom that transcended

[284] Johansson (1985), Lauritsen (1985). It is possible that some of the earlier legislation was inspired by Christian thinking as well: at least one ancient author claims that Philip the Arabian was a Christian. The weight of contemporary scholarly opinion, though, holds that he was not Christian but was later thought to be one because of his religious tolerance (Ensslin, 1965).

[285] N. Q. King (1960:68–69, 102–4).

[286] Last (1966), Raditsa (1980).

credal boundaries. . . . All the organized philosophical traditions of the West grew increasingly intolerant of sexual pleasure
under the late Empire, and it is often impossible to distinguish
Christian ethical precepts from those of pagan philosophy during the period.[287]

We, too, conclude that negative attitudes toward sex developed in the late
Empire, differing from Boswell primarily in seeing economic and political
developments as precipitating this trend, rather than the deurbanization
they occasioned.[288] We have already seen a great deal of evidence indicating
that pagan sexual morality was becoming more restrictive in some circles in
the first two centuries of the Empire. The jurists whose rulings criminalized some forms of homosexual behavior were all pagan. The protection
Paulus extended to slaves is especially revealing. Since slaves enjoyed very
little protection under Roman law, his opinion suggests that at least some
Romans considered coerced homosexuality so ignominious that even slaves
deserved to be protected from it.[289]

Nevertheless, there were differences between Christians and pagans.
Even where pagans viewed sex or homosexual acts negatively, it was rarely
with the extreme feelings that Christians expressed. The emperor Julian,
for example, was celibate. On taking office, he discharged much of the palace staff, including some eunuchs, and insisted that the priests of the state
religion conform to his own ascetic way of life. He loathed Christianity because its bishops lived in idleness and luxury, supported by revenues from
church property. Yet he launched no persecutions of libertines, whatever
their sexual preferences, and proclaimed religious toleration.[290]

The comparison between Libanius and John Chrysostom is especially revealing. Both were born in Antioch and lived in Constantinople around the
same time, and both wrote about homosexuality, Libanius as a pagan phi-

---

[287] Boswell (1980:127–28).

[288] One problem with an analysis that emphasizes the role of deurbanization is that the East
was relatively immune from it. Constantinople in the age of Justinian had a population estimated at 600,000 (Downey, 1960:21). Antioch was a thriving metropolis when John Chrysostom
wrote his diatribes against homosexuality.

[289] Some of these figures could have been influenced by Christian ideas. Alexander Severus,
who ruled from 222 to 235, considered taking steps to end male prostitution (Syme, 1968:107),
but refrained for practical reasons. Though pagan, he held Christianity in high regard. Still, to
be influenced by Christianity one has to be receptive to its message.

[290] J. H. Smith (1976:102), Bowersock (1978:14, 79–80). Of course, Julian's reign was short
and embattled. Had he lived longer, perhaps he would have done something about behavior
he considered immoral. But while he had the chance, he didn't even try. Likewise, the Greek
Stoic philosopher Epictetus (late first century A.D.) recommended sexual self-restraint, but
added, "do not be offensive and censorious to those who indulge in it, and do not be always
bringing up your own chastity" (Halliday, 1925:114). Here the Christians diverged.

losopher and pedagogue, Chrysostom as a bishop. In several passages of his *Orations*, Libanius denounced boys who offer their bodies for gain and wanted boys excluded from the Olympic banquets lest they tempt the men to seduce them.[291] Yet he himself may have had an affair with one of his male students,[292] and wrote that bitterness at the destruction of a city by an earthquake could easily be assuaged in the arms of a male lover.[293] Chrysostom's vehemence is of a totally different order.[294] Though his feelings may have been extreme even among Christians, they were not eccentric in their general thrust. Pagan writings may have deplored homosexuality, but none thought it caused the gods to destroy cities (Sodom). None threatened sinners with gruesome tortures in the afterlife. These themes are unique to Christian writings.

Given the vast extent of the Empire, the variability of its socioeconomic conditions, and the many cultural traditions it supported, attitudes toward homosexuality undoubtedly varied with region, and within region, according to class, ethnicity, and religion. Whereas Salvian found male homosexuality to be quite extensive in early-fifth-century Carthage,[295] Athenaeus, writing from early-third-century Egypt, implies that institutionalized pederasty was part of the remote past in Greek civilization.[296] Some Christians denounced homosexuality; others engaged in it.[297] Too little is known at present to permit even a rough sketch of these variations. However, there is no doubt that the most hostile Jewish and Christian writings are substantially more hostile than those written by unfriendly pagans.

This greater hostility could mean only that people who were especially upset about homosexuality, or rigid in their outlook on sex, tended to convert. Once they did, they were exposed to sermons and literature claiming divine authority for condemnation of homosexuality, and threatening dire sanctions against those who participated in it. These teachings may have grown out of the social and economic conditions of the Empire, but they would surely have reinforced and intensified the antihomosexual effects of those conditions. The consistency of the Christian defamation of homosexuality could hardly have fostered tolerance. Still, as Boswell emphasizes, there is little reason to think that the Christian laity were obsessed with

[291] *Orations* 28.8–11, 39.5–6, 53.6; Festugière (1959:201–4).

[292] Norman (1965:160).

[293] *Orations* 61.23.

[294] A.H.M. Jones's (1961:972) assertion, repeated by Greenberg and Bystryn (1982), that Libanius and John Chrysostom were equally passionate in their denunciation of homosexuality is thus quite misleading.

[295] Salvian (1930), 7.15, 16, 19.

[296] Athenaeus (1854:904), *The Deipnosophists* 13.16.

[297] Laistner (1951:87, 94, 110–11, 136).

homosexuality.[298] Many probably disapproved of it, but not necessarily with vehemence. Even the patristic literature, which expresses strongly negative views, does not devote a great deal of space to the subject.

The Imagery of Homosexuality

As antipathy to homosexuality grew, the imagery used to express it changed. These images, which we have encountered incidentally, are of interest in their own right. The mainstream perception of homosexuality in Greece during the classical age is well illustrated by the statement of the pederast in Xenophon's *Hieron* that he wants from his young male lover "what perhaps human nature compels us to want from the beautiful."[299] Male sexual attraction to other males was considered normal, perhaps inevitable. Even those who thought that the impulse should be curbed (e.g., Plato in *Laws*) considered the impulse itself to be unexceptional. Only when homosexual attraction manifested itself in ways that were immoderate or gender-inappropriate was abnormality imputed.[300]

For the Stoic and Epicurean philosophers, love and lust were deplorable distractions from the *vita contemplativa*, but had no profound moral connotations. Sexual desire may have been an obstacle to the achievement of imperturbability, but that was equally true whether the object of desire was male or female. Standards of sexual conduct purporting to derive from nature, and transcending custom or opinion, had a normative character, but they did not generally imply that homosexual attraction was physiologically or psychologically pathological.

The patristic literature of the fourth and early fifth centuries shifted the focus by making virginity a major component of personal purity. Sexual abstinence replaced martyrdom as the prescribed method of imitating Christ.[301] Unchastity was a sin; for many writers, equally a sin whether homosexual or heterosexual.

The perceptual difference between Greek philosophy and Christian moral teachings is all the more striking in that some of the patristic literature drew heavily on Greek sources. For example, Gregory of Nyssa's essay *On Virginity*[302] borrowed Greek rhetorical devices, identified virginity with the absence of passion, praised it as a way of avoiding the burdens of married life,

---

[298] Boswell (1980).

[299] Quoted in Dover (1975:213).

[300] In addition to the many other examples we've considered, note Athenaeus (1854:904) who, in *The Deipnosophists* 13.18 quotes Diogenes as saying to one man who had shaved his body, presumably to make himself more attractive to men, "I am afraid that you think you have great ground to accuse nature, for having made you a man and not a woman."

[301] Malone (1950), Vööbus (1960a:99).

[302] Gregory of Nyssa (1967).

and equated the life of the Christian ascetic with that of the philosopher. Yet the notion that violations of chastity are moral blots or blemishes for which a god would hold one responsible was something new.

Justinian's language was different again. In his legislation, homosexuality threatens not the individual sinner, but the entire community. According to his *Novella* 77, "because of such crimes, there are famines, earthquakes and pestilences."[303] The tone is reminiscent of Leviticus, where the prohibited defilements, including male homosexuality, threaten the people with being vomited out of the land.

The anthropologist Mary Douglas has proposed a provocative theory of the way in which people experience their bodies that can be used to explain these shifts.[304] Douglas's approach is based on the writings of the French sociologist Emile Durkheim, who argued that the categories through which people think about the world are derived from the structure of the society in which they live.[305] A generation earlier, Marx had already realized that social experience influences the way people think. But Durkheim went farther, by suggesting that the categories of thought reflect the objective structure of society; in other words, that there is a homology between thought and social structure. To know one is to know the other.

Douglas develops this notion by postulating a correspondence between a society's social structure and the way those who live in that society experience their bodies. To make this postulate concrete, she conceptualizes society in terms of two variables, *group* and *grid*. *Group* refers to the strength of people's identification with the group to which they belong; *grid*, to the existence and stability of formally recognized, differentiated social roles. Each of these variables can have high or low values in a given society or collectivity. Douglas thinks these variables influence whether people feel positively or negatively about their bodies, and the kinds of social control they apply to the body.

Where *grid* is high, Douglas argues, we should expect an affirmation of society and its institutions. Where, in addition, *group* is low, religious syncreticism would be expected. This is so because the ideological boundaries that would interfere with external religious influences will be weak. The existence of formalized social roles implies that public behavior is subject to some sort of social control; therefore one would not necessarily expect sexual expression to be uninhibited. But neither would we expect it to be denied or repressed altogether. Instead, we would expect it to be institutionalized through ritual. This seems like a good characterization of the

---

[303] Bailey (1975:73), Bullough (1976:171–72).
[304] M. Douglas (1970).
[305] Durkheim (1963, 1965:474–88).

polytheistic agrarian societies of the ancient Near East, and perhaps of Greece and Rome in their early stages.

These societies are classified as high on *grid* because they were economically and politically stratified, and socially expected behavior depended in generally accepted ways on age, gender, and social status. These societies are classified as low on *group* even though nationalities were socially recognized, because commerce among different groups facilitated social interaction and the diffusion of cultural items. Intermarriage appears to have been acceptable, and it was sometimes possible to change one's national affiliation. Just as the theory predicts, male homosexual relations were associated with the religious rituals of the ancient Near East.

Where *group* and *grid* are both weak, religion loses its social character and magical qualities and becomes personal. So does morality. The universe comes to be seen as benign, or possibly indifferent. The blurring and instability of social roles lead to the weakening of social control over sexuality. Where the universe is conceived as benign, individuals feel relatively uninhibited sexually. The hippie counterculture, with its slogan of "Do your own thing!," provides a modern example.

Where the universe is considered indifferent, sexuality may be subject to self-regulation but can take many forms. Classical and Hellenistic Greece, and Rome under the Republic and early Empire, provide reasonably good examples.[306] In these societies, pederasty could be pursued without social disapproval as long as it conformed to norms concerning gender and the age of one's partner. The religious context of the tribal world was gone, and it had not been replaced by legal prohibitions. The state intervened only when behavior incompatible with citizenship was involved, e.g., when there was prostitution on the part of citizens. Thus, even when some individuals disapproved of homosexuality, or thought that someone was acting in a manner inappropriate for his age, they did little of consequence about it. An adult effeminate man may have been laughed at or scorned, but he was not otherwise punished.

Where *group* is high and grid is low, the most important social distinction is whether someone is inside or outside the group. Dualistic philosophies, ascetic life-styles, and doctrines of personal purity will prevail.

---

[306] The classification of the classical Greek city-states as societies in which group was low is adopted on the following rationale. Citizens had a sense of belonging to a particular city-state, but were divided by tribal loyalties, political commitments (democratic or oligarchic), and an ethos of male competition for status. Moreover, the Greeks shared a common identity that distinguished them from the barbarians. Thus loyalties were cross-cutting and tended to weaken identification with any single group. When it seemed politically or personally advisable, citizens of one city-state emigrated to others, and in some cases even defected to the Persians.

A personal preoccupation with what goes in and out of the body will parallel the social concern with diet, excretion, and sexuality. Lapses will be treated as sins and associated with the powers of evil in the universe.

The Christian church of the third and fourth centuries illustrates this pattern. Persecution at the hands of the Romans, and the need to differentiate the new cult from Judaism, paganism, and heresy, made group membership extremely important. The disorders of the Empire—invasions and economic crises—were weakening traditional markers of social status such as class and kinship. According to Brown,

> The Christian communities in the third and fourth centuries had grown up in precisely those classes of the great cities of the Mediterranean that were most exposed to fluidity and uncertainty.[307]

The Christians were geographically and socially mobile. For many, the church became an alternative community to the one being abandoned as a result of this mobility. The social services it provided substituted for those available earlier from extended kinship networks.[308] Moreover, in its attempt to be universal, the church systematically downgraded other sources of personal identity, such as kinship, race, or town.[309] During these first few centuries, lines of authority within the church were still fluid and ambiguous. Holy men, for example, were seen as rival authorities to the bishops.[310] As expected, sex was looked upon with fear and loathing. And though Jewish dietary restrictions had been dropped on Jesus' authority, many of the church fathers advocated abstention from meat and alcohol.

Consistent with Douglas's analysis, thoughts could be sins in Christian doctrine even if they were not accompanied by action. Jesus had warned, "Whosoever looketh on a woman to lust after her hath committed adultery with her already in his heart."[311] Cassian, who brought Christian monasticism to the West, reported that Saint Basil had once announced, "I have never known women, but still I am not a virgin."[312] He was not confessing to bestiality or a homosexual escapade, but to lustful thoughts. Such thoughts, according to Cassian, were not necessarily one's own: the devil could introduce them into someone's mind if he did not guard against them (another indication of boundary anxiety).

Last, when *group* and *grid* are both high, we expect a "complex, regula-

[307] P. Brown (1972:134).
[308] P. Brown (1972:136), S. L. Davies (1980).
[309] P. Brown (1978:56, 74).
[310] P. Brown (1971:80–101).
[311] Matt. 5:28.
[312] Cassian (1965), *Monastic Institutions* 6.19.

tive cosmos." Body control will be important, because fixed social roles will be accompanied by strong social control. However, there will be less concern with intentionality or subjective states of mind and more with overt visible behavior. Instead of ascetic doctrines of self-discipline and personal striving for spiritual perfection, elaborate ritualized codes will govern behavior. Violations will be seen less as personal blemishes and more as threats to collectivity. The perception that an individual's misbehavior jeopardizes the well-being of the community results in deviants' being considered outsiders, aliens.

The Hebrews who returned to Palestine from the Babylonian exile provide one illustration. Under Ezra, foreign wives were divorced and expelled, and the cult was renewed and purified by the exclusion of those considered contaminated by foreign ways. The priests became a new governing class. It was at this time that rules of purity having to do with sex, food, and bodily secretions (semen, menstrual blood) were codified in Leviticus. Violations had the potential of causing the land to "vomit out" the entire people. Later, when the Pharisees were trying to weaken *grid* by democratizing Jewish religious life while maintaining the solidarity of group identification, they elaborated the rules of ritual purity, but also wrote of them in ways that do not suggest a collective threat connected with violations.

The Eastern Roman Empire in the age of Justinian provides a second test case. Two centuries earlier, Diocletian had attempted to fix people in their occupations and bind cultivators to the soil. Barbarian invasions in the West had led to the breakdown of an organized, imperial society, but in the East, where defenses against the invasions had been more successful, society remained "firm and well-ordered,"[313] though threatened by border conflicts on several fronts. Disastrous earthquakes, droughts, fires, floods epidemics, and visitations of locusts, leading to destruction on an immense scale and to enormous loss of life, added to the sense of personal insecurity. Just two years before Justinian's second novella on homosexuality, one of the worst recorded outbreaks of bubonic plague took place.[314]

In the conventional interpretation, Justinian enacted harsh legislation against heretics and non-Christian religion because he regarded himself as responsible for the fate of the Eastern Empire, and this depended on collective conformity to God's will. There is much to support this view. Justinian declared that decisions made by the four great Ecumenical Councils were valid as imperial law. His *Novella 77*, which proscribed male homosexuality (remaining silent about lesbianism), also forbade "swearing and blas-

[313] Barker (1966:13).
[314] Vasiliev (1950:344–50), Ure (1951:131).

phemy."[315] Adultery was a capital offense. In an attempt to earn God's favor and bring prosperity, Justinian ordered clerics not to gamble or go to the theater or the races.

These laws and prohibitions, and the fear of divine punishment for collective guilt, cannot be dismissed as the idiosyncracies of a caesaropapist ruler: the belief that "natural" disasters were a supernatural response to the neglect of divinely imposed obligations was extremely widespread among pagans, Jews, and Christians in the late Empire.[316] Tertullian remarked in the *Apologeticus* that the pagans

> suppose the Christians are the cause of every public disaster, every misfortune that happens to the people. If the Tiber overflows or the Nile doesn't, if there is a drought or an earthquake, a famine or a pestilence, at once the cry goes up, "The Christians to the lions."[317]

Justinian's legislation seems to reflect the same mentality; only the target is different.

The general correspondence between the perceptions of homosexuality found under different social conditions in late antiquity and those expected on the basis of Douglas's theory is impressive and suggests that there is something to her ideas. At the same time, a critical examination raises questions about them. One difficulty is that Douglas does not specify how ideas about the body or sexuality are brought into correspondence with the structure of society. Her writings lack a social psychology of cognition. Durkheim attempted to justify the equation of conceptual categories and social structure by arguing that society is the only source of general ideas, but that is surely untrue: generally held ideas can have many sources. Even if metaphors of the body are socially derived, they need hardly reflect the structure of society as a whole.

Her two variables, *group* and *grid*, do not seem sufficient for explaining the imagery of homosexuality. *Grid*, for example, specifies the existence and stability of social roles, but does not deal with the nature of those roles and the way those roles are valued or disvalued. To address the uneasiness that lesbianism evoked among men in some societies, including those of antiquity, or the stigma attached to males performing sexual roles defined as female (but not those defined as male) requires, at a minimum, some notion of unequal power relations, domination, and exploitation.

Consideration of societies that have institutionalized slavery makes the limitation of Douglas's scheme especially obvious. Such societies generally

[315] Ure (1951:62).
[316] Ste. Crois (1963), A.H.M. Jones (1966:321).
[317] Quoted in Ste. Croix (1963).

have stable, well-differentiated social roles (high *grid*), but it is doubtful that the slaves feel positively about their roles, or about society and its institutions. While the polytheistic societies of the ancient Near East were slave societies, slaves, as far as we know, did not participate in sexual rituals. They were, however, subject to the sexual demands of their masters. There was nothing ritualistic about sex between slaves and masters. Durkheim took into account the possibility that a society's division of labor could be forced and exploitative,[318] but this insight, shared by Marx, has been overlooked in Douglas's work. It is this oversight that limits the applicability of her work to such phenomena as gender stereotypes, slavery, and prostitution.

These limitations are seen not only in the study of the complex, stratified ancient empires, but even in smaller, more primitive societies. Studies discussed in chapter 2 indicated that in certain New Guinea cultures, homosexual practices help to secure a fragile cohesion among men to facilitate the domination of women. These practices, and the ideology that supports them, cannot be explained by noting that New Guineans identify strongly with their own groups (they do), or that gender roles are sharply differentiated (they are). Douglas's conceptualization is too impoverished to deal with these issues.

This impoverishment is particularly evident when considering societies where overt group conflict is present, e.g., between the sexes, or among classes or political factions. Here one may identify with a group, but the group need not coincide with the entire society. Social roles may be recognized, but may be unstable; or if they are stable, it is because a dominant group's power prevents change. Under these circumstances it can be grossly misleading to speak of the sexual perceptions of a *society*, for different groups can have quite different perceptions.

Justinian's antihomosexual legislation bears reexamination from the point of view of social conflict, for Procopius, Justinian's court historian, claims that it enjoyed little popular support.[319] He maintains that Justinian's motives were not religious but political: homosexuality charges were a convenient pretext for arresting people he or his wife wanted out of the way.

This accusation need not be taken at face value: Procopius was hostile to Justinian, and so may be suspected of bias, but other sources confirm his claim that homosexuality prosecutions were brought with little attention to procedural niceties. Nonetheless, careful scrutiny makes an exclusively political motivation doubtful. The same sources indicate that two bishops were arrested and tortured before Justinian's legislation was adopted. His

[318] Durkheim (1964:374–88).
[319] Bullough (1976:335–37), Boswell (1980:72–74).

wife, Theodora, had someone arrested, tortured, and castrated without trial on homosexuality charges. If the emperor and empress were able to do these things in the absence of legislation, we must wonder why they needed or wanted a law to legitimate them. We must wonder as well why the charge had to be homosexuality. If the aim was to discredit those arrested by bringing false charges, it would have made more sense to choose something the masses considered detestable rather than unimportant. Conceivably, Justinian was not well informed about public opinion (always a possibility for an autocratic ruler); or perhaps Procopius exaggerated popular indifference. The laws could have been a propaganda effort, intended to persuade an urbane, cosmopolitan population of Justinian's provincial, stricter morality; but if so, then Justinian believed what he wrote, and *his* views might be explained by Douglas's scheme (or by some other), even though those of the rest of the population are not explainable in such a way. In this particular instance, it is ultimately unclear how telling a political or social-conflict critique of a *grid-group* analysis is. The important point is that the critique suggests possibilities that the two-variable analysis neglects. Whether or not consideration of these possibilities generates valid insights into any concrete situation requires that they be examined.

We may conclude that Douglas's ideas about the origins of bodily experience in the structure of society provide a provocative beginning for the study of how images of homosexuality vary among times and places. Yet her scheme, despite its insights, leaves out much that is important in the phenomenology of homosexuality, and in the conceptualization of society. We will keep in mind both the insights and the limitations of Douglas's perspective as we examine perceptions of homosexuality in feudal, competitive capitalist, and reform capitalist societies in subsequent chapters.

6   *Feudalism*

Several of the master social institutions of medieval Europe—serfdom, vassalage, and hereditary fiefs—had roots in both late-Roman and German tribal society. Large, self-sufficient agricultural manors worked by serfs had already become prevalent in the late Empire. They subsequently spread to purely German areas, though without entirely eliminating the free peasantry.[1] Flight from the cities began under the Empire and continued after it collapsed. Except in northern Italy, where town life survived, society became almost entirely rural. Forms of personal dependency among the nobility evolved from the patron-client relationships of Roman society, as well as from the personal bodyguards and military retainers of the German nobility.[2]

By the latter part of the first millennium the distinctive configuration of institutions we call Western feudalism had developed from these Roman and Germanic roots.[3] Here we consider social responses to homosexuality in feudal societies. We will be concerned primarily with feudalism as it existed in Western Europe, where the documentation is fullest, but for comparative purposes we will also examine homosexuality in Japan.

The German Heritage

We have already examined the evolution of attitudes toward homosexuality in the late Roman Empire; now we consider the German contribution to the medieval synthesis of the two traditions. At first sight, the sources that deal with German responses to homosexuality seem contradictory. Tacitus reports that it was the German custom to bury alive those guilty of *corpore infames* (bodily infamy) in a swamp.[4] His usage of this phrase in other con-

---

[1]The Germans had some slaves before they conquered Rome, but they were probably not numerous enough to be important antecedents of serfdom.

[2]Gummere (1892:261–69), P. Anderson (1974:130–31, 148, 160–63).

[3]Wiener (1915). The earliest description of an act of homage connected with the granting of a fief comes from Flanders in 1127 (Herlihy, 1970).

[4]*Germania* 12.

texts makes clear that he meant male homosexuality.[5] Much later, Salvian, a fifth-century presbyter of the church at Marseilles, described the Goths, Alans, Saxons, and Vandals as strictly chaste. Unlike the Romans, he added, the Vandals were not tainted by effeminacy, nor did they tolerate it.[6]

Alongside these reports we have others that imply much more positive views of homosexuality. Quintilian depicts the Germans as favoring it.[7] On the day of his baptism, Clovis, king of the Salian Franks from 481 to 511, confessed to this sin and received absolution for it.[8] Ammianus Marcellinus's late-fourth-century *History* has the Taifali, a tribe associated with the Goths, practicing pederasty with young boys until they earned adult status by killing a boar or a bear.[9] Procopius implies that the Heruli, whose young men had to serve their elders until they had proved their courage in battle, had a similar practice.[10] In fact, men's societies (*Männerbünder*) within which pederasty was practiced in connection with the transition from youth to manhood appear to have been common among the Indo-Europeans.[11] We have already seem comparable practices in ancient Greece and in Melanesia.

Tacitus tells of a quite different practice in his description of the worship of divine twins among the Naharvali, a people of the northeast region between the Oder and the Vistula, who, it is thought, later joined the Vandals:

> Among the Naharvali a wood consecrated to an ancient cult is to be seen. It is presided over by a priest dressed as a woman. The gods he tends, it is said, are according to a Roman interpretation Castor and Pollux: such is the value of these divine persons, and their name is Alcis. They have no statue and offer no sign of foreign influence; it is as brothers, as young men that they are worshipped.[12]

The kings of the Vandals served as priests in the worship of the two brother-deities.[13]

Cult transvestism persisted for centuries in Scandinavia, along with other pagan religious practices and a traditional way of life. Adam of

[5]D. J. Ward (1970a), Bleibtreu-Ehrenberg (1981:17).
[6]Salvian (1930:209–17), 7.6, 7.15.
[7]*Declamation de milite Mariano* 3.16 (Bleibtreu-Ehrenberg, 1981:36–37).
[8]Lever (1985:41).
[9]Ammianus Marcellinus (1935:443–45) 31.9.5.
[10]Procopius (1914:1.487, 2.14), Bremmer (1980), Bleibtreu-Ehrenberg (1981:43–45).
[11]Weiser-Aall (1927), Höfler (1938), Przyluski (1940), Widengren (1969:52), Bremmer (1980). The Irish had similar groups, but there is no evidence linking them with homosexual practices (McCone, 1986).
[12]*Germania* 43; Dumézil (1973a:115).
[13]Saussaye (1902:336), Dumézil (1973a:117–18).

Bremen, a church historian of the eleventh century, reports that ritual human sacrifices were carried out every nine years at Uppsala, during which obscene incantations were sung.[14] The nature of these incantations is suggested by Saxo Grammaticus, a Danish historian of the late twelfth century, who mentions that Starkather, a Dane, lived in Sweden "with the sons of Frø" (probably a reference to the royal family, which claimed descent from the God Frø, or Freyr) for seven years and then returned to Denmark,

> for, living at Uppsala in the period of sacrifices, he had become disgusted with the womanish body movements, the clatter of actors on the stage, and the tinkling of bells.[15]

In light of what we have learned about male-to-female transvestite priests in the service of the goddess in other societies, it is likely that these accounts derive from cult homosexuality, though it is not mentioned explicitly.

Numerous references to effeminacy and homosexuality in the Old Norse *Eddas* and Icelandic sagas show reactions of loathing similar to Starkather's.[16] Thus, when Odin insults Loki in the *Lokasenna*, one of the poems of the *Poetic Edda*, he recalls that:

> Eight winters you were in the underworld,
> a lactating cow and a woman,
> and there you bore children,
> and in that I find the marks of one who is *argr*.[17]

The terms *argr*, *ragr*, and *ergi* all refer to receptive male homosexuality, and carry connotations of cowardice and effeminacy. They were among the most powerful terms of abuse: under Norse, Icelandic, Swedish, and Langobardian law one could be outlawed simply for using these words.[18] With this meaning attached to receptive homosexuality, men could be humiliated by subjecting them to it.

Even a religiomagical context did not secure effeminacy from contempt. In the sagas of an inconclusive war between two groups of gods, the Aesir and the Vanir, Freya, one of the Vanir, came to live with the Aesir as a hos-

[14] Adam of Bremen (1959:208), *Gesta* 4.28; J. S. Martin (1972:57).
[15] Saxo Grammaticus (1979:1.172, 2.101), *Gesta Danorum* 6.5:9; see also Dumézil (1973a:115).
[16] Vanggaard (1972:76–81), Bleibtreu-Ehrenberg (1981:102–4), Sørenson (1983).
[17] Vanggaard (1972:77), Bleibtreu-Ehrenberg (1981:103). The word *argr* may be related to the Hittite *hurkilaš* (a type of demon) or to *hurkel* (a grave sexual crime such as bestiality or incest) (Puhvel, 1971).
[18] Hirschfeld (1914:535), Weisweiler (1944), Turville-Petre (1964:131), Dumézil (1969:271, 1973a:67 n. 14), Markey (1972), Vanggaard (1972:76–81), Pizarro (1979), Bleibtreu-Ehrenberg (1981:134), Gade (1984).

tage following a negotiated settlement. She taught Odin, an Aesir, the magical technique known as *seidr*:

> It was by this means that he could fathom the fate of men and of events still to come, and also to speak to men of their deaths or misfortunes or illnesses, and also to take away from men their intelligence or strength in order to give it to others. But the use of this magic is accompanied by so great a degree of effemination (*ergi*) that men (*viri, karlmonnum*) were of the opinion that they could not give themselves up to it without shame, so that it was to the priestesses (*gydjunum*) that it was taught.[19]

Except for Odin and Loki, the Aesir held *seidr* in contempt.[20]

The intensity of feeling against *seidr* may be gauged from an episode in another saga, the *Heimskringla*. When Haraldr of the Shining Locks learns that his son Rögnvaldr Rettilbeini had become a *seidr* master, he sent another son, who "burned his brother Rögnvaldr together with eighty *seidmenn*, and this action was much praised."[21]

It is more than a little puzzling that a practice associated with major deities (Freya, Odin) and institutionalized in a religious cult should be the subject of such profound contempt and violent repression. Several scholars have proposed solutions to the puzzle based on the observation that the Vanir and Aesir are associated with different realms of human concern and activity.[22] The Vanir are gods of fertility, prosperity, and sensual pleasure, while the Aesir are concerned with government and arms-bearing affairs (warfare, hunting). Some of these scholars interpret the war between the gods as an euhemeristic representation of an actual war between a neolithic farming population and a tribe of nomadic warriors; others, as an expression of latent tension between functionally differentiated strata (farmers and ruler-warriors) of early Indo-European society. In the former view, the war ended in compromise and political unification, but the religious and cultural differences between the antagonists persisted. In the latter view, these differences reflect the divergent values of the two social strata.

A reconstruction of Germanic social structure by Price points to the latter interpretation.[23] Among many German tribes, though not all, land was not

---

[19] *Ynglingsaga* 7 (Dumézil, 1973a:68; 1973b:26–48). *Seidr* is derived from *sei*, binding (Bleibtreu-Ehrenberg, 1981:88). Strömbäck (1935); see also Dumézil, 1973a:62) reconstructs the *seidr* ritual from Lapp and Siberian sources and finds that it closely resembles the ceremony described by Saxo Grammaticus.

[20] Dumézil (1973a:621), Bleibtreu-Ehrenberg (1981:153).

[21] *Heimskringla* 34; Dumézil (1973a:70).

[22] Philippson (1953), Turville-Petre (1964:156–60), Dumézil (1973a), Polomé (1974), Strutynski (1974), Bleibtreu-Ehrenberg (1981:55–144).

[23] Price (1969, 1974, 1980).

divided at death. Only the son who inherited his father's land could marry. Other sons left the homestead, underwent hazardous initiation rites at adolescence, and if they passed, joined a religious society or club of ranked warriors dedicated to Wotan. They wore animal skins, engaged in sword dancing, and spent their time hunting, fighting on foot, robbing, and in idleness. In fighting, they intimidated foes with their ecstatic, possibly drug-induced, frenzies. If they inherited the family homestead (e.g., through the death of a brother) they left the club, and only then were they allowed to marry. Otherwise they remained bachelors for life. Because women were expected to abide by strict rules of chastity and were punished severely for violating them, heterosexual outlets were virtually foreclosed. This division between farmers who could marry and hunter-warriors who could not may have had adaptive value in limiting population growth during the centuries when the German tribes failed to expand their agricultural lands by clearing forests. It is presumably within the warrior clubs that institutionalized pederasty was practiced. It is a reasonable inference that it had common antecedents with ritualized pederasty in archaic Greece.[24]

In either interpretation, discrepant attitudes toward male effeminacy originated in the differences in values between planters and hunters. *Seidr*, which involved sex change and homosexuality, was associated with the Vanir, or fertility function, and thus found a place among the planters. The Naharvali, whose transvestite priest Tacitus described, lived far from the border with Rome and attached less importance to military matters than to agriculture.[25] Professional soldiers often hold women and womanly things in contempt; and the low status of the goddesses among the Aesir compared to that of their counterparts among the Vanir[26] suggests that this was true of the Norse and German aristocratic warriors. To the latter, to be a woman, or like one, was to be an inferior being. Thus Flosi mocks Skarp Hedin in *Njal's Saga* by claiming that his beardless father Njal looks like a woman.[27] The sex change that was acceptable among the farmers was repugnant to the warriors devoted to the Aesir.

[24] Remarkably similar groups for unmarried men who either married and settled down or retained their membership were found in Norse (Weiser-Aall, 1927:44–45) and Irish Celtic society, where entry into the *fianna* occurred at about age fourteen, when fosterage ended (McCone, 1981). The sources do not discuss homosexuality within the *fianna*, only sexual license and rape, hunting, fighting, and extortion by youths living in the wild (much like Spartan youths). However, the priests may have been selective in what they reported.

[25] Polomé (1970). The twin gods the Naharvali worshiped appear in many Indo-European myths as differentiated: one responsible for the military function, the other for agriculture and fertility (Ward, 1970b). It is likely that the transvestite priests were particularly connected with the agricultural twin.

[26] Bleibtreu-Ehrenberg (1981:122).

[27] Vanggaard (1972:78–79).

Farmers are often reluctant to go to war because they are needed at home to tend crops. This reluctance was manifest in Scandinavian culture: Tacitus described the Suiones (Swedes), whose chief god was Freyr (a Vanir) as peace-loving,[28] and indicated that during the annual fertility ceremonies the Germans were required to put away all weapons. Warfare was prohibited during this period. Full-time warriors might have seen this antipathy to war as due to cowardice.

The American Indian cultures demonstrate that warfare and hunting need not always entail the subordination of women or the stigmatization of male effeminacy. But among the ancient Norse and German bachelor warriors they did. Their contempt for women may have been a psychological adaptation to enforced lifelong bachelorhood, necessitated by inheritance rules under conditions of land shortage.

Odin's acceptance of *seidr* remains curious; as an Aesir and a war god, he should have wanted nothing to do with it. Yet he became a practitioner. A passage in the *Havamal* provides a clue:

> I ween that I hung on the windy tree,
>   Hung there for nights full nine;
> With the spear I was wounded, and offered I was
>   to Othin, myself to myself.
> On the tree that none may ever know
>   What root beneath it runs.
> None made me happy with load or horn,
>   And there below I looked;
> I took up the runes, shrieking I took them,
>   And forwith back I fell.
> Then began I to thrive and wisdom to get,
>   I grew and well I was;
> Each word led me to another word,
>   Each deed to another deed.[29]

In one view, sacrifices to gods are always symbolic representations of the sacrificer, who gives up his self only to have it returned to him strengthened.[30] Here Odin sacrifices himself to himself, thus gaining the ability to understand the runes. A careful analysis of the sources for this myth demonstrates that Odin did not sacrifice his entire self, just his semen, which he had stored up before the ordeal through sexual abstinence.[31] Comparable techniques for gaining mystical power occur in Hindu mythology. In a warrior society, power is associated with masculinity, which se-

[28] Phillpotts (1967).
[29] *Havamal* 139–42, quoted in Bellows (1923:60–61).
[30] Beattie (1980), O'Keefe (1982:214–17).
[31] Tally (1974).

men represents. It stands for the essence of the male individual. Special powers are ingested by acquiring the semen of someone who already has these powers.

Because Odin was heterosexually active, he was in danger of depleting his semen, the source of his powers, and therefore he had to replenish his supply from time to time. The myths tell us that he did this by visiting corpses hanging from gallows. On these visits Odin drank the semen ejaculated by the hanged men.[32]

As an Aesir who could change his shape (usually into that of an animal),[33] and who gained arcane knowledge by swallowing semen, there was only a small step to changing sex and playing a female role in homosexual encounters. Moreover, though Odin was a war god, he fought with magic rather than physical prowess and thus had nothing to lose from feminization. His followers, who fought with muscle and magic, did.[34]

---

[32] Consistent with this interpretation, German folk tradition dating back to antiquity held that the mandrake which grew from the semen of gallows victims had magical powers, including the ability to confer fertility (Tally, 1974). This may be why the human sacrifices in Germanic fertility cults were often carried out by hanging (Glob, 1971). The provision in *Theodore's Penitential* 4.ii.3, c. A.D 670, forbidding the drinking of semen for magical purposes (D. S. Bailey, 1975:102 n. 1; Payer, 1984a), probably concerns related ritual practices, perhaps involving *seidr*.

[33] The warriors who fought under Odin's patronage clothed themselves in the skins of wolves (Odin's animal) or bears, and fought with the furor of ones possessed by the spirits of those animals (Davidson, 1967:100; Dumézil, 1969:10, 141). The English word "berserk" stems from the Old Norse *berserkir*, "having a bear garment," which referred to the uncontrollable frenzy of these animal-skinned fighters. Related practices can be identified in other Indo-European cultures. At initiation, Irish Celtic youths were given animal names, and old Irish literature refers to possession by animal frenzies and the changing of human shapes into those of wolves. The story of Romulus, founder of Rome (and a twin), who was suckled by a she-wolf and led bachelors in hunting and warfare is very likely derived from related customs. A Spartan equivalent is suggested by the name of the legendary Spartan lawgiver Lycurgus, "man of wolf deeds" (Reinhard and Hull, 1936; McCone, 1986, forthcoming). Gerstein (1974) shows that the werwolf (*warg*) was originally a *berserkir* whose uncontrolled wildness endangered his own society as well as the foe's. This social role may date back to the Hittites (Puhvel, 1971).

[34] Noting the many resemblances between Odin's powers and activities and those of the subarctic shaman, Bleibtreu-Ehrenberg (1981:99–102) concludes that shamanism was a third component of Indo-European religion, in addition to the two elements already mentioned here. The fertility-cult themes in Teutonic culture could have percolated up from the Near East in late antiquity, but could also have been acquired much earlier. Some recent work in historical linguistics suggests that the Proto-Indo-Europeans originated in the ancient Near East before 3000 B.C., a hypothesis that explains the existence of so many Semitic loan-words in the Indo-European languages (Bomhard, 1977; Gamkrelidze and Ivanov, 1985). De Vries's (1933:215–33) suggestion that Odin might originally have been hermaphroditic would certainly be compatible with this hypothesis. De Vries also suggests a linkage with the Athenian Oschophoria, a ceremony described by Farnell (1909:2.628ff.), in which boys dressed as girls. While this is possible, brief cross-dressing of youths on special occasions is sufficiently com-

As war became more important to the Germans, the male warriors and their culture became dominant, and the status of women declined.[35] Effeminacy and receptive homosexuality were increasingly scorned and repressed, along with the magical and religious practices associated with them. The effeminate homosexual came to be identified with the werewolf, the sorcerer, and the outlaw and was depicted as a foul monster.[36] The English words *ragamuffin*, originally the name of a demon[37] (derived from *ragr*, effeminate), and *bad* (originally *baedling*, effeminate), reflect this development.

At first this stigmatization did not extend to active male homosexuality. To take revenge on the disloyal priest Bjorn and his mistress Thorunnr in the *Gudmundar Saga*, "it was decided to put Thorunnr into bed with every buffoon, and to do that to Bjorn the priest, which was considered no less dishonorable."[38] Dishonorable to Bjorn, not to his rapists. In the *Edda*, Sinjotli insults Gudmundr by asserting that "all the *einherjar* (Odin's warriors in Valhalla) fought with each other to win the love of Gudmundr (who was male)."[39] Certainly he intended no aspersions on the honor of the *einherjar*. Then Sinfjotli boasts that "Gundmundr was pregnant with nine wolf cubs and that he, Sinfjotli, was the father." Had the active, male homosexual role been stigmatized, Sinfjotli would hardly have boasted of it.

If Procopius, who wrote in the early sixth century, is to be believed, even the passive role remained acceptable for youths. He tells how the Vandals captured Rome by selecting three hundred boys of good birth "whose beards had not yet grown, but who had just come of age," and sent them to Roman patricians to serve as house slaves,[40] a capacity in which they would have been subject to sexual exploitation.[41] On a predetermined day they killed their masters, facilitating the capture of the city. Evidently the Vandals' horror of effeminacy, on which Salvian commented,[42] did not preclude submission to pederasty when it was militarily advantageous—and probably in other circumstances.

The Christianity to which the Germans and Scandinavians converted

---

mon in kinship-structured societies that one would hesitate to draw a connection in the absence of stronger evidence.

[35] Boulding (1976:320).

[36] Gerstein (1974), Bleibtreu-Ehrenberg (1981:123).

[37] *Piers Plowman* B xvi.89, C xix.122, xxi.283.

[38] *Gudmundar saga dyra*, ch. 20, quoted in Gade (1986).

[39] Quoted in Vanggaard (1972:76).

[40] Procopius (1914:1.13–15), *The Vandalic War* 2.14–15.

[41] Scroggs (1983:39–40).

[42] Salvian (1930:26–27) was writing a century earlier. Unless the Vandals' morals changed a great deal in the subsequent century, Salvian was exaggerating their chastity. He is generally thought to have inflated the virtues of the pagans, the better to castigate the church for its failings.

was officially opposed to all forms of homosexuality.[43] Thus the distinction between active and passive roles dissolved.[44] The association among passive male homosexuality, *seidr*, and moral and physical monstrosity that developed among the pagan Germans as their way of life became increasingly military was extended under Christianity to all forms of homosexuality, and to all forms of magic except those practiced by Christian saints and priests.[45] This association between sorcery and sexual perversity was to persist well into the Middle Ages.

Germanic Law

As the seminomadic Germans settled down, they established monarchies and gradually absorbed Roman ideas. The *Leges Barbarorum*—the various legal codes of the Germanic kingdoms—were products of this exposure. Written in a barbarized Latin, they embody the customary laws of the German tribes. Committed to writing at various times between the late fifth and the ninth centuries, some betray evidence of Roman influence, while others are entirely free of it.[46] At first, the codes applied only to the German population in each territory, while Roman law remained in effect for the conquered Roman population; later they became applicable to both.

With a single exception, none of the early codes mentions homosexuality. The literary and historical sources suggest that, gender stereotypes aside, this is because there was no prejudice against it. In 744, for example, Saint Boniface, the Benedictine missionary, wrote to the king of Mercia, "the people of England have been living a shameful life, despising lawful marriages, committing adultery and lusting after the fashion of the people of Sodom."[47] *nor new a rf'a h homosonlity*

The sole exception is the law of Visigothic Spain. Shortly after King Chinaswinth issued the first territorial code for Spain (applicable to both Goths and Hispano-Romans), he introduced new legislation c. A.D. 650 providing castration for "those who lie with males, or who consent to participate passively in such acts."[48] This secular penalty was to be followed by

---

[43] Manselli (1975:48), Salisbury (1985b).

[44] The distinction between active and passive roles did not by any means disappear overnight. That it remained alive at the end of the sixth century is clear from Gregory of Tours's *Historia Francorum* 4.26(39), which tells how Count Palladius insulted Bishop Panthenium by calling him *mollem* and *effeminatum* (i.e., weak like a woman), who had many male lovers (*mariti*) (Pizarro, 1979). Some of the translations, e.g., Gregory of Tours (1927:147–48), obscure the homosexual themes of the accusation. The older role stereotypes persisted in secular literature well into the Middle Ages (Custer and Cormier, 1984).

[45] Dumézil (1973a:69), Bleibtreu-Ehrenberg (1981).

[46] T. J. Rivers (1977:11–38).

[47] Coleman (1980:131).

[48] *Lex. Visigoth.* 3.5.4.

excommunication. These penalties were later strengthened by a canon adopted at the Sixteenth Council of Toledo in 693 calling for degradation of clergy, followed by exile. Laymen were to receive a hundred lashes in addition. King Egica, who had convened the Toledo Council, supplemented this ecclesiastical legislation with an edict calling for castration, to be followed by execution.[49]

This legislation by no means indicates that the Visigoths were less accepting of homosexuality than the other Germanic peoples prior to their contact with the Roman world. The Visigoths had longer and more extensive contact with the Romans than any of the other Germans. Euric's code (of which only fragments survive), completed around 475, drew heavily on Roman sources. A generation later, Alaric issued a new code for the Roman population; it was prepared by a committee of jurisconsults, drew on the Theodosian Code, the *novellae* of the Western emperors, the *Institutes* of Gaius, and the *Sentences* of Paulus, and was submitted for approval to an assembly of Roman noblemen and priests.[50]

Contact with Byzantium was substantial during this period, particularly after Reccard converted to Catholicism in 587, and as a result there were extensive cultural borrowings.[51] The penalty of castration for male homosexuality, which was also imposed by Justinian, reflects Byzantine influence.

The texts of the laws suggest that religious considerations were paramount. The bishops were ordered to play an active role in their enforcement, and the edict of Egica cited the Bible as authority. Yet it was the kings, not the church, who took the initiative, and Bailey suggests that their motives may have been political.[52] The Visigothic kingdom was torn by persistent conflict (Arianism v. Catholicism, Romans v. Goths, rivalries over succession to the throne). In this atmosphere, a charge of homosexuality could have been an easy way to discredit an adversary.[53] Yet Visigothic kings freely executed their opponents, seemingly without the need to discredit them first. Moreover, an accusation of homosexuality could

[49] *Lex. Visigoth* 3.5.7; D. S. Bailey (1975:92–94), E. A. Thompson (1969:260), Bleibtreu-Ehrenberg (1981:232–33).

[50] Livermore (1971:121–22, 131), P. D. King (1972:9), T. J. Rivers (1977:20), Bleibtreu-Ehrenberg (1981:232).

[51] E. A. Thompson (1969:20–21), P. D. King (1972:12).

[52] D. S. Bailey(1975:94).

[53] Boswell (1980:175) speculates along related lines that the Visigothic rulers enacted stern measures against Jews and homosexuals to deflect social tensions stemming from the cultural diversity of the population. Even if this was so, the choice of these two groups still requires explanation. Just as there is no evidence of popular antagonism to those who engaged in homosexuality, so there is none of popular anti-Semitism (E. A. Thompson, 1969:208; Edward James, 1982:102–3).

discredit someone only if it were already thought bad, and it is unlikely that such was the case with the Goths, or the Celts living in Spain, or the Romans, whom Salvian describes as the lewdest of people.[54] Christian morality took root in the villages only slowly, and probably had little impact on popular pagan sexual mores during this period.[55]

Even if the Spanish bishops did not sponsor the antihomosexual legislation, the role of Christianity in its enactment should not be minimized. King Reccared had converted to Catholicism to gain control of the organizational and ideological resources of the church, hoping they would help him consolidate his rule. His successors depicted themselves as delegated by God to create a Christian society, and used law for this purpose. They summoned church councils and gave them their agendas. At some they presided. Participation was not restricted to bishops, but also included lay aristocrats and royal officials.[56] The king appointed the bishops. The passages in the antihomosexual edicts ordering the bishops to enforce secular law measure the extent of his power over the church. In a de facto sense, he was its head.[57] The kings may have assumed that role for political reasons, but having done so, they took their responsibilities seriously. Their antihomosexual edicts were part of a broader effort to foster Christian family and sexual morality.[58]

How systematically this legislation was enforced is something we do not know. Since implementation depended on clerical cooperation, which was not always forthcoming, enforcement may not have been systematic or vigorous.[59] Whatever enforcement there was came to an end soon, when the Moors overran Spain in 711.

The Frankish kings also sought to reconstitute their kingdom on a religious basis. In 742, Karlmann, the mayor of the palace, and son of Charles Martell, convened a council of bishops to obtain advice about how to establish the *"lex Dei et ecclesiastica religio"* for his *populus Dei.*[60] After deposing

[54] Salvian (1930:196) 7.7.
[55] Salisbury (1985b).
[56] Wallace-Hadrill (1967:123).
[57] Not until the papacy of Gregory VII was the principle of separation of church and state tenuously established. Until then, kings identified themselves as "vicars of Christ," while the pope only called himself "vicar of St. Peter" (Berman, 1983:87). The Ervigian Code, adopted toward the end of the seventh century, explicitly made the king God's agent on earth (P. D. King, 1972:23).
[58] Anti-Jewish legislation, designed to encourage conversions to Christianity, was a necessary component of this strategy, for religion could not serve as the basis of political authority or national unity as long as a substantial non-Christian minority remained (P. D. King, 1972:132, 157).
[59] P. D. King (1972:138), Boswell (1980:174–76).
[60] Ullman (1969:21).

the last of the Merovingian kings and taking the Frankish throne for himself, Karlmann's brother, Pepin the Short

> presented himself as minister of God responsible for recon-
> structing society according to Christian ideals. Foremost in his
> program was translating Christian teachings on marriage into
> secular legislation.[61]

Charlemagne and other Carolingian kings continued to refer to their subjects as "people of God" (implicitly substituting a religious for a national
identity), and issued capitularies (edicts) based on theocratic principles.
Several of Charlemagne's capitularies concerned sins against nature, sodomy, and homosexual relations among monks, but they prescribed no
penalties; violators were simply admonished to desist.[62]

This comparative mildness reflected the superficiality of the Gallic population's conversion to Christianity. The Franks, whom the Gauls converted,
were even more superficially Christian.[63] Though they called themselves
Catholics and subscribed to church doctrine, their ethics remained those of
a pagan, tribal society of warriors, remote from those of the New Testament.[64] The Frankish laws of marriage remained "remarkably free from the
influence of Christianity" under the Merovingians.[65] Polygyny, divorce,
and concubinage were all permitted. Abortion and sexual freedom for
women were not, but this had less to do with Christian morality than with
concern for population growth and the desire to eliminate feuds arising
from quarrels over women in a patriarchal society. In secular matters, a
man could do more or less what he wanted as long as he did not infringe on
the rights of other men.[66]

Between 823 and 828, most of the Spanish Mark was lost to rebel vassals
who had allied with the Moors; and in 828 the Vikings and Hungarians
mounted invasions against which an effective defense could not be organized. These calamities were universally regarded as divine retribution for

[61] Wemple (1981:2).

[62] D. S. Bailey (1975:94–95), Bullough (1976:353), Boswell (1980:177–78).

[63] G. F. Jones (1963:135–38).

[64] Even though organized pagan cults had all but disappeared from the Frankish kingdom
by the end of the sixth century, pagan rites and customs survived for some centuries in rural
areas, where the population was often only nominally Christian. Some of these customs involved male-to-female transvestism at New Year's festivals, probably a survival of earlier German transvestism associated with fertility ceremonies (J. B. Russell, 1972:57–68; A. Evans,
1978:69–71; Bleibtreu-Ehrenberg, 1981:236–37).

[65] Wemple (1981:75).

[66] Wemple (1981:41). As an example, even though "unnatural" intercourse was a serious sin
as far as the church was concerned, a woman who charged her husband before an assembly of
bishops and lay nobles with forcing her to have sex in a forbidden manner was turned away
without a remedy (Wemple, 1981:104).

sins. The Synod of Paris, meeting in 829, blamed them specifically on homosexuality, bestiality, and the survival of heathen practices.[67] Since the church itself was too weak to extirpate them, the assembly called on the king to stop these abuses.[68]

Encouraged by the theocratic visions of the Carolingian rulers, devout but dishonest Christians took advantage of the poor quality of official record-keeping to forge royal documents advancing the transformation of the realm into a corporate Christian kingdom. The *Donation of Constantine*, fabricated at the end of the eighth century, and the *Pseudo-Isidoran Decretals* from the mid-ninth, conceded land and power to the church on a large scale. The *False Capitularies* of Benedict Levita (a pseudonym meaning deacon), written between 847 and 852, are a product of the same workshop. Benedict published a collection of the capitularies of the Frankish kings from 569 to 829. Although some were authentic, most were derived from Roman legal sources, Bavarian and Visigothic customary law, and ecclesiastical texts (patristic writings, confession books, canons, and decretals), misattributed to the Carolingian rulers. Some of the capitularies advanced the political goals of the church, e.g., by maintaining that the bishops could judge an emperor, but that the emperor could not judge bishops. Others were intended to help eliminate immorality.[69]

Three of the forged capitularies mention homosexuality. The first two draw on the document issued by the Synod of Paris, and on the *novellae* of Justinian, to warn that homosexuality imperiled the continued existence of the kingdom and the church. Because of sins against nature, cities had been consumed by heavenly fire and swallowed up in Hell, and 40,000 Benjaminites put to the sword. Yet they mention no penalty other than repentance and temporary excommunication—the standard ecclesiastical penalty. The third capitulary went farther. Construing the Saracen invasion as God's punishment for sin, it called for the Roman penalty of burning to be reinstituted in cases of sodomy.

Although these forgeries carried little weight at first, in an era when precedent was considered legally important, the belief that they were authored by Charlemagne gave them greater influence later on.[70] They turned

---

[67]The synod also denounced blood vengeance and voiced grievances against the nobility. A military crisis of the late eighth century, also interpreted as a divine warning, had earlier led Charlemagne to issue the Capitulary of Herstal (A.D. 779) dealing with administrative, judicial, and ecclesiastical matters (Ganshof, 1965).

[68]M. Bloch (1961:1.54–55), Bleibtreu-Ehrenberg (1981:219–21).

[69]Ganshof (1955:57, 191, 1958:71), Ullman (1962:184–89, 1969:28–29, 43–70), Bleibtreu-Ehrenberg (1981:218–31).

[70]In the absence of an official edition of the royal capitularies, the forgeries were in great demand. The church kept them in circulation to legitimize its claims to land and power.

sodomites and other violators of Christian sexual morality[71] into traitors who bring on invasions and threaten the survival of the kingdom. Against such miscreants no penalty could be too severe.[72]

As in the reign of Justinian a few centuries earlier, sexual conduct had become a matter appropriate for public intervention because it posed a collective threat. There is little concern in the Visigothic legislation or the forged Carolingian capitularies with intent or subjectivity. This is the pattern expected for societies high on *group* and high on *grid* in Mary Douglas's scheme.[73] Unfortunately, it is difficult to characterize the Visigothic or Carolingian kingdoms in this way. Visigothic Spain was ethnically and religiously divided. Charlemagne extended the borders of his Empire by conquest, but was unable to bring about a strong sense of social cohesion based on membership. This inability points to another weakness in the group-grid scheme: it is static. Douglas takes as given whether a society is high in group or grid; but these characteristics are achievements whose accomplishment cannot be taken for granted. The character of a society—the degree of stratification or rigid role definition, and the kind of identifications that define group membership—can be the subject of social conflict. In establishing a state religion, the Visigothic rulers were trying to create an ideological basis for unity that nationality could not then provide. The forgers of the Carolingian capitularies do not appear to have been responding to massive grass-roots concern that sodomy would provoke divine wrath; the documents they circulated were attempts to create that concern in what appears to have been a largely indifferent population. There is no reason to think that this attempt was cynical; in all likelihood they believed the Bible and the Byzantine Christian documents that told them homosexuality was dangerous.

FEUDALISM AND HOMOSEXUALITY

Attempts by Charlemagne (emperor of the West from 800 to 814) and Otto I (Holy Roman Emperor, 962–973) to establish a unified administration over

[71] In addition to homosexuality, the second of the forged capitularies complained about adultery, fornication, incest, and illegitimate marriages, as well as the mistreatment of priests, and the theft and destruction of church property.

[72] Boswell (1980:177 n. 30), Bleibtreu-Ehrenberg (1981:218–26). Bleibtreu-Ehrenberg (1981: 228–29) notes that a seventh-century edict of Rothari and an eighth-century Salic law, both pre-Christian, specified that witches should be burned. Although this might suggest a possible pagan source for Benedict's forgeries, his capitularies do not accuse sodomites of witchcraft or sorcery. At best one might argue that the existence of a precedent making burning an appropriate penalty for serious crimes that threatened the community made Germans more receptive to the revival of the Roman penalty for Christian reasons at a time when external threat that could not be met militarily created a sense of impending doom.

[73] See chapter 5.

a vast territory were never more than temporarily successful. Unable to field an army of their own, the Carolingian rulers responded to the Arab invasions by granting land to knights in return for military service. In so doing, they established the linkage between benefice and vassalage that characterized European feudalism and at the same time weakened the state further. Civil wars of succession, followed by Norse and Magyar invasions, destroyed centralized government altogether. By default, local rule was assumed by a new aristocracy of armored knights, supported by serfs who owed labor services and paid rent in cash or kind, receiving protection in return.[74] Much of Europe thus came to be organized on a feudal basis.[75]

The developments that had given rise to asceticism in late antiquity were now long past. The collapse of the Roman Empire had not had the same meaning for the conquering Germans as for the defeated Romans. The urban lower and middle classes who had suffered in the economic collapse of the fourth century had ceased to exist in the new society of serfs and lords living on almost self-sufficient manors. The Roman citizenry, having lost the power to govern itself under the Empire, did little to resist the German invaders;[76] this was left to the army, made up mostly of mercenaries. By contrast, the armored warriors who lived in and around the fortified castles of medieval Europe were able to do so. They were therefore less attracted to passive contemplation or asceticism.

Tendencies in the direction of asceticism and passivity developed in response to the invasions of the ninth century; the forgeries of Benedict Levita show evidence of them. When the army could not be counted on to respond to the invasions, there was little to do but repent and pray.[77] However, as a decentralized feudalism emerged, the population was better able to defend itself, and the tendency toward disengagement from the tem-

---

[74]This abbreviated account is necessarily a gross oversimplification. Developments in Europe varied with time and place. A detailed survey cannot be presented here, but P. Anderson (1974) sketches the main dimensions of variation.

[75]Definitions of feudalism vary. Some scholars emphasize serfdom or the coerced extraction of surplus in the form of rent paid by those who possess and work the land; some consider vassalage and fealty among the knights to be the essence of feudalism; and some fail to single out any one attribute as critical (Coulbourn, 1956; M. Bloch, 1961; Hindess and Hirst, 1975: 221–22; Critchley, 1978). Although Marxists have usually defined feudalism as an economic system, in *The German Ideology* Marx and Engels (1975:176) define feudalism as "the *political* form of the medieval relations of production and intercourse." We take feudalism to be a political-military system, as this approach gives us more leverage in understanding homosexuality and social responses to it. The relationship between the manorial economy and feudalism as a political system is a subject that cannot be pursued here. The reader should, however, keep one thing in mind: having defined feudalism in this way, we cannot take for granted that feudalism prevailed everywhere in Europe during the Middle Ages.

[76]Ste. Croix (1981).

[77]M. Bloch (1961:1.55).

poral world of carnality was blunted. Moreover, the decentralization of politics and the administration of justice diluted the impact of national legislation (genuine or forged).

C. A. Tripp has remarked that when social survival depends on the personal traits of individual, competitive men, their traits become culturally prized and acquire erotic significance for men as well as women.[78] This was the case for medieval warfare, which featured hand-to-hand military combat with little or no central coordination.[79] In the *chansons de geste* the knight's highest goal was to win fame and glory by displaying personal valor in martial combat.

This stress on male virtues implied a corresponding lack of interest in women. In the *Song of Roland*, a French mini-epic given its final form in the late eleventh or twelfth century, women appear only as shadowy, marginal figures:

> The deepest signs of affection in the poem, as well as in similar ones, appear in the love of man for man, the mutual love of warriors who die together against odds, and the affection between the vassal and the lord or within the church, between two clergy, usually an older and younger.[80]

The *Song of Roland* is generally considered to reflect the values of the time in which it was written down, not necessarily those of its late-eighth-century setting. The work was composed for oral presentation and had to conform to popular values to appeal to audiences. The work was quite popular, not only in France but, in translation or in derivation, in neighboring Christian countries as well.[81] Thus its treatment of male relationships was probably not eccentric.

The chanson that commemorates the life of William Marshall (1145?–1219) also gives short shrift to women, while playing up male-male love. In it, King Henry II loves his page, who is his first cousin. After expelling William from his court for having an affair with his wife, Henry got rid of his wife and displayed great affection for William.[82] *NOT equal to homosexuality*

---

[78] Tripp (1973:68–69).

[79] G. F. Jones (1963:129), Verbruggen (1977:81–82).

[80] Bullough (1973b:165), paraphrasing C. S. Lewis (1959:9).

[81] G. F. Jones (1963:2–4).

[82] Duby (1986:48–54). Even the literature of courtly love, which is on its face heterosexual, contains strong overtones of homoeroticism. The knight's love for a married lady is supposed to inspire him to deeds of valor, but her beauty is never described. He is remarkably lacking in jealousy of her husband. Could it actually be the husband he wants? In *Lancelot*, Sir Gawain prays that God turn him into a beautiful woman so that he will be loved by the unknown knight (Marchello-Nizia, 1981; Duby, 1986:47). One specimen of lesbian troubador verse, from Provence, survives (Bogin, 1976:132–33, 176–77; Matter, 1986).

Arrangements for training knights would have encouraged the development of close emotional ties between them. A prospective knight left home at a young age and was taken into the household of an overlord, where he was raised with other future knights:

> Usually, the young noble youth was incorporated into a group of friends who were taught to love one another as brothers, who were led by an older man, and whose every waking moment was spent in each other's company. Sometimes these groups stayed together for as long as 20 years, from age 11 or 12 until 30 or so, when they were supposed to marry. Sometimes marriage was further delayed, for eligible women were not particularly plentiful.[83]

Primogeniture, adopted to prevent the fragmentation of landholdings, swelled the ranks of these groups with younger sons who had no land of their own, especially during the population growth of the eleventh century. They hoped to win wealth, land, and wife through knightly exploits.[84]

The bonds of affection that developed among companions, or between a youth and the overlord who raised him, were distinct from those of vassalage and were often stronger than ties of blood. Roland and each of the Twelve Peers in the *Song of Roland* had a special companion of this sort.[85] When Tristan went into exile with Isolde, he remembered with regret the young men he had trained for knighthood and feared that he might never be able to rejoin them.[86]

To be sure, deep affection and close emotional ties need not imply a sexual relationship; medieval sensibilities valued nonsexual friendships highly.[87] The French tale of the love of two kings, Amis and Amile, describes bonds of exceptional intensity without referring to sex at all.[88] When the king in Marie de France's *Lay of the Were-Wolf* embraced his knight, magically transformed from wolf into human shape, "and kissed him

---

[83]Bullough (1976:399–400); see also Duby (1968) and Verbruggen (1977:28–29).

[84]Ben-Ami (1969:55), Payen (1970:27–28), Verbruggen (1977:25), Goodich (1979:20–21). It is estimated that by the late Middle Ages men married about ten years after puberty, women about five years (Duby, 1962:1.208–19; Herlihy, 1974, 1983; Flandrin, 1976a:184–87; Shahar, 1983:228–29). I know of no estimates for earlier periods.

[85]Sayers (1971:37).

[86]Payen (1970:27–28). Absent such personal bonds, the receptive male role was stigmatized. Thus in Castile after the Reconquest, it was a terrible insult to say to someone that he had been fucked in the ass (or cuckolded); the *fueros* (law codes) prohibited such inflammatory name-calling (Dillard, 1984:170).

[87]Jaeger (1983).

[88]Boswell (1980:239–40). The eleventh-century "Legend of Boris and Gleb" is a Russian parallel (Karlinsky, 1976).

fondly, above a hundred times,"[89] he was not necessarily expressing erotic interest.

The heterosexual deprivation of young aristocratic males can also be exaggerated. Even if it is true that women eligible for marriage were in short supply, other women were not necessarily unavailable.[90] King Arthur's knights, who often displayed deep devotion to one another, managed many dalliances with women. Nevertheless, in the absence of vigorous repression, intense emotional ties can only increase the likelihood of sexual relations. There was, moreover, little internalized sense of guilt to restrain those who were tempted. The knightly literature of the day was concerned with sin not as the occasion for guilt, but as occasioning the loss of salvation;[91] the concern was practical, not moral.

There is evidence that homosexual relations did develop within aristocratic circles of young males. Duby notes that among the wandering groups of bachelor knights, "morals were far from strict. . . . When Roger and his companions left the household of Chester [in twelfth-century England] . . . Ordericus Vitalis describes them as coming back *quasi di flammis Sodomiae.*"[92] Duby points out that other contemporaries also portrayed these youth gangs as having "depraved habits." Contemporary historians take the prevalence of homosexuality within these groups as well established.[93]

Medieval writers commonly associated the male aristocracy with homosexuality. According to the satirist Walter of Chatillon, young noblemen learned homosexuality when they came to France to study. Kings Edward II, William Rufus, and Richard the Lion-Hearted of England, Frederick II of Germany, Philip II of France, and Conradin of Sicily were all linked with homosexuality, as were prominent members of the nobility, including Robert, duke of Normandy (brother of William Rufus) and William Atheling (son of Henry I of England). Although some of these attributions may have been mistaken, others were almost certainly accurate.[94] The example of Richard, a crusader, demonstrates that these attributions did not necessarily involve an effete, indolent aristocracy; they grew out of and were consistent with the life of a warrior devoted to hand-to-hand combat.

[89] Marie de France (1911:90).

[90] The restoration of town life in the high Middle Ages brought with it a tolerated population of women prostitutes (Burford, 1976; Otis, 1985). Less is known about sexual opportunities in the early Middle Ages, but the attention given to sex in the penitentials suggests that many who were not married chose not to abstain. The texts convey the impression of fairly free sexual expression among the newly converted peoples of Western Europe (Payer, 1984a:121).

[91] G. F. Jones (1963:89–90).

[92] Duby (1977:115).

[93] Payen (1970:27–28).

[94] Bullough (1976:398–400), Goodich (1979:11), Boswell (1980:228–32, 235).

Since it was the aristocracy that made secular law, we should expect the homophile tendencies that arose from its unique circumstances to have been free from legal prohibition. In fact, European secular law contained few measures against homosexuality until the middle of the thirteenth century.[95]

Feudal Japan

Feudal Japan provides us with the opportunity of verifying that similar social arrangements give rise to similar sexual customs and ideologies. Following the Heian period (A.D. 794–1185), political power in Japan shifted from the emperor to leading warrior families in the countryside, and a social order closely resembling that of feudal Europe emerged. Mounted and armored samurai were given land in return for military service to an aristocrat, in a relationship of lordship and vassalage. As in Europe, governmental administration and military affairs were decentralized, and subinfeudation introduced a hierarchy of allegiances. In combat, the samurai usually fought alone against a single opponent of comparable rank, the divided loyalties of the various samurai precluding any coordination of troops. By the twelfth century, an ethical code of chivalry (*bushido*) had developed, prescribing unqualified devotion and loyalty to the master.[96]

Male homosexuality was known in Japan even in the Heian period, and during the feudal age it flourished among the military aristocracy. A samurai warrior went to battle accompanied by a favorite youth, who also served as a sexual partner; for many he may have been the primary, though not necessarily exclusive, sexual outlet. Literary sources depict the relationships as highly romantic, sustained by undying loyalty. Sometimes samurais fought duels on behalf of their lovers. The relationships were not only accepted, but considered extremely desirable, especially in those regions of Japan where physical strength and military prowess were highly prized.[97]

Our expectation that the social organization of military combat in a feudal society is conducive to male homosexuality is fully confirmed. Homosexuality among knights was fully institutionalized in Japan—as far as we can

---

[95]That aristocrats were not personally antagonistic to male homosexuality is suggested by an episode in which Hugh Capet, ruler of France toward the end of the first millennium, encountered two men carressing in a corner of a church. He took no action against them (Lever, 1985:41–42).

[96]Reischauer (1956), Varley (1970:22–23, 29), Morton (1973:49–63). This was more true in Japan than in Europe, where contractual norms of reciprocal obligation qualified a vassal's allegiance to his lord. If the lord did not live up to his obligations, the vassal was excused from his. In Japan, a vassal's obligations were more absolute (M. Bloch, 1961:2.447).

[97]Jwaya (1902), Ebara (1927), M. Daniel (1959), De Vos (1969:269–70), Shiveley (1970), Varley (1970:103), Ihara (1972), Louis (1972:37–38), Childs (1977), Hirayama and Hirayama (1986).

tell, much more so than in Europe. The medieval European literature of knightly combat and chivalry (*chansons de geste, lais*) refers to homosexuality only occasionally, and when it does, the references are rarely favorable.[98] However, these literary works come to us from a time when attitudes toward homosexuality were already changing. Favorable references to homosexuality in the legends on which some of these works are based may well have been deleted in editing or disguised. The late medieval story in which Blancheflor visits Perceval at night and is invited "chastely" into his bed on account of the cold came from an earlier Celtic folktale in which the invitation was not chaste.[99] It may be that the homoeroticism that lies just under the surface in the literature of *amour courtois* is not more explicit because it was becoming less admissible.[100]

A comparison of feudal Japan and feudal Europe must take the role of organized religion into account. Soon after its arrival from China around A.D. 600, Buddhism came to dominate Japanese religious life. Buddhist monks were not allowed to have intercourse with women; but, as male partners were not explicitly prohibited, many monks took youthful male lovers, a practice that was considered quite acceptable.[101] The Jesuit missionary Francis Xavier registered his shock at the indifference of the populace to the open homosexuality of the Buddhist priests on the occasion of his visit to Japan in 1549.[102] Legal codes of the period do not even mention homosexuality.[103]

The Medieval Church

Though the medieval Roman Catholic church continued to value sexual continence, it also maintained the qualified acceptance of sexual activity endorsed by Saint Augustine.[104] This position, a legacy from the early church, was of course radically antagonistic to homosexuality. That the earlier hostility persisted into the Middle Ages is clear from the penitentials.

[98] R. Levy (1948), Herman (1976).

[99] G. R. Taylor (1954:4).

[100] Marchello-Nizia (1981).

[101] (Childs, 1980). Chinese Buddhism considered homosexuality to be a minor transgression, no worse than adultery or transvestism (Eberhard, 1967:29–32; Bullough, 1976:294–95). Japanese Buddhism appears to have disregarded it altogether. Karlen (1971:231) raises the possibility that Japanese monastic homosexuality was a manifestation of temple prostitution, but that is most unlikely. Temple prostitution in the ancient Near East involved gender transformation and service to paying clients. Monastic homosexuality in Japan was transgenerational, not transgenderal.

[102] Pinkerton (1811:629–30), Jwaya (1902), Varley (1970:103), Karlen (1971:231), Spence (1984:224).

[103] J. C. Hall (1979).

[104] d'Avray and Tausche (1980), Cadden (1985).

These booklets were manuals for confessors, to be used as guides in the imposition of penances for different sins. They first appeared in the Celtic churches of Ireland in the sixth century and then spread to England, France, Germany, and Italy. Possibly based on a monastic practice, they mark a transition from public penance, permitted only once in a lifetime, to a more private penance, based on confession.[105] Several dozen of the penitentials have survived.

Taking the penitentials as a whole, 4 to 8 percent of the rules concern homosexuality. This is a substantial proportion, but not so high as to suggest an extraordinary obsession with the subject. Several mention lesbian practices, but most discuss only male homosexuality. Treatment of the subject differs from that in biblical or patristic literature in its detail. Typically, there are separate provisions for different methods of stimulation (mutual masturbation, interfemoral intercourse, fellatio, anal intercourse); and penalties are graded according to the age of the participants, their clerical rank, whether involvement was casual or habitual, and the role played in the episode (active or passive).[106] Priests obviously encountered, and were familiar with, a wide range of homosexual practices among their parishioners.

The penitentials vary widely in the penances they assign. The *Penitential of Theodore*, written by the seventh-century archbishop of Canterbury, specifies a penance of ten years for fornication with a male, while the twelfth-century *Penitential of Thorlac Thorhallson* (the bishop of Skalholt, in Iceland) calls for penances of nine to ten years in cases of homosexuality and bestiality. However, the *Corrector and Physician* of Burchard of Worms is far more lenient.[107] Sometimes inconsistent penalties for seemingly identical offenses appear within the same penitential. Thus the seventh-century *Penitential of Cummean* specifies penance for a year for men guilty of a first homosexual offense and two years for a repetition; but in another passage we are told that it is to be two years if they are boys, three or four years if men, and seven years if it is habitual. The penances were compiled from earlier materials whose disagreements are preserved in the compilations or were based on earlier decisions in specific cases where penalties differed for reasons not stated in the texts. No authorities are cited for the penalties, nor are reasons for them given. The penitentials were created for practical purposes, not theoretical ones.[108]

---

[105] Watkins (1920:2.761–63), Payer (1984a:7).

[106] McNeill and Gamer (1938), D. S. Bailey (1975:100–107), Gauthier (1977), Payer (1984a).

[107] McNeill and Gamer (1938:184–85, 335, 355). Scholars have identified two traditions of ecclesiastical discipline in the penitential literature, one harsh, the other lenient. Burchard is a representative of the latter (Oakley, 1932).

[108] McNeill and Gamer (1938:114), D. S. Bailey (1975:103–4), Bullough (1976:360–63), Payer (1984a).

Penances could involve restriction of diet, prayer, attendance at mass, or an act of public contrition, such as standing barefoot at the church door or going on a pilgrimage. Although the duration of penances may be taken as an indication of the relative gravity of different sins, they did not always last as long as the text indicates, for some penitentials permitted the commutation of penances through prayer or the giving of alms.[109] For example, the *Penitential of Thorlac Thorhallson* permits fasts to be commuted by saying the paternoster fifty times or by performing a hundred genuflexions a day. Some penitentials do *not* explicitly authorize commutation, but the practice may have gone on informally.[110]

Even where the penalties were severe and the sin was regarded as grave, the penitent was still regarded as a member of the community, not as an alien or a monstrosity. He had erred, and required chastisement, but in accepting penance he demonstrated his commitment not to deviate again from the straight and narrow. After completing his penitence he was reconciled with the community, not expelled from it. Like all men, he was a sinner, but he was to be forgiven if he repented. He was not "a homosexual"—a distinct type of person—but someone who had engaged in a homosexual act.

The Carolingian monarchs considered penitentials so essential that they ordered every priest to have one, but the bishops were less enthusiastic. Several ninth-century synods condemned the penitentials for their inconsistencies, lack of ecclesiastical authority, and liberality in allowing commutations; in 829 the Council of Paris went so far as to order them burned.[111] There was little call for penitentials in Spain, where collections of the canons adopted at earlier church councils were readily available, or in Gaul, where councils were held regularly, but in regions where missionaries worked, e.g., the British Isles and Germany, the demand for them was so great that suppression was impossible. Regino, bishop of Prüm, whose compilation enjoyed great authority in the tenth century, wanted bishops to ensure that every priest had a copy. A council of Mainz ordered priests to get them, and a similar requirement was imposed on priests in pre-Norman England.[112] Penitentials were also in use in Verona.[113]

Boswell has argued that the impact of the penitentials was limited because their use was largely confined to the vicinity of cathedrals and to areas controlled by religious orders and because few laypersons attended

[109] Payer (1984b).
[110] McNeill and Gamer (1938:355), Oakley (1932), Boswell (1980:180–82).
[111] Oakley (1932), McNeill and Gamer (1938:26–27), Frantzen (1979), Boswell (1980:182), Payer (1984a:9).
[112] Oakley (1923:14).
[113] Lea (1896:102).

confession regularly.[114] Indeed, in the sixth and seventh centuries, when
the penitentials were first issued, the church had great difficulty in per-
suading sinners to confess and submit to penance. Many waited until they
were about to die to confess. Only in 1215 did the Fourth Lateran Council
require confession at least once a year.[115] The trend toward greater leniency
over time may well have been a strategy to reduce the disincentives to confess. Nonetheless, the fact that so many penitentials were compiled suggests that there was considerable demand for them on the part of priests.

Although the penitentials were intended primarily for guidance in private penance, their use was not limited to voluntary confessions, but also
governed the coercive imposition of penances on recalcitrant sinners. In
802, Charlemagne ordered his counts and *missi dominici* to force sinners to
perform the penances assigned by their bishops when they refused to do
so voluntarily.[116] Thus the impact of the pentitentials need not have been
small; their cumulative impact on moral standards over a period of several
centuries may have been profound.[117]

Even if the organizational weakness of the early medieval church limited
the immediate impact of the penitentials, they nevertheless show us the
moral standards the compilers wanted to set. The fact that the penitentials
were not handed down by a remote superior, but reflected the "grass
roots" sentiments of the priesthood, strengthens their value as indicators
of popular morality. While the penances for homosexuality vary in the penitentials, none suggests that it is not sinful, and most regard it as among
the more serious sins.[118]

Perhaps more to the point, the severe penances for homosexual offenses

[114] Boswell (1980:182).

[115] Lea (1896:110–11), Oakley (1937, 1938). This requirement was by no means novel; many
bishops had earlier ordered regular confession; the council's decision simply gave the requirement greater authority (Teatler, 1977:20–22). Nevertheless, in much of Europe, observance
may have been lax for the uncloistered population (Lenman, 1984).

[116] Lea (1896:107).

[117] Oakley (1937).

[118] Boswell (1980:180) is somewhat misleading in suggesting that "viewed comparatively,"
homosexuality "appears to have been thought less grave than such common activities as
hunting." He cites in support of this claim the eighth-century penitential of Pope Gregory III
in which the penance for priests who went hunting was to be three years, while that for male
homosexual acts ranged from one to ten years, depending on circumstances. But hunting was
not a sin at all for laymen, and the penalty for homosexual activity on the part of a priest was as
low as three years only for those ignorant of its gravity. For the others, the penance was to be
seven years or ten, not exactly less than the three imposed for hunting (Bullough, 1976:
362–63). Boswell is also misleading in asserting that only long after the eighth century did the
penitentials specifically deal with homosexual acts among the unmarried. The seventh-
century *Penitential of Cummean* (an Irish abbot) specifically discusses homosexual acts among
boys, as does the *Penitential of Pope Gregory III*.

are matched in a number of the penitentials by equally severe penances for heterosexual sins. Thus the Irish *Penitential of Cummean* calls for seven years' penance for men guilty of habitual homosexual practices (less for a first offense) and seven years' penance for heterosexual adultery. The book of ecclesiastical discipline issued by Regino of Prüm specifies a penalty of three years for anal intercourse whether the anus is that of a male or a female and also three years for heterosexual fornication. Similarly, the *Book of David* (c. 500–525) states that those who have committed fornication with a woman who has been vowed to Christ or a husband, or with a beast or a male "for the remainder of their lives dead to the world shall live unto God"—presumably in perpetual encloisterment. The *Penitential of Theodore* requires three years' penance if a woman practices vice with another woman—or with herself and also demands equal maximum penalties of fifteen years in cases of heterosexual or homosexual fornication.[119]

There are other penitentials in which harsher penances are imposed on those guilty of sodomitical fornication than on those who commit the conventional kind,[120] but these references to sodomy do not necessarily concern homosexuality alone. In the eighth century, the Venerable Bede referred to anal intercourse with a wife as a sodomitical crime, and later church authorities also adopted this usage.[121] Many of the references to sodomy or to oral sex in the penitentials suggest that the authors had heterosexual contacts in mind. The penalties for these heterosexual offenses are no less severe than those for homosexual ones. For example, the *Penitential of Theodore* demands fifteen years of penance in the worst cases of unnatural intercourse with a wife (*"si in tergo nupserit"*).[122] As in the early church, homosexuality was not the primary category for distinguishing acceptable sex from unacceptable; the principal distinction had to do with the potential for conception. As applied to sexual acts, homosexuality was a subsidiary category of nonreproductive sex.

The attitudes of individual churchmen varied quite widely. Some were quite punitive. We have already mentioned Benedict Levita, who in the mid-ninth century forged a Carolingian capitulary calling for "sodomites" to be incinerated. However, this was exceptional for its time. Later, in the middle of the eleventh century, Peter Damian railed against homosexuality, particularly among priests. Many sinners, he insisted, escaped serious

---

[119] McNeill and Gamer (1938:102–3, 1973), Bieler (1963:61), D. S. Bailey (1975:105–6), Roby (1977), Boswell (1980:182–83), Payer (1984a:170 n. 110), Gade (1986).

[120] The seventh-century *Penitential of Columban* and the eighth-century *Burgundian Penitential* treat homosexual infractions more severely than heterosexual ones (McNeill and Gamer, 1938; Bullough, 1976:361; Payer, 1983:29, 41).

[121] Noonan (1966:166).

[122] McNeill and Gamer (1938:197).

penalty by confessing to priests who were also their lovers. In his *Book of Gomorrah*, he urged Pope Leo IX to establish severe uniform penances to be imposed on everyone, without mitigation. Clerics were to be expelled from their orders for a single violation.

On the whole, though, less repressive views prevailed. Alcuin, an Anglo-Saxon scholar at the court of Charlemagne (and later abbot of Tours) deplored adultery and incest in his writings, but said nothing about homosexuality.[123] Although his silence may have reflected only his own romantic feelings toward his male students,[124] Peter Lombard, the twelfth-century Italian theologian and bishop of Paris, who is not similarly suspected, also said virtually nothing about homosexuality, though he discusses other sexual sins in his writings.[125] Saint Anselm, the twelfth-century archbishop of Canterbury, urged that the ecclesiastical penances for homosexuality adopted at the Council of London in 1102 be moderated because "this sin has been so public that hardly anyone has blushed for it, and many, therefore, have plunged into it without realizing its gravity."[126]

The homophilic poetry of the tenth and eleventh centuries strongly suggests that the moderate position articulated by Anselm was the dominant one. Latin poets, many of them monks, wrote unselfconsciously of their romantic feelings toward men or boys.[127] Two examples are particularly noteworthy because they were written by men who either were or were about to become bishops. Marbod, who lived in the eleventh or early twelfth century, headed the school attached to the cathedral at Angers, and later became the bishop of Rennes, wrote:

> My mind did stray, loving with hot desire . . .
> Was not or he or she dearer to me than sight?
> But now, O winged boy, love's sire, I lock thee out!
> Nor in my house is room for thee, O Cytherea!
> Distasteful to me now the embrace of either sex.

His contemporary, Baudri, abbot of a monastery and later an archbishop in Britanny, wrote:

> This their reproach: that wantoning in youth,
> I wrote to maids, and wrote to lads no less.

---

[123] G. R. Taylor (1965).

[124] Boswell (1980:188–91).

[125] Goodich (1979:32–33).

[126] H. Ellis (1936:40), H. M. Hyde (1970), D. S. Bailey (1975:125).

[127] P. S. Allen (1928:149–51), Curtius (1953:114–16), Dronke (1968:1.195–201, 218–19, 2.495), Bullough (1976:370–72), Herman (1976), Goodich (1979:11), Boswell (1980:235–39, 370–74), Stehling (1983, 1984), Kuster and Cormier (1984). Some romantic verse written by nuns to one another has also survived; see Southern (1953:24), Dronke (1968:1.225–26, 2.478–81), Boswell (1980:220–21), Hart (1980:105–6), Matter (1986).

> Some things I wrote, 'tis true, which treat of love;
> And songs of mine have pleased both he's and she's.[128]

Evidently, Baudri was being reproached for his youthful indiscretions; probably they were considered inappropriate for someone who had become an abbot. He does not even hint that his homosexual interests were considered more objectionable than his heterosexual ones. Neither poet shows fear of being punished for confessing to past homosexual interests or intimates that it was wrong to have had them. Some of the homophile poetry of their day circulated widely, and there is no evidence that its authors suffered from the publicity.

Boswell has identified this poetry as the product of an urban-based male homosexual subculture distinct from that of the military aristocracy.[129] It flourished particularly among clergy and university students; its literary products were concerned with beauty and romance and draw on classical sources. The extent of this subculture, and its freedom from repression, can be gauged from the comment of Henry, abbé of Clairvaux, to Pope Alexander III, that "ancient Sodom is reborn from its ashes,"[130] and from Jacques de Vitry's description of Paris in 1230 as filled with sodomites.[131] At the start of the next century, Dante had his teacher, Brunetto Latini, in hell for sodomy, comment on the large number of clerks and famous men of letters there with him because they had committed the same offense while they lived.[132]

In the early part of this period, the church still exercised exclusive jurisdiction over homosexuality. Evidently it lacked the will or the capacity to

---

[128] Curtius (1953:115–16) gives both poems in the original and in translation.

[129] Boswell (1980:236–66). The application of the term "subculture" to medieval urban homosexual life is problematic. In sociology this term refers to a variant version of a dominant culture that is socially learned and transmitted. The development of a distinct argot in this instance is suggestive, but Boswell does not demonstrate that the specialized terms were restricted to a subset of the population. Richard of Devizes lists *molles*, *mascularii*, and *pusiones*, all words with homosexual connotations, as London outsiders in his 1192 *Chronicon de tempore regis Richardi Primi*, but it is unknown how widely these terms were used, or whether they would have been recognized by those to whom he applied them. The existence of male homosexual brothels in France tells us something about the demand for homosexual partners (though some of the quotations Boswell interprets as referring to prostitution could as easily be read as referring to sexual relations between patrons and clients), but tells us little about the clients and their self-concepts. Literary defenses of homosexual desire and relationships do suggest a consciousness and sexual ideology at odds with that of the church. But the jocular poetry of late-thirteenth-century Siena describes a social world in which gamblers, prostitutes, drunkards, and sodomites mix freely. Here there is a subculture of marginality, not one based on homosexuality (Marti, 1956; Dall'Orto, 1983; Johansson, 1984b).

[130] Lever (1985:41).

[131] Quoted in Karlen (1971:85) and Courouve (1980).

[132] *The Inferno*, canto 15, 106–8.

deploy punitive measures effectively enough to destroy the social world of medieval male homosexuality.

THE GROWTH OF REPRESSION

Hostility toward homosexuality intensified during the twelfth and thirteenth centuries. It came in part from ecclesiastical sources, but was not confined to the clergy, for some of the secular literature of the twelfth century—the epic *Eneas*, the *Lai de Lanval* of Marie de France, the fabliau *Der Prestre et du chevalier*—shows that laymen viewed homosexuality with revulsion. Alain of Lille's twelfth-century *De planctu naturae* (The Complaint of Nature) condemns homosexuality, along with other sexual vices, on philosophical grounds, without invoking religious arguments. Other literature of the period, such as the *Roman de Renart*, takes a less serious (but hardly affirmative) view of homosexuality[133]—a sign that opinions were still in flux. The thirteenth-century *Roman de la rose* contains a long diatribe against sodomites, who are denounced for their sterility.[134]

The literature of the period often linked male homosexuality with Islam or religious nonconformity.[135] As early as the tenth century, German writers depicted Christian men as facing martyrdom rather than submit to Arab sexual demands.[136] The perceived association between Islam and homosexuality was strengthened as the Crusades and the reconquest of Spain brought Christians into protracted conflict with the Arab world. Propaganda on behalf of the First Crusade at the end of the twelfth century accused the Turks of homosexuality and also heterosexual rape. At the end of the thirteenth century, William of Adam argued that trade with Moslem Egypt should be restricted on the grounds that Christian children were sold into slavery there and forced to become male prostitutes.[137]

The association between heresy and homosexuality dates to the early twelfth century, when the Henricians were accused of immorality with women and boys. Around the same time, heresy accusations from the French village of Bucy-le-long featured men having intercourse with women from behind, as well as men with men and women with women. The confessions of a thirteenth-century heretic describes a cult whose ritual involved an orgy at which intercourse "*masculi in masculos et feminae in feminus*"

---

[133] Herman (1976).

[134] Dynes (1985c). This is also a theme in an anonymously edited collection of verse denunciations of the growing male homosexual urban subcultures translated by Boswell (1980:261–63).

[135] Boswell (1980:279–82).

[136] Goodich (1979:3).

[137] N. Daniel (1979:153, 223–25). From A.D. 1249 on, Egypt was ruled by the Mamlukes, a foreign military caste. To preserve their isolation from the native Arab population, they imported boys from Central and Eastern Europe for purposes of pederasty (S. O. Murray, 1987g).

took place.[138] In the early fourteenth century, charges of homosexual initiation rites and more general homosexual promiscuity figured in the prosecution of the Templars, a monastic order of knights, for heresy and sacrilege.[139]

As Robert Lerner comments, it is hardly conceivable that all the charges of licentiousness leveled at the heretics were true.[140] Most of the documents that describe the sexual beliefs and practices of heretical sects were written by their enemies, and many were probably smear attempts, listing everything orthodox Christians were supposed to abhor. However, some of the accusations, such as those directed at the Albigensians, may have had a factual foundation. The Albigensian heresy originated in Bulgaria, where Bogomil, an early-tenth-century priest, developed a dualistic religion with roots in Manichaeanism, a Gnostic religion of late Roman antiquity. Bogomil's followers, who called themselves Cathars, appeared in France in the mid-eleventh century, disappeared for fifty years, and then reemerged as an organized presence in the twelfth century. The Cathars considered life to be evil, and thus condemned procreation. Although the elite *perfecti* were reported to be celibate, the "believers" were allegedly free to practice forms of intercourse that could not lead to conception. Although sex was considered sinful, forgiveness could be attained by undergoing the simple ritual *consolamentum*, after which abstinence was required. Most believers waited until just before death before taking this step.[141] The English word "buggery," a corruption of "Bulgarian," reflects these medieval beliefs about the Cathars. Initially the French form, *bougerie*, referred to the heresy, but later took on the connotation of the sexual practice believed to be associated with the sect.[142]

Church Policy

The highest levels of the church hierarchy responded cautiously to the growth of hostility toward homosexuality. When Peter Damian demanded

[138] Karlen (1971b), Bullough (1974b), J. B. Russell (1972:95), A. Evans (1978:55), Goodich (1979:7). Witchcraft cults were also accused of holding orgies in which incubi and succubi had intercourse with humans, but it was usually heterosexual (J. B. Russell, 1972:219, 239, 250). Where homosexuality is mentioned, it is usually in a nonexclusive context. Thus Pope Gregory IX's letter to King Henry of Germany, written in 1232, describes an alleged witchcraft cult in northern Germany in which, after a banquet and ceremony, "the lights are put out and those present indulge in the most loathsome sensuality, having no regard to sex. If there are more men than women, men satisfy one another's depraved appetites (Kors and Peters, 1972:49; see also A. Evans, 1978:56).

[139] Legman (1966), Partner (1982).

[140] R. E. Lerner (1972:10–34).

[141] J. B. Russell (1965:192–203), Karlen (1971b), Bullough (1974b), Noonan (1966:180–89), A. Evans (1978:52–61).

[142] Some passages in thirteenth-century secular legislation, such as the *Coutume de Touraine-*

a crackdown on homosexuality among the clergy in the middle of the eleventh century, Pope Leo IX was less than enthusiastic. Although he agreed that it was a grave sin that could not be ignored, he reminded Damian that justice must be tempered with mercy and serious penalties reserved for the worst cases. For the next fifty years, complaints about homosexuality were rare and failed to evoke any institutional response from the church beyond the system of penances long in effect. Told that the man named to be bishop of Orleans was the lover of the archbishop of Tours, Pope Urban II did nothing to stop the installation at the end of the eleventh century.[143]

Several of the twelfth-century church councils did adopt measures dealing with homosexuality. In 1102, the Council of London threatened to excommunicate "those who commit the shameful sin of sodomy" until they confessed and showed penitence. Clerics were to be degraded and laymen were to lose their legal status (presumably, free men were to be forced into serfdom). Except for monks, who came under the authority of their abbots, only the bishop could grant absolution. The council was held shortly after the death of William Rufus and may have been a response to debauchery at the royal court during his reign.[144]

Eighteen years later, in the kingdom of Jerusalem, the Council of Nablus, in which both clergy and royal officials participated, stipulated that sodomites were to be burned, though those who confessed before being accused were to be spared. The penalty, which is almost unique in its severity in the twelfth century, reflects familiarity with Roman law, which was being rediscovered at that time.[145]

The circumstances of the crusader states suggest an explanation for this severity. The crusaders had come without women, and vigorous attempts were made to prevent them from socializing with Moslems and Byzantine Christians. Fear that, in the absence of Roman Catholic women, the Crusaders would turn to Moslem or Byzantine men must have motivated the

---

Anjou, the *Livres de Jostice et de Plet*, and the *Coutumes de Beauvoisis*, have occasionally been interpreted as dealing with homosexuality, though a careful reading makes clear that the target was heresy, not sex (Philippe de Remi, 1842:1.157, 2.85; D. S. Bailey, 1975:141–42).

[143]D. S. Bailey (1975:111–14), Bullough (1976:363–64), Goodich (1979:28–31), Boswell (1980:210–15).

[144]D. S. Bailey (1975:124), Bullough (1976:383), Goodich (1979:42), Boswell (1980:215–16). Boswell (1980:229–30) questions the usual identification of Rufus as a homosexual, but not the general atmosphere of sexual license that a number of contemporary sources attributed to his entourage. It was in response to the measures adopted at this council that Anselm, quoted earlier in this chapter, cautioned moderation and possibly suppressed the publication of the decree (Boswell, 1980:216).

[145]Even earlier, the Frisian *Sendrecht*, promulgated in the eleventh century, provided that someone guilty of "breaking the law of Octavianus and Moses and the whole world" was to be given a choice of being burned, buried alive, or castrating himself (Gade, 1986).

legislation. Since the Moslems were a subject population religiously tied to enemy forces, sexual relations with them would have threatened the cohesion and loyalty of the ruling Catholic minority. To prevent this would have required only a prohibition against non-Catholic partners, but religious considerations, made more salient by the conflict with the Moslems, required the broader prohibition.[146]

The legislation adopted at the Council of Nablus applied only locally and is thus significant more as a harbinger of future repression than for its immediate influence. The Third Lateran Council of 1179, however, was ecumenical. Citing passages in both Old and New Testaments, it adopted a canon against "incontinence which is against nature" and provided penalties of degradation from office and encloisterment for clerics, as well as excommunication for laymen—a penalty far milder than had been adopted at Nablus. Pope Gregory IX made this provision a permanent part of common law, and it was reiterated by many thirteenth-century synods, a number of which declared sodomy to be a sin that could be absolved only by a higher ecclesiastical authority, such as a bishop.[147]

Under Pope Innocent III (1198–1216), the twelfth-century penalty for heresy was increased from exile and confiscation of property, to death.[148] Then, in 1233, Pope Gregory IX created the Inquisition (Holy Office) to coordinate the repression of heresy. As heretics were believed to practice sodomy, the Inquisition gained jurisdiction over sodomy cases as well as heresy. At first it appears to have concerned itself with sodomy only where heretical beliefs were at stake,[149] but later, as antihomosexual sentiment grew, it was less restrained. Where given a free hand, as in Spain, it played an active role in the prosecution of homosexual activity.[150] Inquisitors inter-

---

[146]Ben-Ami (1969:119), D. S. Bailey (1975:95, 97), Goodich (1979:42–43), C. Davies (1982). In relation to Mary Douglas's scheme for explaining sexual ideology (which we reviewed in chapter 5), the kingdom of Jerusalem seems best classified as one that was high on *group* (because the distinction between Roman Christianity and other religions was so important), and high on *grid* (its social structure was formally feudal). This leads to the prediction that violations of ritualized behavior codes embodying ascetic norms would have been seen as threats to the community. The prediction is confirmed, at least in the retrospective view of the local church officials, for the Council of Nablus opened with a sermon that attributed a recent military defeat at the hands of the Saracens to sins of the flesh (D. S. Bailey, 1975:96; Goodich, 1979:42). This explanation of the defeat was, of course, one that was in the interest of the church to promote; it provided external, objective confirmation of the necessity of observing the moral standards taught by the church. It did this, moreover, without criticizing the military leadership or its tactics. The defeat would, of course, have intensified feelings of vulnerability to betrayal.

[147]D. S. Bailey (1975:95), Bullough (1976:384), Gauthier (1977), Goodich (1979:43, 46), Boswell (1980:277).

[148]Kidd (1933:40).

[149]Boswell (1980:285–86).

[150]Perry (1980:132).

rogated and tortured suspected sodomites, then delivered those found guilty to the secular authorities to be executed.

Secular Legislation

Beginning in the mid-thirteenth century, French secular legislation adopted stiff new measures against homosexual relations. *Li livres de jostice et de Plet,* probably written around 1260 in Orleans, called for the amputation of the testicles of first-time male offenders, the removal of the penis for a second offense, and burning of third-time offenders. Women were to be mutilated for the first two offenses and burned for a third.[151] The *Coutumes de Beauvoisis* provided that those guilty of "sodomiterie" shall be burned (along with those who err against the faith and refuse to acknowledge the truth).[152] Other customals (collections of customary law) which had adopted measures against *bougerie* were soon interpreted as having made sodomy a capital offense—even though this may not have been the original intent.[153]

Parallel developments took place outside France. For example, the *Siete Partidas,* drawn up under Alfonso the Wise of Castile and Leon around 1265, provided that those found guilty of male homosexual acts be castrated and then stoned to death.[154] The code drew on Roman, biblical, and canon law, somewhat adopted to Castilian conditions. However, resistance from localities that preferred to keep their own customary law blocked this centralizing effort for almost a century; only in 1348 did it become part of the law of Castile.[155]

In addition to this body of national legislation, starting in the mid-twelfth century, the self-governing towns of northern Italy, northern France, Flanders, and the Rhine Valley began to enact municipal statutes dealing with sodomy. Many of the laws, such as that adopted in Perugia in 1342, provided fines for first and second offenses and execution by burning for third-timers. Amputation of hands or feet, exile, and confiscation of goods were common provisions.

With time, penalties tended to escalate. In a law of 1250, the first statute known to deal with homosexuality, Bologna permitted men banished from the city because of a sodomy conviction to pay a fine and return, but in 1259, banishment was made permanent. Later that year, sodomy was made a capital offense.[156] Frequent amendments show that the issue remained a

[151] D. S. Bailey (1975:142), Crompton (1980/81).
[152] Philippe de Remi (1842).
[153] Goodich (1979:77–78), Boswell (1980:290–91).
[154] Karlen (1971a:89), Boswell (1980:289). That other penalties could also be applied is clear from an eyewitness: "Leaving Madrid . . . in 1495, Münzer saw the corpses of two men taken in sodomy and hanged with their genitals strung around their necks" (T. Miller, 1972:90, 192).
[155] Kleffens (1968:155–56, 207–13).
[156] Blansher (1981).

live one.[157] At first, enforcement was entrusted to associations of pious laymen organized by the Franciscans and Dominicans; later, provisions were made for enforcement by city officials.[158] The new towns were often religious fraternities, whose members believed that God would favor their political and economic goals if the residents were sufficiently virtuous.[159] They didn't hesitate to use coercion to achieve collective virtue, a major component of which was sexual.

The trend did not take hold everywhere. The Old Norwegian *Gulapings-log*, introduced some time in the twelfth century, specified permanent out-lawry for two men convicted of enjoying the pleasures of the flesh (with one another), with their possessions to be divided between the king and the bishop. This innovation probably did not derive from church law—the procedure it provided for clearing oneself against common rumor (ordeal by hot iron) was not ecclesiastical. Gade suggests that the measure could have been derived from the Justinian Code, which was known in Conti-nental law schools visited by Scandinavian clerics.[160] She suggests that it was introduced into Norwegian law as part of a compact between the king and the bishop, to enable them to take possession of their enemies' prop-erty. The measure was incorporated into twelfth- and thirteenth-century Norwegian church law, but not into other Scandinavian legislation. Bes-tiality became a capital offense, but homosexual relations did not.

The Sicilian *Constitutions of Melfi*, issued by Frederick II in 1231, did not mention homosexuality—possibly because of Frederick's own homosexual leanings, possibly because of his religious skepticism and exposure to Arab culture while growing up in Southern Italy. Nor did the thirteenth-century German law codes, the *Sachsenspiegel* and the *Schwabenspiegel*.[161]

England, too, failed to adopt secular legislation dealing with homo-sexuality.[162] Instead, sodomy cases were prosecuted in ecclesiastical courts,

[157] For example, Florence amended its act of 1325 with additional legislation in 1403, 1418, 1432, and again in the 1490s under Savonarola (*Atti criminali provvisioni* 92, ff. 9r–10r, April 23–24, 1403; Brucker, 1971:201–4; Goodich, 1979:83–84).

[158] Goodich (1976, 1979:80–86).

[159] D. Weinstein (1970).

[160] Gade (1986).

[161] Schevill (1936:112), Boswell (1980:286–87).

[162] Assertions to the contrary found in the literature (Goodich, 1979:77; Boswell, 1980:292) are mistaken. Several English legal treatises dating from around 1290 assert that sodomy should be punished by death. Two of them, *The Mirror of Justices* and *Fleta*, say that the sanc-tion for sodomy is burial alive, a penalty reminiscent of Tacitus. However, much of *The Mirror* is known to be false. Though more credible, *Fleta* is not trustworthy on every point. The work attempts to summarize the main points in *Bracton*, an earlier treatise on English law, and to bring *Bracton* up-to-date by taking Edward I's legislation into account. It draws on other con-temporary writings, as well as on Roman law. However, the passage dealing with sodomy does not appear in *Bracton*, and none of the statutes of Edward I deals with the subject. No

where the penalties involved some sort of penance—prayer, pilgrimage, standing barefoot at the church door, and the like. However, the medieval church courts rarely prosecuted sodomy cases; if the English church dealt with sodomy at all it was through the confessional, not the courts.[163] Even where antisodomy legislation was on the books, it was not necessarily applied consistently or vigorously. The customals, for example, were not always systematically enforced.[164] Some were compiled as a way of asserting royalist, centralizing claims that could not always be made good. Court records show that no one was convicted, much less executed, for sodomy in the secular courts during the reigns of Louis IX (1226–70) and Philip IV (1285–1314).[165] When trials were held, they were probably for reasons that did not occur regularly—there was something unusual about the event, the people, or the time.

In those exceptional cases, though, the law could be stringent. A knife-maker was burned to death in Ghent in 1292 for a homosexual act. Jehan le Bel records an instance of total castration for sodomy and heresy in his mid-fourteenth-century chronicle of the Hundred Years' War.[166] Although records of convictions for thirteenth-century Italy have not been published, trials and sentences from Florence beginning in the late fourteenth century leave no doubt that the sodomy statutes were enforced.[167]

The Meaning of Sodomy

It is often assumed that medieval references to sodomy refer to homosexuality alone. For a few figures that assumption is correct. Albertus Magnus, the thirteenth-century Dominican theologian, for example, defined sodomy

---

sodomy cases are recorded in the voluminous *Notebooks* of cases heard in the royal courts from that period or any later one. A third treatise, *Britton,* specifies the penalty for sodomy (along with sorcery and heresy) to be burning alive. This work claims the authority of Edward I, but in the words of Plucknett (1966:3), this claim "deceived nobody" (Plucknett, 1922:80, 1956: 265–67; Ogg, 1925:191–97; D. S. Bailey, 1975:145–47). A fourth, unpublished treatise, the *Summa* of Gilbert de Thornton, now in the Harvard Law Library, does not mention homosexuality (personal communication, Samuel Thorne). The fact that three of the four treatises claimed that sodomy was a capital offense is revealing, even if the claim did not reflect the actual state of English law, for it tells us that several authors thought this penalty to be appropriate and believed that readers would find the assertion unsurprising.

[163] Personal communications, Barbara Hanawalt and Richard Helmholz.

[164] Boswell (1980:290 n. 58).

[165] D. S. Bailey (1975:142–43), Bullough (1976:391), Goodich (1979:78). Bullough (1976:410 n. 65) implies that no one was convicted under Philip V (1316–22) either, but Courouve (1979) cites one execution in Laon in 1317, and another trial, whose outcome is uncertain, the following year.

[166] Godefroy (1961:464).

[167] Brucker (1971:204–6) summarizes two court cases in detail. The Florentine prosecutions will be discussed further in chapter 7.

as "unisexual intercourse" of men with men or women with women.[168] His pupil, Thomas Aquinas, adopted the same usage.[169] Bede, on the other hand, described anal intercourse in marriage as a "sodomitical crime."[170] Peter Cantor classified coitus interruptus as sodomy, and the *Book of Vices and Virtues* (1375) makes clear that the "sin so foule and so hideous that it should not be named" could be committed by married couples as well as same-sex partners.[171] A fifteenth-century handbook for confessors prepared by Antoninus, a fifteenth-century Dominican friar, includes male and female homosexual and heterosexual intercourse "outside the fit vessel" in its definition of sodomy.[172] A Dutch writer of the sixteenth century, Joost den Damhouder, even counted intercourse with Turks, Saracens, and Jews as sodomitical, on the grounds that Christian faith counted these infidels as equivalent to "dogs and animals."[173]

The growth of commerce and the expansion of royal and municipal government generated a demand for education beyond that given to priests. Universities established in various European towns filled that need, creating a stratum of literate intellectuals equipped to enter the professions and the ranks of state bureaucracies. The increased orderliness of society, an achievement of the royal pacification of the countryside, helped to create a sense that the cosmos itself was orderly and could be understood through the sustained application of systematic reason, without invoking miracles to explain anomalies. Rational judicial procedures began to replace trial by ordeal. Whereas early Christianity rejected the vain concerns of the world and had little reason to encourage efforts to understand its secrets, Christian theologians of the first half of the twelfth century saw in the regularities of the world a manifestation of divine reason and valued efforts to comprehend it.[174]

It was against this background that the rediscovery of Stoic writings (notably Cicero) and Roman legal texts resurrected "nature" as a standard for judging sex.[175] Lacking any tradition of empirical science, the philosophers and theologians invoked an idealized or theoretical nature that had little

---

[168] Bullough (1976:379–80).
[169] Thomas Aquinas, *Summa Theologica* Q. 154, art. 11.
[170] Noonan (1966:166).
[171] Francis (1942:43a), Bullough and Brundage (1982).
[172] Bullough (1976:381).
[173] Frankel (1964).
[174] A. Murray (1978:63–67), Stiefel (1985).
[175] For example, Justinian's *Digest* defines "natural law" as that which "is taught to all living creatures by nature itself, laws which apply not only to mankind but to every living creature on the earth, in the heavens or in the seas. It is this that sanctions the union of man and woman, which is called marriage, and likewise the bearing and upbringing of children: we can see that other living creatures also possess understanding of this law" (A. Murray, 1978).

relationship to anything they encountered in the world around them. It was not observed patterns of sexual conduct that were to establish criteria for normalcy, but God-given reason that was to decide which animal behaviors were natural for humans and which were not.[176]

The deduction of complex systems of ideas from unquestioned, pre-given premises offered much room for ill-founded assumptions, dubious logic, and the common prejudices of the day.[177] For the scholastic theologian, though, the conclusions to be reached about sexuality were predetermined by church teachings, not by independent reason. It is inconceivable, for example, that Aquinas could have come to the conclusion that oral sex was a positive good. Had his reason led him to that conclusion, he would have revised his reasoning. When the twelfth- and thirteenth-century sermons and theological treatises began to describe a number of human sexual activities as "contrary to nature," they simply took the sexual prohibitions of the penitentials and provided rationales for them that were absent there.

Homosexual acts were among those classified as unnatural, but so were other nonprocreative acts such as heterosexual anal and oral intercourse, and coitus interruptus. Gratian's twelfth-century *Decretum* refers to "what is done contrary to nature, as when a man wishes to use a member of his wife not conceded for this," and Saints Catherine and Bernardino of Siena both bemoaned the frequency of the sin against nature among married couples of their day (the fourteenth and fifteenth centuries, respectively). One French archbishop of the fourteenth century classified masturbation as a sin against nature so serious that priests could not absolve it. Some writings even considered heterosexual genital intercourse in a position other than male-superior as unnatural, ostensibly because it reduced the chances of conception.[178]

These notions filtered down into popular consciousness and can be found in secular literature of the day. The fourteenth-century Middle English verse narrative, *The Seven Sages of Rome*, says of King Seneschalus, "Wimmen he louede swithe lite, / And used sinne sodomizte." Chaucer, in the *Parson's Tale*, defined "unkyndely synne" as intercourse in which "a child may not be conceived."[179] In the *Merchant's Tale*, January asserts the

---

[176]Noonan (1966:240). Thus Peter Damian wrote, "God . . . took care to enlighten man through the individual natures and instinctive behavior he bestowed on lower animals: from animals people may learn what behavior should be imitated, what avoided; what may wisely be borrowed from them, and what should rightly be avoided" (quoted in Boswell, 1980:304).

[177]O'Connor (1968), Boswell (1980:303–30).

[178]Noonan (1976:174, 223–26), Flandrin (1972).

[179]The *Seven Sages of Rome*, ll. 1553–54 (Brunner, 1933:66), Bullough (1976:388), Bullough and Brundage (1982:66).

principle, radically at odds with church teachings, that "You can no more sin with your own wife than you can cut yourself with your own knife." The use of obviously fallacious reasoning alerts us to Chaucer's irony.[180]

Fairly broad definitions of sodomy also prevailed in the courts. In 1396, a robber was decapitated in Florence for sodomizing a seven-year-old girl.[181] Wives were urged to resist unnatural sex "even unto death."[182] One Venetian wife did resist—unto her husband's death. A fisherman, he was beheaded in 1481 for "frequent sodomy with his own wife."[183] Heterosexual sodomy was prosecuted in early-sixteenth-century Florence, and preachers denounced the practice regularly.[184] According to the sixteenth-century jurist Farrinaci, married couples were burned at the stake in Rome for sodomy.[185] Men tried for bestiality in sixteenth- and seventeenth-century France were also prosecuted as sodomites.[186] In 1549, a woman was permanently banished from Saragosa, in Aragon, for "imperfect sodomy" (lesbianism).[187]

Evidently, the distinction between heterosexual and homosexual intercourse was less important than the distinction between sex that is potentially reproductive and sex that is not. The sex of one's partner was not altogether inconsequential: Thomas Aquinas, for example, distinguished masturbation, sodomy (with a partner of the same sex), improper intercourse with a partner of the opposite sex, and bestiality, as distinct forms of unnatural vice, each with its own degree of seriousness.[188] Yet the legal prosecution of heterosexual sodomy, even if infrequent,[189] shows that the distinction among these forms was not so sharp or clear as it would be today. For some people, it was almost irrelevant.[190]

[180] P. Field (1970).
[181] *Atti criminali* ACP 2044, ff. 87r–90r.
[182] Erickson (1976:197).
[183] Ruggiero (1985).
[184] Personal communication, Gene Brucker.
[185] R. Becker (1964:119), Hahn (1979:22).
[186] Hernandez (1920).
[187] Bennassar (1979:348).

[188] *Summa Theologica* 2a.2ae. Q. 154, art. 12. Masturbation was the least serious, bestiality the most. It is not entirely clear whether sodomy was worse than unnatural heterosexual sex.

[189] Differences in the ways homosexual and heterosexual sodomy cases came to someone's attention probably contributed to this infrequency. If married couples were discreet about their sexual practices during confession, others would not ordinarily have learned about them. Homosexual sodomy probably took place more often under conditions of reduced privacy.

[190] For the different categories of unnatural sex to have been altogether irrelevant, sexual actors would have had to make no distinctions among human male, human female, and non-human animal partners. There may have been such people: a man who seems to have been as happy with a sow or mare as with a human male is known to us from seventeenth-century

Whether their partners were of the same or opposite sex, the dominant, church-backed ideology defined sodomites by their behavior, not their inclinations. Someone who wanted to engage in sodomy but did not do so was no sodomite, and someone who had done so but had stopped was one no longer. The category was defined by the act, not the person.

It is tempting to suppose that this voluntarism reflected only the inability of a prescientific culture to understand behavior in any terms other than voluntaristic. This supposition would be entirely mistaken, for there were at least two materialist frameworks for explaining sexual behavior available to the medieval world, astrology and mechanical medicine.

As early as the second century A.D., the Alexandrian scientist Ptolemy, who devised the geocentric model of the universe, explained sexual preferences in terms of the configurations of heavenly bodies.[191] The Arabs inherited and added to the astrological knowledge of late antiquity. In the twelfth and thirteenth centuries, Arab astrological texts started to become available in Europe, and in the Renaissance astrology became very popular. But as far as I've been able to discover, sexual preferences were not explained astrologically in the Middle Ages.

From Hippocrates to Galen, Greek medicine explained conditions we would classify as psychological conditions or as mental illnesses in physiological terms. Some of this literature dealt with particular homosexual roles.[192] The Arabs preserved the Greek texts and transmitted them to medieval Europe. Some physicians and scholars were influenced by these writings. The famous surgeon William of Bologna, for example, was probably drawing on classical literature when he attributed lesbianism to a growth emanating from the mouth of the womb and appearing outside the vagina as a pseudopenis.[193] This was obviously not a notion derived from clinical observation. Gentile de Foligno and Peter of Abano took over the explanation of pathic homosexuality given in pseudo-Aristotle.[194] Albertus Magnus, the Dominican scholastic (1193–1280), drew on Arab sources to suggest that a powder prepared from the fur of a hyena and applied to the anus would cure a patient of desire for sodomy (presumably anal penetration).[195]

England (Quaife, 1978:75–77; Bray, 1982:70, 76). This was probably uncommon, but the poetry of Marbod and Baudri quoted earlier shows us men who showed an equally lively interest in partners of both sexes.

[191] Claudius Ptolomy (1976:113–16), 3.18–19. One configuration of the planets leads to effeminacy and wantonness, another makes men "debauchers of women" as well as "corrupters of youths." As a generic and exclusive category, homosexuality does not appear. This was also true of other astrological writings in late antiquity (Boswell, 1980:52 n. 28).

[192] Pseudo-Aristotle, *Problemata physica* 4.24–26.

[193] Lemay (1982). See also Linnhoff (1977).

[194] Jacquart and Thomasset (1985:215), Siraisi (1970).

[195] Boswell (1980:316–18).

More commonly, though, physiological explanations of homosexuality were deleted in translation from the Arabic or Greek. Though the *Prose Salernitan Questions* (an anonymous collection of writings on science and medicine dating from around 1200) draws on the *Problemata,* it omits the passage dealing with pathic homosexuality.[196] When it came to homosexuality, few thinkers were able to overcome the ideological hegemony of the church. It maintained that unnatural vice stemmed not from corporeal causes but from vice. The problem was in the soul, not the body.[197]

It may be that this voluntaristic conception of homosexual behavior was particularly attractive because many of those who engaged in it did not do so exclusively. To a man who could respond erotically to both males and females, homosexual conduct was voluntary. If the attraction itself was common, it would not have been seen as calling for an explanation.

Notwithstanding this voluntarism and the firmly established Roman Catholic doctrine that repentant sinners are forgiven, the association between sodomy and heresy or Islam was beginning to transform the sodomite into an alien who had to be destroyed rather than forgiven.

EXPLAINING THE SHIFT

By the year 1300, Europe had become distinctly less hospitable to those who engaged in homosexual acts than it had been two hundred years earlier. Philosophy, theology, and literature of the late Middle Ages display a dread of homosexuality; canon law was antagonistic, and secular law highly repressive.

This turn toward repression can be explained in part by the greater ability of church and state to carry it out. In the centuries following the barbarian invasions, the church wasn't able to do much about sexual practices it disapproved because it had its hands full trying to restore order and convert the heathen. The invasions of the tenth century renewed these difficulties. But as Europe was converted and pacified, the church became better able to impose its will. The decentralization of political power under feudalism had also interfered with the exercise of secular state functions. Then when the royal houses began to rebuild centralized political power, they were able to enact and enforce legislation in a wider range of matters.[198]

Yet the sources we examined suggest that it was not just policies that were becoming less tolerant in this period, but attitudes, too. Church priorities for dealing with homosexuality cannot be fully explained in terms of

---

[196] Lawn (1979), Jacquart and Thomasset (1985:214).

[197] Jacquart and Thomasset (1985:214).

[198] On this line of reasoning, the absence of thirteenth-century-German secular legislation dealing with homosexuality reflects the extreme weakness of the emperor, whose authority over the various states of the Holy Roman Empire was little more than nominal.

a greater capacity to act on traditional beliefs. Moreover, repression was not always initiated by church or state; at times it was demanded by grass-roots movements. Thus, while organizational capability was obviously necessary for carrying out a program of repression, it cannot be the whole story.

The increased repression of homosexuality in the late Middle Ages can be traced to two distinct but related sources: church-state conflict and class conflict. With regard to the former, it will be argued that the growing preoccupation with homosexuality was an indirect and unanticipated consequence of the efforts of church reformers to establish sacerdotal celibacy. With regard to the latter, it will be suggested that a popular hostility toward homosexuality was part of a broader middle-class morality that became increasingly forceful in its opposition to a life-style of luxury and excess as class divisions widened.

Church Reform

In much of Europe, the mid-eleventh-century church had recovered from the depredations of the previous century, and through bequests, it had come into possession of vast tracts of land. The prospect of a good living attracted men—especially younger sons deprived of an inheritance by the primogeniture rule—to church office despite their lack of a strong religious vocation. The secular rulers were more than willing to make them abbots, bishops, and even archbishops in return for cash payments.[199]

By official Christian standards, the morals of the clergy were appalling. Although clerical marriage had been prohibited long before (e.g., by Pope Leo I in the fifth century), many clergy were married. The prohibition of marriage for priests had never been formally rescinded; it appeared in the canonical collections of Regino of Prüm, Abbon of Fleury, and Burchard of Worms. But enforcement was not easy, and from the time of Gregory the Great (c. 600) to the tenth century, the majority of priests in the West were married or had concubines. Some church authorities explicitly permitted marriage, or else qualified the prohibition.[200] Nor were the sexual activities of the clergy restricted to women:

> Raoul II, Archbishop of Tours, was notorious for his original code of morals and the younger clergy composed songs on his relations with John his archdeacon, whom he succeeded in promoting to a bishopric.[201]

[199] Petit-Dutaillis (1936:86).

[200] Macdonald (1932:29), Amann and Dumas (1942:476–77), G. R. Taylor (1954:35), Brooke (1972:84, 1975:254), Frazee (1972), Burford (1976:102–3), Martines (1979:15–16), Jochens (1980), Wemple (1981:129–36). By contrast with Roman Catholicism, the Eastern Orthodox church had never insisted on celibacy for the lower clergy.

[201] Petit-Dutaillis (1936:87); see also Goodich (1979:31–32).

The wholesale neglect of celibacy posed a number of problems for the church. In the feudalism of the time, offices were becoming hereditary, and priests often wanted to pass their positions—and their churches—on to their sons. In the tenth and eleventh centuries, priests in Northern Italy, Normandy, Britanny, Wales, and Iceland were conveying church property to their children. When their sons preferred a lay career, they appropriated church resources to help them get started. Alarmed by the magnitude of the losses, Pope Gregory VII (1073–85) concluded that they could be halted only if priests were not married.[202]

Popular discontent with clerical incontinence was also a problem. In some places incontinence came to be considered customary, but in most it scandalized the laity and contributed to the anticlerical feelings of the poor, many of whom resented the wealth and privilege of the church.[203] Some believers began to stay away from masses celebrated by married priests. At a time when heretical movements were beginning to attract followers, disgust at corruption within the church became sufficiently widespread to threaten a potentially serious legitimacy crisis.[204]

Throughout the tenth and early eleventh centuries, individual bishops and local synods had tried to discourage priests' sexual activities by threatening degradation from orders, but in many regions they could do little, for too many priests were incontinent.[205] The problem had to be addressed at a churchwide level. By the middle of the eleventh century, energetic reformers like Cardinal Humbert, Peter Damian, and Hildebrand were attempting to do so. They had concluded that the prime causes of all the evils of the church were the meddling of secular rulers in spiritual affairs and the abandonment of celibacy on the part of the clergy. The two problems were linked, because the church could not maintain effective discipline over priests and monks unless it regained the power to appoint and depose them. Moreover, the church's claim that it, rather than the secular rulers, should exercise spiritual authority, was not easy to maintain while the moral standards of the clergy were so vulnerable to criticism.[206]

The reformers hoped to strengthen the moral authority of the church by drawing a sharper line between the clergy and the laity and were thus eager to end clerical marriage. Moreover, the theology of the time was placing greater emphasis on the sacraments, and thus attention was drawn to the purity of the priest who administered them. The question of whether sac-

[202] Lea (1884:65), A. J. Macdonald (1932:28), Amann and Dumas (1942:480), Brooke (1972: 72), Frazee (1972).

[203] Marriage was much more common among the richer priests of the cities than among country clerics, who were often "beggarly and serflike" (Martines, 1979:16).

[204] Amann and Dumas (1942), R. I. Moore (1977:65, 76–77).

[205] Amann and Dumas (1942:48–82).

[206] Cantor (1969:275).

raments administered by priests who were in a state of sin were valid (the issue in the controversy over the Donatist heresy) again came to the fore.[207]

The reform program tackled both problems—secular interference in spiritual affairs and clerical incontinence—at once. In 1054, Pope Leo IX presided over a council at Mainz that condemned simony (the purchase of ecclesiastical office) and priestly marriages. Popes Nicholas II (1059–61), Alexander II (1061–73), and Gregory VII (Hildebrand) (1073–85) went so far as to forbid attendance at masses celebrated by simoniac or incelibate clergy.[208] It was a populist measure, calling on the laity to judge the moral qualifications of the priests.

When Gregory first assumed the papal throne, he had hoped that the secular princes would cooperate in carrying out the reform program, but soon discovered that he could not persuade them to accept the elimination of their prerogatives and a reduction in their revenues. Conflict between church and state over rights and privileges quickly developed.[209] Gregory's vision of the role of the church in the world was grandiose: he saw the pope as head of a worldwide Christian empire, to whom the secular rulers were clearly subordinate. Their resistance to his claims (as well as the resistance of the bishops, who were reluctant to give up some of their own traditional prerogatives),[210] gave him further reason for wanting to tighten the organizational discipline of the church. If the clergy were to become foot soldiers for the pope, it was important that their loyalty be to the church alone, undiluted by allegiance to secular authorities, or by affection for wives, concubines, and children. Thus the elimination of simony, lay investiture, and priestly marriage became even more important.[211]

The campaign against priestly marriage continued over a span of decades. Urban II (1088–99) declared sons of priests ineligible for the clergy.[212] Papal decrees against attending masses celebrated by the clergy who were married or who had concubines were issued on a regular basis. The First

[207] The church ultimately ruled that such sacraments were valid, a decision it could hardly have made otherwise, for the Donatist position would have left worshipers in the untenable situation of not knowing whether the sacraments they had received were valid. Nevertheless, several of the reformers, including Hildebrand and Cardinal Humbert, came quite close to endorsing the Donatist heresy, without actually doing so.

[208] Lea (1884:192–94), Brooke (1975:254), R. I. Moore (1977:54).

[209] Fliche (1944:75, 413–14).

[210] Thus, Anselm, a powerful supporter of the Gregorian reform movement who had convened the Council of London on behalf of the reform program, resisted the sending of a papal legate to his archdiocese while he served as Archbishop of Canterbury. The primacy of the pope was all very well in principle, but when traditional prerogatives were at stake, it had its limits.

[211] Lea (1884:193).

[212] Brooke (1972:72).

Lateran Council reiterated this prohibition in 1123, as did the Second Lateran Council in 1139. Pope Innocent II took up the issue again in 1215 at the Fourth Lateran Council.[213]

The celibacy rule met with strenuous and sometimes violent resistance from clerics and their wives. When the archbishop of Rouen announced that priests had to become celibate, they "rioted, attacked the soldiers of the archbishop, and fought to drive them out of the cathedral."[214] After the bishop of Brescia was almost killed, some Italian bishops "did not dare to announce the decrees."[215]

The elimination of heterosexual outlets for priests could only have fostered the development of homoerotic feelings. Sexual experiences are not merely a way of releasing physiological tension, or a source of physical pleasure; they are also a way of establishing and maintaining emotional intimacy with others.[216] In some people—the proportion is not known, but it is probably substantial—the psychological need for such relationships is stronger than the orientation toward partners of a particular sex. Thus when people are deprived of the opportunity to satisfy the need for emotional intimacy heterosexually, some of them will seek the fulfillment of that need homosexually.[217]

This is especially likely to happen in a single-sex milieu, where contact with members of the opposite sex is entirely cut off. It is well known that in prison some inmates who had no homosexual interests on the outside develop them inside.[218] For similar reasons, high levels of homoeroticism develop in boarding schools,[219] monasteries,[220] isolated rural regions,[221] and on ships with all-male crews.[222]

The association between homosexuality and Christian monasticism dates back to the early history of cenobitic communities in late antiquity. Refer-

[213] J. B. Russell (1965:7), Brooke (1972:75–77), R. I. Moore (1977:53), Fliche, Thouzellier, and Azais (n.d.:143).

[214] Frazee (1972).

[215] Schimmelpfennig (1979); see also Wishart (1900:182–86), Brooke (1972:84, 1975:253), Martines (1979:15), H. J. Berman (1983:95).

[216] Benjamin (1978).

[217] This reasoning occasionally cropped up in the Middle Ages. The prevention of male homosexuality was sometimes given as an argument for tolerating female prostitution (Trexler, 1981; Otis, 1985:211 n. 19). The argument rests implicitly on the assumption that men would readily substitute one sex for the other.

[218] Buffum (1973), Shore (1981), O'Brien (1982:90–100, 136), Scacco (1982), Wooden and Parker (1982).

[219] A. Freeman (1960), Gathorne-Hardy (1977:163–64), Bullough and Bullough (1980), Chandos (1984), Vicinus (1985:187–89).

[220] Lea (1884:137), Brunel (1955:203–4), Prince Peter (1963:458), Childs (1977).

[221] Kinsey, Pomery, and Martin (1948:455–57, 630–31), J. Katz (1976:508–12).

[222] J. Katz (1976:467–80), Burg (1983).

ences to homosexuality are almost completely absent from the earliest monastic literature, but in subsequent generations measures to curb it received increasing attention. Augustine cautioned nuns that they should love each other spiritually, not carnally,[223] while an *Epistle* of Paul Helladicus, sixth-century abbot of Elusa, "one of the most unsavory documents of Christian monasticism," warns of the need to take precautions against lesbianism in convents.[224] Egyptian monks were warned against bringing boys into their communities, and the *Rule of Saint Pachomius* (early fourth century) prohibits any physical contact between monks. In some parts of the Thebaid, it became necessary to lock monks into their cells at night. Late Syrian monastic documents urge monks not to spend too much time in one another's cells, or to accept young boys.[225] Basil, the fourth-century church father who brought monasticism to the West, warned:

> At meals take a seat far away from your young brother; in lying down to rest, let not your garments be neighbor to his; rather, have an elderly brother lying between you. When a young brother converses with you or is opposite you in choir, make your response with your head bowed lest perchance by gazing fixedly into his face, the seed of desire be implanted in you by the wicked sower and you reap sheaves of corruption and ruin. At home or in a place where there is no witness of your actions, be not found in his company under the pretext of meditation on the Divine Word or for any other excuse, even the most urgent need.[226]

The Second Council of Tours, held in 567, forbade monks and priests from sleeping two-to-a-bed;[227] the *Benedictine Rule*, adopted to regulate the monastic life, also calls for specific measures to prevent homosexual relations among monks.[228]

Considering how easy it was to find sexual partners on the outside, men and women with strong homosexual proclivities would hardly have been attracted to the ascetic communities of the early church. Rather, homosexual interests developed within the communities. The repeated references to the subject indicate that even the most extreme precautions and vigilance brought only limited success. While many monks and nuns may never have developed homosexual feelings—or may not have acted on

---

[223] *Epist.* 211.14 (D. S. Bailey, 1975:85; Bullough, 1976:195).
[224] Bury (1923:21).
[225] Vööbus (1960b), Chitty (1966:66–67), Randers-Pehrson (1983:241).
[226] Bullough (1976:195).
[227] D. S. Bailey (1875:91).
[228] Delatte (1950, Bullough (1976:372), Horn and Born (1979).

them if they did—the persistent warnings and rules tell us that some continued to do so.

The same pressures that gave rise to monastic homosexuality in the early Christian monasteries were generated again by the closing off of heterosexual relationships for the medieval clergy. The emotional consequences of this measure can be seen in the homophile poetry and letters of passionate male friendship and love written by twelfth-century clergy to one another. When Anselm wrote to two of his relatives, whom he may never have met, on the occasion of their deciding to become monks,

> My eyes eagerly long to see your face, most beloved; my arms stretch out to your embraces. My lips long for your kisses; whatever remains of my life desires your company, so that my soul's joy may be full in time to come,[229]

or to a monk transferred to another monastery after spending several months in Anselm's, "we cannot now be separated without tearing apart our joint soul and severing our heart,"[230] he was expressing the human need for shared intimacy and love that monastic institutions tried hard to suppress but could not. That the recipient of the first letter existed for Anselm only as a fantasized figure does not detract from the power of his feelings; rather, it testifies to their strength, and the force of his need to express them.

It bears emphasizing that powerful feelings of love and intimacy do not necessarily imply awareness of sexual interest or attraction. Although the intensity of Anselm's expressions of friendship was unconventional in his generation, it is not clear that his contemporaries would have read his letters with our sensibilities.[231] He himself organized the Council of London to deal with clergy who failed to live up to the higher moral standards required by the reform movement. It was this council that adopted the first canonical rules against clerical homosexuality for the English church.[232] Anselm would undoubtedly have taken violent exception to any claim that his letters expressed a sexual interest; he himself loathed sex.[233]

Nevertheless, even if strong feelings of love and intimacy are sometimes free from any sexual element, often they are not. Just as it would be wrong to read a sexual meaning into every expression of love, it would be a mistake to dismiss the possibility of sexual interest in the entire body of

---

[229] Quoted in Southern (1963:69).
[230] Southern (1963:74).
[231] Southern (1963:69–72).
[232] Church (1937:311–12), Goodich (1979:42).
[233] McGuire (1974).

homophile poetry and letters of passionate friendship and love written by eleventh- and twelfth-century monks and priests.[234]

The many reports of homosexuality in the medieval monasteries suggest that monks and nuns often gave their feelings sexual expression. Salimbene di Adamo, a nobleman of thirteenth-century Parma, wrote that homosexuality was widespread, particularly among clerks, nuns, and scholars,[235] and Cardinal Henry of Susa wrote in the mid-thirteenth century that sodomy was a common vice among the clergy.[236] Other writers of the late twelfth and thirteenth centuries who associated the clergy with homosexuality include Gilles de Corbeil, Guiot de Provins, Gautier de Metz, Alexander de Roes, Walter Mapes, and Thibaut I, king of Navarre.[237] William of Langland's fourteenth-century *Vision of Piers Plowman* also thought homosexuality to be the special vice of friars and nuns.[238]

The precautions the church took to deal with clerical homosexuality are the best evidence that these attributions were not simply a reflection of anticlerical sentiment. In a canon that also dealt with clerical marriage, the Third Lateran Council decreed deposition from office and confinement to a monastery for clergy "involved in that incontinence which is against nature," and the Fourth Lateran Council strengthened the penalty.[239] In 1212 the local Council of Paris forbade nuns from sharing a bed, and stipulated that a lamp burn all night in dormitories—an extension to convents of the *Benedictine Rule* for monks that the Council of Rouen reenacted two years later.[240] In 1221, the Cistercians began to expel monks for sodomy.[241]

This response was dictated by the same considerations that made priestly involvement in heterosexual relations intolerable. Scripture had long been understood to condemn all homosexuality, and patristic authority had been unequivocal in its denunciation of same-sex love. The laity were insisting that priests adhere to a higher standard of morality, and this excluded homosexual as well as heterosexual activity. The legitimation needs of the church made tolerance of priestly homosexuality impossible. Then, too, the reformers' desire to build a priestly army unencumbered by personal or worldly attachments was inconsistent with homosexuality in its ranks. There was, then, a confluence of moral and practical or organizational considerations at work.[242]

---

[234] Many of them are reproduced in English translation in Boswell (1980:218–26, 370–74).

[235] Cleugh (1963:91), Karlen (1971:90), Bullough (1976:393).

[236] Lea (1896:8, 243).

[237] Irsay (1925), Herman (1976), Goodich (1979:10), Kuster and Cormier (1984).

[238] Bullough (1976:387), Bullough and Brundage (1982:66).

[239] Goodich (1979:43–45).

[240] D. S. Bailey (1975:132–33), Bullough (1976:384).

[241] Goodich (1979:46).

[242] The attribution of hidden pragmatic motives for church policies may elicit skepticism from those who prefer to think of the church as untainted by pragmatic considerations, but a

With these considerations all present, it is hardly surprising that the ex-
tirpation of homosexuality among the clergy was part of the reformers'
larger agenda. Peter Damian, whose vitriolic attack on clerical homosexuality we noted earlier, was a firm opponent of simony, clerical marriage,
and concubinage.[243] Anselm, who was responsible for the Council of London's decree against homosexuality (which gave particular attention to clerics), fought with William Rufus and Henry I over lay investitures.[244] Pope
Innocent III, who continued Gregory VII's policy of seeking papal supremacy over the state, initiated an investigation into clerical sodomy in Macon
in 1203.[245] When Pope Gregory IX ordered a crackdown on clerical fornication in the German church in November of 1231, he included those engaged
in homosexual activity among those who were to be compelled to be continent.[246] The campaign to eliminate homosexuality from the clergy was thus
an essential component of the Gregorian reform movement. It was because
this campaign was shaped by the reform movement that it paid so much
attention to the morals of the clergy. The reform Councils of Paris and
Rouen were concerned with homosexuality exclusively among priests and
nuns; they had nothing at all to say about the laity.

Despite the reformers' denunciations, their responses to homosexuality
were often restrained. Thus, accusations of homosexuality against church
officials were sometimes ignored. Anselm urged in correspondence that
sodomites not be admitted to the priesthood and wanted those already admitted warned to desist; but he also favored moderation in punishment.[247]
In a similar spirit, Pope Honorius III wrote in 1227 to the archbishop of
Lund that in cases involving incest, bestiality, and "that sin which should
neither be named nor committed, on account of which the Lord condemned
to destruction Sodom and Gomorrah,"

> divine mercy is greater than human perverseness and since it is
> better to count on the generosity of God than to despair of the
> magnitude of a particular sin, we order you herewith to repri-
> mand, exhort and threaten such sinners and then to assign

---

number of other medieval church policies regarding marriage and family appear to have been
shaped by institutional interests (Goody, 1983). I do not suggest that efforts to discourage homosexuality were merely cynical and lacked a moral dimension, only that pragmatic concerns
were also at work and gave backbone to moral conviction. Some reformers themselves articulated pragmatic reasons for adopting strict moral standards. Peter Damian worried that "each
of the faithful seems to be, as it were, a lesser church" (quoted in Cantor, 1969:274), and went
on to argue, as did other eleventh-century reformers, that only by leading a morally superior
life could the clergy justify the special powers they claimed for themselves.

[243] Brooke (1972:72), Little (1978:72).

[244] Church (1937), Southern (1963).

[245] Goodich (1979:17).

[246] Little (1978:142).

[247] Goodich (1979:41–42), Boswell (1980:215).

them, with patience and good judgment, a salutary penance, using moderation in its devising, so that neither does undue leniency prompt audacity to sin, nor does unreasonable severity inspire despair.[248]

Honorius was writing in a century in which the church backed the burning of heretics, and so his letter cannot be dismissed as a simple expression of Christian charity and forgiveness. Boswell suggests that in many instances, clerics may have been reluctant to endorse or participate in the persecution of others like them.[249] This may have been so, but there were also clear political and organizational reasons for giving higher priority to the ending of simony, lay investiture, and clerical marriage. Homosexual relationships, for example, did not result in progeny, and therefore did not threaten the preservation of church property.

Nevertheless, as time went on, the church became more uncompromising in its stance. Whereas Lateran III in 1179 treated clerical homosexuality as comparable in gravity to clerical marriage and imposed a purely ecclesiastical penalty (degradation from rank, penance in a monastery), Lateran IV, in 1215, called for secular penalties to be imposed as well—establishing a precedent for lay authorities to act on their own. Several monastic orders required abbeys to build prisons for sodomites and other offenders, and the church cooperated fully in the prosecution of accused sodomites under the new municipal and royal statutes. The Council of Angers (1216/19) portrayed pederasts as monsters, and as time went on, this imagery was to become more and more prevalent.[250]

This development followed almost inevitably from the success of the reform movement. The more the church suppressed priestly marriage and concubinage, the stronger must have been the homosexual drive it aroused within its ranks. The organizational suppression of sexuality, made more effective by the strengthening of monastic discipline, would have prevented many priests from giving expression to their homosexual impulses. As official pronouncements insisted on the incompatibility of homosexuality with clerical status, it would have been psychologically risky for priests to acknowledge their own homosexual desires even to themselves. To have done so would have required an open acknowledgment that the church was suppressing an important part of themselves.

When a conflict such as this cannot be eliminated or recognized, it does not disappear but is driven underground and lives in the unconscious. Psychological defense mechanisms develop to prevent knowledge of the

[248] Quoted in Boswell (1980:380).
[249] Boswell (1980:211–12).
[250] Goodich (1979:43–46).

conflict from reaching the level of awareness. Projecting one's own unacceptable desires onto someone else is one such mechanism; reaction formation, in which one reassures oneself against the suspicion of having a forbidden desire by an exaggerated repudiation and hostility, is another. Knowledge that someone else has the tabooed desire and acts on it places the repression from consciousness of one's own desire in jeopardy, and thus evokes the punitive reaction. It is fueled by the energy of the repressed impulse.[251]

Clinical psychologists claim to have identified these processes in their patients' responses to real or imputed homosexuality.[252] Yet the skeptic may wonder how we can be sure that a subconscious conflict is present when it cannot be observed directly. How does one know it is there? Conflict can be assumed when it makes better sense of behavior patterns than alternative explanations and when it can be inferred from experimental evidence. If intolerance of homosexuality stems from fear of one's own hidden homosexual impulses, hostility toward those believed to be homosexual should be greater if they are one's own sex, for it is they who as potential sexual partners should arouse the greatest anxiety. This is exactly what researchers have found.[253] It would be difficult to explain this pattern except in terms of a psychological defense mechanism, for normally we expect people to be *more* tolerant of those who are most like them, not less.[254]

If subconscious psychological processes contribute to hostility toward homosexuality in modern times, it is not unreasonable to think that they did so in earlier eras as well. It may be suggested, then, that fear and loathing of homosexuality developed in the Middle Ages as a psychological defense mechanism against the inner conflict created by the imposition of clerical celibacy and the rigid repression of all sexual expression.[255] The irra-

---

[251] In a naïve view, those who succumb to temptation and violate a rule should have more guilt than those who conform, but experimental evidence suggests that the reverse may be true. Resistance to temptation can feed energy to the conscience and lead to higher levels of guilt (MacKinnon, 1938).

[252] Mahl (1971:117–22).

[253] San Miguel and Millham (1976), Weinberger and Millham (1979). These experimental studies are particularly significant because their subjects were not psychiatric patients. As for the connection psychologists have postulated between paranoia and the repression of homosexual desire, it has been confirmed empirically in some psychological or psychiatric studies, but not in others (for a review of this work see Kline, 1972:265–75). However, almost all these studies involve patients diagnosed as schizophrenic and thus do not bear directly on our concern with people who would not be considered psychotic, no matter how irrational their views of homosexuality.

[254] Black (1976:73–78).

[255] The repression of priestly heterosexuality created conflicts that were no less intense. These conflicts, reflected at first in the Mariolatry of the thirteenth century, contributed to the

tional and at times hysterical tone in which homosexuality was discussed in the late Middle Ages can thus be understood as a manifestation of reaction formation and projection originating in organizationally induced psychological conflict.

The deepening of hostility in the High Middle Ages is consistent with this explanation. Initially, homosexuality was not a great source of anxiety. It was disapproved but in most instances it was not punished more severely than a number of other sexual sins. Then monkish reformers began a campaign to refurbish the moral image of the church by insisting on clerical celibacy. Some of those reformers (e.g., Peter Damian) were deeply antagonistic to homosexuality, but they concentrated their fire on the clergy, not the laity. Their writings were candid in expressing organizational as well as purely moral or religious concerns, and their preoccupation was not with homosexuality alone, but with all forms of sexual expression. Once heterosexual outlets were shut off, concentration on homosexuality intensified and, at least at first, focused particularly on the clergy.[256]

The notion that someone who denounces homosexuality, or persecutes those who engage in it, is a "latent" homosexual whose hostility derives from panic at his own homosexual impulses has long been a cliché of pop psychology. Though not necessarily wrong, this belief does not take us far enough to be helpful. Apart from its reliance on the questionable concept of a "latent" homosexual, it fails to tell us who is especially likely to experience this panic, or under what circumstances it appears. The present analysis does this by situating the source of homosexual impulses and the need to repress them in the institutional arrangements the medieval church was establishing for clergy. These arrangements added up to an unintended but efficient machine for generating hostility to homosexuality. Thus, while the argument looks Freudian, it has nothing whatsoever to do with family configurations or oedipal complexes.

Although the church devoted its greatest efforts to controlling homosexuality among the clergy, it was also concerned with the morals of the laity. Some of this concern would have been due to the indiscriminate nature of psychological defense mechanisms. A priest trying to repress his

---

increased misogyny of the later Middle Ages, and were thus a factor in the witchcraft persecutions, which were directed largely at women.

[256] Given the trend toward greater repression of homosexuality, it is a bit surprising to find as late as the end of the fifteenth century that some reformers still treated priests who took concubines, and those who were guilty of homosexuality, on an equal footing. Yet Savonarola, a firebrand active in Florence between 1482 and 1498, complained in a letter that "this one goes at night to his concubine, the other to his youthful male lover and then in the morning they go to say mass" (Lea, 1884:399).

own homosexual desires would have felt as much anxiety over a lay-person's homosexuality as over another priest's or nun's.

The political-ideological context of the High Middle Ages made this anxiety especially consequential. Perhaps more than at any other time in its history, the early-thirteenth-century papacy strove to create a single, unified Christian society. Clothed with prestige won in the Crusades, and at least partly successful in the investiture controversy, the popes sought to establish the primacy of Rome in all spheres. Earlier medieval political theory had held church and state to be separate but equal, each having jurisdiction over its own affairs. But by the early thirteenth century, Pope Innocent III was advancing the radical claim that the pope was superior to civil rulers even in secular matters, and asserted this claim actively, by excommunicating, deposing, and crowning Holy Roman Emperors.[257]

The pope's political claims made sense only if all subjects were members of the church, and attempts were therefore initiated to bring outsiders into the fold. New efforts were mounted to convert the Jews and to exile those who refused conversion. The new urban communes founded in the High Middle Ages were typically religious fraternities bound together by a common allegiance to Latin Christianity; they were amenable, therefore, to the adoption of legislation derived from church teachings. The newly founded Franciscans and Dominicans were sent out to preach Christian doctrine and morality to the secular world.[258] This activist role was novel: earlier orders of monks had retreated from the turmoil of the world to their monasteries, where they devoted themselves to prayer and contemplation. Instead of avoiding the world, the mendicant orders invaded it and tried to change it. The sexual morality of the laity thus became one of their concerns.

At the time, few other views of morality were being disseminated. Most of Christian Europe learned about homosexuality from the sermon and the confessional—that is, from Roman Catholic sources alone. Churches made their teachings visually salient by installing sculptures infaming sodomites and other sexual nonconformists in full view of worshipers.[259] It was Catholic doctrine, then, that shaped popular consciousness. Dante, Chaucer, the Pearl Poet, and William Langland, all writing in the fourteenth century, expressed conventionally orthodox repugnance for homosexuality in their writings.[260]

The situation in the Byzantine Empire was quite different. There the

[257] Schevill (1961:95–96).
[258] J. Cohen (1982).
[259] Weir and Jerman (1986:84, 101).
[260] Bullough (1976:387–89), Cawley and Anderson (1976:81–82).

lower clergy were married, and because church and state were integrated, the dynamic of church reform seen in the West was not present. Though the Justinian prohibition remained in effect, it became little more than a dead letter. Though homosexuality was frowned on, the ready availability of eunuchs at court, and of slaves until the twelfth century, facilitated the indulgence of homosexual tastes among men.[261]

GENDER AND CLASS CONFLICT

Strictly speaking, Christian teachings prohibited homosexuality in all its forms, whether or not those who engaged in it violated broader gender norms. But some of the church fathers shared the views of male effeminacy held by their pagan contemporaries. Chrysostom repeatedly denounced any changes in customary gender roles as acts against nature, even when they did not involve homosexuality. One of his objections to male homosexuality was that it entailed "losing one's manhood" and "becoming a woman."[262]

The persistence of stigma against effeminacy can be seen in the complaints of the clergy of late-eleventh- and twelfth-century England and Normandy about homosexuality in the royal entourage of the Norman rulers. The young men of the royal court had begun to wear long hair and women's clothing, and adopted effeminate mannerisms; it was this the monks found offensive. Ordericus Vitalis (Orderic) deplored the court of William Rufus, son of the Conqueror, where "the effeminate predominated everywhere and revelled without restraint, while filthy catamites, fit only to perish in the flames, abandoned themselves to the foulest practices of Sodom."[263] Similar passages appear in the writings of Orderic's contemporaries, including William of Malmesbury. In 1108, the Council of Westminster condemned men's wearing their hair long, and several leading churchmen not only preached against the effeminacy of the court, but also cut the hair of the king and nobles with their own scissors.[264]

[261] Jenkins (1967:88, 165–66, 198–99, 301). These remarks must be qualified by the observation that the subject of Byzantine homosexuality has not received the careful study that the subject deserves.

[262] Laistner (1951:94, 136 n. 11), E. A. Clark (1979:12, 25 n. 37).

[263] D. S. Bailey (1975:123–24), H. M. Hyde (1970:33), Herman (1976). Boswell (1980:229–31) questions the credibility of Orderic's attribution of homosexuality to William Rufus and other Normans, pointing out that other sources charge him and his followers with fornication and adultery, but do not mention homosexuality. However, there is no reason to think that sexual preferences in this circle had to be exclusive. For our purposes, the accuracy of the attribution is unimportant. What is significant is the view of gender the accusations display.

[264] E. A. Freeman (1882:1.159, 2.330, 340–41), Tatlock (1950:350–53), Kuster and Cormier (1984). It is possible that long hair for men was not a new style at all. To the early medieval Germans it was a sign of potency. When a Merovingian king was deposed, he was humiliated

Only incidentally do these clerical passages deplore homosexuality; their deepest preoccupation is with men dressing and acting like women. Sexual stratification in the feudal aristocracy had been sharp. Although there were a few women warriors,[265] this was rare. When Joan of Arc insisted on wearing men's clothing, she was executed. The new styles of clothing and bodily appearance cultivated by the men of the post-Conquest Norman aristocracy were incompatible with their traditional pastimes (hunting, fighting); gender conservatives interpreted them as involving the imitation of women, who had traditionally been subordinate to men. The clergy found this voluntary adoption of the life-style of a subordinate sex repugnant, perhaps incompatible with the expectations of a ruling class.

Disgust with the voluptuous, sybaritic life of the court also figured prominently in writings about homosexuality among the laity. The English cleric John of Salisbury evoked this life in the following passage, written in 1159:

> When the rich lascivious wanton is preparing to satisfy his passion he has his hair elaborately frizzled and curled; he puts to shame a courtesan's make-up, an actor's costume. . . . Thus arrayed he takes the feet of the figure reclining by him in his hands, and in plain view of others caresses them and, not to be too explicit, the legs as well. The hand that had been encased in a glove to protect it from the sun and keep it soft for the voluptuary's purpose extends its exploration. Growing bolder, he allows his hand to pass over the entire body with lecherous caress, incites the lascivious thrill that he has aroused, and fans the flame of languishing desire. Such abominations should be spat upon rather than held up to view.[266]

As this passage indicates, complaints about homosexuality were beginning to serve as a vehicle for the expression of popular discontent with the growing social gap between the court and the rest of the population. The

---

by having his head shorn (Wallace-Hadrill, 1967). The English priests may have interpreted long hair as effeminate on the basis of 1 Cor. 11:14, even though it did not have that meaning to the Normans.

[265] Boulding (1976:443–44).

[266] Quoted in Karlen (1971:87). Boswell (1980:216 n. 30) notes that "the passage is a pastiche of classical quotations" and, citing John's expression of intense feeling toward Pope Hadrian IV, suggests that it "most probably does not represent John's personal feelings about gay relationships, which may have been quite different." However, feelings are one thing, lust another. The fact that medieval homophile poetry drew on classical sources does not mean that the sentiments it expressed were inauthentic, and the same is true of hostile writings. We cannot interrogate John as to his convictions, but if he was writing what was expected of him rather than what he really thought, the passage remains valuable for what it shows of the mentality of the time.

hand encased in a glove to protect it from the sun belongs to a member of the leisured aristocracy, not to someone who does manual labor. John is believed to have been of modest social origins; he feared that the new wealth was eroding traditional morality,[267] and resented those who possessed it. (At the same time, the almost pornographic seduction scene suggests fascination as well as aversion.)

Sodomy was also linked with wealth in the class conflicts that accompanied economic growth in the cities of northern Italy, northern France, Flanders, and the Rhine Valley, beginning in the middle of the twelfth century.[268] Many of the details of these conflicts remain unstudied, but at least in Italy, where they erupted in scores of city-states, their broad outlines can be traced.

The early Italian communes were dominated by knights who owned land near the city proper and also engaged in commerce and industry. These lesser nobles, joined by wealthy nonnoble merchants (*popoli grassi*), who often intermarried with them, constituted the *magnati*, the politically most powerful group. This urban patriciate led the fight for communal self-government and independence from the Holy Roman Empire. Although antagonistic to the great lords of the countryside, their ethos remained largely feudal. Violent vendettas between leading families plagued the communes for generations.[269]

The merchants aped the social customs of nobility, including concubinage and conspicuous consumption. Perhaps because their financial dealings so often entailed the charging of interest on loans—officially defined by the church as usury, a grave sin—they had little use for orthodox religion and were uninterested in persecuting heretics.[270]

By the early thirteenth century, this ruling stratum came under political pressure from artisans and shopkeepers who sought broader participation in city government. The growth of commerce heightened inequality of wealth and exacerbated class tensions. The *popoli minuti* raged against the great bankers and merchants who demanded usurious interest rates and sought relief from imprisonment for debt. Where the middle classes were able to take political power (Lombardy in the early, and Tuscany in the late thirteenth century), they enacted legislation against both practices.[271]

A class defines itself in opposition to other classes culturally by turning its own traits and standards into universal values. Scorned by the hereditary aristocracy, these small-scale entrepreneurs, who lacked a well-defined

---

[267] Cantor (1969:356).
[268] Goodich (1979:79–85).
[269] Brucker (1962:35), Waley (1969:165), Martines (1979).
[270] Schevill (1961:67, 72), Waley (1969), Goodich (1982:80–81).
[271] J. K. Hyde (1966:21), Goodich (1979:79).

social place in the feudal order, embraced utilitarianism as the basis for status and privilege, praising their own industriousness and self-reliance, while criticizing the aristocracy as lazy and parasitical.[272] The *popoli minuti* castigated the aristocracy, and the *popoli grassi* who mimicked them, for their profligate life-styles and vulgar ostentation. In essence, they were attacking those vices that their own class position did not allow them to indulge: adultery, prostitution, gambling, and sodomy (by which they meant all nonprocreative sexual activity, heterosexual or homosexual.

Sodomy came to be seen as an unproductive self-indulgence that expressed lust, not love or the desire for children; it became a metonym for excessive indulgence of sensuous desires, evoking connotations that went far beyond sexuality. It represented a going beyond natural limits in the same way that unrestricted greed did in the economic sphere. As usury was a sin in Christian thought, interest-takers were sometimes called *bougres,* that is, heretics. Probably because the urban patriciate engaged in both practices, and because heretics were already believed to favor sodomy, usury and sodomy also became linked in the popular mind:[273] Dante placed usurers and sodomites together in the same circle of hell.[274]

In northern Europe, to attribute sodomy to the great Italian bankers who lent to the royal houses of England and Europe at high interest rates was to depict lenders who were unscrupulously "screwing" their debtors financially as doing so literally through sexual domination and exploitation of weakness.[275] The first time the English parliament mentioned sodomy was in 1376, in a request to Edward III to banish "Lombard brokers," along with Jewish and Saracen merchants, on the grounds that their practice of sodomy and usury endangered the kingdom.[276] Sodomy and exploitation were also linked in the writings of the Anonimo Genovese, a mystical religious

---

[272] Cantor (1969:412–14), Gouldner (1970:61–65).

[273] Just as sodomy acquired extensive connotations in popular usage, usury came to mean more than a technical violation of a rule against taking interest; it implied an antispiritual amassing of wealth and the use of this wealth in ways that upset older forms of sociality and undermined traditional morality or stratification systems. For example, the great lords, whose revenues from land were inadequate to purchase luxury goods from the Orient that became available after the Crusades, or who wished to host sumptuous entertainments, often borrowed from moneylenders and were forced to give up their lands when they could not repay the loans (Schevill, 1961:293). Moneylending was practiced by all classes in late-thirteenth-/ early-fourteenth-century Padua, but evoked hostility only when lenders amassed huge fortunes in a short time, threatening the stability of the class structure (J. K. Hyde, 1966:189). It was these connotations that the equation of sodomy and usury evoked.

[274] Koffler (1979). Like others of his age, Dante often used the term "sodomy" very loosely. For example, he characterized blasphemy and the refusal to write poetry in the vernacular as "spiritual sodomy"—the latter because the refusal to communicate violates the natural order (Pézard, 1950:294–311; Kay, 1969, 1978).

[275] Goodich (1979:86), Koffler (1981).

[276] H. M. Hyde (1970:36).

poet who wrote c. 1295–1311 that the four worst sins were homicide, sodomy "which is so filthy and grave that anyone who commits it deserves death by fire"), harming orphans or the poor, and not paying one's workers.[277]

It was the middle strata of artisans and shopkeepers that had provided the backbone of support for the Gregorian reforms. It was they who favored harsher criminal laws and more impersonal, bureaucratic law enforcement[278]—probably to prevent the wealthy from flouting the law with impunity. Middle-class hostility toward the magnates was exceeded only by its antagonism toward corruption within the church. Clergy who lived in affluence on the contributions of the laity and whose personal morality was inconsistent with the claims of the church to a privileged status in spiritual matters were detested no less intensely than the sybaritic aristocracy. Bourgeois demands to be free from compulsory tithes added a material dimension to this cultural enmity.[279] The antagonism went far beyond a bit of grumbling: in Milan around 1060, the *popolo*, in alliance with the papacy, attempted to overthrow the established church hierarchy. Noncelibate clergy were forced to flee the city when mobs beat them and plundered their homes.[280] It is a measure of the importance that the Gregorian reformers attached to the reconstitution of the spiritual life and organizational structure of the church that to advance these goals they were willing to countenance violent attacks on obdurate clergy.

Though antagonistic toward corruption within the church, the middle class was not irreligious, but intensely pious. Indeed, the Franciscans and Dominicans came largely from nonnoble families, whose involvement in the forging of new types of social relations based on the cash nexus encouraged the mendicant friars to move into and remake the world, rather than withdraw from it as the Benedictines and Cistercians had done.[281] When riots broke out, they sided with the *popolo*.[282] The moral standards they sought to realize had as much to do with their social class backgrounds as with traditional Christian doctrine.

To be sure, *leaders* of the mendicant orders often came from wealthier backgrounds. Saint Francis's father was a wealthy merchant of Assisi. Faced with the eruption of political opposition in the early-thirteenth-

---

[277] Martines (1979:87).

[278] Blansher (1981).

[279] These material conflicts persisted; in the fourteenth century, rebels attacked the church in its role as proprietor and landlord, directing their attacks particularly at the higher clergy living in luxury (Mollat and Wolff, 1973:288–89).

[280] Brooke (1975:343), Butler (1969:66–67), Schimmelpfennig (1979), Berman (1983:95, 578–79 n. 11).

[281] Goff (1968, 1970), Freed (1977), J. Cohen (1982:41).

[282] Blansher (1981).

century Italian city-states, some of the sons of the *popoli grassi* came to regard the emphasis on profit-making and the accumulation of wealth in the new commercial economy as incompatible with the antimaterialism of traditional Christianity. Unlike their fathers, they worried about the growth of social inequality and took concrete steps to ameliorate the lot of those less well-off. They attributed Mongol victories in Poland and Hungary, and the defeat of the papacy at the hands of Frederick II, to the moral weaknesses of their parents' generation.[283]

Abandoning the privileges of their class, these youths joined with reformed-minded members of the lower classes to campaign for a moral reawakening.[284] As leaders of the Dominicans and Franciscans, they campaigned in the cities against abortion, heresy, prostitution, and sodomy.[285] They intervened often on behalf of the Guelphs, the party supported by the middle classes and, in Francis's generation, by the renegade sons of wealthy merchants. Much of the restrictive morals legislation of the thirteenth century was enacted under Guelph rule, with input from the friars.

The friars supported the Guelphs for geopolitical as well as moral considerations related to their class backgrounds. The Hohenstaufen ambition of subjugating all of Italy ran directly contrary to papal political interests, for Rome would not have been able to maintain its political independence had it been surrounded by the forces of the Holy Roman Empire. To prevent this, Rome supported the popular anti-imperial parties in the northern Italian cities (i.e., the Guelphs).[286] They furnished the troops that, under the political leadership of Pope Alexander III, defeated the imperial armies at Legnano in 1176.[287]

[283] Goodich (1982:80–81, 101).

[284] That these campaigns served the long-term interests of the wealthy by reducing popular discontent is sufficiently obvious as to require little belaboring.

[285] Some of their writings make their class concerns explicit. In a commentary on the Gospel of Luke, the Dominican scholastic Albertus Magnus concluded that homosexual acts are more objectionable than other sins for several reasons, one of them being its greater prevalence among the upper classes (Boswell, 1980:316 n. 52). The friars also led anti-Jewish campaigns. Most of the Dominicans and Franciscans shared the prejudices of their class, which grew out of commercial rivalry (J. Cohen, 1982:43–44). In Spain, the highest levels of the aristocracy and the church were relatively tolerant of the Jews—though they did sponsor some conversion campaigns—but "the most determined enemies of the Jews were the new mendicant orders" (G. Jackson, 1972:144). Boswell (1980) notes that the medieval repression of Jews and those who engaged in homosexual acts intensified at the same time, but fails to perceive the class dynamics responsible for both developments.

[286] Their opponents, the Ghibellines, favored the Empire, and drew their support from forces sympathetic to the old feudal aristocracy; however, rivalries between cities or noble families sometimes led to allegiances that departed from this general pattern (Herlihy, 1958: 55, 177–83; Waley, 1969:206).

[287] Herlihy (1958), Cantor (1969:430–31).

These highly popular campaigns, led by friars, culminated in the adoption of new antisodomy legislation (described above) by the ruling Guelph parties. The earliest surviving criminal statutes of medieval Bologna, enacted in 1250 under popular rule, expelled sodomites and heretics from the city. In 1259, another statute, enacted in response to a request from a Dominican, had sodomites burned to death.[288] In some cities, officials were granted special powers to enforce these statutes: in Florence, "the podesta, captains of the people, and other officials were given complete license to investigate, torture, and punish in any way they saw fit and to ban all suspects from the city."[289] To aid them in this task, the Franciscans and Dominicans created and supervised virtuous laymen (Tertiaries) who supported the reform efforts and helped to enforce morals legislation.[290] Thus the municipal campaigns against sodomy of the thirteenth century were part of a much broader, class-based program of social reform.[291] The repression of sodomy was justified by reference to the early Christian interpretation of the story of Sodom, but the energies that drove the campaign were those of class hatred.

[288] Blansher (1981).

[289] Goodich (1979:84).

[290] Goodich (1979:79, 1982:152–55).

[291] The scope of the campaign is indicated by Goodich (1982:152). In addition to sumptuary legislation and laws freeing imprisoned debtors and forbidding excessive usury, the communes enacted measures against abortion, magicians, sodomites, public prostitutes, and adulterers.

II The Construction of Modern Homosexuality

7 Repression and the
Emergence of Subcultures

The Decline of Feudalism

Over a period of centuries, political centralization and the expansion of a cash economy eroded feudal social relations in Western Europe. Increasingly, cultivators raised crops for the market instead of for local consumption, while a larger and larger proportion of the working population engaged in manufacturing and trade. Serfdom had almost entirely disappeared in England before being abolished altogether by Elizabeth I. By the time of the Revolution, almost all French peasants were legally free— though they were still burdened by a host of quasi-feudal, traditional obligations to their landlords. Production came to be carried out primarily by laborers working for wages, on behalf of those who owned land, machinery, or raw materials, and who sold their products for cash on the market. Still, a middle class composed of self-employed small farmers, artisans, craftsmen, and tradesmen played a growing role in the economy.

Defeated militarily by the centralizing monarchs, the aristocracy was forced—first in England under Henry VIII, then on the Continent—to withdraw from its military functions. Some nobles took up capitalist agriculture or commerce; some became courtiers or staffed the upper levels of the royal bureaucracies. Wealth eventually brought the bourgeoisie social respectability, and later, political power. As the commercialization of agriculture drove peasants and laborers from the land, the control of the dispossessed became an urgent concern for the upper classes.

Scholars of the fourteenth century disputed Aristotelian explanations of motion, and with the Renaissance, science mounted wider challenges to medieval explanations of natural phenomena. The Reformation made Western Christianity officially pluralistic; and subsequently, political philosophies based on contractualism and utilitarianism became the basis for novel moral theories. Despite these developments, traditional Christian teachings dominated sexual ideology throughout most of the early modern era.

The Repression of Homosexuality

From the fourteenth to the beginning of the nineteenth century, homosexuality continued to be described as a sin or crime contrary to nature. After invoking the destruction of Sodom and Gomorrah, the preamble to anti-sodomy legislation adopted in Venice in 1458 recalled that "our most wise ancestors [who had promulgated earlier statutes against sodomy] sought with all their laws and efforts to liberate our city from such a dangerous divine judgment."[1] The attorney general who prosecuted the earl of Castlehaven on sodomy charges in 1631 described his crimes as being "of that pestiferous and pestilential nature that if they be not punished they will draw from heaven heavy judgments upon this kingdom."[2] A century later, the author of *Satan's Harvest Home* feared that the growth of sodomy would "make us more ripe for *Divine* Vengeance." The logic and language remained that of the Justinian Code.[3]

Statutory Provisions

In essence, the legal status of homosexuality remained that of the late Middle Ages. Italian cities of the Renaissance continued to prosecute sodomy under statutes adopted in the thirteenth century or amended in only minor ways later on.[4] In Spain, Ferdinand and Isabella confirmed the thirteenth-century death penalty for male homosexuality, but brought the sanction into line with Roman precedent by changing the penalty from castration followed by stoning to burning at the stake.[5] The Afonsine Ordinances, promulgated in Portugal in 1446 by Afonso V, also called for sodomites to be burned.[6]

In the Holy Roman Empire, the *Bambergische Halsgerichtsordnung* of 1510

---

[1] Quoted in Ruggiero (1985:ch. 6).

[2] C. Bingham (1971).

[3] 1949:52. Emphasis in original.

[4] Florence enacted a new statute against sodomy in the 1490s in the midst of the fervor of Savonarola's campaign against extravagant life-styles, with further legislation in 1502, four years after his death, and still more in 1506 (Wittkower and Wittkower, 1963:169; Goodich, 1976, 1979:84). Venice adopted supplementary legislation in 1458 and 1467 (Ruggiero, 1985:ch. 6); and Cosimo I enacted still another antisodomy statute in the Grand Duchess of Tuscany in the 1540s (Monter, 1976:196–97 n. 13). But for the most part, the Italian cities continued to prosecute under their earlier, medieval legislation.

[5] Isabella had some personal interest in homosexuality, as she succeeded to the throne of Castile because of strong suspicions that her uncle, Henry IV, known for his close involvements with young men, could not have been the father of his wife's daughter (M. Daniel, 1960; G. Jackson, 1972:134–35; T. Miller, 1972; Phillips, Jr., 1978). However, her devout Catholicism probably had more to do with the legislation; it was Ferdinand and Isabella who ordered the Jews expelled from Spain in 1492.

[6] Trevisan (1986:66–67).

and the *Constitutio Criminalis Carolina* of Charles V (1532) provided that "unchastity contrary to nature" between two men, two women, or with an animal be punished by burning.[7] According to an eighteenth-century French source, those convicted of homosexual acts in Switzerland were dismembered alive over a period of several days and then incinerated.[8] In Russia, homosexuality had long been under church jurisdiction, but at the start of the eighteenth century Peter the Great, who often slept with his soldiers, hypocritically made the prohibition secular.[9] Where the initial legislation applied only to men, as in Spain, it was sometimes extended by interpretation to include women as well.[10]

As in medieval times, sodomy cases in early modern England were handled by ecclesiastical courts on the rare occasions where they were prosecuted at all. Their traditional leniency persisted: William Franklin, convicted of bestiality in Tittleshall, Norfolk, in 1525, was ordered to walk in a procession and offer a penny candle as penance.[11] However, in 1533, "the detestable and abominable vice of buggery," defined as "carnall knowledge . . . by mankind with mankind, or with brute beast, or by womankind with brute beast," was made a capital offense, punishable by hanging.[12] This new legislation had less to do with a change in attitude toward homosexuality or bestiality than with Henry's break with Rome, which had just taken place;[13] offenses previously heard in church courts were now to be

---

[7] Kohler and Scheel (1968a:43, 56; 1968b:1.62).

[8] Crompton (1978a).

[9] Nabokoff (1905), Karlinsky (1976).

[10] Crompton (1980/81).

[11] Hair (1972:152).

[12] 15 Henry VIII, c. 6. The law was repealed and reenacted several times in the next few decades; Gigeroff (1968:8) and H. M. Hyde (1970:40) detail the legislative history.

[13] Knowles (1959:204–5) suggests a more devious motive for the legislation. In 1540, Henry VIII advised his nephew, James V of Scotland, to "augment his revenue" by confiscating monasteries, as he himself had done already. In a subsequent letter to the Scottish regent, he recommended sending an investigatory commission to the religious houses to "get knowledge of all their abominations" in order to create a pretext for the confiscation. In 1534–35, the teams of investigators Thomas Cromwell had sent to the English monasteries on Henry's behalf found some cases of homosexuality, especially in the North. Henry presented their report to Parliament, and the text of the Act of 1536, which dissolved the smaller houses, referred to their "vicious, carnal and abominable living" as the reason for the dissolution. Nevertheless, it is not clear that the report was needed to legitimate the confiscation, for complaints about debauchery in the monasteries had circulated in England for at least 150 years and had been confirmed more than once by bishops' visitations. While Cromwell's agents did find some homosexuality in the monasteries, they also publicized cases of heterosexual fornication, laziness, and profligacy. Some prominent monks were prosecuted for treason when they resisted Henry, but as far as is known, none were charged with buggery, not even those named in the commissioner's reports for practicing it (Gasquet, 1892:37–39, 364; Froude, 1915:109–40; Coulton, 1930:84–107; Dickens, 1959; Bowle, 1964:194–200). Lemberg (1970:185) takes

handled by the state. The secular penalty was harsh, but that was equally true of almost all Tudor criminal legislation. The commonly cited figure of 78,000 executions during the reign of Henry VIII is mythical, but the death penalty was imposed very generously—for example, on vagabonds who refused to work on three occasions. Women convicted of prostitution with a soldier could be branded on the face with a hot iron.[14]

New World legislation was equally sanguinary. In Nouvelle-France (now Canada), homosexuality was a capital offense under French law. It carried the death penalty in New Netherlands (later New York), where, under Dutch rule, the legislation of Holy Roman Emperor Charles V was in effect. The Portuguese extended their death penalty to Brazil in 1521, broadening it to include lesbian acts in 1603. English law dealing with buggery was assumed to be in effect in Virginia and the Southern colonies, or else was explicitly enacted, making it a capital crime. Lesbianism was not, because it was not mentioned in Henry VIII's legislation. Male homosexual acts were also capital in New England:[15] however, the Puritan settlers derived the penalty not from English law but from the Old Testament. They considered themselves to be new Israelites, building a theocratic Christian society in the wilderness, and made the Hebrew Bible the foundation of their criminal laws.[16]

With the advance of time, statutes were less likely to refer to specific biblical passages as the basis for their prohibitions: the New Jersey law of 1683, drawn up by predominantly Quaker landowners who had purchased the colony, simply listed sodomy, along with other offenses displeasing to God (the list included cursing, swearing, drinking to someone's health, and using obscene words) as illegal, each to be punished appropriately. Massachusetts changed its prohibition from "sodomy" to "buggery" (Christian wine in a secular bottle) when it revised its statutes in 1697, adding that the crime was "contrary to the very Light of Nature."[17] But this represented only a slight degree of secularization: behind Nature stood Nature's God,

---

the denial of benefit of clergy in the buggery statute as evidence that the act had been drafted with the impending visitation of the monasteries in mind, but much Tudor legislation denied benefit of clergy (Bellamy, 1984:143).

[14]Burford (1976:120).

[15]Between 1655 and 1665, New Haven law, which was based on the New Testament as well as the Old, extended the death penalty to lesbianism, heterosexual anal intercourse, and male masturbation to orgasm in someone else's sight (J. Katz, 1976:22–23). Lesbianism was not a capital offense elsewhere in the colonies. For a detailed account of the colonial North American statutes see Crompton (1976) and J. Katz (1983:23–133).

[16]Crompton (1976), J. Katz (1976:14–23, 1983:23–133), Oaks (1978, 1979/80), Trevisan (1986:66–67).

[17]J. Katz (1983:120–22).

more impersonal perhaps, but still willing to sanction the annihilation of those who broke her laws.

Quaker aversion to killing led Pennsylvania to repeal the death penalty for all offenses except willful homicide in 1682; nevertheless, cursing, gambling, drunkenness, fornication, and the performance of stage plays all remained illegal. Sodomy was punishable by whipping, a fine, and six months of imprisonment for a first offense; by life in prison for a second. Penalties for adultery were comparable—whipping and imprisonment for a year for a first conviction, life imprisonment for a second. However, in 1700 the death penalty was reinstated for Negroes, and in 1718, upon demand from England, for whites. England was not concerned specifically with sodomy; it simply wanted to bring Pennsylvania law into line with that of the colonial power.[18]

Enforcement—Europe

The existence of highly punitive legislation was unable to prevent the emergence—or the persistence from medieval times—of urban social networks within which male homosexual transactions could take place. Benvenuto da Imola found the University of Bologna "infested" by sodomites in 1375; he denounced them, but, warned by a sodomite priest, many got away.[19] According to Saint Bernardino of Sienna, Florence and other early-fifteenth-century Tuscan cities had such a reputation for sodomy that Genoa would not hire Tuscan schoolmasters, and boys walking down the streets of Florence were in greater danger than girls of being sexually assaulted.[20] In Venice, a coterie of homosexual sodomites came to light in 1406.[21] In a sermon of 1494, Savonarola charged that Florence had become infamous for sodomy,[22] a charge that literary figures of the time, including Sabadino and Bandello, confirmed.[23]

That sodomy was coming to be accepted by some elements within the church is suggested by Montaigne's discovery on a trip to Rome in 1580 that the Church of Saint John was performing marriages of male couples.[24] Others in official positions were not so happy about the high levels of ho-

[18] H. E. Barnes (1968:31–39), Crompton (1976).

[19] Dall'Orto (1983).

[20] Herlihy (1969). He attributed the high rate of sodomy to several factors. One of them was delayed marriage for men. Men commonly married at thirty, girls at much younger ages. He also blamed parents for dressing their sons in revealing fashions and permitting them to prostitute themselves for money (Origo, 1962:197–99, 289 n. 42).

[21] Ruggiero (1980:36).

[22] Bedoyere (1958:162), D. Weinstein (1970).

[23] Peyrefitte (1963).

[24] Montaigne (1948:954–55). This practice may have reflected Byzantine influence. John Boswell (1982) has discovered what he calls a "gay marriage ceremony" from the Greek Ortho-

mosexuality. The city government of Florence was sufficiently concerned about the declining birthrate, which it blamed on sodomy, to recruit female prostitutes from other cities. Like Venice, Florence outlawed female-to-male transvestism to stop streetwalkers from dressing like boys to attract male clients.[25] In 1488, the authorities sealed off the porch of Santa Maria Mater Domini, a church in Venice, to stop the sodomites from using it as a gathering place.[26]

Lesbianism was known; Antoninus, archbishop of Florence, mentioned it in a list of sins in the late fifteenth century, and Cardinal Cajetan argued in the early sixteenth that it was no different from male-male sex. Cardinal Carlo Borromeo, the reformist archbishop of Milan, included it in a late-sixteenth-century manual for confessors; and in *Peccatum Mutum* (The Secret Sin), the misogynist Friar Ludovico Maria Sinistrari described women whose "mutual touches" lead to "voluntary pollution . . . produced by rubbing their privy parts together." Yet sexual relations between women received so little discussion in secular and religious sources that they could not have been common or publicly visible. Sinistrari drew on Seneca, not on the behavior of women of his own day, when he wrote of women raping men anally with their enlarged clitorises.[27]

The men who made up the urban homosexual networks were at some risk, for the capital statutes were enforced, even if only sporadically.[28] Fifteenth-century Bologna punished sodomy, rape, infanticide, and heresy with cas-

---

dox church of the ninth or tenth century. This ceremony, however, solemnized "spiritual friendship" and was not intended to legitimate carnal relations.

[25] Trexler (1981), Labalme (1984), Ruggiero (1985:ch. 6). A fair number of working women were prosecuted on these charges. It was feared that clients of such prostitutes would want oral or anal sex, which was illegal (Goodich, 1979:83–84; Trexler, 1981).

[26] Dall'Orto (1983).

[27] Sinistrari (1958), Kleinberg (1982). *Peccatum Mutum* was never published because the church placed it on its Index of prohibited books. My observation that there could have been little publicly visible lesbianism is not meant to imply that it did not exist at all. Some prostitutes undoubtedly became involved in lesbian relationships as an adaptation to the working conditions of the occupation (McCaghy and Skipper, 1969), but the only direct evidence of this known to me comes from the trial records of two women who worked in a Florence bordello (*Atti criminale* AEOS. 2045, ff. 15r–16r, Dec. 12, 1424). I am grateful to Gene Brucker for sharing this case with me. For convent lesbianism, see J. C. Brown (1984, 1985).

[28] The infrequent but harshly repressive campaigns against male homosexuality raise questions about the continuity of urban homosexual networks that cannot be fully resolved at this time. It is possible that episodes of repression disrupted the networks to the point where they had to be reconstituted more or less from start when persecutions died down. On the other hand, survivors may have been able to start them up again. Noting that the homosexual networks evident in fifteenth-century-Venice trial records were far more extensive and much more visible than those in the fourteenth-century records, Ruggiero (1985:ch. 6) suggests that the subculture took time to recover from the persecutions of the thirteenth century. Monter (1974, 1980/1981) and Trumbach (1977, 1984) debate the possible existence of a continuous clandestine homosexual network in early modern Geneva.

tration, blinding, cutting off of a hand, or burning to death.[29] At least fifty cases were prosecuted in Florence between 1348 and 1461, with death sentences carried out in approximately 20 percent.[30] Fourteenth-century Venice prosecuted sodomy only infrequently, but burned those convicted. The level of sodomy prosecutions rose by an order of magnitude in the fifteenth century, with no reduction in the severity of penalties. By contrast, fornication and adultery were treated with great leniency. Most of the sodomy cases involved male homosexuality, with many young teenage boys being raped. But the number of men prosecuted for sodomizing their wives or other female partners was by no means negligible.[31] In late-sixteenth-century Rome, the male couples who had been married in church were burned when it was discovered that they had been living together as spouses.[32]

One reason enforcement was not more consistently harsh is that, until the Counter-Reformation, many of the urbane, sophisticated members of the Italian elite—both secular and ecclesiastical—considered it little more than a peccadillo. Moral standards at the highest levels of the Church relaxed to the point that courtesans and bishops' mistresses attended papal social gatherings.[33] Rumor had it that Pope Leo X (1513–21) died in the middle of a sexual act with a boy.[34] Pope Julius III (1550–55) was widely

---

[29] Frati (1900:81–82).

[30] I have computed these figures from Gene Brucker's notes on the court records found in the Archivio di Stati, which he has generously made available to me. All but two of the cases involved male homosexuality. One of the others concerned bestiality; the second, a woman who had forced her daughter to enter a house of prostitution. Most of the death sentences were for cases where force was used, where small children were partners, where the offense was repeated, or where there were collateral charges such as murder or housebreaking. An additional number of death sentences were imposed in absentia on defendants who had escaped to another Italian city; the absence of extradition arrangements gave them de facto immunity. Most of the remaining penalties were fines, with imprisonment in the local jail for nonpayment. The pattern of penalties suggests that death was rarely imposed on first-time consensual offenders except where flight made the sentence impossible to impose. Even multiple offenders could be treated with leniency. The first time the painter Benvenuto Cellini was convicted of sodomy he was fined; the second time, sentenced to four years imprisonment, commuted by Duke Cosimo de Medici to house arrest (Saslow, 1986:156).

[31] Ruggiero (1975, 1980:36–37, 205 n. 6, 1985:ch. 6), Pavan (1980), Labalme (1984), Rocke (1987). Evidently this was a common practice, for in 1461 there were complaints in Venice that wives were increasingly consenting to sodomy, and in the last decades of the fifteenth century a bordello catered to men who wanted to sodomize women (Pavan, 1980). Heterosexual anal intercourse was a recurrent theme in the pornography of the time. The Italian reputation for this mode of entry reached the point where a French lawyer suggested to the mother of Cellini's mistress that she accuse Cellini of sodomizing her daughter "al modo italiano" (Saslow, 1986).

[32] Montaigne (1948:954–55), Spence (1984:226).

[33] A. von Martin (1944:81).

[34] T. Wagner (1977).

believed to be a lover of males,[35] while one writer called Pietro Aloiso, the son of Pope Paul III (1534–49) "the prince of Sodomy."[36] Antonio Beccadelli's widely read *Hermaphroditus*, which depicted brothel scenes of all kinds in prose of classical elegance, was made court poet at Pavia and was knighted at Naples, where the emperor Sigismund presented him with poet's laurels.[37] Cellini's sodomy convictions did not stand in the way of his receiving commissions from the church for his sculptures, or his being buried in church with full honors when he died.[38] World-wise clergy penned pornography, some of it homoerotic.[39]

The reform campaigns that attacked sodomy, such as those led by Savonarola, drew support primarily from nonelite strata and didn't last long. After Savonarola's death, one member of the Council of Ten remarked, "And now we can practice sodomy again!"[40] In this bawdy milieu, the more adventurous advertised their sexual preferences openly. The painter Giovanni Bazzi (1477–1549), for example, signed his tax returns "Il Sodoma," and sang pederastic songs on social occasions.[41] A market developed for paintings of classical scenes with homoerotic content, e.g., portraits of Zeus and Ganymede, or Caravaggio's "The Boy Bitten by a Lizard."[42] Prosecutions were still possible: in 1476, the young Leonardo da Vinci was arrested after an anonymous accusation of sodomy. Though the charges were later dismissed for lack of evidence,[43] and even though death was not the usual sentence for those convicted, the possibility of a capital sentence gave the more cautious good reason to be discreet. Still, some of their activities were sufficiently well-known for artists to develop a reputation for sleeping with their teenage apprentices, and, scattered references suggest, nobles with their pages. Early in the fourteenth century, Perugia poets often wrote of same-sex love,[44] and in the sixteenth century, literary works praised sodomy.[45]

Even in this atmosphere, one cannot speak of a homosexual subculture analogous to the modern one. Many of the homosexually active men were also actively heterosexual. A sermon of Fra Bernardino speaks of the un-

[35] Bullough (1976:420).
[36] R. Thompson (1979:138).
[37] Wittkower and Wittkower (1963:165).
[38] Saslow (1986:144).
[39] A. von Martin (1944:81).
[40] Wittkower and Wittkower (1963:169), Lorenzoni (1976).
[41] Wittkower and Wittkower (1963:172–75), Bullough (1976:419–20), Dall'Orto (1983). Notwithstanding his flagrancy, Pope Leo X awarded him the title of *cavaliere* in 1518 (Canaday, 1969:262–65).
[42] Posner (1971), Hibbard (1983), Saslow (1986).
[43] Wittkower and Wittkower (1963:171), Bullough (1976:417).
[44] Marti (1956:633–712), Dall'Orto (1983).
[45] Karlen (1971:107–8), R. Thompson (1979:125), Dall'Orto (1983).

happiness of sodomites' wives.[46] Cellini had affairs with women and eventually married.[47] Caravaggio lived for years with one of his male models, but later had a relationship with a woman. The model married and fathered a son.[48] Pietro Aretino seduced a married woman, but also chased boys.[49] After giving up women of ill-repute, Cardinal Francesco Maria Del Monte (1549–1626) sampled male youths.[50] Many of these individuals probably identified themselves and were considered by others as libertines, not homosexuals or sodomites. In the impoverished strata, homosexuality was part of a criminal subculture, not a gay one: Francesco Scambrilla, a man of the fifteenth century, noted that near a certain church one could find spies, thieves, traitors, murderers, and sodomites.[51]

Yet it would be an exaggeration to say that sexual tastes were totally undifferentiated, or that this differentiation was never recognized. In a novella of Sabadino, for example, a man informs his priest that he has never sinned with a woman because "women disgust me to the point that when I just look at them I want to vomit." When he wanted diversion, he confessed, he turned only to boys.[52] The fifteenth-century Platonist Marsilio Ficino observed that some men "naturally love males," while others do not because they are more strongly motivated by "the pleasure of sexual intercourse, and the achievement of corporeal reproduction." Still, he immediately concedes, "the reproductive drive of the soul, being without cognition, makes no distinction between the sexes" and is "naturally aroused for copulation whenever we judge any body to be beautiful." For this reason, "it often happens that those who associate with males, in order to satisfy the demands of the genital part, copulate with them." Backtracking once again, he comments that this is especially true of those "at whose birth Venus was in a masculine sign and either in conjunction with Saturn, or in the house of Saturn, or in opposition to Saturn."[53] While anyone could become a sodomite, some seemingly were more disposed than others by the astrological conditions prevailing at their births.

Many of the male homosexual relations of the time were pederastic. Salai

[46] It must be conceded, though, that the wives could have been unhappy because their husbands were *not* heterosexually active. Bernardino blamed sodomy and infanticide for Florence's alleged population decline, but need not have been thinking only of homosexual sodomy in that context. His sermons made clear that he considered all nonprocreative sex to be unnatural (Origo, 1962:146, 198; Bullough, 1976:380, 407 n. 10). It seems unlikely that there were no real-life heterosexual instances.

[47] Saslow (1986:14, 144).

[48] Hibbard (1983:87).

[49] Karlen (1971:108).

[50] Hibbard (1983:29–30).

[51] Dall'Orto (1983).

[52] Sabadino (1963).

[53] Ficino (1985:135), speech 6, ch. 14.

was ten when he began living with the thirty-eight-year-old da Vinci; Michelangelo was fifty-eight when he took up with the young Roman nobleman Tommaso Cavalieri.[54] Some of these relationships endured, but many must have ended when the youthful partner reached adulthood. In the absence of other institutions (like gay bars) that could have helped to forge a homosexual identity, this instability was not conducive to the formation of an identity or a subculture based on male-male love.

As the tensions and social conflicts of the Renaissance subsided, so did the sodomy prosecutions. Sodomy remained a capital offense in all the Italian states, and executions occurred into the eighteenth century, though infrequently. Under ordinary circumstances, nothing was done about it. Travelers had long commented on the Venetians' lax morality, which neither the Counter-Reformation nor the fall of the Republic in 1798 was able to repress. George Sand, who visited Venice in 1833–34, noticed the young men dressed as women who openly solicited strollers on religious holidays; Byron, William Beckford, and August von Platen, who all had to leave their native lands to avoid prosecution on homosexuality-related charges, found the city a safe haven.[55]

In seventeenth-century Rome, pimps in the Piazza Novona offered boys to customers.[56] The Scottish traveler William Lithgow found "beastly Sodomy" to be "as rife" in early-seventeenth-century Padua

> as in Rome, Naples, Florence, Bullogna, Venice, Ferrara, Genoa, Parma not being exempted, nor yet the smallest Village of Italy; a monstrous filthiness, and yet to them a pleasant pastime, making songs, and singing Sonets of the beauty and pleasure of their Bardassi, or buggerd boys.[57]

Italy's reputation for sodomitical practices spread across Europe.[58]

Of more than 30,000 cases prosecuted between 1536 and 1821 by the Portuguese Inquisition, just under 900 were for *pecado nefando* (unmentionable sin), i.e., sodomy. This could be heterosexual or homosexual; in some cases wives accused their husbands. Most of those prosecuted, however, were clerics, adolescents, or slaves. Those who turned themselves in were released with a warning, but roughly 50 of those accused were burned at the stake. After the decision in the middle of the seventeenth century that true sodomy required "penetration with ejaculation of semen," prosecution of lesbian cases ended. Heterosexual buggery, though, was prosecuted.[59]

---

[54] Wittkower and Wittkower (1963:151, 172–73), Saslow (1983:156–57), Rocke (1987).
[55] Morand (1977), Crompton (1985).
[56] Dall'Orto (1983).
[57] Lithgow (1906:38).
[58] Bussy-Rabutin (1868), Burton (1927:651–53).
[59] Mott (1984), Amiel (1986). It is of interest to compare these figures with those of Italy,

Even in this atmosphere of terror, male homosexual social networks were able to function. Mott's research on seventeenth-century Lisbon revealed that "there were inns openly patronized by sodomites, balls where transvestites danced and played instruments, much street prostitution, and men who served as go-betweens for male sexual encounters. . . . All classes participated,"[60] with the clergy heavily represented. Whether these networks constituted a single homosexual subculture or several subcultures, or were parts of subcultures defined in terms other than homosexuality, is unclear without further study.

As part of their effort to Christianize India, the Portuguese publicly burned men caught committing sodomy in sixteenth-century Goa. The executions were authorized by the Inquisition, which dealt with Hindus as well as European clerics, and carried out under the supervision of the royal tribunals.[61]

Spain was quite repressive. Though the Inquisition was primarily concerned with religious apostasy, it put the heat on sexual deviation, too. Pedro de Leon, a Jesuit prison chaplain, recorded fifty-two executions for sodomy in Seville alone between 1578 and 1616. Between 1566 and 1620, Valencia burned seventeen, Zaragoza thirty-four, and Barcelona a mere two.[62] Among the executions were those of two nuns who used "material instruments," presumably on each other. However, women convicted of lesbian relations in mid-sixteenth-century Granada were merely given a whipping and sent to the galleys, presumably because they had not met the legal requirements of completed sodomy.[63]

Those convicted were not always torched; in Barcelona between 1566 and 1620, only 2.3 percent of those convicted of sodomy were burned. The percentages were higher in Valencia and Zaragoza—13.7 percent and 19.1 percent, respectively.[64] In one remarkable case, a man who confessed to homosexual intercourse at a Black Mass attended by several other Satan-worshipers was given six years in the galleys.[65] The clergy, who made up

---

where secular rulers were less willing to surrender jurisdiction over sodomy cases to the Inquisition. For roughly the same time period, the Venetian Inquisition had 16 sodomy cases out of 3,592. There were no cases at all in Friuli, Naples, and Sicily (Monter and Tedeschi, 1986).

[60] Mott (1984).

[61] A. Wright (1982:144), Spence (1984:223).

[62] Crompton (1978a), Perry (1980:67, 72, 84), Carrasco (1985:76). For purposes of comparison, the number of executions for bestiality in Zaragoza was 57, in Valencia, 11, and in Barcelona, 0. By comparison with the 168 sodomy prosecutions in Valencia between 1571 and 1630, there were 2,543 prosecutions of Moriscos (Moors practicing Islam) (Carrasco, 1985:71, 76).

[63] Crompton (1980/81), Perry (1980:84). How effectively they could row after the two hundred lashes they received in Seville is not indicated in the records.

[64] Carrasco (1985:76). The percentages killed for bestiality were somewhat higher.

[65] Contreras and Henningsen (1986).

almost 20 percent of the Valencia cases, were generally not burned unless they had first been warned to desist a number of times.[66] This leniency could have been a practical measure to preserve the priesthood from extermination; according to Pedro de Leon, sodomy was widely practiced by priests and monks.[67] Even though many sodomites were not killed but simply sentenced to the galleys or forced labor, the percentage executed was very high compared to that for Moriscos[68]—evidence of exceptional concern about sexuality. The humanism that helped to create a more casual sexual morality in upper-class circles of the Italian Renaissance did not take hold in Spain to nearly the same extent. Literary evidence suggests that by the sixteenth century there were strata of the population for whom homosexuality was no longer feared, but instead an entertaining subject.[69] Nevertheless, while the Holy Office remained active, the subject was necessarily treated with great caution. A clandestine subculture did emerge in the cities, with an elaborate system of signals by which men could recognize one another, but the threat of prosecution restricted its scope and visibility.[70]

The Reformation brought no respite, as Protestant leaders were as committed as Catholics to the restriction of sex to the marriage bed. In fact, they outdid the Catholics in this respect, by curbing female prostitution, which had led a tolerated existence in much of Catholic Europe. One of the reasons Protestants abolished priestly celibacy was the belief that it encouraged homosexuality. Despite their supposed endorsement of religious individualism, Protestant clergy, who still feared that divine wrath would doom an entire city for the sins of a few, continued to impose stern sanctions as a deterrent. Late-sixteenth-century Strasbourg drowned men for bigamy, beheaded or burned them for incest, and sent them to the stake for sodomy.[71] Between 1555 and 1678, Geneva saw sixty-two prosecutions and thirty executions for sodomy, almost as many as for infanticide.[72]

In comparison with Renaissance Italy or Spain, prosecutions were infrequent in the Low Country, but they did occur. The president of the States-General was beheaded for sodomy in 1446—the highest official to be executed for this offense anywhere in Europe,[73] and in the following century, two-dozen monks from Ghent and Bruges were burned to death.

---

[66] Kamen (1968:201), Carrasco (1985:167).

[67] Perry (1980:132).

[68] In Valencia between 1571 and 1630, only 1 percent of Morisco defendants were burned (Carrasco, 1985:71).

[69] Bradbury (1981).

[70] Carrasco (1985:135).

[71] Abray (1985:190, 219).

[72] Monter (1980/81).

[73] Römer (1978), Murray and Gerard (1987).

Then the pace slackened: there were three capital sentences in the entire seventeenth century, one of them being the artist Jerome Duquesnoy, who was strangled in 1652 for committing sodomy in a chapel of the Cathedral of Bruges.[74] Leiden had only five sentences for sodomy between 1533 and 1700; in addition, two women were flogged and banished for lesbianism and transvestism.

Beginning in 1689, occasional trials began to reveal the existence of male homosexual networks, cross-dressing, and specialized argot, from which a public image of an urban homosexual subculture began to form. Then in 1730, the Dutch Republic mounted a major antihomosexual campaign involving secret denunciations and extraction of confessions through torture. When completed anal intercourse with ejaculation could be proved, execution by hanging, burning, beheading, garroting, or drowning followed. Possibly as many as a hundred boys and men were executed and denied burial. Lesser acts such as mutual masturbation or anal intercourse without ejaculation were punished by imprisonment for as long as forty years— without parole. Further waves or prosecution followed in 1764–65 and 1776–79.[75]

The magnitude of the Dutch onslaught—exceptional on the Continent in the eighteenth century—has seemed to call for a special explanation. The rationale given for the prosecutions—to forestall divine wrath—was traditional, but tradition alone can hardly explain a quantum leap in the level of repression. Meer suggests that the disclosure of a subculture of wide extent may have been a factor, for it must have been more frightening to discover networks joining men of different social classes and linking different cities than to learn of isolated incidents. However, the authorities had not responded in like manner when information about the homosexual underworld came to light a generation earlier.[76]

A number of developments in Dutch society may account for the greater interest shown in 1730. Shortly before the trials began there had been a peasant revolt in the East and a worrisome epidemic of cattle plague. An infestation of woodworms created a sense that the very foundations of the country were rotting (in the western third of the country houses were built on poles). Though the average standard of living remained the highest in

[74] Wittkower and Wittkower (1963:175).

[75] Crompton (1978), Gerard (1981), Boon (1983), Noordam (1983), Spierenberg (1984:125–26), Huusen (1985), Meer (1985, 1988). The rare cases of lesbianism that came to light puzzled the authorities because they didn't fit into a familiar conceptual framework. The women were punished, but much more lightly than the men. I've not been able to examine Dekker and van de Pol (1987), which analyzes 114 Dutch cases of female transvestism in the seventeenth and eighteenth centuries.

[76] Meer (1985).

Europe, the Dutch economy was being overtaken by the English and French, which created a subjective sense of economic decline. As production fell in major sectors of the economy, poverty and unemployment rose. The share of income going to financiers also increased, so that inequality of wealth and power grew in the towns.[77]

In this atmosphere, a stricter moral climate took hold. The orthodox Calvinist clergy instigated prosecutions for prostitution and adultery to undermine the more liberal political and economic elites, who were often Catholic, and, as merchants and bankers, tolerated individual idiosyncracies that were not relevant to the conduct of business.[78] A major pogrom in the 1720s virtually eliminated gypsies from Dutch life. The sodomy prosecutions were another manifestation of aggression generated by the succession of frustrating events. They were not, however, a simple knee-jerk reflex; the response was mediated by the imagery of sodomy present in Christian teachings.[79] It is likely that the emphasis given to God's sovereignty in Calvinism enhanced the punitive character of that response. Medieval Catholicism did not necessarily ascribe every natural occurrence to God's will; the role of Fortune, or chance, in human affairs was recognized.[80] Calvin's *The Institutes of the Christian Religion* explicitly denied this role, attributing everything that happens to God. The doctrine of predestination undercut any rationale for leniency. To live a sinful life was to exhibit an innate, irrevocable depravity. God was not merciful to those he had damned; there was no need for people to be.

Male homosexual networks have been documented for the larger French cities of the fifteenth and early sixteenth centuries, including Paris, Rouen, and Cologne; comedies celebrating male homosexuality, a product of these subcultures, were performed as street theater during the annual Carnival season.[81]

Here, too, there was repression, though its magnitude is not clear. Trial records from late-medieval and early-modern lower French courts are incomplete, because, at least officially, sodomy was considered so heinous that the transcripts of the proceedings were sometimes burned along with the offenders.[82] Records for one fourteenth-century case involve a complaint by two youthful servants of a procurator of the Parlement of Paris (an

---

[77] Blok (1912:52, 75), J. L. Price (1974:212–15), personal communication, Kent Gerard.

[78] Shetter (1971).

[79] Gerard (1981), Huusen (1985).

[80] K. Thomas (1971:84–89, 110–11).

[81] I. Bloch (1908), I. Nelson (1977), Goodich (1979:14–15), Murray and Gerard (1988). A survey of Cologne's pastors in 1484 led to estimates that approximately 1 percent of the population engaged in unnatural sexual activity and discloses the existence of male prostitution.

[82] M. Daniel (1957:46–50).

appellate court) that their employer had pressured them into having inter-crural sexual relations. Because he had taken minor orders, he was tech-nically a cleric, and so was turned over to the church, but he escaped from prison before he could be tried. Others were not so lucky; in the preceding year a man was burned alive for sodomy at Chambery. Others, however, were merely fined.[83] In subsequent centuries, prosecutions appear to have been infrequent: there are no prosecutions on sodomy charges in the court records of Lyon between 1500 and 1789.[84] However, the Parlement of Paris processed 176 sodomy cases between 1565 and 1640, including 121 cases in which death sentences were being appealed.[85]

As elsewhere, the great majority of prosecutions were directed at men, but occasionally women were charged. For example, two Frenchwomen were tried for tribadism in 1533, but acquitted for lack of evidence. Several women commoners of the same century, who disguised themselves as men, worked at male occupations, and married other women, were burned when their deceptions were discovered.[86] As the "wives" in these mar-riages were not prosecuted, it is clear that the punitive response was evoked not by lesbianism, but by gender-crossing. Women who tried to appropri-ate male identity and its powers for themselves were killed. There were ar-guments for treating both partners on an equal basis: Jean Gerson, rector of the University of Paris in the fifteenth century, and author of a manual for confessors, referred to sexual relations between women as indescribably horrible, and sixteenth-century works of jurisprudence state that those guilty of it are to die; however, no executions are known except where transvestism was involved.[87]

The law notwithstanding, memoirs show the atmosphere of the French court of the late-sixteenth and early-seventeenth centuries to have been irre-ligious, with male homosexuality and tribady open and well represented.[88] Men of the court aristocracy treated sexual relations between women with

[83] M. Daniel (1972).

[84] P. T. Hoffman (1984, personal communication).

[85] Soman (1978), Coward (1980a), Monter (1980/81). Incomplete information is available about later cases. Hernandez (1920) summarizes ten cases between 1540 and 1726, drawing on judicial documents preserved in the Bibliothèque Nationale, most involving the use of force (one involved the anal rape of a married woman, the rest were for heterosexual sodomy). But there were certainly more prosecutions than these. Jousse, a French penologist of the late eighteenth century, reports nine sodomy executions, including that of the rector of the Uni-versity of Paris, whose hanging in 1584 is not mentioned by Hernandez (Crompton, 1978). Courouve (1978) lists still more cases. In addition, Fleuret (1920) records forty convictions for bestiality between 1540 and 1649. Hernandez was Fleuret's pen name.

[86] Crompton (1980/81), Bonnet (1981:36–37, 49–51, 53–55), Everard (1982).

[87] Bonnet (1981:14, 54–55). There may have been some in Calvinist Geneva (Monter, 1980/81).

[88] Brantôme (1933), Rat (1955:62–65).

amused indulgence,[89] so that lesbianism began to figure in pornography. Nicholas Chorier's *The Dialogues of Luisa Sigea*, published in 1660, contains a sapphic seduction scene.[90]

Henri III, a bisexual transvestite who ruled from 1574 to 1589, surrounded himself with "ruffled mignons" who disgusted the public by flaunting their effeminacy and homosexuality.[91] His successor, Henri IV, tried to set a better example by having two of his courtiers burned at Saint-Germain-en-Laye for engaging in sodomy with his pages, but according to De L'Estoile, writing in 1607, sodomy remained sufficiently prevalent at court that it was "best to keep one's hands in one's trousers."[92]

It was widely believed that Louis XIII, king from 1610 to 1643, was slow to produce an heir because his sexual interests were in males, not females.[93] Though the homosexual affairs and flagrant transvestism of Philip, duc d'Orleans (brother of Louis XIV) were an embarrassment at the court late in the century, they did not arouse nearly so much scandal as Louis XIV's illegitimate children.[94] Court society attached great importance to decorum and observance of an elaborate protocol; it was outward appearance that counted, not inner feelings or hidden behavior. In the absence of occupational or functional differentiation among the court nobility, rank-specific ceremonial roles and rules of etiquette served to mark status.[95] As long as extramarital affairs were conducted with discretion, no one made much of them, whether they were heterosexual or homosexual. Though Louis XIV found male homosexuality personally distasteful, he continued his patronage of the composer Jean-Baptiste Lully, whose homosexual leanings were common knowledge.[96]

Following the "Poison Affair," which involved several of Louis's sons, the atmosphere at Versailles became more austere, but not terribly repressive. In 1670, Louis issued a royal ordinance removing sodomy cases to the royal court to ensure that the regional Parlements would not apply the incendiary medieval penalties across the board.[97] When several scandals broke around 1692, one of them implicating abbés and great lords in a ring

[89] de Beauvoir (1952:407), Brantôme (1933), Sole (1976:209–10), Monter (1980/81).

[90] Chorier (1890).

[91] Römer (1902), Brézol (1911), L'Estoile (1943:7–28, 61–82, 142, 181, 191, 200–205, 444, 544, 569, 575–607), Robin (1963, 1964a, b, c), Karlen (1971:110–11), Bullough (1976:448–50), Lacroix (1937:1250–74).

[92] Lacroix (1937:1340).

[93] Daniel (1961c), Karlen (1971:111).

[94] Rowse (1977).

[95] Elias (1983).

[96] Prunières (1929:45, 142–43), Amar (1968). Nevertheless, Lully thought it advisable to marry; the king was godfather to his oldest son.

[97] Desmon (1963).

of boy prostitution, the reaction was quite restrained. Twenty years later, when a homosexual orgy was discovered taking place right under Louis XIV's windows, little was done.[98]

The Catholic Reformation, or Counter-Reformation, which began in France around 1620 and continued for several decades, disrupted the accommodation of homosexuality only slightly. The Counter-Reformation had begun in response to the disaffection of lay people and the lower clergy from corruption at the highest levels of the church, and in an effort to stem defections to Protestantism.[99] In France, royal officials and wealthy urban merchants who hoped that the suppression of popular culture and the inculcation of a work ethic would put an end to rebellions, joined the church in trying to impose a stricter sexual morality. Nudity in art was banned; illegitimacy, concubinage, prostitution, immodest clothing, and mixed nudity at public baths were repressed.[100]

During this period, since homosexuality could not be known about publicly at court, its practitioners were left the options of exile or secrecy. Even during this wave of repression, however, those close to the king enjoyed a de facto immunity. Thus, the duc de Vendôme, a cousin of the king and a distinguished general, had no trouble despite his public transvestism and homosexuality. The poet Théophile de Viau was sentenced to burn in 1623, but the sentence was annulled. His partner, known as Des Barreaux, remained a magistrate and patron of letters, and despite public knowledge of his homosexuality, became a councillor to Parlement.[101]

Those who did not enjoy noble status or protection did not fare so well.

[98] Erlanger (1953:55, 195–98), M. Daniel (1957:10, 27, 51, 1961c), Karlen (1971a:110–11), Rowse (1977), Hahn (1979:20–21).

[99] Kidd (1933), Elton (1963), Spitz (1984). Homosexuality was one of the points of criticism. It was widely believed that two popes of the fifteenth century, Paul II and Sixtus VI, engaged in homosexual relations, and Karlen (1971:89), usually skeptical about such claims, concludes that in these instances they were well founded. In the following century, similar allegations were made about Popes Leo X, Adrian VI, and Julius III (Bullough, 1976:420; T. Wagner, 1977; Martines, 1979:310). Toward the end of the fifteenth century, Savonarola prophesied that a revitalized Florence, free from poetry, public sports, intoxication, usury, sodomy, and indecent dress would usher in a new spiritual age, displacing the hopelessly corrupt Roman curia from the leadership of the Catholic church (D. Weinstein, 1970:26–27, 155–73). In Italy the Counter-Reformation began much earlier, spearheaded by the Council of Trent (1545–63). Pope Paul IV got the movement off to a good start by ordering clothing to be painted on Michelangelo's nudes in the Sistine Chapel. In this chillier climate Cellini married and wrote an autobiography that understated his earlier homoerotic adventures. Fewer portraits of Ganymede were painted, and they became less erotic (Bullough, 1976:441; Saslow, 1986:161, 172, 175).

[100] P. T. Hoffman (1984:92–95).

[101] Perrens (1896), Schirmacher (1897), Lachèvre (1909, 1911). M. Daniel (1957:14, 17), A. Adam (1965).

In 1586, a master at the Collège Cardinal was sentenced to be hung and burned for sodomizing one of the children in his charge,[102] and in 1645, the schoolmaster Vigean was burned alive for sodomy. Sixteen years later two old men were executed for supplying youths to aristocrats, who were not even prosecuted. The deaths of Richelieu and Louis XIII brought some relief, though the piety of the queen regent, Anne of Austria, prevented a full return to tolerance.[103]

As among the German and Russian nobility of the eighteenth century, homosexuality was not uncommon among the French.[104] According to one observer, by 1724, *"le péché philosophique"* had become "ultrafashionable in aristocratic circles."[105] Throughout the eighteenth century the aristocracy was the prime audience for erotic literature, and the most popular works "gave equal attention to all types of sexual activity, natural or perverse."[106] In this century as in the preceding one, the aristocracy treated homosexual interests with the same broad tolerance accorded heterosexual affairs, so long as they were expressed discreetly.[107]

Even indiscretion was not necessarily catastrophic. The bishop of Laon was temporarily banished to his seminary after being implicated in the Deschauffours affair in 1725,[108] but in the 1730s he played an active role in religious disputes. The duc de la Tremoile, exiled in 1724 because of his affair with the king's governor, later became a hero for his military exploits.[109] Nobility conferred a de facto immunity from prosecution.

The urban male-homosexual subculture of late medieval Paris was still a going concern in the seventeenth and eighteenth centuries.[110] At the start of the reign of Louis XV, the Paris police began the systematic surveillance of those they knew to be involved and of locations used for solicitation, using informants or provocateurs, some of whom had previously been ar-

---

[102] Coward (1980a).

[103] M. Daniel (1957:17–30).

[104] Herberstein (1969:40), Rowse (1977).

[105] Coward (1980a). Edmond Barbier (1689–1771), who belonged to the Parisian *haute bourgeoisie*, noted in his journal that the "vice of the ass" had long been popular in France, in his own time more than ever; "to the chagrin of the ladies of the court, the young lords devote themselves to it with a vengeance" (quoted in Courouve, 1980).

[106] Marchand (1933:149, 213).

[107] V. Lee (1975:12–15).

[108] Benjamin Deschauffours was tried and convicted for supplying the French and English upper classes with French boys, some of whom were raped and beaten; one died. Over two hundred men were implicated, but Deschauffours was the only one executed. Most participants were not prosecuted; those who were drew sentences of three to six months (Hernandez, 1920; Coward, 1980a).

[109] Coward (1980a).

[110] Courouve (1978), Rey (1984/85, 1985).

rested on sex charges, to identify and entrap men. Police concerns were more pragmatic than religious. They were after pederasts (using the term in a way that did not imply adolescence of the partner), not sodomites, and were mainly worried about potential threats to the public order. Female prostitution was just as much a concern to the police for identical reasons.[111]

Given the nature of police concerns, few of those detected were arrested: "action was taken only when specific complaints were laid, when behavior outrageous to public decency was reported, and when offenses were committed which involved the corruption of minors;[112] political intrigue, or involvement in related crimes, such as kidnapping, also risked a more active police response.[113] In the absence of these elements, one could boast loudly in the street about the previous night's adventures and earn no more than an admonition from passers-by.[114]

To protect the reputation of families and to avoid publicizing the offense, men arrested were rarely brought to trial.[115] When the police wanted to intervene, they used their discretionary authority to refer to a confessor, conscript, exile to the West Indies (as was done with female prostitutes), or commit to the asylum at Bicêtre.[116] Solicitations and attempts were treated just like completed sexual acts, suggesting that it was the deviant desire or inclination that evoked the preventive measure, not the violation of a provision in the criminal code.[117]

More stringent penalties could still be imposed. In 1691, Antoine Fenelle, surprised in the act of sodomy, was, as an act of royal mercy, confined to the Hôpital Général for life, his parents to pay the expenses.[118] In 1750, an eighteen-year-old journeyman joiner and a twenty-four-year-old butcher caught in the act in a public street were burned at the stake to serve as an example at a time when homosexuality was believed to be spreading. But this was quite exceptional. The public was coming to regard the death pen-

---

[111] Courouve (1981), Rey (1982, 1985).

[112] Coward (1980a).

[113] M. Daniel (1957).

[114] Rey (1985). In one's own neighborhood, a violation of etiquette, as might occur through an overly bold solicitation, could earn a public reprimand or shaming; only rarely were the police called.

[115] In 1784 the police commissioner Pierre-Louis Foucault showed some friends a book containing the names of 4,000 pederasts, almost as many as female prostitutes. It would have been extremely difficult to try that many defendants (Courouve, 1981). Courouve (1979) lists fewer than fifty trials between 1611 and 1783.

[116] Commitments to Bicêtre could also be initiated by family members who wanted to avoid scandal (Desmon, 1963).

[117] M. Daniel (1961c), Coward (1980a), Rey (1982).

[118] Courouve (1981).

alty as excessive, and it was imposed quite infrequently. More typical was the two-month sentence handed down in 1726, or the case of the priest who, the previous year, was set at liberty after a month in Bicêtre, with a warning not to say mass for a while.[119] Of the 108 death sentences issued by the Parlement of Paris in 1775, only one involved sodomy.[120] All but two of the seven men executed in the eighteenth century (the two just mentioned) were accused not merely of sodomy, but also of homicide, rape, theft, or blasphemy.[121] Effeminate men were still ridiculed, and homosexuality continued to be viewed somewhat negatively[122]—the *bougre*, for example, was revived as a term of indecent abuse—but it was no longer horrifying. Beginning in the early 1700s, Paris cafés catering to men with homosexual tastes flourished free from police interference through the rest of the century even though their existence was widely known.[123] Although some writers deplored the decline of moral standards, this leniency is a strong indication that public feelings about homosexuality were not passionate.

Toward the latter part of the century, "tribadism had become almost fashionable,"[124] especially among actresses and women of the court. Its adherents patronized certain cafés—some of them also frequented by participants in the male homosexual subculture—and met at private social gatherings from which men were excluded.[125] Their incomes and independent social lives enabled these women to create an urban lesbian subculture, in all probability for the first time in history.[126]

[119] Courouve (1981).

[120] The last execution took place on October 1, 1783. The condemned man, who was broken on the wheel, was a defrocked Capuchin monk who had raped and stabbed a young chimney sweep to death.

[121] Kaplow (1972:141–42), Courouve (1979), Coward (1980a), Bonnet (1981:51–52), Ariès (1982), Rey (1982).

[122] Rousseau, who had experienced a frightening attempt at homosexual seduction while still a youth, found it disagreeable; and Voltaire described it in his *Philosophical Dictionary* as a "disgusting abomination"—but he tried it once so that he could judge from personal experience (Coward, 1980a). On several occasions in 1781, mobs chased young dressed in outlandish, effete outfits interpreted as effeminate (Rey, 1985).

[123] Coward (1980a), Rey (1985).

[124] Coward (1980b).

[125] Reuilly (1909).

[126] Marriages of the French nobility and upper bourgeoisie were arranged between families, with partners having little choice; consequently ties of love and affection were often lacking. Many husbands encouraged their wives to develop an independent social life so that they could spend time with their mistresses. Since the wives had independent incomes and did not need to work for a living, they were able to conduct lesbian affairs free from familial control or the time constraints of those who did. Brantôme (1933) suggests that many husbands found this less upsetting than their wife having an affair with another man. Actresses had incomes of their own, both as performers and courtesans. This was a fairly recent development: only

Though formally subject to the death penalty, lesbianism was not severely punished in the eighteenth century. In the early years of the century, tribades were sometimes detained by the police or through *lettres de cachet,* as prostitutes were, but this was rare. They were scorned, and toward the end of the century, the subject of occasional scandals and ostracism, but none was ever executed. On the whole, the response was mild.[127]

Those groups that advocated a more repressive policy—notably the Compagnie du Saint-Sacrement under Louis XIII and the Jesuits under Louis XIV—did so largely on the basis of religious considerations, which still weighed heavily in the seventeenth century. However, secular arguments in favor of liberalization were starting to appear. Louvois, war minister under Louis XIV, suggested that homosexuality might not be so bad, for men devoted to it would not be as reluctant to go to war as men with wives and mistresses at home. It was said that while underpopulation might have made the biblical prohibition of homosexuality necessary in ancient times, population growth since then had made the prohibition unnecessary. And since God had not punished anyone for it since the destruction of Sodom and Gomorrah, the prohibition was evidently no longer in effect![128] In earlier centuries, a remark like that would have been dangerously heretical.

Eighteenth-century arguments in opposition to homosexuality were also increasingly secular, reflecting the rationalism of the Enlightenment. French military strength depended on its manpower; those who engaged in homo-

---

since the seventeenth century were women permitted to perform in public, and the occupation remained so highly stigmatized that actresses were automatically excommunicated by the church. Women of other classes were more constrained: lower-class women had to spend most of their time working, and since they were paid less than men, they remained dependent on their husbands. Middle-class women often worked alongside their husbands in shops or businesses, and lacked the opportunity to carry on an independent social life (V. Lee, 1975:9–12, 18, 20–27, 36–38; Maclean, 1977:88; E. Jacobs, 1979). Though from the time of the Renaissance the larger cities afforded a fair number of women enough freedom to have made discreet lesbian relationships feasible (Sachs, 1971:42–43), access to the more attractive positions was achieved through husbands. And when economic change removed production from the household, women were forced out of the market, leaving them even more dependent on men for support (M. Howell, 1986). Of the eleven women prosecuted for "dirty acts" with one another in Amsterdam 1795–97, only one was affluent and married. The others were peddlers, collectors of dry wood, or prostitutes. When one was asked why she had not married, she replied, "Just to fuck? If that's all I'm missing I can do it myself" (Meer, 1984:143–44, 1988).

[127] V. Lee ((1975), E. Jacobs (1979), Coward (1980a, b). Bonnet (1981:165) disagrees, arguing that when Mme de Lamballe, the lover of Marie Antoinette, was executed in 1792 and her genitals mutilated, the real target was Lesbos. However, the ferocity of this response can hardly be understood without taking into account the class hatred present in the French Revolution. There is no record of commoners being attacked in this way.

[128] M. Daniel (1957:57–58), Karlen (1970:134), Coward (1980a).

sexual relations were accused of shirking their duty to the nation in this respect.[129] But the philosophes also criticized men who remained celibate, kept mistresses, or patronized prostitutes, on exactly the same grounds.

Renaissance and Enlightenment pornography, court memoirs, and philosophical writings open a window on conceptions of homosexuality outside those of religious and legal discourse. Those discourses were concerned with acts and consequently little concerned with the persons who engaged in those acts. For the most part that remained true in these nonlegal, nonecclesiastical contexts, but not entirely. Nicholas Chorier's *The Dialogues of Luisa Sigea*, published in 1660, implies that erotic attraction to persons of the opposite sex is innate, but does not exclude the possibility of a same-sex choice: "He who seeks Venus in a boy offers violence to his own natural propensity." This seeking, he insists, is not natural but due to "corrupt morals."[130] A woman in one of the dialogues initially loathed tribady but, after being seduced by a female friend, found that she liked it.[131] Here the

---

[129] The same accusation was raised in Germany, where the Protestant theologian Johann Michaelis argued in his *Grundliche Erklärung des Mosaischen Rechts in Sechsen Theilen*, published in 1770–75,

> If one considers how dreadfully damaging sodomy is for the state, and how much this disgusting vice spreads secretly, the death penalty does not seem too hard. Once this vice develops a hold, striplings begin to seduce striplings, not adults. It knows no rest, indeed, once its shamefulness and ugliness is lost and becomes a mark of gallantry and pride in the nation, it will become the greatest force of depopulation and weakness, not in its initial stages but three or four generations later. Not only does sodomy weaken marriage (as does whoredom, though this is sometimes procreative) and aid and abet he who refuses to raise a family, or is incapable of doing so, . . . bringing the nation (Rome of the Caesars) through this unsuitable vice to the brink of destruction (quoted in Heinsohn and Steiger, 1982).

This theme has continued to lend a note of unintended hilarity to the writings of credulous historians. Listen to Norman Cantor (1963:31):

> The civilization of the Roman empire was vitiated by homosexuality from its earliest days. A question, uncomfortable to our contemporary lax moralists, may be raised: Is not the common practice of homosexuality a fundamental debilitating factor in any civilization where it is extensively practiced, as it is a wasting spiritual disease in the individual? It is worth considering that another great and flourishing civilization, the medieval Arabic, where homosexuality was also widespread, similarly underwent a sudden malaise and breakdown. Is there some moral psychological causation, resulting from the social effects that has been ignored?

In the second edition, published six years later, Cantor adds twentieth-century England to the list of great civilizations brought down by homosexuality. Crompton (1978b) delightfully refutes the "decline of civilization" thesis; Demandt (1986) offers a historiographic survey.

[130] Chorier (1890:82–83), dialogue 6, "Frolics and Sports." According to Havelock Ellis (1936:2.67), an Italian priest named Carretto also declared, in 1676, that homosexual tendencies are innate, but I've not been able to locate the original source.

[131] Chorier (1890), in the dialogue "Tribadicon."

taste is acquired, the behavior voluntary. Presumably any woman could indulge. Many of the tribades in Brantôme's memoirs have husbands or male lovers, or turn to them because women cannot truly satisfy them. Some turned to women to avoid the scandal of a man, or, in countries where women are secluded, for lack of men.[132] Though he cannot resist repeating stories about women with enlarged clitorises, most of the women he describes are depicted as altogether normal. Yet Brantôme also quotes Angelo Firenzuola's early-sixteenth-century *Dialogue on the Beauty of Women* as saying that Jupiter makes some women lovers of women, others lovers of men. Here we have the sapphist as a distinct type of person, one who flees from marriage because she can't stand men.

Partisans of unnatural sex were beginning to contribute to discussions of these questions. Giovanni della Casa, the archbishop of Benevento, and papal secretary to Pope Paul IV, applauded sodomy in his *Capitolo del Forno* (1538) and *De laudibus sodomia sev pederastiae* (1550). The prosodomitical dialogue, *Alcibiade Fanciullo a Scola*, was published at Oranges in 1652.[133] The tenor of the arguments raised by apologists for same-sex love is apparent from Chorier's remark that he was not persuaded by the arguments of "buggers and catamites . . . in defense of their cause, from nature, morals, or from the dignity or renown of certain men."[134]

Enforcement—England

In England, the Buggery Act of 1533 was at first invoked only in connection with religious or political prosecutions. Thus Walter Lord Hungerford was beheaded in 1540 on charges of sodomizing his servants over a period of several years, but not for this reason alone: he was also convicted of harboring a traitor, and of ordering his chaplains to prophesy the date of the king's death and whether he would defeat his enemies.[135] The following year, the headmaster of Eton confessed to sexual relations with his male students and a servant, but since there were no political issues at stake, he was not even prosecuted. He did lose his headmastership, but later held

[132] Brantôme (1933:128–36), First Discourse, ch. 15. In the eighteenth century, Montesquieu, Diderot, and Voltaire all attributed homosexual eroticism to the segregation of the sexes, which they considered pernicious (Coward, 1980a).

[133] R. Thompson (1979:125), Karlen (1971:107).

[134] Chorier (1890:84).

[135] Salmon (1941:149), T. B. Howell (1816:483), Murray and Gerard (1988). One might wonder whether the sodomy charge had been added to the others to smear the reputation of one of the king's enemies, but this is unlikely. A number of aristocrats were executed in 1541 for treason, but none of the others was charged with sodomy. In light of contemporary discussions about whether homosexual preferences were generally exclusive in the premodern era, it may be worth noting that Hungerford had married three times and fathered four children (Stephen and Lee, 1964:260).

prominent positions in the Anglican church and was appointed head-master at Westminster.[136]

The next execution took place almost a century later, in 1631. It was not a simple case of consensual homosexuality, but involved group rape, and the defendant—the earl of Castlehaven—was a Roman Catholic, whose prose-cution was an indirect attack on Charles I, whom Protestants considered overly sympathetic to Rome.[137] The execution ten years later of an Anglican bishop in Dublin also had more to do with his involvement in political and religious controversies of the day than with the homosexual offense of which he may have been convicted by a predominantly Catholic jury.[138]

The moral tone set by the English court varied over the course of the sev-enteenth century. James I (king of Scotland as James VI from 1567 to 1625, of England from 1603 to 1625) was linked romantically with a number of men (as well as with various women)—as was his lord chancellor, Francis Bacon—and understandably did not wish to initiate a policy of repression; his court was noted for its moral laxity.[139] His son and successor, Charles I (king, 1625–49) frowned on sexual license of any kind, perhaps having taken too seriously his father's (tongue-in-cheek?) admonition that sod-omy, like witchcraft and willful murder, was unforgivable.[140] In the somber atmosphere of the court, one observer wrote,

> the fools, bawds, mimics and catamites of the former court, grew out of fashion, and the nobility and courtiers, who did not quite abandon their debaucheries, yet so reverenced the King as to retire into corners to practice them.[141]

---

[136] H. M. Hyde (1970:41).

[137] It is the exceptional nature of the Castlehaven case that renders Bingham's (1971) use of it as the sole basis for drawing conclusions about early-seventeenth-century English attitudes toward homosexuality quite inappropriate.

[138] H. M. Hyde (1970:44–57), Bingham (1971), Burg (1983:6–9), A. Simpson (1984). The sources disagree as to Atherton's charge. Those contemporary with the trial say he was con-victed of sodomizing his servant (H. M. Hyde, 1970:58; Bullough, 1976:476). Later and pre-sumably less reliable sources say he was believed guilty of bestiality with a cow, and of debauchery with parishioners' daughters (*The Case of Atherton*, 1710; Barnard, 1710, Benbow, 1823:25–26). These later sources also portray Atherton as the victim of a malicious prose-cution brought in connection with a dispute over church property. The fact that the chief witness against him later recanted before his own later execution lends credence to the con-tention that he was convicted on the basis of perjured testimony (H. M. Hyde, 1970:58; A. Simpson, 1984).

[139] Akrigg (1962:157–76), Karlen (1971:114), Bingham (1981:3–4, 83–86, 124–25, 130), Burg (1983:5), Duchein (1985).

[140] Bingham (1971). Charles may have had some homosexual experiences as a youth, but this is not certain (Carlton, 1982).

[141] Quoted in Bingham (1971).

Thomas Carew, a dissipated courtier, alluded to this newly austere atmosphere in his masque *Coelum Britannicum*, performed before the king and his gentlemen in 1633. The character Momus, describing reforms that Jupiter is establishing in heaven, announces, "Ganimede is forbidden the Bedchamber, and must onely minister in publique. The gods must keep no Page, nor Groomes of their Chamber under the age of 25. And those provided of a competent stocke of beard."[142] Yet Charles took no steps to initiate the prosecution of buggers. Prominent literary circles were widely suspected of homosexuality, but their members were not molested in any way.[143]

The treatment of male homosexuality in Elizabethan and Jacobean literature was equally mixed. Many authors linked sodomy with papist sympathies, treated it as a form of monstrosity that threatened to upset the natural order of the universe, and destroyed Sodom and Gomorrah over and over again.[144] Yet some authors—William Drummond and Richard Barnfield among them—published homoerotic verse celebrating the love of shepherd boys in imagined Arcadian settings.[145] While this minority viewpoint was not actively persecuted, its adherents could hardly have remained unaffected by the prevalent condemnation of sodomy.[146]

During the Interregnum (1649–60), the ruling Puritans tried to impose a strict and quite unpopular morality on the rest of the population. They

[142] Carew (1949:159).

[143] Kleinberg (1983).

[144] Bray (1982:8–25).

[145] Fone (1983). Bray (1982:60–61) argues that seemingly homophile poetry was often written as a literary exercise and had no emotional significance for its authors, but his evidence for this claim is weak. As we have repeated several times, the use of classical models does not imply that the imitation lacks personal meaning. Nor does the fact that its authors later wrote heterosexual pornography. As Bray acknowledges, much of the antihomosexual writing of the time—which he takes as expressions of the authors' views—was equally derivative and formulaic.

[146] Evidence that coteries of homosexually inclined writers were not fully able to shield themselves from the pejorative views of the majority can be found in their writings. Thus, Antonio, who loves Bassanio in *The Merchant of Venice*, describes himself (4.1. 114–16) as "a tainted wether of the flock, / Meetest for death." A tainted wether is a diseased castrated sheep, and Antonio was melancholic because Bassanio was leaving him to marry Portia for her money. Shakespeare's treatment of this homophile relationship suggests that homoeroticism, not necessarily exclusive, was unexceptional among the aristocracy, but could still lead to self-disgust. If interpreted autobiographically, Shakespeare's sonnets suggest that his own homosexual feelings evoked shame and guilt (Fiedler, 1972:31–38; Shell, 1979; Kleinberg, 1983). The pastoral setting of so many of the explicitly homophile poems is readily explained by the impossibility of realizing an idealized homosexual romance in a world where the law, even if laxly enforced, made homosexuality a capital offense, and where men came under strong family pressure to marry heterosexually. One of the first references to lesbianism in English literature, in Philip Sidney's (1912) *Arcadia*, written 1580–81, no doubt places it in a pastoral setting for similar reasons.

closed theaters, alehouses, brothels, and gambling houses, and banned traditional village entertainments such as bearbaiting and cockfighting.[147] Though the Puritans' rejection of homosexuality was total, they do not seem to have considered it worse than many other vices. Paul Bunyan's *Pilgrim's Progress*, published in 1678, considered an accurate reflection of seventeenth-century Puritan thought, pays it very little attention.[148]

This lack of interest is reflected in the court records. Of the 8,557 assize and quarter-sessions indictments in Essex between 1620 and 1680, only one involved homosexuality, and the case was dropped for lack of evidence.[149] Court records for Somerset between 1601 and 1660,[150] and for Kent, Sussex, Hertfordshire, and Essex for the years 1559–1625 yield only a handful of sodomy indictments.[151] The few cases that did come to public attention during the Interregnum were handled with little more than a wrist-slapping. For example, the Reverend John Wilson, vicar of Arlington, confessed to buggery with more than a dozen partners, but was not prosecuted— merely deprived of his benefice.[152] Far greater attention was paid to such religious offenses as blasphemy and Sabbath breaking; and since the costs of supporting illegitimate children were paid out of local taxes, to premarital fornication.[153]

So far as is known, Charles II, king from 1660 to 1685, was entirely heterosexual, but his libertine personal life set the tone for a frivolous and sexually freewheeling court.[154] According to Pepys, many of the courtiers engaged in homosexual relations with impunity.[155]

Weary of Puritan sobriety, the upper classes gladly followed their sovereign's example in tolerating sexual variance.[156] Their more relaxed attitude can be seen in literature. Though never favorable in its treatment of homo-

---

[147] Maurois (1960:320), Straka and Straka (1973:56–57), Burg (1983:10).

[148] Burg (1983:30–33).

[149] Sharpe (1983:66). By comparison there were nine indictments and three hangings for bestiality in the same period. Since Essex was predominantly rural, the preponderance of animal partners in the indictments is not especially surprising. On the basis of the paucity of homosexual indictments, Sharpe concludes that "however common in London or in court circles, [it] was not a widespread phenomenon in rural Essex," but it is also possible that people simply didn't care about it very much. The absence of references to homosexuality in court cases involving sexual slander (personal communication, J. A. Sharpe) is consistent with the latter possibility. Ingram (1976) found no defamation cases involving homosexuality in the diocesan court of Salisbury for the years 1615–29, or in the Liberty of Ely 1571–95, 1610–39.

[150] Quaife (1979:175–77).

[151] Bray (1982:71, 127–28 n. 44).

[152] I. Bloch (1958:393), H. M. Hyde (1970:59).

[153] Bray (1982:47).

[154] G. R. Taylor (1954:189).

[155] H. M. Hyde (1970:60).

[156] R. Porter (1982).

sexuality, Restoration drama, written largely for aristocratic audiences, portrays it with moral indifference. *Sodom or the Quintessence of Debauchery,* a crude verse comedy by John Wilmot, earl of Rochester, was performed at the court of Charles II. In it, the king of Sodom proclaims "that bugg'ry may be us'd / Through all the land, so cunt be not abus'd."[157] Coupler, an elderly homosexual matchmaker in Sir John Vanbrugh's play *The Relapse, or Virtue in Danger* (1696), is treated as an amusing figure, not by any means horrifying.[158] Lampoons against prominent political figures referred to their sexual habits, but in a mocking tone totally lacking in moral outrage.[159] A market developed for Italian and English pornography, some of it dealing with lesbian or male homosexual encounters.[160]

Homosexual relations within the male aristocracy were generally pederastic, in congruity with the explicit inequalities that constitute an aristocratic order.[161] George Villiers, duke of Buckingham, who shared James I's bed, was twenty-five years his junior. Sir Francis Bacon's lover was "a very effeminate-faced youth . . . his catamite and bedfellow."[162] Pages, being close at hand, were often chosen as partners. John Wilmot boasted in one of his poems that "There's a sweet, soft page of mine / Does the trick worth forty wenches,"[163] and the passage already quoted from *Coelum Brittanicum* is premised on the sexual compliance of pageboys.[164]

Homosexual interests within these circles were generally not exclusive. Elizabethan and Jacobean satires, Bray tells us, "are remarkably consistent: the sodomite is a young man-about town, with his mistress on one arm and his 'catamite' on the other."[165] Wilmot patronized female prostitutes.[166] Rakish characters of Restoration plays were enamored of both male youths and women.[167] Even Francis Bacon, whose interests for a long stretch of his life appear to have been exclusively pederastic, eventually married.[168]

[157] H. M. Hyde (1970:60–61), Bullough (1976:476–77).

[158] Bingham (1971), Berkowitz (1981:8–9), Burg (1983:13–20).

[159] O'Neill (1975). For example, Samuel Parker's *A Reproof to the Rehearsal Transposed,* published in 1673, ridiculed Andrew Marvell by describing him as an impotent homosexual. *The Popish Courant,* a weekly that began publication in 1679, circulated the story that Pope Sixtus IV had authorized his cardinals to engage in sodomy during the three hottest months of the year (R. Thompson, 1979:43, 140–41).

[160] R. Thompson (1979).

[161] Saslow (1986), Trumbach (1987).

[162] Karlen (1971:15), Bullough (1976:147).

[163] Veith (1968:51), Bray (1982:50).

[164] Carew (1949:159), Saslow (1986).

[165] Bray (1983:34).

[166] Karlen (1970:131).

[167] Trumbach (1987) gives as examples Aphra Behn's "The Amorous Prince" (1671), Thomas Otway's "The Souldier's Fortune" (1680), and Nathaniel Lee's "The Princess of Cleve" (1680).

[168] Karlen (1970:115), Bullough (1976:447).

This lack of exclusivity was an obstacle to the formation of a homosexual personal identity, or the creation of a subculture organized around homosexual choice. Special institutions to find partners were not needed as long as dependent servants, who could not easily say no, were available. If there was a subculture, it was one of libertinage, not homosexuality.

The Revolution of 1688 brought William of Orange to the throne, stirring up the religious sentiments that had lain dormant during the Restoration. To pious Puritans and orthodox churchmen, Providence had arranged the defeat of James II to prevent the restoration of Catholicism. Politically and militarily insecure, they worried that continued divine protection might be withdrawn unless England remained morally worthy. But by the 1690s, many feared that this worthiness was being jeopardized by the spread of gambling, drinking, blasphemy, lewdness in the theater, prostitution, and male homosexuality. Commentators wrote that sodomy, formerly rare, was becoming much more common. As far as the male aristocracy was concerned, the Englishman who in 1698 told Elizabeth Charlotte, duchess of Orleans, that "nothing is more ordinary in England than this unnatural vice,"[169] may not have been exaggerating. According to the December 1, 1715, entry in the diary of twenty-four-year-old Dudley Ryder at Oxford, where it was customary for students to share their beds,[170] "among the chief men in some of the colleges sodomy is very usual . . . it is dangerous sending a young man who is beautiful to Oxford."[171] In *For God or Satan* (1709), the Anglican clergyman Thomas Bray warned that "the sodomites are invading our land."[172] Some said that Charles II and his entourage had introduced the practice after learning it while in exile in France.[173]

Legislation dealing with these various forms of vice was already on the books, but in the absence of a full-time, salaried police force, enforcement was necessarily ineffective. Private individuals could prosecute, but to do

---

[169]Orleans (1924:1.217), G. R. Taylor (1954:189), H. M. Hyde (1970:62).

[170]Mosse (1985:76).

[171]G. R. Taylor (1974:274). Judging from the remarks of William Cowper, who attended Westminster in the mid-eighteenth century, little had changed in half a century (Trumbach, 1978:266; see also *A Faithful Narrative*, 1739). The French colleges may have been no different. The November 1731 issue of *Gentleman's Magazine* (1:498) announced that "At Bordeaux no less than eleven Fellows of the Jesuit College have been detected of Sodomy, and are fled."

[172]Bahlman (1957:1–4), Malcolmson (1973:90).

[173]The attribution of homosexuality to foreigners has been a persistent theme in discussions of the subject. Marie de Medici was blamed for introducing it into the France of Henri IV, and eighteenth-century French and English sources often spoke of it as an Italian vice (Coward, 1980a). Thus Daniel Defoe wrote in *The True-Born Englishman: A Satyr* (1701) that sodomy originated in Turkey or "the Torrid Zone of *Italy* where / Blood ferments in Rapes and Sodomy" (G. S. Rousseau, 1985). See also Lacroix (1937:1250–54). Present-day Jewish Israelis often associate homosexuality with Arabs, and in Algeria it is associated with the French (personal communications, Michael Goodich and Marnia Lazreg).

so was costly and time-consuming. Few individuals had the resources to attack a problem that, at least in London, had grown to substantial proportions. The solution was to pool resources, and with the threat of Catholicism eliminated, men obsessed with the state of morals did just that. The first Society for the Reformation of Manners was founded in London's East End in 1690, and within a few years others were established elsewhere in England.

Though some of the reforming societies had elite leadership, members came primarily from the lower middle classes—artisans, apprentices, retailers. It was they who were distressed by the crudity and uninhibited sexual manners of the urban poor and resented the profligate displays of the wealthy. As Lofland points out, they were also less able than the wealthy to shield themselves from the crime, drunkenness, and public display of lewdness that London nurtured.[174] With paid staffs, the reforming societies were able to search out offensive behavior, bring complaints to the constables, and pressure officials not to drop cases. Between 1692 and 1725, the London Society alone took credit for more than 90,000 arrests.[175]

The reforming societies were mainly concerned with illegal drinking establishments, bawdy houses, Sabbath breaking, swearing, and to some extent the theater, but in London they also instigated prosecutions on sodomy charges. The distinctive character of homosexual life-styles in London helps to explain the efforts to repress it there.

Literary sources and the few court records dealing with homosexuality prosecutions in the smaller towns and villages suggest that it was well integrated with the institutions of conventional, everyday life. Servants of the same sex often slept in the same bed; sometimes one attempted to seduce the other.[176] Pamela, a paragon of virtue, shared her bed with a female servant in Samuel Richardson's novel, *Pamela, or Virtue Rewarded*, published in 1740.[177] Masters took advantage of their servants, sometimes male as well as female; and teachers developed sexual relations with their students. As many of those indicted were married fathers,[178] homosexual relations were probably not exclusive for most of the participants.[179]

Every piece of evidence available suggests that these communities were

[174] Lofland (1973:65).
[175] Bahlman (1957:14–40), C. Hill (1961:296–97), E. N. Williams (1962:82), Malcolmson (1973:100–162), Curtis and Speck (1976), Bristow (1977:14).
[176] Quaife (1979:175).
[177] Mosse (1985:76).
[178] Trumbach (1977) mentions that 35 percent of the defendants in the trial records he examined in an unspecified sample were married fathers. About a third of the men arrested in early-eighteenth-century France were married (Rey, 1985), as were many of those arrested in Holland around the same time (Huusen, 1985).
[179] Bray (1982).

completely lacking in homosexual subcultures or specialized institutions serving men with distinctive sexual tastes. Involvement in homosexual relations did not become the basis for self-identification: participants probably did not think of themselves as "buggers" or "sodomites." Their genders— that is, their identification of themselves as male—was conventional. In all likelihood, a fair amount of this casual sexual activity went unnoticed or was handled informally. George Dowdeney, a married innkeeper in Somerset, tried to seduce a number of men over a period of years before he was finally brought to trial in 1722.[180] In 1716, when rumors spread that a tenant farmer had seduced an out-of-town servant in Gloucestershire, a number of the villagers gathered in a festive mood to shame the culprit. They reenacted the seduction, subsequent birth, and mock baptism of a straw baby—and left things at that.[181]

The small towns of rural England did not grow significantly in this period, but as wealth poured in from overseas and farmers displaced from the land sought employment in the city, London and some of the industrial cities grew rapidly.[182] In the metropolis, it was possible to prevent families or work associates from learning of one's sexual proclivities—a necessity as long as homosexuality was a capital felony. Small towns, where everyone knew everyone else, afforded much less privacy.

Rudimentary homosexual networks formed even in some of the smaller towns. Eighteenth-century Bath had "its own topography of sodomy; safe-fields, pick-up streets."[183] Kent Gerard's research, still in progress, points to the existence of similar networks in Dublin, York, Bristol, Exeter, and Norwich.[184] But, by comparison with London, these were rudimentary. By the end of the seventeenth century, there were London parks and walks where men seeking homosexual partners could meet. Responding to a demand created by the rapid growth of a cash economy and population in an expanding mercantile capitalist economy, coffeehouses serving the public had opened in London in the last half of the seventeenth century; within fifty years there were hundreds of them, serving specialized clienteles,[185] some of them homosexual. Clubs and taverns known as molly-houses,

---

[180] Quaife (1979:175–77), Bray (1982:70).

[181] Rollison (1981).

[182] Estimates of London's population in the 1630s range from 225,000 to 340,000; by contrast, the populations of the six major provincial capitals—Bristol, Norwich, Exeter, Salisbury, York, and Newcastle—had populations of 8,000 to 12,000 (Bridenbaugh, 1968:118–19 n. 1, 128). London's population roughly doubled between 1600 and 1700 and increased by another 50 percent in the following century (Wrigley, 1967).

[183] Polly Morris (1985), quoted in Trumbach (1985).

[184] Trumbach (1985).

[185] Carswell (1973:64).

where men with homosexual interests could socialize, served as more sheltered meeting spots, particularly for the middle and lower classes.[186]

The molly subculture was entirely male. Though Elizabethan London afforded some women enough freedom to permit them to live independently
of men,[187] there is no evidence that a lesbian subculture formed. However,
by the early part of the eighteenth century, lesbian relationships were developing. In the fourth book of *Gulliver's Travels,* published in 1726, Jonathan
Swift remarks on "those unnatural Appetites in both Sexes, so common
among us." John Cleland's *Memoirs of a Woman of Pleasure (Fanny Hill)* takes
whorehouse lesbianism for granted.[188]

Eighteenth-century court records tell of a few cases where women imper-
sonated men and married women—allegedly deceitfully—to defraud them
of their money. Some of these illegal marriages did involve lesbian practices. The November 1746 issue of *Gentleman's Magazine* reports the conviction of Mary Hamilton, who had married fourteen wives in succession, the
last of whom deposed that she had lived for three months with the defendant, "during which time she thought the prisoner was a man, owing to
the prisoner's vile and deceitful practices." In addition to seducing women
while disguised as a man, Hamilton picked up soldiers at the theater while
dressed as a woman. At least one of her female lovers left her for "a real
man."[189] Altogether, two-dozen such cases can be identified from the *Annual
Register* and other published sources for the period 1735–1833.[190] A self-help
medical guide for women, published in 1740, discusses the case of a girl who
had been taught to masturbate by her mother's maid; for seven years they
tried "all means to pleasure each other, and heighten the titillation."[191]
There is no evidence in any of these cases for the existence of a lesbian
subculture; each event seems to have occurred spontaneously and in isolation from the others. The anonymous sex reformer's tract, *Satan's Harvest
Home,* hints at the existence of a network of upper-class lesbians in the
middle of the century, but unfortunately says virtually nothing about it.[192]

In 1780, Eleanor Butler and Sarah Ponsonby, young Irish aristocrats, refused to marry and began living together and sharing a bed in Wales.
Though there were newspaper hints that their relationship was unnatural,
they were widely celebrated for their life of simplicity and "perfect friendship." Their main difficulties were financial: their families tried to cut off

[186] Bristow (1977:29), Trumbach (1977, 1984, 1987), Bray (1982:81–89).
[187] Bridenbaugh (1968:169–70, 193), Stenton (1977:218).
[188] Faderman (1981:28).
[189] 16:612; I. Bloch (1934:131–34).
[190] Knapp and Baldwin (1819:395), G. R. Taylor (1974:10–11), A. Simpson (1984).
[191] Faderman (1981:27).
[192] *Satan's Harvest Home* (1749:60–61).

their incomes. Other women, too, developed powerful romantic attachments—perhaps in response to the severe restrictions placed on upper-
class women, which resulted in a large cultural gap between women and
men. However, family pressures and financial obstacles often prevented
the women from living together independently. A number of novels publicized such relationships, and in some instances, couples knew about, and
were in communication with others.[193]

These relationships, and perhaps others, helped to make the existence
of lesbianism common knowledge. Jack Cavendish probably knew of it
from personal observation as well as from classical sources.[194] Indeed, London's reputation for lesbianism spread to Europe: in 1773, the Frenchman
Bachaumont wrote in a letter that the opera star Mlle Heinel was settling in
England; "her taste for women will find there attractive satisfaction, for
though Paris furnishes many tribades it is said that London is herein superior."[195] He may have been correct: Hester Thrale's diary for December 9,
1795, observes that "hundreds of French and English women practice vice
with one another of which Juvenal was ignorant. . . . 'tis a Joke in London
now to say such a one visits *Mrs.* Damor. Bath is a Cage of these unclean
Birds I have a Notion, and London is a Sink for every Sin."[196] Toward the
end of the century, German travelers wrote of lesbian clubs in London;[197]
one of them may have been devoted to flagellation.[198]

A man who patronized a molly-house reduced his risk of accidentally approaching a hostile stranger on the street, but the houses were not entirely
secure, as they could be penetrated by the curious or the hostile. Outsiders
who described the houses were especially impressed by the effeminacy of
the patrons. Edward Ward sketched the men who frequented one of the
molly-houses in *The Secret History of Clubs:*

> They adopt all the small vanities natural to the feminine sex to
> such an extent that they try to speak, walk, chatter, shriek and
> scold as women do, aping them as well in other respects. In a
> certain tavern in the City, the name of which I will not mention,
> not wishing to bring the house into disrepute, they hold parties
> and regular gatherings. As soon as they arrive they begin to be-

[193] Mary Gordon (1936), Mavor (1973), Faderman (1981).
[194] Cavendish (1771).
[195] Mavor (1973:80).
[196] Balderston (1951:2.949, see also 740, 770). Thrale was a friend of Butler and Ponsonby
and visited them several times (Mary Gordon, 1936:187); presumably she did not suspect
them of being "unclean Birds."
[197] Archenholz (1787:1. 269–70), I. Bloch (1958:183–84), Faderman (1981:40).
[198] Karlen (1971:142).

have exactly as women do, carrying on light gossip as is the custom of a merry company of real women.[199]

A number of houses featured dancing and had private rooms for sexual activity, including male prostitutum. Jonathan Wild, the notorious fence and thief-taker attended a party at one, at which he found "He-Whores . . . rigg'd in Gowns, Petticoats, Head cloths, fine lac'd Shoes, Furbelow Scarves, and Masks." They were "tickling and feeling each other, as if they were a mixture of wanton Males and Females."[200] In some molly-houses, patrons enacted marriages, births, and baptisms.[201]

Though possibly exaggerated for rhetorical purposes, the descriptions are too consistent to be dismissed as fictitious.[202] They spotlight the spontaneous creation of a new social role based on the fusion of gender transformation and homosexuality.[203] Effeminacy had previously been linked with male homosexuality in attacks on the vices of the aristocracy, but it was not an important element of the medieval conception of sodomy, or a common feature of urban male homosexuality in the Middle Ages or the Renaissance. Artistic representations of men accused of sodomy in these periods do not show cross-dressing or effeminacy, and written accounts rarely mention these themes.[204] The fops and beaux of the seventeenth and

[199] E. Ward (1709:284–300), H. M. Hyde (1970:63).

[200] Howson (1970:49), Castle, 1987).

[201] E. Ward (1709:284–300), *Hell upon Earth* (1729), *Satan's Harvest Home* (1749), Holloway (1813:11), G. R. Taylor (1974:97 n. 53), McIntosh (1968), Trumbach (1977, 1987), Bray (1982:81–114).

[202] What is remarkable—and therefore suspect as exaggeration—about the English accounts is that they describe *all* the patrons of the molly-houses as effeminate cross-dressers. If the descriptions are accurate, *both* partners of the mock marriages were, in contemporary terminology, transvestites or transsexuals. This seems implausible. Some instances of effeminacy are also known outside the molly-house subculture. The politician and author John, Lord Hervey, who combined a passionate devotion to his male lovers with active heterosexuality (he fathered eight children), was attacked by Pope for his effeminate, androgynous manners. His enemies hinted obliquely at his interest in boys, but were explicit about his unconventional gender (Dubro, 1976).

[203] McIntosh (1968), Bray (1982), Trumbach (1987). By the late nineteenth century, this fusion began to inform fiction. The pornographic novel, *The Sins of the Cities of the Plain, or the Recollections of a Mary-Anne* (1881), involves an effeminate man, and *Letters from Laura and Eveline* describes a mock marriage and wedding trip. But effeminacy was still not considered an invariant correlate of homosexuality, especially by those who engaged in it. Neither *Teleny, or the Reverse of the Medal*, published anonymously in 1893 (but sometimes attributed to Oscar Wilde), nor E. M. Forster's semiautobiographical novel, *Maurice*, written in 1913 (but published only decades later, after his death), reflects the stereotype.

[204] The phenomenon existed and was recognized even by Regino of Prüm (d. 915), who wrote of "*viri corpus muliebriter constitutum*," and in twelfth-century London (Johansson, 1984b, Kuster and Cormier, 1984), but is not mentioned in most reports. The French language

early-eighteenth centuries were sometimes mocked for effeminacy, but were not usually considered homosexual; on the contrary, they were primarily suspected of overly strong attraction to women.[205] Thus Donne: "Thou callest me effeminate, for I love women's joys."[206]

There is evidence that the development of a molly subculture had international parallels. As already noted, there were transvestite balls in seventeenth-century Lisbon.[207] In early-eighteenth-century France there were circles of men who wore ribbons and powder, curtsied, and called each other by women's names. Some men with homosexual interests were put off by this and avoided those circles.[208] Transvestism was sometimes found in association with male homosexuality in the eighteenth-century Dutch Republic, and some sodomites had female nicknames.[209] J. Baptiste della Porta, the founder of "human physiognomy," tells of meeting a transvestite in Naples and seeing many in Sicily.[210]

Unlike berdaches and their counterparts in other primitive societies that did not repress transgenderal homosexuality, the mollies' gender transformation was episodic. They mimicked women in the molly-houses, and probably in more private settings as well, but in public they conformed to conventional gender roles. In the absence of diaries or letters written by mollies, we cannot say how they perceived their own effeminacy. Was it a playful toying with conventional gender distinctions? A means of mutual recognition, analogous to a password for a semisecret society? Or was it a more serious expression of identification with women, which might have led to a more stable transformation of gender had there been no threat of arrest or stigma? We do not know, but I will offer a speculation at the end of chapter 8. Whatever was responsible for this flowering of male effeminacy, whatever it meant to the mollies themselves, it could not have become the basis for a subculture in an atmosphere of hostility in the absence of private spaces where gender-crossers could gather;[211] hence the centrality of spe-

---

began to distinguish gender-based homosexual roles between the sixteenth and eighteenth centuries. The effeminate role was called *bardache,* the masculine role *bougre* (Courouve, 1982). Although the term *buggery* appeared in English usage as early as the fourteenth century, *bardache* was used very infrequently. It was not until *molly* entered the English vocabulary that there was a special term for the feminine role in that language.

[205] Staves (1982), A. Simpson (1984), Trumbach (1987).

[206] Trumbach (1987). A few fops had boy lovers as well as mistresses.

[207] Mott (1984).

[208] Rey (1985).

[209] Meer (1984), Huusen (1985).

[210] Porta (1971:813), Dall'Orto (1983).

[211] When effeminately dressed young men appeared on Paris streets in the late eighteenth century, they were attacked by mobs (Rey, 1985). In early-eighteenth-century London they were arrested (Trumbach, 1987).

cialized taverns to the subculture. Medieval life did not afford comparable privacy.

Even though it was not shared by all members of the homosexual networks, the high cultural salience of gender and the conspicuousness of gender-linked mannerisms, clothing, and coiffure led observers to regard effeminacy as a key component of male homosexuality. John Armstrong, the Scottish physician, expressed the identification of gender deviance with unnatural sex (heterosexual or homosexual) in his "The Oeconomy of Love, a Poetical Essay":

> For Man with Man
> And Man with Woman (monstr'ous to relate!)
> Leaving the natural Road, themselves debase
> With deeds unseemly, and Dishonour found.
> Britons, for shame! Be Male and Female still.[212]

So firmly had the stereotype of the male homosexual as effeminate become established that when thirty men were arrested in a raid on the White Swan Tavern in London in 1810 (the "Vere Street scandal"), people seemed genuinely surprised that many had physically demanding blue-collar occupations.[213]

Eighteenth-century discussion of the mollies helps to illuminate the currently contested question of when the notion of a homosexual person first appeared.[214] Though the Renaissance sodomite was depicted as a monster whose vice signified a repudiation of God and nature, no one suggested that he suffered from a disease and required therapy. No one proposed that eugenic measures be taken to prevent him from having children. His repudiation of God and morality was considered volitional; it was his acts, not his physiology or psychology that made him monstrous.

Numerous authors from eighteenth- and early-nineteenth-century England modify this picture in only minor ways. In 1811, the anonymous author of *Hints to the Public* warned that "the monsters must be crushed or vengeance will fall on the land."[215] As late as mid-century, another anonymous writer referred to the growth of "monsters in the shape of men, commonly designated *Margeries*, *Pooffs*, etc."[216] But, however disturbing or disgusting most men found the mollies, they probably did not see them as diabolical. Visitors to the molly-houses did not fear for their lives or try to

---

[212] P. Wagner (1987). The poem dates from 1736.
[213] Harvey (1978).
[214] McIntosh (1968), J. Weeks (1977a), Bray (1982:134–37 n. 18).
[215] *Hints to the Public* (1811:101).
[216] *Yokel's Precepter* (1850).

exorcize the devil.[217] The narratives read more like those written by a jungle explorer who has just discovered an exotic new species, or by an anthropologist revealing a tribe with a new kinship system.

Discussions of why the mollies exist became more complex in this period. A poem included in Edward Ward's *Secret History of Clubs* suggests—possibly for the first time in English, and only in jest—that homosexual desire is innate. Male sodomites and turds

> Were born the very self same Way,
> From whence they draw this cursed Itch,
> Not to the Betty but the Breech;
> Else who could Woman's Charms refuse,
> To such a beastly Practice use?[218]

However, even in this pre-Lamarckian era, innate traits were evidently considered modifiable, for the poem continues:

> For he that is of Woman born,
> Will to her Arms again return;
> And surely never chuse to play
> His Lustful Game, the backward Way.

Ward's fleeting glance at biology was quite atypical. The author of *Hell Upon Earth* commented that the mollies are "much fonder of a new *Convert* than a Bully would be of a new *Mistress*,"[219] implying that homosexual attraction is learned. *Hints to the Public* insists that mollies must receive "instant death" to prevent contagion.[220] Parallel views can be found in penological discussions of crime. Throughout the century, reformers objected to the indiscriminate jailing of criminals together on the grounds that more experienced criminals corrupted novices.[221]

A more extended discussion in *Satan's Harvest Home* explains homosexuality as the product of defective upbringing. Boys were coming to be raised at home rather than apprenticed or sent away to boarding schools. Pampered by their mothers and kept from the rough-and-tumble play of boys, they were growing up effete, never having had the chance to acquire the manly traits that would enable them to dominate, and thus satisfy, women.

---

[217] As discussed below, neighbors of the molly-houses sometimes knew their character but elected to take no action against them. In one instance, a raid was initiated not by neighborhood bigots but by a patron irritated when none of the other customers accepted his propositions (Howson, 1970:49). Some of the Dutch defendants were known to their neighbors for a long time before being arrested (Meer, 1984).

[218] E. Ward (1709:299–300).

[219] *Hell Upon Earth* (1729:43).

[220] *Hints to the Public* (1811:101).

[221] Hanway (1776:39), Howard (1784:8, 211), Hinde (1951:15, 34).

Such men, "unable to please the Women, chuse rather to run into unnatural Vices with one another, than to attempt what they are but too sensible
they cannot perform."[222] In other words, the sodomite is an unsuccessful
heterosexual.

Gender-crossing and homosexuality remain choices in these writings,
but the choices are shaped by socialization, accidents of seduction, and the
availability of female partners. Except for Ward, writers saw mollies as anatomically and physiologically normal. But their effeminacy and sexual preferences set them apart from other men, even if not irrevocably.

References to the exclusiveness of sexual choice suggest a degree of confusion. Sometimes men arrested on sodomy charges in England defended
themselves by bringing witnesses to testify to their heterosexual interests,
a strategy that rested implicitly on the notion that sexual preferences must
be exclusive. But this defense did not always work. We know that quite a
few mollies were married and had children, and that transvestite male
prostitutes sometimes had girlfriends;[223] undoubtedly some people knew it
then, too.

The diversity of eighteenth-century perceptions shows that it was a period of cognitive transition. Some continued to view homosexuality as
a vice anyone might find attractive. Those who thought that found homosexuality especially frightening, because they believed it had the potential for spreading and reaching epidemiclike proportions. Others began to
see effeminacy and homosexuality as defining a distinct type of person
whose sexual orientation was fairly stable, and whose distinguishing essence was determined in some way by factors outside his own control.[224]
The nineteenth century was to develop these ideas more systematically and
explicitly.

Predictably, the London reforming societies made the local homosexual
subculture one of its targets. They disrupted outdoor meeting places and
sent informers to the molly-houses to gather evidence for use in prosecutions. The societies organized small raids in 1699 and 1707, and in 1726
broke up more than twenty houses. Although these efforts were sporadic
and were given low priority in the overall agendas of the societies, a number of men were hanged or pilloried as a result of the prosecutions they
initiated.[225]

[222] *Satan's Harvest Home* (1749:49–50).

[223] Holloway (1813:12), *Yokel's Precepter* (1850:6–7), *Sins of the Cities* (1881:1.87).

[224] The very long prison sentences given to Dutch defendants not executed might suggest a
simultaneous belief in both positions. Some defendants seemed to confirm that their homosexual desires were deepseated and stable, but others admitted only a single experience
(Noordam, 1983; Meer, 1985).

[225] Bray (1982:89–91). Most of the executions in the early part of the eighteenth century

Weakened by a number of factors, the societies became less active after 1730, and soon they disappeared altogether. The societies had been able to get the evidence needed for prosecution only by using informers, who were highly unpopular. The rural gentry opposed the societies' attempts to suppress popular entertainment and traditional leisure pastimes,[226] while bishops and judges resented their attacks on the church and the government for not doing more to stop vice. Though publicly sympathetic with moral reform, King William felt threatened by the societies' willingness to accept religious dissenters as members, and may have feared exposure of his own homosexual involvements. Possibly the lower-middle-class members had difficulty paying staff and investigators on an ongoing basis. Once the societies dissolved, prosecutions fell dramatically.[227]

For the next half-century, prosecutions on felony charges were infrequent, and most of them involved homosexual rape. Private prosecutions for consensual sodomy were rare; they were mostly for acts taking place in public. When such cases were brought, magistrates were usually reluctant to prosecute and dismissed many accusations.[228] It is fair to assume that most of those who brought prosecutions were hostile to homosexual expression, but they did not necessarily seek executions, and, to avoid a possible capital sentence, sometimes refused to testify. Reluctance to send sodomites to the gallows may explain why something like 75 percent of the prosecutions were on misdemeanor charges of attempted sodomy rather than on felony charges of completed sodomy; in heterosexual-rape cases the ratio of felonies to misdemeanors was just the reverse.[229]

Nevertheless, sodomy was not regarded as altogether trivial. When Earl Strutwell propositions Roderick Random in Smollet's *The Adventures of Rockerick Random,* published in 1748, Random is horrified and ends the conversation by quoting Smollett's earlier satirical *Advice,* "Eternal infamy to the wretch confound / Who planted first this vice on British ground."[230]

---

stemmed from prosecutions that were *not* initiated by the reforming societies. For reasons discussed below, most of the society-initiated prosecutions were for attempted sodomy.

[226] The lower classes also opposed these efforts, but they were less able to express their opposition effectively.

[227] Bahlman (1957:9, 28–33, 69, 79–81, 84–86, 95–97), C. Hill (1961:196–297), E. N. Williams (1962:82), Malcolmson (1974:162), Bristow (1977:29), Trumbach (1978:283), Isaacs (1982), Porter (1982), A. Simpson (1984).

[228] One noted jurist, Sir William Eden, detested homosexuality, but thought that prosecutions and executions should be discouraged so as not to give the vice unnecessary publicity. It is unlikely that the lower rate of prosecutions was due to the destruction of the homosexual networks at the hands of the reforming societies, for in London in the 1750s there were clubs at which members engaged in group masturbation (P. Wagner, 1985).

[229] A. Simpson (1984:445–48, 453, 462–63).

[230] Day (1982), G. S. Rousseau (1985).

John Armstrong's "The Oeconomy of Love," quoted earlier in this chapter, admonishes British readers to

> Banish this foreign Vice; it grows not here,
> It dies, neglected; and in Clime so chaste
> Cannot but by forc'd Cultivation thrive.

Armstrong was overly optimistic, but the public response to prosecutions on charges of assault with intent to commit sodomy shows that the repugnance he and Smollett expressed was widely shared. Sometimes these charges were brought where an act of consensual sodomy had been consummated, and the evidence too weak to sustain a sodomy conviction. But men were also prosecuted where there was no evidence that anal intercourse was even contemplated, e.g., in cases of mutual masturbation, oral copulation, kissing "with intent to stir up Unnatural Lusts and Desires," and "exposing their private parts to each other with intent to excite and stir up in each other filthy and unnatural Lusts and desires."[231] Technically, these cases should never have been permitted to proceed, as the acts described in the complaint were not illegal except by a conjectural relationship to anal intercourse.

Sodomy attempts were punished at law by exposure in the pillory for a few hours, or by prison sentences—typically of seven months or less in the period 1741–70, and two years after that.[232] Burg points out that the pillory was the lightest sentence available to the courts and that its use signified an attitude of considerable tolerance.[233] In a century when even minor thefts could be punished by hanging, brief public exposure would seem to have been an exceptionally mild penalty, one suggesting that the offense was regarded as quite trivial.

In practice, the pillory was not always a minor penalty, for antagonistic crowds frequently pelted pilloried sodomites with anything at hand. Guards had to be posted to protect the men, but they were not always able to do so: in 1763, a man pilloried for sodomy was killed by a mob, and another man may have suffered the same fate in 1780. In other cases, serious injuries were inflicted.[234]

---

[231] Bristow (1977:29), J. Weeks (1977:12), Harvey (1978), Bray (1982:98), A. Simpson (1984: 471–72, 739–40).

[232] Gilbert (1977), A. Simpson (1984:505).

[233] Burg (1983:25).

[234] Archenholz (1787:2.267), I. Bloch (1958:389), A. Simpson (1984:760–69), Crompton (1985:21–22). Deaths are reported in *Annual Register* 6, pt. 1:67 (1763) and 13, pt. 1:207–9 (1780). Injuries are reported for 1751 in *New Newgate Calendar* 2:376–78, and for 1809 in 3:64–65 (Knapp and Baldwin, 1819), as well as in *Annual Register* 53, pt. 1:28–81 (1810) and 64, pt. 2:425–32 (1822). This last case involved an Anglican bishop who was detected in the act in the backroom of a public house. I am indebted to Antony Simpson for these cases. In another

Burg has argued that mob violence did not necessarily occur because of popular hatred of homosexuality.[235] The London mob rioted at the drop of a hat and attacked men who were pilloried for all kinds of offenses, more for amusement than from hatred of the men attacked. Yet London crowds, however volatile, did not choose their targets completely at random. Most of the other men killed at the pillory had infuriated the public by giving perjured testimony that led to the wrongful execution of defendants. When the crowd sympathized with defendants, as it sometimes did in political trials, its behavior was by no means so unruly. Thus, when Daniel Defoe was pilloried for publishing a pamphlet, the crowd brought him flowers. Thousands turned out to cheer Daniel Eaton, who was pilloried in 1812 for circulating the writings of Tom Paine. These cases were far from exceptional: many defendants were treated kindly while in the pillory.[236]

The more plausible interpretation of the mob response is that it reflected popular loathing of homosexuality. Episodes of summary punishment inflicted on suspected sodomites who had not been charged in court demonstrate that expressions of popular antagonism were not confined to the crowds that gathered at the pillory. Moreover, allegations that the victim-prosecutor in a criminal case was homosexual often gained an acquittal for defendants.[237] Enlightened intellectuals remained just as unfriendly: Blackstone found support for the death penalty in "the voice of nature and of reason, and the express law of God" when writing his commentary on English law.[238]

Bray points out that despite popular disgust, people who knew of homosexual activity or of the molly-houses often seem to have done nothing about them.[239] The names of popular molly-houses were published in books in the early eighteenth century without any apparent repercussions. The situation was no different on the Continent. Neighbors in some of the French cases reported by Hernandez knew of ongoing homosexual activity for long periods of time, but did not inform the authorities.[240] Some of the eighteenth-century Dutch defendants had long had reputations for sod-

---

case, an under-marshall named Hitchen was apprehended in the act of sodomy in a Charing Cross tavern. Sentenced to a fine of £20, an hour in the pillory and six months in jail, he had to be taken down from the pillory after half an hour because the mob treated him so roughly that it was feared he would die (Howson (1970:288).

[235] Burg (1983:35–36).
[236] Cobbett (1812), Minto (1879:40), E. P. Thompson (1963:604–5).
[237] A. Simpson (1984:770–74).
[238] Blackstone (1769:4.216).
[239] Bray (1982).
[240] Hernandez (1920).

omy; neighbors even observed them in sexual acts without going to the authorities.[241]

To explain the seeming incongruity of simultaneous hostility and inaction, Bray speculates that the stereotypical image of monstrosity disseminated by Christian teachings about Sodom and Gomorrah was central to popular conceptions of homosexuality. This image was so extreme that it could not readily be connected with an acquaintance who seemed normal in every way except for his sexual habits and leanings. Nor could people easily apply it to themselves. One of the characters in the January eclogue of Spenser's *The Shepherd's Calendar* illustrates this difficulty when he marks that pederasty was "much to be preferred before gynerastice, but yet let no man thinke, that herein I stand with Lucian or his develish disciple Unico Aretino, in defence of execrable and horrible sinnes of forbidden and unlawful fleshlinesse . . ."[242]

Once someone was arrested, however, he was exposed to crowds who did not know him personally, and whose responses were consequently governed by the stereotype. Bray's argument makes sense of the comparative paucity of prosecutions outside London: in small towns where people know one another they are less prone to see each other in terms of stereotypes.

Though not as prone to violence as the lower classes who mobbed the pillories, the aristocracy began to show a distinct distaste for homosexuality. Early in the eighteenth century, when the upper classes had an "absolutely uninhibited and guilt-free attitude to sexual pleasure," homosexuality was all the rage at Oxford.[243] But by the latter part of the century, men stopped kissing one another lest they be considered homosexual.[244] Gentlemen were ostracized if their homosexual interests became known, and some chose to go into exile.[245] The German traveler von Archenholz, who visited England at this time, commented that "unnatural pleasures are held in great abhorrence with the men. In no country are such infamous pleasures spoken of with greater detestation."[246]

This shift in attitudes had its origins in the bourgeoisification of the aristocracy. The middle class was growing numerically relative to the aristocracy and was rising in the ranks of government bureaucracies, inevitably, it was becoming more influential in questions of public policy. Living in the

[241] Meer (1984, 1988).
[242] A. Barton (1983).
[243] G. R. Taylor (1974:272, 274).
[244] I. Bloch (1958:396).
[245] H. M. Hyde (1970:70–77).
[246] R. Porter (1982).

cities, it had greater cultural influence than did the rural aristocrats and gentry. Through business dealings and intermarriage, the upper classes were exposed to middle-class values. By the late-eighteenth century, the more straight-laced middle class was beginning to set the moral tone for its social superiors. Even when the upper classes did not internalize middle-class sobriety, they felt it advisable to conform to restrictive moral standards in public.[247] The Augustan Age was becoming "Victorian."[248]

This tightening of sexual morality can be seen in the court records: the 1780s saw an upsurge in prosecutions for attempted sodomy. Unlike the first half of the century, when most such prosecutions were for attempted rape, most of the cases were now consensual. As noted earlier, legal standards for conviction were often ignored in practice, so that acts bearing no obvious relationship to the statutory definition of sodomy were being prosecuted successfully.[249] England was becoming more intolerant of sexual—indeed, emotionally intimate—relations between men.

Enforcement—the Americas

For three hundred years, colonial Brazil was subject to Portuguese anti-sodomy legislation providing the death penalty for sodomy and for "sins against nature" between women. Those guilty of mutual masturbation were to be exiled to the galleys. Transvestites could be whipped in public, then exiled for three years. Anyone who knew of sodomy and failed to denounce it could be exiled for life; those who did so received half the guilty party's possessions. Witnesses could testify in secret, and suspects were tortured to reveal the names of others. The courts were ordered not to mitigate the penalty even for nobles or officials of the court. As if that weren't enough, between 1536 and 1765, the Inquisition sent commissioners to Brazil to deal with a number of problems including sodomy.[250]

They had their work cut out for them. European settlers' morality was dissolute; some had been convicted of sodomy in Europe. The institutionalization of male homosexuality among some of the Brazilian Indians enabled colonists to take Indian men as wives; some did. Black slaves brought from Africa persisted in the homosexual practices they'd learned in Angola and the Congo.[251]

In practice, the law was not enforced with full rigor. Domingo Pires, con-

---

[247] G. R. Taylor (1974:44–61).

[248] It is now recognized that English morals were becoming restrictive long before Victoria's coronation in 1837 (E. N. Williams, 1962:163; G. R. Taylor, 1974).

[249] A. Simpson (1984:435, 471–72, 739–40).

[250] Trevisan (1986:47–54, 66–67).

[251] Trevisan (1986:23, 55).

victed of sodomy in Pernambuco in 1593, was sentenced to penances of prayer and fasting, followed by instruction in a monastery for one month. The following year, Salvador Romero, a multiple offender, was sentenced to burn, but because of his repentance the sentence was commuted to a public whipping followed by eight years of galley slavery.[252]

This laxity permitted homosexuality to flourish among men and women of all classes to an extent that European visitors found remarkable. The aristocratic governor of Brazil from 1602 to 1607 was a reputed sodomite. In 1761 the bishop of Rio de Janeiro complained that many priests lived with male lovers; one had confessed to sexual relations with more than forty people. As late as the beginning of the nineteenth century, homosexuality was "scandalously common . . . in cities such as Rio de Janeiro—especially among small shopkeepers, where immigrant Portuguese predominated, often keeping their sales clerks as lovers."[253]

In Mexico, the Holy Office also shared jurisdiction over sexual perversions with civil authorities, and gave much attention to sodomy; the transcripts of the proceedings "leave no detail of the crime to the reader's imagination."[254] A number of the defendants were burned to death.[255]

In Nouvelle-France, where the Inquisition did not operate, the maximum statutory penalty was probably never imposed. In the first known case, a man was convicted and sentenced to death on a sodomy charge in 1648, but the sentence was commuted when the condemned man agreed to become the colony's official executioner.[256] In another case, in 1691, an army officer was fined and banished from the colony for having sexual relations with two of his men.[257]

The New Netherland antisodomy law was implemented with particular faithfulness to the Bible. In 1646, Jan Creoli, a Negro slave of the New Netherland Company, was strangled and then burned for forcibly sodomizing a ten-year-old Negro boy, Manuel Congo. Because the court interpreted Leviticus as calling for the punishment of both partners in a sexual relationship of two males, even when one's participation was involuntary,

[252] Trevisan (1986:58).

[253] Trevisan (1986:46, 52, 97).

[254] Greenleaf (1961:33–34).

[255] C. Taylor (1987). The executions seem to have been ineffective, for only four years after the public garroting and burning of fifteen men the Inquisitors wrote to their Spanish superiors that "we have discovered a great number of people, primarily clergy, who engage in homosexuality and have passed into bestiality." With permission to proceed against them denied, the burnings ended.

[256] Séguin (1972:346–47), Kinsman (1987:75). Curiously, the source says nothing about his partner. Could it have been a juvenile who was not prosecuted because of his youth?

[257] Sylvestre (1983:37–43), Kinsman (1987:75).

the court punished Congo, too. On account of his youth and innocence he was not executed, but tied to a post with wood piled around him, beaten with rods, and made to watch Creoli being killed. In another episode, fourteen years later, the perpetrator of a homosexual rape was tied in a sack and thrown in the river to drown, while the boy he raped was privately whipped and expelled from the colony. One wonders whether the judges feared that the rape victims might have enjoyed the experience, and wanted to warn them against returning to it.[258]

The English colonies lacked the population base needed to sustain the sodomitical subcultures of the Old World cities, and the emphasis placed on family life in a society that needed to procreate to sustain its precarious foothold in hostile territory afforded little scope to homosexual expression. Several of the New England colonies went so far as to require unmarried men to live as servants or boarders in the homes of families headed by a married couple; to prevent "sin and iniquity" they were not permitted to live alone or with one another.[259] Puritan ideology frowned on sensuality of any kind that might jeopardize commitment to work and family. The family was perceived to be the core social institution, responsible for production, reproduction, and the transmission of property from one generation to the next. Nothing could be permitted to jeopardize it.[260]

The colonists brought with them the Christian belief that all men are sinners. It followed that anyone could commit sodomy; the act was not characteristic of a distinct type of person and did not connote effeminacy. Colonists feared that one sodomite would corrupt others, but only by example, not by modifying their partners' psyches.[261]

Prosecutions were conducted along fairly legalistic lines. If anal penetration was proved, a defendant was convicted of sodomy; if not, not.[262] Attempted sodomy and other forms of carnal homosexual behavior not involving penetration were punished more lightly. In 1637, shortly after Plymouth Colony made sodomy a capital offense, the "notoriously guilty" John Alexander was sentenced to be whipped, burned in the shoulder with a hot iron, and banished from the colony; his partner, an indentured ser-

---

[258] Brief summaries of these and several other cases can be found in O'Callahan (1968:4.103, 113, 115, 8.201, 9.213, A.319), J. Katz (1983:90, 103) and Brooke (1984). More extended accounts appear in the colonial *Council Minutes* 4 and *Fort Orange Council Minutes* 2, published by Geneological Publishing Co. in its series of *New York Historical Manuscripts: Dutch*.

[259] J. Katz (1983:32).

[260] J. Katz (1983:23–65).

[261] J. Katz (1983:23–65).

[262] Some thought that emission had to be proved, too, but that view never became dominant. Only the New Haven law of 1656 included public masturbation or solicitation to masturbate in its definition of sodomy, and made them capital offenses.

vant, was whipped, but not burned or banished. They had been convicted of "often spending their seed upon the other," technically not sodomy. Comparable penalties were imposed for heterosexual offenses like adultery.

Only in part does this legalism explain the tiny number of executions— no more than a handful in roughly two hundred years—for some of those convicted of sodomy were spared the noose. Where the death penalty was imposed, it appears to have been on account of aggravating circumstances. William Cornish, a shipmaster, was hanged in Virginia in 1624 for forcibly sodomizing one of his crew. William Plaine, executed in New Haven in 1646, though married, had sodomized two men in England, and "corrupted a great part of the youth of Guilford by masturbations . . . above a hundred times," and questioned the existence of God. John Knight, who was hanged in New Haven in 1655, had a previous conviction, and his partners were young boys and girls. By contrast, men found guilty of bestiality *were* executed; it was considered a form of sodomy, as were sexual relations with a prepubescent girl. The New Haven law of 1656 extended the definition of sodomy to include "abusing the contrary part of a grown woman, or child of either sex." The heterosexual violations either went unpunished, or were treated more leniently than the same-sex violations. Women, however, could not commit sodomy with one another, though they could be "unchaste" or "lewd" together."[263]

Few of the colonists who came to America were aristocrats; consequently, the libertine philosophy that prevailed in some noble circles in Europe had no social base in America. With the exception of convicted felons, slaves, and indentured servants, most of the immigrants were middle class and upheld its restrictive sexual morality. However, they were not necessarily fanatics. A few attempts were made to start societies for the reformation of morals on the English model, but they garnered little support, and quickly died.[264] No doubt life on the frontier was difficult, but the absence of flagrant displays of wealth and immorality in the first century of colonial life, along with the unorganized quality of homosexual relations, may have made most colonists less anxious about sex morality than their British counterparts. As in the smaller English towns, the settlers were probably reluctant to prosecute their neighbors. When two men were accused of sodomy in 1635, the governor of New Hampshire declined to try them. In 1677, a citizen of Windsor, Connecticut merely had to post bond for future good behavior after repeated and widely known attempts at sodomy with a number of different men over a period of thirty years.[265]

[263] Crompton (1976), J. Katz (1976:16–23, 1983:66–133), Oaks (1978, 1979/80), Chapin (1983).
[264] Flaherty (1971).
[265] J. Katz (1983:73, 111–19).

Nowhere in these reports from seventeenth- and eighteenth-century North America do we find evidence of a homosexual subculture. This is so even though the majority of the colonists came from England, where, by the early eighteenth century, the existence of such subcultures in the major towns was widely known. Their absence in North America cannot be attributed to a stricter criminal code; English law was just as strict. Nor is selective immigration a likely explanation. North America, however, lacked towns large enough to sustain specialized establishments, such as taverns. Nor could the small American towns insure the anonymity participants needed to avoid stringent legal sanctions. By contrast, urban subcultures were able to form in early modern Mexico and Brazil, where cities were larger. Not until the nineteenth century did American cities grow to the point where homosexual subcultures could form.[266]

[266] In 1790 the populations of Boston, New York, and Philadelphia were, respectively, roughly 18,000, 33,000, and 42,000, the New York and Philadelphia populations having increased greatly over the previous few decades (U.S. Bureau of the Census, 1909:11). In the same year, the population of Mexico City was 131,000 (B. R. Mitchell, 1983:98). A rough estimate of the population of Bahia, Brazil, in 1699 is 100,000 (Boxer, 1964:127). A century later, the population of Rio de Janeiro was 43,000 and of Salvador, Brazil, about 100,000 (B. R. Mitchell, 1983:106).

8   *The Rise of Market Economies*

The conjuncture of extremely harsh legislation justified primarily on religious grounds, erratic enforcement, and popular indifference, punctuated by infrequent episodes of repression, remained characteristic of social responses to homosexuality from the Renaissance through the eighteenth century, but began to change in the modern era. The nineteenth and twentieth centuries saw the appearance of novel ideas about homosexuality and the introduction of new methods of control.

This chapter, and the next two argue that three developments were particularly important in shaping a distinctly modern response to homosexuality: the growth of competitive capitalism, the rise of modern science, and the spread of bureaucratic principles of social organization. The effects of these developments were contradictory, but their net effect was to strengthen antihomosexual beliefs and attitudes. The further development of capitalism in the decades following World War II has moderated those beliefs and attitudes, but only to a degree.

COMPETITIVE CAPITALISM AND HOMOSEXUALITY

The mercantile economy of early modern England was highly regulated: justices of the peace set wages and prices, and vigorous efforts were made to restrict the geographical mobility of labor. Royal charters still granted guilds and other corporate bodies monopoly rights to engage in many lines of trade. As the economy expanded, the number of small entrepreneurs engaged in trade or manufacture also grew. Beginning in the early seventeenth century, this burgeoning middle class began to campaign for the repeal of these restrictions on contractual freedom, though with only limited success until 1832, when laissez faire was elevated to a fundamental principle of English social policy.[1]

[1]Polanyi (1957), Humphries and Greenberg (1981).

France took a similar direction. According to the economic historian Georges d'Avenal:

> Richelieu's administration appointed officials to deal with every conceivable person or object. People, animals, goods, voyages, all negotiations of public or private life, all coming and going, the simplest activities, were matters for the administration: crossing a bridge, cutting a tree, a bale of hay. . . . Regulations existed for the most everyday affairs.[2]

Since pay and working conditions were subject to direct government control, strikes were treated as revolts. In large and small industries alike, "regulation reigned supreme, not only regulation of labour but regulation of the goods made, a system hostile to every innovation and every attempt to perfect machinery or to make any alteration in the employment or combination of raw materials."[3]

Following the defeat of the sans-culottes, the radical bourgeoisie who triumphed in the post-Thermidorian Revolution dismantled much of this regulatory machinery. The guilds were abolished, special privileges eliminated, and the regulation of commerce and industry cut back, though strikes and workers' organizations remained illegal under the Le Chapelier law of 1791. The Napoleonic Code consolidated these trends by placing contractual freedom at the heart of French private law.

On paper, the economies of the North American colonies were also highly regulated, but not always effectively; the high demand for labor made wage control impossible to enforce. In the decades following Independence, government-granted franchises and monopolies in the United States continued to restrict competition, as did private agreements among employers. As in England, these restrictions came under attack from entrepreneurs whose ambitions were thwarted by the advantages regulation gave to "old" capital; by the 1830s these forces had become strong enough to give a free-market slant to Jacksonian economic policy.[4]

The ideological hegemony of Christian teachings on sexuality made it conceptually difficult for Renaissance sodomites to protest calumny and judicially sanctioned slaughter. Leonardo da Vinci, one of the greatest intellects of the Italian Renaissance, wrote in one of his private notebooks, that "the bat, owing to unbridled lust, observes no universal rule in pairing, but

[2] Quoted in Jacoby (1973).

[3] Hauser (1933).

[4] Cochran (1959), Commons (1968), Hofstadter (1957:55), W. Nelson (1975), Horwitz (1977), J.R.T. Hughes (1977:34–44).

males with males and females with females pair promiscuously, as it may happen,"[5] echoing Church propaganda against witches.

The revival of classical learning familiarized the intelligentsia with the pederastic practices of ancient Greece and Rome, enabling them to refute the alleged monstrosity of sodomy by naming the writers, philosophers, and military heroes who engaged in it. Only a few risked the horrible deaths that awaited those who dared to challenge Christian doctrine directly. One of them, Christopher Marlowe, was accused of atheism and blasphemy for saying, among other things, that Christ and Saint John the Evangelist were bedmates.[6] But the power of Christianity, backed up by secular judicial authorities, was too strong to make that kind of challenge effective.

The molly-houses brought together men who shared a common legal risk, making a collective response possible. In 1725, the patrons of one London molly-house fought back when the house was raided. But a weakly organized minority was in no position to conduct a military struggle. The battle had to be won ideologically, if at all.

The rise of science and the extension of a market economy offered new conceptual possibilities for constructing a coherent argument. Science was important at this time not for any new discoveries about homosexuality, but for introducing materialist explanations of human behavior. To the sixteenth-century Puritan scholar John Rainolds, sodomy was something to which "men's natural corruption and viciousness is prone."[7] Natural law furnished rules for behavior that right reason could deduce, but it was through free will that one acted according to reason, or in conflict with it. Galileo broke halfway with this medieval idea by arguing that the motion of inanimate matter is subject to mechanical, lawlike causality. This mechanistic philosophy was developed further in Italy by Toricelli and Viviani, in France by Mersenne and Descartes, and in England by Boyle, Hooke, Oldenberg, Hobbes, and with some qualifications, Newton. The development and dissemination of complex pieces of machinery for practical purposes may have helped to gain credibility for this new conception of the universe.

Eighteenth-century French philosophers extended materialism to human behavior. To Holbach, man "exists in Nature. He is submitted to her laws. He cannot deliver himself from them."[8] It followed that free will is delusory. "It is the structure of the atoms that forms [man], and their motion

[5] "Fantastic Tales" 1234 (Richter, 1972:321).
[6] Karlen (1971:116–17), Bray (1982:63–65).
[7] Bray (1982:17).
[8] Randall (1940:274), Cassirer (1955:69), Matson (1964:29–30).

propels him forward; conditions not dependent on him determine his nature and direct his fate." La Mettrie concluded that "man is a machine."[9]

Sodomites began to realize that, if all actions were governed by natural laws, then their sexual conduct could not possibly be unnatural. The inevitable dialogue between proponents of the two world-views took place in seventeenth-century Italy when a confessor told a sodomite, "That is a sin against nature," and was told in reply, "Oh father, but it is very natural to me."[10] In a remarkable anonymous homophile play, *L'Ombre de Deschauffours,"* written around 1739, characters discuss the causes of homosexual tastes. "In nature," one says, "everyone has his own inclination." Another contends that the direction of this inclination is formed at birth.[11] Diderot's more eclectic *Suite de l'entretien* allows environmental influences: "those abominable tastes" come from "the abnormal nervous systems in young men and from decaying of the brains of old men. From the lure of beauty in Athens, the scarcity of women in Rome, the fear of the pox in Paris." His speculations about the causes of homosexuality among the American Indians ranged from the hot climate to the status of women and the morphology of their genitalia.[12]

The Enlightenment carried to other lands, including Russia, the notion that homosexuality might stem from an illness. In 1785 the Senate issued a ukase at the request of Catherine II, a friend of Voltaire, telling judges to treat sodomy cases "with the utmost clemency and mercy" because "the victims must be considered to have been more temporarily out of their wits, than really criminal."[13]

De Sade's 1795 essay, "Yet Another Effort Frenchmen, If You Would Become Republicans," draws on this new positivist conception of nature and homosexuality to defend the normalcy of all nature's works and to denounce the savagery of punishing homosexuality:

> It makes absolutely no difference whether one enjoys a girl or a boy, . . . no inclinations or tastes can exist in us save the ones we have from Nature. . . . she is too wise and too consistent to have given us any which could ever offend her. The penchant for sod-

[9] La Mettrie, *L'homme machine,* quoted in Needham (1955:236) and Matson (1964:29).

[10] Dall'Orto (1983). A similar dialogue occurs even earlier in fiction, in one of the bawdy novelle of Matteo Bandello (1963), a Dominican bishop of the sixteenth century.

[11] Courouve (1981). Paris police records from the 1720s record conversations in which people say such things as "He had this taste all his life," or "From an early age he did not do anything else but amuse himself with men; these pleasures were in his blood" (Rey, 1983). There is a clear recognition here of highly stable, specialized homosexual orientations.

[12] Quoted in Delon (1985). In the third section of *La rêve de d'Alembert,* Diderot questions the meaningfulness of terms like "normal" or "natural" as applied to human sexual behavior.

[13] Braun (1966:29).

omy is the result of physical formation, to which we contribute nothing, and which we cannot alter. . . . Sometimes it is the fruit of satiety, but even in this case, is it less Nature's doing? Regardless of how it is viewed, it is her work, and in every instance, what she inspires in us must be respected by men.[14]

The capitalist emphasis on the rational pursuit of material gain tends to undercut, or at least restrict, religious authority. The laissez-faire doctrines that flourished during the competitive stage of capitalism asserted the desirability of leaving people free to negotiate their own contractual arrangements so long as no one else was injured. William Brown, brought to trial in London in 1726 on charges of attempted sodomy, argued along these lines when he announced, "I think there is no crime in making what use I please of my own body."[15] An anonymous French pamphlet of 1790 with the humorous title of *Les petits bougres au manège* (The Little Buggers at the Riding School) not only endorsed the slogan "all tastes are natural," but drew explicitly on the new political economy to argue that because people possess their own bodies, they should be free to do with them what they will—including engage in homosexual relations.[16]

Some of the leading thinkers of the eighteenth and early nineteenth centuries adopted or were influenced by these ideas. Though Montesquieu found homosexuality personally distasteful, he maintained in *The Spirit of the Laws* (1748) that it was punished to excess. Beccaria, writing with an eye on the Florentine censors, hinted cautiously in his *Dei delitti e delle pene* (1764) that laws against homosexuality should be repealed because it was harmless.[17] Bentham, the philosopher of rational hedonism, argued that same-sex love was thoroughly innocuous, and rebutted one argument after another for its criminalization. Fearing the prejudices against homosexuality would jeopardize his reform program—and possibly his life—he never published these writings.[18] Charles Fourier went even further: in his *The New Amorous World* (1818), a sexual utopia based on anarchist principles of voluntarism, homosexuality is not merely tolerated but accommodated. There are special associations for those with minority sexual tastes such as

[14] Quoted in Aron and Kempf (1979). De Sade was, of course, an interested party. His argument had been circulating in France for some time; one of the characters in de Boyer's pornographic novel *Thérèse philosophe* indicates that monsters who prefer *plaisir antiphysique* defend their tastes with exactly that argument (J. B. de Boyer, 1975:159–60).

[15] Bray (1982:114).

[16] Dynes (1981).

[17] Beccaria's Dutch disciple Abraham Perrenot was more cautious still. Accepting the argument that sodomy did little harm, he responded to a wave of prosecutions in 1776 by recommending the substitution of long imprisonment for capital punishment (Huusen, 1985).

[18] Bentham (1978/79), Crompton (1983, 1985:19–57, 251–83).

flagellation and male and female homosexuality.[19] Unpublished until long after Fourier's death, it could not have had any influence at all on the Fourierist utopian socialist movement.

The French Penal Code of 1791 and the Napoleonic Code both took freedom of contract to its logical conclusion by decriminalizing homosexual relations between consenting adults.[20] Conquest brought French law to many other European and Latin American countries, extending the decriminalization of homosexuality quite widely. Russia, Prussia, Austria, and Tuscany all dropped the death penalty for homosexuality in the late eighteenth century.[21] A new Criminal Code for Brazil, based on Benthamite principles and the Napoleonic code, ratified in 1830, eliminated all reference to sodomy. This step influenced Spanish law, and so Latin America.[22] By the early twentieth century, Belgium, France, Italy, Luxemburg, Monaco, Portugal, Rumania, Spain, the Netherlands, Mexico, Guatemala, Bolivia, Brazil, Paraguay, Uruguay, and Venezuela had no criminal prohibition of consensual homosexual acts in private between adults.[23]

Decriminalization by no means eliminated all prejudice, or even legal repression. The Portuguese Imperial Code, applicable to Brazil, continued to prohibit crimes "offending morality and good custom" in public; by interpretation this included homosexual relations.[24] In 1824, the revelation of an aristocrat's homosexuality threw France into an uproar, and under the Restoration he was ostracized. In the same year police regulations barred brothel-keepers from permitting their prostitutes to sleep together; those who did could be jailed briefly. One madam lost her license when an inspector surprised her in bed with one of her women.[25] In 1826 and 1845, the Paris police raided clubs frequented by men and women with homosexual

[19] Fourier (1967:389–91), Beecher and Bienvenue (1971:54).

[20] Zeldin (1979:313–14) suggests that the omission of homosexual offenses from the Napoleonic criminal code was the achievement of the archchancellor Cambaceres, who was a homosexual. He is mistaken. Cambaceres helped to prepare the civil code, but had nothing to do with the criminal code, which was compiled by a committee of five jurists not known for a sexual interest in men. They, like the earlier committee of seven jurists who prepared the penal legislation of 1791 eliminating the death penalty for sex offenses, were liberals influenced by the rationalist philosophy of the Enlightenment. They did not necessarily approve homosexuality, but considered it a matter inappropriate for the criminal law (Daniel, 1961a, b). The same principle continued to govern French legislation through the nineteenth century. F. Richardson (1972) attributes the laxity of French law to Napoleon's alleged homosexual tendencies, but this explanation, too, wrongly reduces a broad trend in conceptions of the role of government to a matter of one person's idiosyncratic leanings.

[21] Crompton (1983).

[22] Trevisan (1986:68).

[23] Hirschfeld (1914:841–69).

[24] Trevisan (1986:68).

[25] Parent-Duchatelet (1857:167).

interests. A supposed increase in homosexuality was attributed to French troops who had been contaminated by Arab vice while serving in Algeria.[26] The Second Empire (1848–70) brought the limited tolerance of the July Monarchy (1830–48) to a sudden end. Notwithstanding the ostensible protection of the criminal code, dozens of men were arrested in raids or harassed by the police.[27] Between 1850 and 1870, the repression was severe enough to cause something of a panic.[28] In those years, Parent-Duchatelet described tribades as having "fallen to the last degree of vice to which a human being could possibly attain,"[29] while Proudhon referred to sodomy as the last degree of human depravity, the foundation of crime, a monstrosity, that all of society must pursue with iron and fire," and wondered whether it would lead to cannibalism.[30] Prison discipline was tightened to prevent homosexuality.[31] To avoid suspicion, Emile Zola published his *Novel of a Born Invert* only in Italian.[32]

By the 1920s, repression had lessened to the point where a gay subculture could flourish in Paris, and literary figures like Proust and Gide could write of homosexuality.[33] But same-sex eroticism remained stigmatized, and men were still sent to jail for distributing pornography or participating in homosexual acts in public urinals.[34]

Legal reform came more slowly to England. The outbreak of the French Revolution, at a time when the English laboring class was on the edge of revolt, struck terror into the hearts of the upper classes. Determined not to show any sign of weakness, they stifled reform for a generation.[35] As they saw it, the way to the French Revolution had been prepared by moral decay. The Society for the Suppression of Vice was founded in 1802, largely by upper-class members, with the stated goal of shoring up the polity by improving morality. With an urgency derived from the guillotine across the Channel, they tried to persuade aristocrats to set a better example for the lower orders and used the state to uphold their high standards of public decency and decorum. Taking the reforming societies of the early eigh-

---

[26] Karlen (1971:161–62).

[27] Zeldin (1979:313).

[28] Aron and Kempf (1978:48).

[29] Parent-Duchatelet (1957:167).

[30] Quoted in Aron and Kempf (1978:85). This view was by no means universal. Flaubert, who seized every opportunity to get in bed with a woman on his tour of the Middle East, was curious about homosexuality and used the opportunities his travels presented to try it out (Aron and Kempf, 1978:86; Flaubert, 1979:111).

[31] O'Brien (1982:90).

[32] Barbedette and Carassou (1981:94).

[33] Barbedette and Carassou (1981:94).

[34] Barbedette and Carassou (1982:111, 123, 146–47).

[35] Quinlan (1941:2, 68; Trudgill, 1976:166).

teenth century as a model, they prosecuted Sabbath breakers, stage dancers and tumblers, ballad singers, and nude sea bathers.[36] Although some of the reformers' legislative proposals failed to overcome libertarian opposition in Parliament, they were powerful enough to impart a repressive tone to the moral climate.

The 1780s saw an upsurge in sodomy prosecutions that continued for half a century, especially in London (the provinces saw no comparable increase). More than fifty executions took place in the first third of the nineteenth century; and in 1828 the evidentiary standard for proving sodomy was relaxed so as to make proof of emission unnecessary. Although no one was executed after 1836, an attempt to abolish the death penalty for homosexual acts failed in Parliament in 1841. Only in 1861 was the penalty replaced by imprisonment from ten years to life.[37] The death penalty had been abolished for most other previously capital offenses several decades earlier. Although felony prosecutions were rare after that, intermittent scandals kept male homosexuality before the public.[38] Even though the risk of prosecution was small, some members of the upper classes preferred to live abroad, where they were not in legal jeopardy.

Sodomy remained criminal in the United States following Independence, but most states abolished the death penalty as part of a broader movement to replace executions with imprisonment.[39] Prison sentences were typically long (five to ten years in Pennsylvania, ten in New York, twenty in Massachusetts), but because the scope of the law had been limited by judicial interpretation to anal intercourse alone, prosecutions were uncommon. As a defendant could not be convicted of a felony on the basis of the unsup-

[36]Quinlan (1941:100), E. N. Williams (1962:82–84), E. P. Thompson (1963:56–57, 402–3), J. Weeks (1981a:27), A. Simpson (1984:96–111).

[37]H. M. Hyde (1970:91–92), Harvey (1978), J. Weeks (1981a:100–101). Scotland followed suit in 1889.

[38]H. M. Hyde (1970:93–170).

[39]The movement was not as strong in the South as in the rest of the country. North Carolina replaced the death penalty for sodomy with imprisonment for up to sixty years only in 1869; South Carolina eliminated its death sentence for homosexuality four years later, with a much lower maximum prison sentence: five years (Crompton, 1976). The abandonment of the death penalty for most offenses is conventionally attributed to Enlightenment humanitarianism, but a number of scholars have traced this development to efforts on the part of the propertied classes and their political representatives to meet the political and economic problems of an emerging capitalism (Rothman, 1971; Takagi, 1975; Melossi and Pavarini, 1977:143–237; M. B. Miller, 1980). A shift in Protestant theology away from Calvinist doctrines of predestination probably did contribute to the movement, but this shift itself can be explained as a consequence of economic growth, which increased opportunities for upward social mobility. With economic status open to individual striving, the fate of the soul comes to seem less fixed. Similar factors played a role in the English and French campaigns against the death penalty (Foucault, 1977; Ignatieff, 1981).

ported testimony of an accomplice—a rule derived from English procedure—minimal precautions to insure privacy would have eliminated the
risk of prosecution for most cases.[40]

Notwithstanding constitutional barriers to the establishment of a state
religion, theology continued to inform legal rhetoric. Thus an indictment
for attempted sodomy in Baltimore County, Maryland in 1810 described the
defendant as "not having the fear of God before his eyes, but being moved
and seduced by the instigation of the Devil . . .," and characterized the offense as displeasing to Almighty God as well as being in violation of an act
of the state assembly.[41]

The nineteenth century was one of explosive urban growth and commercial expansion, developments with enormous repercussions for the sex
lives of American city-dwellers. The familial and neighborly social control
of the small town could not function in the larger cities, particularly for the
young single men and women who came to the city to find jobs.[42] Employees no longer lived in their employers' homes and consequently found
it easy to maintain a "private" sex life without an employer's knowledge.
Even before rental apartments came on the market, boardinghouses and
hotels made it possible to conduct a clandestine pre- or extramarital affair.

These conditions permitted male homosexual networks akin to those
found in early-eighteenth-century London to emerge in New York City.[43]
There were recognized cruising grounds and, from the 1830s on, all-male
social clubs. Notwithstanding stringent legislation on the books, homosexuality was not vigorously persecuted. A New York City policeman was dismissed from his job in 1846 for molesting other men while on duty, but he
was not prosecuted.[44] The first known conviction of a sodomy charge in
New York occurred only in 1861, more than two centuries after the last one![45]
The few sodomy cases prosecuted in subsequent years almost always involved coercive anal intercourse with a minor. Consenting adults were
occasionally prosecuted for indecent exposure if discovered having sexual
relations in public, but not for sodomy.[46]

[40] H. M. Hyde (1970:77), Bullough (1976:578).

[41] J. Katz (1976:26).

[42] The larger cities had an exceptionally high number of young, unmarried men in the mid-
century decades (P. Boyer, 1978:109). In the absence of informal social control or economic
disincentives, small towns can be just as liberal sexually as larger cities; in nineteenth-century
Germany, the rural proletariat led the way to a less restrictive heterosexuality (Phayer, 1977).

[43] Lynch (1985a).

[44] J. Katz (1976:29–33). Gay (1986:206–212) points to the diary of Albert Dodd, who gradu-
ated from Yale in 1838, as further evidence that the period was not highly repressive. Dodd
wrote of both male and female love interests without any sense of guilt or sin.

[45] L. Murphy (1985a).

[46] Lynch (1985a).

The public showed no signs of panic over homosexuality in these years. On the few occasions when New York City newspapers tried to sensationalize an arrest on homosexuality-related charges, their efforts fell flat.[47] The moralists who denounced the wickedness of city life complained primarily about saloons, gambling halls, brothels, obscenity in the theater, and irreligiosity, not about homosexuality. Still, some stigma remained. The Reverend Horatio Alger, Jr., had to flee Brewster, Massachusetts, in 1866 when his sexual involvements with boys came to light, and Walt Whitman lost his job at the Interior Department when *Leaves of Grass* was published.[48]

The new capitalist order contributed to this stigmatization and to the intensification of prosecutions which occurred late in the century in the United States, England, and Europe. It did so by intensifying competition between men, by sharpening the sexual division of labor and strengthening the ideology of the family, and by stimulating the invention of medical explanations of social deviance.

COMPETITION AND CHARACTER

As the nineteenth century advanced, productive and distributive economic activities came to be organized predominantly through competitive markets driven by supply and demand.[49] With the development of transportation, U.S. markets became regional or national rather than local, greatly increasing the intensity of competition. The economies of early-nineteenth-century France and England also became increasingly competitive.[50]

In an unregulated market economy composed of small-scale capitalist or petit-bourgeois enterprises, owners pursuing profits compete for customers and workers compete for jobs. To succeed they *must* do so: the market is impersonal; it is concerned with the balance sheet alone and bestows profits only on those who compete most effectively. Like it or not, an entrepreneur who permits ties of affection, solidarity with competitors, or sympathy for employees and customers to temper his competitiveness risks losing out to someone who pursues profits more singlemindedly. Thus the market favors certain character traits and disfavors others.

A disciplinary mechanism that influences character formation through direct conditioning is thus built into the very structure of competitive capitalism. By rewarding competitiveness, foresight, discipline, and instru-

---

[47] Lynch (1985a).

[48] J. Katz (1976:33–34), Lynch (1985b).

[49] Competitive firms can be organized on capitalist principles (division between owners and workers), as petit-bourgeois units (family farms and shops), or along socialist lines (worker cooperatives). Only the first two of these three forms had a significant presence in the nineteenth-century American economy.

[50] Polanyi (1957), E. J. Evans (1978).

mental rationality, the market provides positive reinforcement to these traits, just as it negatively reinforces any traits that interfere with successful competition.

Even though extremes of wealth made early capitalist competition highly unequal and chance factors must have influenced outcomes in individual cases, the abolition of surviving feudal restrictions on the attainment of wealth and status gave all free men a formally equal chance to succeed. The claim of *Poor Richard's Almanack* that "early to bed, early to rise" was sufficient to make a man "wealthy" as well as "healthy and wise" was untrue most of the time, but a handful of spectacular "rags to riches" careers gave credibility to the claim that anyone could prosper if he worked hard enough and resisted the temptation to squander his earnings.[51] It must have been equally obvious that those who failed to work hard, or did not save their earnings, tended to fall into poverty, or remained there. Thus the attribution of success to personal character, though ideological, had an experiential basis—as well as an obvious appeal to those who succeeded. Popular adages and works of fiction, such as the stories Horatio Alger, Jr., wrote in the post-Civil War decades, magnified the direct effects of market outcomes in shaping the male character. The direct effects were limited to the individuals who succeeded or failed and to those who knew them personally; the indirect effect was cultural and permeated the entire society.

Once incorporated into popular culture, notions of how to succeed influenced character formation through their effect on the way children were brought up. In every generation, parents who care about their children's futures will attempt to mold them in directions they believe will help them succeed as adults. They will be especially prone to do so when they identify strongly with their children. This identification is easiest when there are fewer children in a family, and when the odds of a child surviving infancy are high. In the absence of these conditions, parents have been remarkably indifferent to their children, if not destructive.[52] But fertility rates were declining steadily in the United States throughout the nineteenth century—as they were in the English middle class after mid-century[53]—and infant mortality rates were dropping.[54] These conditions favored parental investment in their children's future.

Research suggests that parents attempt to prepare their children for the kinds of jobs they are likely to hold when they grow up. Contemporary middle-class parents value autonomy more than lower-class parents, not just for themselves, but for their children as well; by contrast, lower-class

[51] Pessen (1971).
[52] Lorence (1974), Mause (1975).
[53] Banks (1981).
[54] Shorter (1975: 199–204, 353–56).

parents value conformity more. On the average, middle-class parents are more permissive, with class differences in mother-child interaction appearing when the child is only six months old. These are just the differences one might expect if lower-class parents are preparing their children for jobs that are highly supervised and require strict conformity to instructions, and middle-class parents are readying their children to be more independent and self-directing.[55]

To be sure, parental ability to shape a child's character is always constrained. Their resources are limited, and they always have multiple goals that may conflict, e.g., to manage their families with minimal inconvenience, maintain familiar gender distinctions, prepare their children for future careers, etc. The pursuit of some goals may interfere with the ability to attain others. Knowledge as to what traits will be advantageous, and how to foster them, is often poor, especially in periods of rapid social change. Efforts may even be counterproductive: sometimes children rebel against excessive parental pressures.[56] Even under the best of circumstances, outcomes in individual cases are never entirely predictable.

Nevertheless, parents try. We can reasonably assume that on the average such attempts are at least moderately successful, and produce at least a rough correspondence between character types and anticipated occupational prospects. On this assumption, early-nineteenth-century middle-class parents would have begun raising their male children in ways that fostered self-assertiveness and competitiveness, while discouraging such traits as emotional expressiveness, dependence, and nurturance—traits that would have been dysfunctional in the competition.

The unusual degree of independence that de Tocqueville had noted in young boys during his visit to the United States in 1831 has been attributed to just that sort of socialization.[57] Harriet Martineau, an Englishwoman who visited the States a few years later, commented favorably on "the independence and fearlessness of children"; other foreign visitors noted the same traits but were less favorably impressed: they thought the children were excessively unruly and rebellious.[58]

---

[55] B. C. Rosen (1956), Sears, Maccoby, and Levin (1957), Kohn (1977).

[56] Dubbert (1979:18–26).

[57] Pessen (1969:90–92).

[58] Wishy (1968:13). Similar methods of child-raising were being advocated in Great Britain in response to the Industrial Revolution. Thus Andrew Combe (1834): "the child ought as far as possible to be allowed the choice of its own occupations and amusements and to become the chief agent in the development and formation of its own character. In later life, the independent child will show far more promptitude and energy than the 'puppet' dominated by parents and trained in moral slavery." To prepare an entrepreneur, some degree of autonomy and independence had to be permitted.

This was something new. Seventeenth- and eighteenth-century Puritan-evangelical methods of child-rearing had been authoritarian. The infant was regarded as evil; its will had to be broken by relentless parental domination so that a spiritual rebirth could take place later. Rigorous discipline was used to enforce strict obedience to parental instructions. Colonial parents were slow in abandoning these harsh methods, but gradually they did so. They were appropriate for a stable, hierarchical community with little social mobility, not for a world in which it was necessary to exercise initiative and invention to make one's way. By the 1820s to the 1830s, even evangelical families were placing greater emphasis on the fostering of children's independence. Other traits suitable for an entrepreneur in a competitive capitalist society, such as industriousness, sobriety, and self-control, were also stressed. Children's books promised material benefits for good behavior, rather than the spiritual rewards held out to earlier generations.[59]

The competitiveness instilled in boys through parental upbringing, as well as through direct participation in a competitive market economy, would have tended to discourage the acceptance of emotionally intimate relationships between men—whether or not they involved sex. Emotional intimacy is incompatible with competitiveness because intimacy requires trust, sharing, and the willingness to expose vulnerability, all of which weaken a competitor. Thus middle-class men of late-eighteenth-century England objected to the custom of men greeting one another with an embrace, while in Europe and the United States, where the economy had not developed as far in the direction of competitive capitalism, the practice remained acceptable as an expression of friendship.[60] It is tempting to see in the difficulty Thoreau had in expressing his romantic feelings toward men—so apparent in his diaries[61]—just this sort of upbringing.

While competitiveness might have inhibited emotionally intimate sexual relationships between men, it would not have stood in the way of casual or impersonal sexual transactions, such as take place in twentieth-century public restrooms or baths.[62] Nor would it have precluded transgenerational

[59] A. L. Kuhn (1947:94), Kiefer (1948:52–53, 83–85, 226), Wishy (1968:20, 23, 32–33, 42, 46–47), Greven (1973:4–5, 1977).

[60] G. R. Taylor (1974:275), Lynch (1985a). It was still possible in the 1880s for American heterosexual male friends to lie together in the same bed with arms around one another, entirely free from any suggestion of eroticism, but the practice was probably not common (Duberman, 1986:41–48).

[61] J. Katz (1976:481–94).

[62] Humphreys (1970), Weinberg and Williams (1975), Delph (1978). The practice of having sexual relations with strangers is documented for the United States around 1850 in recently discovered poetry of Walt Whitman (Peters, 1984); in Europe, from the eighteenth century. This practice cannot plausibly be linked to capitalism; rather, it was an adaptation to the difficulty of sustaining ongoing relationships under conditions of severe repression.

homosexual relations such as thrived in classical Athens, where men were highly competitive.[63] Because the Greek *erastes* and *eromenes* belonged to different generations, they were not in competition with one another. Nor were Roman slaves and masters. To understand why neither impersonal homosexuality between adult partners nor homosexuality structured along lines of age or class was acceptable, we must look to other factors.

CAPITALISM AND SELF-RESTRAINT

Self-control becomes more important in market economies because of the conflict the petit bourgeoisie faces between consumption and investment. Entrepreneurs must use their capital as efficiently as possible, for if they spend it unproductively, their resources will be depleted and their businesses will fail. Where entrepreneurs are labor-intensive, employers can minimize their costs by keeping wages down. This gives them an incentive to bargain for low wages, and to encourage their workers to adopt a standard of living compatible with a modest income. In addition, where personal savings constitute a major source of capital, entrepreneurs have an incentive to restrict their own consumption so that they can invest their savings. This is also true for those members of the working class who are trying to enter the ranks of the lower-middle class by opening small businesses of their own.

In the Middle Ages and in the early modern era, statutory restrictions on wages limited laborers' consumption levels, and sumptuary laws served the same purpose for the middle classes. But in modern times these constraints could not have been enforced very effectively. In the absence of external control, restraints on consumption had to be internal. To meet their need for internalized restraints, the petit bourgeoisie, which grew up in the interstices of feudalism and expanded as the feudal economy disintegrated, created a morality that placed a high premium on self-discipline and frugality. The Calvinist emphasis on hard work, sobriety, and the stifling of impulse exemplifies this morality. Its appeal to yeoman farmers, craftsmen, and small tradesmen stemmed from the ways in which it corresponded to their material needs.

By placing comparatively inexpensive mass-produced goods within reach of workers and the middle class at the same time wages were being deregulated and sumptuary laws repealed, the Industrial Revolution created historically unprecedented temptations. On their own in an uncertain economy, the fear of losing everything plagued clerks, artisans, shopgirls, and ambitious merchants. The saloons, gambling houses, and brothels offered additional opportunities for losing money and respectability. Lodg-

[63] Gouldner (1966).

ing houses indiscriminately threw newcomers to the city into close contact with those already corrupted, making it harder to avoid temptation[64] and intensifying the need for self-restraint.

These restraints materialized in just those classes that had the most use for them. The English trading class "was emphatically frugal and expenditure on anything which was not absolutely necessary was condemned on religious as well as economic grounds."[65] It could not easily enjoy an activity unless it was useful for business or health.[66] By contrast, the gentry were uninhibited in their conspicuous consumption, and laborers enjoyed life with a clear conscience to the extent that their limited incomes permitted. In America, "the patrician elites took a more relaxed attitude toward alcohol, gambling, and the pleasures of the flesh than did the rising commercial class with its evangelical creed and self-disciplined habits."[67]

The denial or self-control of impulses had been an important emphasis in Protestant childrearing outside the aristocracy in the early American colonies.[68] It acquired greater importance with the rise of factory production in the 1820s and 1830s, and the growth of cities, so that the 1830s and 1840s saw a new emphasis in child-rearing on resistance to temptation.[69] Reformers opened Sunday schools and lobbied for the expansion of public education, in part to help prepare the next generation to live a life of self-control.[70]

The temperance movement was one manifestation of this bourgeois emphasis on austerity and self-restraint;[71] a preoccupation with sexual excess and restraint was another. This preoccupation has had a long history. The archaic belief that semen is a material substratum for the manly virtues informs the writings of Greek physicians of late antiquity advising sexual

---

[64] Boyer (1978:60, 110).

[65] G. R. Taylor (1974:76).

[66] E. N. Williams (1962:78–79).

[67] Boyer (1978:77).

[68] Greven (1977).

[69] Wishy (1968:46–47).

[70] Kuhn (1947:95), Boyer (1978:61–64).

[71] H. Levine; Humphries and Greenberg (1981). That the critical factor was class rather than ethnicity or the rise of a "Protestant" ethic is evident from the comment of Barber (1955:79) that in France even before the Revolution enthroned "middle class respectability in all its aspects, the bourgeoisie disapproved of the lax sexual morality for which the eighteenth century was famous." This was as true of the Catholic bourgeoisie as it was for the Calvinists. The persistence of these attitudes into the next century is noted by Freedeman (1978), who writes about the French bourgeoisie of that era, that

> the tendency toward stratification was reinforced by the social attitudes and collective psychology of the class: the emphasis on success, social ascension, and moderation in personal habits; unique attitudes toward work, thrift, marriage, family, children and education. These attitudes give the bourgeoisie an originality, which clearly distinguishes them from both the nobility and the people . . .

moderation.[72] Shakespeare evidently held the same belief. In *All's Well that Ends Well*, Paroles encourages Bertram, who refuses to consummate his reluctant marriage to Helen, with these words:

> To th' wars, my boy, to th' wars!
> He wears his honour in a box unseen
> That hugs his kicky-wicky here at home,
> Spending his manly marrow in her arms,
> Which should sustain the bound and high curvet
> Of Mars's fiery steed.[73]

A century later, Hermann Boerhaave, the great Dutch physician of the early eighteenth century, spelled out the clinical consequences of male sexual excess in his *Institutes of Medicine*, published in 1708, when the Dutch Republic had been a thriving commercial nation for a century.

> the semen discharged too lavishly occasions a weariness, weakness, indisposition of motion, convulsions, leanness, dryness, heat and pains in the membranes of the brain, with a dullness of the senses, more specifically of the sight, a *tabes dorsalis*, foolishness and disorders of the like kind.[74]

This and later medical writings of the eighteenth and nineteenth centuries viewed men as having a limited amount of bodily energy; excessive discharge of this energy through sexual release, it was said, would deplete the supply available for other purposes and would thus lead to enervation and lethargy, if not more dire consequences. Ejaculation was described as "spending" the semen, a metaphor that would have made sense to those who had been taught that "a penny saved is a penny earned." The comparison was made explicit in the writings of the French physician who wrote during the reign of Louis Philippe that the wasteful loss of semen through masturbation was no different from throwing away money.[75]

It followed from this view of sex that intercourse between spouses should not take place too frequently. Some marriage manuals recommended coitus no more than once a month, and then only for purposes of procreation.[76]

---

[72] Foucault (1984b: 164–65). Nonetheless, the few references to masturbation are positive, not negative.

[73] 2.2.295–300.

[74] Quoted in Foucault and Sennett (1982); see also Bullough (1976: 496).

[75] Quoted in Mosse (1985: 34).

[76] Haller and Haller (1974), McLaren (1976), Dubbert (1979: 42), W. S. Johnson (1979), Fellman and Fellman (1981a). Other manuals were not so restrictive: William A. Hammond's *Sexual Impotence in the Male*, published in 1883, allowed a frequency as high as once a week, but cautioned that it was necessary to take account of variation in individual vigor. It must be emphasized that by contrast with the early Christian ascetics, the Victorian purveyors of sex-

Though couched in strictly physiological terms, these recommendations were rational from a point of view not mentioned at all, that of the household economy. With the decline of the family farm and the introduction of mass education, children were becoming an economic liability. Since effective contraception was not generally available, parents had to practice self-restraint.[77] And indeed they did, for the birthrate fell substantially in England, France, and the United States over the course of the nineteenth century.[78]

That more was involved than a rational restriction of fertility is clear from the large volume of antimasturbation literature that began to circulate in the eighteenth century.[79] To be sure, attempts to discourage masturbation were not altogether new. It was a sin in Christian religion, and most of the penitentials dealt with it. Yet the thirteenth-century French physician Arnold of Villanova had recommended it on medical grounds.[80] By the early modern era, it was given little attention. Jean Gerson, the author of a fifteenth-century confessional, says that many adults did it without realiz-

---

ual advice did not advocate total celibacy. Sex was all right as long as excess was avoided; some stressed that some sexual release was necessary for health. Authors differed as to what constituted excess. Even those who, like Elizabeth Blackwell, challenged some of the premises of Victorian sexual ideology, accepted the notion that male sexuality had to be restricted to save energy for socially important endeavors (Fellman and Fellman, 1981a,b). Neale (1972: 121–42) and W. S. Johnson (1979) summarize the views of some of the dissenters from mainstream Victorian sexual ideology.

[77] Trudgill (1976:17), Prothero (1979:203–9). In addition to abstinence, parents limited family size by practicing coitus interruptus and abortion. Lenders of money denied loans to businesses owned by parents who had too many children, giving small entrepreneurs a direct incentive to restrict their fertility. The need to accumulate capital to start a business also helped to reduce the birthrate by delaying marriage. In her study of Oneida County, New York, before the Civil War, Ryan found that only half the men had married by ages twenty-five to twenty-nine (1981:155–57, 179).

[78] Shorter (1973), Phayer (1977). Banks (1981:67–75) argues that middle-class parents in mid-nineteenth-century England began to curb their fertility because they were preparing their sons for careers in the state bureaucracy. This required extended education, and that was expensive. In America, where opportunities for state employment were more limited, that was probably not a major consideration. McQuillan (1984) calls attention to additional factors. When peasant landholdings are small (as they were in nineteenth-century France), only a few children can be supported on the land; thus small-scale peasant agriculture encourages the restriction of fertility unless child mortality is extremely high. By opening up opportunities for child labor, the early stages of capitalist development may have made it financially attractive to have many children. Only when formal education became a necessity and child-labor laws were adopted did children become a financial liability.

[79] Spitz (1952), Hare (1962), Cominos (1963), R. H. MacDonald (1967), Szasz (1970:180–206), Barker-Benfield (1972a, 1976), Engelhardt (1974), Haller and Haller (1974:295–311), Gilbert (1975), Neumann (1975), Aron and Kempf (1978).

[80] Ussel (1977:136).

ing that it was a sin; and characters in sixteenth-century French fiction show no guilt over it.[81] The sixteenth-century Italian anatomist Gabriello Fallopio even *recommended* masturbation as a way to enlarge the penis.[82] Saint Ignatius of Loyola did not mention the subject in his seventeenth-century *Spiritual Exercises*, an omission that suggests he did not consider it important.[83] Nonclerical sources rarely mention masturbation before 1750.[84]

The new secular literature on masturbation dates from around 1723, when the anonymous pamphlet *Onania*, devoted entirely to the pernicious moral and medical consequences of masturbation, was published in England. The work was known to Tissot, a prominent Swiss physician whose *L'Onanisme: Dissertation sur les maladies produites par la masturbation*, more scientific in tone than *Onania*, was published in Latin in 1758, and in French, English, German, and Italian translations soon after. While some late-eighteenth- and early-nineteenth-century physicians challenged the extravagant claims of Tissot, most seem to have accepted them. Though the immediate impact of the antimasturbation literature was restricted to the literate strata, visual representations disseminated its doctrines more widely. In 1775, a wax museum opened in Paris with exhibits depicting the noxious medical consequences of masturbation for men and women.[85]

Although Benjamin Rush, the American Revolutionary-War physician, endorsed the claims of European medical writers that masturbation was physiologically harmful,[86] he was less extreme in his treatment of the topic than later writers. Fears intensified in the 1830s in the United States, and in England after 1857, when William Acton's highly popular *The Functions and Disorders of the Reproductive Organs*, devoted to male sexuality, was published. Following the "discovery" of adolescence in the 1830s, the prevention of masturbation in juveniles was given more explicit attention,

[81] Flandrin (1972, 1976b: 151, 160–62).

[82] Plumb (1975). Several other physicians of the early modern era, including Johann von Wesel (fifteenth century) and Paul Zacchia (seventeenth century), also advised masturbation on the same grounds as Arnold of Villanova: it rid the body of decaying semen.

[83] Spitz (1952).

[84] For example, it is not discussed in the anonymous *Aristotle's Masterpiece*, published in England in 1684, or in Nicolas Venette's (1688) *Tableau d'amour*, or in the early modern literature on madness (M. MacDonald, 1981). Shorter (1975) argues on this basis that masturbation rarely occurred, but few historians agree. It is difficult to imagine why clerical literature was concerned about masturbation if it was so infrequent. More plausibly, secular literature did not mention the subject because the laity were indifferent to it.

[85] Hare (1962), MacDonald (1967), G. R. Taylor (1974:327–28), Flandrin (1975:160–62, 1976a: 186), F. B. Smith (1977), Aron and Kempf (1978:160–62), Donzelot, 1979:14), Banks (1981: 91–92), Doerner (1981:137), La Barre (1985:120–25), Mosse (1985:11–12).

[86] His comments appear in his book, *Medical Inquiries*, published in 1812. Rush had been educated at Edinburgh, and may have become aware of the Anglo-European literature on masturbation while there. Tissot was not published in the United States until 1832.

ostensibly because immature nervous systems are more vulnerable to abuse.[87]

As the masturbation literature evolved, the emphasis shifted from preventive measures such as cold baths and a moderate diet, to more extreme measures such as mechanical restraints and surgery.[88] These preoccupations continued throughout the nineteenth century and into the early twentieth. As late as 1912, Lord Baden-Powell contended, in his *Scouting for Boys*, that masturbation led to hysteria, insanity, blindness, paralysis, and loss of memory.[89]

Of course, the Victorians were not completely unanimous in thinking that seminal loss was dangerous,[90] but few dissented in print. Undoubtedly sexual practices did not conform to the ideal standards expressed in purity manuals and in the medical literature, witness the large number of women prostitutes found in nineteenth-century England—many more than in the eighteenth century.[91] But diaries, private correspondence, and the large market for popular literature urging sexual restraint indicate that the proponents of self-control were not preaching to an indifferent audience. What is significant is not that men of the middle class conformed to rigid norms of self-restraint, but rather that they thought they should, tried to do so, and felt guilty when they failed.[92]

A clue as to the reasons masturbation provoked so much anxiety can be gleaned from Acton's discussion of its consequences:

> The frame is stunted and weak, the muscles undeveloped, the eye is sunken and heavy, the complexion is sallow, pasty, or covered with spots of acne, the hands are damp and cold, and the skin moist. The boy shuns the society of others, creeps about alone, joins with repugnance in the amusements of his schoolfellows. He cannot look anyone in the face, and becomes careless in dress and uncleanly in person. His intellect has become

[87] Shryock (1931), Rosenberg (1973), Walters (1974), Dubbert (1979:41).

[88] Spitz (1952), Hare (1962), Duberman (1986:30–32).

[89] MacDonald (1967), Hynes (1968:168), Rosenthal (1985).

[90] B. Harrison (1967), F. B. Smith (1977), P. Gay (1980).

[91] Degler (1974), G. R. Taylor (1974:87–88), F. B. Smith (1977), Banks (1981:86), Gay (1983, 1986:357–58).

[92] Carroll Smith-Rosenberg (1978) points out that preoccupation with the physical and mental effects of masturbation appears to have been entirely male. Women of the Jacksonian Age who wrote about sexuality focused on the dangers of being seduced and abandoned and attacked the double standard; they were not the least concerned with what men did to themselves. Nevertheless, the persistent indoctrination in a particular sexual ideology had its long-term effects. Two-thirds of the forty-five married women in the Mosher survey (conducted between 1892 and 1920), most of them well educated and married to upper-class men, believed that conception was the primary purpose of sex (Sokolow, 1983:33).

sluggish and enfeebled, and if his habits are persisted in, he may end in becoming a drivelling idiot or a peevish valetudinarian. Such boys are to be seen in all stages of degeneration, but what we have described is but the result towards which *they all* are tending.[93]

For Acton, the consequences of masturbation are social withdrawal and the loss of aggressiveness or self-assertiveness. Masturbation threatened virility, which was "necessary to give a man that consciousness of his dignity, of his character as head and ruler, and of his importance, which is absolutely essential to the well-being of the family, and through it, of society itself."[94] The masturbator risks losing the personal qualities needed to dominate wife and children and to compete successfully in the capitalist economy. The discipline needed to limit the expression of sexuality to the potentially procreative was also the discipline needed to resist the temptation to indulge in all the pleasures offered by the capitalist city. Thus the repression of masturbation in children was seen as character training for resistance to other temptations later in life.[95] To a contemporary reader, the fear that men will abandon the world of work so that they can spend all their time masturbating must seem fantastical. The strength of nineteenth-century fears that this could happen testifies to the anxieties men felt a hundred years ago about their adequacy to compete in the business world.[96]

Although the ease with which anyone could engage in masturbation without others knowing may have made it especially worrisome, other forms of sexual pleasure were also anathema. Marital intercourse for enjoyment, and homosexuality, were both considered outside the pale as "unproductive" forms of sexuality. French socialists of the nineteenth century opposed birth control on the grounds that a life devoted to the pursuit of pleasure—a pursuit that would have been financially disastrous for the left's working-class constituency—was morally wrong.[97] If spouses could

[93] Quoted in Marcus (1964:19), Marcus's italics.

[94] Acton (1865:74), L'Esperance (1977).

[95] Fellman and Fellman (1981b:85, 91). Parents' letters to their college-age students in mid-nineteenth-century America stress the importance of prudence, sobriety, good work habits, and self-control; in 1837 the Utica Maternal Association held discussions on how to teach these habits to their children (Ryan, 1981:173–76).

[96] During the first half of the century, these fears concerned men and boys only, not women or girls. Up to 1860, the American masturbation literature was devoted almost entirely to males (Barker-Benfield, 1976:167). Female masturbation will be discussed briefly below.

[97] Maclaren (1976). German Social Democrats took a similar position: Clara Zetkin and Rosa Luxemburg both opposed contraception and urged workers to have more children (R. J. Evans, 1979:242). Similarly, prominent English socialists of the nineteenth century attacked

engage in sex for enjoyment, what would they do next? Paul Claudel asked this question out loud in a letter to André Gide in 1914:

> The line between acceptable and bad, deviant sex must be the possibility of issue. Otherwise where do you draw the line? If one pretends to justify sodomy, another will justify onanism, vampirism, rape of children, cannibalism, etc. There is no reason to stop.[98]

Claudel simply takes for granted that people will want to engage in all these activities.

As early as 1796, the German physician Johann Valentin Müller wrote of masturbation as a precursor of same-sex love.[99] Nineteenth-century Anglo-American masturbation literature repeated this claim, seeing in "the solitary vice" the first step along a path that led eventually to unnatural relations with a partner of the same sex.[100] Rev. John Todd, author of popular books of advice to boys and men, wrote that contraception and abortion in marriage, practices that made sex for pleasure alone possible, would lead inevitably to homosexuality. Masturbation, marital coitus, and homosexuality all used up energy that should be saved for other purposes. Pleasure was the primary threat; the source of the please—one's own body, a wife, or another male—was secondary.[101] Physiological theory was reproducing the Augustinian criteria for acceptable sex! It was, however, doing so in a radically different discourse.

The clinical evidence behind the antisex-pleasure writings was almost entirely anecdotal and, to contemporary readers, not very persuasive. Much of it is laughable. It is tempting, therefore, to infer that physicians were simply conservative guardians of an old Christian sexual morality at a time when religion was losing the ability to perform that function. But the rhetoric employed shows that more was involved than the defense of religious teachings. Anxieties about downward mobility in society that lacked

---

birth control as a ruling-class scheme to restrict the growth of the working class (Heath, 1982:10–11).

[98] Claudel and Gide (1949:220), Lanteri-Lauri (1979:24).

[99] Müller's *Entwurf einer gerichtlichen Arzneiwissenschaft* (Outline of Forensic Medicine) is reprinted in Hohmann (1977).

[100] Bullough and Voght (1973), Bullough (1976:547), J. Weeks (1977:25), Mosse (1985:29). Since boys sometimes learned to masturbate from older youths or men and engaged in mutual masturbation with them, the suggestion was not without some foundation, even if it was largely fanciful. The widespread concern that household servants would initiate the children of the house into sexual vice focused primarily on heterosexual seduction, but may have had a homosexual component as well.

[101] Barker-Benfield (1976:179, 211–12).

"safety nets," and about the fatigues and exhaustions to which the mind and body were susceptible under the alienating work conditions of capitalist production,[102] left their print on sexual ideology.

It was in the interests of physicians to elaborate and disseminate that ideology. Acton and some of the other leading British contributors to the masturbation literature did not come from the most prestigious or reputable ranks of the medical profession, and may have been pandering to public fears to make money with their advice books.[103] For others this was probably not an issue. Tissot came from a patrician Swiss family,[104] and Benjamin Rush was one of the most prominent American physicians of his day. However, all physicians faced the difficulty that nineteenth-century medical knowledge was too limited to permit the diagnosis and treatment of many diseases. Because almost all patients had had some previous history of masturbation, doctors could plausibly attribute almost any mysterious illness or death to it. This enabled them to avoid having to confess their ignorance and professional impotence.[105] At a time when physicians were trying to improve their social standing, masturbation fears were a godsend.

The rise of a parallel medical preoccupation with masturbation and homosexuality occurred alongside the intensification of hostility toward male homosexuality in eighteenth-century England. Middle-class parents began to show more concern with the prevention of homosexuality in their adolescent children, and the more expensive boarding schools began to make it possible for youths to have beds of their own, instead of sharing beds. Prior to the 1770s, this does not appear to have been of any concern.[106] Similar measures were taken in boarding schools on the Continent around the same time.[107]

We have already noted the upswing in homosexuality-related prosecutions in England in the late eighteenth century; the next chapter will document a comparable increase in late-nineteenth-century America. As more of the population was drawn into the capitalist economy, preoccupation with homosexuality grew.

FAMILY AND GENDER

Though restricted in a number of ways by church, state, and popular ideologies of female inferiority, the medieval woman was nevertheless an active

---

[102] Rabinbach (1982).
[103] L. A. Hall (1986).
[104] Portmann (1980).
[105] Gilbert (1977).
[106] Trumbach (1978:256), L. Stone (1979:332).
[107] Foucault (1980:28–29).

participant in the world around her.[108] Husbands and wives of the feudal manor formed a cooperative economic unit, jointly overseeing the production of almost everything consumed at the manor. Merchant guilds accorded them trading rights, though not always full membership.[109]

Upper-class women of the Renaissance and early modern era were able to gain an education, and a number made noteworthy contributions to cultural life.[110] As queen, Elizabeth I of England appointed women to prominent positions, and her example encouraged some women to dress as men, and to protest male privilege.[111] From the fifteenth century on, women's occupational activities were increasingly restricted in much of Europe, yet the wives of craftsmen, peasants, and small tradesmen were still able to make major contributions to household production and the production of commodities.

Despite their contributions to the economy, women were far from being equals of men. At law they were badly disadvantaged, and in peasant villages, men who could not control their wives were encouraged to do so through collective public shamings.[112] Yet, though a customary division of labor prevailed between spouses, it was flexible. The wives of gentry and aristocrats routinely managed their husbands' estates when they were away; craftsmen's widows knew their husbands' businesses well enough to run them. In all classes, the house itself served as the center of production, facilitating the contribution of both husband and wife to the same task.[113] Women's power and status reflected these contributions.

In the early American colonies, men dominated religious and political life,[114] but in household production, sexual stereotypes and the division of labor were poorly defined. There was no distinct domestic sphere. The virtues considered desirable in the sermons of New England ministers were not gender-specific: men and women were both expected to be pious and meek.[115]

Though details and timing varied with place, the impact of the rise of capitalism broadly transformed the relationship of men and women to production and consumption, thereby changing their relationship to one another. Capitalism reorganized the family, sharpened gender stereotypes,

[108] Herlihy (1976), Stuard (1976).

[109] V. Lee (1975:42–43), Boulding (1976:420), R. Hamilton (1978:25, 33–37).

[110] C. Silver (1973), R. Thompson (1974:4–5).

[111] S. C. Shapiro (1977), B. J. Baines (1978), André (1981).

[112] N. Z. Davis (1971, 1975:97–123), E. P. Thompson (1972), Flandrin (1976a:122).

[113] A. Clark (1919:5–12, 291–306), Sachs (1971:42–43), George (1973), R. Thompson (1974:4–5), R. Hamilton (1978:28–29).

[114] Barker-Benfield (1972b), Koehler (1974).

[115] Ryan (1979:28–29), Ulrich (1979), J. Katz (1983:50–51).

created and disseminated new ideologies of love and sex, and established new methods of socializing children. All these developments had an impact on social responses to homosexuality.

The enclosure of the common lands, which began in England and Spain in the sixteenth century with the introduction of sedentary animal husbandry (primarily the raising of sheep whose wool could be sold), contributed, along with the other factors, to the exodus of large numbers of peasants from the land. In seventeenth-century France, high taxes and rents drove peasants into poverty, and many lost their lands. As it became possible to purchase household items for cash, production for use on the great estates was discontinued, and servants were dismissed. The supervisory responsibilities of the lady of the house diminished, while her husband began spending more time away from home, in business or politics.

Most of the dispossessed peasants and craftsmen became wage-laborers, leaving their homes every day to go to work. The entry of so many landless peasants into the labor market depressed wages, making it possible for middle-class families to afford household servants. In consequence, middle-class wives were relieved of many of their household tasks. By the early eighteenth century, middle-class wives in London and the larger provincial English towns were becoming ladies of leisure, while their husbands worked outside the home.[116] In France and the United States, the rise of female domesticity did not occur until the nineteenth century.[117]

The ideal that respectable wives should not work filtered down to the upper levels of the working class. In 1875, the Secretary of the (English) Trade Union Congress could identify woman's "proper sphere" as the home. To prevent women who were paid less from undercutting men's wages, the unions opposed their employment.[118] This does not mean all working-class women became housewives. Many male workers earned too little to permit their wives to stay home, and when they lost their jobs, their wives' incomes were essential. Still, by the late nineteenth century, most English workers' wives did not hold steady jobs outside the home.[119]

In addition to sharpening the sexual division of labor and creating rigidly separated public and private spheres of lives, capitalism meant greater geographic mobility, which tended to weaken extended kinship ties. Newlyweds were beginning to live in their own homes, away from parents; and the family was being redefined as the conjugal unit (father, mother, and

---

[116] Watt (1957:44–45), George (1973), K. Moore (1974:xiv–xxi), R. Thompson (1974:74–75), N. Z. Davis (1975:176), R. Hamilton (1978:42–44).

[117] C. Silver (1973), Baron (1981), B. G. Smith (1981:45–46).

[118] Benenson (1984).

[119] B. Taylor (1979), E. Ross (1984).

their children), excluding the household servants and assorted relatives who populated the extended patriarchal family which succeeded the medieval patrilineage.[120]

Marriage was also being redefined. Under the impact of economic individualism, marriage was being reconstituted as a contractual union of free individuals, rather than a strategic alliance between lineages or extended families. Women were winning the right to decline a marriage proposal, and the notion that marriage should involve love and affection between the spouses was gaining ground[121]—earlier in England than in France. With the contraction of the household, the emotional intensity of the relationship between spouses heightened. It became more important to choose a wife who was emotionally compatible (and capable of performing wifely duties), and thus the notion that marriage involves intense emotional bonds between the spouses took hold.[122]

As ties to distant kin and to neighboring villages weakened, Christianity elevated the importance of the family. In Puritan thought, the abolition of intermediaries (priests, saints) between humans and God required each family to become a miniature church, and every member to be as holy as a priest. Marriage was sanctified, and the restriction of sexual expression to marriage given greater importance. Prostitution, previously tolerated, was suppressed. Chastity became the supreme virtue, and the double standard came under attack, especially in the middle class.[123] In 1650, adultery was made a capital offense in England, as it had been under Calvin in Geneva.[124]

Nor were these developments confined to Protestantism. The Catholic church also began to spiritualize marriage, for example, by requiring that it be performed by priests (a requirement that dates only from the Counter-Reformation), and campaigning against concubinage, which had become

[120]Watt (1957:139–40), Barker-Benfield (1976:24), Flandrin (1976b:14–15), Trumbach (1978:3).

[121]Goody (1983) takes exception to this assertion, arguing that consent was always required of a Christian marriage, and pointing out that love was not invented in modern times. Yet parents can coerce their children's consent by such means as withholding inheritance rights, and often did. While romantic love sometimes led to marriage in premodern times, it was neither necessary nor sufficient. It was probably not even expected. References to love in early modern writings suggest that it was a duty akin to loyalty, not a passion, and was expected to develop after marriage, not to precede it (R. Thompson, 1974:116–21), Shorter (1975:56–65, 148–49), Maclean (1977:88), Trumbach (1978), B. G. Smith (1981). Medieval courtly love was, of course, entirely adulterous.

[122]Watt (1957:155), G. R. Taylor (1974:3–7), Flandrin (1976b:150–58), Shorter (1975:65), Trumbach (1978:3), L. Stone (1979), M. Anderson (1980:52, 208).

[123]R. Thompson (1974:155), R. Hamilton (1978:67).

[124]Watt (1957:156–57), Karlen (1971a:125–26).

widespread in France by the sixteenth century, among the bourgeoisie as well as among the aristocracy.[125]

In the short run, the cultural elevation of love had only a limited impact on sexual ideology. In 1546 the Council of Trent backed away slightly from the Augustinian position that marital intercourse became sinful when pleasure overcame reason (which was almost always) by proclaiming that concupiscence was only the "tinder of sin." By implication, it was not itself sinful. Saint Alphonsus Liguori, the founder of the Redemptorist Order, wrote in his highly influential *Theologia Moralis* of 1748 that a woman was allowed to stimulate herself to prepare for intercourse, or if her husband climaxed before her.[126] Yet the Catholic church continued to restrict the legitimate grounds and partners available for intercourse and warned against excessive passion in marriage.[127]

In repudiating the Catholic ideal of celibacy, Protestantism stopped derogating sex. It broadened the acceptable grounds for it to include, in the words of the seventeenth-century Anglican prelate Jeremy Taylor, "a Desire of children, or to avoid fornication, or to lighten and ease the cares and sadness of household affairs, or to endear each other."[128] Yet lust remained suspect, even a potential threat to the stability of the family. The valorization of pleasure seemed to recognize no limits, and thus it threatened the stability of monogamous marriages. Although extramarital sex need not be a threat to some types of family arrangements, it is arguably a threat to families held together primarily by emotional ties, which can be fragile.[129]

In a world in which the conjugal family was becoming the primary social unit, political theorists found this fragility worrisome. They saw the family as a socializer: they wanted children to grow up in a family governed by a patriarchal father according to strict moral precepts so that they would more readily accept rule by absolute monarchs and autocratic employers when older. Thus a threat to the family was a threat to the social order itself, and this could not be tolerated. The reformers of the late eighteenth

[125] Flandrin (1976b:177–78), Trumbach (1978:121).

[126] Gardella (1985:13).

[127] Flandrin (1976b:150–59), M. Anderson (1980:43–44).

[128] Quoted in Schucking (1929:38–39) and R. Hamilton (1978:59).

[129] This was especially true once divorce became possible, as it did among Protestants. The introduction of new inheritance rules strengthened the ideological restriction of heterosexual expression to marriage. Under feudalism, the eldest son inherited the entire estate, a provision that prevented the fragmentation of landholdings. Because middle-class property could be divided more easily, the bourgeoisie abandoned primogeniture. Whereas the lord who was concerned that his land be passed on to his own son, not someone else's, did not need to be concerned about his wife's adultery after their first son was born, the bourgeois husband had to worry about the paternity of all his children (Trudgill, 1976:17; R. Hamilton, 1978:100).

and early nineteenth century in England saw a direct connection between the moral regime of the family and the political stability of the realm.[130]

These developments offered no possibility of a rethinking of the traditional prohibition against homosexuality. Had love become a sufficient rationale for sex, then at least some sexual liaisons between persons of the same sex might have become acceptable. But the social importance of the family ruled out this possibility. Had sexual pleasure been redefined as a positive good, whether or not within marriage, an even broader acceptance of homosexual experience might have become possible. But this could not happen when such a high premium had to be placed on sexual restraint and on the preservation of the nuclear family.[131]

GENDER STEREOTYPES AND LESBIANISM

Stereotypes linking lesbianism with masculinity date back to the Romans. In Martial's epigrams, women who make love to women lift weights and engage in men's sports. A female character in Lucian's *Dialogues of the Courtesans* brags of being "a man in every way."[132] With the fall of Rome, classical learning declined, and the stereotype of lesbians as masculine disappeared. It does not inform the few references to sexual relations between women in early Christian and medieval writings.

With penetration considered the essence of "the sex act," some writers even thought sexual relations between women to be impossible. When Fiorispina, a character in Ariosto's *Orlando Furioso*, discovers that the object of her affections is not male, but a woman dressed as a man, she laments that she may "hope for no reliefe" from her passion. Likewise in Philip Sidney's late-sixteenth-century *Arcadia*, the heroine considers her passion for a stranger she (erroneously) thinks female to be an "impossible desire."[133]

Sixteenth-century Continental sources begin to tell of women who left home, disguised themselves as men, found employment, and married women. Eventually their true sex was discovered and they, but not their gender-normal spouses, were executed. They called the women tribades, a

---

[130] A. Simpson (1984), Amussen (1985). The physicians who wanted to restrain male sexuality also favored the restriction of sex to marriage. They reasoned that marital sex was less exciting, hence less dangerous than extramarital sex (Gardella, 1985:57).

[131] Significantly, no Protestant denomination went so far in its acceptance of emotional rationales for sex as to endorse sexual contacts that were not at least potentially procreative. Protestantism thus did not even break with genital supremacy in marital heterosexual relations, much less accept homosexual relations.

[132] 5.3. Bullough (1976:146), Boswell (1980:77).

[133] Sidney (1912:174–75), Faderman (1981:35), J. H. Foster (1985:35–37).

term derived from the Greek verb *tribein*, "to rub," and carrying connotations of masculinity. The publication of the Roman poet Martial in translation led some authors to portray tribades as having abnormally large clitorises.[134]

This was not a universally shared stereotype. Brantôme, the chronicler of the "gallant" life of the sixteenth-century French court, described the techniques of women who made love to women without any reference to unusual anatomy. The seventeenth-century poet Bensserade thought his lover's choice perplexing when she left him for a woman, but he did not consider her morphology to be odd.[135]

By the end of the seventeenth century, French physicians recognized for the first time that clitoral pleasure was physiologically normal. Nicolas Venette referred to the clitoris poetically as "the fervor and rage of Love. . . . It is there that Nature has placed the throne of her pleasures and voluptuousness, as she has done in the male gland."[136] Perhaps that recognition influenced the fictional portrayal of lesbian relations. The mother superior in Diderot's *La Religieuse* (The Nun) (1780), who used her position to seduce the nuns of her convent, was portrayed unsympathetically, but her attraction to women was caused by isolation from men, not by her anatomy. In the *Erotika Biblion* (1780) Mirabeau referred to male and female same-sex relations as perfectly normal. As Bonnet remarks, a conception of erotic response that broke with earlier religious and medical understandings was developing in late-eighteenth-century French freethinking circles.[137] Still, such standard references as Larousse's *Dictionnaire universal du XIXᵉ siecle* kept earlier fantasies alive by attributing enlarged clitorises to tribades.[138]

With only a few exceptions, fiction and poetry of the early and mid-nineteenth century fails to attribute masculine anatomy, dress, or comportment to women involved in sapphic relations. Courbet's painting, *Sleep* (1866), depicts a decadent lesbian eroticism entirely free from gender stereotypes.[139] Nonetheless, real-life episodes of gender-boundary transgressions kept the earlier image alive. Butler and Ponsonby wore men's hats,

[134] This fanciful notion may have been sparked by the rediscovery of the clitoris by medical anatomists after some centuries in which the dissection of the body had been banned (Bonnet, 1981:22–55, 76–77). One of the early English-language contributions to the genre is the anonymous *Rare Verities* (1657:12–13), which attributes the dilation of the clitoris to arousal (perhaps a reference to female masturbation?). The consequence, it says, is "feminine congression, . . . a thing that happens too too common and frequent."

[135] "Sur l'amour d'Uranie avec Philis," in Bensserade (1698:213–18).

[136] Venette (1696:20–21).

[137] Bonnet (1981:111–12).

[138] Bonnet (1981:170).

[139] Faderman (1981:254–76), J. H. Foster (1985:51–99).

shoes, and coats (as well as petticoats) in public.[140] From adolescence, the French painter Rosa Bonheur wore male attire, possibly in imitation of George Sand, who shocked the French middle-class by wearing trousers and smoking cigars.[141] Writers of fiction sometimes used these figures as models; the lead character in Théophile Gautier's 1835 novel, *Mademoiselle de Maupin*, who sometimes dressed as a man and made love to a woman, was based on the early-eighteenth-century opera singer Mme. Madeleine d'Aubigny. The great popularity of the novel in the last few decades of the century helped to convey the image of the mannish lesbian to a wide audience.[142]

The exclusion of middle- and upper-class women from a direct, remunerative role in the cash economy had consequences for the way men of the nineteenth century thought about female sexuality. These perceptions shaped social responses to lesbianism.

Between the sixteenth and eighteenth centuries, women's education was gradually restricted in England. Women continued to lose ground in the early nineteenth century: Georgian women had been socially more equal to men than Victorian women—they read the same books, discussed politics, and enjoyed considerably more freedom.[143] Women of Victorian England were rarely able to obtain an advanced education and were barred by law from many occupations; unless they were independently wealthy they had to marry to preserve their class position. At law a married woman was a *feme covert;* all her legal rights were vested in her husband. Only in 1857 did she gain the right to sue for divorce, and then only on grounds of cruelty or desertion (not adultery, which was an acceptable ground for a man seeking divorce). Since divorce was costly, and a married woman had no legal right to property—not even to her own earnings—her dependence on her husband was virtually total and inescapable.

American women were not quite as restricted, but they too were rarely able to gain access to higher education, and exclusion from many occupations left them limited opportunity to achieve financial self-sufficiency.[144] In France, the Napoleonic Code restricted female independence, limited

---

[140] Mavor (1973:198–99).

[141] Ashton and Hare (1981:31–32, 53–57).

[142] A. E. Carter (1958:39).

[143] E. N. Williams (1962:51), George (1973), R. Thompson (1974:75–76).

[144] G. Lerner (1969), K. Moore (1974:xiv–xxiv), R. Evans (1979:44–45). More than legislation was involved in the exclusion of women from certain occupations. Opposition from male co-workers played a role, as did the growing spatial separation of home and workplace associated with large-scale production and capitalist rationalization. This separation interfered with women's child-care responsibilities, forcing many of them to relinquish employment (B. Taylor, 1979; B. Smith, 1981:47; Baron, 1981).

women's property rights, and made obedience to their husbands a legal obligation.[145] With other possibilities so drastically foreclosed, women on both sides of the Atlantic had to please men in order to maintain the standard of living of the families in which they had grown up.[146]

The last thing men who faced rigorous competition at work wanted was more competition at home. On the contrary, they wanted home to be a haven, and their wives to care for their material and psychic needs while making few demands on them. Thus women became "homemakers" and child-rearers, responsible for the reproduction of life on a day-to-day basis, as well as from one generation to another. They cultivated the interpersonal traits appropriate to these roles: gentleness, nurturance, docility, and self-abnegation.[147] The inability to do men's work became an ideal: "The backwash of the late eighteenth-century Romanticism had produced an exaggerated respect for refinement and sensibility, so that the further removed from toil of any kind, the more delicate and empty-headed, the more of a lady was a woman held to be."[148]

Asexuality was part of this constellation of ideal female traits.[149] Fearful of depleting their sexual energies—energies that defined them as male, as superior—men worried about the sexual demands their wives might make on them. Although the ideal wife was to be sexually available when her husband wanted her, she was not to take the initiative herself. Whereas love and marriage manuals of the seventeenth, eighteenth, and even early nineteenth century instructed husbands on how to maximize female sexual pleasure, nineteenth-century medical advisors denied that respectable women were capable of it. William Acton, one of the most influential, wrote:

> I should say that the majority of women (happily for society) are
> not very much troubled with sexual feeling of any kind. . . .

[145] C. Silver (1973), B. Smith (1981:47).

[146] Working-class women *did* work for wages, but since their wages were substantially lower than men's, they could not easily live independently (Tannahill, 1980:354).

[147] Welter (1966), Smith-Rosenberg (1972), Shade (1978).

[148] K. Moore (1974:xiv).

[149] This was not a traditional view. Men of the sixteenth and seventeenth centuries believed that women's sex drive was much stronger than men's. Robert Burton (1927:55) asked in *The Anatomy of Melancholy*, first published in 1621, "Of women's unnatural, unsatiable lust, what country, what village does not complain?" The *Compleat Midwifes Practice Enlarged* (1659) recommended that widows masturbate to obtain the orgasms their husbands could no longer provide, and suggested that if necessary they seek the assistance of midwives in this task! (Easlea, 1981:79). The 1690 and 1791 editions of *Aristotle's Masterpiece*, a popular sex manual, provided detailed descriptions of the external female genitalia, which it said were for "titillation and delight." It described the clitoris as "the seat of greatest pleasure in the act of copula-

> Many of the best mothers, wives, and managers of households know little or are careless about sexual indulgences. Love of home, of children, and of domestic duties are the only passion they feel.[150]

The *Westminster Review* published this opinion: "Nature has laid so many burdens on the delicate shoulders of the weaker sex: let us rejoice that this at least is spared them." The author's anxiety that it might be otherwise is clear from his remark that if this were not so, "sexual irregularities would reach a height of which, at present, we have happily no conception."[151] Though dissenting voices were raised, this was the predominant opinion.[152] Simply to be a sexually active female was, to a degree, deviant; but then it was also deviant to be socially active in spheres men were appropriating to themselves. The male students of the Edinburgh School of Medicine rioted when women were admitted in 1869.[153] Women who became active in movements to abolish slavery, gain the right to vote, or enter the professions were denounced and vilified.[154]

Although the notion that women are sexless was developed by men, women's ignorance of sex, their fears of childbirth and venereal disease, and their husbands' indifference to their satisfaction must have made sexual abstinence welcome for many women.[155] Then, too, the social and intellectual distance between men and women was large and growing. Marriage virtually ruled out careers for women. Lillian Faderman observes that under these conditions it must have been difficult for many women to meet their emotional needs heterosexually.[156] Some turned to other women and became involved in emotionally powerful, sensuous, committed ro-

---

tion," called, for that reason, "the sweetness of love, and the fury of venery." These passages were omitted from mid-nineteenth-century revised editions (Blackman, 1977).

[150] Quoted in Haller and Haller (1974:99).

[151] Quoted in Karlen (1971a:165).

[152] Barker-Benfield (1976), Hamowy (1977), Cott (1978), J. Weeks (1981:40–44), Gorham (1982), Chauncey (1982/83). Michael Ryan's (1837:152–53) *The Philosophy of Marriage*, which claims that women enjoy intercourse more than men, represents a survival of the older view. George Drysdale's (1861) *The Elements of Social Science*, which advocated the equality of men and women and the use of contraception so that women could enjoy sex without worrying about unwanted children, was given a negative review in the *Lancet*, a leading British medical journal (Blackman, 1977).

[153] Boulding (1976:648).

[154] R. Evans (1979), Easlea (1981:138–49).

[155] Cott (1978). Almost half the women in the Mosher survey indicated that the ideal frequency of intercourse for them was 0–1 times a month; another 25 percent said 2–3 times a month (Landale and Guest, 1986).

[156] Faderman (1981).

mantic relationships of the sort that Ponsonby and Butler pioneered. The feelings and endearments they expressed in letters to one another signal erotic interest to our twentieth-century ears, but it is not always easy to tell whether these effusive epistles represented more than a literary convention. Even less can we say how many of these relationships were expressed sexually, though it can hardly be doubted that some were.[157]

These intimate female friendships encountered surprisingly little hostility. In France, Germany, Holland, and Great Britain, a few financially independent female couples lived together for long periods of time—quite infrequently in the eighteenth century, more often in the nineteenth—but seem to have aroused little suspicion.[158] Men had so firmly committed themselves to seeing women as nonsexual that they resisted evidence to the contrary. Despite highly persuasive testimony, the House of Lords ruled in a libel suit in 1819 that two schoolmistresses accused of a lesbian relationship could not have been guilty; according to one of the judges, "No such case was ever known in Scotland, or in Britain. . . . I do believe that the crime here alleged has no existence." Another remarked, "according to the known habits of women in this country, there is no indecency in one woman going to bed with another." Indeed, girls were then still sleeping two-to-a-bed in boarding schools—a practice that had already been discontinued for boys.[159]

By the late nineteenth century, the development of the American economy and the establishment of private colleges for women were making it possible for a limited but growing number of professional and academic women to achieve financial independence from men. Some lived in "Boston marriages" with other women, or had close relationships with them; and this, too, attracted little more than a passing comment.[160]

Toward the end of the century, the belief that normal women are blessed by sexual anesthesia was being challenged by the contention that erotic interest is a normal component of romantic love, for women as well as for men. Free-love advocate Annie Besant was almost alone when she wrote in

[157] Havelock Ellis (1859–1939) indicated that, in his day, actresses and prostitutes often indulged in lesbianism, but that lower- and middle-class girls were often too inhibited to carry a romantic attachment to another woman to its sexual conclusion (I. Bloch, 1958:425). It is testimony to what our generation considers important in a relationship that this question constantly arises in discussions of romantic friendships among women of the past. Women of a previous century may not have considered it so important.

[158] Wells (1978), Ashton and Hare (1981), Faderman (1981:190–238), Mavor (1973), Meijer (1983), Schwarz (1983), Grumbach (1984), Jeffreys (1985).

[159] Faderman (1981:147–49, 152, 1983).

[160] Taylor and Lasch (1973), Smith-Rosenberg (1975), Degler (1980:165), Faderman (1981:190), D'Emilio (1983a:92–95), Leonardo (1983).

1877 that celibacy was insalubrious to both men and women, but over the next half-century she was joined by many other voices on both sides of the Atlantic. Advanced thinkers were coming around to the view that sexual satisfaction was a woman's birthright. Reformers championed contraception to enable women to engage in sexual relations without worrying about pregnancy, implicitly severing the relationship between sexual expression and procreation. By the 1920s, Vatican sex expert Arthur Vermeersch pronounced simultaneous orgasms desirable.[161]

The restoration of female sexual response to normalcy applied only to its heterosexual manifestations. Indeed, with female sexuality more openly recognized, passionate friendships among women attracted more attention. Intimate relationships previously considered unremarkable or even praiseworthy were now suspected of being sexual, and were stigmatized.[162] American women's colleges tried to suppress romantic relationships among their students,[163] and beginning in the early twentieth century, schoolgirl "raves" in English boarding schools drew criticism for encouraging a degree of independence that could not be reconciled with heterosexual marriage.[164] Attempts were made to extend the English prohibition of "gross indecency" between men to include lesbian relations. Speakers deplored the homes and families broken by this "dreadful degradation" which threatened the fundamental institutions of society and the perpetuation of the race.[165]

New thrusts in the medical literature contributed to the late nineteenth-century reconceptualization of relationships between women.[166] Throughout the century, nonprocreative activity was considered abnormal, but only masturbation received much attention. In the last few decades of the century, however, physicians began to contribute articles to medical journals dealing with other forms of abnormal sex. They gave particular attention to violation of gender roles, which they considered biologically determined.

---

[161] J. Katz (1983:139–42), Gardella (1983:37–38), Jeffreys (1985:44, 48).

[162] Faderman (1981:233–38), R. Rosenberg (1982:200–204), J. Katz (1983:137–74), Jeffreys (1985:102–27).

[163] Sahli (1979).

[164] Vicinus (1983, 1985:206–10).

[165] S. Edwards (1981:43), Jeffreys (1985:113–15). The attempt was defeated by members of parliament who feared that the law would spread lesbianism by publicizing it.

[166] Several other factors probably contributed to the discrediting of women's intimate friendships: toward the end of the nineteenth century, feminists seeking entry into male-dominated professions were putting greater emphasis on the intellect, implicitly devaluing passion (Sahli, 1979). By the 1920s, increased acceptance of heterosocial arrangements and heterosexual sex also became important (Chauncey, 1983). Dating and the use of contraceptives became acceptable in many circles, so that the norm became heterosexuality, not marital procreative

For several centuries men had fantasized that women who loved women did so in the male mode, with enlarged clitorises. But this image was difficult to sustain in the face of contrary evidence. For example, Bianchi dissected the corpse of an Italian woman who had dressed for eight years as a man and was shot while trying to elope with a woman. He found no anatomical abnormality. The English translator of his essay remarked that "this irregular and violent inclination . . . must either proceed from some error in nature or from some disorder or perversion in the imagination."[167] As clinical observation came to play a larger role in medical education and clinical practice in the aftermath of the French Revolution,[168] other physicians must have made similar discoveries, contradicting the stereotype. The focus in the new literature shifted away from pseudomale anatomy to behavior regarded as masculine.

One of the first doctors to adopt this new perspective explicitly was the German physician Karl Westphal. In 1870 he wrote of a patient with "contrary sexual feelings," who, when young, "was particularly fond of boys' games, and liked to dress as a boy. Since her eighth year had a liking for young girls—not all, but certain ones. Made love to them, kissed them, embraced them, at times succeeded in touching their genitals. From her eighteenth to her twenty-third year had frequent opportunity to gratify her desire." At the age of thirty-five she "still had a great desire to be a man."[169]

As these writings became known in the United States, similar imagery appeared in the American medical literature. The neurologist George Beard wrote that

> long-standing masturbators of either sex care little for the opposite sex; are more likely to fear than to enjoy their presence, and are especially terrified by the thought of sexual connection; similarly, excess in a normal way tends to make us hate the partners in our excess. . . . The subjects of these excesses go through the stages of indifference and of fear, and complete the circle; the sex is perverted, they hate the opposite sex, and love their own; men become women, and women men, in their tastes, conduct, character, feelings, and behavior. Such . . . is the psychology of sexual perversion, whenever and wherever found.[170]

---

sex. These trends weakened the boundaries separating male and female spheres, and made women who preferred to associate with women in their private lives seem more deviant.

[167] Bianchi (1751:66), quoted in Friedli (1987).

[168] Foucault (1973).

[169] Westphal (1869), quoted in Shaw and Ferris (1883) and J. Katz (1983:188).

[170] Beard (1884:106–7). Beard here makes explicit the connection, only hinted at in most other writers, between masturbation and homosexuality.

It was not merely sexual preference that constituted perversion for Beard, but "tastes, conduct, character, feelings, and behavior"—all the components of gender. One could be perverted simply because of one's desires, without ever doing anything about them; and this perversion was a gross affliction of the self, not merely a matter of a wrong sexual object choice.[171]

Other writings embodying the same thinking depicted women who wore men's clothing, drank, smoked, and whistled (men's habits), shunning stereotypically female pastimes such as needlework, and living independently of men. They took the initiative in their sexual relations with women and could attain orgasm only in the superior position. To Havelock Ellis, "the principal character of the sexually inverted woman is a certain degree of masculinity."[172] Allan Hamilton, a physician, described the masculine partner in a lesbian relationship in these gender-defined terms:

> The offender was usually of a masculine type, . . . [holding views that were] erratic, "advanced," and extreme, and she nearly always lacked the modesty and retirement of her sex.[173]

The physicians responsible for these writings did not invent these women; as already mentioned, transvestite women were part of the scene in late-nineteenth-century Paris. Everyone knew about them. Physicians saw some of them as patients in their offices, or in psychiatric asylums. Nevertheless, they were doing more than recording what they saw. In a number of ways they were simplifying and classifying in the process of seeing and recording. Some of the women who achieved notoriety for wearing men's clothing were never linked romantically or sexually with other women. Jane Dieulafoy was married, and both she and Rosa Bonheur said they had taken to wearing men's clothing because it was more practical for their work.[174] Stella Browne, a disciple of Havelock Ellis, published the case of a woman she called homosexual in the absence of any romantic or erotic interest in women, solely on the basis of gender stereotyping. She had "a decided turn for carpentry, mechanics and executive manual work. Not

[171] Note that Beard assumes an interest in the opposite sex to be normal for girls as well as boys. The loss of this interest, with accompanying shyness and subsequent social isolation, would have sufficed to make masturbation abnormal even in the absence of subsequent homosexuality. Other writings, dealing more specifically with female masturbation, consider flirtatiousness and self-assertion—behaviors inappropriate to a Victorian girl—as its undesirable outcomes (Haller and Haller, 1974:105; Barker-Benfield, 1976). In both sets of writings the key issue is the violation of gender norms, but the norms are different.

[172] Quoted in Bonnet (1981:184–85).

[173] A. Hamilton (1896), quoted in J. Katz (1976:60–64).

[174] Stanton (1910:363), O. P. Gilbert (1932:141–42), Ashton and Hare (1981:31–32, 53–57), Casselaer (1986:39–47).

tall; slim, boyish figure; very hard, strong muscles, singularly impassive face, with big magnetic eyes. The dominating tendency is very strong here."[175]

That in most instances the association between gender and lesbian love was not nearly as strong as many physicians indicated is suggested by the comments of Julian Chevalier that "there is a *little* of the man in the lesbian . . . In a host of ways, feeings, conceptualization, actions, there is a resemblance. Among other qualities, she acquires coarseness of feelings, disdain for detail, strength of conviction, a certain breadth of viewpoint, respect for one's word; she is unaware of small feminine deceits." Yet he concluded these remarks, which themselves betray strong gender-stereotyping, with the remark that "between this and the achievement of true virility, there is a gulf fixed: the lesbian is and can only be a sexless being."[176] The many firsthand accounts of lesbian literary and artistic circles in *fin-de-siècle* Paris[177] also lead to the conclusion that most lesbians were not highly masculine.

The female partners of the masculine lesbians, who did not cross gender lines, received comparatively little attention, and were not considered true perverts. Iwan Bloch and Havelock Ellis called them "pseudohomosexuals."[178] Allan Hamilton described "the passive agent" in a lesbian relationship as "decidedly feminine, with little power of resistance, usually sentimental or unnecessarily prudish. . . . [T]he weak victim can be made the tool of the designing companion."[179] While there may have been couples who fit such stereotypes, other writers suggest that most did not. Coffignon noted that while "sapphists appear to be conspicuous most often for their boyish looks, their short hair and the masculine cut of their clothes . . . nearly all [are] both active and passive."[180]

In any event, the "feminine" partner, having done nothing to challenge male prerogatives sexually or socially, could be pitied as a manipulated victim. Her masculine partner was feared: she symbolized the possibility of disrupting the gender system through withdrawal and noncompliance. Her visibility made her a potential example to other women, and so she had to be singled out for special repressive measures. With time, the press, and later, works of fiction such as Radclyffe Hall's best-selling novel, *The*

[175] F.W.S. Browne (1923), quoted in Jeffreys (1985:118).
[176] Chevalier (1893:247–48), quoted in Casselaer (1986:21).
[177] Casselaer (1986).
[178] H. Ellis (1897:262), I. Bloch (1926), quoted in Jeffreys (1985:108).
[179] A. Hamilton (1896), quoted in J. Katz (1976:60–64).
[180] Coffignon (1890:306–7), quoted in Casselaer (1986:11). Likewise, Compton Mackenzie (1928:248) noted that while one woman sometimes assumes a masculine role in courting another, it usually doesn't last long. At one time or another, she observed, both may be "reluctant madams."

Well of Loneliness, published in 1928, communicated these gender-based stereotypes of "inverted" or "perverted" lesbians to a wide audience.[181]

GENDER STEREOTYPES AND MALE HOMOSEXUALITY

Though organized effeminate male homosexuality was present in several European countries in early modern Europe, the eighteenth-century English writings on the molly-houses gave it greater prominence. The phenomenon was familiar enough in France for Balzac to take it for granted in his 1843 novel, *Splendeurs et misères des courtesans.*[182] In America, however, the connection was slow in coming. Edward Hyde, Lord Cornberry, the colonial governor of New York and New Jersey between 1703 and 1708, appeared regularly in public dressed in women's clothing, but was never suspected of being a sodomite on that account.[183] Nor were sodomites accused of being like women. Sources discussing male homosexual relations in the United States in the decades before the Civil War are not plentiful, but none point to the existence of anything like London's molly subculture.

Male effeminacy first became a collective phenomenon in the United States in the late nineteenth century. This timing suggests that as cities grew, urban male homosexual networks grew along with them, differentiated, and came to include circles of cross-dressers. In an atmosphere that was even moderately hostile to homosexual relations, the London molly subculture could not spread to the United States until cities were large enough. This point was reached only after the Civil War. In 1871, a physician wrote of "restaurants frequented by men in women's attire, yielding themselves to indescribable lewdness."[184] Toward the end of the century, Colin Scott revealed more of this strange social world. It included

> coffee-clatches, where the members dress themselves with aprons, etc., and knit, gossip and crochet; balls, where men adopt

---

[181] Baker (1985:227–55). Mackenzie's (1928) novel, *Extraordinary Women,* published in the same year, also helped to sustain the stereotype by having one of its characters, Rosalba Donsante dress like a young man (pp. 38–41); it describes another, Aurora Freemantle, as looking like a man dressed in a woman's clothing (p. 45).

[182] When the director of a Paris jail declines to show Lord Durham, whom he is taking on a tour of the institution, one building, he points to it in disgust and remarks, "'I shall not take Your Lordship there, . . . it is where the *queens* hang out . . .' 'Hao!' said Lord Durham, 'And what are they?' 'They are the third sex, my Lord'" (quoted in Aron and Kempf, 1979). Descriptions of the confluence of male homosexuality and effeminacy in Germany can be found in Steakley (1975:14, 27), in Paris in Barbedette and Carassou (1981:11–87), and in American cities in J. Katz (1976:39–53). In rural areas, male homosexual relations did not usually involve effeminacy (J. Katz, 1976:508–12).

[183] J. Katz (1976:570 n. 23, 1983:125–27).

[184] Napheys (1871:29), quoted in J. Katz (1983:157); Reade (1970:173).

the ladies' evening dress are well known in Europe. . . . The av-
ocations which inverts follow are frequently feminine in their
nature. They are fond of the actor's life, and particularly that
of the comedian requiring the dressing in female attire, and
the singing in imitation of a female voice, in which they often
excel.[185]

While Scott may have been doing nothing more than amateur ethnography,
the treatment of cross-dressing in other reports makes clear that selective
perception was at work. A decade later, the St. Louis physician Charles H.
Hughes reported:

Male negroes masquerading in woman's garb and dancing with
white men is the latest St. Louis record of neurotic and psycho-
pathic sexual perversion. . . . All were gowned as women at the
miscegenation dance and the negroes called each other feminine
names. . . . The names of these negro perverts, their feminine
aliases and addresses appeared in the press notices of their arrest, but the names of the white degenerates consorting with
them are not given.[186]

Though Hughes refers to the whites, who evidently did not cross-dress, as
"degenerates," he gives most of his attention to the black men, who did.

    These passages linking male homosexuality with effeminacy represent
a new development in medical literature. True, Giuseppi Baptiste della
Porta, the seventeenth-century Italian physician who founded physiognomy, had made such a connection,[187] but his passing comments had little
or no influence. Johann Valentin Müller's 1796 treatise on forensic medicine
claimed a somatic basis for homosexuality, but it was not one that attributed
female bodies to sodomites.[188] The Swiss milliner, Heinrich Hössli, who
wrote a two-volume defense of male-male love, entertained the kabbalistic
teaching, based on belief in the transmigration of souls, that "female souls
in male bodies are repelled by women," but pointed out its inadequacy:
there was nothing about some of the brawny practitioners of male-male
love to suggest the possession of a female soul.[189] By the middle of the nineteenth century, however, more definitive statements were beginning to
appear, perhaps derived from literary sources or firsthand knowledge
of homosexual patterns. Thus, in 1849, the French forensic psychiatrist
Claude François Michea proposed that male homosexuality might be due

---

[185]C. Scott (1896), quoted in J. Katz (1976:44).
[186]C. H. Hughes (1907), quoted in J. Katz (1976:49).
[187]Porta (1652:508–11).
[188]The work is reprinted in Hohmann (1977).
[189]Hössli (1836:1.296), quoted in Kennedy (1988).

to a rudimentary uterus that caused some men to become effeminate.[190] But doctors were slow to accept this formulation. Only in the last few decades of the nineteenth century did European and American medical journals begin to discuss male homosexuality in terms of gender deviance. Just as the lesbian was masculine, the male homosexual was effeminate. In a case from Philadelphia in 1886, a young man was described as "effeminate from childhood." He took the name of Jane, said he was a girl, spoke in a "squeaking, effeminate voice," and liked "to fondle men, both with his hands and mouth."[191] A certain Dr. Witry wrote in the *Revue de l'hypnotisme* that "many homosexuals are attracted toward an occupation which corresponds to their quasi-feminine character."[192] The Swiss psychiatrist Auguste Forel contended that male homosexuals

> feel the need for passive submission, they become easily enraptured over novels and dress, they like to occupy themselves with feminine pursuits, to dress like girls and to frequent women's societies. . . . They generally, but not always have a banal sentimentalism, they are fond of religious forms and ceremonies, they admire fine clothes and luxurious apartments; they dress their hair and "fake" themselves with a coquetry which often exceeds that of women.[193]

To others, the male homosexual had a female brain, or was a type of hermaphrodite or androgyne.[194] Called in to examine a defendant in a sodomy trial, Krafft-Ebing, who specialized in forensic psychiatry, concluded that he could not have been guilty of receptive homosexuality:

> he possessed neither the peculiarities of the male prostitute nor the clinical marks of effemination; and he had not the anthropological and clinical stigmata of the female-man. He was, in fact, the very opposite of this.[195]

The passage assumes a perfect relationship between anatomy and sexual orientation. This assumption enabled Havelock Ellis to write of one married man in 1895 that his voice and considerate manner identified him as one "who might easily have been attracted to his own sex,"[196] even though he had no evidence that he was so attracted. Dr. Blumer, a physician at the New York State Lunatic Asylum, described one of his patients as having

[190] Michéa (1849a,b).
[191] Leidy and Mills (1886), quoted in J. Katz (1983:204–5).
[192] Quoted in Barbedette and Carassou (1981:96–97).
[193] Forel (1933:242–43).
[194] Krafft-Ebing (1965:363–71), Chauncey (1982/83).
[195] Krafft-Ebing (1965:620).
[196] Quoted in Chauncey (1982/83).

"contrary sexual feeling" even though he found the idea of sex with another man loathsome; the diagnosis was made on the basis of his long eyelashes, womanlike voice and intonation, an occasional lisp, his talent in writing fiction, and his excellence at playing the piano and composing music—unmanly interests.[197] One of the patients Westphal considered sexually inverted was a man who had never had sexual relations with men, but who had been imprisoned several times for dressing like a woman.[198]

THE IMPORTANCE OF GENDER

Why was gender so important in late-nineteenth-century medical writings on homosexuality? Part of the answer is obvious: patients were coming to their doctors and telling them that they felt like, and experienced the desire to behave like, members of the opposite sex.[199] Yet, though transgenderal homosexuality was novel among white Americans in the late nineteenth century, it was nothing new in England or Europe. Doctors of the Old World could hardly have been unaware of it; it received too much publicity. It was new that patients were turning to doctors for advice on this condition. Their doing so reflects the belief not only that their condition was problematic, but also that doctors could help them with it. Neither the English mollies nor their doctors would have thought so.

Still, as I've already stressed, doctors were doing more than just describing what they saw. In singling out one element of a complex and differentiated phenomenon for particular attention, an element of selective perception was obviously at work. One factor that may have made gender professionally salient to physicians of the late nineteenth century is that biologists had only recently made important discoveries regarding sexual differentiation in mammalian embryos. These discoveries and their impact will be considered in the next chapter.

A second important factor is that rigid gender divisions in society were beginning to weaken. Some American women were beginning to gain access to advanced education and were entering the professions of law and medicine. Elementary-school teaching was well on its way to becoming a predominantly female occupation.[200] Following the 1870 Education Act in

[197] G. A. Blumer (1882), excerpted in J. Katz (1983:183–84).

[198] Westphal (1869).

[199] These remarks implicitly take exception to Foucault's (1980:43) treatment of this subject, which is concerned almost exclusively with the history of ideas and techniques of control. By neglecting the possible contribution of changing patterns of sexual behavior and identification to these ideas, he misleadingly suggests an exclusively top-down process that is altogether arbitrary. Foucault never tells us why Westphal should have written about his patients in terms of gender anomaly.

[200] By 1890 the United States had 250,000 women teachers, and 4,500 women physicians.

Great Britain, job opportunities for middle-class women opened up in a number of fields.[201] Women on both sides of the Atlantic were demanding to vote and campaigned on behalf of a multitude of social reforms. Opponents of these reforms often attacked the reformers for violating gender roles; they described abolitionists, for example, as long-haired men and short-haired women. Physicians who opposed greater freedom for women argued that sharp sex distinctions were biologically based and, if violated, would injure women's reproductive capacities.[202] Some of the women-led campaigns—those against prostitution and in favor of prohibition—seemed to be directed against elements of male culture. Men felt that women were trying to feminize them, and they sponsored organized sports to shore up boys' beleaguered masculinity.[203]

Lillian Faderman's suggestion that the growing hostility to lesbianism, and its confusion with female masculinity in the late nineteenth century, were responses to the threat that women were beginning to pose to male domination is entirely plausible.[204] Julian Chevalier, the author of *Inversion sexuelle*, who attributed homosexuality to congenital hermaphroditism, went on to suggest that it was increasing because women were achieving independence from men and pursuing careers.[205] Some of the most prominent sexologists, including Edward Carpenter, Havelock Ellis, and Maria Stopes, criticized lesbianism and feminism for encouraging women to abandon marriage and motherhood.[206] Members of the English Parliament who debated in 1921 whether to make "gross indecency between female persons" a misdemeanor, as it had been for males since 1885, feared that women who engaged in lesbianism would then have "nothing whatever to do with the opposite sex," and thought that the abandonment of traditional feminine morality had been responsible for the downfall of the Greek and the Roman civilizations.[207]

The preservation of male domination in the face of women's aspirations

[201] Faderman (1981:185–86), Jeffreys (1985:111).
[202] Easlea (1981:138–43), Smith-Rosenberg (1983).
[203] Dubbert (1974).
[204] Faderman (1981).
[205] J. Chevalier (1893:219–25), Casselaer (1986:12–13).
[206] Jeffreys (1985:107–10, 115–21).
[207] Jeffreys (1985:114). Even if exaggerated, the fear that lesbianism would attract women away from men was not altogether without a rational basis. Faderman (1981:186) notes that "Of the 977 women appearing in the 1902 edition of *Who's Who*, almost half did not marry, and of women who received Ph.D.'s in American universities from 1877 to 1924, three-fourths did not marry." A striking percentage of English Victorian women who won acclaim in various fields were also spinsters (Auchmutz, 1975:9–19; Jeffreys, 1985:86). The conditions of middle-class marriage made a career or sustained political activism difficult; consequently, many women who followed those directions refrained from marriage and lived with other women.

to equality depended on men possessing qualities that clearly differentiated them from women. It consequently became necessary to police men who lacked those qualities just as much as women who exhibited them. Continued male rule required that male effeminacy be repudiated.

While these developments may have enhanced the salience of gender, defensiveness over an insecure masculinity appeared in England long before Victorian feminism. Dueling, which had virtually disappeared in the early part of the eighteenth century, revived in the 1770s and persisted for half a century. No man could decline a challenge, no matter how trivial the cause, lest he appear cowardly and effeminate. And though dueling had previously been confined to the upper classes, now everyone engaged in it.[208] Gillis describes the generation of university students of the 1820s as one that "could still weep without fear of being called effeminate, could embrace without taint of sexual deviation."[209] But by 1860, "men no longer dared embrace in public or shed tears."[210]

Changes in child-rearing arrangements may have contributed to this pre-feminist concern with masculinity. As men's work was relocated outside the home, men played a correspondingly smaller role in raising children. By default, children were raised almost entirely by women (mothers, female relatives, nurses, governesses), with implications for the formation of gender identity—the process by which people come to consider themselves male or female and give meaning to those identities.

One way gender identification develops is through modeling, or imitation of adults—whether or not they are of the same sex as the infant. Children cannot readily identify with their father when he is away from the household during most of the hours they are awake. On the other hand, identification with the mother (or her surrogate) is encouraged when it is she who takes care of all the infant's needs. Moreover, a mother who is emotionally deprived by her husband's absence, and frustrated by her exclusion from prestigious and rewarding extradomestic endeavors is likely to make her children the focus of her emotional life.[211] Inevitably she will become the focus of theirs. As might be expected from what we know of contemporary American work and child-rearing arrangements (now changing), children of both sexes tend to identify with their mothers more than with their fathers throughout childhood.[212]

---

[208] A. Simpson (1984:675–92).
[209] Gillis (1974:106).
[210] J. Weeks (1981a:40).
[211] In extreme cases mothers may even try to feminize their sons.
[212] J. H. Williams (1977).

It has been considered important in almost all societies for boys to grow up thinking of themselves as male, as so many aspects of life have hinged on a person's gender. Thus small boys must relinquish their initial female identification and acquire a male identity if they are to live a life that is considered normal for persons of their sex.

In extreme cases the transition is never made, and the boy grows up thinking of himself as a female trapped in a male body—in contemporary language, a transsexual. It is quite possible that the mollies were men who never gave up a primary female identity based on very early childhood identification with a mother. Writings of the time almost suggest as much: the author of *Satan's Harvest Home*, for example, attributed the rise in sodomy to boys being educated at home, where they were pampered and sheltered from the rough-and-tumble of boys' play by their mothers.[213] Unfortunately, we lack the biographical data needed to confirm lifelong femininity and female self-identification on the part of the mollies.[214]

Most boys manage the transition. Their fathers are usually not altogether absent; and when they are, other adult males may substitute. Mothers can encourage male children to think of themselves as male and to behave in ways they define as masculine. However, much research on the development of gender identities suggests that even when a boy abandons a primary identification with his mother and acquires a male identity, a residual female identity remains latent. In the early modern era this identity would have been uncomfortable to acknowledge, for as gender role differences crystallized, it became shameful for a man to be feminine. Women's exclusion from many occupations and from a role in public life was legitimized by doctrines of female inferiority. For a man to identify himself as partly female would have been to announce that he was to some degree inferior.

The transition from female to male identity would have been especially difficult in eighteenth-century England, for little boys typically wore girl's clothing until they were sent away to boarding school—undoubtedly a traumatic occasion.[215] We would thus expect pronounced sexual-identity conflicts among eighteenth-century English men, and that is exactly what historians have found.[216] Similar conflicts have also been reported for

---

[213] *Satan's Harvest Home* (1749:45–61).

[214] The testimony of contemporary gays warns us that cross-dressing can have other meanings. One of the subjects interviewed by Carol Warren differentiated between transvestism and camp. Practitioners of the latter may dress in drag in a spirit of caricature or spoof of gender stereotypes, without actually believing themselves female (Warren, 1974:103–5); see also Newton (1972).

[215] Trumbach (1978:281–83).

[216] G. R. Taylor (1974), Trumbach (1978:281–83), A. Simpson (1984).

American colonists outside the aristocracy,[217] and for the nineteenth-century Anglo-American middle class.[218]

Eighteenth- and nineteenth-century hostility toward male femininity, I suggest, was to a substantial degree a psychological defense against gender-identity conflict. In early-eighteenth-century England this hostility took the form of diatribes against fops and beaux—men who wore fancy clothes, paid excessive attention to their appearance, and spent too much time courting women.[219] Later it showed itself in hostility to, alongside fascination with, effeminate homosexuality. Men's clothing, which had been frilly in the Elizabethan Age, became more sharply differentiated from women's from the 1770s on.

No comparable dynamic was at work vis-à-vis lesbianism. Though it may have challenged men's presumption that all women were placed on earth to gratify men's sexual desires[220] and, when coupled with transvestism and financial independence, male supremacy in other spheres, it did not threaten male identity as such. Henry Brewster told the lesbian composer and suffragette Ethel Smyth that "whereas in the case of two males he found 'the brutal outrage' indefensibly ugly, in the case of two women, 'the woman being a caressing animal,' his feeling was tolerant sympathy."[221] Nor did it threaten women's gender identity, at least not to any great extent. Whereas a boy had to relinquish his early identification with his mother to become an adult, a girl did not; her sexual identity was thus more secure. As an adult she was not threatened by masculine women as men were by feminine males: she had never been forced to give up a strong childhood identification with her father. His absence from the home did not permit a strong identification with him to develop.[222]

[217] Greven (1977:124–40, 243–50). Even though boys of the colonial aristocracy wore girls' clothing and hairstyles until age six, they do not seem to have suffered from sexual-identity conflict in later years. With adult males present on the plantation to serve as role models, they later experienced no anxiety at wearing wigs, long hair, or elegant clothing, and were less inhibited in their heterosexual relations (Greven, 1977:26)—and possibly in their homosexual relations as well (Duberman, 1982/83).

[218] Barker-Benfield (1976:203–26).

[219] E. Ward (1709:138–46), *Hell Upon Earth* (1729:32–36), Staves (1982), A. Simpson (1984: 742–45).

[220] Even this threat was reduced in the last half of the nineteenth century and in the early twentieth by substantial surpluses of women in Germany, England, and the United States (Faderman, 1981:183–84; Jeffreys, 1985:86–89).

[221] Casselaer (1986:72).

[222] Chodorow (1968). Exceptions could occur when mothers took little interest in their daughters, but their fathers did, and, treating their daughters as substitute sons, encouraged them to develop interests then defined as masculine. Several scholars have identified this family configuration in the biographies of nineteenth-century feminists (Riegel, 1963; Welter, 1976).

Because it provoked little anxiety, lesbianism drew comparatively little attention. No one raised an eyebrow at Phoebe's whorehouse affair with Fanny Hill in John Cleland's novel, *Memoirs of a Woman of Pleasure*. When women were pilloried for disguising themselves as men and marrying other women to get their money, they were pelted by crowds of women, but that was because they had defrauded and deceived their spouses, not because they had had sexual relations with them.[223] The member of parliament who argued against criminalizing lesbian relations in 1921 gave practical reasons—to avoid "introducing into the minds of perfectly innocent people the most revolting thoughts."[224] But the fact that no one had argued against publicizing sexual acts between males by criminalizing them suggests that there was a double standard.

Since male involvement in child-rearing remains minimal in all advanced industrial nations, one might legitimately expect gender-identity conflicts to continue to explain social responses to homosexuality. By general agreement, lesbians still do not evoke the same hostility as homosexual men. The literature is divided on the question of whether effeminate homosexual men evoke a stronger hostile response from heterosexuals than gay men whose gender is conventional,[225] and on the relationship between these responses and the respondent's psychological conflicts. However, a number of studies have found that people who hold rigid gender stereotypes are more likely to be hostile to homosexuality.[226]

Though child-rearing arrangements may have been a relatively stable source of hostility to male effeminacy in recent centuries, other developments have intensified this hostility at particular conjunctures. The antifeminist backlash in late-nineteenth-century America may have been one of these; militarism has been another.

A number of historians have commented on the anxieties aroused in the

---

[223] *Gentleman's Magazine* 16:612 (November 1746), Knapp and Baldwin (1819:395), A. Simpson (1984).

[224] Parliamentary Debates, Commons (1921) 145:1805, quoted in Jeffreys (1985:114).

[225] Compare MacDonald and Games (1974) and Laner and Laner (1979) with Storms (1978). M. D. Murphy (1984) found that Andalusian youths in Spain feared masculine homosexual men (*guarrones*) more than effeminate *maricas*. The latter were pitied but not feared; boys could look at them and say with reassurance, "I'm not like that, therefore I'm okay." The former resembled them more. Murphy suggests that *guarrones* were more of a threat because of their normal appearance. If they could be homosexual then so could anyone. His findings suggest that here gender-identity conflicts do not seem to play a large role in structuring feelings about male homosexuality; however, Murphy's respondents may have feared that the *guarrones* would turn them into *maricas*.

[226] Morin and Garfinkle (1978). The similarity of the mean scores of overt male homosexuals and heterosexuals who are hostile to homosexuals on the MF (inversion) scale of the M.M.P.I. is consistent with the argument presented here (Sanford, 1951; M. Lewin (1984).

1880s and 1890s by the new attraction of the British upper middle class to imperialist ideology and its diffusion by the end of the century to the working class. The foreign mercenaries of the eighteenth century had been abandoned; now British youth were to fight for empire and rule the colonies. To do this, they had to steel themselves, and that meant suppressing nurturant, "feminine" traits.[227]

It was important, too, that government officials be morally qualified to lead the troops. However, military defeat in the first Boer War (1881) and at Khartoum in 1885 under the leadership of General Gordon, who was known as a homosexual, cast doubt on the adequacy of the military. The Gladstone government was blamed for Gordon's death in the Sudan in 1885, and during the same year a major sodomy scandal in Ireland, involving high government officials, discredited the government. Male effeminacy was taken as a sign that the nation was losing its ability to sustain imperial expansion. The poor health of working-class recruits in the second Boer War at the end of the century tended to confirm doubts about the physical and moral fitness of British youths.

Riots of the unemployed in the 1890s amplified this concern.[228] Publicity given to Max Nordau's *Entartung* (published in English as *Degeneration* in 1895), which portrayed European civilization as decadent, nourished the belief that "only a chaste leadership can survive challenge from the infidel lower classes."[229] Campaigns against masturbation intensified.

It was in this atmosphere of shaken confidence that Lord Baden-Powell founded the Boy Scouts to strengthen the moral fiber of England's youth, and made sexual purity a major component of its program. Much of the public hostility toward Oscar Wilde, who was convicted on sodomy charges in 1895, stemmed not from his homosexuality, but from his flamboyant and contemptuous manner, and reflected concern that he was cor-

---

[227] Pearce and Roberts (1973), F. B. Smith (1977), J. Weeks (1981a), Macleod (1983:36).

[228] Statesmen saw imperialist expansion as a solution to the unemployment problem. To avoid a "bloody civil war," Cecil Rhodes announced, "we colonial statesmen must acquire new lands to settle the surplus population, to provide new markets for the goods produced by them in the factories and mines. The Empire, as I have always said, is a bread and butter question. If you want to avoid civil war, you must become imperialists" (quoted in Semmel, 1960:16). This concern points to a flaw in B. Adam's (1987a:34) argument that nineteenth-century British hostility to nonprocreative sex "proved functional to a system" that "required an immense supply of labor power." Adam refers, of course, to capitalism. However, capitalist economies don't always expand; from time to time they contract. The great industrial depression that began in the mid-seventies and lasted with only slight interruptions almost through the eighties led to a great deal of concern about *surplus* labor. There is little reason to think that the repression of masturbation and homosexuality had, or were intended to have, a significant impact on the supply of labor in Great Britain.

[229] F. B. Smith (1977).

rupting his youthful partners, not just sexually, but through exposure to his "artistic" life-style. An editorial in the *London Evening News* on the day Wilde was convicted denounced him as

> one of the high priests of a school which attacks all the whole-some, manly, simple ideals of English life, and sets up false gods of decadent culture and intellectual debauchery. The man him-self was a perfect type of his class, a gross sensualist veneered with the affectation of artistic feeling too delicate for the appre-ciation of common clay. To him and such as him we owe the spread of moral degeneration amongst young men with abilities sufficient to make them a credit to their country. At the feet of Wilde they have learned to gain notoriety by blatant conceit, by despising the emotions of healthy humanity and the achieve-ments of wholesome talent.[230]

In short, effete snobs were taking over, undermining older, more robust virtues. A new emphasis on marriage and motherhood appeared at the same time: women were supposed to breed soldiers for imperialism, not demonstrate for the vote or compete with men for jobs.[231] Many of these concerns lessened in the aftermath of the British victory in World War I.

A similar preoccupation with masculinity developed in the United States in the 1890s as America began to assert itself as a world power with expan-sionist ambitions. Theodore Roosevelt warned of the pernicious effects of peace: "The greatest danger that a long period of profound peace offers to a nation is that of [creating] effeminate tendencies in young men."[232] Similar anxieties were aroused by the high failure rate for physical exams given re-cruits in World War I (and later in World War II). The U.S. Supreme Court approved protective labor legislation for women to prevent factory work from ruining their health and thereby weakening the race.[233] And, as the

---

[230] Quoted in Pearce and Roberts (1973). This was also the atmosphere in which the Va-grancy Act of 1898 made homosexual "soliciting" illegal (J. Weeks, 1977a:15). Wilde's trial is discussed in more detail in H. M. Hyde (1956) and Ellman (1988).

[231] Rowbotham and Weeks (1977:172–74), J. Richards (1987).

[232] Quoted in Dubbert (1979:167), see also Dubbert (1974).

[233] In *Muller v. Oregon* (208 U.S. 412, 1908) the court held:

> Even if all restrictions on political, personal, and contractual rights were taken away, and [women] . . . stood, so far as statutes are concerned, upon an abso-lutely equal plane with [men] . . . it would still be true that . . . her physical structure and a proper discharge of her maternal functions—having in view not merely her own health, but the well-being of the race—justify legislation to pro-tect her from the greed as well as the passion of man. The limitations which this statute places upon her contractual powers, upon her right to agree with her employers as to the time she shall labor, are imposed not only for her benefit, but also largely for the benefit of all. . . . The two sexes differ in structure of the body, in the amount of physical strength, in the capacity for long-continued la-

figures cited in the next chapter show, prosecutions for homosexuality escalated.

Perhaps because America's involvement in World War I was brief and not very threatening, anxiety over masculinity was not as great as in Britain. Popular culture exploited stereotypes of masculine women and effeminate men,[234] but the blurring of gender boundaries in the 1920s (e.g., "flapper girls," universal suffrage) made these social types less deviant. In the "Jazz Age," well-attended drag balls in New York, Chicago, and New Orleans were reported without alarm in the newspapers; high-society "straights" like the Astors and Vanderbilts came to admire the costumes. At least in a controlled setting, gender impropriety was more a source of entertainment than a threat.[235]

Gender differences in late-nineteenth-century Germany were widely considered innate and absolute, with "male" traits regarded as superior to female.[236] The all-male German Youth Movement, which began in 1901, glorified a robust, out-of-doors manliness and attacked city life, modernity, and bourgeois decadence.[237] Middle-class opinion largely opposed equality of the sexes, seeing feminism as a leftist program.[238] The *Mutterschutz* movement, which began in 1905, dropped most of the goals of the earlier women's movement to concentrate on the protection of motherhood.[239] Even feminists made use of traditional stereotypes of women in arguing that women's suffrage would benefit the nation.[240]

German characterizations of homosexual men depicted them as lacking the few positive female traits (nurturance, gentleness) and exaggerating the less favorable ones; to Maximilien Harden, a liberal journalist, they "almost always have the unpleasant sides . . . of femininity."[241] He had read Emil Kraepelin's *Psychiatrie,* a standard textbook of pre-Freudian German psychiatry, which characterized them as

> weak, suggestible, dependent. . . . Undependability, lack of veracity, tendency to boastfulness, and petty jealousy are typical

---

bor, the influences of vigorous health upon the future well-being of the race, the self-reliance which enables one to assert full rights, and in the capacity to maintain the struggle for subsistence. This difference justifies a difference in legislation (quoted in J. A. Baer, 1978:421–23; Steinberg, 1982:80–81).

The decision is discussed in N. S. Erickson (1982).
[234] J. Katz (1983:313–18).
[235] Chauncey (1986).
[236] Steakley (1975:49).
[237] Mosse (1985:45–47).
[238] Steakley (1975:49).
[239] Jeffreys (1985:136).
[240] Mosse (1985:111).
[241] Hull (1982:134).

vices. In cases of predominant homosexuality the manner of living frequently changes in the direction of the opposite sex. The man becomes feminine in his movements, walk, bearing, taste. He shows a sickly sweet, fragile essence, becomes vain, flirtatious, lays much worth on externals, clothes himself with care . . . writes tender letters on perfumed paper . . . etc. There is not the slightest doubt, that contrary sexual tendencies develop from the foundation of a sickly degenerate personality.[242]

Against this backdrop, several scandals involving homosexual affairs and orgies among the kaiser's close associates were instigated for political reasons in the first decade of the new century, and threatened to implicate Wilhelm II himself. With revelation after revelation, it began to appear that a large part of the military might be involved, as well as many high civilians in government.[243] Under pressure to defend his credentials as a healthy heterosexual, Wilhelm abandoned his goal of achieving a rapprochement with England and adopted a posture of bellicose militarism. Unmarried army officers married to avoid suspicion. The outbreak of war only intensified gender stereotyping, as unyielding firmness and aggressivity were held out as the essence of masculinity.[244] The Nazis later embraced that militaristic conception of masculinity and its corresponding equation of femininity with motherhood.[245]

Although the association between homosexuality on the one hand and male effeminacy and female masculinity on the other had its origins within the homosexual social worlds of large Anglo-European and American cities, it was given wider currency by physicians, who were displacing the clergy as arbiters of sexual morality, and writers of fiction. In an era of firm gender stereotyping, much of it male supremacist, the effect was to impart a new stigma to homosexuality. But to those willing to brave the stigma, overstepping gender boundaries was a way to express defiance of restrictive conventions, as well as to identify oneself as homosexual to potential partners. Homosexual men and women whose public appearance conformed to accepted gender codes may have been protected from suspicion of homosexuality by public belief in the stereotype.[246]

Gender stereotyping of homosexuality may have kept some men and

[242] Hull (1982:134).
[243] Harden let his imagination run wild: "Everywhere there are men of this trade, in courts, in high positions in the army and navy, in ateliers, in the editorial rooms of large newspapers . . . merchants, teachers and even judges. All united against a common enemy [heterosexuals]" (Hull, 1982:136). He claimed that "entire cavalry regiments [were] infested with homosexuality" (Steakley, 1983).
[244] Bullough (1976:575–77), Hull (1982), Steakley (1983), Nye (1984:336–37).
[245] Mosse (1985:153–80).
[246] Chauncey (1986).

women who did not fit the stereotype from thinking of themselves as homosexual despite their attraction to others of their sex. Some prospective entrants into homosexual subcultures may have been repelled by behavior they considered aberrant. For others, the stereotypes provided defined social roles, in effect telling novices what it meant to be homosexual. One of the sailors recruited into a male homosexual network at the Newport Rhode Island Naval Training Station shortly after World War I was originally heterosexual and masculine in manner, but he began to use makeup and took a woman's name "because the others did." [247]

[247] Chauncey (1983).

9   *The Medicalization of Homosexuality*

The Rise of Reform Capitalism

Beginning in the late nineteenth century, Western capitalism entered a new period of growth, crises, and consolidation. The Industrial Revolution began to provide a higher standard of living for an expanding middle class, while workers responded to their still-precarious position by organizing trade unions, going on strike, and forming political parties with socialist programs. Large trusts and combines began to dominate major sectors of national, and sometimes international, economies. The European powers scrambled to acquire colonies, ushering in a new age of imperialism.

So long as Britain remained the leading industrial power, free-trade ideology dominated British economic policy. On the other hand, the economists of the late-developing nations such as Germany sought protection for infant home industries. As these countries began to catch up to England, British manufacturers faced greater competition on the world market, and the largest of them sought assistance from the state. When businesses had been small, owners feared an overly powerful state and thus favored laissez-faire principles. After they had become larger, though, they could exercise more leverage on state action and consequently had less to fear from politicians.

The political mobilization of the working class also helped to expand the state's role in civil society. As workers grew in number, and began to organize, they became more militant, posing a potential threat to the survival of capitalism.[1] Although force could be—and was—used to repress workers, some reformers recognized that repression would intensify their hostility to the prevailing order. The fear of an explosion, together with the need

---

[1] Militant Parisians established a revolutionary government in 1871, and by the late nineteenth century, anarchist movements and social-democratic parties were beginning to enliven European politics. In the last decades of the century, class conflict in the United States became militant and violent.

to gain the cooperation of the working class, which furnished the foot soldiers of imperialist conquest, argued for co-optation rather than repression.[2] American populists campaigned for government control of monopolies; and though cautious about turning for help to probusiness legislatures, some unions lobbied for protective legislation, especially for women and children.[3]

By the time World War I broke out, the limited protection of workers' welfare was everywhere becoming an explicit goal of state policy, and steps were being taken to regulate the terms of employment through legislation dealing with wages and hours and occupational health and safety. The English working class, whose sacrifices had subsidized the Industrial Revolution, had, by 1914, become "relatively prosperous . . . fairly well protected by laws which not only guaranteed trade union security, but also provided national insurance and old-age benefits."[4] Germany under Bismarck and Italy under Giolitti adopted social-welfare policies with the explicit aim of weakening the socialist movement. Commitment to laissez-faire doctrines slowed change in the United States, but major steps toward a more interventionist state were taken during the Progressive Era.

The expanded role of the state in mediating the relationships among classes and solving social problems is so central to the social dynamics of the late-nineteenth and twentieth centuries—and to our analysis in particular—that we refer to the period as one of "reform capitalism," rather than the more conventional and problematic Marxist term, "monopoly capitalism."[5] The transition to reform capitalism, together with the growth of bureaucratic organizational forms, which will also be discussed in the next chapter, had major implications for social responses to homosexuality. One of these was the medicalization of homosexuality.[6]

---

[2]Freitag (1985).

[3]Steinberg (1982:186–88).

[4]Semmel (1960:234).

[5]An overview of the American developments, in more detail than can be furnished here, can be found in Schwendinger and Schwendinger (1974:11–20, 135–40). Other useful discussions are those of Hopkins (1940), Fine (1956), Wiebe (1962, 1967), J. Weinstein (1968), D. Levine (1971), and Wolfe (1977). E. Evans (1978) points out that in England the contrast between laissez faire and intervention was not absolute: there was a degree of state intervention in the economy even in the 1830s and 1840s (e.g., the Factory Acts), though the predominant thrust of reform then was the abolition of mercantile restrictions on contractual freedom. In the latter part of the century the scope and accepted purposes of state intervention broadened.

[6]Conrad and Schneider (1980) introduced the phrase "medicalization of deviance," but did not define it precisely. I use the term when a physiological or somatic explanation is given for a condition considered pathological. Medicalization ordinarily entails treatment and prevention to be performed by or under the supervision of a physician.

One of the many consequences of economic growth and greater state involvement in civil society was a drastic transformation in the life circumstances of juveniles. As the commercial and industrial revolutions increased the educational requirements for many jobs, middle-class parents began to keep their children in the French lycées and English public schools longer. First in the United States, then in other countries, the democratic ethos led petit bourgeois and some working-class parents to seek expanded, publicly funded educational opportunities for their children. New paternalistic labor legislation barred children from working in many occupations and forced them into school.[7] Economic dependency kept them at home longer. The decline of apprenticeships and family farms, paralleling the rise of factory production and administrative offices, left juveniles more excluded from adult life than ever before.

These developments reduced opportunities for sexual connections across generational lines. Moreover, as children were being redefined as asexual (and manifestations of childhood sexuality, such as masturbation, labeled pathological or pathogenic), the law was stepping in to place them "off limits" to adults. In England, the Criminal Law Amendment Act of 1885 raised the age of consent for girls; and many states of the United States raised the minimum age for marriage. The homosexual seduction of "innocent minors" became even more abhorrent than relations between adults.

These trends restructured homosexual relations. In the early modern era, the standard form of male homosexual relationship seems to have been transgenerational (though other forms, such as transgenderal, were also present). To this day, pederastic relations have not disappeared; in fact, they have vocal advocates.[8] However, over time, the egalitarian form, involving relations between persons of approximately the same age, or in which age differences, where present, are unimportant, has become the norm. Even the molly subculture seems to have been one of adults alone. This was largely true of the late-nineteenth-century urban male-homosexual subcultures and of their post-Civil War counterparts in the United States. These subcultures were sufficiently visible that foreign visitors could find them readily; but prejudice (and in the case of England and the United States, statutory penalties) required that participants protect themselves from public identification.

---

[7] Ariès (1962), Berg (1970), Gillis (1974), Panel on Youth (1974), D. F. Greenberg (1977), O'Donnell (1985).

[8] O'Callaghan (1961), Drew and Drake (1969), Rossman (1976), Mitzel (1980), Plummer (1981), Tsang (1981), Hannon (1982), O'Carroll (1982).

The Medicalization of Homosexuality

Though stigmatized, male homosexuality was not a major public concern in England in 1885 when the Labouchère Amendment to the Criminal Law Amendment Act extended the scope of the legal prohibition of buggery to include "any male person who, in public or private, commits, or is a party to the commission of, or procures or attempts to procure the commission by any male person of, any act of gross indecency with another male person."[9] Though often described as a legal watershed, criminalizing oral sex for the first time, the legislation actually had little practical significance, in that the sexual acts prohibited by the amendment were already being prosecuted as "attempted sodomy" in the eighteenth century.[10]

Since few prosecutions were brought under the act, the government apparently had little interest in trying homosexuality cases. But scandals and prosecutions toward the end of the century, including the Cleveland Street Scandal in 1889 and the prosecution of Oscar Wilde in 1895, show evidence of mounting fear. On the whole, homosexuality was still considered a monstrous vice, and as the *London Evening News* editorial quoted in the previous chapter indicates, it was thought that one person could teach or communicate it to another. Homosexuality remained lawful in countries like Holland or France, but as in England, hostility grew.

In the decades following 1879, most American states amended their sodomy statutes or passed new legislation for the first time criminalizing oral sex and, in some cases, mutual masturbation.[11] Physicians played a particu-

---

[9]The passage of the amendment has generally been attributed to strong antihomosexual sentiment, but F. B. Smith (1976) shows that this attribution has been made too casually. Labouchère was a libertarian and personal friend of Oscar Wilde, who is unlikely to have favored antisodomy legislation. He tacked his amendment onto a statute that raised the age of consent for females as a joke to discredit the act. The purity organizations that campaigned for the adoption of the act had never mentioned homosexuality in their pamphlets. The late-night debate over Labouchère's Amendment came at the end of a two-year period of parliamentary debate that never mentioned homosexuality. The debate itself was extremely superficial, and according to H. M. Hyde (1970:135–36) and Plummer (1975), it is uncertain whether the members of Parliament who approved it understood its provisions. Ten years later, Labouchère wrote that he had copied the text of the amendment from the French criminal code, but if so, he miscopied it. French law prohibited only sexual relations between adults and children, while Labouchère's amendment prohibited consensual sex between adults as well (Pearson, 1937:242–43). As the original act concerned sexual relations between men and girls, this account is certainly plausible. The popularity of Wilde's conviction would have made it difficult for Labouchère to acknowledge his earlier error publicly.

[10]A. Simpson (1984).

[11]Some of this legislation may have been a response to appeals-court decisions acquitting defendants charged with these acts on the grounds that they were not illegal at common law or under state antisodomy statutes (L. R. Murphy, 1985a).

larly active role in campaigning for this legislation.[12] As a result of these new laws, the number of people in prison for "unnatural crimes" increased by a factor of 3.5 between 1880 and 1890, even though the population increased by just 25 percent.[13]

The legislation drew on the older Christian execration of sodomy, but incorporated Victorian fears of masturbation and the belief that it was a prelude to more "advanced" techniques of unnatural intercourse. For example, Indiana's first sodomy statute, adopted in 1881, states:

> Whoever commits the abominable and detestable crime against nature by having carnal knowledge with mankind or beast; or who, being a male, carnally knows any man or woman through the anus; and whoever entices, allures, instigates or aids any person under the age of twenty-one to commit masturbation or self-pollution is guilty of sodomy, and upon conviction thereof, shall be imprisoned in the State prison not more than fourteen nor less than two years.[14]

This statute, like many others, continued to criminalize heterosexual as well as homosexual sodomy. A court decision interpreted the statute as prohibiting fellatio.[15]

This medical attention to homosexuality was not altogether lacking in precedent. Since the seventeenth and eighteenth centuries, European judges had been calling on specialists in forensic medicine or psychiatry to help illuminate cases of transvestism and homosexuality, initially to determine from a physical examination whether a defendant had engaged in anal intercourse.[16] Their involvement with homosexuality was limited, however, and their contribution to wider discussions of homosexuality minimal. Most early-modern discussions did not give it a somatic basis.

The prominence of late-nineteenth-century physicians in efforts to gain adoption of the late-nineteenth-century American statutes signals a new activism for an old profession. Doctors were not simply speaking up when called upon; they were actively seeking to shape society's control apparatus. Why this new involvement?

Physicians came primarily from the middle class and would have shared the general sexual ideology of that class.[17] Since the medical profession was

[12] Hamowy (1977).

[13] J. Katz (1976:36–39).

[14] *Revised Statutes*, 1881, para. 2005, quoted in Hamowy (1977).

[15] Glover v. State, 179 Ind. 459, 101 S.E. 629 (1913).

[16] Zacchia (1688), J. V. Müller (1796).

[17] Of course specialized professional training can swamp the diffuse ideology acquired in the course of growing up in a particular social class. There is little evidence that this occurred in relation to normative questions in nineteenth-century medicine.

highly competitive in Victorian England, France, and America,[18] physicians would have been subject to the same social and psychological pressures as the rest of their class. In 1889 one medical journal described the
majority of New York physicians as living in "dignified starvation."[19] The
majority of their British contemporaries struggled unsuccessfully to maintain a gentleman's standard of living from their fees. Many had to delay
marriage to finance a medical education and establish a practice—making
sex a particularly important source of anxiety. In fact, physicians were
heavily involved in drawing up and lobbying for other sorts of sex-related
legislation, e.g., against prostitution, contraception, and abortion.[20]

It needn't be assumed that the physicians most involved in shaping homosexuality legislation were living on the edge of poverty. The medical
profession was stratified, and some were well off. A detailed study of the
doctors specifically concerned with homosexuality remains to be carried
out; however, clinicians working hard to earn a living rarely have the time
to write journal articles or lobby legislators. One of those involved, William
Hammond, had been a surgeon general of the U.S. Army; another, Charles
Hughes, edited a psychiatric journal. George Beard was a prominent neuro-
logical researcher. They were presumably in the upper ranks of the profession. However, an expanded jurisdiction for physicians was very much in
the interests of the entire profession; it meant not only potential sources of
income but also greater prestige. This was a time when leaders of the medical profession were trying to upgrade its respectability. It was in their interest to associate themselves with a conservative sexual morality.[21]

Remarkable advances in medicine and industrial technology, and the
dissemination of scientific modes of thought, which seemed to undermine
the voluntaristic assumptions of law and religion, brought into being a

[18]Markovitz and Rosner (1973), Larson (1977:20–21), Sussman (1977), Peterson (1978:
215–24), Weisz (1978), G. Rosen (1983:58).

[19]Quoted in Shryock (1947).

[20]Hamowy (1977), Mohr (1978), Smith-Rosenberg (1983), Luker (1984). Luker argues that
physicians sought the legal prohibition of abortion to eliminate the alternative medical practitioners—herbalists and midwives—who performed most abortions. But if income had been
the sole consideration they could instead have lobbied for the restriction of the right to perform abortions to physicians. They did not, largely because they shared nativist concerns
about declining fertility among white, Anglo-Saxon Protestants. This was a subject of substantial anxiety at a time when immigrants with high birthrates were entering the country in large
numbers. Demographic trends were a particular source of anxiety in France and helped to
erode traditional French tolerance for sexual variety. Between 1872 and 1911, the French population grew by a mere 10 percent, an alarming figure when compared with the rates for Germany (58 percent), Great Britain (43 percent), and European Russia (78 percent). The French
birthrate fell, and in some years after 1890, the growth rate was actually negative (Nye, 1984:
134, 155). Nonprocreative sex came in for a hard time.

[21](P. Gay, 1983:315–16).

large public constituency for ambitious scientists who sought to create a scientifically based and scientifically directed culture purged of metaphysics and religious superstition.[22] Medical leaders took advantage of this opportunity by laying claim to a variety of social problems. In 1852, for example, the Swedish physician Magnus Huss coined the word "alcoholism," a new "disease" that medical research claimed to have discovered; before that there had only been drunkenness, condemned from the pulpit and managed by the policeman. By calling heavy drinking a disease, Huss was reclassifying it as a condition that physicians should treat.[23]

Medicine is of necessity a normative science, and its standards of health must come largely from outside itself. In late-nineteenth-century America, doctors drew heavily on the moral standards of their class in specifying criteria of normalcy, while at the same time introducing new theories of causation and strategies of treatment.

Immigration from abroad and, internally, to the cities made it more difficult for people to obtain moral guidance from their neighbors, whom they did not always know. By default they turned for advice to physicians, who, in a sense, had become a kind of secular clergy. In France, physicians imbued with a technocratic philosophy sought public office with considerable success: between 1870 and 1900, almost a third of the French Chamber of Deputies consisted of physicians.[24] In America, influence was primarily indirect. Physicians wrote books and articles expounding their ideas, gave leadership to social-purity organizations, and called on legislators to consult medical experts.[25] Writing in a weekly medical journal in 1884, a Dr. George Shrady argued in relation to men and women with "abnormal instincts" that "conditions once considered criminal are really pathological, and come within the province of the physician. . . . The profession can be trusted to sift the degrading and vicious from what is truly morbid."[26] In ways they did not specify (and because of their ignorance could not have specified), physicians were to take over the process of what should be done with those suffering from morbidity.

Though physicians were asserting the "superiority of their medical expertise over that of legislators, lawyers and judges,"[27] their advice was not always adopted. In the United States, their efforts to establish state-regulated prostitution were defeated by abolitionist forces.[28] In Germany,

[22] Burrow (1966), F. M. Turner (1974).
[23] Nye (1984:155).
[24] Drinka (1984:62), Nye (1984:44, 68).
[25] Burnham (1960, 1971), Pivar (1973), J. Katz (1976:137), Hamowy (1977).
[26] J. Katz (1983:198).
[27] J. Katz (1983:154).
[28] Pivar (1973).

physicians supported attempts to repeal the infamous Paragraph 175, which criminalized male homosexual acts, but the Reichstag was hostile and refused to go along.[29]

Homosexuality as Innate

The notion that homosexuality or a specific homosexual role could be biologically based has appeared and reappeared over the centuries. In chapter 4 we noted the Aristotelian school's explanation of pathic homosexuality, and in chapter 6, its revival in the Middle Ages. The conception of homosexuality as a relatively stable condition, possibly innate, characteristic of a distinct minority population with largely exclusive sexual tastes, appeared with greater frequency in the early modern era,[30] but was still a minority perspective. When the Roman physician Paulus Zacchia published his *Questionum Medico-Legalium* in 1688, its treatment of homosexuality conformed to church doctrine.[31] Even where a somatic basis for homosexuality was postulated, the break with voluntarism did not necessarily go far. The enlarged clitorises some writers attributed to tribades merely made sex with another woman possible; it didn't require it. Ultimately, the vice was still located in the spirit, not the body; and some writers suggested that the enlargement of the clitoris was itself the result of friction, i.e., vice.

An 1824 report on the state of French prisons by the physician Louis-René Villermé distinguished the "circumstantial" homosexuality of inmate "pederasts," who played the "male" role, from that of their "female" partners, called *gironds* or *petits jesus*, whose involvement was instinctive or preferential.[32] The report may indicate that in some medical circles the inheritance of some forms of homosexual desire was already taken for granted, but it does not seem to have had wide impact on thinking about the causes of homosexuality. Adolphe Henke's textbook of legal medicine referred to homosexuality as an "abominable vice," and described its medical consequences (so that guilty parties could be identified in court), but not its causes.[33]

The phrenological school of psychology, which flourished in the late eighteenth and early nineteenth centuries, began to develop a different approach to the biological causes of homosexuality.[34] The school took as its fundamental premises that the strengths and weaknesses of the various brain functions corresponded to the sizes of different regions of the brain

[29] Steakley (1975).
[30] See chapter 7 and S. O. Murray (1987a).
[31] Zacchia (1688).
[32] Villermé (1824:95).
[33] Henke (1832:105–6).
[34] Lynch (1985b).

and that the shape of the skull reflected the brain's contours.[35] The originator of the school, Franz Joseph Gall (1758–1828), suggested that one of the brain functions was "adhesiveness," the faculty responsible for the instinct of friendship.

That several of the leading figures of the phrenology movement lived in long-term, intense relationships with other men may explain the attention they gave to same-sex attachments as manifestations of adhesiveness. One of them, the Scottish physician Robert Macnish, wrote that a deficiency of amativeness and a high degree of adhesiveness could make women prefer the company of other women to that of men, and gave Achilles and Patroclus, and Jonathan and David, as examples of "beautiful pictures of friendship between men."[36]

Like other faculties, adhesiveness was vulnerable to pathological excess. In the August 1836 issue of the *Lancet*, a British medical journal, Macnish published a brief note reporting the following case:

> adhesiveness.—I knew two gentlemen whose attachment to each other was so excessive, as to amount to a disease. When the one visited the other, they slept in the same bed, sat constantly alongside of each other at table, spoke in affectionate whispers, and were, in short, miserable when separated. The strength of their attachment was shown, by the uneasiness, amounting to jealousy, with which the one surveyed any thing approaching to tenderness and kindness, which the other might show to a third party.[37]

The note is striking because it invokes the metaphor of disease without altogether embracing it, and because issues of gender are never raised. There isn't the slightest imputation of effeminacy. The report locates the diseaselike excess in emotional attachment, not in sexual behavior, about which nothing explicit is said. Subsequent phrenological writings continued to write of excess adhesiveness as giving rise to overly strong feelings of friendship, while remaining quite silent about sex. These writings had an enormous impact on the American poet Walt Whitman, who found in the vocabulary of adhesiveness a language to express the comradely love of men which he was championing in poetry and prose as especially suitable for a democracy.[38]

Had this approach been taken further, it might have provided a basis for thinking about relationships in terms of their emotional qualities, rather

[35] Fink (1938:2–19), J. D. Davies (1955).
[36] Lynch (1985b).
[37] Quoted in Lynch (1985b).
[38] Lynch (1985b).

than the sex and gender identities of the partners alone. But that was not to be. After a period of faddish enthusiasm, phrenology came to be regarded as quackery and died out,[39] only to be resurrected in slightly different form by Lombroso, whose work is discussed below.

At mid-century, the French physician Claude François Michéa revived the notion that "Greek love" was an "instinctive passion" with a somatic basis. Perhaps independently, the German physician Johann Ludwig Casper proposed just a few years later that homosexuality could be innate, but did not think that was necessarily so in every case. In some people "the taste for this vice has been acquired in life, and is the result of oversatiety with natural pleasures"; in others, he said, the condition was congenital.[40] But he did not develop his ideas, and had little immediate influence. American physicians of the late nineteenth century were still attributing homosexuality to masturbation.[41]

Some French writers had already begun to attribute various forms of *crime* to heredity in the first half of the nineteenth century. Eugene Sue's enormously popular novel *Les mystères de Paris* (1842–43) featured hereditary criminals. Lauvergne's *les forçats*, written under the influence of phrenological treatises that linked human behavior with the shape of the skull, attributed crime to impulse, an undeveloped will, and innately brutal instincts. Prosper Lucas's *Traité physiologique et philosophique de l'hérédité naturelle* also discussed crime in terms of heredity.[42] It was no extraordinary extension of these ideas, then, for Tardieu to describe the supposedly distinctive anatomical features of active and passive male homosexuals,[43] or for Westphal to maintain that his patients' homosexuality was inborn.[44]

An early-nineteenth-century French novel hinted as to what was distinctive about innate homosexuality; in *Mademoisselle de Maupin*, published in 1835 by Théophile Gautier, Mlle de Maupin, a lover of both women and men who has "the body and soul of a woman, the spirit and strength of a man," proclaims herself "a third sex which has not yet got a name."[45]

[39] Shapin (1975, 1979), Cooter (1984).

[40] Michéa (1849a, b), Casper (1852:56–78), H. Ellis (1897:25), Karlen (1971a:185–86).

[41] Burnham (1973).

[42] Lauvergne (1841), Lucas (1947), Schafer (1969:141).

[43] Despite these remarks, he commented that he did not pretend to understand the causes of pederasty and asked whether it is anything other than a moral perversion: "Perhaps only unrestrained debauchery and jaded sensuality can explain pederastic practices in married men and fathers of families" (Tardieu, 1857:126).

[44] Westphal (1869), Karlen (1971a:186), Bullough (1976:638), Hahn (1979:193–228).

[45] Quoted in Barbedette and Carassou, 1981:91, Faderman, 1981:266, Courouve, 1985:215, Foster, 1985:64–65). This was not the first time that the phrase "third sex" had been used. As early as 1722, Mary Wortley Montagu had referred to her androgynous, bisexual friend John, Lord Hervey, as belonging to a third, intermediate sex, but without suggesting that the condi-

Most recent discussions of the nineteenth-century medical writings on homosexuality contrast them with the voluntarism and behaviorism of medieval and early modern writings on sodomy.[46] In the premodern literature, it is argued, sodomy was the significant category, and it could be performed with a male or female partner. Anyone could potentially be tempted to engage in it, though of course a virtuous person would abstain.

Explanations of homosexuality in terms of vice distanced themselves only a little from this voluntarism. Even if the homosexual outcome was not freely chosen, the early stages were. With a strong enough will it was possible to refrain from masturbation and other vices. The French and German physicians who began in the late nineteenth century to write of homosexuality as innate are supposed to have broken radically with this belief system. They proposed to classify people, not conduct, on the basis of biological attributes that could not be changed. It is said that this development brought into being "the homosexual" as a category of thought and speech, sharply distinguished from the rest of the population (though the word "homosexual" was not to be introduced until a little later; see below).

A careful examination of the full range of materials from the Middle Ages, Renaissance, and early modern eras makes clear that this position oversimplifies a more complex history.[47] It is true that the dominant discourse on sexuality in the Middle Ages and Renaissance was voluntaristic, and that sodomy, the principal category of prohibited sexual acts, could be heterosexual or homosexual. But distinctions among sodomitical acts were sometimes made on the basis of the sex of the partner. A few Renaissance authors wrote of sexual orientation as a relatively stable trait and discussed it within a framework of causal determinism. Most significant, men of the Renaissance who engaged in sodomitical relations with other men sometimes spoke of their sexual desires in these terms. This way of thinking became more common in the early modern era, where it formed part of an

---

tion was congenital (Dubro, 1976). The phrase also appears in J. V. Delacroix's (1777:1.34–43) *Peinture des moeurs du siècle*, but it is unclear from the context that the reference is to homosexuality (Courouve, 1985:215). Somewhat later, in 1852, a Protestant minister named Mandeville referred to women attending a feminist convention in Rochester, New York, as a "hybrid species, half man and half woman, belonging to neither sex" (Gay, 1983:190); and in 1886, Senator J. J. Ingalls of Kansas referred to reformers as "the third sex" and described them as singing falsetto. They were, he said, the sort of men usually selected to guard Oriental harems (*Congressional Record*, 49th Congress, 1st Session, March 26, p. 2786), quoted in Pugh (1983: 103–104). Neither mentioned homosexuality explicitly, but Ingalls implies a lack of heterosexual interest or capability.

[46] Among others, J. Weeks (1977:23–32), Foucault (1980:23–32), Chauncey (1982/1983), J. Katz (1983:137–74), Adam (1987:14–16), and Kinsman (1987:45–47) endorse this position.

[47] See S. O. Murray (1987a) and chapter 7 of this book.

incipient group consciousness. The significance of the nineteenth-century medical literature was not so much the novelty of its ideas as the greater credibility those ideas enjoyed.

The medical claims, conflicting as they did with the voluntarism long taken for granted in law and religion, touched off a protracted debate on the role of heredity in the etiology of crime and insanity; and when it came to homosexuality, at first represented a distinctly minority opinion. Though Tardieu's work was known to specialists, it had only limited dissemination, and even more limited influence. Like the general public, most physicians continued to regard homosexuality as acquired, or simply as an evil.

It was not until several decades later that the phrase "third sex" was introduced again—possibly independently—by Karl Heinrich Ulrichs, an assessor for the kingdom of Hanover. Ulrichs had been impressed by the recent discovery that the human embryo has both male and female sex organs, losing one of them as it develops in the uterus. He conjectured that sexual preferences were just as innate as the sex organs themselves. Homosexuality resulted when an accident in the differentiation of the fetus associated a preference for male partners (which Ulrichs defined as a female preference) with a male body, or vice versa.

To avoid the unsavory connotation of existing terms like "sodomite" or "pederast," Ulrichs called men who belonged to the "third sex" Uranians.[48] Though he considered the condition to be congenital, he thought it neither hereditary nor disadvantageous apart from its legal implications. In 1864, protected by the fact that homosexual relations were not illegal in Hanover, Ulrichs began to issue a series of pamphlets calling for the decriminalization of Uranian love elsewhere and for the recognition of same-sex marriage. These writings were the first in modern times to develop systematically the contention that same-sex love was caused by cross-sex identification, and that it was invariably congenital.

Though they are not well documented, German cities almost certainly had male homosexual subcultures by the time Ulrichs was writing. One might think, then, that he simply applied the new embryological research findings to male effeminacy within the subcultures he knew. This is possible, but according to Hubert Kennedy, at the time Ulrichs began writing, he did not know any other men with Uranian interests. His belief that all men who experienced same-sex eroticism were in some sense female may have reflected the rigidification of gender roles then underway.[49] His social

[48] Numantius (1864), Steakley (1975:4–8), Kennedy (1980/81). Ulrichs used the German *Urning;* the reference is to Aphrodite Uranus in Plato's *Symposium.* Women who loved women were called *Dionings.*

[49] Kennedy (1980/81). Because Ulrichs regarded himself as psychologically female, his theory has generally been taken as an explanation of his own condition. However, Ulrichs wrote

isolation may have prevented him from correcting this misconception. Even though homosexual relations were not illegal in Hanover, they were stigmatized, and Ulrichs published his first pamphlets under a pen name.

A number of authors adopted Ulrichs's terminology, but eventually it was supplanted by the modern word "homosexual," coined by the Vienna-born writer Karoly Maria Benkert, who shared Ulrichs's ideas about psychic hermaphroditism.[50] Like the French and German physicians who wrote of homosexuality as innate, Ulrichs and Benkert viewed same-sex preferences as reflecting an underlying and ineradicable trait. For them, though, this trait was not necessarily revealed in anatomy, but in urges or desires.

Ulrichs's conclusion that uranians are born, not made, may have been inspired by embryological discoveries as he claimed; conveniently, it was an attractive position for someone arguing against the criminalization of homosexual relations. If homosexual desire is congenital and therefore beyond control, one could argue for legal immunity in a criminal-law system that viewed crime voluntaristically. "They can't help what they do," the argument went; "therefore they shouldn't be punished for it." Rightly fearing that German reunification would extend the Prussian prohibition of male homosexuality to all of Germany, Ulrichs made exactly this argument. Edward Stevenson, writing as Xavier Mayne, repeated it to an English-speaking audience a few decades later.[51]

The "third sex" theory of homosexuality influenced the growing psychiatric literature on sexual problems. Otto Weininger's *Geschlecht und Charakter* (Sex and Character) and G. Herman's *Libido und Mania*, both published in 1903, saw mankind as fundamentally bisexual and homosexuality as an intermediate form that combines male and female elements.[52]

---

that he had been unaware of his female qualities until after arriving at his theory (Kennedy, 1980/81). Thus a large amount of self-labeling based on a theory or stereotype appears to have taken place. Alternatively, he may have been trying to cover up his prior acquaintance with a Hanover subculture. Only a few decades after Ulrichs began writing, male homosexual subcultures were quite visible in the major German cities.

[50]Bullough (1976:637), Féray (1981), Courouve (1985:222–25), Herzer (1985). For a time other terms were also used in the medical and psychiatric literature, two of the more popular being "inversion" (Courouve, 1985:142–47) and "perversion" (Moll, 1893).

[51]Mayne (1908). The strategy may have had some success. Hirschfeld (1935b:xviii) estimated that as a defense witness his testimony to that effect had saved defendants from 6,000 years of imprisonment. In Italy, the repeal in 1889 of criminal legislation against consensual homosexual relations between adults may have been due to the efforts Lombroso made to influence public opinion on this issue (Grosskurth, 1964:283).

[52]Weininger (1903, 1906:45–48), Ellenberger (1970:293, 503), Heller (1981). This point of view, which had already been taken up by Krafft-Ebing and Julien Chevalier, had been criticized a decade earlier by Raffalovich (1895, 1896) for its failure to correspond to the gender

The "third sex" theory also carried considerable weight in the early German homosexual-liberation movement. Magnus Hirschfeld and other leaders of the Scientific Humanitarian Committee, founded in 1897, accepted the theory and published an annual, whose name, the *Jahrbuch for sexuelle Zwischenstufen* (Annual for Intermediate Sexual Types), advertised it. Like Ulrichs and Benkert, they hoped to use the argument that homosexuality is congenital to end its legal persecution. It was a controversial strategy among German homosexual activists; those in the antifeminist wing of the movement viewed male homosexuality as an expression of male superiority and considered the Ulrichs-Hirschfeld position insulting.[53]

Hirschfeld offered a sociologically astute explanation for the emergence of the committee and for its success in attracting support from leading intellectuals. At the end of the nineteenth century, Germany faced a host of social problems associated with poverty and rapid urbanization. The educated middle class was unable to participate directly in a government controlled by Junkers and industrialists, yet it found the working-class socialist movement politically unacceptable as an alternative. Avoiding both, it initiated single-issue reform movements that operated as pressure groups. Even though male homosexuality was illegal under Paragraph 175 of the criminal code, German homosexuals were able to organize such a movement because the traditional tolerance of the Berlin police, dating back to the eighteenth century, had permitted homosexual bars to operate. By 1914 the city had forty, with clientele drawn primarily from the middle class. The social interaction in the bars facilitated political mobilization, just as it did in the United States during the 1970s.[54]

The growth of a comfortable middle class that found sexual repression economically less necessary helped create a larger constituency for the committee. As some of the early psychoanalytic case histories demonstrate, this shift may not have advanced very far by the end of the century. But the trend continued over the next few decades to the point where Berlin in the 1920s sustained a libertine nightlife renowned throughout the world. Within some segments of the population, punitive attitudes toward sexual expression weakened, making the Scientific Humanitarian Committee's petition campaigns possible.

---

identities of many homosexuals. Himself an invert who converted from Judaism to Roman Catholicism, he considered both acquired and innate homosexuality to be natural, but thought violations of chastity to be immoral (Healy, 1978; Hilliard, 1982).

[53] Friedländer (1904), Steakley (1975: 16, 48–49), G. Schmidt (1984). Hirschfeld had read the major medical sources on homosexuality, including August H. Niemeyer, J. L. Casper, Ulrichs, Moll, and Krafft-Ebing.

[54] Hirschfeld (1904), Steakley (1975: 24–40), Wolff (1980: 73–73), A. Meyer (1981), D'Emilio (1983a), Berlin Museum (1984), Schoppman (1985).

In Great Britain, Havelock Ellis, a physician whose wife was a lesbian, led the movement, along with Edward Carpenter, a poet, socialist, and homosexual. Ellis argued in his *Sexual Inversion* that the appearance of strong homosexual drives at an early age—documented in many of the case histories he collected—was inconsistent with environmental causation; and the large numbers of men of great talent and creativity who were homosexual could not be reconciled with hereditary degeneration[55] (a theory of homosexuality discussed below). He concluded that most cases of homosexuality were inborn and involved an anomaly of gender, but were not pathological. Sexual differentiation was a matter of degree, as each sex had the recessive traits of the other. Inverts were simply an extreme case of a possibility that was latent in everyone. While Ellis acknowledged that some cases of inversion might be acquired, he thought them rare and believed that even these cases may have involved a congenital predisposition (since not all youths seduced by older men persist in homosexuality as adults).

Though Ellis presented homosexuality in a largely favorable light, he had not fully shaken off conventional attitudes. For example, he maintained that society had a right to prevent homosexuality from being acquired through corruption; it was only congenital inverts who had a right to tolerance.[56]

Carpenter generally shared Ellis's views on homosexuality, but was less concerned with working out the biological details. Instead he collected anthropological reports showing the pervasiveness and acceptance of homosexuality among primitive peoples. Noting that many shamans were homosexual, he suggested that inverts tended to have special mental powers, possibly representing a higher stage of human evolution.[57] The writings of Ellis and Carpenter guided and inspired sex reform efforts in England in the early part of the century.[58]

Degeneracy Theory

Ulrichs, Benkert, Ellis, and Carpenter had advanced the hypothesis of psychic hermaphroditism in the hope of improving the social and legal status of homosexuals. The physicians who promoted degeneracy theory, however, incorporated the notion into a vision of new forms of social control. The theory formalized the loose ideas about heredity and environment that informed discussions of crime on both sides of the Atlantic in the late nineteenth century. One of its earliest proponents, B. A. Morel, head physi-

[55] H. Ellis (1897:41–42, 129).
[56] H. Ellis (1897), Robinson (1976:4–10), J. Weeks (1977a), Brome (1979:62–101), Grosskurth (1980), Chauncey (1982/83).
[55] Carpenter (1908, 1914), Rowbotham (1977).
[58] J. Weeks (1977a:68–83, 1977b, 1981:171–75), Adam (1987:35–38).

cian at a French provincial mental asylum, drew from the then-current Lamarckian doctrine regarding the inheritability of acquired characteristics the most pessimistic conclusions imaginable.[59] He translated the biblical story of the Fall of Man into secular terms by postulating that many medical, psychiatric, and social problems were due to the deterioration of the human body from an initially perfect state, under the impact of an unhealthy environment. The pathologies brought about by poverty, drink, and poor diet, he believed, could be transmitted genetically to offspring, resulting in progressive degeneracy. Because progeny weakened by hereditary taint tended to live in unsatisfactory environments, morbid deviations from normalcy tended to grow from generation to generation.[60]

Degeneracy theory was first propounded by French physicians who found in it a justification for expanding the role of physicians in the prevention and treatment of crime, alcoholism, and poverty. Their entry into national politics after 1875 gave them a forum from which to publicize the theory, while the defeat at the hands of the German army in 1870–71, the stagnation of the economy at a time when Germany's was booming, the decline in the French birthrate, and the growth of alcoholism,[61] crime, and suicide gave credibility to the notion that the French population was indeed deteriorating. New discoveries in cell biology and medicine made the attribution of this deterioration to a physiological process believable. Eighteenth-century doctors had known almost nothing about the causes and treatment of diseases, but the discoveries of Pasteur, Koch, Reed, and Lester built public confidence in physicians.[62]

Soon degeneracy theory acquired prominence in French criminological literature.[63] Emile Zola's novels gave it wider publicity.[64] Professional and lay organizations with local chapters sponsored lectures on degeneracy, distributed pamphlets, and lobbied for preventive measures.[65]

Degeneracy theory quickly spread beyond France. It has been argued that the theory's determinism made it particularly appealing to Calvinists,[66] but its popularity among lay people owed far more to middle- and upper-class anxieties over urbanization, economic decline, class conflict, and im-

[59] Morel (1857, 1860), Friedlander (1973), S. C. Gilman (1985).

[60] Walter (1956), Semadini (1960), Burgener (1964), Duesterberg (1979), S. L. Gilman (1985: 192).

[61] The phylloxera blight destroyed most of the French vineyards, shifting alcohol consumption from wine to hard liquor.

[62] Duesterberg (1979), Nye (1982, 1984), Drinka (1984:62).

[63] Moreau (1882), Feré (1884, 1888), Laurent (1893), Magnan (1893), Magnan and Legrain (1895), Talbot (1899), Duprat (1909), Genil-Perrin (1913).

[64] G. Wright (1983:117).

[65] Nye (1982).

[66] Walter (1956).

migration. In the context of England in the 1880s and 1890s, the theory of hereditary degeneration had "widespread middle-class support" due to "the agricultural depression, the rural exodus, the growing predominance of urban England, the increase of working-class discontent, fears about foreign competition and doubts about free trade."[67] Riots on the part of workers left unemployed by the downturn in the economy seemed to confirm fears that civilization was collapsing. Degeneracy theory provided "a mental landscape within which the middle class could recognize and articulate their own anxieties about urban existence." In addition, it reassured them of their own normalcy by confining social pathology to a restricted class of "degenerates." By contrast, masturbation theory put virtually everyone at risk for horrific disease and decline. Implicitly, degeneracy theory endorsed Havelock Ellis's position that by itself masturbation did not play a significant role in causing homosexuality.

Degeneracy theory came to public attention in the United States when physicians testifying on behalf of the defense in the 1881 trial of Charles Guiteau for the assassination of President Garfield contended that he was not responsible for his actions because he was a hereditary degenerate. But it was American social conditions—not unlike those of England—that gave the theory its appeal to the middle class.[68] The high demand for scarce labor had driven wages up and attracted streams of immigrants from Europe and the Orient. Toward the end of the century, violent labor disputes and the participation of the immigrant population in the urban political machines threatened the dominance of the native-Protestant middle and upper classes. Coming just at the time of the closing of the western frontier, these developments stirred uneasiness about the future of the Republic. Some writers attributed the Depression of 1893 to the biological deterioration of the population.[69]

In Europe, a flock of physicians wrote of homosexuality as a manifestation of congenital degeneracy without entirely denying circumstantial environmental influences in some cases.[70] In America, dozens of physicians wrote journal articles based on degeneracy theory.[71] Most of these writings

[67] G. S. Jones (1971:127–28, 150). See also Bannister (1979:144).

[68] C. E. Rosenberg (1968).

[69] Hofstadter (1968:161), C. E. Rosenberg (1974).

[70] Krafft-Ebing (1877, 1965), Charcot and Magnan (1882), Magnan (1885), Tarnowsky (1886), Moreau (1887), Moll (1891), Feré (1899), Forel (1905), Wettley (1953), Gindorf (1977). As early as 1770, J. B. Pressavin had adopted the term "degenerate" in his *Nouveaux traité des vapeurs* to describe men who have "taken on the slackness, the habits and tendencies of women; all that is wanting is the similarity of their bodily constitutions," a process he thought was accelerated by drinking coffee (Doerner, 1981:109–10). However, he did not regard this degeneracy as innate or link it with homosexuality.

[71] J. N. Katz (1976, 1983).

were unknown except to physicians, but Krafft-Ebing's *Psychopathia Sexualis*, first published in 1886 and revised many times, reached a wider audience. His interest sparked by Ulrichs's pamphlets, Krafft-Ebing compiled hundreds of case histories of unusual sexual behavior or interests. In common with the psychiatric practice of the day, he devised dozens of labels for distinguishing his cases, discussing such varied "perversions" as sadism and masochism, and assorted fetishisms, as well as "antipathic sexual instinct," his term for congenital homosexuality.[72] The vocabulary for discussing sexuality expanded to encompass terms for these rapidly multiplying categories, giving us "transvestite," "urolagnia," "necrophilia," etc. Though the terminology and scientific scaffolding were new, the fundamental opposition between normal sex and abnormal paresthesias was largely based on traditional oppositions. Sex was perverse if reproduction was not its goal.[73] No surprise: Krafft-Ebing was Catholic.

In cases where homosexuality was fully developed, Krafft-Ebing wrote, "feeling, thought, will, and the whole character . . . correspond with the peculiar sexual instinct, but not with the sex which the individual represents anatomically and physiologically."[74] Often it was accompanied by cross-sex dressing. The earlier editions left this abnormality unexplained except in terms of degeneration, but in later editions, Krafft-Ebing endorsed a proposal of Chevalier—not very different from that of Ulrichs— that in prenatal development, conflict between the male and female sexual elements resulted in the conquest by the "wrong" element, resulting in an inconsistency between anatomical sex and sexual instinct.[75]

A common objection to claims that homosexuality is inherited is that parents of homosexuals are rarely homosexual—never exclusively so. However, according to Krafft-Ebing,

> In almost all cases where an examination of the physical and mental peculiarities of the ancestors and blood relations has been possible, neuroses, psychoses, degenerative signs, etc. have been found in the families.[76]

It was not homosexuality that was inherited, but degeneracy, and it could take many forms.

Krafft-Ebing endorsed the repeal of Paragraph 175 in the German criminal code and called for tolerance. His homosexuality cases are presented

[72] Krafft-Ebing (1965).
[73] Lanteri-Laura (1979:39–41).
[74] Krafft-Ebing (1965:357–58).
[75] Wettley (1959), Krafft-Ebing (1965:369–70), Karlen (1971a:191–95), Bullough (1976:641–43), Sulloway (1979:293), Kennedy (1980/81), Caplan (1981), Chauncey (1982/83).
[76] Krafft-Ebing (1965:361).

more sympathetically than those involving other "perversions of the sexual instinct."[77] Most came from middle- and upper-class families and are depicted as moral beings who are no danger to others. One advocate of homosexual emancipation, Edward Stevenson, thought Krafft-Ebing's contribution so salutary that he dedicated his own book, *The Intersexes*, to him.[78] Still, Krafft-Ebing's insistence that homosexuality was a manifestation of hereditary degeneration could not have done too much to eliminate stigmatization.

Darwinian Theory

An alternative to degeneracy theory that shared much in common with it also gained currency in this period. Inspired by Darwin's theory of evolution, including its extension to humans in *The Descent of Man* (1871), Cesare Lombroso, an Italian-Jewish physician, proposed in 1876 that criminals were biological atavisms—throwbacks to an earlier stage of evolution—who were incapable of functioning adequately in the modern world. The American physicians James Kiernan and Frank Lydston extended this explanation to homosexuality by recalling that, in the remote past, the primitive organisms from which the human race evolved were hermaphroditic or bisexual.[79] It seemed to follow that contemporary homosexual humans were congenital throwbacks to the period before monosexuality was established in the animal kingdom.[80]

The Darwinian theory appealed to the middle and upper classes because it legitimated the existing distribution of property and power. Earlier in the century, when business concerns had been small in scale (often no larger than partnerships), poverty and its associated "pathologies" such as crime could be attributed to moral inadequacies such as laziness and insufficient "willpower" with some degree of plausibility, in that a sufficiently penurious worker could conceivably save enough capital to open his own business.

As occupations became specialized and required technical skills, which often had to be acquired through costly advanced education, as work increasingly involved employment in bureaucratic organizations, and as larger amounts of capital were required to open a business, *moral* deficien-

---

[77] Lanteri-Laura (1979:44).

[78] Mayne (1908).

[79] Kiernan (1884), Lydston (1889). Lombroso (1911:418) himself had indicated that some homosexuals were "born criminals," while in other cases, such as those in which there was deprivation of female companionship, their tastes were situational. However, he never treated the subject in greater detail, and in particular, never stated what it was that was distinctive about homosexuality.

[80] Krafft-Ebing (1965:365).

cies no longer provided a plausible explanation for failure. Indeed, workers came increasingly to blame their difficulties on the class system, which severely limited their opportunities and threw them out of work at every downturn in the business cycle. This, however, was an uncomfortable thought to those who were relatively privileged; they found it far more attractive to explain failure in terms of innate intellectual deficiencies.[81]

The rediscovery of Mendelian genetics after 1900 gave renewed strength to hereditary explanations of social problems. The growing social distance between middle-class respectability and the "dangerous classes" in whom deviance was concentrated made theories that considered deviance to be hereditary seem more plausible. It is easier to "write off" members of culturally alien social groups as innately depraved than to acknowledge deviance among one's familiars.

Finally, Darwinian doctrine legitimated imperial expansion at the expense of "inferior" peoples, giving it an added appeal at the point when the United States was beginning to challenge the European powers for world dominance. The European powers were also building empires in Asia and Africa at this time and found Darwinian doctrine attractive for the same reason.

Much of the degeneracy-theory/evolutionary-theory literature on homosexuality appeared in medical journals or in books that were not readily accessible to the public. The more salacious passages of *Psychopathia Sexualis* were printed in Latin. The first English edition of Ellis's *Sexual Inversion* was suppressed,[82] and retail sales of the American edition were at first restricted to doctors and lawyers. Newspaper and magazine coverage was virtually nonexistent.

As with other radical new ideas, the interpretation of homosexuality as a form of innate pathology was at first resisted. When Lombroso's writings first appeared in the United States, they were opposed on religious grounds.[83] The *Lancet,* England's leading medical journal, refused to review *Sexual Inversion* lest lay people read it, and observed that the editors were unconvinced that "homosexuality is anything else than an acquired and depraved manifestation of the sexual passion."[84]

The extent to which the medical conception of homosexuality penetrated

---

[81] Gonzalez (1977).

[82] Following the arrest and conviction of a bookseller for retailing *Sexual Inversion* on the grounds that it was "a lewd, wicked, bawdy, scandalous libel," the book became difficult to obtain, and subsequent editions of Ellis's *Studies in the Psychology of Sex* were not released in Britain.

[83] Rosenberg (1968:69).

[84] Quoted in Hynes (1968:162).

the educated classes over the next decade or so can be gauged from an article that appeared in 1909 in the French *Revue de l'hypnotisme;* it commented that

> today we see a curious phenomenon: the Catholic Church and Protestant Church rank themselves, in relation to homosexuality, on the side of medicine; they declare that sexual inversion is an anomaly of nature, a sickness, and that the paragraphs [of the criminal code] against the inverts are unjustified.[85]

Educated inverts devoured this literature, and some were strongly influenced by it. At one stage of his life, for example, Oscar Wilde was "continually reading and talking about" Krafft-Ebing's *Psychopathia Sexualis.*[86] After reading Ellis and Krafft-Ebing, Radclyffe Hall reconstructed her biography to fit the "third sex" theory.[87] Reading Havelock Ellis's *Sexual Inversion* "brought home" to F. O. Mathiessen that he was inverted "by nature," not because he had been seduced by older boys at school. Notwithstanding his conventionally masculine appearance, his reading taught him that he had a "female sex element."[88] Physicians complained that homosexuals used this literature to justify their resistance to change, or to gain sympathy.[89]

The popular press and writers of fiction began to adopt the new terminology and theories. Writing in the *New Statesmen* at the start of World War I, George Bernard Shaw denounced Berlin's "forty tolerated homosexual brothels," taking for granted that his readers would know what he meant.[90] A writer in the *Atheneum* observed that criminal-law reform might be needed because research linking "intersexes intermediate between male and female" to chromosome abnormalities was suggesting that "what we thought was the deepest moral obloquy is in reality a congenital misfortune."[91] The novels of Marcel Proust and Radclyffe Hall disseminated images of congenital effeminate male and masculine female homosexuals to a wider audience.[92]

---

[85] The journalist J. Ernest-Charles (1910) was less certain. In an article published in a literary review the following year, he referred to pederasty as a "vice or malady" (quoted in Gay, 1986:201).

[86] H. M. Hyde (1984:225). After his conviction, Wilde described his condition, somewhat self-servingly, as "a disease" (J. Weeks, 1981a:105), something neither he nor his prosecutor had claimed during the trial.

[87] Baker (1985:248).

[88] L. Hyde (1978:47, 87).

[89] Kiernan (1884), Mayne (1908).

[90] Shaw (1914).

[91] J.S.H. (1921).

[92] Proust's series of novels, *A la recherche du temps perdu,* was published between 1913 and

Nonetheless, outside educated circles the whole area remained conceptually murky. When the young T. C. Worsley, a British literary figure, tried to make sense of his lack of erotic interest in women, and his powerful attraction to young boys, he lacked the vocabulary to classify himself. "We had . . . in our provincial back-water, no word for those who nowadays would be summarily described as 'Queer' or 'Bent.'"[93] Military authorities were completely ignorant of medical theories of homosexuality when a major scandal erupted at a U.S. naval training center just after World War I.[94]

The Interventionist State

Since degeneracy and evolutionary theories seemed to explain a very wide range of social problems, including poverty, insanity, idiocy, drunkenness, crime, labor strife, and sexual pathology, the scope of government intervention they called for was also wide. Reformers advocated public health and sanitation measures, and the restoration of a traditional sexual division of labor.[95] For existing degenerates or atavistic criminals they sought long-term incarceration to protect the public. Thus Lombroso proposed that "homosexual offenders who are born such, and who manifest their evil propensities from childhood without being determined by special causes . . . should be confined from their youth," presumably for life, to prevent innocent youths from being corrupted.[96] Moreau had called for a similar policy some years earlier.[97]

Others feared that homosexuals would marry and then have degenerate children.[98] Feré reported the case of an invert who married and whose chil-

---

1928; it appeared in English under the title *Remembrance of Things Past.* Proust knew personally some of the men who developed the idea that homosexuality was a congenital pathology; Tardieu and Brouardel had been colleagues and friends of his father. He had read Krafft-Ebing and Havelock Ellis and drew on these writings in his novels, but only went so far as to posit a hereditary disposition to homosexuality, whose realization could depend on imitation and conditioning (Rivers, 1980:157–59). Radclyffe Hall's *The Well of Loneliness* was published in 1928. Earlier English homophile literature, from the second half of the nineteenth century, shows very little evidence of medicalization (Reade, 1970). Havelock Ellis was one of the first to call the attention of English-speaking readers to the Continental medical literature (in his 1897 *Sexual Inversion*).

[93] Worsley (1967:74). John Marshall's (1981) interviews with older Englishmen show that many who "fooled around" with each other in the 1920s and 1930s lacked a vocabulary to talk about their sexual feelings and actions.

[94] Chauncey (1985).

[95] Talbot (1899), Kevles (1984).

[96] Lombroso (1911:418).

[97] Moreau (1887).

[98] Because it takes time for new ideas to gain acceptance, not all physicians worried about this. Many encouraged homosexual patients to marry in the hope that they would eventually take to heterosexuality (Mayne, 1908:530–54).

dren were epileptic, imbecilic, inverted, or died in infancy.[99] Despite his own sympathies with inverts, and his warning that Feré's case might not be typical, Ellis cautioned that attempts at a cure should generally be avoided, for the cure might be superficial, and the children will "for the most part . . . belong to a neurotic and failing stock."[100] An essay published in 1903 under the auspices of the Scientific Humanitarian Committee in Germany, and distributed in English translation under the title "The Social Problem of Sexual Inversion" by the British Society for the Study of Sex Psychology (founded as a reform society just before World War I, with Carpenter as its first president), warned that descendants of "third sex" parents "are especially liable to nervous and mental trouble."[101] Forel thought the law should prevent homosexuals from marrying for exactly this reason.[102]

Some physicians thought that, instead of imprisoning homosexual patients, they could be castrated or vasectomized to prevent them from procreating;[103] others thought such measures unnecessarily extreme. Krafft-Ebing, for example, thought that castration would not work and that "sexual perverts in general by no means constitute the worst type of degeneration."[104] He noted that no one proposed to stop libertines or drunkards from having children; and from his experience, he added, the children of homosexuals were not likely to be congenitally inferior (a remark seemingly at odds with comments he makes elsewhere in *Psychopathia Sexualis*).

Despite these reservations on the part of leading specialists, many states in the United States adopted compulsory sterilization provisions for sex offenders and included homosexuals in the categories of offenders to which they could be applied.[105] Sterilization was also being applied—logically from the point of view of degeneracy theory or Lombrosianism—to habitual criminals, "defective delinquents," the mentally retarded, and the

---

[99] H. Ellis (1897:143).

[100] H. Ellis (1897:146–47).

[101] Quoted in J. N. Katz (1976).

[102] Forel (1933:245–46).

[103] F. E. Daniel (1893), Ellis and Talbot (1896), Sharp (1909).

[104] Krafft-Ebing (1965:478). Because Krafft-Ebing could hardly have doubted that castration would effectively prevent procreation, this statement shows that it was homosexuality that troubled him, not the possibility of transmitting degeneracy to the next generation. Interestingly, German physicians performed unilateral castrations on at least eleven men between 1916 and 1921 and transplanted testicular material from other men into them, in the hope of "curing" their homosexuality. They did not perform complete castrations because they wanted their patients to be able to reproduce. The experiments failed, in that none of the men abandoned homosexuality (G. Schmidt, 1984). From the end of the nineteenth century, American men sought castration or sterilization to get rid of their unwanted homosexual desires, but these operations do not appear to have been very successful either.

[105] J. N. Katz (1976:140–46), Hamoway (1977).

insane. The practice was international.[106] The aura of prestige conferred on the medical profession by advances in the prevention and treatment of illness, and the image of benevolence associated with traditional medical care, helped to gain public acceptance of these new "therapeutic" practices.

Although a strict Darwinian analysis might have suggested that "defectives" should be left alone to die out, reformers feared that a laissez-faire policy toward natural selection and evolution would fail. Medicine and charity, they argued, were keeping alive degenerates who would otherwise die.[107] To make matters worse, the educated and prosperous classes were bearing fewer children than the uneducated and impoverished. Market forces were no longer capable of solving the problem.

Warmed by a Hegelian vision of the positive state that could intervene actively to improve social conditions, reformers called on the government to assist nature in weeding out the unfit. If this required coercive measures, they were justified by the benefits they would bring to the rest of society. Questions of guilt, sin, and desert were dismissed as metaphysical irrelevancies.

The mass influx of immigrants to the United States undoubtedly encouraged these ideas among well-off descendants of earlier waves of immigration, but similar ideas were also advanced in England and Europe,[108] where there was no comparably large immigrant population. In 1912, Havelock Ellis published *The Task of Social Hygiene,* an argument favoring the voluntary creation of a genetic aristocracy, a measure he thought essential to the success of socialism. Without it, he thought, socialism would undermine civilization by enabling the unfit to survive and multiply.[109]

Leading members of the British professional-middle class (PMC) promoted eugenicism for reasons of status and class closely related to those that led elite American physicians to promote sex legislation.[110] Eugenicism explained social failure and deviance as the inevitable consequence of individual flaws and attributed achieved success to innate personal merit. It thus legitimated the PMC as a natural-born elite. Eugenicism called for state-run programs that would place members of the PMC in positions of power and responsibility, able to determine who could marry and have children. It was in their interests to promote such a doctrine.

The corporatist ideology of the Progressive reformers provided the vision that gave added impetus to American efforts. Faced with class conflict, they sought to inhibit greediness among rich capitalists and also among workers. Their goal was to achieve recognition of the mutual dependence

---

[106] Kopp (1938).
[107] Feré (1888:90), G. S. Jones (1971:287).
[108] Keuls (1984).
[109] Brome (1979:159–60).
[110] D. A. MacKenzie (1981).

of classes, to bring about greater cooperation among classes, and to imbue public life with greater spirituality and selfless motivation. Male lust, as manifested in masturbation, homosexuality, and the patronizing of prostitutes, epitomized the selfishness and exploitation that reformers strove to stamp out.[111] Sexual restraint had become less a matter of self-control for a penny-pinching small bourgeoisie than part of a broad strategy for transforming conflict between men and women, and between the bourgeoisie and the working class, into social harmony.

The prevention of homosexuality was but a small component of this strategy, but the steps taken on its behalf cannot be fully understood apart from it. It was a strategy that depended on quite new understandings about the proper role of the state in society and the relationship of the individual to the collective. An early-nineteenth-century liberal would have allowed anyone to have children who could support them; an end-of-the-century reform Darwinist argued that some people could legitimately be prevented from having children in the interests of the society as a whole.

The Progressive expansion of state powers extended to a range of deviant and marginal populations. "Classical school" criminologists of the late eighteenth and early nineteenth centuries had leaned on contractual, libertarian, social-contract principles in advocating legislatively determined prison sentences of fixed duration to deter crime. By contrast, criminologists of the late nineteenth century under the sway of the medical conception of crime abandoned the rational-choice model of the classicists and advocated sentences of indefinite extent, with release only when the individual pathology assumed responsible for criminality had been cured. This preventive orientation could, in principle, mean incarceration for much longer than possible under classical principles, which held that the severity of punishment should be proportional to the gravity of the offense. It could also mean that offenders convicted of the same crime could receive widely disparate sentences if treatment considerations so dictated. The late-nineteenth-century state sodomy statutes typically gave judges great discretion to take treatment "needs" into account in sentencing offenders; the Indiana sodomy statue of 1881 provided a minimum of two years and a maximum of fourteen. Later, another Progressive-era reform, parole, introduced an additional layer of quasi-judicial discretion in sentencing, ostensibly to adjust dispositions on the basis of treatment considerations even more finely.

Psychoanalytic Theory

Two further explanations of homosexuality have influenced treatment and control strategies in the twentieth century—psychoanalysis and behav-

---

[111] Pivar (1973), J. Weeks (1977a:16), Chauncey (1982/83), Jeffreys (1985).

iorism. As developed by the Viennese psychiatrist Sigmund Freud and extended and modified by later theorists psychoanalytic theory provides explanations for homosexuality in purely psychological terms—a radical departure from the somatic emphasis of nineteenth-century theories of degeneration or evolution. Yet Freud drew extensively on late-nineteenth-century neurology and psychiatry as he formulated his own ideas.[112]

One of the insights Freud appropriated from his predecessors and contemporaries was the notion of childhood sexuality. Its existence had been taken for granted in the Renaissance, but was gradually reinterpreted as undesirable. The Victorians recognized that children were capable of sexual arousal, but thought this response infrequent, abnormal, and pernicious. They attributed frightful diseases to childhood masturbation.[113]

By the late 1870s, psychologists who had begun to study children systematically were beginning to abandon this denial of the normalcy of childhood sexuality.[114] George Romanes, a friend of Darwin, wrote in 1888 that sexual response appeared in infants from the age of seven weeks. This work was cited by writers on child development, including James Baldwin, whose work Freud knew. Freud's intimate friend and correspondent Wilhelm Fliess discussed children's sexuality in a monograph that considered sucking, bedwetting, and hemorrhoids to be expressions of sexuality—an important development in extending the notion of sex beyond genital response;[115] it led directly to the Freudian notion of erotogenic zones. In 1900, Havelock Ellis suggested that breastfeeding should be seen as a sexual experience for both infant and mother.

Albert Moll drew out the implications of the normalcy of childhood sexuality for theories of homosexuality.[116] His case histories of subjects who were not psychiatric patients or abnormal in any obvious way showed that childhood sexual experience, including masturbation, did not necessarily lead to inversion in adults—as had been claimed by Alfred Binet and other proponents of the view that homosexuality was largely acquired. Researchers who had made that claim had restricted their studies to subjects with a history of homosexual involvements. Finding masturbation or seduction in their early backgrounds, the researchers concluded that these events were decisive, simply assuming their absence in everyone else. Yet Moll found that most children have some sort of sexual experience. If that sufficed to produce sexual inversion, then everyone would be homosexual.

[112] Sulloway (1979).
[113] Ariès (1962:100–127), chapter 8 of this work.
[114] Hale (1971:105–6).
[115] Fliess (1897).
[116] Moll (1891, 1897).

Some physicians argued that, if most children masturbated without becoming inverted, those who did must have been hereditarily vulnerable. This argument seemed to strengthen the case for congenital homosexuality. Freud could never quite bring himself to repudiate this logic and always acknowledged the possible contribution of constitutional elements to sexual development.[117] Yet neither could he bring himself to endorse the claim that homosexuality was in itself a sign of hereditary degeneration. Degeneracy theory was being used in anti-Semitic campaigns, to which Freud was quite sensitive.[118] He was aware of his own erotic attraction to Fliess, which he would surely have been reluctant to label a sign of degeneracy.[119] Nor could he easily label his patients degenerate. Most of the European doctors who developed degeneracy theory were specialists in forensic medicine and obtained their subjects from the courts. Often they and their families had the lengthy medical, psychiatric, and legal histories common to low-income criminal offenders, which made it easy to conclude that they suffered from hereditary degeneration. By contrast, Freud's patients were unusually affluent (his fees were high) and often intelligent, cultured, and talented. Apart from their sexual idiosyncracies, they and their families showed no signs of degeneration. Confronted with this evidence, even Krafft-Ebing abandoned degeneracy theory toward the end of his life, and influential later writers repudiated it.[120]

Like Ulrichs, Chevalier, Krafft-Ebing, and Fliess, Freud was influenced by the discovery that vertebrate embryos have both male and female sex organs, one of them disappearing in the course of development. As a student, Freud had assisted one of his teachers in research on sex alternation in crustacea and was thus quite familiar with these findings. They were widely interpreted as demonstrating that sexuality was complex, consisting even in normal persons of both male and female components, one of them subordinate to the other.

Ernest Haeckel, Darwin's German disciple, had proposed that each individual's development retraces the evolution of the species ("ontogeny re-

[117] The strength of Freud's early commitment to a hereditary explanation of psychological problems can be gathered from his remark of 1888 that the etiology of hysteria "is to be looked for entirely in heredity. . . . Compared with the factor of heredity all other factors play a second place and play the part of incidental causes, the importance of which is as a rule overstated in practice" (Freud, 1953–74:1.50; L. Stewart, 1976). These early writings set out as a major task for psychiatry the determination of how much degeneracy contributed to psychological problems and how much other factors were responsible (S. L. Gilman, 1985:205–7).

[118] L. Stewart (1976).

[119] Heller (1981), Freud (1985:2–4).

[120] Krafft-Ebing (1901), Sulloway (1979:171–74, 248–50, 263–64, 273, 295, 298–304, 390–411), I. Bloch (1926:490–91).

capitulates phylogeny"). Both Fliess and Freud accepted this principle. Interpreting the embryological findings in its light, they concluded that homosexuality was a developmental disorder. The idea that such a disturbance could occur after birth as well as before had already been proposed by Moreau, Ellis, and Feré in works that Freud had read.

In the model of sexual development that Freud synthesized from these sources, a newborn infant is assumed to be "polymorphously perverse," or ambisexual,[121] deriving pleasure from tactical sensations anywhere on its body. In subsequent development the sexual drive is invested in the mouth, then the anus, and finally in the genitals, leaving a residue of responsiveness in the abandoned zones.[122] Each stage involves the choice of a new love object: first the self, then the mother, the father, and normally someone else of the opposite sex. The model makes homosexuality an element of everyone's psychological history. Moreover, it is never fully eradicated: even the heterosexual adult preserves elements of homosexual interest in the form of same-sex friendship.[123]

For Freud, the process of maturation from stage to stage is complex and not always executed perfectly. Someone can become fixated at one of the intermediate stages and regress to it as the result of a later traumatic event:

> Accentuation of anal eroticism at the stage of pregenital organization gives rise in a man to a marked predisposition to homosexuality, when the next stage of the sexual function, that of genital primacy, is reached.[124]

Freud postulated the Oedipus complex to be a particularly important cause of regression. He concluded that a young lesbian patient he analyzed had at puberty wanted a child from her father. At that time her mother, whom she hated, actually gave birth to another child.

> Furiously resentful and embittered, she turned away from her father, and from men altogether. After this first great reverse she foreswore her womanhood and sought another goal for her libido. . . . She changed into a man, and took her mother in place of her father as her love-object. Her relation to her mother had certainly been ambivalent from the beginning, and it proved easy to revive her earlier love for her mother. . . . Since there was

---

[121] Ambisexuality is the better term, since in Freudian theory the notion of perversity is technically inapplicable to a newborn infant.

[122] The theory postulates an additional substage for females: from clitoral to vaginal response.

[123] Freud (1905).

[124] Freud (1913).

> little to be done with the real mother, there arose from the con-
> version of feeling described the search for a mother-substitute to
> whom she could become passionately attached.[125]

This solution had the advantage of angering her father, and thus proved to be an effective way of revenging her wounded feelings on him. A further contributing factor, Freud suggested, was her envy of an older brother's penis, an envy that led her to feminism.

In cases of male homosexuality, Freud added, strong attachment to the mother makes involvement with other women difficult.[126] By pursuing other men, the son notifies his father that he will not compete with him for the love of his mother and reassures his mother that he will not abandon her for another woman. Identifying himself with her, he chooses partners he can love narcissistically, imagining that he is the partner, receiving the love he wants from his mother. Freud mentions castration anxiety, de-preciation of women for their deficient genitalia, and hostility toward same-sex siblings, converted by parental pressure into feelings of love, as further contributing factors.

It is fundamental to Freudian theory that, even though unacceptable impulses can be repressed so that they never come to consciousness, they can nevertheless continue to exercise a potent influence on mental processes. Thus someone can be a "latent" homosexual without ever having been aware of homosexual desires. This entails a considerable extension of what the word "homosexual" means.[127]

Though rooted in somatic theory, these explanations no longer posit a physiological basis for homosexuality. Freud's theory made heterosexuality just as much the product of family interaction as homosexuality, and thus implicitly removed the latter from the category of pathological. Freud made this explicit in his "Letter to an American Mother," where he commented that whatever its origin, homosexuality is not a sickness. One could live with it happily and productively. In most cases psychoanalysis could not

---

[125] Freud (1920).

[126] Freud (1920). Freud's thinking here bears a striking resemblance to the folk theory of the Swahili in present-day Mombasa, in Kenya. The Swahili say that boys or young men who become receptive homosexuals for a period are especially likely to come from households which are headed by a mother and which include several sisters but no brothers. However, this may have less to do with the psychodynamics Freud postulates than with the associated poverty that would lead a young male to become a prostitute or client of an older, wealthier man (Shepherd, 1987).

[127] This innovation had been anticipated by Charles Fourier a century earlier, in his book *The New Amorous World*. He suggested that cruelty could arise from the suppression of homosexual passions of which the subject was completely unaware (Beecher, 1986:238–39).

be expected to produce heterosexual orientations, but it could resolve conflicts and eliminate unhappiness and inhibition.[128]

Freud held to this view consistently over many decades. In 1905 he told a newspaper reporter that "homosexuals must not be treated as sick people, for a perverse orientation is far from being a sickness." He refused to analyze patients because of their homosexuality unless they were also neurotic and opposed attempts to bar homosexuals from becoming analysts. At the same time he vigorously opposed the prosecution of homosexuality in the criminal courts. In 1930, he signed a statement stating that to punish homosexuality was an "extreme violation of human rights." Nevertheless, there are implicit standards of normalcy in his model of psychosexual development and thus an implicitly pejorative evaluation of homosexuality as immature.[129]

Though Freud may have built on the scientific discoveries of others, the particular emphases in his work reflect the culture and political milieu of *fin-de-siècle* Vienna.[130] The Austrian aristocracy of the late nineteenth century had neither been defeated by the *haute bourgeoisie* nor assimilated to it. As the latter became more affluent, they began to emulate the sensuosity and aestheticism of the aristocracy as an investment in "cultural capital" that would pay off in upward social mobility. This purpose imparted a peculiarly self-conscious quality to the cultivation of the senses. Middle-class attitudes toward sex became less rigid; eroticism pervaded the art of Gustav Klimt, Egon Schiele, and Oscar Kokoschka. Upper-middle-class fathers encouraged their sons to learn about sex from prostitutes or working-class girls, but the double standard still prevailed: young women of the middle class were still heavily chaperoned and kept ignorant of sex. For many it remained laden with guilt and anxiety. With the machinery of government kept hidden from the public by censorship, "secretiveness blanketed public life, prompting a search for latent meanings behind every event."[131]

Freud's influence, of course, extended far beyond the Austrian border; he became especially popular in early-twentieth-century America. It has been suggested that this popularity stemmed in part from the sorts of problems psychoanalysis purported to cure: nervousness, lack of self-confidence, over-conscientiousness, feelings that life was meaningless—all problems one might expect to encounter in the professional classes in a society that encouraged hard work, had a high level of geographic and social mobility,

[128] Freud (1935).

[129] Spiers and Lynch (1977), Caplan (1981), T. Murphy (1983/84), Abelove (1986), Isay (1986), Dynes (1987a:559).

[130] Zweig (1943:73–75). Barbu (1952), Bry and Rifklin (1962), Shick (1968/69), W. M. Johnston (1972:117–18), 239–40), Schorske (1980), Lerman (1986:27–33).

[131] W. M. Johnston (1972:239).

and was absorbing immigrants whose traditional culture failed to provide interpretive meanings and behavioral guideposts in the New World.[132] It has also been suggested that Freud's explanations of these problems meshed well with the New England spiritualism of Unitarian Christianity and transcendentalist philosophy, but that hardly explains his particular appeal to Jews.

Perhaps more important, America was moving from an economy of scarcity to one of abundance. The need for self-repression was diminishing; controlled enjoyment, including sexual pleasure, could now be allowed, even encouraged, and Victorian prudery put aside. Yet residual sexual repression remained. Freud demonstrated a new willingness to come to terms with sexual drives in his remark that some masturbation was probably necessary in childhood if the genitals were to become the main locus of adult sexual response.[133] Only a few decades earlier, physicians thought masturbation endangered normal adult sexuality and would have reacted with outrage and indignation to Freud's ideas.

Freud's acceptance of female sexuality as normal would also have shocked the previous generation; it came at a time when women were entering the labor force and beginning to have premarital affairs.[134] The weakening of gender roles implied by these developments may have made it possible for Freud to separate gender identity from sexual object choice. This separation, made only incompletely in Freud's writings on women,[135] meant that a male homosexual was no longer assumed to be feminine on the basis of his sexual preference alone. Conversely, a woman could be identified as a lesbian even if she did not adopt the masculine dress and behavioral traits that had distinguished the stereotypical lesbian a few decades earlier.[136]

Despite the derogatory view of homosexuality in much psychoanalytic thought, many men and women troubled by their homosexual feelings or involvements have gone to analysts or read psychiatric writings and learned to interpret these experiences in light of Freudian theory. In its emphasis on early-childhood experience and its unquestioning acceptance of gender stereotypes, this interpretation was in some ways a conservative one.

[132] Hale (1971:401). One problem with this argument is that France, Germany, and England had similar problems (Rabinbach, 1982). Yet France was unreceptive to psychoanalysis until after 1968 (Turkle, 1978).

[133] Freud (1905), Patten (1912:11–17, 25–26, 147–58, 164), Hale (1971:250), Rieff (1959:338), Sulloway (1979:314).

[134] Hale (1971:477), Trimberger (1983).

[135] For example, in the case history quoted earlier in this chapter, Freud (1920) has the woman "become a man," a process that results in her being attracted to women. Gender identity is being confused with object choice. G. Schmidt (1984) cites several other examples.

[136] Chauncey (1982/83).

Freud attributed his lesbian patient's feminism to penis envy, not to envy of male status and prerogatives, implying that it was irrational and pathological to be a feminist. Psychoanalysts have not been known for encouraging their homosexual patients to organize against societal oppression of homosexuals, or to fight against male supremacy.[137]

The wide dessemination of Freud's ideas, often in vulgarized form, altered perceptions of same-sex relationships. All-female couples came to be looked upon with greater suspicion than in the Victorian Age, when women were thought to be asexual; and lesbians found it more difficult to live together unobtrusively.[138]

In tracing virtually every aspect of human life back to sex, Freud implied a vast expansion of the sexual sphere. In his writings all roads lead to sex; it provides the secret of our innermost existence. It follows that our sexual orientations are not merely one attribute of many that characterize us, but the key to who we really are. Degeneracy theorists had viewed homosexuality as merely one manifestation of a deeply pathological inner essence. Freud dropped their contention that this essence was inherited, but retained their belief in the existence of a hidden core identity and gave sexuality a much greater role in revealing that identity. Thus the normative judgment of psychoanalysis that homosexuality is pathological was, notwithstanding Freud's letter to an American mother, a judgment that homosexuals are pathological in a profoundly fundamental sense. It is not just their sexual preferences that are wrong, but everything about them. This notion, introduced into a society that saw homosexuality as undesirable, intensified social rejection.

Early in the history of the psychoanalytic movement, challenges to Freud's theories became the basis for new schools of psychiatric thought. Many of these schools devised their own models for the formation of sexual object choice, though most involve only slightly variations on themes already present in Freud.[139] In almost all psychodynamic theories,

> the homosexual behavior is regarded either as involving the gratification of some major pregenital infantile drive (most often the wish for symbiotic fusion with the mother) or as reflecting a

[137] A number of psychoanalysts did speak out in favor of decriminalizing homosexuality. Their stance can be seen at least in part as a jurisdictional claim. The psychotherapists wanted to take over from the courts the primary responsibility for controlling homosexuality.

[138] Sahli (1979), Faderman (1981:233–38), R. Rosenberg (1982:200–204), J. N. Katz (1983: 137–74), Jeffreys (1985:102–27).

[139] Bieber (1962), Wiedeman (1962), Karlen (1971a:284–303, 405–37), and R. C. Friedman (1986) provide major reviews of this literature. A host of thorny methodological problems have stood in the way of definitive empirical testing of psychoanalytic explanations of homosexuality.

reparative adjustment to a phobic avoidance of oedipally-tinged heterosexuality, based either on the dread of the "close-binding" mother or retaliation from the hostile father.[140]

It remains a form of psychopathology, with a pejorative evaluation made more explicit than in Freud's own writings. Bieber, for example, summarizes the findings of a large-scale study of male-homosexual psychiatric patients in terms that are blatantly normative:

> The data reveal the homosexual to be the interactional focal point for extraordinary parental psychopathology. . . . the parental constellation most likely to produce a homosexual son or a heterosexual one with severe homosexual problems is a detached, hostile father and a close-binding, intimate, seductive mother who is a dominating, minimizing wife. In a few cases, the mother is seemingly detached, rejecting, and overtly hostile to her son, but the majority of mothers form a possessive, controlling, inappropriately intimate relationship with their sons.[141]

Because it is so wrapped up with psychopathology, "homosexuality is incompatible with a reasonably happy life." Yet psychoanalysis holds out the hope of an eventual heterosexual adjustment—a more "optimistic" view than Freud's. Another psychiatrist wrote that "homosexuality, like these other manifestations of 'dis-ease' [impotence, frigidity, pornography, masochism, promiscuity] is a symptom of a disturbed personality."[142] Patients who have undergone psychotherapy based on these antihomosexual premises have sometimes come to hate themselves. In a letter broadcast in November 1948 on a New York-radio-station panel dominated by psychiatric perspectives, one self-identified homosexual man "in this pathetic mental condition" confessed, "I detest it!"[143]

In 1973, the American Psychiatric Association seemingly rejected this view of homosexuality by removing it from its *Diagnostic and Statistical Manual of Psychiatric Disorders*, an official listing of mental illnesses. But the

[140] Mitchell (1978).

[141] Bieber (1965). Bieber's reliance on a sample of psychiatric patients to sustain claims about homosexuality in the general population has been widely questioned (e.g., by Churchill, 1967:260–68). the relationship between family configuration and process in childhood and later sexual orientation has also been studied in nonpatient populations, with discrepant findings; see, for example, Chang and Block (1960), R. B. Evans (1969), Snortum et al. (1969), N. L. Thompson et al. (1973), Saghir and Robins (1973), and Bell, Weinberg, and Hammersmith (1982). Abelove (1986) concludes that Bieber's views have been widespread in American psychoanalysis.

[142] Kronemeyer (1980: vii). For similar views, see Bychowski (1945, 1954), Rado (1949), Bergler (1957), Socarides (1968, 1978).

[143] Duberman (1986:194–98).

step was taken under pressure from gay-liberation activists and did not stimulate a rethinking of the theory of sexual preferences. In fact, most psychiatrists disagreed with the removal; just under 70 percent of the 2,500 psychiatrists who responded to a survey conducted by the journal *Medical Aspects of Human Sexuality* opposed it.[144] The eminent senior psychoanalyst Abram Kardiner complained that the decision was mistaken because "the suspicion with which middle America views homosexuality cannot be voted out of existence."[145] Newspaper-advice-columnist Ann Landers was also unpersuaded:

> I fought for the civil rights of homosexuals twenty years ago and argued that they should be regarded as full and equal citizens. However, I do not believe homosexuality is "just another life style." I believe these people suffer from a severe personality disorder. Granted some are sicker than others, but sick they are and all the fancy rhetoric of the American Psychiatric Association will not change it.[146]

Behaviorism

A second school of psychology, behaviorism—also known as learning theory—abjures the psychological constructs of Freudian theory. It invokes no subconscious, no id, no superego, no fixation; instead it limits itself to visible behavior, which it explains as a response to external stimuli.[147] Behaviorism asserts that pleasure positively reinforces behavior, encouraging its repetition; pain, on the other hand, is a negative reinforcer, or aversive conditioner.

Behaviorism has its roots in utilitarian psychology (which views people as seeking pleasure and avoiding pain) and has appealed particularly to scientists favorable to social engineering. It was developed by John B. Watson, an American psychologist of the Progressive Era, who saw in it an alternative to the mysticism of Christian introspective psychology as it was taught in turn-of-the-century colleges. His refusal to consider biological explanations for differences in people's behavior was at odds with the domi-

---

[144] Kronemeyer (1980:4–5); see also Fort, Steiner, and Conrad (1971), and for a comparable British survey, Philip Morris (1973).

[145] Quoted in Bayer (1981:193). The passage is remarkable for its explicit advocacy of psychiatry's taking its standards of health and illness from popular and probably ill-informed prejudice.

[146] Quoted in Bayer (1981:193). It is doubtful that Landers could have taken a more radical position without jeopardizing the distribution of her syndicated column in newspapers that sell to conservative readers.

[147] In recent years learning theorists have abandoned their strictures against explaining behavior in terms of mentalistic concepts, and have thus been able to include the cognitive and symbolic dimensions of learning in their theories.

nant intellectual currents of the time, but was not entirely perverse, for when Watson was formulating his ideas a crisis in evolutionary theory was leading prominent research biologists to repudiate the doctrine of natural selection. It was in this atmosphere that such cultural anthropologists as Alfred Kroeber and Margaret Mead began to argue for the preeminence of nurture over nature, of culture over biology.[148]

Insofar as it repudiated doctrines of racial superiority and congenital degeneracy, behaviorism was a distinctively democratic theory. It shared the optimism of the Progressive reformers. Nevertheless, its applicability to social problems was premised on the existence of a small elite who could use it to manipulate the masses.[149] It was a doctrine for technocrats, not participatory democrats.

In learning theory, sexual choice is not instinctual. There is no innate preference for heterosexuality or homosexuality: the majority preference for opposite-sex partners is simply the result of consistent encouragement given to heterosexual choices and consistent discouragement of homosexual ones. No matter how strongly someone has been conditioned to one type of response, reconditioning to another always remains possible.[150]

Learning theory does not even implicitly suggest that homosexuality is pathological; on the contrary, it regards it as completely normal. The psychological processes that lead to it are assumed to be the same as those that lead to heterosexuality. Nevertheless, behavior therapists have been heavily involved in attempts to eliminate their patients' homosexual behavior through aversive conditioning. The first reported effort along these lines was undertaken by a Dr. Louis Max, who administered electric shocks to a young man while displaying homosexual stimuli. Later, therapists used chemicals to induce convulsive shock in homosexual patients.[151]

Often behavioral therapy has been sought by patients seeking to escape the social and legal penalties attached to homosexuality in a repressive society. Over the past fifteen years, gay activists have questioned the ethics of administering behavioral therapy. Therapists contend that they themselves are neutral and merely carry out the wishes of patients who wish to change.[152] Critics argue that a choice coerced by society's punitive attitudes and sanctions is not truly voluntary.

[148] D. Freeman (1970).

[149] Birnbaum (1964).

[150] Churchill (1976:100–120), Akers (1977:189–200).

[151] M. P. Feldman (1966), Feldman and McCulloch (1967), Blitch and Haynes (1972), J. N. Katz (1976:164–67), Birk (1980).

[152] It is clear, though, that some behavioral therapists have considered homosexuality to be highly undesirable (Karlen, 1971:587–92).

A Plethora of Perspectives

Once a new theoretical perspective in the behavioral sciences gains adherents, it tends to perpetuate itself through schools, training programs and institutes, and journals. Even after promising new ideas appear, students trained in the old continue to draw on them in their research and in therapy. Even after Raffalovitch, Freud and others showed that a homosexual object choice did not necessarily imply an unconventional gender identity, the stereotype that male homosexuals are similar to feminine women persisted. Research findings called it into question; for example, in one study, the psychologist E. Lowell Kelly found a correlation of only 0.09 (very small) between scores on an "inversion scale" and those on a "masculine/feminine" scale, but subsequent psychologists continued to write of the "feminine" personalities of homosexual men.[153]

At least in the United States, the marketplace for therapists is sufficiently diverse and extensive to permit the survival of many therapeutic systems, based on a variety of mutually inconsistent assumptions. Consequently, twentieth-century biological and psychiatric analyses of homosexuality have been characterized by a multiplicity of theoretical schools. Until recently these medical and psychiatric perspectives collectively dominated scholarly work on homosexuality. All but three of the eighteen contributors to Marmor's 1965 collection of review essays on different aspects of homosexuality were biologists or M.D.'s.[154]

From time to time new ideas arise within these established cognitive frameworks and inspire new treatments. Thus the discovery of male and female hormones stimulated a revival of attempts to link sexual orientation with sex-related physiological abnormalities, and gave rise to hormone-injection therapy.[155] West German physicians of the 1960s and 1970s revived the "third sex" theory of homosexuality and gave it a new twist by performing brain surgery on homosexual men—some thirty between 1962 and 1979—destroying part of the hypothalamus, where they hypothesized the "female center" of the brain to be located.[156]

The recent renaissance of sociobiology, which tries to explain human traits and behaviors as the outcome of natural selection, has resurrected the idea that homosexuality can be inherited[157]—an idea that had lost favor

[153] M. Lewin (1984:166–67, 179–83, 263).

[154] Marmor (1965).

[155] J. N. Katz (1976:164–65, 167–69).

[156] G. Schmidt (1984).

[157] G. E. Hutchinson (1959), Weinrich (1976, 1987), E. Wilson (1978:149–53), Pillard, Poumadere, and Carreta (1981), Kirsch and Rodman (1982), Ruse (1984), Goodman (1987). Wilson responds to the usual criticism of the inheritability of homosexuality—that it would place an

after Freud turned to psychological explanations of sexual development without ever completely disappearing. In an age of gay liberation, however, the assumption that homosexuality is pathological, which is explicit in the degeneracy literature, has been abandoned. Wilson notes that in modern societies homosexuals tend to have higher-than-average intelligence and speculates that they may carry genes for altruism. This makes them a social asset, not a liability.

---

organism at a competitive disadvantage, and so should disappear over time through the standard evolutionary process of survival of the fittest—by pointing out that a homosexual who has no children may be able to provide his or her relatives with resources that help them survive. Thus homosexual genes could be favored even if homosexuals do not themselves procreate. The higher-than-average intelligence found in samples of homosexuals is also consistent with this hypothesis. Wilson's reasoning makes assumptions about the way resources are distributed in kinship-ordered, primitive societies that need to be confirmed and is based on the questionable assumption that homosexuality among primitives is restricted to certain people who avoid heterosexual intercourse. As we have seen in chapter 2, this is a very dubious proposition except for those instances where homosexuality also entails gender transformation.

10 *Bureaucracy and Homosexuality*

The early-twentieth-century German sociologist Max Weber abstracted from the features of bureaucracies he knew, to imagine an ideal bureaucracy,[1] operating on the basis of officially defined areas of jurisdiction "which are generally ordered by rules, that is, by laws or administrative regulations." The authority to give commands is hierarchical, but "strictly delimited by rules." The administration of the office is sharply distinguished from the private affairs of the officeholder: "Bureaucracy segregates official activity from the sphere of private life." This administration is governed by general rules:

> The reduction of modern office management to rules is deeply embedded in its very nature. The theory of modern public administration, for instance, assumes that the authority to order certain matters by decree—which has been legally granted to public authorities—does not entitle the bureau to regulate the matter by commands given for each case, but only to regulate the matter abstractly. This stands in extreme contrast to the regulation of all relationships through individual privileges and bestowals of favor.[2]

Administration on the basis of general rules that regulate the rights and duties of officeholders implies that an employee's dealings with clients and other officeholders are to be impersonal rather than governed by subjectively determined criteria, personal favoritism, or mere whim. Loyalty is owed to the organization rather than to particular superordinate individuals, and recruitment and promotions are to be based on objective merit.[3]

---

[1] A Weberian ideal type is not a standard to be attained, but an analytical construct to be used in theorizing. It refers to a "pure" case of something. It is recognized that in real life there may be no pure cases.

[2] Weber (1946:198).

[3] Weber (1968:3.956–1005).

Weber's ideal type was derived in large measure from the Prussian state bureaucracy and cannot be taken as a literal description of how organizations operate today. A bureaucracy where everyone had to act like a faceless automaton would undoubtedly be highly alienating. Employee cooperation is facilitated by friendliness and congeniality, which tends to undercut impersonality. To keep up employee morale, build loyalty to the company, and enhance productivity, managers have had to be less formal and authoritarian.[4] Even so, Weber's principles may be taken as at least a recognizable first-order approximation of how many real-life bureaucracies function.

BUREAUCRACY AND SOCIAL CONTROL

Social control takes on a distinct character when society is organized bureaucratically. In kinship-based societies, social control is primarily a matter of self-help: the injured party and his kin seek compensation for an injury. Should they fail to receive it, they may retaliate. Other parties may mediate a dispute, but do not ordinarily impose penalties on wrongdoers. In a feudal society such as that of Japan or early medieval Europe, the decentralization of political power continues to leave social control primarily to the parties directly involved, along with their vassals and lords. By contrast, when bureaucracies become important, rule enforcement is increasingly taken over by salaried full-time staffs. In large-scale complex societies, where most occupations are full-time and specialized, this is almost a necessity.

Even in a bureaucratic society, the individual role in social control persists; it takes such forms as ridicule and criticism, ostracism, law suits and dismissal of employees, and the bringing of complaints to the social-control bureaucracies. However, the costs to private individuals of exercising social control on their own can be formidable: it takes time and energy to find out about hidden vice and to do something about it. In the face of these disincentives, only those who feel deeply threatened or profoundly outraged will take action. On the other hand, when a bureaucracy acts, the costs to complaining individuals are greatly reduced. Thus the existence of an enforcement bureaucracy removes obstacles to the repression of activities that are only mildly offensive to the general population.

Tax revenues provide official enforcement agencies with resources for surveillance and prosecution far beyond those available to private individuals, making possible the hiring of salaried, full-time staffs to carry out a campaign of repression. Since costs are distributed to all taxpayers, they

---

[4]Miller and Swanson (1958:52–53).

are not excessively burdensome to any one person, and even those who are not particularly in favor of repression are unlikely to protest.[5]

Because campaigns against consensual offenses can be conducted so much more readily by public agencies, it is not surprising that the great prosecutions of homosexuality in the past five hundred years have been carried out by the bureaucracies of church and state. When the Spanish Inquisition received jurisdiction over sodomy cases in 1451, prosecution was stepped up. By contrast, in those regions of Italy where the Inquisition did not receive this jurisdiction, travelers reported that homosexual relations were carried on quite openly.[6] In France, the establishment of the Paris police force under Louis XIV, with its vast network of secret informers, greatly enhanced the capacity of the state to ferret out unreported homosexual activity. Police files of the period show that they made use of this capability, keeping records on hundreds of men who participated in homosexual liaisons.[7]

The McDonald Report on the Canadian Royal Mounted Police, released in August of 1981, reveals that the mounties have kept files on alleged homosexuals on an even larger scale in recent years. The massive deportation of homosexuals to Nazi extermination camps[8] could not have been carried out except by means of a vast bureaucratic organization. Police entrapments and arrests on charges related to homosexuality in public places—a pattern of enforcement that has prevailed in twentieth-century England and in North America—are also greatly facilitated by bureaucratic organization.

Although bureaucracies may be necessary for sustained campaigns of persecution, their staffs do not necessarily have strong personal feelings about the enforcement of the orders their superiors give them. Often they are simply doing the job they have been assigned or have taken as a source of income. Though some of the vice-squad detectives who loiter in public restrooms may be there because of personal preoccupation with homosexuality, most are probably not passionately devoted to arresting men who fellate one another; they do it because that's their job. Vigor in enforcement is not usually demanded; what is required is only enough activity to forestall criticism. Under these circumstances, an official policy of repression is commonly mitigated by the indifference or corruption of the

[5]Private associations are an intermediate case. The example of the moral-reform societies of eighteenth-century England (see chapter 7) indicates that, even though private associations can pool members' resources to finance prosecutions, they may have difficulty in securing adequate funding on a long-term basis.

[6]Lea (1907:4.361, 364), Lithgow (1906), Karlen (1971a:109–10, 122).

[7]M. Daniel (1957). Rey (1982, 1985).

[8]Heger (1980), Lautmann (1980/81), Rector (1981), Stümke and Finkler (1981), Schilling (1983), Plant (1986).

enforcement staff. This is a pattern often seen in the enforcement of "victimless crime" legislation.[9]

BUREAUCRACY AND IMPERSONALITY

The principles of bureaucratic administration enunciated by Weber contrast sharply with those found in societies where kinship is the dominant form of affiliation. In such societies, loyalty is to a clan or lineage, not to an organization of interchangable, anonymous individuals. Bureaucratic principles likewise clash with those operative in a feudal society, which is structured on the basis of vertical ties of personal loyalty. The feudal vassal swears an oath of homage and fealty to his lord, not to his office. The administration of the patrimonial ruler of a feudal kingdom is staffed by members of the king's household and is properly influenced by personal loyalty to his family and vassals. There may be no distinction between the king's personal wealth and the national treasury. The distribution of land to followers is from the king's own patrimony and is not subject to evaluation on the basis of universalistic criteria.

By contrast, bureaucratic organizations are expected to be universalistic or impartial in the way they make decisions. This feature of bureaucracies requires a degree of impersonality in the way employees deal with outsiders and with one another. Impersonality is potentially threatened when one member of an organization is linked to others, or to outsiders, by ties of affection or sexual attraction, in which cases an organizational decision might be influenced by extraneous personal considerations. Moreover, jealousy within an organization on the part of those excluded from a sexual or romantic relationship could easily make it difficult for employees to work together harmoniously.

Even when decision-makers actually remain uninfluenced by personal loyalties, the appearance of impartiality that a bureaucracy must maintain to preserve its legitimacy can be threatened if intimate relationships are

[9]Schur (1965). It is precisely under this pattern of enforcement that a semicovert deviant subculture comes into being. As we've been arguing, informal social controls are not as effective in large cities as in small towns and villages; the greater variety of sexual tastes found in large cities and the inattention of a salaried enforcement apparatus make the existence of such subcultures possible. Until the advent of gay liberation, they were the predominant form of organized homosexual social life in the West. Even in the USSR, where male homosexual relations are illegal and law enforcement is more efficient than in the United States, a subterranean gay social life can be found in the larger cities. It is necessarily much more restricted than in the United States or in Western Europe (Schuvaloff, 1976; Stern, 1979:217; G, 1980; Boyd, 1987). In those Warsaw Pact countries where homosexuality is not illegal, it remains severely constricted by the absence of available public spaces and the inability to organize formally without the approval of the state (B. Adam, 1987a:139–41). There is also a small but very clandestine gay subculture in the People's Republic of China (Cabral, 1982).

publicized. To avoid this threat, Mary Cunningham, a vice president at Joseph E. Seagram & Sons, had to resign her position a few years ago when rumors surfaced that she was having an affair with the chairman of the company. For the same reason, judges are supposed to disqualify themselves when they have personal ties to one of the parties in a trial.

Some contemporary bureaucracies—notably business firms and universities—promulgate nepotism rules to prevent heterosexual relationships among employees from interfering with the functioning of the organization. Others make no formal rules, but simply fire one of the lovers.[10] By analogy, we might expect that bureaucracies would have introduced a prohibition against male homosexuality (or preserved one if it already existed) for the same reason at a time when bureaucracies were staffed only by men.[11] Since women were excluded from public and private bureaucracies before the twentieth century, lesbian and heterosexual relationships would not have excited the same degree of public concern as male homosexuality—as indeed they did not in most periods of Western history.[12]

Just these considerations were invoked by Heinrich Himmler in a speech to the SS leadership in November 1937. He announced that there could be no homosexual men in the state service because they would tend to award positions to one another instead of on merit.[13] From that time on, any SS member convicted of homosexuality was executed. Women were to be kept out for the same reason, though lesbianism did not pose a comparable threat to Nazi goals and was never even made criminal.[14]

[10] Fulman (1982).

[11] C. Davies (1982) has also suggested that organizational considerations, such as the need to preserve authority, maintain morale, and distinguish between insiders and outsiders, might explain rules against homosexuality; however, he does not qualify his argument, as we do below. The ideas developed in this section were first presented in Greenberg and Bystryn (1984).

[12] Now that women are being employed in bureaucracies to an increasing extent, concern over heterosexual romances at the workplace is rising, and Margaret Mead (1978) has gone so far as to call for the creation of a taboo against such relationships. On the other hand, Mary Cunningham, having lost her job because there is such a taboo, has called for its abandonment (as reported in the May 17, 1982, issue of the *New York Times*).

[13] Like many of his era whose fear of homosexuality reached paranoid proportions, Himmler believed that homosexuals could recognize one another, making it possible for them to aid or conspire with even secret homosexuals and bring down the *Männerstaat* (Mosse, 1985: 166–68).

[14] Organizational considerations were, however, not the only factors shaping Nazi policy toward homosexuality: a party statement issued in May 1938 condemned it in the name of masculinity, might, and discipline (Steakley, 1975:84; Plant, 1986:50). Yet in practice, homosexuality within party ranks was tolerated, and Hitler even defended Röhm against charges of homosexuality, saying it was his own private affair. Igra (1945) presents evidence suggesting that, in his youth, Hitler himself may have indulged. In any event, in the early 1930s Hitler reversed his policy of toleration. Within a month of his appointment as chancellor of Germany

The special features of Ottoman government make it especially suitable for testing our reasoning about bureaucratic imperatives and homosexuality. Prior to the nineteenth century, much of the Ottoman state administration was staffed by janissaries—male children of Christian parents, conscripted at an early age and trained collectively by palace eunuchs for military and political careers. Training lasted until age twenty-five or thirty, during which time they were not allowed to marry. Advancement was based on seniority and merit rather than birth, and in this respect the Ottoman state resembled a modern bureaucracy. We should thus expect to find homosexual relations prohibited to the janissaries, and they were. During the period of training, when the all-male environment would have created strong pressures toward homosexual attachments, the youths were subjected to strict surveillance and punished severely for violating the prohibition of homosexuality.[15]

In one respect, the Ottoman state differed from a modern, rational bureaucracy: government officials were personal slaves of the sultan, who ruled as an absolute monarch. In this respect, the administration was patrimonial, and loyalty was to the person of the sultan, rather than to his office or to the law. In this state structure, homosexual relationships between the sultan and his high officials would have posed no organizational problems: they would not have undermined universality because it did not exist and was not expected. In fact, Ottoman sultans often had homosexual relationships with their high officials.[16] With the exception of state functionaries, the Turkish population was not bureaucratized and not trained for future employment in a bureaucracy. Here, too, homosexuality would have posed no structural problem. According to numerous Western travelers, it was extremely widespread among the men, especially the rich.[17]

The Chinese Empire was also a patrimonial bureaucracy. For long periods, palace eunuchs played a large role in state administration, serving as a counterweight to the politically contentious mandarins. While not all eu-

---

in January 1933, the government banned homosexual-rights organizations. Later in the same year it instigated raids on gay bars and sponsored the vandalizing of Magnus Hirschfeld's Institute of Sexual Science. The following year it had Röhm shot (Plant, 1986:50–51, 53–70). These steps were taken when it became necessary to present an image of respectability to the middle class whose political support Hitler was trying to win. The contrast between the image of sexual purity projected by the Nazis and the decadence of Weimar Berlin's nightlife, where male and female homosexuality were highly visible, may have gained the Nazis some support (Mosse, 1985).

[15] Lybyer (1966), Eton (1972:29).

[16] Creasy (1877:34–35, 85–86), Lybyer (1966:75–77, 122, 244–45, 263), Eton (1972), Inalcik (1973:74–75).

[17] Blanch (1983:110), Crompton (1985). The penalty at law was trivial (Heyd, 1973:102–3).

nuchs participated in homosexual relationships, emperors and princes sometimes had affairs with them, as well as with men who were not eunuchs.[18]

By early modern times, Chinese law did prohibit sexual relations between consenting men, but treated them as a type of fornication—not a very serious offense.[19] Participation appears to have been widespread, throughout all ranks of society, and evoked no moral outrage whatsoever. Male prostitution was practiced openly and without interference in the larger cities.[20] However, officials who engaged in fornication (whether heterosexual or homosexual) with inhabitants of their own districts received a penalty two degrees higher than that for civilians. This provision was evidently an attempt to preserve the impartiality of state administration in a society that, with the exception of the state, was not bureaucratized and did not generally stigmatize homosexuality.

Soviet-type societies provide further test cases. In Russia, homosexual relations had been criminal under the absolutist regime of the czars.[21] However, the new Bolshevik government repealed this legislation in December 1917, shortly after taking office.[22] While some high government officials viewed homosexuality as a type of illness—a view they shared with many educated non-Marxist contemporaries in the West—official policy, as formulated by Dr. Grigorii Batkis, director of the Moscow Institute of Social Hygiene, was

> the absolute noninterference of the state and society into sexual matters, so long as nobody is injured, and no one's interests are encroached on. . . . Only when there's use of force or duress . . . is there a question of criminal prosecution.[23]

[18] Matignon (1899), Gulik (1961:62), Cheng (1963:157–58), Coser (1964).

[19] When and how this legislation was adopted is not known.

[20] Alabaster (1899), Matignon (1899), Karsch-Haack (1906:1–62), Jacobus X (1896:1.91), Spence (1984:220–23).

[21] Nabokoff (1903).

[22] Karlinsky (1976) has argued that the Bolshevik repeal of antihomosexual legislation was merely incidental to a total repeal of all existing laws, a measure taken to make the repression of political opponents easier (by freeing the state from the constraints of the criminal code), but this contention is misleading. Faced with the chaos brought about by the Revolution and subsequent civil war, the new leaders had no intention of eliminating all rules. In a decree of December 7, 1917, the courts were instructed to take the law of the overthrown government as binding where it had not been explicitly repealed and was not contradictory to the Revolution's conception of justice (Juviler, 1976:20). The decriminalization of homosexuality was not an incidental by-product of broader legal reforms, but a conscious act of state policy. The policy remained in effect for almost two decades.

[23] Quoted in Lauritsen and Thorstad (1974:62–64). Nonetheless, by 1928, Batkis spoke of homosexuality as a sexual perversion when he spoke in Copenhagen at the Second International Congress for Sexual Reform (Wolff, 1986:261).

The extensive new criminal legislation of the 1920s did not mention homosexuality; and Magnus Hirschfeld was met with accolades when he visited the USSR in 1926–27.[24] However, recriminalization did take place under Stalin. In a statute promulgated in March 1934 and still in effect today, the government introduced a maximum penalty of five years for consensual male homosexuality.[25] This was a time of major bureaucratization in state and economy.[26] Official policy toward homosexuality in the highly bureaucratized People's Republic of China has also been hostile.

Here, however, the evidence seems more ambiguous. The Soviet legislation was part of a broader legal initiative to end abortion, increase the birthrate, and strengthen male domination of the family. The recriminalization of homosexuality was part of a counterrevolution in gender roles, fueled at least in part by Stalin's sexual puritanism, not an attempt to preserve the impartiality of the government bureaucracy. The Chinese Communist repugnance to homosexuality is part of a much broader suppression of sensuality. Although one might expect a society trying desperately to limit its fertility to favor nonprocreative sexual outlets, the government seems to fear—perhaps correctly—that the acceptance of pleasure as a sufficient justification for a social relationship will open the door to an individualism that might threaten the collective ethic and to consumer demands that the economy cannot easily meet.

Cuba is another test case. A certain amount of bureaucratization has taken place since the Castro government was formed in 1959, and policy toward homosexuality has been repressive. Criminal legislation provides a fine of three to nine months of imprisonment for the public practice of homosexuality or for soliciting, with heavier penalties when the partner is under eighteen. In 1965, homosexual faculty at the University of Havana were dismissed, and a number of writers lost their jobs. Three years later, bars in the La Rampa district of Havana were closed, and men suspected of homosexuality on the basis of their style of clothing and haircut were arrested indiscriminately on the streets and inducted into special militarized work units.[27] Homosexuals have been barred from important sectors of the

[24] Wolff (1980:242).

[25] Lauritsen and Thorstad (1974:68–70), Stern (1979:214, 218–19), Jong (1985). Lesbianism was not mentioned.

[26] Schachtman (1962), Lefort (1974/75), Arato (1978).

[27] Protests from the Union of Writers and Artists (and from intellectuals and leftists abroad) eventually led to the practice being stopped and the units abolished, but harassment on grounds of homosexuality has continued, with local Committees for the Defense of the Revolution playing a large role in identifying targets. Arguelles and Rich (1984) allege that the CIA has exacerbated Cuban prejudices by recruiting many homosexuals for counterrevolutionary projects and inducing them to emigrate to the United States, but they provide no evidence to support these allegations. In the absence of considerable prejudice and discrimination, it is

economy: medicine, culture, education, the army, and at least formally, though not always in practice, from party membership. Public statements refer to homosexuality as a form of counterrevolutionary bourgeois depravity and question the loyalty of those who engage in it.[28]

Yet other factors than bureaucracy seem to be at work. The tourist trade under Batista supported male (and female) prostitution, giving it an unsavory reputation.[29] The provisions of the criminal code dealing with homosexuality date back to 1939, cite the Bible, and refer to Sodom, suggesting the continuing influence of Roman Catholicism, rather than a new development.

Cuban contempt for male effeminacy (and to a more limited extent, female masculinity) is also traditional.[30] Yglesias tells of a man who was sent to a labor camp when caught being "speared" anally, while nothing was done to his partner, "the spearer." He explains, "most Cubans would have taken for granted . . . that the partner was not a homosexual."[31] An exile who appears in the film *Improper Conduct*, released in New York in 1984, reports that homosexuals were tolerated in the Cuban government, even in the police force, as long as they were manly in appearance and deportment. This gender-specific tolerance is not a manifestation of bureaucratic rationality, but a survival of Latin American machismo,[32] reinforced by the value the government places on the cultivation of military virtues in the male population. An official statement issued in 1965 makes this gender-stereotyping explicit:

---

hard to see why Cuban homosexuals would be especially recruitable or amenable to leaving Cuba. It is true, though, that the exodus of many Cuban homosexuals has increased popular feelings against homosexuality.

[28] Karol (1970:395), Cardenal (1974:21), Salas (1979:150–77), Young (1982), Boogaard and van Kammen (1985).

[29] The revolutionary government set out to abolish prostitution by criminalizing pimping and by training prostitutes for other kinds of work (Olmo, 1979).

[30] Arguelles and Rich (1984).

[31] Yglesias (1968:275). Similar assumptions prevail in Nicaragua. The anally receptive male partner has a distinct and somewhat stigmatized identity, *el cochon*. Participation as an active partner in a homosexual relationship is not incongruous with manliness, is not stigmatized, and leads to no distinct identity (Lancaster, 1986; B. Adam, 1987b). For Brazil, see Young (1973); for Mexico, Carrier (1976, 1977).

[32] Traditional sexist stereotyping is just as evident in Cuban medical writings on homosexuality (which differ little from contemporaneous American writings). One psychiatric report of 1965 explained male homosexuality as the result of the physical or emotional absence of the father, the child spending too much time surrounded by women, or his being overprotected, all factors leading to a weak masculine identification. Its recommendation: "the father should behave as such and the mother should occupy her place within the home" (quoted in Salas, 1979:163). If the Family Act of 1975 succeeds in reducing the sexual division of labor, gender-stereotyping, such as is seen here, may diminish, and with it, intolerance of homosexuality that violates traditional gender norms (Boogaard and van Kammen, 1985).

> No homosexual represents the Revolution, which is a matter for men and not feathers, of courage and not trembling, of certainty and not intrigue, of creative valor and not of sweet surprises.[33]

The state of seige imposed on Cuba by the U.S. government is likely to perpetuate this cultural emphasis, but a few years ago, under the influence of American and European sympathizers critical of Cuba's homosexuality policy, some tentative signs of relaxation began to appear.[34]

The Gregorian reforms of the medieval church more clearly support the argument. As was emphasized in chapter 6, these reforms were undertaken to draw sharper lines between clergy and laity and to preserve clear lines of hierarchical authority within the church. The repression of homosexuality, suppression of clerical marriage, and attacks on simony were all means to this end.

The examples of the church and the Ottoman and Chinese empires make clear that rules or laws against homosexuality have sometimes been adopted to serve organizational goals of rationality and legitimacy. It is equally clear that this is not the only reason homosexuality has been prohibited and that some contemporary bureaucracies fail to ban homosexuality. These examples warn us that a functionalist argument to the effect that rules against homosexuality are absolutely necessary for the functioning of bureaucratic organizations is wrong. Perhaps personal ties between officeholders, or between staff and outsiders, interfere with rational decision-making and raise doubts about impartiality. Yet organizations where ties of this sort develop are familiar enough. Decisions may or may not be influenced by these ties; fellow employees may grumble at real or imagined favoritism, but the organization continues to operate.[35] Since management cannot easily spy on employees to learn about office romances, it often elects to do nothing until publicity forces it to take action.[36]

There is another reason why many organizations can easily remain indifferent to homosexuality. As long as officeholders segregate their work from their personal lives, restricting their romantic and sexual involvements to outsiders who have no dealings with the organization, the impartiality of organizational decisions will not be threatened even in appearance. The large size of modern cities has made this sort of segregation easy to maintain. In fact, many homosexuals have kept their positions in just this way,

---

[33] Quoted in Salas (1979:166).

[34] Arguelles and Rich (1984), Boogaard and van Kammen (1985).

[35] There is no evidence, for example, that promotions given to the owner's son in a family firm destroy business morale. At worst they may lead employees who aspire to head the firm to leave.

[36] Quinn (1977), Dullea (1982), Fulman (1982).

in effect withholding information about their sexual preferences from possibly hostile organizational superiors.[37]

It is a different matter when the "total" quality of an organization precludes significant outside relationships. Where people's lives are encompassed by an organization, and the efficient and impersonal functioning of the organization is important, the relationships of members become important, too. One bureaucracy that meets these criteria is the military, and it has shown an exceptional preoccupation with homosexuality. In 1914, the German minister of war, von Einem, ordered homosexual officers dismissed from the army.[38] Buggery was a capital offense under the Articles of War for the British navy, which punished it with execution more consistently than it punished mutiny or desertion. By contrast, the British army, in which life was not as totalized as on a ship, relied more heavily on whippings.[39] In 1967, when the legal prohibition against homosexuality was lifted, men in the armed forces were explicitly excluded. The public discussion of decriminalization and the parliamentary debates focused on the maintenance of lines of authority within the military, and on the problems of demoralization that might occur were officers to use their positions to demand sexual favors from the men under their commands.[40] Men in the military were likewise exempted in Spain when its sodomy law was repealed in 1976. Article 356 of the Military Code of Law permits sentences up to six years in prison and discharge from the service for homosexual acts between men.[41]

U.S. military policy toward homosexuality has been variable. It was grounds for court-martial during World War I, but no special efforts were made to prevent the induction of homosexual men into the military. Though Freud was by then becoming known within educated circles,[42] military officials still did not conceive of homosexuality as something characteristic of a distinct minority that could be detected and excluded. By the time of World War II that notion was much more prevalent. Draftboard members and medical doctors at induction centers tried to screen recruits by looking for effeminate mannerisms and asking about prior homosexual experience. Nonetheless, much homosexuality occurred within the military—a product of inefficient screening, heterosexual deprivation, the intense bonding

[37] Zoglin (1979).
[38] Wolff (1986:157).
[39] A. N. Gilbert (1977).
[40] Bentley (1980), C. Davies (1975:119–23, 1982).
[41] International Association (1985:166).
[42] By 1915, Walter Lippman and Max Eastman were writing articles on Freud for popular consumption, and as of the following year there were 500 psychoanalysts in New York (Leuchtenberg, 1958).

that develops under combat conditions, and leaves that could not be supervised. Although disciplinary considerations should have led the military to suppress all homoeroticism, the importance of not demoralizing the troops dictated a policy of tolerating private consensual relationships so long as they were not disruptive and did not create an open scandal.[43]

Once the war ended, thousands of soldiers were given dishonorable discharges. In fact, a Senate subcommittee investigating the employment of homosexuals in government noted that the armed services had been much more aggressive than the civilian branches in attempting to exclude homosexuals.[44] In one case that went to court, the conviction of a navy officer for fraternizing with an enlisted man was upheld on appeal because "some acts are by their very nature palpably and directly prejudicial to the good order and discipline of the services."[45] The judge was evidently concerned that the hierarchical line of command would be subverted by a personal relationship between an officer and an enlisted man.

This difference in policy between the military and civilian branches persists to this day. Although few civilian agencies bar employment on grounds of homosexuality,[46] hundreds of men and women are discharged from the armed services—most of them from the navy—each year.[47] As late as 1984, 2d Lt. Joann Newak was given a seven-year sentence by a military court for her off-base, off-duty affair with another airwoman.[48] The severe sentence does not necessarily mean that high-ranking military officers are especially prejudiced against homosexuality (though many probably are)—similar actions are taken in cases of prohibited heterosexual conduct. In 1983, a male marine lieutenant was court-martialed for courting the corporal who became his wife, on charges of violating a policy against fraternization. The Marine Corps considers dating between officers and enlisted personnel to be "prejudicial to good order and discipline."[49]

---

[43]Bérubé (1981). Laxity seems to have been greatest toward lesbians. Sailors were sent to a naval psychiatric hospitality for homosexuality or to prison. In 1941, a quarter of the new admissions at the two principal naval prisons were for male homosexuality. As in the British Royal Navy, enforcement was especially vigorous when relations linked officers and enlisted men (Costello, 1985:93–98, 151–58, 167–68).

[44]U.S. Senate Subcommittee (1950).

[45]Quoted in Pearce (1973).

[46]The FBI is one of the few.

[47]Williams and Weinberg (1971), Gibson (1978), Willens (1986). An estimated 40,000 to 50,000 men and women were discharged from the U.S. military on charges of homosexuality between 1950 and 1980 (Bourdonnay, 1983).

[48]*Citizen Soldier*, May 1983, p. 2, and June 1984, p. 7.

[49]*New York Times*, September 7, 1983.

Bureaucracy and Personality

There is reason to think that bureaucratization has also shaped attitudes toward homosexuality through its effect on personality. Bureaucracies can ensure employees' compliance with organizational rules by making pay and promotions contingent on performance. In so doing, they mold what has been called "the bureaucratic personality"—methodical, rational, prudent, disciplined, unemotional, and preoccupied with conformity to expectations.[50] Through consistent reinforcement, the cold impersonality of the bureaucrat's "working personality" can become internalized. Someone who is conditioned to respond at work like an automaton, or to manipulate other employees as if they were inert objects, may have difficulty being warm or emotionally intimate away from the office.

By contrast, in a social system in which legitimate authority is exercised primarily on the basis of tradition or personal charisma there is nothing to reinforce these bureaucratic personality traits. A traditional or charismatic leader can throw a temper tantrum, but modern bureaucrats are expected to contain their emotions (or to feel none).

Until quite recently, bureaucratic employment was restricted almost entirely to men. It is thus hardly a coincidence that what sociologists have called the *bureaucratic* personality is essentially what students of gender have portrayed as the *male* personality.[51] One psychological study found being unemotional, objective, logical, unexcitable in minor crises, hiding emotions, and never crying to be traits valued by men, whereas women valued being gentle, empathic, and expressing tender feelings.[52]

Until recently, girls in the Western world have been socialized to encourage the expression of traits that are alien to bureaucratic administration (nurturance, emotional expressiveness), but that are important in tasks carried out in the home or in such occupations as elementary education and nursing, where women have been employed in large numbers. Of course this linkage between sex and personality traits is imperfect and would not be so pronounced in strata or social groups where the sexual division of labor is weak.

These differences are widely recognized. In a critique of Leninist political parties, with their top-down, authoritarian hierarchies, Sheila Rowbotham relates the austere image of the revolutionary held by these groups to the aspects of male socialization we are emphasizing:

[50] Merton (1957:195–206).
[51] Sawyer (1970), Jourard (1974), R. A. Lewis (1978), Nichols (1979).
[52] Rosenkrantz et al. (1968).

The individual militant appears as a lonely character without ties, bereft of domestic emotions, who is hard, erect, self-contained, controlled, without the time or ability to express loving passions, who cannot pause to nurture, and for whom friendship is a diversion. . . . It's a stark vision of sacrifice and deprivation. . . . It surely owes something to the strange things done to little boys in preparing them for manhood in capitalism. . . . Leninist groups still tend to reduce the criteria for success to an old-style managerial concept of efficiency.[53]

Because the formation of the bureaucratic personality in men entails the suppression of affective emotional responses toward males, men will tend to experience anxiety in the presence of expressions of emotional intimacy or sexual contact between men—or even at the thought of intimacy.[54] It is this anxiety, I contend, that lies behind irrational anger toward male homosexuality. The violence directed toward gay men walking along city streets with their arms about one another may be provoked not so much by their sexual preference or conduct—about which an observer can only speculate—as by their open exhibition of affection toward one another.

If Freud is right in maintaining that everyone has some degree of homosexual feeling, even if only in the form of friendly sentiments, then someone who has internalized the belief that these feelings are improper and shameful will undergo anxiety-provoking psychological conflict when he notices men walking down the street displaying their feelings toward one another. Violence toward those whose presence evokes this conflict serves as a psychological defense mechanism; it reassures the person who engages in it that *he* is not homosexual and has none of the threatening feelings toward men that he sees in others.

This general line of reasoning receives support from an experimental study of aggression toward homosexuals.[55] The study found that male-heterosexual college students who had negative views of homosexuality were more aggressive toward homosexual targets they believed to be simi-

[53] Rowbotham (1979).

[54] The inhibitions against emotional intimacy may be greater than those discouraging sexual relations. Young male hustlers who do not consider themselves homosexual are able to manage sexual relations with older men for money by denying any emotional response or involvement (Reiss, 1961). The impersonality of many homosexual transactions (Delph, 1978) may be due not merely to the obstacles social discrimination and legal repression pose to stable personal relationships, but also to the difficulties many men have in expressing emotion. In heterosexual relationships it is typically the female partner who is responsible for the emotional work necessary to maintain a viable relationship.

[55] San Miguel and Millham (1976).

lar to themselves than toward those they considered dissimilar. When the targets were heterosexual, the response pattern was just the opposite: subjects were far more aggressive to those they believed to be dissimilar to themselves than to those they believed similar. This difference in patterns of aggressiveness suggests that hostility toward homosexuals may be provoked by an irrational sense of personal threat aroused by unconscious homosexual impulses. The greater the resemblance of the supposed homosexual to the subject, the greater the threat.[56]

My argument that the internalized prohibition against male-male intimacy stems to a significant degree from work-related socialization in bureaucratic organizations carries implications for historical change in attitudes toward homosexuality. To pursue these implications we must examine the process by which social organization in the West became bureaucratized.

THE SPREAD OF BUREAUCRATIC ORGANIZATION

Bureaucratic organization was introduced to Western Europe slowly over a period of centuries.[57] The innovations adopted by the papacy during the investiture struggle to prevent the feudalization of the church established it as a transnational bureaucracy governed by a formal hierarchy according to the rational logic of canon law at a time when national states were not bureaucratized at all.[58] National states began to bureaucratize much earlier than private business enterprises, and different state functions were bureaucratized at different times.

To defend their claims against the church, increase their revenues from court fees, and regularize their relationships with the nobility, medieval kings began to systematize secular law, rationalize the administration of justice, and introduce principles of constitutionalism. To a lesser extent, the free cities of the Middle Ages followed a similar course after gaining rights of self-government. However, resistance from feudal lords and tech-

[56] In another study, Millham, San Miguel, and Kellogg (1976) found that males have higher levels of anxiety over male homosexuality than over lesbianism and are more repressive toward it. Though female subjects preferred male homosexuals to lesbians, they were neither more anxious nor more repressive toward lesbianism than toward male homosexuality. Other studies have shown that, even though males and females share the same general cultural beliefs about homosexuality, males feel more negatively toward it, or more threatened by it, when in close proximity to an actor they believe to be homosexual (Nungesser, 1983:5).

[57] Bureaucracy had developed even earlier, in the Roman Empire—first in the army, then later in the state administration—but implementation of bureaucratic principles as Weber conceived of them remained severely limited by the strength of elite patronage systems. The collapse of the empire in the West put an end to even this limited degree of bureaucracy (Antonio, 1979).

[58] Berman (1983).

nical limits on administrative capacity prevented the bureaucratization of government from proceeding very far.

The transformation of military combat began in the early fourteenth century when pikemen recruited from the ranks of burghers in the urban communes (or in the case of the Swiss, from communities of peasant farmers with common meadowland) defeated the armored cavalry of the feudal armies, ending the military supremacy of the medieval horseman.[59] Combat in the feudal armies had been primarily hand-to-hand, and discipline was weak. Each contingent of knights fought under the banner of its lord, complicating the task of coordinating the troops. For the new armies, on the other hand, "strict discipline was absolutely necessary . . . and they had to move in units on the march and on the battlefield."[60] The invention of the gun in the late fourteenth century reinforced these tendencies.

Seventeenth-century France marked the rise of the military engineer. Under the leadership of the great fort-builder Vauban and of Louvois, "the technician of war," the age of siege warcraft began and with it the necessity of orchestrating huge numbers of men, supplies, and equipment. To meet this requirement, the army, which under the reign of Louis XIII had been "feudal in spirit and mercenary in composition,"[61] was restructured. Official chains of command were established and uniforms, wages, and equipment standardized.

These developments were giving warfare the character of a contest between mass armies composed of interchangable, anonymous soldiers deployed by commanders on the basis of strategic considerations that took no account of personal ties among them. The new spirit was exemplified by Cromwell's New Model Army, "with its rigid camp discipline, its elaborate rules against every imaginable sin from looting and rapine to blasphemy and card-playing and finally its workmanlike and efficient military tactics."[62] Discipline was enforced through both individual self-control and mutual surveillance.

Major steps toward the bureaucratization of the English state were undertaken in the latter part of the reign of Henry VIII, following the fall of Cardinal Wolsey in 1529. Until then, no distinction had been made between the royal purse and the national treasury, and the king supervised the administration of government personally. By the end of his reign the state had been separated from the king's personal household, and public accounting was reorganized. Members of the privy council functioned with

[59] Bean (1973), Verbruggen (1977:99).
[60] Verbruggen (1977:151).
[61] Treasure (1972).
[62] Walzer (1974:13).

clear-cut formal responsibilities as heads of bureaucratic agencies. Summarizing these developments (which, however, did not include the conduct of military and foreign affairs for another century), a leading student of British government noted that "Henry VIII ascended the throne of a medievally governed kingdom, while Elizabeth handed to her successor a country administered on modern lines."[63]

The turning point in France came during the reigns of Louis XIII and Louis XIV and their ministers Richelieu, Mazarin, and Colbert. With the rise of royal absolutism, steps were taken to rationalize and bureaucratize a number of state functions. When Louis XIII came to the throne, ministers acted in the name of the king. Courts had to wait for a letter from the king before executing a minister's order. By the reign of Louis XIV, ministers had obtained delegated authority and acted in their own names. A similar shift can be seen in the role of the *intendants* (overseers for the crown). At first they had acted chiefly as investigators, being sent to the scene and returning to the king with a report. By the 1660s and 1670s they had taken up permanent residence in the provinces, had developed their own bureaus, and were granted a great deal of authority.[64] As rulers were sometimes reluctant to give up personal supervision of government, this process did not always proceed smoothly. But the vast expansion in state functions needed to implement mercantilist economic policy made the result inevitable.

Rationalization also took place in other areas. The French criminal code of 1670 brought together and codified preexisting legislation. Archives were organized and provisions made for gathering social statistics. Colbert's administration introduced a kind of public accounting and a tax-roll system. It was at this time that age-grading, rationalization of the curriculum, classification, individualized ranking, surveillance, and discipline were introduced into the schools, hospitals, and factories.[65] Similar steps were being taken in eighteenth-century Prussia.[66]

Although the centuries during which the bureaucratization of state administration were taking place were marked by official antagonism toward homosexuality, there is no evidence that these developments had much to do with one another. The absolutist desire for public order did try to stop men from having sexual relations in public, but as we noted in chapter 7, upper-class attitudes toward homosexuality were by no means consistently negative in the early modern era. Heads often turned the other way, and courtiers were not infrequently involved in homosexual activity. But at that

---

[63] Elton (1953:3–4).
[64] Perkins (1886), Rule (1969).
[65] Ariès (1962), Foucault (1977).
[66] H. Jacoby (1973:28–35).

time the implementation of bureaucratic organizational principles was still extremely limited. The purchase and inheritance of offices—the standard practice in both France and England—profoundly limited the rationalization of the state. Outside of government, bureaucracy was almost completely unknown.

Only in the twentieth century did a large fraction of the male population come to be employed in bureaucracies and thus exposed to the kinds of experiences that would inhibit emotional or sexual involvement with other men. As late as 1840 there were no American business firms in which middle-level managers supervised other managers and reported to salaried senior executives: virtually all top managers were owners—either partners or major stockholders. Even after that date most businesses were organized as partnerships of two or three close associates, often family members. The large manufacturing plant remained atypical until quite late in the nineteenth century. However, the years between 1880 and 1920 saw an appreciable growth in the average number of employees per plant, a rationalization of work organization (including the introduction of the Ford assembly line), and the tightening of hierarchical authority.[67] These innovations, introduced to cope with technical problems of large-scale operations, cut costs, and better control labor, were facilitated by the shift from family-held businesses to the more impersonal corporation, with its separation of ownership (in the hands of stockholders) and management.[68] They came no earlier to other countries than they did to the United States.

Rapid economic change was one of the factors leading to a growth in governmental administrative capacity. Demands for regulation coming from diverse sectors of business and labor whose interests were jeopardized by the giant corporations and trusts, as well as from some of the major corporations themselves, led to the creation of the Interstate Commerce Commission in 1887, the Federal Trade Commission in 1914, and dozens of other federal agencies in subsequent decades. State governments were expanding their supervisory roles at the same time.[69]

Civil-service reform, which came to the United States with the Pendleton Act of 1873, entailed the adoption of such bureaucratic principles as hiring on the basis of competitive examinations instead of political-party affiliation, political neutrality in government administration, and formal rules for

[67] Miller and Swanson (1958:44) chart the growth of the enterprise over a longer time-span. In the first half of the nineteenth century, the typical manufacturing concern employed 50 to 100 people; by 1948, almost half of all employees worked in plants that employed 500 or more, and slightly more than a third in plants that employed 1,000 or more.

[68] K. Stone (1974), D. Nelson (175), Chandler (1977), Hounshell (1984).

[69] G. D. Nash (1957), Kolko (1963, 1965), J. Weinstein (1968), G. H. Miller (1971), Skowronek (1982), Freitag (1985).

promotion and pay. This depoliticization of government hiring had the support of business associations as well as of a college-educated patrician elite advocating the professionalization of government. Both feared the economic power of the large corporation and the political power of the corrupt urban machine. Similar steps were taken at roughly the same time by other industrializing nations: England in 1870, Germany in 1873 (extending to the newly unified Germany the system that had been in effect in Prussia since 1810), Canada in 1882, and Japan in 1887.[70]

In the aftermath of the Boer War (1899–1902) and the Spanish-American War (1898), England and the United States moved toward reorganization of the army along lines that had enabled Prussia to defeat France, Denmark, and Austria in the late nineteenth century: a large army of conscripted citizens commanded by a staff of professional officers who in peacetime plan and prepare for war. Dissatisfaction with the performance of state militia in the strikes of the late nineteenth century (in several states they sided with workers) added to the impetus for army reorganization.[71]

With these changes taking place more or less simultaneously around the turn of the century, bureaucratic principles spread to large numbers of worksites, so that for the first time in history most men began to experience the sort of adult socialization that we have argued would lead to antipathy to homosexuality.

Major changes in the socialization of children were also taking place. Formal schooling was gradually being extended to the entire juvenile population and made mandatory under pressure from "manufacturers and professionals" who sought "a universal agency of socialization which would insure a self-disciplined, deferential, orderly, punctual and honest citizenry and labor force which would work well in manufacturing or bureaucratic units characterized by administrative hierarchies, and in nonworking hours go about business in an orderly fashion."[72] In the United States public-school enrollments more than doubled between 1890 and 1910. The proportion of the juvenile population attending school daily increased from 44 percent to 67 percent, and the school year was extended from 135 to 173 days over these decades.[73] School attendance continued to rise in subsequent years, as did the school-leaving age. Other Western na-

[70] Skowronek (1982:47–59), W. Nelson (1982:119–22).

[71] Skowronek (1982:85–99). W. Nelson (1982:114–33) details other dimensions of the bureaucratization in the post-Civil War years, such as competitive bidding for contracts, the depoliticization of customs, reorganization of the congressional system to reduce the influence of political parties, and greater use of formal, rational reasoning in court decisions.

[72] A. J. Field (1974:ii–iii).

[73] Edwards and Richy (1971).

tions saw similar extensions of schooling. Exposure to the reward contingencies of a bureaucracy increasingly began not in adulthood, with employment, but at a very early age.

As bureaucracies became major sources of employment, parents and schools inevitably began to prepare their children to meet the expectations of future employers. Studies of child-raising suggest that parents try to encourage their children to develp the personal traits they think will be useful to them in occupational settings later in life. Successive editions of *Infant Care*, a manual for parents published by the U.S. Children's Bureau, gave less and less emphasis to the suppression of children's impulses and desires in the years between 1914 and 1951. Play came to be considered desirable as long as other people's rights were respected.[74] This is the sort of change one would expect as individual entrepreneurship gave way to bureaucratic employment, where it is important to cooperate with fellow employees.

In a survey of Detroit mothers, Miller and Swanson found that wives of entrepreneurial husbands raised their children differently from those married to men employed in bureaucracies.[75] These differences were just those predicted on the assumption that parents try to encourage their children to develop the traits that they themselves have found useful. Unfortunately, they did not ask about the specific traits of interest to us.[76]

With occupational careers in modern times increasingly open to all—to children of workers as well as to those of the middle and upper classes, to blacks as well as whites, and now to women as well as to men—entrepreneurial and working-class parents might reasonably anticipate that their own children would eventually be employed in bureaucracies and prepared them accordingly. So the trend has been a broad one, affecting many children who ultimately end up working outside a bureaucracy.

The persistence of antihomosexual attitudes well into recent times has very likely been due at least in part to these developments. The concentration of these attitudes in the middle class during the early years of this century lends strength to this claim. We do not have survey data for earlier generations, but scattered evidence suggests that casual involvement in male homosexual relations and a comfortable acceptance of same-sex physi-

[74] Wolfenstein (1951).

[75] Miller and Swanson (1958).

[76] In a cross-national study of the United States and Poland, Kohn, Slomczynski, and Schoenbach (1986) have shown that, in both countries, parents' values regarding occupational self-direction are related to their positions in a social-stratification system, and that they effectively transmit these values to their children. All this is consistent with the ideas proposed here.

cal contact were characteristic of nineteenth-century British working-class life. Men with money had little difficulty finding soldiers and sailors or working-class youths willing to take money for sex, even though their own preferences were not homosexual.[77] Daniel Guerin was easily able to find sexual partners among working-class youths in France during the 1930s and in the United States after World War I.[78] Though some American sailors beat up "fairies" who solicited them just after World War I, many—including quite a few married men—made themselves available.[79] Boys from proletarian family backgrounds, of course, had a much more limited exposure to formal education, and unlike their middle-class peers, were not destined for bureaucratic employment. The same is true, obviously, for the Swiss and Russian peasants who also seem to have had few inhibitions about male homosexuality[80]—and for the many peoples living in nonbureaucratic tribes or civilizations described in the earlier chapters of this book.

The Kinsey survey findings also bear this out. In their sample, boys whose education stopped at grade school had, on the average, four of five times as many homosexual experiences as those who went to college. Although education is not a direct measure of parents' social class (or of the type of employment the subject has or will have), it is strongly related to it and was probably even more so a generation ago when the Kinsey survey was conducted.[81]

[77] H. Ellis (1897:9–11), Ackerley (1968:110, 135), J. Weeks (1977a:39–41).
[78] Sedgwick (1982/83).
[79] Chauncey (1985).
[80] H. Ellis (1897:9–11).
[81] Kinsey, Pomeroy, and Martin (1948).

11   *Gay Liberation*

THE ADVENT OF GAY LIBERATION

Despite the growing acceptance of a medical or psychological understanding of homosexuality, homosexual acts remained felonious in every state of the United States until well past mid-century under nineteenth-century sodomy laws that also criminalized various forms of heterosexual intercourse. Though rarely imposed, the penalties meted out to the few who were unfortunate enough to be prosecuted were sometimes severe. A man who ran a private male-homosexual entertainment establishment from his home in Brooklyn during World War II served a full twenty-year prison sentence on a sodomy conviction despite his having helped the government catch German spies.[1] Men convicted in the Boise, Idaho, scandal in the mid-fifties were sent to prison for long periods, in one case with a maximum sentence of life.[2]

The legal tide began to turn in 1961, when the new Illinois Model Penal Code quietly led the way for a number of states to decriminalize homosexual relations in private between consenting adults. Yet, as of 1986, they remained illegal in twenty-four of the fifty states and in the District of Columbia.[3] In a 1986 decision, the U.S. Supreme Court decided by a 5 to 4

---

[1]L. R. Murphy (1985b). The judge in this case was no right-wing fanatic or Christian zealot; he was a liberal Democrat and a Jew, who in earlier years had served as a defense attorney for the Scottsboro boys, Negro youths who had been framed on charges of raping a white woman in Alabama.

[2]Gerassi (1966).

[3]Rivera (1979, 1982). The states that prohibit both male and female homosexual relations include Alabama, Arizona, Florida, Georgia, Idaho, Kentucky, Louisiana, Maryland, Michigan, Minnesota, Missouri, North Carolina, Oklahoma, Rhode Island, South Carolina, Tennessee, Utah, and Virginia. States that prohibit only relations between males are Arkansas, Kansas, Montana, Nevada, and Texas. Some states, like Illinois and Maine, have repealed their sodomy statutes with little or no publicity in the course of a revision of the entire criminal code. Adoption of the model penal code prepared by the American Law Institute, which deleted prohibitions against consensual sodomy to avoid "overcriminalization" and court

455

majority that such laws do not infringe the constitutional right to privacy, even when the prohibited acts take place at home.[4] However, in recent years prosecutors have shown little interest in these cases. Charges against the Atlanta man whose challenge to the Georgia antisodomy statute was rejected by the Supreme Court were dropped despite the availability of the arresting officer's eyewitness testimony.[5]

The situation in Great Britain remained somewhat repressive well into mid-century, with the police staging a major drive against male homosexuality in the 1950s. Decriminalization came only in 1967, a decade after the recommendation of the prestigious Wolfenden Report. Nevertheless, prosecutions on charges of indecency, made easier by new legal provisions for summary trials, rose by a factor of three in the next six years.[6] French legislation under Petain and de Gaulle strengthened penalties against indecent exposure and sexual relations with minors; in the 1960s and early 1970s some hundreds were arrested each year on these charges.[7] In the Federal Republic of Germany, prosecutions under the infamous Paragraph 175 of the criminal code, still on the books after the war, rose between 1953 and 1965, sending survivors of the Nazi extermination camps to prison with sentences as long as six years.[8]

Notwithstanding legal penalties, by the early decades of the twentieth century there were neighborhoods and social milieux in the larger Ameri-

---

crowding, made liberalization possible in a number of states by avoiding controversial public discussions of the issue. Often the press did not discover that decriminalization had occurred until after it had taken place (Cohen and Gallagher, 1984). In other states, such as New York, the statutes were struck down by state appeals courts.

[4]Bowers v. Hardwick, 106 S. Ct. 2841 (1986).

[5]Even though prosecutors have been reluctant to press charges under the antisodomy statutes, they seem to want them on the books. In Georgia and New York, district attorneys have appealed to higher courts when antisodomy statutes were declared unconstitutional.

[6]Walmsley (1978), Dodd (1981).

[7]Earlier legislation had treated homosexual and heterosexual relations with minors on an equal basis.

[8]Stümke and Finkler (1981:368–70), Schilling (1983), Witzel (1985), Adam (1987a). Trends in other countries have been variable. Homosexual relations between consenting adults are not illegal in any of the Scandinavian countries, and in 1981 Norway banned public defamation on grounds of homosexuality (Pederson, 1985). Austria and Finland both decriminalized consensual sexual relations among adults in 1971, but legal harrassment has occurred in both countries on the basis of substitute legislation forbidding the incitement or encouragement of homosexuality (Hosi-Wien Collective, 1985; Mansson, 1985). In Israel, those who have "carnal knowledge of a person against the order of nature" or permit someone to do so with them are vulnerable to a prison sentence of ten years under a law originally put into effect by the British under the Protectorate (Sofer, 1985). The law is not enforced, but the parliamentary strength of the religious parties makes repeal unlikely.

can cities where same-sex couples could live relatively unmolested and wider homosexual social networks could be sustained. These expanded in the decades following World War II.[9] Nonetheless, the atmosphere was repressive. Jill Johnston's observation that in the 1950s "there was no lesbian identity except a criminal one" held true for male homosexual identities as well.[10] Most of those who wanted to engage in homosexual relations on a regular basis were forced into a life of hiding. Fear of ostracism, divorce, unemployment, hellfire, or a guilty conscience kept others to the straight and narrow. Though allusions to homosexuality occasionally made their way onto the stage, Hollywood shunned the subject.[11] Popular attitudes, reflecting stereotypes that could not be corrected by observing people who did not fit them, or through secondhand exposure in the mass media, remained sharply negative. In a national survey conducted in 1970 for the Institute for Sex Research, 49 percent of the respondents agreed with the statement that "homosexuality is a social corruption which can cause the downfall of a civilization."[12]

Attitudes shifted during the 1970s in the direction of greater tolerance. A 1977 Harris Poll survey found that Americans favored legislation prohibiting job discrimination on the basis of sexual orientation by a 2 to 1 majority, though many respondents favored exempting specific occupations such as teaching.[13] The following year California voters defeated a referendum (the Briggs Initiative) that would have barred homosexuals and those publicly advocating homosexuality from employment as teachers.[14] Some Protestant denominations began ordaining gay ministers. Bishops of the Roman Catholic church denounced discrimination against gays, while priests and nuns formed counseling and support groups.[15] Openly gay politicians were elected to public office, and in 1982, Vice-President Walter Mondale addressed a gay-rights dinner. Despite initial misgivings, colleges recognized gay student organizations, allowed gay dances on university premises, offered courses on homosexuality, and granted tenure to openly gay pro-

[9] Mayne (1908), Vice Commission (1911:295–96), J. N. Katz (1976:39–53, 1983:235, 297–99), Bérubé (1981), Garber (1982), Sprague (1985), Chauncey (1986), J. Meyerowitz (1986). Hirschfeld (1934) discusses the comparable effect of World War I in stimulating the growth of male homosexual communities in Europe.

[10] J. Johnston (1973:58).

[11] Tyler (1974:157), Dyer (1980), Russo (1981), Bronski (1984:92–132). On the rare occasions when homosexual characters did appear in film, they were presented in the most extreme stereotypes.

[12] Levitt and Klassen (1974).

[13] Paul (1982), Rueda (1982:4–13).

[14] D'Emilio (1981).

[15] Rueda (1982).

fessors. Major film studios released films that depicted homosexuality nonjudgmentally and advertised them to a general audience.[16] The gay-liberation movement played a critical role in bringing about these changes.

Efforts to promote homosexual rights go back to the late nineteenth century in Europe and in the United States, to the twenties. Following World War II, the Mattachine Foundation (later renamed the Mattachine Society), ONE, Inc., and Daughters of Bilitis contested discrimination and issued educational materials, for the most part working quietly and unobtrusively, just as civil-rights groups did for blacks.[17] By the 1960s these pioneers were joined by newcomers who broadened the goals and tactics of the small but growing movement to include picketing and boycotts.[18]

The Stonewall Riot in New York's Greenwich Village on June 27, 1968— in which the patrons of a gay bar, joined by community residents, fought back against police who raided the bar—ushered in a new militancy. Gay-liberation groups sprang up seemingly out of nowhere. Comparable groups appeared in England and Europe. Identifying themselves openly as gay, activists displayed an assertiveness and self-confidence rarely seen in the older groups. Gay protests, demonstrations, and parades now confronted the public with angry and determined homosexual men and women who came out of their closets and boldly flaunted traditional stereotypes or demonstrated their falsity.

Instead of demanding equal treatment for yet another minority, the more radical groups called for a rethinking of human sexuality and its place in society. They insisted that everyone was capable of homosexual response and argued that homosexuality could achieve equal status with heterosexuality only when that capability was realized. Only then could crippling gender distinctions between men and women break down. And so they called for the "liberation of homosexuality" in everyone.[19]

The nascent gay movement drew inspiration from black militancy, and both members and tactics from the white fraction of the New Left, a social movement of reformers and revolutionaries opposed to racism, capitalism, imperialism, militarism, and large-scale bureaucratic forms of social organi-

[16]Stabiner (1982), Barol et al. (1984).

[17]In Europe, the prewar homosexual-rights movement cautiously reconstituted itself in the decade following the end of the Nazi occupation (Adam, 1987a:65–66).

[18]Bérubé (1981), Marotta (1981), J. Levin (1982), D'Emilio (1981, 1983a), S. O. Murray (1984), Escoffier (1985), B. Adam (1987a).

[19]Altman (1971, 1979:16, 74), Shelley (1972). The history of the gay-liberation movement in the United States is well documented in Teal (1971), Humphreys (1972), Martin and Lyon (1972: 238–94), Licata (1980/81), Marotta (1981), D'Emilio (1983a), and B. Adam (1987a). J. Weeks (1977a) discusses the British movement, Girard (1981) the French movement, Tielman (1982) the Dutch.

zation. It called for "participatory democracy," an implicitly antibureau-
cratic form of governance, and protested the administration of universities
by computers as dehumanizing. It was at its peak influence at the time of
Stonewall. New Left activists were largely college youths who either lacked
clear vocational goals or anticipated careers in the nonbureaucratic sectors
of the economy (e.g., as teachers or independent professionals). Toward
the end of the sixties the women's-liberation movement had developed a
critique of the gender-role system and the male-dominated monogamous
family and projected an androgynous future. This is exactly the segment of
the population one would expect to be most favorable to the gay movement
if our explanation of hostility to homosexuality is correct.[20]

Influential though the gay movement has been, its success must itself be
explained. Back in 1924 when Henry Gerber founded an organization to
promote homosexual rights, the Chicago police arrested the officers, Gerber
lost his job at the post office, and the organization fell apart. No one came
to its defense, not even the inverts Gerber had hoped to mobilize, and it
disappeared without a trace.[21] Half a century later everything had changed.

How can we account for the difference? The gay movement arose toward
the end of an exceptionally long period of economic prosperity. The generation of students with middle- and upper-class backgrounds entering
college in the 1960s had never known scarcity and were relatively unconcerned about their future occupational prospects. As children, they had
been indulged by their moderately affluent parents, who put much less
emphasis on self-discipline and self-restraint in raising their children than

---

[20]To be sure, there was some opposition to gay rights even within the New Left. Some of
the disciplined, hierarchical Leninist groups and Communist parties dismissed the gay issue
as bourgeois and insisted that homosexuality was a type of psychopathology caused by capitalism. The older, more conservative members of the women's-liberation movement feared
that it would be tarnished by association with lesbianism. Still, the left gave stronger support
to the gay movement, especially in its early years, than any other part of the political spectrum. In pointing to the disproportionate recruitment of the early gay-liberation groups from
the New Left, I do not mean to imply that persons with black, Hispanic, Oriental, and Amer-
indian backgrounds were not also involved. The connection between gay liberation and the
New Left has also been close in Holland, France, and West Germany (Mehler, 1979; B. Adam,
1987a:76).

[21]J. N. Katz (1976:385–97). It should be noted that some tentative hints foreshadowing later
liberalization were already in evidence even in the early years of the century. The sexually
repressive eugenics movement had, ironically, promoted sex education and discussion, helping to lift taboos on the discussion of sexual topics. In 1912, anarchist and free-love-advocate
Emma Goldman publicly denounced sexual repression and spoke of homosexuality in positive terms (Falk, 1984:159–60), as did Edith Ellis (Havelock Ellis's wife) in carefully guarded
terms in a lecture tour that brought her to several American cities in 1915 (J. N. Katz, 1976:
359–66).

did earlier generations of parents, because the decline in self-employment made these traits less important for adults.[22]

Rather than requiring self-restraint to permit capital accumulation, the economy now required high levels of consumer spending to forestall recessions. Department stores placed a cornucopia of goods on display for shoppers, while television brought them into millions of homes night after night. Students of the 1960s were the first generation to be raised on television. By contrast with the generation of the Great Depression, they were raised in a "culture of abundance."[23] In college, many rebelled against restrictions that appeared to serve no rational purpose and developed a lifestyle of moderate hedonism. This new life-style included the recreational use of drugs and alcohol, the blurring of traditional gender roles (beads, long hair, and colorful clothing for men; short hair and army fatigues for women), and the abandonment of traditional restrictions against sexual expression. They sought self-expression and self-realization, rather than conformity to externally imposed behavioral standards.[24]

These developments occurred against a backdrop of changes in the nature of work and the composition of the labor force. White-collar employment, which increased relative to blue-collar work, was physically undemanding and could be performed equally well by either sex. Women were staying in school longer, and after leaving school were more often taking jobs, both white- and blue-collar.[25] Gender stereotypes were changing fast: in 1967, more than half the freshmen entering college thought that married women should not hold a job, in 1984, less than a quarter agreed.[26] Personality traits like aggressiveness and rationality no longer seemed so strongly associated with one sex or the other.[27] As rigid gender stereotypes weakened,

[22] Flacks (1971), Miller and Swanson (1958).

[23] The phrase is due to Susman (1985).

[24] Potter (1965), Yankelovitch (1981).

[25] E. Klein (1984).

[26] The survey, conducted annually by UCLA and the American Council of Education, polled more than 180,000 students attending 345 schools around the country. The findings were reported in the *New York Times*, January 14, 1985. In that the need for two incomes to sustain a comfortable level of consumption is unlikely to decline anytime soon, the trend can be expected to continue. The vigorous campaign launched after World War II to put working women back in the home, bearing and raising children, bucked the long-term trend for only about a decade (Escoffier, 1985).

[27] Cancian (1987). The weakening of gender differences in society at large and their ideological rejection within the feminist movement have probably been the most important factors in weakening gender distinctions among gays. Many reports indicate that lesbian couples are less likely than in the past to pattern their relationships on the traditional husband-wife model of the heterosexual world, with its sharp role differentiation (Jay and Young, 1977; Califia, 1979, Wolf, 1979). It is also unusual for contemporary gay men to fall into rigid, gender-defined roles (Bell and Weinberg, 1978; Harry and Devall, 1978; Spada, 1979). When they do,

so did resistance to homosexuality. In some circles, it became trendy to be bisexual.

It was important for women who held jobs to be able to control their fertility, and so they organized to repeal legal restrictions on contraception and abortion. Public concern with the "population explosion," particularly on the part of taxpayers vexed by rising welfare costs, helped to weaken the notion that the only acceptable grounds for sex were procreative. Once contraception became readily available, as it had by the late 1960s, the "double standard" quickly fell by the wayside, helped along by men who wanted their dates to be more compliant. Young people quickly came to accept and engage in premarital heterosexual intercourse.[28]

These trends started long before the sixties. The Roaring Twenties had seen youthful rebellion against stifling convention and more open discussion of sex. The automobile helped to establish dating outside of adult supervision as an accepted custom, making premarital sexual exploration more feasible. Over the course of the century, marriage manuals gradually began to endorse sexual pleasure as legitimate in its own right, though they said precious little about how to achieve it.[29] The meticulous laboratory research of Masters and Johnson elucidated that question,[30] throwing cold water on vaginal intercourse and sparking demands for clitoral stimulation. Feminists denounced older distinctions between the normal and the perverse as phallocentric. The newer marriage manuals reflected these developments by providing detailed instruction in technique, directed to all who are sexually active, not just husbands and wives, and aimed at encouraging the exploration of a wider sexual repertoire.[31]

In the 1960s the pace of change accelerated dramatically and received more publicity. Surveys show a substantial rise in premarital sexual experience from the beginning to the end of the decade, and less disapproval.[32]

---

they are more likely to be roles that exaggerate, rather than reverse, conventional gender traits (Humphreys, 1971; Kleinberg, 1978).

[28] Ehrenreich, Hess, and Jacob (1986:54–62) note that the revolution in premarital sexuality was already in progress before the "pill" became available, at least in large cities, where large numbers of young women lived on their own, supporting themselves with jobs, before marrying.

[29] Michael Gordon (1970), Trimberger (1983).

[30] Masters and Johnson (1966).

[31] Michael Gordon (1971), Heath (1984), Ehrenreich, Hess, and Jacob (1986:87–102).

[32] According to a report by the National Center for Health Statistics, the percentage of women who delayed intercourse until marriage was 48 percent among women who married between 1960 and 1964, 42 percent between 1965 and 1969, 28 percent between 1970 and 1974, and 21 percent between 1975 and 1977. The figures were cited in the *New York Times*, April 17, 1985. Approval of premarital sex in the Gallup Poll went from 24 percent to 47 percent in 1973, to 58 percent in 1985. The figures were reported in the *Daily News*, September 23, 1985.

Unmarried heterosexual couples could live together openly and no longer had to keep their affairs secret. Sex was not only becoming valuable for its own sake, it was also becoming detached from marriage. To many, sexual pleasure had become a birthright, maybe even necessary for psychological health.

The acceptance of some forms of sexual experience whose sole purpose is pleasure, sociability, or the expression of love makes it hard, in the absence of rational grounds, to reject others that are equally harmless and consensual. Thus there occurred a reduction in hostility toward homosexuality alongside a relaxation of attitudes toward divorce, premarital sex, contraception, abortion, and pornography.

England experienced comparable, parallel trends over the same time period, for similar reasons. So did Sweden. The decriminalization of homosexual acts in 1944 did little to erase the stigma there. In 1966, the Lutheran bishops reminded Swedes that homosexuality was a sin, and prejudice remained strong enough to prevent openness. With postwar prosperity, the welfare state, and acceptance of premarital fornication, acceptance of homosexuality grew apace. By the late 1970s, the eradication of vestigial discrimination was accepted as a goal by representatives of all political parties, across the spectrum. Controversies revolved around such issues as same-sex marriages and adoptions.[33]

Several other factors made the continuing rejection of homosexuality more difficult to sustain. One was the development of separatism in the women's movement. If men are believed to be the oppressors of women, then heterosexuality for women means consorting with the enemy and undermining female solidarity. Jill Johnston proclaimed that "the continued collusion of any woman with any man is an event that retards the progress of woman supremacy."[34] Not all feminists concurred, but the idea that all women should be sisters made it difficult to criticize separatism or exclude lesbians (though some did so anyway). Other women, not necessarily committed to separatism as a political strategy, found their experience with domineering men to be so embittering that they saw no alternative to personal withdrawal. While celibacy remained an option, many women found it less attractive than involvement with other women. The result: lesbianism became more acceptable.

Over the past few decades people have become more skeptical of established ideas about society. The expansion of higher education to ever larger

---

[33] Linner (1968:2–3, 70), Davies (1975), Mort (1980), Petersson (1985).

[34] J. Johnston (1973:276). Likewise Charlotte Bunch (1975): "Lesbianism is the key to liberation and only women who cut their ties to male privilege can be trusted to remain serious in the struggle against male dominance."

numbers of youths in the post-World War II years has exposed more of the population to unfamiliar ideas and life-styles. Social-science courses, which are required for many students, preach cultural relativism. Students are encouraged to question their taken-for-granted values and beliefs.[35] As they go through college they become more liberal and less rejecting of homosexuality. Surveys of national values show that sexual permissiveness increases with exposure to education.[36]

The delegitimation of accepted authority brought about by the civil-rights and antiwar movements of the sixties added greatly to this skepticism. To movement participants, university heads and political leaders often seemed so slow in responding to transparently just and reasonable demands, so willing to compromise their principles, and so hypocritical in their insistence that activists work through a visibly unresponsive political system, that they lost all credibility. The popularity of R. D. Laing's writings on schizophrenia and of Thomas Szasz's proclamation that mental illness is a myth[37] owed a great deal to the social movements that were projecting a vision of the world and the way it operates that was radically different from the conventional one. This projection carried with it an implied skepticism about all received notions of conventional morality.

Scientific conceptions of homosexuality were also becoming less monolithic during this period. While some psychiatrists continued to regard homosexuality as a form of psychopathology and persisted in studying the usual constellation of its purported biological and familial causes, others abandoned this project as pointless and potentially repressive.[38] Some even turned the tables by branding the irrational fear of, or anger toward, homosexuality "homophobia," a condition one psychologist termed "a disease."[39]

Perhaps the greatest conceptual innovation came from sociology. In earlier decades it had given homosexuality very little attention, but now it began to make up for lost time, bringing to bear on homosexuality new theoretical perspectives and concerns coming to the fore in the 1960s. The new sociology of deviance gave particular emphasis to the subjective as-

[35] Irwin (1977:170–77).

[36] Hyman and Wright (1979), J. A. Davis (1982).

[37] Laing (1964, 1965), Szasz (1961, 1970).

[38] Bayer (1981), B. Adam (1987a:81–83).

[39] G. Weinberg (1973:xi). The term has been criticized on the ground that there is no evidence of the condition being a classical Freudian phobia. The critics go on to argue that the term misleadingly suggests that hostility to homosexuality stems from an abnormal psychological state in particular individuals, rather than reflecting a cultural system of beliefs and practices widely diffused throughout Western societies (Plummer, 1975; Lehne (1976), Bentley, 1980). Nonetheless, it has come into wide usage.

pects of social life. It assumes that people act toward things (including people) on the basis of the meanings those things have for them.[40] These meanings can be invented or learned from others. An especially important category of meanings centers on one's *self-identity*, the answer a person gives to the question "Who am I?" The answer to that question is not necessarily determined by one's behavior, for it is almost always possible to interpret actions in more ways than one. Several studies found, for example, that youths could have homosexual relations on a regular basis without defining themselves as homosexual.[41] They were able to interpret their actions to themselves as motivated only by the need for quick cash or sexual release free from emotional entanglement. Another study noted that some men considered themselves to be homosexual even though they were married and restricted their sexual contacts to their wives; while having intercourse, they imagined their wives to be men.[42] Most psychiatric or psychological writings on homosexuality ignored these self-concepts and classified subjects on the basis of their overt behavior or an unconscious psychodynamic. The Kinsey scale, which places individuals on a continuum that runs from exclusively heterosexual to exclusively homosexual, likewise counts only sexual acts, ignoring the meanings those acts have to the actor or their relationship to the actor's identity.[43]

Sociologists' concern with self-identity led them to study the ways homosexual identities are constructed and maintained, usually in interaction with others who offer interpretations and evaluations of different possible identities. Seen sociologically, becoming homosexual was no longer a matter of having the wrong kind of parents, but of coming to see oneself in a particular way—a way that is not foreordained by sexual desires or behavior alone. It is not that sociologists viewed desires or behavior as entirely irrelevant to homosexual identities; it is only that they were proclaimed neither necessary nor sufficient.[44]

Sociologists interested in meanings generally prefer to study them through intensive interviews or by observing subjects as they go about their everyday routines. They hope in this way to learn their subjects' perspectives and to capture their social worlds. In the 1960s and 1970s, ethnographic work of this kind began to give us a picture of homosexuality, not as a medical or psychological condition, but as a component of a way of life with distinctive manners, customs, and institutions.[45]

---

[40]This is one of the major tenets of symbolic interactionism, an important school of social psychology (Blumer, 1969).

[41]Reiss (1962), Gerassi (1966), Humphreys (1970).

[42]Dank (1974).

[43]Robinson (1976:67).

[44]Plummer (1975), Berger (1983).

[45]The volume of published work is too great to permit comprehensive bibliographical cita-

Research of this kind can be voyeuristic ("look how weird these people are"), but more often it has had a humanizing effect. Instead of studying just one aspect of subjects' lives (such as their early childhoods)—an aspect that perhaps is not even terribly important to them—and from an alien perspective, this approach places an activity society regards as deviant in the context of an authentic social world whose logic and coherence becomes manifest, within which the activity takes its place as viable. It lets subjects speak with their own voices and furnishes them with audiences, inverting the traditional scientific procedure of putting deviant subjects under the microscope, turning them into objects to be classified, and producing discourses that tell supposedly objective truths about them to themselves and others.

The growing popularity of this style of research made it virtually inevitable that it would be adopted in studying homosexuality. At the same time, the proliferation and functional specialization of gay institutions, and the growing visibility of gay culture, made this kind of research easier. And as the stigma attached to homosexuality began to decline, so did sociologists' fears that they might be tainted by studying a suspect subject.

Much of the new historical work on homosexuality reflects similar sensibilities. In demonstrating the historical variability of the cognitive categories through which people think about sex, this research undermines the seeming naturalness and objectivity of our own. Almost inevitably it raises the question: if other times and places have been less repressive, why not ours? Inability to answer on rational grounds calls all dogmatic responses into question.

Teaching based on these new social-science perspectives—in college courses and in elementary and high-school sex-education classes—could hardly have become commonplace had not society already become somewhat more tolerant, though norms of professionalism and academic freedom also helped to protect instructors who taught ideas that ran counter to common prejudices. At the same time, exposure to these perspectives widens acceptance of homosexuality, reducing prejudice further. The two processes have amplified each other.

The magnitude of change should not be overestimated. Where restrictions were dropped, it was often in reluctant response to pressure. Formal change has not always meant greater liberalization in practice; Colorado

---

tion. The more important studies include Hooker (1956, 1965, 1967), Leznoff and Westley (1956), Achilles (1967), Hoffman (1968), Humphreys (1970), Dank (1971), Warren (1974), Weinberg and Williams (1974, 1975), Sweet (1975), Bell and Weinberg (1978), Delph (1978), Harry and Devall (1978), Read (1978), Moses (1979), Ponse (1979), Wolf (1979), Fitzgerald (1986). Most of this work has been American, but the approach has influenced writing on homosexuality as far away as Poland (Pietkiewicz, 1981).

gays were arrested just as often after state legislation criminalizing homosexual acts was repealed as before.[46] In some quarters, liberalization was
viewed with uneasiness or alarm and was fought bitterly. Polls show that
many people still regard homosexuality as immoral.[47]

Despite New York's large gay population, its city council—presumably
responding to constituents in the more conservative boroughs outside
Manhattan—repeatedly rejected antidiscrimination bills over a period of
years, even though they had the strong support of the mayor, before finally
adopting one in 1986. Voters have defeated gay-rights referenda in a number of cities: in Lincoln, Nebraska, and San Antonio, Texas, by margins as
large as 4 to 1.[48] When the Washington, D.C., city council adopted a new
sex-crime code decriminalizing consensual homosexual acts between consenting adults, Congress overturned the vote. In the 1984 elections, some
conservative candidates attacked their political opponents for favoring gay
rights or accepting contributions from gay organizations.[49] Following a 1983
federal-appeals-court ruling that gay and lesbian foreigners could not be
denied admission to the United States on account of their sexual orientation, the Reagan Justice Department ordered the Center for Disease Control to prevent them from entering by imposing a medical quarantee on
"self-professed homosexuals" on psychological grounds.[50]

Violence against homosexuals has claimed numerous lives over the past
decade, often with legal impunity. In 1976, when a gay college student was
beaten to death by teenagers in front of a Tucson bar, the judge imposed no
penalty and praised the teenagers' scholastic records. In the summer of
1984, three teenage boys beat and threw a young man of Bangor, Maine,
into a stream, where he drowned; the judge released the youths to the
custody of their parents.[51] Ongoing violence against gays in New York's
Central Park was highlighted by an incident in 1980 that left five victims
hospitalized. Later that year, a minister's son machine-gunned a gay bar in
Greenwich Village, killing two men.[52] Two years later, a team of New York
police insulted and injured patrons and employees of a gay bar in a raid
whose purpose has never been convincingly explained.[53]

---

[46] H. L. Ross (1976).

[47] Rueda (1982:6–11). As late as 1980, three-quarters of the respondents to NORC's General
Social Survey said they considered sexual relations between two adults of the same sex to be
always or almost always wrong (Singer and Cutler, 1984).

[48] Crawford (1980:152–53), *New York Times*, May 13, 1982, Sablatura (1985).

[49] Bush (1984), Ridgeway (1984). Similar tactics have been used against Labour candidates in
British elections (Marr, 1987).

[50] However, no effort to exclude hypocritical, self-denying homosexuals was called for.

[51] Cort and Carlevale (1984).

[52] Paul (1982).

[53] *New York Civil Liberties* 31 (November–December 1982), p. 4.

These were by no means isolated incidents. A National Gay Task Force survey of eight cities found that a fourth to a third of gay men had been assaulted or threatened with violence. The percentages for lesbians were lower, but still substantial.[54] In San Francisco, more than a hundred assaults were reported in a single three-month period of 1981. The gay organization, Community United Against Violence, reports that

> One man's body was discovered with his face literally beaten off. Another had his jaw smashed into eight pieces by a gang of youths taunting "you'll never suck another cock, faggot!" Another had most of his lower intestine removed after suffering severe stab wounds in the abdomen. Another was stabbed 27 times in the face and upper chest with a screwdriver, which leaves a very jagged scar. Another had both lungs punctured by stab wounds, and yet another had his aorta severed.[55]

Fundamentalist propaganda incites this violence. Anita Bryant, leader of the "Save Our Children" campaign, announced that "God puts homosexuals in the same category as murderers." A mass mailing from Reverend Jerry Falwell, head of the Moral Majority, called on readers to "Stop the Gays *dead* in their perverted tracks." Dean Wycoff of the Santa Clara branch of the Moral Majority stated on television that he believed "that homosexuality should be included with murder and other capital crimes so that the government that sits upon this land would be doing the executing." Episodes of violence jumped following this and an earlier television broadcast portraying gays in an unfavorable light.[56]

Religious groups have led efforts to block the expansion of gay rights. Opposition from the Orthodox rabbinate, elements of the Roman Catholic hierarchy, and the more conservative Protestant denominations has been especially firm. Because Orthodox Jews are geographically concentrated and relatively few in number, their political weight outside of New York is modest. The main opposition has come from the Christian right, which is primarily Protestant, and from elements of the Roman Catholic hierarchy. Major Protestant denominations still consider homosexual relations to be sinful, and refuse to ordain "active" homosexuals as ministers.[57] Fundamentalist evangelical organizations like the Moral Majority and Christian Voice propagandize against homosexuality.[58] Though some Roman Catholic

---

[54] Cort and Carlevale (1984).

[55] Wickliffe (1981), G. R. Edwards (1984:120).

[56] Wickliffe (1981), Paul (1982); Falwell's italics.

[57] G. R. Edwards (1984). *New York Native*, August 10, 1987, p. 4, quotes the president of the Unitarian Universalist Association as saying that, although his denomination ordains gay and lesbian ministers, congregations do not hire them.

[58] Jorstad (1981), Conway and Siegelman (1982).

bishops have denounced antigay discrimination, others resist legal efforts to end it.[59] The tough stand taken by Pope John Paul II on gay issues leaves little hope that significant liberalization will come during his reign.[60]

In survey research, respondents from the South, from small towns, and from rural areas, who are older, poorer, and less well-educated, are more likely to think homosexuality morally wrong and to oppose gay rights, but religion is a more powerful predictor than any other individual trait. Jews and those with no religious affiliation prove to be the most tolerant, followed by Catholics and members of liberal Protestant denominations. Evangelical Protestants are the most likely (88.7 percent) to think homosexuality immoral. Stronger religious commitment and more frequent church attendance are also associated with negative views of homosexuality.[61]

Conservative Christians also oppose abortion, pornography, premarital and extramarital sexual relations, divorce, equal rights for women, and sex education in school. They cite the Pauline epistles to the effect that women should learn in silence and submit to their husbands.[62] Family, sex, and gender issues are absolutely central to the religious right.[63]

Some of the Christian conservative teachings on gender and family issues derive directly from the Bible, but others do not. Much of their appeal can be understood in terms of the social position of adherents, who fall predominantly into the lower- and middle-income brackets. In one survey done in 1978–79, only 7.1 percent of Evangelical Protestants had an income of at least $25,000; in other denominations, the percentages ranged from

[59]Goldstein (1984). In New York, for example, John Cardinal O'Connor led the fight to defeat the gay-rights bill and has barred homophile organizations from meeting in Catholic churches. Other bishops have endorsed legislation to prohibit discrimination against gays in employment and housing. Georgetown University, a Catholic institution, went to court in an unsuccessful attempt to have the Washington, D.C., ordinance barring discrimination on the basis of sexual orientation to be an unconstitutional infringement on Roman Catholic religious beliefs. The university fought attempts of gay students to gain recognition as an official student organization (T. F. Murphy, 1987).

[60]The pope temporarily reduced the powers of Archbishop Hunthausen of Seattle for, among other things, tolerating a mass sponsored by Dignity, an organization of gay Catholics. In October of 1986 he sent a letter to the American bishops stating that a homosexual "inclination" was "a more or less strong tendency toward an intrinsic moral evil" and ordering the withdrawal of support for organizations seeking to "undermine" the teaching of the church on homosexuality (Reinhold, 1987). The letter referred to a "homosexual inclination" as an "objective moral disorder."

[61]Spitze and Huber (1983:201–6), Rueda (1982:8–9), J. D. Hunter (1983:85, 105).

[62]Jorstad (1981), Conway and Siegelman (1982), J. D. Hunter (1983:85, 103–5), J. Simpson (1983). The biblical passages are Eph. 5:22, 1 Cor. 11:3–13, 1 Tim. 2:11.

[63]According to Rev. Jerry Falwell, Moral Majority, Inc., which he headed, limited its program to four issues: defense of life, morality, the traditional family, and America (Fackre, 1982:107 n. 2).

15.8 to 23.1 percent.[64] Occupationally, they were predominantly skilled workers, laborers, and managers, or held lower-level white-collar jobs as clerks, sales personnel, etc. Far fewer had a profession than did members of other religious bodies. They were also not as well educated.

Family ties are especially important to these members of the "old middle class" and upper ranks of the working class. Children may go into a family business or find a job through family contacts. The family serves as a source of support in times of illness or unemployment. By contrast, family connections are less important to the careers of professionals or employees of large-scale bureaucratic organizations—the "new middle class."[65] Pension funds, investments, insurance, and geographical mobility lessen dependence of professionals and executives on their families of origin, even if they do not eliminate it altogether.[66] This is not entirely a matter of income. The owner of a small business may earn as much as a college professor, but his family is much more likely to be involved in his business than hers is in her teaching and research.[67]

This dependence makes preservation of the family especially important to women. Women of the old middle class are less likely to hold jobs and more likely to make being a wife and mother central to their identities. They have much less to gain from legal equality than working-class women or women of the new middle class. They lack the education and capital

[64] J. D. Hunter (1983:53–55). Spitze and Huber also found Protestant fundamentalists to have lower-than-average incomes in their study (personal communication), but this may not be true everywhere. A survey of the Dallas-Fort Worth metropolitan area in 1981 found that 61 percent of Moral Majority supporters had incomes of at least $30,000, compared to 53 percent of nonsupporters and 45 percent of those who were indifferent (Shupe and Stacey, 1983). However, in national direct-mail campaigns, average contributions to such conservative groups as Christian Voice and the antiabortion Life Amendment Political Action Committee are about half those to liberal groups like National Committee for an Effective Congress (Latus, 1983). It seems unlikely that this difference reflects weaker commitment to the cause. Luker (1984) found antiabortion activists to be less affluent than prochoice activists. It is worth keeping in mind, though, that not all Christian conservatives have low incomes. An earlier study found support for a Billy Graham crusade not in the lower economic ranks but among those who were solidly middle class, who had an "old middle class life-style, an individualistic nonintellectual, pietistic, familistic style, definitely at odds with the cosmopolitanism of corporate and intellectual elites . . . [which] cuts across horizontal status levels" (Clelland et al., 1974).

[65] The term is not entirely satisfactory, but has become conventional. Medicine and law, for example, are not new professions, but old; yet if what distinguishes the new from the old middle class is the importance of information and communication (Susman, 1985), these professionals have more in common with the new than with the old middle class.

[66] Oberschall (1984).

[67] That may be why income and occupational prestige are fairly weak predictors of attitudes toward homosexuality (Spitze and Huber, 1983:202, Shupe and Stacey, 1983).

needed to pursue lucrative careers. Should they have to get a job, their wages will be substantially lower than those of their husbands.[68]

For these reasons, the significance of homosexuality to Christian conservatives is not simply that the Bible forbids it. The Bible forbids much else that they ignore. It is that homosexuality is sex outside a family relationship between a man and woman playing distinct but complementary roles. It exemplifies promiscuity, extramarital affairs, and a repudiation of stereotypical gender roles, which are a direct threat to the viability of the way of life that depends on that family. Fear that the destruction of the family will mean the loss of nurturance, stable companionship, and commitment in personal relationships adds another dimension to the defense of the family.[69] In the case of homosexuality this threat may be more symbolic than genuine. But at a time when the conventional nuclear family is being jeopardized by women no longer willing to sacrifice careers and self-fulfillment for husbands and children, the loss of parental authority, escalating divorce rates, the destruction of neighborhoods, and economic pressures that force women to enter the paid labor force on unsatisfactory terms, the broader associations that homosexuality evokes loom large.[70]

Someone might conceivably hold to these views and still do nothing to impose them on others. Several factors, though, have moved conservative Christians into a more coercive posture. Oberschall points out that the stability of family ties is enhanced by shared moral beliefs. It is much easier

---

[68]Himmelstein's (1984) analysis of support for the Equal Rights Amendment, which attempted to make discrimination on the basis of sex unconstitutional, complicates this analysis only slightly. He finds that female opposition to the Equal Rights Amendment reflected a conception of women as vulnerable and dependent on men, regardless of whether the particular woman opposed to the amendment was herself vulnerable or dependent. Solidarity with other women led to a concern with the possible impact of the amendment on the entire class, not just on herself.

[69]Gordon and Hunter (1977).

[70]California State Senator John Briggs tried to appeal to these concerns in his infamous Proposition 6, brought before California voters in a referendum in 1978. The initiative began, "One of the most fundamental interests of the State is the establishment and preservation of the family unit. Consistent with this interest is the State's duty to protect its impressionable youth from influences which are antithetical to this vital interest. . . . This proscription [of employment to teachers] is essential since such activity and conduct undermines the state's interest in preserving and perpetuating the conjugal family unit." Writing in the *New York Times* while an antidiscrimination bill was before the New York City Council, Rabbi Yehuda Levin (1986), a candidate for mayor in 1985 on the Right to Life ticket, called the bill "a dangerous assault on our families and our values . . . which can only pave the way for the general breakdown of family values and moral responsibility." In Britain, one commentator wrote that "a number of well-organized and evil people and groups have, in effect, declared war on the institutions of marriage and the family. . . . It is time that the normal majority declared war in their turn, counter-attack and took the warfare into enemy territory" (P. Johnson, 1986).

to communicate one's convictions to children when they are reinforced, rather than undermined, by teachers, politicians, rock and film stars, and pornographic magazines. Children cannot easily be insulated from these influences without some coercive controls on public behavior.[71]

Much of the focus in referenda on gay rights has therefore been not on homosexual behavior in private (the target of sodomy statutes), but on public actions and words. Antihomosexual crusades of the past decade have devoted far less effort to recriminalizing sodomy where it has been decriminalized than to blocking gay-rights bills. Proposition 6, which California voters defeated in 1977, barred teachers of any sexual orientation from expressing themselves, in or outside the classroom, in ways that could be construed as favorable to homosexuality. This emphasis suggests that for conservatives the core concern is not protecting children from molestation (at the time of the initiative there had not been a single case of a teacher molesting a student homosexually in the state of California), but shielding them from the knowledge that homosexuality exists and that it is not incompatible with intelligence and respectability.

Something similar was at work in 1984 when Archbishop O'Connor of New York announced that the church did not discriminate against gays in hiring for its city-funded social-service programs, but that religious considerations prevented it from signing a statement to that effect. Evidently the sticking point was not employing gays, but acknowledging that the church did so. Under the contested antidiscrimination measure, the church would have to continue employing someone *publicly identified as gay*. Doing so would inevitably make it harder to convey to the faithful the church's teaching that homosexuality is sinful. If the sinner suffers no social penalty, many will assume that no one really cares very much about the sin. "Hate the sin, love the sinner" may be good theology, but it is not an easy principle to communicate.[72]

Not without justification, moral conservatives see the various sex and gender issues as linked; permissiveness about homosexuality therefore implies equal permissiveness on abortion, premarital and extramarital sex, pornography, and the role of women in society. Alarm about liberalization on one of these issues is consequently heightened by the perception that it carries implications for the others.[73] Antigay campaigns thus become in-

---

[71] Oberschall (1984).

[72] This logic makes it easier for the church to provide care to AIDS patients (whose illness can be interpreted as a punishment for violating natural or divine laws) than to act on behalf of healthy homosexuals.

[73] Thus the Church of Jesus Christ of Latter Day Saints officially opposed the Equal Rights Amendment because it would lead to "an increase in the practices of homosexual and lesbian activities" and "strike at the family" (J. T. Richardson, 1984).

vested with the anxieties and agendas associated with sexual permissiveness in all its manifestations. It is not just normative heterosexuality that they defend, but a whole way of life.[74]

Moral conservatism is, of course, nothing new; Protestant fundamentalism has been around for several generations.[75] Why has it mobilized around homosexuality (and other sex and gender issues) just now? There are several reasons. One is that, to a degree, religious conservatives have prospered in the post-World War II decades. In the aggregate they are not yet as affluent as the country as a whole; but the number of conservative blue-collar workers who have entered middle-level income brackets is substantial.[76] A minority of the conservatives have done quite well; after all, the sobriety favored by religious fundamentalism ought to be conducive to success in business. The financial resources and organizational skills this minority has acquired on the way up have facilitated political mobilization. The "old right," which has focused its attention primarily on economic and foreign policy, has lent support in the form of mailing lists, large donations, and strategic advice. As a result, the religious right has been able to raise funds and use the mass media with a sophistication it didn't have a generation ago.[77] Their greater competence, then, helps to explain why religious conservatives abandoned their earlier abstention from politics.

Second, it is only in the past two decades that sex has become a leading public issue. An estimated one or two million abortions were being performed illegally each year before the Supreme Court's 1973 decision in *Roe v. Wade* legalized abortion, but no one picketed or bombed abortionists' offices—a rather frequent happening in the last decade. The visibility of the clinics and public debates about government subsidies for abortions elicited counteraction. There were bars catering primarily to homosexual men and women before gay liberation—usually in areas of the city where they would attract little attention. Men found sexual partners in public restrooms or parks. But no one waged "Save Our Children" campaigns, as Anita Bryant has done. The gay movement, which politicized homosexual

[74] In accord with this claim, Tsai, Heller, and Chalfont (n.d.) find that, in a national survey of Protestants, affiliation with fundamentalist denominations and support for the Moral Majority political platform is highest among those who think that world affairs are deteriorating and public officials are uninterested in the problems of the average man. Several other recent social movements have been analyzed as efforts to defend a life-style, or set of cultural values, e.g., Page and Clelland (1978), Wallis and Bland (1979), Lorentzen (1980), Wood and Hughes (1984), Clarke (1987a, b).

[75] G. Marsden (1980).

[76] This nouveau middle-class tends to affiliate with conservative churches until its middle-class position is consolidated; then it switches to more moderate or liberal denominations (Glock and Stark, 1966:202; Streiker and Stroher, 1972:154; K. Phillips, 1982:21).

[77] Jorstad (1981:138–43), Conway and Siegelman (1982), Liebman (1983), Oberschall (1984).

desire, brought demonstrations, parades, radio and television appearances of gay and lesbian spokespersons, demands for the ordination of gays as ministers, the recognition of gay marriages, and legislation to outlaw discrimination. It denounced psychiatry for considering homosexuality pathological. Sensuous, amorous same-sex couples began appearing in public unashamed. The threat of these developments was not just homosexuality, but its validation. The conservative churches have welcomed repentant sinners who have given up their errant ways and returned to the heterosexual fold. It is gays who persist in asserting their normalcy that the fundamentalists cannot tolerate.

Antigay drives, like the campaigns against the Equal Rights Amendment, have received added impetus from status resentments. The radical and countercultural movements of the sixties challenged many taken-for-granted assumptions of white-middle-class life: racial segregation, the armed forces, marriage, monogamy, the value of education and hard work for upward social mobility. Highly respected public figures, including politicians and religious leaders, began to endorse the challenges. They denounced white racism, demonstrated against the war in Vietnam, advocated egalitarian marriages, endorsed abortion rights and gay rights.

For many Americans, adherence to conventional values and standards was a major component of their claim to respectability. The challenge to conventionality was therefore an implicit—and sometimes explicit—attack on this claim.[78] Every time a feminist argued for opening all-male occupations to women by describing full-time motherhood as mindless and boring, she denigrated full-time mothers. The activists who chanted "gay is twice as good as straight" denied straights their claim to being morally worthy for not being homosexual. People with other sources of self-regard could perhaps shrug off this denial. But to others, such as those whose material success has been limited, moral respectability has been psychologically important.[79] For many it may be the only basis for a claim to be a

[78]Streiker and Stroher (1972:148–49), R. L. Hunter (1983:116–17).

[79]In national surveys, support for Moral Majority positions has been lowest on the part of those who perceive their incomes to be better than average (Singer and Cutler, 1984). Sociologists have invoked "status discontent" to explain other American social movements whose goals involved coercion to morality. For example, Gusfield (1963) argued that the temperance movement was a small-town, middle-class response to a social status that was declining under the impact of the growing political power of immigrants concentrated in large cities and the growth of large industry. By gaining public endorsement of one of its cultural norms, the declining class sought to recover its earlier status. However, this account of Prohibition is no longer considered adequate (Paulson, 1973; N. Clark, 1976; Kyvig, 1979; Rorabough, 1979; Tyrrell, 1979; Humphries and Greenberg, 1981). Status discontent has also been criticized as an explanation of antipornography sentiment. Yet the skeptics do find that manual and lower white-collar workers are significantly more likely than persons in other occupations to oppose

worthy person. In campaigns against gay rights, "middle America" reasserts the moral value of its way of life. Prejudice against blacks on the part of poor-white southerners is commonly understood in the same way: it gives them someone to look down on.

This reassertion is aided and abetted by conservative politicians and religious leaders who publicly identify a "traditional" American or Judeo-Christian way of life and interpret departures from that alleged way as threats, attacks, or insults even when they are not so intended and would not necessarily be so interpreted spontaneously. Speaking to the publishers of the Presidential Biblical Scorecard in Dallas during the 1984 Republican party convention, President Ronald Reagan took a stand against civil-rights legislation to protect against job discrimination on the basis of sexual orientation:

> Society has always regarded marital love as a sacred expression of the bond between a man and a woman. In the Judeo-Christian tradition it is the means by which husband and wife participate with God in the creation of a new human life. . . . In part, the erosion of these values has given way to a celebration of forms of expression most reject. We will resist the efforts of some to obtain government endorsement of homosexuality.[80]

Endorsement is, of course, not at issue in antidiscrimination legislation. In a direct-mail letter distributed during the 1984 campaign, Reverend Falwell informed readers that

> In San Francisco we actually saw homosexuals sharing a public platform in Union Square with transvestites, Communists, Central American terrorists, punk rock anarchists, unionized prostitutes, people who would legalize marijuana, and other radicals. Perversion is open, public, and pervasive. The main streets are dominated by garish, hardcore theaters promoting homosex-

---

pornography (Wood and Hughes, 1984), even when other factors like age, sex, education, rural residence, and membership in a conservative Protestant denomination are taken into account. This is what status-discontent theory would lead us to expect. In any event, I am not arguing that status discontent based on membership in a declining social class is directly responsible for antigay activism. It was a challenge to normative heterosexual monogamy, along with other deeply cherished tenets of American "secular religion," such as patriotism, that gave rise to status discontent. I am suggesting that status discontent may be more intense in the working class and lower-middle class because it is there that familialism and patriotism have been held with particular tenacity, and because members of those classes have few other sources of social status with which to cushion loss of status from the normalization of homosexuality. For male teenagers, masculine status anxiety is another likely suspect (Greenberg, 1977).

[80] Quoted in the *Village Voice*, September 25, 1985.

ual pornography and live, nude, homosexual shows. Sado-masochistic "demonstrations" are carried out on stage. Men kiss, tongues entwined, openly in public. Other men wear women's clothing, makeup, and hair styles. Bathhouses, massage parlors, and leathershops are seen everywhere. City parks have become cesspools of perverted behavior. The smell of marijuana alarms the senses as one walks along sidewalks in front of stores like Macy's and Saks. . . . And you see, what they plan for you and your children is what makes them most dangerous!! . . . and they do have eyes on your children. Remember, since homosexuals cannot have children of their own, the only way for them to expand their ranks is to recruit your children and mine. . . . It is time to take a stand. . . . With your help I will launch a "truth campaign" to counter the homosexual attack on America.[81]

Falwell links the unimaginable sinfulness of Babylon, communism, and implicitly, the Democratic party (which held its convention in San Francisco) with a conspiracy against children and an attack on America. His message warns of all the evils his readers might expect to see if gay rights were to be achieved in their hometowns. To someone living in San Francisco, his prurient prose would probably be laughable, but for readers who live in small towns and in rural states it could well frame debates over public policy in relation to homosexuality.

LOOKING AHEAD

In many respects, gay liberation has made advances over the past two decades far beyond those that could have been foreseen by the liberal, assimilationist leadership of the previous generation. These advances may have led some activists to hope that prejudice against homosexuality would soon disappear and that homosexuality would simply be as accepted as heterosexuality is. This is most unlikely. Our analysis has highlighted two factors as critical to the long-term persistence of antihomosexual prejudice: bureaucracies and the social pressures faced by the lower-middle-class. These are not likely to change very much in the short run.[82]

The economic and social pressures facing the lower-middle-class are not

---

[81] *Village Voice*, September 25, 1985, p. 33.

[82] To single out these two factors is not to denigrate the short-term consequences of religious and psychiatric ideologies that oppose the normalization of homosexuality. The thrust of my analysis, though, is that the appeal and some of the content of these ideologies have much to do with the structural factors highlighted in the text. The movements for change within the more liberal Christian denominations and among some psychiatrists and psychologists show that there is room for flexibility when it is called for.

an inevitable feature of modern civilization. Were these pressures to be reduced, we might not be seeing the kind of reactionary movements that have been active in the United States and England in recent years. Holland and Scandinavia, whose welfare-state systems are more generous than those of America and Britain, are less frightened of homosexuality. However, short-term prospects for an expanded welfare state and the progressive redistribution of income (not to speak of socialism) in the United States and Great Britain are obviously poor. Both have been headed in recent years by conservatives committed to cutting back the welfare state. Long-term predictions are less easily made; they hinge on political developments that cannot be easily anticipated.

Something so central to Western civilization as bureaucracy could hardly be eliminated short of destroying the entire civilization. Yet its effects may be mitigated somewhat by the weakening of gender differences in society. To the extent that someone's sex is less important in work, in politics, in social life, it will have less significance in sexual choice as well. The gender stereotyping that now influences perceptions of homosexuality will decline. If men involve themselves more in raising children, they may become more nurturant and less anxious at the display of affection between persons of the same sex.[83] However, even if economic pressures and career aspirations continue to bring women into the labor market, the sexual segregation of the workplace will prove recalcitrant to feminist attacks in major sectors of the economy; it may diminish, but it is not likely to disappear altogether. Work-related constraints will stand in the way of the genuine sharing of child-care for most parents.

Despite major obstacles, pressure from the gay movement has won important victories in the past. This pressure will continue. One source of gay power has been the vote. An openly lesbian candidate was elected to the Massachusetts state legislature as early as 1974. Since then, gays have been elected to public office in several other cities and states and have held major political appointments, such as judgships.[84] Gay activists spearheaded the referendum that made West Hollywood an independent city. Gay groups have raised funds for sympathetic candidates and worked to turn out votes on election day; in return, politicians have courted gay constituencies, rewarding support with appointments and backing for progay legislation.[85]

[83] Women proved to be more opposed to the Briggs Initiative in California than men, presumably because they were less concerned with upholding sex stereotypes in the raising of their children (Hollibaugh, 1979).

[84] A national gay conference of gay politicians held in West Hollywood in 1985 drew 170 openly gay officeholders or potential officeseekers, including 20 elected officials at the city-council level or higher and many appointed officials (Yoshihashi, 1985).

[85] Altman (1982a, b), Fourt and Riddiough (1982). In 1982, the Human Rights Campaign

The recent proliferation of gay organizations facilitates the mobilization of these constituencies.

The approval in June 1984 by the United States Conference of Mayors of a resolution calling for the legal protection of gay and lesbian rights at all levels of government is one sign of the success of this strategy. The passage of antidiscrimination legislation or the issuing of executive orders barring some forms of discrimination in seventy-six cities, counties, or states as of 1986 is another.[86] Money is another source of gay power. Manufacturers and retailers, aware that gay men have disposable income, have begun to target advertisements to gay consumers.[87] With women's incomes substantially below men's, this development does relatively little to help lesbians.

Gay political and financial strength is concentrated in the larger cities (precisely to what degree we do not know), and even there it may be confined to certain electoral districts. In much of America, there is no organized gay presence to oppose antigay policies or sentiments. The gay movement has been strong enough to prevent major setbacks, such as the Briggs initiative, but not powerful enough to win major new victories. Moreover, individual attitudes are harder to change than public policies, which can be made by a small number of officeholders. A top-level administrator was able to initiate a program to recruit gays to the San Francisco Police Department, but he was not able to protect them from harassment by their fellow officers.[88]

Educational campaigns waged by the gay movement have already reduced prejudice, and these will certainly continue. On the other hand, educational and propaganda efforts may already have reached most of those who are likely to be receptive to them. A Bible-belt preacher is unlikely to read gay literature or to be swayed by it if he does. The gradual replacement of older by younger and less prejudiced cohorts of the population will make a modest difference, but only over a period of years.

Fund, devoted to the advancement of gay rights, raised $609,000 and contributed to more than a hundred congressional campaigns. In 1986, it raised $1.4 million and ranked 39th among 4,586 political-action committees. Gay support has been credited with the electoral victory of Marion S. Barry, Jr., who was an underdog when he ran for mayor of Washington, D.C. in 1978, and with the defeat in 1982 of Sheriff Duane Lowe of Sacramento after he announced that he would not hire gays as deputy sheriffs (Clendinen, 1983; T. Morgan, 1987).

[86] *New York Times*, September 2, 1984.

[87] Stabiner (1982), Hadley-Garcia (1983). One indication of this power is the advertisement placed in the April 1979 issue of the *Advocate*, a gay newspaper with national distribution, by Joseph Coors of Coors Brewery. In the face of a threatened boycott of Coors Beer provoked by allegations of discrimination against gays in hiring, the advertisement advised readers that the brewery did not discriminate on the basis of sexual preference and had never supported Anita Bryant or the Briggs Initiative (Crawford, 1980:215–16).

[88] Kane (1985).

Radical calls for the eradication of exclusive heterosexuality, heard often in the early days of gay liberation, have largely been forgotten. As they did not call on anyone to do anything in particular, they inevitably fell to the wayside in favor of more modest requests of the sort that groups fighting discrimination typically make: the elimination of pejorative newspaper reporting and stereotyping on television, a stop to police harassment, an end to discrimination on the part of government agencies and private businesses, funding for research and social welfare. These are the sorts of demands that concerted pressure can achieve, and since many cost little, they can be granted easily where constituency pressure against them is not too strong. The civil-rights/black-power movement served as a model for a cooptive response to the gay movement: gays could be assimilated to the category of an ethnic minority or interest group.[89] It is with such representation that gays now look to the future.

The AIDS epidemic complicates the future of homosexuality in a number of ways.[90] In the short run it has probably not changed the way most people think about homosexuality. In a Gallup Poll of 1,008 adults taken in November 1985, 59 percent said AIDS had not changed their attitudes toward homosexuals. The number of individuals who think homosexual relations between consenting adults should be legal is about the same now as it was before AIDS became the subject of public concern.[91] In New York City, the passage of an antidiscrimination statute in 1986, after fifteen years of unsuccessful efforts to gain adoption of earlier civil-rights bills, may have reflected sympathy for AIDS patients. On the other hand, the same Gallup Poll found that more than a third of Americans say they have a less favorable attitude toward homosexuals because of AIDS.[92]

AIDS has provided a new focal point for antigay diatribes. Right-wing publicist Patrick J. Buchanan wrote in the *New York Post* that homosexuals "have declared war upon nature, and now nature is exacting an awful retribution."[93] James Anderton, the chief constable of Greater Manchester, in England, attributed the spread of AIDS to "degenerate conduct" in the form of "obnoxious sexual practices" and described gays as "swirling around in a human cesspit of their own making." Lady Saltoun, a member

[89] Altman (1982a, b), Paul (1982), Escoffier (1985), S. Epstein (1987).

[90] AIDS is an acronym for Acquired Immune Deficiency Syndrome. It destroys the immune system, leaving its victim unable to fight infections. At this writing the condition is invariably fatal. In Europe and the United States its victims have been primarily homosexual or bisexual men, their female sexual partners, hemophiliacs, and narcotics users who share needles. In parts of Africa it has struck heterosexuals more extensively.

[91] Shipp (1986).

[92] Shipp (1986).

[93] May 24, 1983, quoted in J. Weeks (1985:48).

of the House of Lords, warned that it was not possible "to get away from the wrath of God."[94] Newspaper columnists sometimes refer to hemophiliacs and infants born to AIDS-infected mothers as the "innocent" victims, implying a contrast with other victims who are, apparently, guilty (of what?). Steady exposure to such a tendentious framing of the AIDS crisis in the mass media has affected attitudes and stimulated assaults against gay men and, in some parts of the country has reduced support for gay rights. The 1985 defeat of a homosexual-rights bill in the Massachusetts House of Representatives, reversing a vote for passage two years earlier, was widely attributed to the AIDS issue.[95]

The prevention of AIDS has provided a new rationale for shutting down gay bathhouses and for discriminating against gay patients in housing, employment, education, and medical care. Fear of contagion, even if irrational—the virus that causes AIDS is not transmitted by casual contact—may be leading some who are unprejudiced to try to isolate those who have been exposed to the AIDS virus, e.g., by barring them from school classrooms. The inimitable William J. Buckley, Jr., has proposed tattooing anyone found to have been exposed to the virus on the arms and buttocks.[96] Theresa Crenshaw, a San Diego sex therapist and member of the Presidential Commission on AIDS, has favored quarantines. In an attempt to shut the barn door after the horse is already in, Mayor Edward Koch of New York has called for the mandatory testing of all foreign visitors to the United States.

Practical considerations make most of these proposals unfeasible. Responsible politicians and office holders, along with gay leaders, have concluded that educational campaigns are a more promising strategy for stopping the spread of AIDS. Realizing that calls for sexual abstinence may not be heeded, yet fearful of the costs of a major medical catastrophe to the public purse, government officials have sought to encourage the adoption of "safe sex" techniques. The result has been an unusually frank public recognition of sexual practices and preferences that in the past could not easily be discussed at all. A generation ago, the sale of contraceptives was still illegal in some states; now a publication of the U.S. government, issued by an administration that has been morally conservative, recommends the use of condoms during vaginal or anal intercourse.[97] New York City public high schools teach students how to use them, and the Board of Education

[94] M. Jones (1986).

[95] *New York Times*, September 24, 1985.

[96] Buckley (1986).

[97] Koop (1986:17), Gross (1987). In England, the Department of Health and Social Security mailed an information leaflet, *Aids: Don't Die of Ignorance*, to every household in the U.K.

is considering distributing them to pupils free. This isn't being done because educators want to encourage teenage sexual activity; it is because they know it goes on and can no longer be ignored or repressed. For practical reasons, homosexuality now has to be accommodated, even by those who would prefer to do otherwise.[98]

To prevent the extensive spread of AIDS to the heterosexual population, the official literature has been targeted to the population at large, not just to gays. The effect has been to make many heterosexuals fearful of being infected—in most instances to a degree not warranted by the very small number of cases transmitted heterosexually. Since AIDS was initially identified in the West as a "gay plague," some resentment against gays has developed on the part of heterosexuals who must now take steps to avoid it. This fear and resentment have figured in violence against gays.

In the larger American cities, some segments of the gay population have been decimated by AIDS. Young men beginning to identify themselves as gay must now come to grips with the necessity of taking precautions—perhaps for the rest of their lives, until a vaccine or cure is found—against a contagious, lethal disease and the knowledge that others may suspect them of harboring it. These circumstances must make it more difficult to think of one's homosexuality in positive terms. We may see men trying to become heterosexual to avoid the risk of AIDS. Collectively, gays have met the AIDS crisis by publicizing techniques for safe sex, cutting back on promiscuity, developing support networks, raising funds for research and treatment, and combating AIDS-related repression. These efforts have generated a stronger sense of social cohesion even as they have channeled political efforts away from some of the gay movement's earlier foci.

Scholars are not likely to come to an agreement anytime soon about the causes of sexual orientation, or its nature. Various disciplines look at sexuality in different ways and rarely confront each other's ideas. In many cases they seem to be altogether unaware of them. Biologists who view most traits as inherited, and psychologists who think sexual preferences are largely determined in early childhood, may pay little attention to the finding that many gay people have had extensive heterosexual experience, and that a fair number of straights have had some homosexual experiences. Sociologists are just as unlikely to know about, or take seriously, research on

[98] There has been some opposition to this accommodation. In both England and the United States, some religious leaders have objected to AIDS-prevention propaganda that emphasizes contraceptive devices rather than abstinence. Right-wing Republican Senator Jesse Helms has introduced federal legislation barring the Centers for Disease Control from financing AIDS education that directly or indirectly promotes or encourages homosexuality. And in Duval County, Florida, teachers have been told that in teaching about AIDS they may not tell students how it is transmitted (*New York Native*, October 12, 1987).

hormones or family structure. Often they are not even cognizant of the journals in which such research is published.

College students, exposed to sociological ideas in their courses, may be influenced by them, but they are also exposed to other, competing ideas. For every lesbian separatist arguing that lesbianism is a political choice that carries feminism to its logical conclusion, there is someone else saying, "I was born that way." Short of definitive evidence, which no theory has thus far received, the disagreement is likely to continue. Cognitive and normative pluralism will persist for the indefinite future.

Epilogue:
Under the Sign
of Sociology

Even though *The Construction of Homosexuality* makes extensive use of historical sources, it is a sociology, not a history. In the conventional division of scholarly labor, the historian's task is to recover the past. In practice, this usually means reconstructing events and ideas from a single region or society in a delimited time frame: Elizabethan England, Renaissance Florence, Jacksonian America. In contrast, the sociologist tries to identify patterns and processes, and to determine their causes and effects. The focus shifts from the unique to the general, from the concrete to the abstract, from the irregular and accidental to the lawlike. It is a focus that calls for comparisons: between classes and people, societies, time periods, systems of meanings.

In practice, this neat division of labor often breaks down. The sociologist interested in change naturally turns to historians for data; if they cannot provide them, he may have to turn historian himself. The demands of the narrative more or less force historians to offer explanations of why history turned out as it did. Some do this by borrowing explanations from sociology and anthropology—sometimes even after they have become discredited in those fields; others improvise ad hoc accounts, or recycle the explanations current in the period they study.

The historian's approach has both strengths and weaknesses; so does the sociologist's. By studying a particular period intensively, a historian is able to learn a great deal about it. This intimate knowledge can suggest theoretical explanations. It immunizes against glib armchair theorizing and casual overgeneralization. These are pitfalls for sociologists, who may know too little about other societies or periods in history to recognize that their explanations make little sense. On the other hand, a historian who studies only a single society or period has no way of verifying that an explanation holds up across the board. Numerous explanations for institutionalized homosexuality, or intolerance of it, devised in relation to a single society, fail to survive the test of comparison.

482   Sociology methodology textbooks dictate a procedure that differs radi-

cally from the historians'. It begins with the formulation of a theory that postulates relationships among a set of variables. A representative sample of units is selected for analysis; these may be people, or cities, or events—such as elections or riots. The variables are measured for each unit in the sample. Statistical tests are then used to determine whether a pattern predicted on the basis of theory is found. If not, the theory is rejected.

Some types of research permit these procedures to be carried out to the letter. But in studying long-term historical change, many obstacles arise. As was frequently true in this study, critical data may be missing and unrecoverable. Often they are qualitative and do not readily lend themselves to quantitative manipulation. The appropriate unit of analysis may be unclear. Most statistical theory assumes that individual observations are independent, but in practice that may not always be true. Cultural transmission virtually guarantees that a society's beliefs and practices are influenced by its past. Laws and religious doctrines—of particular interest in this study—are especially slow to change. Nor do influences stop at national borders. Christian missionaries have carried the teachings of their religion to the farthest corners of the earth. Napoleon's army brought the French Revolution's repeal of criminal legislation against homosexuality to much of Europe. The British imposed their criminal legislation against male homosexuality on their colonies, where it has frequently survived decolonization. All these factors tend to reduce the number of truly independent observations, making the use of conventional multivariate statistical techniques virtually impossible. Under these circumstances, a qualitative comparison of different societies and periods may prove more instructive than a quantitative analysis.

Where little is known about a subject, the textbook procedure is particularly unhelpful in the way it posits the relationship between theory and data. It says nothing about how a theory is to be constructed. The process is simply assumed to have been accomplished before data are collected, much less examined. Theorizing, then, is purely a matter of logical thought, requiring no prior knowledge of a subject. Few sociologists try that approach, because the limitations of the human mind make it difficult to carry out. There are more phenomena under the sun than the uninformed mind ever dreamed.

In practice, theorizing usually begins when something puzzling is encountered. In attempting to explore or test an initial explanation, the theorist may be forced by unanticipated findings to reject or revise it, but equally he or she may discover that the original question was not well formulated. The present study began with the goal of understanding variability in attitudes toward homosexuality. Why were some people tolerant and others highly intolerant? How had Western civilization come to be so repressive? These questions implicitly assumed that homosexuality is entirely presocial, a biological *given*, constant in different periods of history and in different societies. Being the same everywhere, one could simply see how attitudes toward it changed as society changed.

An examination of what was known about homosexuality in different societies quickly shattered this preconception. It became clear that sexual practices and the ways they are socially organized vary greatly from one society to another and that the conceptual categories through which people think about sex are also variable. Homosexuality is not a conceptual category everywhere. To us, it connotes a symmetry between male-male and female-female relationships and makes no distinction between roles within a relationship. It says nothing about the relative ages or genders of the partners. When used to characterize individuals, it implies that erotic attraction originates in a relatively stable, more or less exclusive attribute of the individual. Usually it connotes an exclusive orientation: the homosexual is not also heterosexual; the heterosexual not also homosexual.

Most non-Western societies make few of these assumptions. Distinctions of age, gender, and social status loom larger. The sexes are not necessarily conceived symmetrically. Much the same can be said of earlier periods of Western history. In medieval Catholic doctrine, the sex of one's partner was not as important as whether the sexual contact was potentially procreative. Discovering that this was so shifted the focus of the study to the ways same-sex relationships are conceived, as well as the social responses that accompany these perceptions.

The notion that the categories through which we think are socially constituted has been an important element in certain strands of twentieth-century European philosophy and integral to recent work in the history of science.[1] This insight was taken up by "young Turks" in the sociology of deviance in the 1960s,[2] but was late in reaching sociologists who study sex. As late as 1976, Jonathan Katz could write of berdaches as "gay American Indians," and two years later, Louis Crompton was to characterize the persecution of homosexuality as "gay genocide from Leviticus to the Holocaust."[3] Both failed to grasp that the connotations of "gay," which include a collective, political consciousness, might be inapplicable to American Indian cultures, or the Hebrews in biblical times.

Today, most scholars who carry out historical or cross-cultural studies of homosexuality accept the constructivist axiom that propositions concern-

---

[1] T. S. Kuhn (1962), Schutz (1967), Collins (1981), Law and Lodge (1984).

[2] J. D. Douglas (1970), Schur (1971, 1979, 1980), Scott and Douglas (1972).

[3] J. N. Katz (1976), Crompton (1978). Both authors have been much more sensitive to the historically specific nuances of terminology in their more recent works.

ing sexual acts and actors inevitably make use of conceptual categories that distinguish some acts and actors from others. They also accept the claim that these categories are culturally specific. Nonetheless, the constructivist position has recently come in for criticism from "essentialists," who see greater continuity between earlier historical periods and our own.[4] Some premodern societies, they point out, did recognize specialized, even exclusive, sexual propensities. While conceding that there may have been some changes in the social organization of same-sex sexual relations over time, and in the self-concepts of those who participated in such relations, they see enough similarity to the present to warrant the use of terms like "homosexual" or "gay" even when they are, strictly speaking, anachronistic. Adherents of this position hold that homosexual behavior is a manifestation of some inner essence, perhaps biological or psychological, is relatively stable over time, and characteristic of a distinct minority of the population.

To date, debates among adherents of these positions have failed to recognize that social constructionism entails a number of distinct claims, whose validity must be assessed individually. The most vulnerable claim is that the notion of the homosexual as a distinct "species" originated only about a hundred years ago, an invention of the medical profession or the product of capitalist urbanization.[5] The materials presented in the preceding several chapters make abundantly clear that the world was neither conceptually nor behaviorally polymorphously perverse prior to the Industrial Revolution. Though distinctions between homosexual and heterosexual sodomy were not usual in the Middle Ages or Renaissance, sometimes they were made; for example, inchastity contrary to nature between two men, or two women, or with a beast was forbidden on pain of death by fire in the influential *Constitutio Criminalis Carolina* promulgated for the Holy Roman Empire under Charles V in 1532; unnatural relations between a man and a woman were not mentioned.[6]

Physiological explanations for homosexual desire or distinct homosexual roles have a long pedigree, dating back to the world of classical antiquity. Psychological explanations are not exactly new either: one of the Dutch

---

[4]The position I am labeling as "essentialist" is an ideal type. Social constructionism has been criticized from a number of directions; not all critics would necessarily endorse every argument mentioned here. For representative critiques, see Boswell (1982/83), Dynes (1985d, 1987b), Whitam and Mathy (1985).

[5]For representative examples, see J. Weeks (1977a:25–32, 1980), Foucault (1980), Mort (1980), D'Emilio (1983a, b), J. N. Katz (1983:147–74), Hansen (1985), Adam (1985b, 1987a), Kinsman (1987).

[6]Art. 116. The same prohibition had appeared earlier in article 141 of the *Bamberger Halsgerichtsordnung* of 1507 (Kohler and Scheel, 1968a, 1968b:1.62, 2.56, 3.43).

men arrested for homosexual sodomy in 1730 attributed his inclinations to prenatal influences on his mother.[7] As is obvious from the evidence presented in chapter 7, physicians did not invent the notion of an essential homosexuality. It was a product of the urban male-homosexual networks and subcultures that had developed in European cities well before the late nineteenth century. The participants in those subcultures contributed actively to the development of what eventually came to be called a "medical" conception of homosexuality. Foucault, who held a chair in the history of ideas, assumed too readily that intellectuals are the sole repository of conceptual invention and simply imposed a new hegemonic discourse on passive recipients.

Still, those early writings that understood homosexual desire as a manifestation of a distinct and stable personal trait did not express the predominant views of their day, and it would be misleading to contend that modern science, medicine, and psychology contributed nothing new to the conceptualization of sexuality. Social constructionists have been on solid ground in stressing the historical variability of conceptions of homosexuality, even if they have been mistaken about when changes occurred.

To say this is not to say that every culture is totally unique in the way it conceives of homosexuality. To take one example, the gender-crosser who engages in homosexual relations appears as a distinctive role in many cultures. Though the hijra's place in modern India is not exactly the same as that of the berdache among North American Indians, I believe that each would recognize the other as someone very much like himself, in the same way that members of two Christian denominations recognize their common religious heritage, despite doctrinal or liturgical differences. That a berdache who would similarly recognize himself in a Melanesian inseminator or a modern gay liberationist seems far more doubtful. In orienting us to the study of these culturally specific roles, systems of classification, and explanatory schemes, social constructionism opens the door to lines of investigation not even imagined a short time ago.

Some critics have accused social constructivists of exaggerating the power of society to shape sexuality. The presocial urges of the body, such as are postulated in biological and psychoanalytic writings on sexuality, are treated in social-constructionist writings as more or less a myth. In the absence of a concept of exclusive homosexuality, the premodern world, Foucault argues, had no such critter. It was the production and dissemina-

---

[7]Meer (1985). His father was away from home much of the time his mother was pregnant. The defendant said his father's absence caused his mother to long for a man so intensely that her longing was transmitted to him *in utero*. As a result he, too, ended up desiring men. An early version of the "distant father" thesis.

tion of a medical discourse in the recent past that gave birth not just to the *concept* of a homosexual person, but also to homosexuals themselves, and at the same time, to their antitwins, heterosexual persons. In the beginning was the word!

The years some homosexuals spend trying without success to conform to conventional expectations regarding gender and sexual orientation tell against the most extreme claims of sexual plasticity.[8] However, in the absence of any evidence linking the peculiar sexual practices of Melanesia with genetic difference, it is reasonable to suppose that if a bunch of Melanesian infants were to be transported in infancy to the United States and adopted, few would seek out the pederastic relationships into which they are inducted in New Guinea, or take younger homosexual partners when they reached maturity. Similarly, American children raised in New Guinea would accommodate themselves to the Melanesian practices. Where social definitions of appropriate and inappropriate behavior are clear and consistent, with positive sanctions for conformity and negative ones for nonconformity, virtually everyone will conform irrespective of genetic inheritance and, to a considerable extent, irrespective of personal psychodynamics.[9] If it is assumed that a young *eromenes* will grow up to become an *erastes* and will also marry, then it is likely he will do so.

It is plausible that in a world where sexual orientation is widely thought to be highly stable, a young person may be prone to strive for consistency in choice of partners by seeking out those who fit his or her subjective sexual orientation and suppressing desires incongruent with it.[10] He or she may avoid erotically tinged settings where inappropriate partners might be

[8] Years ago, as the labeling perspective in deviance theory was being formulated, some of its more extreme proponents argued that casual involvement in deviant behavior was extremely widespread, but usually quite transient. Only those who were singled out by the authorities, labeled as deviant, and punished or treated entered into careers of sustained and systematic deviance. Critics pointed out that being labeled was neither necessary nor sufficient to produce a deviant career. Although there is a great deal of transient, youthful homosexual activity, closeted homosexuals can engage in homosexual relations on a long-term basis without ever being labeled as such by others (Mankoff, 1971). More recent work within the labeling tradition recognizes that individuals and groups may self-label, reject labels imputed by others, and negotiate over which labels should be applied (e.g., Matza, 1969; Rogers and Buffalo, 1974; Rotenberg, 1974).

[9] Uniformity in child-rearing practices will, of course, tend to reduce variability in personal psychodynamics and contribute to behavioral uniformity. Even in a tribal society, however, this uniformity cannot be guaranteed (Stoller and Herdt, 1985).

[10] Many people report having feelings that are inconsistent with their self-defined sexual orientation at one time or another, even if they do not act on these feelings (Bell and Weinberg, 1978:56–59, 290). Surveys probably underestimate this phenomenon, because the interpretation of feelings as erotic may itself be governed by the prevailing social belief that erotic choices are exclusive and by our tendency to forget feelings we think we shouldn't have had.

expected. The erotic alternatives someone considers may be influenced by his or her knowledge of what is possible, and whether it can be attained at reasonable cost.[11] Coming to define oneself as a homosexual—a process that includes learning sets of beliefs about what homosexuals are like—may not be necessary for one to engage consistently in homosexual relations and to abstain from heterosexual ones, but it does help.[12]

The essentialist claim that homosexuality is, or can be, constitutional, would not be controversial if the attributes presumed to give rise to it could be observed directly. Of course, they cannot; they must be inferred. When we observe that someone is consistently attracted erotically or romantically to persons of the same sex, over a long period of time, under conditions where opposite-sex partners are available, the imputation is a reasonable one, even if not wholly certain.[13] Conversely, when we find someone whose attraction to same-sex partners ends soon after long-term deprivation of heterosexual opportunities, we may think it more likely that the same-sex interest was produced by the environment and is not constitutional.

To say that inner essences cannot be observed directly, and that proof of their existence is difficult, is by no means to say that they don't exist; some proponents of social constructionism have been remiss in suggesting otherwise. It is generally true in the sciences that essences are not observed di-

---

[11]For example, one woman who became a lesbian as a mature adult tells of marrying when she was sixteen to get away from home. "I wasn't in love with the man. There was no romance involved, it was just a way out. . . . I knew that my marriage was hell, but I just assumed that was the way it was supposed to be, so I just accepted it. I didn't even hear the word *lesbian* until I was thirty-two and had four children. My husband was the first one to use the word with me. He said he thought I was one! I gave it some thought and decided to find out" (S. G. Lewis, 1979:20).

[12]Plummer (1981b), T. Weinberg (1983), Whisman (1986). Defining oneself as a homosexual or a heterosexual seems to have a potent effect on the choice of subsequent sexual partners. It does not follow that all persons could change their sexual orientation at will by mentally redefining themselves.

[13]To see that certainty is not possible consider a woman whose "essence" is perfect bisexuality; she is equally disposed to desire men and women, with her response to particular males and females dictated by traits possessed by some members of each sex, but not all. Purely by chance she might find herself attracted to a string of males in succession, or a string of females. In the first instance we would be inclined to impute heterosexuality; in the second, homosexuality. She would, in fact, draw the same conclusions about herself. The longer the unbroken string, the less likely it could arise by chance for someone who is indeed constitutionally bisexual, provided she encounters males and females in roughly equal numbers. But even if the unbroken string is very long, the eventuality is not impossible, merely highly improbable. Consequently, certainty can never be achieved on the basis of experienced sexual behavior or attraction alone. Every imputation must be treated as provisional. The possibility that someone's "essence" can change makes certainty even less possible.

rectly, but imputed to entities on the basis of their behavior. Newton's postulate that objects have a gravitational mass equal to its inertial mass achieved wide acceptance because it helps to organize observations of the trajectories of material bodies in motion. Sexual orientation is, in this respect, no different. Moreover, most of the evidence collected by sociologists and social anthropologists is inconclusive as far as questions of the etiology of an individual's sexual preferences or orientation are concerned. Cross-cultural variation in sexual practices is equally consistent with cultural and genetic determination.[14]

In the natural sciences, some philosophers have found the constructivist position unsettling because it seems to imply a radical epistemological relativism, in which any set of concepts or theories is just as good as any other.[15] Foucault seemed to endorse this relativism when he spoke at New York University some years ago. A questioner asked him whether he wasn't discouraged by his study of the history of sexuality. With the weight of centuries of sexually repressive thinking bearing down on us, how could we ever free ourselves? Foucault answered that his thinking made him optimistic: what was thought one way can be thought another. By revealing that ideas about sex were human creations, he said, he hoped to neutralize their power and pave the way for emancipation. He seemed to believe that ideas about sex are altogether unconstrained by the objective conditions of the society that produces them or of the body, so that emancipatory ideas could simply be substituted for repressive ones.

This seems wrong on several counts. Metaphors for sexual behavior, though certainly not uniquely determined by the behaviors to which they refer, cannot be totally idiosyncratic if they are to be meaningful. Mostly they are drawn from the familiar.[16] In various combinations, conceptions of homosexuality revolve around gender, voluntarism, internal vs. external

[14] That is because the human population need not be homogeneous with respect to the relevant genes. Long-term isolation of a population in a distinct ecological niche could lead to selection on the basis of factors not selected for elsewhere. However, if sexual practices change rapidly in response to a people's life circumstances (e.g., conversion to Christianity, or an end to warfare between villages), a genetic explanation is excluded. The development of heterosexual interests in adulthood on the part of New Guinea pederasts cannot be reconciled with a highly stable, exclusive homosexual orientation transmitted genetically with little possibility of later social influence.

[15] Collins (1981) suggests as much when he asserts that the natural world has "a small or non-existent role in the construction of scientific knowledge." Thomas S. Kuhn's (1962) contention that cognitive change in science occurs through successive, mutually unintelligible paradigms has been interpreted as an endorsement of this position, though he himself has tried to distance himself from it.

[16] And they occur in predictable combinations (J. Weeks, 1981b; S. O. Murray, 1984:19–20).

determination, and normative notions such as sin and disease. The thrust of the program that has inspired the present analysis has been that these combinations stem from identifiable features of the societies in which they are found.[17] It is not by chance, then, that medical conceptions of homosexuality became influential in nineteenth-century Europe and not in the villages of New Guinea, or that transgenerational male homosexuality became institutionalized in Melanesia and not in modern Europe. To my knowledge, no gay liberationist has proposed that contemporary Americans adopt the Melanesian pattern, or urged the substitution of ritual cult prostitution for Sunday-morning church services. The belief systems that supported those homosexual practices cannot be sustained in the modern Western world. The current adoption of prohibited contraceptive methods by many Roman Catholics despite the church's institutional commitment to perpetuate their prohibition testifies to the tendency of ideas to erode when the conditions required to sustain them no longer exist.

It has long been recognized in the sciences that, even if classification schemes are not wholly arbitrary, they are not totally determined by the phenomena they attempt to classify.[18] We group together in a single class or category entities that seem similar, even if not identical, because we think the differences within the classes less significant than those between. Complex entities differ in a great many ways, and in practice it is necessary to choose which criteria are important. For example, biologists classify a whale as a mammal rather than a fish because they consider being warmblooded and bearing young alive to be more important than being aquatic.[19]

[17] In this respect my agenda is not as radical as that of the deconstructionists, who wish to take apart and disclose the underlying premises in various discourses, without rooting those discourses in social organization. The realization that our conceptions of something—say, homosexuality—are not given automatically by the thing itself is a departure from standard positivist assumptions. However, this departure does not at all imply, as some have contended, that a causal analysis is impossible.

[18] Thus Knorr-Cetina (1982) remarks, "Epistemic relativism is not committed to the idea that there is no material world, or that all knowledge claims are equally good or bad, or to the idea that meter readings can be made to our liking. It is only committed to the idea that what we make of physical resistances and of meter signals is itself grounded in human assumptions and selections which appear to be specific to a particular historical place and time." In this sense it is possible to be simultaneously an ontological realist and an epistemological relativist or constructivist. Much confusion in the debates over social-constructionist writings on homosexuality has resulted from failure to realize that a claim to the effect that homosexuality is a modern invention (Plummer, 1981b; J. N. Katz, 1983:1–19) concerns assumptions and classification schemes; it need not imply that in earlier times there was no one who would be called a homosexual by today's standards.

[19] Bulmer (1967) makes our point in an anthropological context; see also Law and Lodge (1984).

In defining unnatural vice to include masturbation, bestiality, heterosexual and homosexual intercourse, Saint Thomas Aquinas was making a decision that the potentially procreative quality of an act was its most important feature. He recognized that a variety of distinct acts were subsumed under the broader category, but the distinctions among them—e.g., whether there was a partner, whether it was human, and whether it was of the same or opposite sex—were less important. A different structure of relevances would lead to a different classification scheme.

Contemporary scientists assess the utility of a classification scheme not simply on the basis of a subjective judgment as to the similarity of items classed together. They are especially concerned with the predictive power of a scheme. Do the entities classed together behave similarly with respect to criteria considered important? The broader the scope of predictions, and the greater their accuracy, the more satisfactory a classification system will seem. Using this criterion, our contemporary system of classifying someone as either homosexual or heterosexual on the basis of his or her past sexual history leaves a good deal to be desired. If at a given moment we classify individuals as either homosexual or heterosexual on the basis of their sexual history to date, the predictions made regarding the sex of their future sexual partners will undoubtedly be better than predictions made at random, but a fair number of errors will be made.[20] Membership in the classes so defined will also correlate imperfectly with other personal traits, such as gender identity.[21]

There are several likely reasons for this imperfect predictability. If there are "essences" that structure erotic feelings, they may in some people, or even in all, be unstable or subject to environmental influence. Also, the categories homosexual and heterosexual are in some important ways heter-

[20] No one has formulated his or her research findings in just this way, but numerous studies have shown that an appreciable fraction of those who call themselves heterosexual have had some homosexual experience in earlier years, and that persons who call themselves homosexual have often had heterosexual experience, e.g., Reiss (1962), Kinsey, Pomeroy, and Martin (1948), Wolff (1971:210), Saghir and Robins (1973:84–91), Bell and Weinberg (1978:54–61), Ardilla (1985).

[21] Whitam and Mathy (1984) argue that many attributes associated with male homosexuality are culturally invariant, implying good predictability for these variables. But their finding is based on only four societies and a sampling procedure within each society that greatly reduced the heterogeneity of the subjects studied. Several studies (Saghir and Robins, 1973: 18–21, 192–98; Green, 1987) have found a positive relationship between adult homosexuality and some degree of opposite-gender behavior or identification, but their sampling procedures yield correlations larger than would be found in the general population. Storms (1979) found no relationship between sexual orientation and masculinity or femininity in a sample of college students.

ogeneous, grouping together individuals whose sexual orientation arises in diverse ways.[22] And it may be that sexual behavior or response is not the optimal criterion for use in classification.[23]

To some, the social-constructionist position has seemed troublesome because of its political implications.[24] When heterosexual chauvinists have told homosexuals to change, essentialist theories have provided a ready response: I can't. When parents have sought to bar homosexual teachers from the classroom lest their children (horror of horrors!) become homosexual, essentialist theories have provided a seemingly authoritative basis for denying the possibility. The present study is concerned only with scientific concerns and cannot make concessions to such opportunistic considerations. It should be pointed out, though, that nothing in the social-constructivist position legitimates the denial of rights.[25] Although it is well known that people can and sometimes do change their religious convictions, no one argues that people should be denied rights on the basis of their religion, or be forced to convert. Assertive gay liberationists have argued that it may be strategically wiser to concede the possibility that a few students might be influenced to become gay by having an openly gay teacher as a role model, and to say, "So what?"[26] Moreover, the epistemological observation that alternative systems of classifying people are possible has little relevance to those who are now classified as homosexual. Had I been born in a different country or different era, my ideas would no doubt be very different from what they are now, but that doesn't mean that at the snap of the finger I

[22]This possibility was noted by Gorer (1966) and is now stressed in recent sociological and psychiatric literature, e.g., Schofield (1965), Bell and Weinberg (1978), Plummer (1981b), Stoller (1985), Endleman (1986), Knauft (1987). The most obvious heterogeneity is, of course, the dissimilarity of males and females, but there are others as well. This heterogeneity has been an obstacle to the political unity of the gay-liberation movement.

[23]Wolff (1971:209) found that 55 percent of her sample of 106 self-identified lesbians had been physically attracted to men, while only 13 percent had ever been deeply involved with a man emotionally. This finding suggests that if there is an "essence" of lesbianism, it may lie more in emotions and feelings than in sexual response.

[24]Dynes (1987b), S. Epstein (1987).

[25]By itself, neither an essentialist nor a social-constructionist stance has political implications. Their concern is with the origins of sexual orientations and identities, not with the normative question of what should be done about them. However, the assumptions that underlie these perspectives can inform political initiatives. For example, an essentialist who thinks of homosexuality in terms of a discrete minority may advocate legislation extending civil rights to members of that minority. Since many people engage in homosexual relations who, in the opinion of essentialists, are not members of that minority, such legislation might extend rights too narrowly. It would be odd to say that it is illegal to discriminate against homosexuals because of their sexual orientation, but not illegal to do so against heterosexuals or bisexuals who engage in homosexual relations. Such legislation might force the courts to decide who qualifies as a homosexual, a task it is ill-equipped to perform.

[26]D'Emilio (1984).

could begin thinking like a Hindu or a medieval Frenchman. The modern Western system of sexual classification is embodied in social identities, roles, institutions, and ways of life that can hardly be abolished by an arbitrary act of will. Gays who tried to do so would be giving up the resources they provide for self-defense. Few if any social constructionists have advocated doing so.

The analogy with race is instructive. Racial-classification systems place people in categories on the basis of a small number of attributes. At different times and in different cultures, the choice of attributes has been differently made. The significance attached to racial membership has also varied greatly.[27] It hardly follows from this that American blacks could or should stop thinking of themselves as blacks, or that black civil rights efforts should be halted.[28]

In seeking to identify the social sources of perceptions of homosexuality, a number of critical decisions had to be made. Where, after all, does one look? So little attention had been given to this issue that there did not exist much of a theoretical tradition on which to build. For the reasons outlined in chapter 1, what little there was seemed unsatisfactory.

I decided at the outset not to restrict consideration to the macrosociological. This is the term sociologists use to refer to the gross characteristics of entire societies. Though I anticipated that such characteristics might be important, historical events are not wholly determined by macrosociological variables. One could never hope to predict which way the U.S. Supreme Court's decision in *Bowers v. Hardwick* would go from the knowledge that the United States has a capitalist economy. Had the composition of the court been slightly different, or if the attorneys in the case had presented slightly different arguments, the decision might have gone the other way.[29]

One might still hope that, over the long haul, individual idiosyncracies would cancel out, like the random-error terms in a regression equation. Friedrich Engels expressed the hope that such cancellations would occur in a letter of September 21–22, 1890, to Joseph Bloch. Rejecting the contention that economic factors cause everything as a mistaken interpretation of the theoretical tradition that he and Marx had founded, he insisted on the mutual interaction of economics, politics, philosophical theories, and religious doctrines. Nevertheless, "amidst all the endless host of accidents (that is, of things and events whose inner interconnection is so remote or so impos-

[27] Dominguez (1986), Goldberg (1988).

[28] B. Adam (1986).

[29] 106 S. Ct. 2841 (1986). Newspaper accounts following the decision indicate that Associate Justice Lewis Powell, Jr., had originally planned to vote to strike down the Georgia antisodomy statute, but changed his mind. Had he not done so, the case would have been decided differently.

sible of proof that we can regard it as nonexistent, as negligible), the economic movement finally asserts itself as necessary."[30] It is this principle that makes us confident that the Christian church would have rejected homosexuality even if Saint Paul had never said a word about it, in response to the same economic and social developments of the late Hellenistic world that also affected the Stoics and the Jews. However, Engels gave no proof that economic factors would finally assert themselves in every instance. What if the "final moment" never comes?[31]

In the short run even less correspondence can be expected between ideas and economic conditions. Religious teachings, for example, may fail to respond to changed social circumstances because religious authorities do not revise doctrine casually once it has been given divine sanction. To do so would tend to undermine the church's claims that its teachings are sacred, and not just the leaders' personal opinions about how life should be lived. In law, precedent is not always binding, but it does count. Had Napoleon died in childhood, consensual homosexual relations might well have remained illegal in more than one European country a hundred years after the actual date of his death. It is always easier to leave the status quo in place than to attempt the repeal of legislation that on its face harms only a small minority. The repeal of laws prohibiting consensual homosexual relations would almost certainly have come in the long run, but people live in the short run.

These obstacles to ideological and institutional change imply that the ideas about homosexuality circulating at any given moment need not all correspond in a direct, simple way to its gross social structure (e.g., capitalism). Archaic ideas can be dusted off and recirculated, even if in transmogrified form. New ideas may build on, or be introduced in opposition to, earlier ideas (though their appeal should be greatest if they are structurally relevant or appeal to material or ideological interests). In overlooking the resulting ideological multiplicity (especially great in the modern age), structural theorists tend to exaggerate its conceptual uniformity.[32]

It seemed important that a place should be found in the analysis for psychological processes. Sociologists have often been reluctant to incorporate them into their models, perhaps because they don't know much about psychology, perhaps because psychological explanations sometimes focus

[30] Marx and Engels (1959:398).

[31] E. P. Thompson (1978:1–210).

[32] This failing more or less forces them to imagine change as occurring through virtually instantaneous quantum leaps (Foucauldian *coupures*), brought about by no specified process. We have already seen this to be an oversimplification of the way ideas about homosexuality evolved in Europe in recent centuries.

only on the individual mind and its processes, completely ignoring the role of social factors. Without some attention to the social, historical change cannot be explained.[33] Yet the consideration of psychological processes does not preclude an analysis of the social context in which they occur. Psychology and sociology are not mutually exclusive; rather, they complement one another. Institutional change can transform the socialization process and structure the opportunities and costs of satisfying psychological needs or drives. Widely shared psychological processes—or idiosyncratic ones on the part of a strategically placed individual such as a ruler or religious leader—can shape the direction of institutional development and the production of ideologies.[34] Given the transparent limitations of the "goal-directed rational-actor" model on which most sociological work depends, it seems best not to foreclose the consideration of other psychological perspectives.

The antihomosexual bias of much psychiatric writing on the etiology and treatment of homosexuality might make one especially hesitant to turn in that direction in the sort of study presented here. Too often, psychiatric terminology has been used to discredit historical figures by suggesting without sufficient independent grounds that their behavior is irrational or neurotic. But the existence of bias in some, or even most, psychiatric or psychological writings does not in itself invalidate the entire approach. Even if one rejects specific psychological explanations for homosexual orientation, one may still find in the notions of ambivalence, the unconscious, conflict between impulse and prohibition, gender identification, and psychological defense mechanisms conceptual tools whose implications for hostility to homosexuality may be worth exploring. So long as they are ignored, one will never discover any insights that depth psychology might contribute or learn that they do not illuminate one's problem.

Almost by definition, explanations of events that involve unconscious psychological processes will be very different from those the subjects of our study would have provided had they been interviewed. Although we found it important to understand the worldviews of these subjects (absent such an understanding, their actions would have been incomprehensible), we did not limit ourselves to recounting their views. It is axiomatic in psychoanalysis that people are not always aware of the psychological processes that limit and direct their thoughts and actions. The same is true of

---

[33] M. Levine (1988), for example, points out that an exclusively psychological explanation of gender-identity formation cannot explain the change in gender styles that has swept American male homosexual communities in recent years. Effeminacy has to a great extent been replaced by a conventional or even exaggerated manliness.

[34] R. F. Murphy (1959).

social factors. A methodology that examined only the goals and perspectives of subjects themselves would overlook all those influences of which the participants themselves were unaware. The exploration of these hidden factors and their effects is a major part of the task of the sociologist who wishes to understand the origins of deviance-defining rules, or indeed, of almost any other historical development.

In postulating such hidden factors—be they psychological or social—the problem of demonstration arises. Since they are not directly observable, a skeptic may say, it is easy to attribute anything at all to such factors. This is true, but as with any other explanation, plausibility can be attained through indirect evidence that the postulated process and not some other factor is at work. This can be done by developing indicators for the postulated variables, and applying standard methodological canons for the attribution of causality.[35] In essence, one considers possible alternative explanations of an observed pattern and rules them out. When working with nonexperimental data, this procedure rarely permits one to *prove* that a postulated explanation is correct, but it can enhance its plausibility. Comparative data are especially valuable for this purpose. If an explanation is valid, it ought to hold up across the board. If it does not, it may be wrong, or at least require qualification.

With truly good data and large numbers of observations, one might hope not only to synthesize micro- and macrosociological explanations, but also to test and refine complex causal models involving variables drawn from different levels of analysis. In our work, the small number of observations and the crudeness with which some of the critical variables could be measured preclude that strategy.[36]

That is not as great a loss as one might at first think. Let us return to the example of Napoleon Bonaparte, and for the sake of argument, let us accept the contention that if he had died in childhood, the history of criminal prohibitions dealing with homosexuality in Europe and Latin America would have been different. It is difficult to imagine a sociological theory that would predict with good accuracy which eighteenth-century Corsican children would succumb to typhoid fever. If one had such a theory, what would one do with it? Even if one had the required data, one would hardly want a theory of vulnerability to disease to become an integral part of a

---

[35] When X and Y are measured without error, to infer that X is a cause of Y one must show that there is a pattern of association between X and Y, that X precedes Y in time, and that there are no third variables Z whose causal influence on both X and Y entirely explains their observed pattern of association.

[36] For example, we did not even try to quantify such variables—critical to our analysis though they were—as involvement in market relations or the degree of societal bureaucratization.

theory of homosexuality prohibitions; the theory would be a monstrosity. It seems to me preferable to keep theories for different domains of experience distinct, bringing them together when appropriate for a particular problems—or simply to accept some events, such as Napoleon's survival to adulthood and rise to political power, as givens that need not be theorized because their explanations are remote from present concerns. One can reasonably say that the rise of capitalism and the growth of bureaucratic social organizations had important consequences for the history of homosexuality without being required to commit oneself to a particular theory of either development.

The bringing together of microsociology or psychology with macrosociology and mesosociology[37] makes possible the transcendence of the deficiencies in the theoretical perspectives on the creation of deviance categories highlighted in chapter 1. Because these limitations apply quite broadly—not just to the study of homosexuality prohibitions—it is worthwhile returning to them briefly.

As we noted, the scholarly literature that identifies entrepreneurs who campaign to make some activity deviant suffers from voluntarism. It depicts moral fanatics who reach for power, but offers no explanation of where they get their moral standards, or why they want to impose them on others. It depicts a wealthy and powerful minority seeking to enhance its position at the expense of others, but it is unclear as to why the majority permits them to do so. Because the entrepreneurial literature does not adequately conceptualize the society in which the entrepreneur operates, the existence of entrepreneurs, the choice of their goals, and their success or failure in mobilizing constituencies all remain unexplained.

The group conflict perspective that attends much of the entrepreneurial literature also forgets that sometimes people define their own activities as deviant, and seek to control themselves rather than others.[38] It is thus unable to make sense of such episodes as occurred in The Netherlands during the persecutions of 1743, when the twenty-two-year-old Pieter Didding turned himself in to a Dutch court and confessed to an act of sodomy with Willem Knieland, who lived in an orphanage with him. He told the judges that he

> had committed it this one time and never again and also had not given any thought to doing it again, but that after the committed act, he had become very sad and that his conscience could not

[37] Mesosociology is my neologism for institutional or organizational analysis.

[38] Schur (1979:160–61) suggests that people rarely define themselves as deviant. But confessors, psychiatrists, and clinical psychologists routinely encounter penitents and patients who do just that.

rest about it and such was the cause that he, out of remorse of his mind, had made it known to the fathers of the house and that the thing mentioned above had happened some five weeks ago and that he had since prayed day and night to the Lord to prevent him from such sins and that he had only been seduced to this atrocious fact by the before mentioned Willem Knieland.[39]

The functionalist approach posits a relationship between the rules that define deviance and a society's social structure, but does so in such depersonalized and mechanistic terms as to defy credibility. The approach makes sense only if societies are assumed to be omniscient, so that they always know just what they need for their own good and how to obtain it. It is as if society as a whole acts, rather than the people who make up that society. In this respect, the theory reifies society.

Our analysis has tried to overcome the limitations of these two approached without losing sight of the insights they do have to offer. Entrepreneurs certainly appear in our account; they include the Gregorian reformers of the Middle Ages, participants in the purity movements of the eighteenth century, physicians who pioneered in developing degeneracy theory in the nineteenth, and gay-liberation activists of the twentieth. In identifying these entrepreneurs as shaping the course of events, we adopted a strategy radically at odds with that of Michel Foucault, whose depersonalized history of sexuality postulates power without a subject, history without an agent.[40] However, we moved beyond the familiar level of entrepreneurial, interest-group type of analysis in a number of crucial respects. First, we examined the social-structural developments that gave rise to these social movements, gave direction to their goals, and determined their ultimate impact. In so doing, we did not neglect the ideological factors that influenced the character and direction of these movements, but took care not to treat them in a vacuum. Ideology grows out of lived experience and is thus itself a social product. The actions that spring from ideology are conditioned by resources, costs, and opportunities.

By paying attention to these constraining factors, we were able to avoid the misleading assumption that major powerholders (government officials, religious elites, professionals) can do anything they please, and that their pleasure is essentially random. We noted, for example, that the asceticism of the early Christian church and the medieval reform movement were, in part, responses to popular demand, not simple impositions from above. Protagonists in today's debates over sexual morality try to appeal to—and at the same time take cues from—a larger public.

[39]Quoted in Meer (forthcoming).
[40]Foucault (1980).

At the same time, attention to constraints enabled us to avoid the misleading impression conveyed in some of the more voluntaristic deviance literature that every individual is free to negotiate any identity or adopt any life-style whatever. One cannot help but be impressed that, despite the awesome penalties in store for those guilty of homosexual delicts, men and women have, over centuries of Western history, found ways to express their feelings, create new cultural forms, and organize in self-defense. However, subcultures based on homosexual identities have been able to flourish, and homophile political movements to mobilize and win victories, only under very specific historical conditions.

The analysis of the social creation of deviance-defining categories in relation to an institutional (i.e., social-structural) and ideological context by no means entails the adoption of functionalism. We made no assumption that society has moral boundaries that the prohibition of homosexual activity maintains, that society as a whole gains by the prohibition, or that the perceptions and responses we described are explained by their consequences. Researchers would do well to avoid these gratuitous and frequently misleading assumptions.

It is an explicit feature of our work that we allow for the possibility of unanticipated consequences. The Gregorian reformers who campaigned for clerical celibacy do not appear to have expected that their success would later contribute to the execution of sodomites, or that it would intensify misogyny and thus contribute to the witchcraft persecutions, but our analysis suggests that the institutional reforms they carried out may have had this consequence. The nineteenth-century inverts who argued that homosexuality was innate did not anticipate what the degeneracy theorists would make of their claim. Too often in the study of deviance-defining rules it is assumed that measures we now see as repressive were planned to turn out that way. This is a treacherous assumption. Earlier generations were no more omniscient than ours; we make mistakes, so did they.

Years ago, when Edwin Sutherland initiated the study of white-collar crime, he proclaimed that it was not his goal to reform the criminal, only the criminologist.[41] I, too, hope to have an impact on the direction of social research, not just in homosexuality studies. The precepts and sensitizing principles found useful here are potentially relevant to the study of the social construction of other deviance definitions and conceptual categories and should have broader applicability in historical sociology. Methodologically speaking, homosexuality is not *sui generis*.

[41]Sutherland (1961:xiii).

References

Abbott, Lyman (1898). *The Life and Letters of Paul the Apostle*. Boston: Houghton Mifflin.

Abelove, Henry (1987). "Freud, Male Homosexuality, and the Americans." *Dissent* (Winter) 34:59–69.

Aberle, David (1961). "Navaho." Pp. 96–201 in David M. Schneider and Kathleen Gough (eds.), *Matrilineal Kinship*. Berkeley: University of California Press.

——— (1977). "The Psychological Analysis of a Hopi Life History." Pp. 79–138 in Robert Hunt (ed.), *Personalities and Cultures: Readings in Psychological Anthropology*. Austin: University of Texas Press.

Abray, Lorna Jane (1985). *The People's Reformation: Magistrates, Clergy, and Commons in Strasbourg, 1500–1598*. Ithaca, N.Y.: Cornell University Press.

Achilles, Nancy (1967). "The Development of the Homosexual Bar as an Institution." Pp. 228–44 in John H. Gagnon and William S. Simon (eds.), *Sexual Deviance*. New York: Harper and Row.

Achilles Tatius (1947). *Clitophon and Leucippe*. Tr. S. Gaselee. Cambridge, Mass.: Harvard University Press.

Ackerley, J. R. (1968). *My Father and Myself*. London: The Bodley Head.

Ackroyd, Peter R. (1968). *Exile and Restoration: A Study of Hebrew Thought of the Sixth Century B.C.* Philadelphia: Westminster.

Acton, William (1865). *The Functions and Disorders of the Reproductive System*. London: J. & A. Churchill.

Adam, Antoine (1965). *Théophile de Viau et la libre pensée française en 1620*. Geneve: Slatkine.

Adam, Barry D. (1979). "A Social History of Gay Politics." Pp. 285–300 in Martin P. Levine (ed.), *Gay Men: The Social History of Male Homosexuality*. New York: Harper and Row.

——— (1985a). "Age, Structure, and Sexuality: Reflections on the Anthropological Evidence on Homosexual Relations." *Journal of Homosexuality* 11:19–33.

——— (1985b). "Structural Foundations of the Gay World." *Comparative Studies in Society and History* 27:658–70.

——— (1986). "Further Comment on the Toronto Conference and Social Constructionists." *SGC Newsletter* 46 (Jan.).

——— (1987a). *The Rise of a Gay and Lesbian Movement*. Boston: Twayne.

501

—— (1987b). "Homosexuality Without a Gay World: The Case of Nicaragua." *ARGOH Newsletter* 9(3):6–10.

Adam of Bremen (1959). *History of the Archbishops of Hamburg-Bremen.* Tr. Francis J. Tschen. New York: Columbia University Press.

Adams, J. N. (1982). *The Latin Sexual Vocabulary.* London: Gerald Duckworth.

Adkins, A.W.H. (1972). *Moral Values and Political Behavior in Ancient Greece.* London: Chatto and Windus.

Africa, Thomas W. (1982). "Homosexuals in Greek History." *Journal of Psychohistory* 9:401–20.

Akers, Ronald L. (1977). *Deviant Behavior: A Social Learning Approach.* Belmont, Calif.: Wadsworth.

Akrigg, G.P.V. (1962). *Jacobean Pageant, or the Court of King James I.* Cambridge, Mass.: Harvard University Press.

Alabaster, Ernest (1899). *Notes and Commentaries on Chinese Criminal Law.* London: Luzac.

Aldred, Cyril (1968). *Akhenaton: Pharaoh of Egypt—A New Study.* New York: McGraw-Hill.

Alföldi, A. (1963). *Early Rome and the Latins.* Ann Arbor: University of Michigan Press.

Allegro, John M. (1970). *The Sacred Mushrooms and the Cross.* Garden City, N.Y.: Doubleday.

—— (1977). *Lost Gods.* London: Michael Joseph.

Allen, Michael R. (1967). *Male Cults and Secret Initiations in Melanesia.* Victoria, Austral.: Melbourne University Press.

—— (1984). "Homosexuality, Male Power and Political Organization in North Vanuatu: A Comparative Analysis." Pp. 83–127 in Gilbert Herdt (ed.), *Ritualized Homosexuality in Melanesia.* Berkeley: University of California Press.

Allen, Philip Schuyler (1928). *The Romanesque Lyric.* Chapel Hill: University of North Carolina Press.

Altekar, A. S. (1956). *The Position of Women in Hindu Civilization.* Banaras: Motilal Banarsidass.

Altman, Dennis (1971). *Homosexual Oppression and Liberation.* New York: Outerbridge and Dienstfrey.

—— (1979). *Coming Out in the Seventies.* Sydney, Austral.: Wild and Woolley.

—— (1982a). "The Gay Movement Ten Years Later." *Nation* (Nov. 13):494–96.

—— (1982b). *The Homosexualization of America, the Americanization of the Homosexual.* New York: St. Martin's Press.

Amann, Emile, and Auguste Dumas (1942). *L'Eglise au pouvoir des laïques (888–1057).* Paris: Bloud and Gay.

Amar, Robert (1968). "Un sodomite de génie: Jean-Baptiste Lully (1632–1687)." *Arcadie* 172:163–70 and 173:229–35.

Amiel, Charles (1986). "The Archives of the Portuguese Inquisition: A Brief Survey." Pp. 79–99 in Gustav Henningsen and John Tedeschi (eds.), *The Inquisition in Early Modern Europe: Studies on Sources and Methods.* DeKalb: Northern Illinois University Press.

Ammianus Marcellinus (1935). *History*, vol. 3. Tr. John C. Rolfe. Cambridge, Mass.: Harvard University Press.

—— (1937). *Rerum gestarum libri qui supersunt*, vol. 2. Tr. John C. Rolfe. Cambridge, Mass.: Harvard University Press.

Amussen, Susan Dwyer (1985). "Gender and the Social Order in Early Modern England." Pp. 196–217 in Anthony Fletcher and John Stevenson (eds.), *Order and Disorder in Early Modern England*. Cambridge: Cambridge University Press.

Anderson, Michael (1980). *Approaches to the History of the Western Family, 1500–1914*. London: Macmillan.

Anderson, Perry (1974). *Passages from Antiquity to Feudalism*. London: NLB.

André, Caroline S. (1981). "Some Selected Aspects of the Role of Women in Sixteenth Century England." *International Journal of Women's Studies* 2:76–87.

Andrews, Edmund, and Irene D. Andrews (1944). *A Comparative Dictionary of the Tahitian Language*. Chicago: Chicago Academy of Sciences.

Angelino, Harry, and Charles Shedd (1955). "A Note on Berdache." *American Anthropologist* 57:121–25.

Angus, S. (1925). *The Mystery-Religions and Christianity*. New York: Charles Scribner's Sons.

Anton, Ferdinand (1973). *Woman in Pre-Columbian America*. Tr. Marianne Herzfeld. New York: Abner Schram.

Antonio, Robert J. (1979). "The Contradiction of Domination and Production in Bureaucracy: The Contribution of Organizational Efficiency to the Decline of the Roman Empire." *American Sociological Review* 44:895–912.

Arboleda, Manuel (1981). "Representaciones artisticos de actividades homoeroticos en la ceramica Moche." *Boletin de Lima* 16:98–107.

Archenholz, Johann Wilhelm von (1787). *England und Italien*. 5 vols. Leipzig. Dykeschen Buchhandlung.

Ardilla, Ruben (1985). "La Homosexualidad en Colombia." *Acta psiquiatrica y psicologica de America Latina* 31:191–210.

Arguelles, Lourds, and B. Ruby Rich (1984). "Homosexuality, Homophobia, and Revolution: Notes toward an Understanding of the Cuban Lesbian and Gay Male Experience, Part I." *Signs: Journal of Women in Culture and Society* 9:683–99.

Ariès, Philippe (1962). *Centuries of Childhood*. Tr. Robert Bladwick. New York: Vintage.

—— (1982). "Réflexions sur l'histoire de l'homosexualité." *Communications* 35:56–67.

Aristotle (1927). *The Works*. 12 vols. Tr. E. S. Forster. Oxford: Clarendon Press.

—— (1959). *Nicomatchean Ethics*. Tr. J.A.K. Thomson. Penguin: Baltimore.

Arney, William Ray (1982). *Power and the Profession of Obstetrics*. Chicago: University of Chicago Press.

Arnold, Edward Vernon (1971). *Roman Stoicism*. Freeport, N.Y.: Books for Libraries. Orig. pub. 1911.

Aron, Jean-Paul, and Roger Kempf (1978). *La pénis et la demoralisation de l'occident.* Paris: Bernard Grasset.

——— (1979). "Triumphs and Tribulations of the Homosexual Discourse." Pp. 141–57 in George Stamboulian and Elaine Marks (eds.), *Homosexualities and French Literature: Cultural Contexts/Critical Texts.* Ithaca, N.Y.: Cornell University Press.

Artemidorus Daldianus (1975). *The Interpretation of Dreams.* Tr. Robert J. White. Park Ridge, N.J.: Noyes.

Ashton, Dore, and Denise Hare (1981). *Rosa Bonheur: A Life and a Legend.* New York: Viking.

Assyrian Dictionary (1958–71). Chicago: Oriental Institute.

Astour, Michael (1966). "Tamar the Hierodule." *Journal of Biblical Literature* 85: 185–96.

——— (1967). *Hellenosemitica: An Ethnic and Cultural Study in West Semitic Impact.* Leiden: E. J. Brill.

Athenaeus (1854). *The Deipnosophists, or Banquet of the Learned,* vol. 3. Tr. C. D. Yonge. London: Henry G. Bohn.

Auchmutz, Rosemary (1975). *Victorian Spinsters.* Ph.D. dissertation, Australian National University.

Augustine, Saint (1950). *The City of God.* Tr. Demetrius B. Zema and Gerald G. Walsh. New York: Fathers of the Church.

——— (1957). *The Confessions.* Tr. Edward B. Pusey. New York: Pocket Books.

d'Avray, D. L., and M. Tausche (1980). "Marriage Sermons in *ad status* Collections of the Central Middle Ages." *Archives d'histoire doctrinale et littéraire du Moyen Âge* 47:71–119.

Babar, Emperor (1926). *Memoirs of Zehir-Ed-Din Muhammed Baber, Emperor of Hindustan.* Tr. John Leyden and William Erskine. London: Longman, Rees, Orme, Brown, and Green.

Babb, Lawrence A. (1975). *The Divine Hierarchy: Popular Hinduism in Central India.* New York: Columbia University Press.

Bach, G. (1946). "Father Fantasies and Father Typing in Father Separated Children." *Child Development* 17:63–80.

Badayuni, 'Abda-l-Qadir ibn-i-muluk Shah (1973). *Muntakhabu-T-Tawarikh.* Patna, India: Academica Asiatica.

Baer, Judith A. (1978). *The Chains of Protection: The Judicial Response to Women's Labor Legislation.* Westport, Conn.: Greenwood.

Baer, Richard A., Jr. (1970). *Philo's Use of the Categories Male and Female.* Leiden: E. J. Brill.

Bahlman, Dudley W. R. (1957). *The Moral Revolution of 1688.* New Haven: Yale University Press.

Bailey, Derrick Sherwin (1975). *Homosexuality and the Western Christian Tradition.* Hamden, Conn.: Archon. Orig. pub. 1955.

Baines, Barbara J. (1978). *Three Pamphlets on the Jacobean Antifeminist Controversy.* Delmar, NY: Scholar's Fascimiles and Reprints.

Baines, John (1985). *Fecundity Figures.* Chicago: Bolchazy-Cartucci.

Baker, Michael (1985). *Our Three Selves: The Life of Radcliffe Hall.* London: Hamish Hamilton.

Balderston, Katherine C., (ed.) (1951). *Thralania: The Diary of Mrs. Hester Lynch Thrale (Later Mrs. Piozzi) 1776–1809.* Oxford: Clarendon.

Balsdon, J.P.V.D. (1979). *Romans and Aliens.* Chapel Hill: University of North Carolina Press.

Bancroft, Hubert Howe (1874–75). *The Native Races of the Pacific States of North America.* 2 vols. New York: D. Appleton.

Bandello, Matteo (1963). "Premiere Partie—Nouvelle VI." *Arcadie* 111:131–36.

Banerji, Sures Chandra (1980). *Crime and Sex in Ancient India.* Calcutta: Naya Prokash.

Banks, J. A. (1981). *Victorian Values: Secularism and the Size of Families.* Boston: Routledge and Kegan Paul.

Bannister, Robert C. (1979). *Social Darwinism: Science and Myth in Anglo-American Social Thought.* Philadelphia: Temple University Press.

Barbedette, Gilles, and Michel Carassou (1981). *Paris Gay 1925.* Paris: Presse de la Renaissance.

Barber, Elinor (1955). *The Bourgeoisie in Eighteenth Century France.* Princeton: Princeton University Press.

Barbu, Zevedei (1952). "The Historical Pattern of Psycho-Analysis." *British Journal of Sociology* 3:64–76.

Barclay, A., and D. R. Gusmano (1967). "Father Absence, Cross-Sex Identity and Field Development Behavior in Male Adolescents." *Child Development* 38:243–50.

Bargatzky, Thomas (1985). "Person Acquisition and the Early State in Polynesia." Pp. 290–309 in Henri J. M. Claessen, Pieter van de Velde, and M. Estellie Smith (eds.), *Development and Decline: The Evolution of Sociopolitical Organization.* South Hadley, Mass.: Bergin and Garvey.

Barguet, Paul (1967). *Le livre des morts des anciens Egyptiens.* Paris: Cerf.

Barker, John W. (1966). *Justinian and the Late Roman Empire.* Madison: University of Wisconsin Press.

Barker-Benfield, G. J. (1972a). "The Spermatic Economy: A Nineteenth-Century View of Sexuality." *Feminist Studies* 1:45–74.

——— (1972b). "Ann Hutchinson and the Puritan Attitude toward Women." *Feminist Studies* 1:65–96.

——— (1976). *The Horrors of the Half-Known Life: Male Attitudes toward Women and Sexuality in Nineteenth-Century America.* New York: Harper Colophon.

Barnard, Nicolas (1710). *The Case of John Atherton, Bishop of Waterford in Ireland; Who was Convicted of the Sin of Uncleanness with a Cow.* London: E. Cull.

Barnes, Harry Elmer (1968). *The Evolution of Penology in Pennsylvania.* Montclair, N.J.: Patterson Smith. Orig. pub. 1927.

Barnes, Timothy D. (1981). *Constantine and Eusebius.* Cambridge, Mass.: Harvard University Press.

Barol, Bill et al. (1984). "The Fight over Gay Rights." *Newsweek on Campus* (May): 4–10.

Baron, Ava (1981). *Woman's 'Place' in Capitalist Production: A Study of Class Relations in the Nineteenth Century Newspaper Printing Industry.* Ph.D. dissertation, New York University.

Barrett, D. S. (1981). "The Friendship of Achilles and Patroclus." *Classical Bulletin* 57:87–93.

Barton, Anne (1983). "That Night at Farnham." *London Review of Books* 5:(Aug. 15–31).

Barton, George A. (1893–94). "The Semitic Ištar Cult." *Hebraica* 10:1–74.

——— (1914). "Hierodouloi (Semitic and Egyptian)." Pp. 64–66 in James Hastings (ed.), *Encyclopedia of Religion and Ethics,* vol. 6. New York: Charles Scribner's Sons.

Basham, A. L. (1959). *The Wonder that Was India.* New York: Grove.

Bateson, Gregory (1958). *Naven.* 2d ed. Stanford, Calif.: Stanford University Press, Orig. pub. 1936.

Baudin, P. (1885). *Fetichism and Fetich Worshippers.* New York: Benziger Brothers.

Baumann, Hermann (1955). *Das doppelte Geschlecht.* Berlin: Dietrich Reimer.

Baumann, Oscar (1899). "Konträre Sexual-Erscheinungen bei der Neger-Bevölkerung Zanzibars." *Verhandlungen der Berlinger Anthropologischen Gesselschaft* 668–70.

Baumhoff, Martin A. (1963). *Ecological Determinants of Aboriginal California Populations.* Berkeley: University of California Press.

Baxter, P.T.W., and U. Almagor (1978). "Observations about Generations." Pp. 159–81 in J. S. La Fontaine (ed.), *Sex and Age as Principles of Social Differentiation.* A.S.A. Monograph 17. New York: Academic.

Bayer, Ronald (1981). *Homosexuality and American Psychiatry: The Politics of Diagnosis.* New York: Basic.

Beaglehole, Ernest (1957). *Social Change in the South Pacific: Raratonga and Aitutaki.* London: George Allen and Unwin.

Beaglehold, J C. (1961). *The Journals of Captain James Cook on His Voyages of Discovery.* Vol. 1: *The Voyage of the Resolution and Adventure, 1772–1775.* Cambridge: Cambridge University Press.

Beals, Ralph L. (1932). "The Comparative Ethnology of Northern Mexico Before 1750." *Ibero-Americana,* vol. 2. Berkeley: University of California Press.

——— (1934). "Ethnology of the Nisenan." *University of California Publications in American Archaeology and Ethnology* 31:335–76.

Bean, Richard (1973). "War and the Birth of the Nation State." *Journal of Economic History* 33:203–21.

Beard, George A. (1884). *Sexual Neurasthenia.* New York: E. B. Treat.

Beattie, J.H.M. (1980). "On Understanding Sacrifice." Pp. 29–44 in M.F.C. Boudrillon and Meyer F. Fortes (eds.), *Sacrifice.* London: Academic.

Beauvoir, Simone de (1952). *The Second Sex.* Tr. H. M. Parshley. New York: A. A. Knopf.

Becker, Howard (1963). *Outsiders: Studies in the Sociology of Deviance.* New York: Free Press.

Becker, Raymond de (1964). *L'érotisme d'en face.* Paris: Paivert.

Bedoyere, Michael de la (1958). *The Meddlesome Friar: The Story of the Conflict between Savonarola and Alexander VI.* London: Collins.

Beecher, Jonathan (1986). *Charles Fourier.* Berkeley: University of California Press.
———— and Richard Bienvenu (1971). *The Utopian Vision of Charles Fourier.* Boston: Beacon.
Bell, Alan P., and Martin S. Weinberg (1978). *Homosexualities: A Study of Diversity among Men and Women.* New York: Simon and Schuster.
————, Martin S. Weinberg, and Sue K. Hammersmith (1981). *Sexual Preference: Its Development in Men and Women.* Bloomington: Indiana University Press.
Bellamy, James A. (1979). "Sex and Society in Islamic Popular Literature." Pp. 23–42 in Afaf Lutfi Al-Sayyid-Marsot (ed.), *Society and the Sexes in Medieval Islam.* Malibu, Calif.: Undena.
Bellamy, John G. (1984). *Criminal Law and Society in Late Medieval and Tudor England.* New York: St. Martin's Press.
Bellows, Henry Adams (ed.) (1923). *The Poetic Edda.* Tr. H. A. Bellows. New York: American-Scandinavian Foundation.
Belo, Jane (1970). "A Study of Customs Pertaining to Twins in Bali." Pp. 3–56 in Jane Belo (ed.), *Traditional Balinese Culture.* New York: Columbia University Press.
Ben-Ami, Aharon (1969). *Social Change in a Hostile Environment.* Princeton, N.J.: Princeton University Press.
Benbow, William (1823). *The Crimes of the Clergy, or the Pillars of Priest-Craft Shaken.* London: Privately printed.
Benenson, Harold (1984). "Victorian Sexual Ideology and Marx's Theory of the Working Class." *International Labor and Working Class History* 25:1–23.
Benjamin, Jessica (1978). *Internalization and Instrumental Culture: A Reinterpretation of Psycho-Analysis and Social Theory.* Ph.D. dissertation, New York University.
Benko, Stephen (1967). "The Libertine Gnostic Sect of the Phibionites According to Epiphaneius." *Vigilae Christianae* 21:103–19.
———— (1984). *Pagan Rome and the Early Christians.* Bloomington: Indiana University Press.
Bennassar, Bartolomé (1979). *L'Inquisition Espagnole, XVᵉ–XIXᵉ siècle.* Paris: Hachelte.
Bensserade, Le Comte (1698). *Les oeuvres.* Paris: Charles de Secy.
Bentham (1978/1979). "Offenses Against One's Self: Paederasty." *Journal of Homosexuality* 4:389–405 and 5:91–109.
Bentley, Eric (1980). "The Homosexual Question." Pp. 307–17 in Byrne R. S. Fone (ed.), *Hidden Heritage: History and the Gay Imagination, An Anthology.* New York: Avocation.
Benveniste, Émile (1932). "Les classes sociales dans la tradition avestique." *Journal asiatique* 221:117–34.
———— (1938). "Traditions indo-iraniennes sur les classes sociales." *Journal asiatique* 230:529–49.
———— (1973). *Indo-European Language and Society.* Tr. Elizabeth Palmer. Coral Gables: University of Miami Press.
Berg, Ivar (1970). *Education and Jobs: The Great Training Robbery.* Boston: Praeger.
Berger, Raymond M. (1983). "What is a Homosexual? A Definitional Model." *Social Work* 28:132–35.

Bergler, Edmund (1957). *Homosexuality: Disease or Way of Life?* New York: Hill and Wang.

Berkowitz, Gerald M. (1981). *Sir John Vanbrugh and the End of Restoration Comedy.* Amsterdam: Rodopi.

Berland, Cottie (1973). "Middle America." Pp. 143–62 in Philip Rawson (ed.), *Primitive Erotic Art.* New York: G. P. Putnam's Sons.

Berlin Museum (ed.) (1984). *Eldorado: Homosexuelle Frauen und Männer in Berlin 1850–1950, Geschichte, Alltag und Kultur.* West Berlin: Frölich and Kaufmann.

Berman, Harold J. (1983). *Law and Revolution: The Formation of the Western Legal Tradition.* Cambridge, Mass.: Harvard University Press.

Berndt, Ronald M., and Catherine H. Berndt (1951). *Sexual Behavior in Western Arnhem Land.* New York: Viking Fund.

Bertholon, Lucien-Joseph (1909). "Essai sur la religion des Libyans." *Revue Tunisienne* 16:477–89.

Bérubé, Alan (1981). "Marching to a Different Drummer: Lesbian and Gay GIs in World War II." *Advocate* (Oct. 5):20–24. Reprinted, pp. 88–99 in Ann Snitow, Christine Stansell, and Sharon Thompson (eds.), *Powers of Desire: The Politics of Sexuality.* New York: Monthly Review Press.

Besmer, Fremont E. (1983). *Horses, Musicians and Gods: The Hausa Cult of Possession-Trance.* South Hadley, Mass.: Bergin and Garvey.

Bethe, Erich (1907). "Die dorische Knabenliebe, ihre Ethic, ihre Idee." *Rheinische Museum für Philologie* 62:438–75.

Bettelheim, Bruno (1962). *Symbolic Wounds: Puberty Rites and the Envious Male.* Glencoe, Ill.: Free Press.

Beyerlin, Walter (1978). *Near Eastern Religious Texts Relating to the Old Testament.* Tr. John Bowden. London: SCM.

Bianchi, Giovanni Paolo Simone (1751). *An Historical and Physical Dissertation on the Case of Catherine Vizzani.* London: W. Meyer.

Bianquis, Thierry (1986). "La famille en Islam Arabe." Pp. 557–601 in André Burgièrre et al. (eds.), *Histoire de la famille.* Paris: Armand Colin.

Bibring, Grete (1953). "On the 'Passing of the Oedipus Complex' in a Matriarchal Family Setting." Pp. 278–84 in Rudolph M. Loewenstein (ed.), *Drives, Affects and Behavior: Essays in Honor of Marie Bonaparte.* New York: International Universities Press.

Biddle, G. (1968). *Tahitian Journal.* Minneapolis: University of Minnesota Press.

Bieber, Irving (1962). *Homosexuality: A Psychoanalytic Study.* New York: Basic.

——— (1965). "Clinical Aspects of Male Homosexuality." Pp. 248–67 in Judd Marmor (ed.), *Sexual Inversion: The Multiple Roots of Homosexuality.* New York: Basic Books.

Bieler, Ludgwig (1963). *The Irish Penitentials.* Dublin: Dublin Institute for Advanced Studies.

Biggs, Robert D. (1967). *ŠA.ZI.GA: Ancient Mesopotamian Potency Incantations.* New York: J. J. Augustin.

——— (1969). "Medicine in Ancient Mesopotamia." *History of Science* 8:94–105.

Biller, A. B. (1970). "Father Absence and the Personality Development of the Male Child." *Developmental Psychology* 2:181–270.

Biller, Henry B. (1972). *Father, Child and Sex-Role: Paternal Determinants of Personality Development.* Lexington, Mass.: Heath.

—— and Lloyd Borstelmann (1967). "Masculine Development: An Integrative View." *Merrill-Palmer Quarterly* 13:253–94.

Bingham, Caroline (1971). "Seventeenth-Century Attitudes toward Deviant Sex." *Journal of Interdisciplinary History* 1:447–68.

—— (1981). *James I of England.* London: Weidenfeld and Nicolson.

Bingham, Joseph (1844). *Origines Ecclesiasticae; or, The Antiquities of the Christian Church,* vol. 6. London: William Straher.

Birk, Lee (1980). "The Myth of Classical Homosexuality: Views of a Behavioral Psychotherapist." Pp. 376–90 in Judd Marmor (ed.), *Homosexual Behavior: A Modern Reappraisal.* New York: Basic.

Birnbaum, Lucille Terese (1964). *Behaviorism: John Broadus Watson and American Social Thought, 1913–1933.* Ph.D. dissertation, University of California at Berkeley.

Black, Donald (1976). *The Behavior of Law.* New York: Academic.

Blackman, Janet (1977). "Popular Theories of Generation: The Evolution of *Aristotle's Works:* The Study of an Anachronism." Pp. 56–88 in John Woodward and David Richards (eds.), *Health Care and Popular Medicine in Nineteenth-Century England: Essays in the Social History of Medicine.* London: Croom Helm.

Blackstone, William (1811). *Commentaries on the Laws of England.* 4 vols. Oxford: Clarendon.

Blackwood, Beatrice (1935). *Both Sides of Buka Passage: An Ethnographic Study of Social, Sexual and Economic Conditions in the North-Western Solomon Islands.* Oxford: Clarendon.

Blackwood, Evelyn (1984). "Sexuality and Gender in Certain Native American Tribes: The Case of Cross-Gender Females." *Signs: Journal of Women in Culture and Society* 10:27–42.

Blanch, Lesley (1983). *Pierre Loti: Portrait of an Escapist.* London: Collins.

Blansher, Sarah Rubin (1981). "Criminal Law and Politics in Medieval Bologna." *Criminal Justice History: An International Journal* 2:1–30.

Bleibtreu-Ehrenberg, Gisela (1980). *Mannbarkeitsriten: Zur institutionellen Päderastie bei Papuas und Melanesiern.* Frankfurt am Main: Ullstein.

—— (1981). *Homosexualität: Die Geschichte eines Vorurteils.* Frankfurt am Main: Fischer.

—— (1984). *Der Weibmann: Kultischer Geschlechtswandel im Schamanismus.* Frankfurt am Main: Fischer.

Bligh, William (1792). *A Voyage to the South Seas.* London: B. Nicol.

Blitch, J. W., and S. N. Haynes (1972). "Multiple Behavioral Techniques in a Case of Female Homosexuality." *Journal of Behaviour Therapy and Experimental Psychiatry* 3:319–22.

Bloch, Ivan (1908). "Die Homosexualität in Köln am Ende des 15. Jahrhunderts." *Zeitschrift für Sexualwissenschaft* 1:528–35.

—— (1926). *The Sexual Life of Our Time, in Its Relations to Modern Civilization.* New York: Allied. Orig. pub. 1907.

—— (1933). *Anthropological Studies in the Strange Sexual Practices of All Races in All Ages.* New York: Anthropological Press.

—— (1934). *Sex Life in England Illustrated: As Revealed in Its Obscene Literature and Art*. Tr. Richard Deniston. New York: Falstaff.

—— (1958). *Sexual Life in England Past and Present*. Tr. William H. Forstern. London: Arco.

Bloch, Marc (1961). *Feudal Society*. 2 vols. Tr. L. A. Manyon. Chicago: University of Chicago Press.

Bloch, Raymond (1960). *The Origins of Rome*. New York: Praeger.

—— (1969). *The Ancient Civilization of the Etruscans*. Tr. James Hogarth. New York: Cowles.

Blok, Petrus Johannes (1912). *History of the People of the Netherlands*, vol. 5. Tr. Oscar A. Bierstadt. New York: G. P. Putnam's Sons.

Blumer, G. Alder (1882). "A Case of Perverted Sexual Instinct (Conträre Sexualempfindung)." *American Journal of Insanity* 39:22–35.

Blumer, Herbert (1969). *Symbolic Interactionism: Perspective and Method*. Englewood Cliffs, N.J.: Prentice-Hall.

Boardman, John and Eugenio La Rocca (1978). *Eros in Greece*. New York: Erotic Art Book Society.

Boelaars, Jan J.M.C. (1981). *Headhunters About Themselves: an Ethnographic Report from Irian Jaya, Indonesia*. The Hague: Martinus Nijhoff.

Bogin, Meg (ed.) (1976). *The Women Troubadours*. New York: Norton.

Bogoras, W. G. (1904). "The Chukchee." *Memoirs of the American Museum of Natural History* 11. New York: Museum.

Bolinder, Gustav (1925). *Die Indianer der tropischen Schneegebirge: Forschungen im nordlichen Südamerika*. Stuttgart: Strecker und Schröder.

Boling, Robert G. (1975). *Judges*. Anchor Bible Series 6A. Garden City, N.Y.: Doubleday.

Bomhard, Allan R. (1977). "The I.E.-Semitic Hypothesis Re-Examined." *Journal of Indo-European Studies* 5:55–99.

Bonnet, Marie-Jo (1981). *Un choix sans équivoque: Recherches historiques sur les relations amoureuses entre les femmes, XVIᵉ–XXᵉ siècle*. Paris: Editions Denoël.

Boogard, Henk van den, and Kathelijne van Kammen (1985). "'We Cannot Jump Over Our Own Shadow': On Cuban Actions Against Homosexuals and Against Antihomosexuality." Pp. 29–41 in *IGA Pink Book 1985*. Amsterdam: COC.

Boon, Leo J. (1983). "Those Damned Sodomites." In *Among Men, Among Women*. Amsterdam: Conference Papers.

Borgeaud, Philippe (1979). *Recherches sur le dieu Pan*. Geneva: Institut Suisse de Rome.

Borger, Rykle (1971). *Akkadische Zeichenliste*. Neukirchner-Vluyn: Butzon und Bercker Kevelaer.

Borghouts, J. F. (1981). "Monthu and Matrimonial Squabbles." *Revue d'Égyptologie* 33:11–22.

Borneman, Ernest (1977). "Die sogenannte griechische Liebe: Päderastie in Kult und Ritus des alten Hellas." Pp. 61–71 in Joachim S. Hohmann (ed.), *Der unterdrückte Sexus*. Berlin: Andreas Achenbach Lollar.

Bossu, Jean-Bernard (1962). *Jean-Bernard Bossu's Travels in the Interior of North America, 1751–1762*. Tr. Seymour Feiler. Norman: University of Oklahoma Press.

Boswell, John (1980). *Christianity, Social Tolerance, and Homosexuality: Gay People in Western Europe from the Beginning of the Christian Era to the Fourteenth Century.* Chicago: University of Chicago Press.

——— (1982). *Rediscovering Gay History.* London: Gay Christian Movement.

——— (1982/83). "Revolutions, Universals, Categories." *Salmagundi* 58–59:89–113.

Bottéro, J. and H. Petschow (1975). "Homosexualität." Pp. 459–68 in Erich Ebeling and Bruno Meissner (eds.), *Reallexikon der Assyriologie und Vorderasiatischen Archäologie,* vol. 4. Berlin: Walter de Gruyter.

Boucé, Paul-Gabriel (1983). "The Secret Nexus: Sex and Literature in Eighteenth-Century Britain." Pp. 70–89 in Alan Bold (ed.), *The Sexual Dimension in Literature.* Totowa, N.J.: Barnes and Noble.

Bouge, L.-J. (1955). "Un aspect du rôle rituel du 'Mahu' dans l'ancien Tahiti." *Journal de la société des Océanistes* 11:147–49.

Bouhdiba, Abeelwahab (1985). *Sexuality in Islam.* Tr. Alan Sheridan. London: Routledge and Kegan Paul.

Boulding, Elise (1976). *The Underside of History: A View of Women through Time.* Boulder, Colo.: Westview Press.

Bourdonnay, Katherine (1983). "Uncle Sam Doesn't Want You!" *Advocate* 367 (May 12):20–21, 57–59.

Bourke, John G. (1892). "The Medicine Men of the Apache." *Report of the Bureau of Ethnology, 1887–88.* 9:443–603.

Bowers, Alfred (1950). *Mandan Social and Ceremonial Organization.* Chicago: University of Chicago Press.

——— (1965). *Hidatasa Social and Ceremonial Organization.* Bureau of American Ethnology Bulletin 194.

Bowersock, Glen W. (1978). *Julian the Apostate.* Cambridge, Mass.: Harvard University Press.

Bowle, John (1964). *Henry VIII: A Biography.* London: George Allen and Unwin.

Boxer, C. R. (1964). *The Golden Age of Brazil, 1695–1750: Growing Pains of a Colonial Society.* Berkeley: University of California Press.

Boyce, Mary (1975). *A History of Zoroastrianism,* vol. 1. Leiden: E. J. Brill.

Boyd, Malcolm (1987). "Inside Russia." *Advocate* 478 (Aug. 4):28–73.

Boyer, Jean Baptiste de, Marquis d'Argens (1975). *Thérèse philosophe.* Paris: Eurodif. Orig. pub. 1748.

Boyer, Paul (1978). *Urban Masses and Moral Order in America, 1820–1920.* Cambridge, Mass.: Harvard University Press.

Bradbury, Gail (1981). "Irregular Sexuality in the 'Comedia.'" *Modern Language Review* 76:566–80.

Brady, Edward Rochie (1952). *Christian Egypt: Church and People.* New York: Oxford University Press.

Brantôme. Pierre (1933). *Lives of Fair and Gallant Ladies.* Tr. A. R. Allinson. New York: Liveright.

Braun, Walter (1966). *Lesbian Love, Old and New.* London: Luxor.

Bray, Alan (1982). *Homosexuality in Renaissance England.* London: Gay Men's Press.

Breasted, James Henry (1906). *Ancient Records of Egypt.* 5 vols. Chicago: University of Chicago Press.

——— (1912). *Development of Religion and Thought in Ancient Egypt.* London: Hodder and Stoughton.

Brelich, Angelo (1969). *Paides a parthenoi.* Rome: Edizioni dell' Ateneo.

Bremmer, Jan (1976). "Avunculate and Fosterage." *Journal of Indo-European Studies* 4:65–78.

——— (1980). "An Enigmatic Indo-European Rite: Paederasty." *Arethusa* 13: 279–98.

——— (1983). "The Importance of the Maternal Uncle and Grandfather in Archaic and Classical Greece and Early Byzantium." *Zeitschrift für Papyrologie und Epigraphik* 50:173–86.

——— (1987). "Roman Myth and Mythography." In J. N. Bremmer and N. M. Horstall (eds.), *Studies in Roman Myth and Mythography.* London: Institute of Classical Studies.

——— (1988). "Adolescents, Symposium and Pederasty." In O. Murray (ed.), *Sympotica.* Oxford: Oxford University Press.

Brettes, Count Joseph de (1903). "Les Indiens Arhouaques-Kaggabas." *Bulletin et mémoires de la société d'anthropologie de Paris* 4 (5th ser.):318–57.

Brézol, Georges (1911). *Henri III et ses mignons.* Paris: Les Editions de Bibliophiles.

Bridenbaugh, Carl (1968). *Vexed and Troubled Englishmen, 1590–1642.* New York: Oxford University Press.

Brier, Bob (1980). *Ancient Egyptian Magic.* New York: William Morrow.

Briffault, Robert (1927). *The Mothers.* New York: Macmillan.

Bristow, Edward J. (1977). *Vice and Vigilance: Purity Movements in Britain since 1700.* Totowa, NJ: Rowman and Littlefield.

Broch, H. B. (1977). "A Note on Berdache among the Hare Indians of Northwestern Canada." *Western Canadian Journal of Anthropology* 7:95–101.

Brockelmann, Carl (1960). *History of the Islamic Peoples.* Tr. Joel Carmichael and Moshe Perlmann. New York: Capricorn.

Brome, Vincent (1979). *Havelock Ellis: Philosopher of Sex.* Boston: Routledge and Kegan Paul.

Bronner, Leah (1967). *Sects and Separatism during the Second Jewish Commonwealth.* New York: Bloch.

Bronski, Michael (1984). *Culture Clash: The Making of Gay Sensibility.* Boston: South End.

Brooke, Christopher (1972). *Medieval Church and Society.* New York: New York University Press.

——— (1975). *Europe in the Central Middle Ages, 962–1154.* London: Longman.

Brooke, James (1984). "A City's Blight: Riots, Crime, Golf in the Streets." *New York Times,* Aug. 23.

Brooks, Beatrice A. (1941). "Fertility Cult Functionaries in the Old Testament." *Journal of Biblical Literature* 60:246–50.

Brooten, Bernadette J. (1983). "Patristic Interpretations of Rom. i.26." Paper presented to the Ninth International Conference on Patristic Studies, Oxford, Eng.

Broude, Gwen J., and Sarah J. Greene (1976). "Cross-Cultural Codes on Twenty Sexual Attitudes and Practices." *Ethnology* 15:409–29.

Brown, Judith C. (1984). "Lesbian Sexuality in Renaissance Italy: the Case of Sister Benedetta Carlini." *Signs* 9:751–58.

——— (1985). *Immodest Acts: The Life of a Lesbian Nun in Renaissance Italy*. New York: Oxford University Press.

Brown, Judith K. (1970). "Economic Organization and the Position of Women among the Iroquois." *Ethnohistory* 17:151–67.

Brown, Peter (1971). "The Rise and Function of the Holy Man in Late Antiquity." *Journal of Roman Studies* 61:80–101.

——— (1972). *Religion and Society in the Age of Augustine*. New York: Harper and Row.

——— (1978). *The Making of Late Antiquity*. Cambridge, Mass.: Harvard University Press.

Browne, F. W. Stella (1923). "Studies in Feminine Inversion." *Journal of Sexology and Psychoanalysis* 51.

Browne, W. G. (1799). *Travels in Africa, Egypt, and Syria from the Year 1792 to 1798*. London: T. Cadell.

Brucker, Gene A. (1962). *Florentine Politics and Society, 1343–1378*. Princeton, N.J.: Princeton University Press.

——— (1971). *The Society of Renaissance Florence: A Documentary Study*. New York: Harper and Row.

Brundage, Burr Cartwright (1967). *Lords of Cuzco: A History and Description*. Norman: University of Oklahoma Press.

——— (1975). *Two Earths, Two Heavens: An Essay Contrasting the Aztecs and the Incas*. Albuquerque: University of New Mexico Press.

Brunel, René (1955). *Le monachisme errant dans l'Islam: Sidd Heddi et les Heddāwa*. Paris: Larose.

Brunner, Karl (ed.) (1933). *The Seven Sages of Rome* (Southern Version). London: Oxford University Press.

Bry, Isle, and Alfred H. Rifkin (1962). "Freud and the History of Ideas: Primary Sources, 1886–1910." *Science and Psychoanalysis* 5:6–36.

Bryant, Anita, and Bob Green (1978). *At Any Cost*. Old Tappan, N.J.: Fleming H. Revell.

Bryk, Felix (1933). *Voodoo-Eros: Ethnological Studies in the Sex-Life of the African Aborigines*. Tr. Mayne F. Sexton. New York: Falstaff.

Buckley, William F., Jr. (1986). "Crucial Steps in Combating the AIDS Epidemic." *New York Times*, Mar. 18.

Budge, E. A. Wallis (1895). *The Book of the Dead: The Papyrus of Ani in the British Museum*. London: British Museum.

——— (1901). *The Book of the Dead*, vol. 2. London: Kegan Paul, Trench, Trübner.

——— (1909). *The Book of the Opening of the Mouth*, vol. 1. London: Kegan Paul, Trench, Trübner.

——— (1972). *From Fetish to God in Ancient Egypt*. New York: Benjamin Blom. Orig. pub. 1934.

——— (1973). *Osiris and the Egyptian Resurrection*. New York: Dover. Orig. pub. 1911.

Buffière, Felix (1980). *Eros Adolescent: La Pédérastie dans la Grèce Antique*. Paris: Les Belles Lettres.

Buffum, Peter C. (1973). *Homosexuality in Prisons*. Washington, DC: National Institute of Law Enforcement and Criminal Justice.

Bullough, Vern (1971). "Attitudes toward Deviant Sex in Ancient Mesopotamia." *Journal of Sex Research* 7:184–203.

—— (1973a). "Homosexuality as Submissive Behavior: Example from Mythology." *Journal of Sex Research* 9:283–88.

—— (1973b). *The Subordinate Sex*. Baltimore: Penguin.

—— (1974a). "Transvestites in the Middle Ages." *American Journal of Sociology* 79:1381–94.

—— (1974b). "Heresy, Witchcraft, and Sexuality." *Journal of Homosexuality* 1: 183–201.

—— (1976). *Sexual Variance in Society and History*. New York: Wiley.

—— (1979). *Homosexuality: A History*. New York: American Library.

—— and Bonnie Bullough (1980). "Homosexuality in Nineteenth Century English Public Schools." Pp. 123–31 in Joseph Harry and Man Singh Das (eds.), *Homosexuality in International Perspective*. New York: Advent.

—— and James Brundage (1982). *Sexual Practices and the Medieval Church*. Buffalo, N.Y.: Prometheus.

—— and Martha Voght (1973). "Homosexuality and Its Confusion with the 'Secret Sin' in Pre-Freudian America." *Journal of the History of Medicine* 28: 143–55.

Bulmer, R. (1967). "Why is the Cassowary Not a Bird? A Problem of Zoological Taxonomy among the Karam of the New Guinea Highlands." *Man* 2:5–25.

Bunch, Charlotte (1975). "Lesbians in Revolt." Pp. 29–37 in Nancy Myron and Charlotte Bunch (eds.), *Lesbians and the Women's Movement*. Oakland, Calif.: Diana.

Burford, E. J. (1976). *Bawds and Lodgings: A History of the London Bankside Brothels c. 100–1675*. London: Peter Owen.

Burg, B. R. (1983). *Sodomy and the Perception of Evil: English Sea Rovers in the Seventeenth-Century Caribbean*. New York: New York University Press.

Bürgel, J. C. (1979). "Love, Lust and Longing: Eroticism in Early Islam as Reflected in Literary Sources." Pp. 81–118 in Afaf Lutfi al-Sayyid-Marsot (ed.), *Society and the Sexes in Medieval Islam*. Malibu, Calif.: Undena.

Burgener, Peter (1964). *Die Einflüsse des zeitgenossischen Denkens in Morels Begriff der Dégénerescence*. Unpublished dissertation, University of Zurich.

Burkert, Walter (1985). *Greek Religion, Archaic and Classical*. Tr. John Raffan. Oxford: Basil Blackwell.

Burkhardt, John Lewis (1822). *Travels in Syria and the Holy Land*. London: S. Murray.

—— (1829). *Travels in Arabia*. London: Henry Colburn.

Burland, Cottie (1973). "North America." Pp. 107–42 in Philip Rawson (ed.), *Primitive Erotic Art*. New York: G. P. Putnam's Sons.

Burnham, John C. (1960). "Psychiatry, Psychology and the Progressive Movement." *American Quarterly* 12:457–65.

—— (1971). "Medical Specialists and Movements Toward Social Control in the Progressive Era: Three Examples." Pp. 19–30 in Jerry Israel (ed.), *Building the Organizational Society*, New York: Free Press.

—— (1973). "Early References to Homosexuality in American Medical Writings." *Medical Aspects of Human Sexuality* 8:39–49.

Burrow, John W. (1966). *Evolution and Society: A Study in Victorian Social Theory*. London: Cambridge University Press.

Burton, Richard (1886). "Terminal Essay." Pp. 63–302 in *The Book of the Thousand Nights and a Night,* vol. 10. New York: Burton Club.

Burton, Robert (1927). *Anatomy of Melancholy.* New York: Farrar and Rinehart. Orig. pub. 1621.

Burton, Robert V., and John W. M. Whiting (1961). "The Absent Father and Cross-Sex Identity." *Merrill-Palmer Quarterly of Behavior and Development* 7:85–95.

Bury, J. B. (1923). *History of the Later Roman Empire.* London: Macmillan.

Busbecq, Ogier Ghislain de (1744). *Travels into Turkey.* London: J. Robinson.

Bush, Larry (1984). "California Dreams, California Nightmares." *New York Native* (Aug. 27–Sept. 9):20–21.

Bussy-Rabutin, Roger (1868). *Histoire amoureuse des Gaules.* Paris: Garnier. Orig. pub. 1665.

Butler, W. F. (1969). *The Lombard Communes.* Westport, Conn.: Greenwood.

Butt-Thompson, F. W. (1929). *West African Secret Societies: Their Organizations, Officials and Teaching.* London: H. F. and G. Witherby.

Butterworth, E.A.S. (1966). *Some Traces of the Preolympian World in Greek Literature and Myth.* Berlin: Walter de Gruyter.

Buxton, John (1963). "Mandari Witchcraft." Pp. 99–121 in John Middleton and E. H. Winter (eds.), *Witchcraft and Sorcery in East Africa.* New York: Praeger.

Bychowski, G. (1945). "The Ego of Homosexuals." *International Journal of Psycho-Analysis* 26:114–27.

———— (1954). "The Structure of Homosexual Acting Out." *Psychoanalytic Quarterly* 23:48–61.

Cabral, John (1982). "Gay Life in Mainland China: I . . . Very . . . Fear!" *Christopher Street* 6(2):27–32.

Cadden, Joan (1985). "Is Sex Necessary? Late Medieval Scientific Views on Sexual Abstinence." Paper presented to the American Historical Association.

Caelius Aurelianus (1950). *On Acute Diseases and On Chronic Diseases.* Tr. I. E. Drabkin. Chicago: University of Chicago Press.

Calame, Claude (1977). *Les choeurs de jeunes filles en Grèce archaïques.* 2 vols. Rome: Ateneo and Bizzarri.

Califia, Pat (1979). "Lesbian Sexuality." *Journal of Homosexuality* 4:255–66.

Callender, Charles, and Lee M. Kochems (1983a). "The North American Berdache." *Current Anthropology* 24:443–56.

———— (1983b). "Reply." *Current Anthropology* 24:464.

———— (1985). "Men and Not-Men: Male Gender-Mixing Statuses and Homosexuality." *Journal of Homosexuality* 11:165–78.

Campbell, Joseph (1969). *The Masks of God: Primitive Mythology.* New York: Viking.

Canaday, John (1960). *The Lives of the Painters.* Vol. 1: *Late Gothic to High Renaissance.* London: Thames and Hudson.

Cancian, Francesca (1987). *Love in America: Gender and Self-Development.* New York: Cambridge University Press.

Cantor, Norman F. (1963). *Medieval History: the Life and Death of a Civilization.* New York: Macmillan.

———— (1969). *Medieval History: The Life and Death of a Civilization* 2d ed., New York: Macmillan.

Caplan, Jane (1981). "Sexuality and Homosexuality." Pp. 149–67 in Cambridge Women's Studies Group (eds.), *Women in Society: Interdisciplinary Essays*. London: Virago.

Cardascia, Guillaume (1969). *Les lois Assyriennes*. Paris: Cerf.

Cardenal, Ernesto (1974). *In Cuba*. Tr. Donald D. Walsh. New York: New Directions.

Carew, Thomas (1949). *The Poems of Thomas Carew*. Oxford: Clarendon.

Carlton, Charles (1982). *Charles I: The Personal Monarch*. Boston: Routledge and Kegan Paul.

Carlton, Eric (1977). *Ideology and Social Order*. London: Routledge and Kegan Paul.

Carpenter, Edward (1908). *The Intermediate Sex: A Study of Some Transitional Types of Men*. London: Mitchell Kennerly.

———— (1914). *Intermediate Types among Primitive Folk*. London: George Allen.

Carrier, J. M. (1976). "Cultural Factors Affecting Urban Mexican Male Homosexual Behavior." *Archives of Sexual Behavior* 6:53–65.

———— (1977). "Sex-Role Preference as an Explanatory Variable in Homosexual Behavior." *Archives of Sexual Behavior* 5:103–24.

———— (1980). "Homosexual Behavior in Cross-Cultural Perspective." Pp. 100–122 in Judd Marmor (ed.), *Homosexual Behavior: A Modern Reappraisal*. New York: Basic.

Carrasco, Rafael (1985). *Inquisicion y Represion Sexual en Valencia: Historia de los Sodomitas (1565–1785)*. Barcelona: Laertes.

Carroll, Michael P. (1978). "Freud on Homosexuality and the Super-Ego: Some Cross-Cultural Tests." *Behavior Science Research* 13:255–72.

Carstairs, George Morrison (1956). "Hinjra and Jiryan: Two Derivations of Hindu Attitudes to Sexuality." *British Journal of Medical Psychology* 29:128–38.

Carswell, John (1973). *From Revolution to Revolution: England, 1688–1776*. London: Routledge and Kegan Paul.

Carter, A. E. (1958). *The Idea of Decadence in French Literature, 1830–1900*. Toronto: University of Toronto Press.

Carter, Dan T. (1969). *Scottsboro: A Tragedy of the American South*. Baton Rouge: Louisiana State University Press.

Cartledge, Paul (1981). "The Politics of Spartan Pederasty." *Proceedings of the Cambridge Philological Society* 207:17–36.

The Case of Atherton, Bishop of Waterford in Ireland: Fairly Represented Against a Late Partial Edition of Dr. Barnard's Relation and Sermon at His Funeral. London: Luke Stokoe, 1710.

Casper, John Ludwig (1852). *Vierteljahrsschrift für gerichtliche und öffentliche Medizin*, vol. 1. Berlin: August Hirschwald. Excerpt reprinted, pp. 239–70 in Joachim S. Hohmann (ed.), *Der unterdrückte Sexus*. Berlin: Andreas Achenbach Lollar, 1977.

Casselaer, Catherine van (1986). *Lot's Wife: Lesbian Paris, 1890–1914*. Liverpool: Janus.

Cassian, John (1965). *Institutions Cénobitiques*. Tr. Jean-Claude Guy. Paris: Cerf.

Cassirer, Ernest (1955). *The Philosophy of the Enlightenment*. Boston: Beacon.

Cassius Dio (1927). *Roman History*, vol. 8. Tr. Earnest Cary. New York: G. P. Putnam's Sons.

Casson, Lionel (1975). *Daily Life in Ancient Egypt*. New York: American Heritage.

Castle, Terry (1987). "The Culture of Travesty: Sexuality and Masquerade in Eighteenth-Century England." In George S. Rousseau and Roy Porter (eds.), *Liberty's a Glorious Feast: Sexual Underworlds of the Enlightenment*. Manchester: Manchester University Press.

Catlin, George (1973). *Letters and Notes on the Manners, Customs and Conditions of the North American Indians*, vol. 2. New York: Dover. Orig. pub. 1866.

Cavendish, Jack (1771). *A Sapphick Epistle from Jack Cavendish to the Honorable and Most Beautiful Mrs. D.* London: M. Smith.

Cawley, A. C., and J. J. Anderson, eds., (1976). *Pearl, Cleanness, Patience, Sir Gawain and the Green Knight*. London: J. M. Dent.

Chagnon, Napoleon A. (1966). *Yonomamo Warfare, Social Organization and Marriage Alliances*. Ph.D. dissertation, University of Michigan.

———— (1977). *Yonomamo: The Fierce People*. New York: Holt, Rinehart and Winston.

Chalmers, James (1903a). "Notes on the Bugilai, New Guinea." *Journal of the Royal Anthropological Institute of Great Britain and Ireland* 33:108–10.

———— (1903b). "Notes on the Natives of Kiwai Island, Fly River, British New Guinea." *Journal of the Royal Anthropological Institute of Great Britain and Ireland* 33:117–24.

Chambliss, William J. (1964). "A Sociological Analysis of the Law of Vagrancy." *Social Problems* 11:67–77.

Chancer, Lynn (1985). "New Bedford, March 6, 1983: Why Couldn't a Community Separate the Rapists from the Raped?" Unpublished paper.

Chandler, Alfred D. (1977). *The Visible Hand: The Managerial Revolution in American Business*. Cambridge, Mass.: Harvard University Press.

Chandos, John (1984). *Boys Together: English Public Schools, 1800–1864*. London: Hutchinson.

Chang, Judy, and Jack Block (1960). "A Study of Identification in Male Homosexuals." *Journal of Consulting Psychology* 24:307–10.

Chapin, Bradley (1983). *Criminal Justice in Colonial America, 1606–1660*. Athens: University of Georgia Press.

Charcot, Jean-Martin, and Valentine Magnan (1882). "Inversion du sens génital." *Archives de Neurologie* 3:53–60 and 4:296–322.

Charles, R. H. (ed.) (1913). *The Apocrypha and Pseudepigrapha of the Old Testament in English*. 2 vols. London: Oxford University Press.

Charlesworth, James H. (1985). *The Old Testament Pseudepigrapha*. 2 vols. Garden City, N.Y.: Doubleday.

Charlevoix, P.F.X. de (1744). *Journal d'un voyage*. vol. 3. Paris: Pierre-Francois Giffart.

Chauncey, George Jr. (1982/83). "From Sexual Inversion to Homosexuality: Medicine and the Changing Conceptualization of Female Deviance." *Salmagundi* 58–59:114–46.

———— (1985). "Christian Brotherhood or Sexual Perversion? Homosexual Identities and the Construction of Sexual Boundaries in the World War One Era." *Journal of Social History* 19:198–211.

———— (1986). "Gay Male Society in the Jazz Age." *Village Voice* 31 (July 1):29–30, 32.

Ch'en, Paul Heng-chao (1979). *Chinese Legal Tradition under the Mongols: The Code of 1291 as Reconstructed*. Princeton: Princeton University Press.

Chêng, Tê-k'un (1960). *Archaeology in China*. Vol. 2: *Shang China*. Cambridge, Eng.: W. Heffner.

Cheng, W. (1963). *Erotologie de la Chine*. Paris: J. J. Pauvert.

Chenier, Louis de (1788). *The Present State of the Empire of Morocco*. London: G. J. and J. Robinson.

Chevalier, Julien (1893). *Inversion sexuelle*. Paris: Masson.

Childs, Maggie (1977). "Japan's Homosexual Heritage." *Gai Saber* 1:41–45.

——— (1980). "Chigo monogatari: Love Stories on Buddhist Sermons?" *Monumenta Nipponica* 35:127–51.

Chitty, Derwas (1966). *The Desert a City: An Introduction to the Study of Egyptian and Palestinian Monasticism under the Christian Empire*. Oxford: Blackwell.

Chodorow, Nancy (1978). *The Reproduction of Mothering: Psychoanalysis and the Sociology of Gender*. Berkeley: University of California Press.

Chorier, Nicolas (1890). *The Dialogues of Luisa Sigea*. Tr. N. C. Paris: Isidore Liseux.

Christensen, James Boyd (1954). *Double Descent among the Fanti*. New Haven: Human Relations Area Files.

Church, R. W. (1937). *Saint Anselm*. London: Macmillan.

Churchill, Wainright (1967). *Homosexual Behavior among Males: A Cross-Cultural and Cross-Species Investigation*. Englewood Cliffs, N.J.: Prentice-Hall.

Cicero (1927). *Tusculan Disputations*. Tr. J. E. King. New York: G. P. Putnam's Sons.

Cipriani, Lidio (1961). "Hygiene and Medical Practices among the Onge (Little Andaman)." *Anthropos* 56:481–500.

——— (1966). *The Andaman Islanders*. Tr. D. Taylor Cox. New York: Praeger.

Claessen, Henri J. M., and Peter Skalnik (eds.) (1978). *The Early State*. The Hague: Mouton.

Clark, Alice (1919). *The Working Life of Women in the Seventeenth Century*. London: Routledge.

Clark, Charles Allen (1961). *Religions of Old Korea*. Seoul: Christian Literature Society of Korea.

Clark, Elizabeth A. (1979). *Jerome, Chrysostom, and Friends: Essays and Translations*, vol. 2. New York: Edwin Mellin.

Clark, Ross (1979). "Language, " Pp. 249–70 in Jesse D. Jennings (ed.), *The Prehistory of Polynesia*. Cambridge, Mass.: Harvard University Press.

Clark, Grahame (1967). *The Stone Age Hunters*. New York: McGraw-Hill.

Clark, Norman H. (1976). *Deliver Us from Evil: An Interpretation of American Prohibition*. New York: W. W. Norton.

Clarke, Alan (1987a). "Moral Reform and the Anti-Abortion Movement." *Sociological Review* 35:123–49.

——— (1987b). "Moral Protest, Status Defence and the Anti-Abortion Campaign." *British Journal of Sociology* 38:235–53.

Clastres, Pierre (1977). *Society against the State: The Leader as Servant and the Humane Uses of Power among Indians of the Americas*. Tr. Robert Hurley. New York: Urizen.

Claudel, Paul, and André Gide (1949). *Correspondence, 1899–1926*. Paris: Gallimard.

Claudius Ptolemy (1976). *Tetrabiblos*. Tr. J. M. Ashmond. North Hollywood, Calif.: Symbols and Signs.

Clelland, Donald A., Thomas C. Hood, C. M. Lipsey, and Ronald Wimberley (1974). "In the Company of the Converted: Characteristics of a Billy Graham Crusade." *Sociological Analysis* 35:45–56.

Clemens, Titus Flavius, Alexandria (1870). *The Writings of Clement of Alexandria.* Tr. William Wilson. Edinburgh: T. and T. Clark.

Clendinen, Dudley (1983). "Throughout the Country, Homosexuals Increasingly Flex Political Muscle." *New York Times,* Nov. 8.

Cleugh, James (1963). *Love Locked Out: An Examination of Sexuality during the Middle Ages.* New York: Crown.

Cline, Walter (1936). *Notes on the People of Siwah and El Garah in the Libyan Desert.* Menasha, Wis.: George Banta.

——— et al. (1938). *The Sinkaietk or Southern Okanagon of Washington.* Menasha, Wis.: George Banta.

Cobbett, William (1812). *Weekly Political Register* 21 (June 13):748–49.

Cochran, Thomas C. (1959). *Basic History of American Business.* Princeton: D. Van Nostrand.

Cody, Jane M. (1976). "The *Senex Amator* in Plautus' *Casina.*" *Hermes* 104:453–76.

Coffignon, Ali (1889). *Paris vivant: La corruption à Paris.* Paris: Kolb.

Coffin, Tristram (1966). *The Sex Kick: Erotica in Modern America.* New York: Macmillan.

Cogan, Morton (1974). *Imperialism and Religion: Assyria, Judah and Israel in the Eighth and Seventh Centuries B.C.E.* Missoula, Mont.: Scholars.

Cohen, David (1987). "Law, Society and Homosexuality in Classical Athens." *Past and Present* 117:1–21.

Cohen, Jeremy (1982). *The Friars and the Jews: The Evolution of Medieval Anti-Judaism.* Ithaca, NY: Cornell University Press.

Cohen, Ronald, and Elman R. Service (eds.) (1978). *Origins of the State: The Anthropology of Political Evolution.* Philadelphia: Institute for the Study of Human Services.

Cohen, Steven F., and James E. Gallagher (1984). "Gay Movements and Legal Change: Some Aspects of the Dynamics of a Social Problem." *Social Problems* 32:72–81.

Coleman, Peter (1980). *Christian Attitudes to Homosexuality.* London: SPCK.

Colin, Jean (1955–57). "Juvenal et le mariage mystique de Gracchus." *Atti della Accademia delle scienze di Torino* 90(2):114–216.

Collins, Harry M. (1981). "Stages in the Empirical Programme of Relativism." *Social Studies of Science* 11:3–10.

Colson, Elizabeth (1958). *Marriage and the Family among the Plateau Tonga of Northern Rhodesia.* Manchester: Manchester University Press.

Combe, Andrew (1834). *Principles of Physiology Applied to the Preservation of Health, and to the Improvement of Physical and Marital Education.* Edinburgh: Black.

Cominos, Peter (1963). "Late-Victorian Sexual Respectability and the Social System." *International Review of Social History* 8:18–48, 216–50.

Commons, John R. (1968). *Legal Foundations of Capitalism.* Madison: University of Wisconsin Press.

Conrad, Jack (1973). *The Horn and the Sword. The History of the Bull as Symbol of Power and Fertility.* Westport, Conn.: Greenwood.

Conrad, Peter, and Joseph W. Schneider (1980). *Deviance and Medicalization: From Badness to Sickness.* St. Louis: C. V. Mosby.

Contreras, Jaime, and Gustav Henningsen (1986). "Forty-Four Thousand Cases of the Spanish Inquisition (1540–1700): Analysis of a Historical Data Bank." Pp. 100–129 in Gustav Henningsen and John Tedeschi (eds.), *The Inquisition in Early Modern Europe: Studies on Sources and Methods.* Dekalb: Northern Illinois University Press.

Conway, Flo, and Jim Siegelman (1982). *Holy Terror: The Fundamentalist War on America's Freedoms in Religion, Politics and Our Private Lives.* Garden City, N.Y.: Doubleday.

Cook, J. M. (1983). *The Persian Empire.* New York: Schocken.

Cooke, George A. (1903). *A Text-Book of North-Semitic Inscriptions.* Oxford: Clarendon.

Coon, Carleton Stevens (1931). *Tribes of the Rif.* Harvard African Studies IX. Cambridge, Mass.: Peabody Museum of Harvard University.

Cooper, John M. (1917). *Analytical and Critical Bibliography of the Tribes of Tierra del Fuego and Adjacent Territory.* Bulletin of American Ethnology 63. Washington, D.C.: Government Printing Office.

——— (1963). "The Patagonian and Pampean Hunters." Pp. 127–68 in Julian H. Steward (ed.), *Handbooks of South American Indians.* vol. 1. Washington, D.C.: Government Printing Office.

Cooter, Roger (1984). *The Cultural Meaning of Popular Science: Phrenology and the Organization of Consent in Nineteenth-Century Britain.* Cambridge: Cambridge University Press.

Corre, Armand (1894). *L'ethnographie criminelle.* Paris: C. Reinwald.

Cort, Joan, and Edmund Carlevale (1982). "Murder in Maine Renews Interest in Rights Bill." *Advocate* 42 (Sept. 4):12, 13.

Coser, Lewis A. (1964). "The Political Functions of Eunuchism." *American Sociological Review* 29:880–85.

Costello, John (1985). *Love, Sex and War: Changing Values, 1939–45.* London: William Collins.

Cott, Nancy F. (1978). "Passionless: A Reinterpretation of Victorian Sexual Ideology, 1790–1850." *Signs: Journal of Women in Culture and Society* 4:219–36.

Coulbourn, Rushten (ed.) (1956). *Feudalism in History.* Princeton, N.J.: Princeton University Press.

Coulton, G. G. (1930). *Ten Medieval Studies.* London: Cambridge University Press.

Courouve, Claude (1978). *Les gens de la manchette.* Paris: Aleph.

——— (1979). "Sodomy Trials in France." *Gay Books Bulletin* 1:22–23, 26.

——— (1980). *Fragments.* Paris: Privately printed.

——— (1981). *Les gens de la manchette.* Paris: Collections archives unisexuelles.

——— (1982). "The Word 'Bardache'." *Gay Books Bulletin* 8:18–19.

——— (1985). *Vocabulaire de l'homosexualité masculine.* Paris: Payot.

Covarrubias, Miguel (1965). *Island of Bali.* New York: Alfred A. Knopf.

Cowan, Paul (1985). "Pilgrim's Progress." *Village Voice* (Mar. 5):20–22.

Coward, D. A. (1980a). "Attitudes to Homosexuality in Eighteenth-Century France." *Journal of European Studies* 10:231–55.

——— (1980b). "Eighteenth-Century Attitudes to Prostitution." *Studies on Voltaire and the Eighteenth Century* 189:363–99.

Crapanzano, Vincent (1973). *The Hamadsha: A Study in Moroccan Ethnopsychiatry.* Berkeley: University of California Press.

Crawford, Alan (1980). *Thunder on the Right: The "New Right" and the Politics of Resentment.* New York: Pantheon.

Creamer, Winifred, and Jonathan Haas (1985). "Tribe or Chiefdom in Lower Central America." *American Antiquity* 50:738–54.

Creasy, Edward S. (1987). *History of the Ottoman Turks.* London: Richard Bently and Son.

Creed, Gerald W. (1984). "Sexual Subordination: Institutionalized Homosexuality and Social Control in Melanesia." *Ethnology* 23:157–76.

Critchley, John (1978). *Feudalism.* London: George Allen and Unwin.

Crompton, Louis (1976). "Homosexuals and the Death Penalty in Colonial America." *Journal of Homosexuality* 1:277–93.

——— (1978a). "Gay Genocide: From Leviticus to Hitler." Pp. 67–82 in Louie Crew (ed.), *The Gay Academic.* Palm Springs, Calif.: ETC.

——— (1978b). "What Do You Say to Someone Who Claims That Homosexuality Caused the Fall of Greece and Rome?" *Christopher Street* 2(9):49–52.

——— (1980/81). "The Myth of Lesbian Impunity: Capital Laws from 1270 to 1791." *Journal of Homosexuality* 6:11–26.

——— (1983). "*Don Leon,* Byron, and Homosexual Law Reform." *Journal of Homosexuality* 8:53–71.

——— (1985). *Byron and Greek Love: Homophobia in Nineteenth-Century England.* Berkeley: University of California Press.

Cross, F. Moore (1966). "Aspects of Samaritan and Jewish History in Late Persian and Hellenistic Times." *Harvard Theological Review* 59:201–11.

Crowder, Michael (1959). *Pagans and Politicians.* London: Hutchinson.

Crumley, Carole L. (1974). *Celtic Social Structure: The Generation of Archaeologically Testable Hypotheses from Literary Evidence.* Anthropological Papers No. 54. Ann Arbor: University of Michigan Museum of Anthropology.

Cucchiari, Salvatore (1981). "The Gender Revolution and the Transition from Bisexual Horde to Patrilocal Band: The Origins of Gender Hierarchy." Pp. 31–79 in Sherry B. Ortner and Harriet Whitehead (eds.), *Sexual Meanings: The Cultural Construction of Gender and Sexuality.* Cambridge: Cambridge University Press.

Curtis, T. C., and W. R. Speck (1976). "The Societies for the Reformation of Manners." *Literature and History* 3:45–64.

Curtius, E. R. (1953). *European Literature and the Latin Middle Ages.* Tr. W. Trask. New York: Pantheon.

Czaplicka, M. A. (1914). *Aboriginal Siberia. A Study in Social Anthropology.* Oxford: Clarendon Press.

Dall, William H. (1870). *Alaska and Its Resources.* Boston: Lee and Shepard.

Dall'Orto, Giovanni (1983). "Antonio Rocco and the Background of His 'L'Alcibiade Fanciullo a Scola' (1652)." Pp. 224–32, 571–72 in *Among Men, Among Women.* Amsterdam: Conference Papers.

Daniel, F. E. (1893). "Castration of Sexual Perverts." *Texas Medical Journal* 8:255–71. Reprinted, pp. 135–37 in Jonathan N. Katz (ed.), *Gay American History.* New York: Crowell, 1976.

Daniel, Marc (1957). *Hommes du grand siècles: Études sur l'homosexualité sous les regnes de Louis XIII et de Louis XIV*. Paris: Arcadie.

—— (1959). "Les amants du soleil levant." *Arcadie* 66:346–56.

—— (1960). "Henri IV le Guère Galant (Henri IV de Castille, 1425–1475)." *Arcadie* 75:159–72.

—— (1961a). "A propos de Cambacéres." *Arcadie* 95:559–68.

—— (1961b). "Histoire de la législation pénale française concernant l'homosexualité." *Arcadie* 96:618–27 and 97:10–29.

—— (1961c). "A Study of Homosexuality in France during the Reigns of Louis XIII and Louis XIV." *Homophile Studies* 4:125–36.

—— (1963). "Nos ancêtres les Hittites." *Arcadie* 115–16:353–56.

—— (1972). "Un homophile au temps des buchers." *Arcadie* 220:170–73.

—— (1975/76). "La civilisation Arabe et l'amour masculine." *Arcadie* 253:8–19, 254:83–93, 255:142–150, 257:269–74, 258:326–30, 259–60:391–95, 263:619–26 and 267:182–87.

—— (1977). "Arab Civilization and Male Love." Tr. Winston Leyland. *Gay Sunshine* 32:1–11, 27.

—— (1979). "L'Ayatollah et les pelotons d'execution." *Arcadie* 305:388–89.

Daniel, Norman (1979). *The Arabs and Medieval Europe*. London: Longman.

Danielou, Alain (1960). *Le polythéisme hindou*. Paris: Buchet-Castel.

Danielsson, Bengt (1956). *Love in the South Seas*. Tr. F. H. Lyon. New York: Reynal.

Dank, Barry (1971). "Coming Out in the Gay World." *Psychiatry* 34:180–97.

—— (1974). "Symbolic Interactionism and the Homosexual Identity." Unpublished paper presented to the American Sociological Association.

Davenport, William H. (1965). "Sexual Patterns and their Regulation in a Society of the Southwest Pacific." Pp. 164–207 in Frank A. Beach (ed.), *Sex and Behavior*. New York: Wiley.

—— (1977). "Sex in Cross-Cultural Perspective." Pp. 115–63 in Frank Beach (ed.), *Human Sexuality: Four Perspectives*. Baltimore: Johns Hopkins Press.

Davidson, H. R. Ellis (1967). *Pagan Scandinavia*. New York: Praeger.

Davies, Christie (1975). *Permissive Britain: Social Change in the Sixties and Seventies*. London: Pitman.

—— (1982). "Sexual Taboos and Social Boundaries." *American Journal of Sociology* 87:1033–63.

Davies, John D. (1955). *Phrenology, Fad and Science: A Nineteenth-Century American Crusade*. New Haven: Yale University Press.

Davies, Stevan L. (1980). *The Revolt of the Windows: The Social World of the Apocryphal Acts*. Carbondale: Southern Illinois University Press.

Davies, William D. (1948). *Paul and Rabbinic Judaism: Some Rabbinic Elements in Pauline Theology*. London: S.P.C.K.

Davis, James A. (1982). "Achievement Variables and Class Cultures: Family, Schooling, Job, and Forty-Nine Dependent Variables in the Cumulative GSS." *American Sociological Review* 47:569–86.

Davis, Katherine Bement (1972). *Factors in the Sex Life of Twenty-Two Hundred Women*. New York: Arno.

Davis, Kingsley (1961). "Sexual Behavior." Pp. 322–72 in Robert K. Merton and

Robert A. Nisbet (eds.), *Contemporary Social Problems*. New York: Harcourt, Brace and World.

Davis, Natalie Zemon (1971). "The Reasons of Misrule: Youth Groups and Charivaris in Sixteenth-Century France." *Past and Present* 50:51–75.

—— (1975). *Society and Culture in Early Modern France*. Stanford, Calif.: Stanford University Press.

Dawson, Christopher, ed. (1955). *The Mongol Mission: Narratives and Letters of the Franciscan Missionaries in Mongolia and China in the Thirteenth and Fourteenth Centuries*. Tr. A Nun of Stanbrook Abbey. London: Sheed and Ward.

Dawson, Warren (1936). "Observations on Ch. Beatty Papyri VII, VIII and XII." *Journal of Egyptian Archaeology* 22:106–8.

Day, Robert Adams (1982). "Sex, Scatology, Smollett." Pp. 225–43 in Paul-Gabriel Boucé (ed.), *Sexuality in Eighteenth-Century Britain*. Manchester: Manchester University Press.

Deacon, A. Bernard (1934), *Malekula: A Vanishing People in the New Hebrides*. London: George Routledge and Sons.

Deakin, Terence J. (1966). "Evidence for Homosexuality in Ancient Egypt." *International Journal of Greek Love* 1:31–38.

Degler, Carl N. (1974). "What Ought to Be and What Was: Women's Sexuality in the Nineteenth Century." *American Historical Review* 79:1467–90.

—— (1980). *At Odds: Women and the Family in America from the Revolution to the Present*. New York: Oxford University Press.

Deissman, Adolf (1927). *Light from the Ancient Near East: The New Testament Illustrated by Recently Discovered Texts of the Graeco-Roman World*. Tr. Lionel R. M. Strachan. New York: George M. Doran.

Dekker, Rudolf M., and Lotte C. van de Pol (1987). *The Tradition of Female Cross-Dressing in Early Modern Europe*. London: Macmillan.

Delacroix, Jacques-Vincent (1777). *Peinture des moeurs du siècle, ou Lettres et discours sur differents sujets*. Amsterdam: Lejay.

Delafosse, Maurice (1912). *Haut-Sénégal Niger, Soudan Française*, vol. 3. Paris: E. Larose.

Delaporte, L. (1970). *Mesopotamia: The Babylonian and Assyrian Civilization*. Tr. V. Gordon Childe. New York: Barnes and Noble. Orig. pub. 1925.

Delatte, Dom Paul (1950). *The Rule of St. Benedict*. Tr. Dom Justin McCann. Latrobe, Pa.: Archabbey.

Delcourt, Marie (1966). *Hermaphroditea: Recherches sur l'étre double promoteur de la fertilité dans le monde classique*. Brussels: Latomus.

Delon, Michel (1985). "The Priest, the Philosopher, and Homosexuality in Enlightenment France." *Eighteenth-Century Life* 9 (n.s.):122–31.

Delph, Edward William (1978). *The Silent Community: Public Homosexual Encounters*. Beverly Hills, Calif.: Sage.

Demandt, Alexander (1984). *Der Fall Roms: Die Auflösung des Römischen Reiches im Urteil der Nachwelt*. Munich: Beck.

D'Emilio, John (1981). "Gay Politics, Gay Community: San Francisco's Experience." *Socialist Review* 55:77–104.

—— (1983a). *Sexual Politics, Sexual Communities: The Making of a Homosexual Minority in the United States, 1940–1970.* Chicago: University of Chicago Press.

—— (1983b). "Capitalism and Gay Identity." Pp. 100–113 in Ann Snitow, Christine Stansell, and Sharon Thompson (eds.), *Powers of Desire.* New York: Monthly Review Press.

—— (1984). "Making and Unmaking Minorities: The Tensions Between Gay Politics and History." *New York University Review of Law and Social Change* 14: 915–22.

Denig, Edward Thompson (1953). "Of the Crow Nation." Pp. 64–68 in *Anthropological Papers* 33, U.S. Bureau of American Ethnology, Bulletin 151. Washington, D.C.: Government Printing Office. Reprinted in John C. Ewers (ed.), *Five Indian Tribes of the Upper Missouri.* Norman: University of Oklahoma Press, 1961.

Derrett, J. Duncan M. (1973). *Dharmaśāstra and Juridical Literature.* Wiesbaden: Otto Harrassowitz.

Desai, Devagana (1975). *Erotic Sculpture of India: A Socio-Cultural Study.* New Delhi: Tala McGraw-Hill.

Desmon, André-Claude (1963). "Petits homophiles et grand siècles." *Arcadie* 115–16:333–45.

Detienne, Marcel (1979). *Dionysos Slain.* Tr. Mireille Muellner and Leonard Muellner. London: Johns Hopkins University Press.

Devereux, George (1937). "Homosexuality among the Mohave Indians." *Human Biology* 9:498–597.

—— (1948). "The Mohave Indian Kamello:y." *Journal of Clinical Psychopathology* 9:433–57.

—— (1950). "Heterosexual Behavior of the Mohave Indians." Pp. 85–128 in Geza Roheim (ed), *Psychoanalysis and the Social Sciences,* vol. 2. New York: International Universities Press.

—— (1967). *From Anxiety to Method in the Behavioral Sciences.* The Hague: Mouton.

De Vos, George A. (1969). *Socialization for Achievement.* Berkeley: University of California Press.

Dickens, A. G. (1959). *Thomas Crowell and the English Reformation.* London: English Universities Press.

Dickey, Samuel (1928). "Some Economic and Social Conditions of Asia Minor Affecting the Expansion of Christianity." Pp. 393–416 in Shirley Jackson Case (ed.), *Studies in Early Christianity.* New York: Century.

Dickson, Donald T. (1968). "Bureaucracy and Morality: An Organizational Perspective on a Moral Crusade." *Social Problems* 16:143–56.

Dickson, H.R.P. (1949). *The Arab of the Desert: A Glimpse into Bedawin Life in Kuwait and Sau'di Arabia.* London: George Allen and Unwin.

Dietrich, B. C. (1974). *The Origins of Greek Religion.* Berlin: Walter de Gruyter.

Dillard, Heath (1984). *Daughters of the Reconquest: Women in Castilian Town Society, 1100–1300.* New York: Cambridge University Press.

Dillon, Myles, and Nora K. Chadwick (1967). *The Celtic Realms.* London: Weidenfeld and Nicolson.

Dinnerstein, Dorothy (1976). *The Mermaid and the Minotaur: Sexual Arrangements and the Human Malaise.* New York: Harper and Row.

Dio Chrysostom (1951). *Works*, vol. 5. Tr. H. Lamar Crosby. Cambridge, Mass.: Harvard University Press.

Diogenes Laertius (1891). *Lives and Opinions of Eminent Philosophers*. Tr. C. D. Yonge. London: George Bell and Sons.

Dionysius of Halicarnassus (1950). *The Roman Antiquities*, vol. 4. Tr. Earnest Cary. Cambridge, Mass.: Harvard University Press.

Divale, William Tylio (1975). "An Explanation for Matrilocal Residence." Pp. 99–108 in Dana Raphael (ed.), *Being Female: Reproduction, Power and Change*. The Hague: Mouton.

——— (1984). *Matrilocal Residence in Pre-Literate Society*. Ann Arbor: UMI Research Press.

Dodd, Charles (1981). "The Legal Problems of Homosexuals." Pp. 139–48 in John Hart and Diane Richardson (eds.), *The Theory and Practice of Homosexuality*. London: Routledge and Kegan Paul.

Dodds, E. R. (1965). *Pagan and Christian in an Age of Anxiety: Some Aspects of Religious Experience from Marcus Aurelius to Constantine*. New York: Cambridge University Press.

Doerner, Klaus (1981). *Madmen and the Bourgeoisie: A Social History of Insanity and Psychiatry*. Tr. Joachim Neugroschel and Jean Steinberg. Oxford: Basil Blackwell.

Döllinger, John J. I. (1862). *The Gentile and the Jew in the Courts of the Temple of Christ: An Introduction to the History of Christianity*. Tr. N. Darnell. London: Longman, Green.

Dominguez, Virginia (1986). *White by Definition: Social Classification in Creole Louisiana*. New Brunswick, N.J.: Rutgers University Press.

Donzelot, Jacques (1979). *The Policing of Families*. Tr. Robert Hurley. New York: Pantheon.

Doré, Henri (1916). *Recherches sur les superstitions en Chine*, part 2, vol. 11. Varieties Sinologiques 46. Shanghai: Mission Catholique à l'Orphelinat de T'ou-sè-wé.

Dorsey, James Owen (1894). "A Study of Siouan Cults." Pp. 351–544 in *Eleventh Annual Report, 1889–90*. U.S. Bureau of American Ethnology. Smithsonian Institution. Washington, D.C.: Government Printing Office.

Douglas, Jack D. (ed.) (1970). *Deviance and Respectability: The Social Construction of Moral Meanings*. New York: Basic.

Douglas, Mary (1970). *Natural Symbols: Explorations in Cosmology*. New York: Pantheon.

Dover, Kenneth J. (1978). *Greek Homosexuality*. Cambridge, Mass.: Harvard University Press.

Downey, Glanville (1960). *Constantinople in the Age of Justinian*. Norman: University of Oklahoma Press.

Drake, C. T., and D. McDougall (1977). "Effects of the Absence of a Father and Other Male Models on the Development of Boys' Sex Roles." *Developmental Psychology* 13:537–38.

Drake, Jonathan (1966). "'Le Vice' in Turkey." *International Journal of Greek Love* 1:13–27.

Drew, Dennis, and Jonathan Drake (1969). *Boys for Sale: A Study of the Prostitution of Young Boys for Sexual Purposes*. Deer Park, N.Y.: Brown.

Driberg, J. H. (1923). *The Lango: A Nilotic Tribe of Uganda*. London: T. Fisher Unwin.

Drinka, George Frederick (1984). *The Birth of Neurosis: Myth, Malady, and the Victorians.* New York: Simon and Schuster.

Driver, G. R., and John C. Miles (1935). *The Assyrian Laws.* New York: Oxford University Press.

——— (1952–55). The Babylonian Laws, 2 vols. Oxford: Clarendon.

Driver, Harold E. (1969). *Indians of North America.* 2d Ed. Chicago: University of Chicago Press.

Dronke, Peter (1968). *Medieval Latin and the Rise of European Love-Lyric,* 2 vols. Oxford: Clarendon.

Drucker, Philip (1941). "Cultural Element Distributions: XVII, Yuman-Piman." *Anthropological Records* 6:91–230.

Drysdale, George R. (1861). *The Elements of Social Science; or, Physical, Sexual and Natural Religion,* 4th ed. London: E. Truelove.

Dubbert, Joe L. (1974). "Progressivism and the Masculinity Crisis." *Psychoanalytic Review* 61:443–55.

——— (1979). *Man's Place: Masculinity in Transition.* Englewood Cliffs, N.J.: Prentice-Hall.

Duberman, Martin (1979). "Hopi Indian Sexuality." *Radical History Review* 20: 99–130.

——— (1982/83). "'Writhing Bedfellows': 1826—Two Young Men from Antebellum South Carolina's Ruling Elite Share 'Extravagant Delight.'" *Journal of Homosexuality* 6:151–70.

——— (1986). *About Time: Exploring the Gay Past.* New York: Sea Horse.

Dubois, Abbe Jean Antoine (1906). *Hindu Manners, Customs and Ceremonies.* Tr. Henry K. Beauchamp. Oxford: Clarendon.

Du Bois, Cora (1944). *The People of Alor: A Social-Psychological Study of an East Indian Island.* Minneapolis: University of Minnesota Press.

Dubro, James R. (1976). "The Third Sex: Lord Hervey and His Coterie." *Eighteenth-Century Life* 2:89–95.

Duby, Georges (1962). *'L'économie rurale et la vie des campagnes dans l'occident médiéval.* Paris: Aubier.

——— (1968). "The 'Youth' in Twelfth-Century Aristocratic Society." Pp. 198–209 in Frederic L. Cheyette (ed.), *Lordship and Community in Medieval Europe.* New York: Holt, Rinehart and Winston.

——— (1977). *The Chivalrous Society.* Tr. Cynthia Postan. Berkeley: University of California Press.

——— (1986). *William Marshall: The Flower of Chivalry.* Tr. Richard Howard. London: Faber and Faber.

Ducey, Charles (1956). "The Life History and Creative Psychopathology of the Shaman." Pp. 173–230 in Werner Nuensterberger (ed.), *The Psychoanalytic Study of Society,* vol. 7. New Haven: Yale University Press.

Duchein, Michel (1985). *Jacques I Stuart: Le roi de la paix.* Paris: Presses de la Renaissance.

Duchesne, Edouart Adolphe (1853). *De la prostitution dans la ville d'Alger depuis la conquête.* Paris: Baillière.

Duchesne-Guillemin, Jacques (1969). "The Religion of Ancient Iran." Pp. 323–76 in J. Jouco Blecker and Geo Widengren (eds.), *Historia Religionum: Handbook for the History of Religions*. Vol. 1: *Religions of the West*. Leiden: E. J. Brill.

—— (1983). "Zoroastrian Religion." Pp. 866–908 in Ehsan Yarshater (ed.), *The Cambridge History of Iran*, vol. 3(2). New York: Cambridge University Press.

Duesterberg, Thomas (1979). *Criminology and the Social Order in Nineteenth Century France*. Ph.D. dissertation, Stanford University History Department.

Dulaure, Jacques-Antoine (1825). *Histoire abrégée de différens cultes*, vol. 1. Paris: Guillaume.

Dullea, Georgia (1982). "The Issue of Office Romances." *New York Times*, May 17.

Dumézil, Georges (1958). *L'idéologie tripartie des indo-européens*. Brussels: Latomus.

—— (1966). *Archaic Roman Religion*, 2 vols. Tr. Philipp Krapp. Chicago: University of Chicago Press.

—— (1969). *Loki*. Darmstadt: Wissenschaftliche Buchgesellschaft.

—— (1973a). *From Myth to Fiction: The Sage of Hadingus*. Tr. Derek Coltman. Chicago: University of Chicago Press.

—— (1973b). *Gods of the Ancient Northmen*. Berkeley: University of California Press.

—— (1974). "'Le Borge' and 'Le Manchot': The State of the Problem." Pp. 17–28 in Gerald James Larson (ed.), *Myth in Indo-European Antiquity*. Berkeley: University of California Press.

Dundes, Alan (1976). "A Psychoanalytic Study of the Bullroarer." *Man* 11:220–38.

——, Jerry W. Lead and Bora Özkök (1970). "The Strategy of Turkish Boys' Verbal Dueling Rhymes." *Journal of American Folklore* 83:325–49.

Dupouy, E. (1906). *La prostitution dans l'antiquité*. 5th ed. Paris: F. R. de Rudeval.

Duprat, Guillaume Léonce (1909). *La criminalité de l'adolescence, causes et remèdes d'un mal social actuel*. Paris: F. Alcan.

Dupree, Louis (1973). *Afghanistan*. Princeton: Princeton University Press.

Dupuy, R. Ernest, and Trevor N. Dupuy (1970). *The Encyclopedia of Military History from 3500 B.C. to the Present*. New York: Harper and Row.

Durkheim, Emile (1963). *Primitive Classification*. Tr. Rodney Needham. Chicago: University of Chicago Press.

—— (1964). *The Division of Labor in Society*. Tr. George Simpson. New York: Free Press.

—— (1965). *The Elementary Forms of the Religious Life: A Study in Religious Sociology*. Tr. J. W. Swain. New York: Free Press.

Du Toit, Brian M. (1975). *Akuna: A New Guinea Village Community*. Rotterdam: A. A. Balkema.

Dyer, Richard (1980). *Gays and Film*. New York: British Film Institute.

Dynes, Wayne (1981). "Privacy, Sexual Orientation and the Self-Sovereignty of the Individual: Continental Theories, 1762–1908." *Gay Books Bulletin* 6:20–23.

—— (1983). "Homosexuality in Sub-Saharan Africa: An Unnecessary Question." *Gay Books Bulletin* 9:20–21.

—— (1985a). *Homolexis: A Historical and Cultural Lexicon of Homosexuality*. New York: Gay Academic Union.

—— (1985b). "'Debasing the Sterling Coin of Nature': Philo's Inscription of Tribal Prohibitions on the Universal Horizon of Ethics." Paper presented to the "Sex and the State" Conference, Toronto.

—— (1985c). "Christianity and the Politics of Sex." Pp. 8–15 in *Homosexuality, Intolerance, and Christianity: A Critical Examination of John Boswell's Work.* 2d ed. New York: Gay Academic Union.

—— (1985d). "'Sex and the State' in Toronto: Historians Coming of Age?" *SGC Newsletter* 45 (Oct.).

—— (1987a). *Homosexuality: A Research Guide.* New York: Garland.

—— (1987b). "Wrestling the Social Boa Constructor." Unpublished paper.

Eakin, Frank E. Jr. (1971). *The Religion and Culture of Israel: An Introduction to Old Testament Thought.* Boston: Allyn and Bacon.

Earl, Donald (1967). *The Moral and Political Tradition of Rome.* Ithaca, N.Y.: Cornell University Press.

Easlea, Brian (1981). *Science and Sexual Oppression: Patriarchy's Confrontation with Women and Nature.* London: Weidenfeld and Nicolson.

Ebara, Saikaku (1927). *Contes d'amour des Samouraï.* Tr. Ken Sato. Paris: Stendhal et Cie.

Eberhardt, Wolfram (1967). *Guilt and Sin in Traditional China.* Berkeley: University of California Press.

Edwardes, Allan (1959). *The Jewel in the Lotus: A Historical Survey of the Sexual Culture of the East.* New York: Julian Press.

—— (1967). *Erotica Judaica: A Sexual History of the Jews.* New York: Julian Press.

Edwards, George R. (1984). *Gay/Lesbian Liberation: A Biblical Perspective.* New York: Pilgrim.

Edwards, Newton, and Heiman G. Richy (1971). *The School in the American Social Order.* Boston: Houghton Mifflin.

Edwards, Susan M. (1981). *Female Sexuality and the Law.* Oxford: Martin Robinson.

Eggan, Dorothy (1943). "The General Problems of Hopi Adjustment." *American Anthropologist* 45:357–73.

Eggan, Fred (1966). *The American Indian.* Chicago: University of Chicago Press.

Eglinton, J. Z. (1964). *Greek Love.* New York: Oliver Layton.

Ehrenfels, Baron Omar Rolf (1941). *Mother-Right in India.* Hyderabad: Oxford University Press.

Ehrenreich, Barbara (1973). *Witches, Midwives and Nurses: A History of Women Healers.* Old Westbury, N.Y.: Feminist.

——, Elizabeth Hess, and Gloria Jacobs (1986). *Re-Making Love: The Feminization of Sex.* Garden City, N.Y.: Anchor Doubleday.

Eichrodt, W. (1961). *Theology of the Old Testament.* Tr. J. A. Baker. London: S.C.M.

Eisenstadt, S. N. (1956). *From Generation to Generation: Age Groups and Social Structure.* New York: Free Press.

Eissfeldt, Otto (1965). *The Old Testament: An Introduction.* Tr. Peter Ackroyd. New York: Harper and Row.

Eliade, Mircea (1962). *The Forge and the Crucible.* Tr. Stephen Corrin. New York: Harper and Row.

———— (1964). *Shamanism: Archaic Techniques of Ecstacy.* New York: Pantheon.

———— (1965). *Rites and Symbols of Initiation: The Mysteries of Birth and Rebirth.* Tr. Willard R. Trask. New York: Harper and Row.

Elias, Robert (1983). *The Court Society.* Tr. Edmund Jephcott. New York: Pantheon.

Ellenberger, Henri F. (1970). *The Discovery of the Unconscious: The History and Evolution of Dynamic Psychiatry.* New York: Basic.

Ellis, A. B. (1890). *The Ewe-Speaking Peoples of the Slave Coast of West Africa.* London: Chapman and Hall.

Ellis, Havelock (1897). *Sexual Inversion.* London: Wilson and Macmillan. Reprinted by Arno Press, New York, 1975.

———— (1936). *Studies in the Psychology of Sex,* vol. 2(2). New York: Random House. Orig. pub. 1910.

————, and Eugene S. Talbot (1896). "A Case of Developmental Degenerative Insanity, with Sexual Melancholia, Following Removal of Testicles, Attempted Murder and Suicide." *Journal of Mental Science* 42:341–44. Reprinted, pp. 140–43 in Jonathan Katz (ed.), *Gay American History.* New York: Crowell, 1976.

Ellis, William (1969). *Polynesian Researchs.* Vol. 1: *Polynesia.* Rutland, Vt.: Charles E. Tuttle, Orig. pub. 1831.

Elton, G. R. (1953). *The Tudor Revolution in Government.* London: Cambridge University Press.

———— (1963). *Reformation Europe, 1517–1559.* New York: Harper and Row.

Elwin, Verrier (1947). *The Muria and Their Ghotul.* Bombay: Oxford University Press.

———— (1949). *Myths of Middle India.* London: Oxford University Press.

Ember, Melvin, and Carol R. Ember (1961). "The Conditions Favoring Matrilocal Versus Patrilocal Residence." *American Anthropologist* 73:571–94.

Embree, Scotty (1977). "The State Department as Moral Entrepreneur: Racism and Imperialism as Factors in the Passage of the Harrison Narcotics Act." Pp. 193–204 in David F. Greenberg (ed.), *Corrections and Punishment.* Beverly Hills, Calif.: Sage.

Encyclopedia Judaica (1971). New York: Macmillan.

Endleman, Robert (1986). "Homosexuality in Tribal Societies." *Transcultural Psychiatric Research Review* 23:187–218.

Engelhardt, Tristan (1974). "The Disease of Masturbation: Values and the Concept of Disease." *Bulletin of the History of Medicine* 48:234–48.

Engineer, Asghar Ali (1980). *The Origin and Development of Islam.* Bombay: Orient Longman.

Ensslin, W. (1965). "The Senate and the Army." Pp. 57–95 in S. A. Cook, F. E. Adcock, M. P. Charlesworth, and N. H. Baynes (eds.), *Cambridge Ancient History.* Vol. 12; *The Imperial Crisis and Recovery,* A.D. *193–324.* Cambridge: Cambridge University Press.

Epstein, A. L. (1979). "Tambu: The Shell-Money of the Tolai." Pp. 149–205 in R. H. Hook (ed.), *Fantasy and Symbol: Studies in Anthropological Interpretation.* London: Academic.

Epstein, I. (ed.) (1935). *The Babylonian Talmud. Seder Nezikin,* vol. 3. London: Soncino.

———— (1936a). *The Babylonian Talmud. Seder Nashim, Tractate Yebamoth.* London: Soncino.

———— (1936b). *The Babylonian Talmud. Seder Nashim, Tractate Kiddūshin.* London: Soncino.

———— (1938a). *The Babylonian Talmud. Seder Mo'ed, Tractate Shabbath.* London: Soncino.

———— (1938b). *The Babylonian Talmud. Seder Mo'Ed, Tractate Sukkah.* London: Soncino.

Epstein, Louis M. (1967). *Sex Laws and Customs in Judaism.* New York: Bloch.

Epstein, Steven (1987). "Gay Politics, Ethnic Identity: The Limits of Social Constructionism." *Socialist Review* 93/94:9–56.

Erickson, Carolly (1976). *The Medieval Vision: Essays in History and Perception.* New York: Oxford University Press.

Erickson, Nancy S. (1982). "Historical Background of Protective Labor Legislation: Muller v. Oregon." Pp. 55–86 in D. Kelly Weisberg (ed.), *Women and the Law: The Social Historical Perspective.* Cambridge, Mass.: Schenkman.

Erlanger, Philippe (1953). *Monsieur, Frère de Louis XIV.* Paris: Librairie Hachette.

Ernest-Charles, J. (1910). "La vie littéraire." *La Grande Revue* 62:399.

Escoffier, Jeffrey (1985). "Sexual Revolution and the Politics of Gay Identity." *Socialist Review* 81/82:119–54.

Estermann, Carlos (1976). *The Ethnography of Southwestern Angola.* New York: Africana.

Eton, William (1972). *A Survey of the Turkish empire.* 2d ed. Westnead: Gregg International. Orig. pub. 1789.

Euripides (1959). *The Complete Greek Tragedies,* vol. 5. Tr. William Arrowsmith, ed. by David Grene and Richmond Lattimore. New York: Modern Library.

Eusebius (1890). *The Life of Constantine.* Tr. Arthur C. McGiffert and Ernest C. Richardson. Select Library of Nicene and Post-Nicene Fathers, n.s., vol. 1. New York: Charles Scriber's Sons.

Evans, Arthur (1978). *Witchcraft and the Gay Counterculture.* Boston: Fag Rag.

Evans, Eric J., ed. (1978). *Social Policy, 1830–1914: Individualism, Collectivism and the Origins of the Welfare State.* Boston: Routledge and Kegan Paul.

Evans, Ray B. (1969). "Childhood Parental Relationships of Homosexual Men." *Journal of Consulting and Clinical Psychology* 33:129–35.

Evans, Richard J. (1979). *The Feminists: Women's Emancipation Movements in Europe, America and Australia, 1840–1920.* New York: Barnes and Noble.

Evans-Pritchard, E. E. (1951). *Kinship and Marriage among the Nuer.* Oxford: Clarendon.

———— (1970). "Sexual Inversion among the Azande." *American Anthropologist* 72:1428–34.

———— (1974). *Man and Woman among the Azande.* London: Faber and Faber.

Everard, Myriam (1982). "Tribade of zielsvriendin." *Groniek* 16:16–20.

Fackre, Gabriel (1982). *The Religious Right and Christian Faith.* Grand Rapids, Mich.: William B. Eerdmans.

Faderman, Lillian (1981). *Surpassing the Love of Men: Romantic Friendship and Love between Women from the Renaissance to the Present.* New York: William Morrow.

———— (1983). *Scotch Verdict: Dame Gordon vs. Pirie and Woods.* New York: Morrow.

———, and Brigitte Eriksson (1980). *Lesbian Feminism in Turn-of-the-Century Germany.* Weatherby Lake, Mo.: Naiad.

Fages, Pedro (1970). *A Historical, Political, and Natural Description of California.* Tr. Herbert Ingram Priestley. Berkeley: University of California Press.

A Faithful Narrative of the Proceedings in the Late Affair between the Rev. Mr. John Swinton, and Mr. George Backer, Both of Wadham College, Oxford . . . to which is prefix'd, a particular account of the proceedings against Robert Thistlewayte, late Doctor of Divinity, and Warden of Wadham College, for a sodomitical attempt upon Mr. W. French, commoner of the same college (1739). London: Privately printed.

Fairservis, Walter A., Jr. (1983). "The Script of the Indus Valley Civilization." *Scientific American* 248:58–66.

Falk, Candace (1984). *Love, Anarchy, and Emma Goldman.* New York: Holt, Rinehart and Winston.

Falk, Kurt (1920). "Gleichgeschlechtliches Leben bei einigen Negerstämme Angolas." *Archiv für Anthropologie* n.s. 20:42–45.

Falkner, Thomas (1935). *A Description of Patagonia and the Adjoining Parts of South America.* Chicago: Armann and Armann.

Farah, Madelain (1984). *Marriage and Sexuality in Islam: A Translation of al-Ghazali's Book on the Etiquette of Marriage from the Iḥyā.* Salt Lake City: University of Utah Press.

Farb, Peter (1968). *Man's Rise to Civilization as Shown by the Indians of North America from Primeval Times to the Coming of the Industrial State.* New York: E. P. Dutton.

Farnell, Lewis Richard (1909). *The Cults of the Greek States.* Oxford: Clarendon.

Faron, Louis C. (1964). "Shamanism and Sorcery among the Mapuche (Arucanians) of Chile." Pp. 123–46 in Robert A. Manners (ed.), *Process and Pattern in Culture: Essays in Honor of Julian H. Steward.* Chicago: Aldine.

Farquhar, J. N. (1929). *Modern Religious Movements in India.* London: Macmillan.

Faulkner, Raymond O. (1969). *The Ancient Egyptian Pyramid Texts.* Oxford: Oxford University Press.

——— (1973). *The Ancient Egyptian Coffin Texts.* Warminster: Aris and Phillips.

Feldman, M. P. (1966). "Aversion Therapy for Sex Deviations: A Critical Review." *Psychological Bulletin* 65:65–79.

———, and M. J. McCulloch (1967). "Aversion Therapy in Management of 43 Homosexuals." *British Medical Journal* 2:594–97.

Fellman, Anita Clair, and Michael Fellman (1981a). "The Rule of Moderation in Late Nineteenth-Century American Sexual Ideology." *Journal of Sex Research* 17:238–55.

——— (1981b). *Making Sense of Self: Medical Advice Literature in Late Nineteenth-Century America.* Philadelphia: University of Pennsylvania Press.

Féray, Jean-Claude (1981). "Une histoire critique du mot homosexualité." *Arcadie* 325:11–21, 326:115–24, 327:171–81 and 328:246–58.

Feré, Charles (1884). "La famille neuropathique." *Archives du neurologie* 7:10–13.

——— (1888). *Dégénerescence et criminalité: Essay physiologique.* Paris: Félix Alcan.

——— (1899). *L'instinct sexuel: Evolution et dissolution.* Paris: Félix Alcan.

Ferguson, John (1959). *Moral Values in the Ancient World.* New York: Barnes and Noble.

Fernbach, David (1976). "Toward a Marxist Theory of Gay Liberation." *Socialist Review* 28:29–41.

Festugière, A. J. (1959). *Antioche Païenne et Chrétienne: Libanius, Chrysostome et les Moines de Syrie*. Paris: E. de Boccard.

Ficino, Marsilio (1985). *Commentary on Plato's* Symposium *on Love*. Tr. Sears Jayne. Dallas: Spring.

Fiedler, Leslie A. (1972). *The Stranger in Shakespeare*, New York: Stein and Day.

Field, Alexander J. (1974). *Educational Reform and Manufacturing Development in Mid-Nineteenth Century Massachusetts*. Ph.D. dissertation, University of California at Berkeley.

Field, P.J.C. (1970). "Chaucer's Merchant and the Sin Against Nature." *Notes and Queries* n.s. 17:84–86.

Figueira, Thomas J. (1986). "Initiation and Seduction: Two Recent Books on Greek Pederasty." *American Journal of Philology* 107:426–32.

Filip, Jan (1982). "Early History and Evolution of the Celts: The Archaeological Evidence." Pp. 33–50 in Robert O'Driscoll (ed.), *The Celtic Consciousness*. New York: George Braziller.

Fine, Sidney (1956). *Laissez Faire and the General Welfare State*. Ann Arbor: University of Michigan Press.

Finger, F. W. (1947). "Sex Beliefs and Practices among Male College Students." *Journal of Abnormal and Social Psychology* 42:57–67.

Fink, Arthur E. (1938). *The Causes of Crime: Biological Theories in the United States, 1800–1915*. Philadelphia: University of Pennsylvania Press.

Finley, Moses I. (1983). *Ancient Slavery and Modern Ideology*. New York: Penguin.

Firmicus Maternus, Julius (1970). *The Error of the Pagan Religions*. Tr. Clarence A. Forbes. New York: Newman.

Firth, Raymond (1936). *We, the Tikopia: A Sociological Study of Kinship in Primitive Polynesia*. New York: American.

Fiser, Ivo (1966). *Indian Erotics of the Oldest Period*. Prague: University Karlova.

Fisher, Saul H. (1965). "A Note on Male Homosexuality and the Role of Women in Ancient Greece." Pp. 165–72 in Judd Marmor (ed.), *Sexual Inversion: The Multiple Roots of Homosexuality*. New York: Basic.

Fitzgerald, Frances (1986). "The Castro." *New Yorker*, July 21 and July 28.

Flaceliere, Robert (1962). *Love in Ancient Greece*. Tr. F. Muller. New York: Crown.

Flacks, Richard (1971). *Youth and Social Change*. Chicago: Rand McNally.

Flaherty, David H. (1971). "Law and the Enforcement of Morals in Early America." *Perspectives on American History* 5:201–53.

Flandrin, Jean-Louis (1972). "Marriage tardif et vie sexuelle: Discussions et hypotheses de recherche." *Annales E.S.C.* 27:1351–78.

——— (1975). *Les amours paysannes: Amour et sexualité dans les compagnes de l'ancienne France (XVIᵉ–XIXᵉ) siècle*. Paris: Editions Gallimard Hulliard.

——— (1976a). *Familles, parenté, maison: Sexualité dans l'ancienne société*. Paris: Hachette.

——— (1976b). *Families in Former Times: Kinship, Household and Sexuality*. Tr. Richard Southern. Cambridge: Cambridge University Press.

——— (1977). "Repression and Change in the Sexual Life of Young People in Medieval and Early Modern Times." *Journal of Family History* 2:196–210.

Flaubert, Gustave (1979). *The Letters of Gustave Flaubert, 1830–1857*. Tr. Francis Steegmuller. Cambridge, Mass.: Harvard University Press.

Fletcher, Alice C., and Frances La Flesche (1911). "The Omaha Tribe," *U.S. Bureau of American Ethnology. Twenty-Seventh Annual Report, 1905–1906*. Washington, D.C.: Government Printing Office. Reprinted, University of Nebraska Press, Lincoln, 1972.

Fleuret, Fernand (1920). *Les procès de bestialité aux XVIᵉ et XVIIᵉ siècles*. Paris: Bibliothèque des Curieux.

Fliche, Augustin (1944). *La réforme Grégorienne et la reconquête Chrétienne (1057–1123)*. Paris: Bloud and Gay.

——, Christine Thouzellier, and Yvonne Azais (n.d.), *La Chrétienté Romaine (1198–1274)*. Paris: Bloud and Gay.

Fliess, Wilhelm (1897). *Die Beziehungen zwischen Nase und weiblichen Geschlechtsorganen*. Leipzig: Deuticke.

Flornoy, Bertrand (1956): *The World of the Incas*. Tr. Winifred Bradford. New York: Vanguard.

Foley, M. (1879). "Sur les habitations et les moeurs des Neo-Caledonians." *Bulletin de la société d'anthropologie de Paris* 2:604–6.

Fone, Byrne R. S. (1980). "Hidden Heritage: History and the Gay Imagination." *Journal of Homosexuality* 8:13–34.

Font, Pedro (1930–31). *Font's Complete Diary of the Second Anza Expedition*. Tr. Herbert Eugene Bolton. Vol. 4: *Anza's California Expeditions*. Berkeley: University of California Press.

Ford, Clellan S., and Frank A. Beach (1951). *Patterns of Sexual Behavior*. New York: Harper and Row.

Forde, C. Daryll (1931). "Ethnology of the Yuma Indians." *University of California Publications in American Archaeology and Ethnology* 28:83–278. Berkeley: University of California Press.

Forel, Auguste Henri (1905). *Die sexuelle Frage: Eine naturwissenschaftliche, psychologische, hygienische und soziologische Studie für Gebildete*. Munich: E. Reinhardt.

—— (1933). *The Sexual Question: A Scientific, Psychological, Hygienic and Sociological Study*. Tr. C. F. Marshall. Brooklyn: Physicians and Surgeons.

Forgey, Donald G. (1975). "The Institution of the Berdache among the North American Plains Indians." *Journal of Sex Research* 11:1–15.

Forster, E. S. (1928). "The Pseudo-Aristotelian Problems: Their Nature and Composition." *Classical Quarterly* 22:163–65.

Fort, Joel, Claude M. Steiner, and Florence Conrad (1971). "Attitudes of Mental Health Professionals toward Homosexuality and Its Treatment." *Psychological Reports* 29:347–50.

Fortune, Reo F. (1932). *Sorcerers of Dobu*. New York: E. P. Dutton.

Foster, Jeannette H. (1985). *Sex Variant Women in Literature*. Tallahassee, Fla.: Naiad. Orig. pub. 1956.

Foster, Stephen Wayne (1985). "Bibliography of Homosexuality among Latin-American Indians." *Cabirion and Gay Books Bulletin* 12:17–19.

Foucault, Michel (1973). *The Birth of the Clinic: An Archaeology of Medical Perception*. Tr. A. M. Sheridan Smith. New York: Pantheon.

—— (1977). *Discipline and Punish: the Birth of the Prison.* Tr. Alan Sheridan. New York: Pantheon.

—— (1980). *The History of Sexuality.* Vol. 1: *An Introduction.* New York: Vintage.

—— (1984a). *Histoire de la sexualité.* vol. 2: *L'usage des plaisirs.* Paris: Gallimard.

—— (1984b). *Histoire de la sexualité.* vol. 3: *Le souci de soi.* Paris: Gallimard.

——, and Richard Sennett (1982). "Sexuality and Solitude." Pp. 3–21 in David Rieff (ed.), *Humanities in Review,* vol. 1. New York: Cambridge University Press.

Fourier, François Marie Charles (1967). *Le nouveaux monde amoureux. Oeuvres Complètes,* vol. 7. Paris: Éditions Anthropos.

Fourt, Martha, and Chris Riddiough (1982). "From Closet to Ballet." *Democratic Left* 10(6):8–10.

Francis, W. Nelson (ed.) (1942). *Book of Vices and Virtues.* London: Oxford University Press.

Francke, Herbert (1981). "Tibetans in Yüan China." Pp. 296–328 in John D. Langlois, Jr. (ed.), *China under Mongol Rule.* Princeton: Princeton University Press.

Frankel, F. E. (1964). "Social History of Sex Crime." *Journal of the History of Ideas* 25:333–52.

Frankfurt, Henri (1948). *Kingship and the Gods: A Study of Ancient Near Eastern Religion as the Integration of Society and Nature.* Chicago: University of Chicago Press.

Frantzen, Allen J. (1979). "The Significance of the Frankish Penitentials." *Journal of Ecclesiastical History* 30:409–21.

Frati, Ludovico (1900). *La Vita Privata di Bologna dal Secolo XIII al XVII.* Bologna: Ditta Nicola Zanichella.

Frazee, Charles A. (1972). "The Origins of Clerical Celibacy in the Western Church." *Church History* 41:149–67.

Frazer, James G. (1962). *Adonis, Attis, Osiris: Studies in the History of Oriental Religion.* Part 4 of *The Golden Bough: A Study in Magic and Religion.* 3d ed. New Hyde Park, N.Y.: University Books. Orig. pub. 1914.

Freed, John B. (1977). *The Friars and German Society in the Thirteenth Century.* Cambridge, Mass.: Medieval Academy of America.

Freedeman, Charles E. (1978). "A la recherche de la bourgeoisie française." Working Paper, Fernand Braudel Center, State University of New York at Binghamton.

Freeman, Arthur (1960). "Schoolboy Homosexuality." *Mattachine Review* 6(5): 12–20.

Freeman, Derek (1967). "Shaman and Incubus." Pp. 315–43 in *The Psychoanalytic Study of Society,* vol. 4. New York: International Universities Press.

—— (1970). "Human Nature and Culture." Pp. 50–75 in *Man and the New Biology.* Canberra: Australian National University Press.

Freeman, E. A. (1882). *The Reign of William Rufus.* 2 vols. Oxford: Clarendon.

Freeth, Zahra, and H.V.F. Winstone (1978). *Explorers of Arabia: From the Renaissance to the End of the Victorian Era.* London: George Allen and Unwin.

Freitag, Peter J. (1985). "Class Conflict and the Rise of Government Regulation." *Insurgent Sociologist* 12(4):51–65.

Freud, Sigmund (1905). "Three Essays on the Theory of Sexuality." *Standard Edition* 7:125–243. London: Hogarth, 1953.

—— (1911). "Psychoanalytic Notes on an Autobiographical Account of a Case of Paranoia (Dementia Paranoides)." *Standard Edition* 12:59–79. London: Hogarth, 1958.

—— (1913). "The Predisposition to Obsessional Neurosis: A Contribution to the Problem of Choice of Neurosis." *Standard Edition* 12:313–26. London: Hogarth, 1958; pp. 87–96 in Philip Rieff (ed.), *Sexuality and the Psychology of Love*. New York: Collier, 1963.

—— (1920). "The Psychogenesis of a Case of Homosexuality in a Woman." *Standard Edition* 18:146–72. London: Hogarth, 1955; pp. 133–59 in Philip Rieff (ed.), *Sexuality and the Psychology of Love*. New York: Collier, 1963.

—— (1935). "Letter to an American Mother." Pp. 1–2 in Hendrick M. Ruitenbeck (ed.), *The Problem of Homosexuality in Modern Society*. New York: E. P. Dutton, 1963.

—— (1953–1974). *The Standard Edition of the Complete Psychological Works of Sigmund Freud*. 24 vols. London: Hogarth.

—— (1953). "On Narcissism: An Introduction." *Collected Papers* 4:40–59. London: Hogarth. Orig. pub. 1914.

—— (1964). *A General Introduction to Psychoanalysis*. Tr. Joan Rivière. New York: Washington Square. Orig. pub. 1920.

—— (1985). *The Complete Letters of Sigmund Freud to Wilhelm Fliess, 1887–1904*. Tr. Jeffrey Moussaieff Masson. Cambridge, Mass.: Harvard University Press.

—— (1970). *An Outline of Psycho-Analysis*. Tr. James Strachey. New York: W. W. Norton.

Freyne, Sean (1980). *Galilee from Alexander the Great to Hadrian, 323 b.c.e. to 135 c.e.: A Study of Second Temple Judaism*. Wilmington, Del., and Notre Dame, Ind.: Michael Glazer and University of Notre Dame Press.

Freyre, Gilberto (1946). *The Masters and the Slaves: A Study in the Development of Brazilian Civilization*. Tr. Samuel Putnam. New York: Alfred A. Knopf.

Friedländer, Benedict (1904). *Renaissance des Eros Uranios*. Schmargendorf-Bedin: Renaissance.

Friedlander, Ruth (1973). *Bénédict-August Morel and the Development of the Theory of Dégénérescence*. Ph.D. dissertation, University of California at San Francisco.

Friedli, Lynne (1987). "'Passing Women'—A Study of Gender Boundaries in the Eighteenth Century." In George S. Rousseau and Roy Porter (eds.), *Liberty's a Glorious Feast: Sexual Underworlds of the Enlightenment*. Manchester: Manchester University Press.

Friedman, Jonathan (1979). *System, Structure and Contradiction in the Evolution of "Asiatic" Social Formations*. Copenhagen: National Museum of Denmark.

Friedman, Richard C. (1986). "Toward a Further Understanding of Homosexual Men." *Journal of the American Psychoanalytic Association* 34:193–206.

Friedrich, Johannes (1971). *Die Hethitischen Gesetze*. Leiden: E. J. Brill.

Friedrich, Paul (1966). "Proto-Indo-European Kinship." *Ethnology* 5:6–36.

—— (1978). *The Meaning of Aphrodite*. Chicago: University of Chicago Press.

Frischauer, Paul (1969). *L'archéologie de la sexualité*. Tr. Remi Laureillard. Zurich: Stock.

Froude, James Anthony (1915). *The Reign of Henry VIII.* New York: E. P. Dutton.

Fry, Peter (1985). "Male Homosexuality and Spirit Possession in Brazil." *Journal of Homosexuality* 11:137–53.

Fryer, John (1697). *A New Account of East-India and Persia.* London: R. Chiswell.

Fulman, Ricki (1982). "Office Affair." *New York Daily News,* Feb. 7.

Fürstauer, Johanna (1965). *Eros im Alten Orient.* Stuttgart: Hans E. Gunther.

Futuyma, Douglas J., and Stephen J. Risch (1984). "Sexual Orientation, Sociobiology, and Evolution." *Journal of Homosexuality* 9:157–68.

G (1980). "The Secret Life of Moscow." *Christopher Street* 4 (June):15–22.

Gade, Kari Ellen (1986). "Homosexuality and Rape of Males in Old Norse Law and Literature." *Scandinavian Studies* 58:124–41.

Gajdusek, Daniel Carleton (1963). *New Guinea Journal: June 10, 1959 to August 15, 1959.* Bethesda, Md.: National Institutes of Health.

——— (1968). *New Guinea Journal: Oct. 2, 1961 to August 4, 1962, Pt. 2.* Bethesda, Md.: National Institutes of Health.

Gamble, Clive (1983). "Culture and Society in the Upper Paleolithic of Europe." Pp. 201–16 in Geoff Barley (ed.), *Hunter-Gatherer Economy in Prehistory: A European Perspective.* Cambridge: Cambridge University Press.

Gamkrelidze, T. V., and V. V. Ivanov (1985). *Indoevropejskyjazuk i Indoevropejcy.* 2 vols. Tbilisi, Georgia: Tbilisi University Press.

Gamst, Frederick C. (1967). "Review of *Wax and Gold: Tradition and Innovation in Ethiopian Culture.*" *Journal of Developing Areas* 1:544–45.

——— (1969). *The Qemant: A Pagan-Hebraic Peasantry of Ethiopia.* New York: Holt, Rinehart and Winston.

Ganshof, F. L. (1955). *Was Waren die Capitularia?* Brussels: Palais der Academiën.

——— (1958). *Recherches sur les Capitulaires.* Paris: Sirey.

——— (1965). "The Impact of Charlemagne on the Institutions of the Frankish Realm." *Speculum* 40:47–62.

Garber, Eric (1982). "'Tain't Nobody's Business: Homosexuality in Harlem in the 1920s." *Advocate* (May 13):39. Reprinted in Mike Smith (ed.), *Black Men/White Men.* San Francisco: Gay Sunshine.

Garde, Noel I. (1964). *Jonathan to Gide.* New York: Vantage.

Gardella, Peter (1985). *Innocent Ecstacy: How Christianity Gave America an Ethic of Sexual Pleasure.* New York: Oxford University Press.

Garlan, Yvon (1975). *War in the Ancient World: A Social History.* Tr. Janet Lloyd. London: Chatto and Windus.

Garstang, J. (1910). *The Land of the Hittites.* London: Constable.

Gasquet, Francis Ardan (1893). *Henry VIII and the English Monasteries,* vol. 1. London: J. Hodges.

Gaster, Theodore (1950). "The Religion of the Canaanites." Pp. 111–43 in Vergilius Ferm (ed.), *Ancient Religion.* New York: Philosophical Library.

Gathorne-Hardy, Jonathan (1977). *The Public School Phenomenon, 597–1977.* London: Hodder and Stoughton.

Gauthier, Albert (1977). "La sodomie dans le droit canonique médiéval." Pp. 111–22 in Bruno Roy (ed.), *L'érotisme au Moyen Âge.* Montreal: Aurore.

Gay, Judith (1985). "'Mummies and Babies' and Friends and Lovers in Lesotho." *Journal of Homosexuality* 11:97–116.

Gay, Peter (1980). "Victorian Sexuality: Old Texts and New Insights." *American Scholar* 49:372–77.

——— (1983). *The Bourgeois Experience—Victoria to Freud.* Vol. 1: *Education of the Senses.* New York: Oxford University Press.

——— (1986). *The Bourgeois Experience—Victoria to Freud.* Vol. 2: *The Tender Passion.* New York: Oxford University Press.

Gazeau, Francis (1981). "Le Pharaon pas comme les autres, ou un cas unique d'homosexualité en Égypte." *Arcadie* 325:41–42.

Geertz, Clifford (1960). *The Religion of Java.* Glencoe, Ill.: Free Press.

Geffcken, Johannes (1978). *The Last Days of Greco-Roman Paganism.* Tr. Sabine MacCormack. Amsterdam: North-Holland.

Geiger, Wilhelm (1882). *Ostiranische Kultur im Altertum.* Erlangen: Andreas Deichert.

Gell, Alfred (1975). *Metamorphosis of the Cassowaries: Umeda Society, Language and Ritual.* London: Athlone.

Genil-Perrin, Georges P. H. (1913). *Histoire des origines et de dégénérescence en médicine mentale.* Paris: A. Leclerc.

Gentile, B. (1976). "Il Partenio di Alcamane e l'amore omerotico femminile nei tiasi spartani." *Quaderni Urbinati di Cultura Classica* 12:59–61.

George, Margaret (1973). "From 'Goodwive' to 'Mistress': The Transformation of the Female in Bourgeois Culture." *Science and Society* 37:152–77.

Gerard, Kent (1981). "The Tulip and the Sodomite: An Antihomosexual Pogrom in the Netherlands, 1730–31." Paper presented to the Kroeber Anthropological Society.

Gerassi, John (1966). *The Boys of Boise: Furor, Vice, and Folly in an American City.* New York: Macmillan.

Gernet, Jacques (1959). *La vie quotidienne en Chine à la veille de l'invasion Mongole.* Paris: Hachette.

Giacomelli, Anne (1980). "The Justice of Aphrodite in Sappho Fr. 1." *Transactions of the American Philological Association* 110:135–42.

Gerstein, Mary R. (1974). "Germanic *Warg:* The Outlaw as Werwolf." Pp. 131–56 in Gerald James Larson (ed.), *Myth in Indo-European Antiquity.* Berkeley: University of California Press.

Gibson, Laurence (1978). *Get Off My Ship: Ensign Berg vs. The U.S. Navy.* New York: Avon.

Gide, André (1950). *Corydon.* Tr. Hugh Gibb. New York: Farrar, Straus.

Giedion, S. (1964). *L'éternal présent: La naissance de l'art.* Washington, D.C.: Bollingen.

Gifford, E. W. (1934). "The Cocopa." Pp. 257–334 in *University of California Publications in American Archaeology and Ethnology* 31 (5).

Gigeroff, Alex K. (1968). *Sexual Deviations in the Criminal Law: Homosexual, Exhibitionistic and Pedophilic Offenses in Canada.* Toronto: University of Toronto Press.

Gilbert, Arthur N. (1975). "Doctor, Patient, and Onanist Diseases in the Nineteenth Century." *Journal of the History of Medicine and Allied Sciences* 30:217–34.

——— (1976). "Buggery and the British Navy, 1700–1861." *Journal of Social History* 10:72–98.

———, and Michael Barkun (1981). "Disaster and Sexuality." *Journal of Sex Research* 17:288–99.

Gilbert, Oscar Paul (1932). *Women in Men's Guise*. London: Bodley Head.

Giles, F. J. (1972). *Ikhnaton: Legend and History*. Rutherford, N.J.: Fairleigh Dickinson University Press.

Gillis, John R. (1974). *Youth and History: Tradition and Change in European Age Relations, 1770-Present*. New York: Academic.

Gilman, Sander L. (1985). *Difference and Pathology: Stereotypes of Sexuality, Race, and Madness*. Ithaca, N.Y.: Cornell University Press.

Gilman, Stuart C. (1985). "Political Theory and Degeneration: From Left to Right, From Up to Down." Pp. 164–98 in J. Edward Chamberlain and Sander L. Gilman (eds.), *Degeneracy: the Dark Side of Progress*. New York: Columbia University Press.

Gilmore, Margaret, and David Gilmore (1979). "'Machismo'": A Psychodynamic Approach." *Journal of Psychoanalytic Anthropology* 2:281–99.

Gimbutas, Marija (1981). "Vulvas, Breasts, and Buttocks of the Goddess Creatress: Commentary on the Origins of Art." Pp. 16–42 in Giorgio Buccellati and Charles Speroni (eds.), *The Shape of the Past: Studies in Honor of Franklin D. Murphy*. Los Angeles: University of California, Los Angeles Institute of Archaeology.

—— (1982). *The Goddesses and Gods of Old Europe. Myths and Cult Images*. Berkeley: University of California Press.

Gindorf, Rolf (1977). "Wissenschaftliche Ideologien im Wandel: Die Angst von der Homosexualität als intellektuelles Ereignis." Pp. 129–44 in Joachim S. Hohmann (ed.), *Der unterdrückte Sexus*. Berlin: Andreas Achenbach Lollar.

Ginzberg, Louis (1913–28). *The Legends of the Jews*. 6 vols. Philadelphia: Jewish Publication Society of America.

Girard, Jacques (1981). *Le mouvement homosexuel en France, 1945–1980*. Paris: Éditions Syros.

Gladwin, Thomas, and Seymour Sarason (1953). *Truk: Man in Paradise*. New York: Wenner-Gren Foundation.

Glanville, S.R.K. (1955). *Catalogue of Demotic Papyri in the British Museum*. Vol. 2: *The Instructions of 'Onchsheshonqy (British Museum Papyrus 10508)*. Part I. London: British Museum.

Glob, P. V. (1971). *The Bog People: Iron-Age Man Preserved*. Tr. Rupert Bruce-Mitford. New York: Ballantine.

Glock, Charles Y., and Rodney Stark (1966). *American Piety: The Nature of Religious Commitment*. New York: Harper and Row.

Gnoli, Gherardo (1980). *Zoroaster's Time and Homeland: A Study on the Origins of Mazdeism and Related Problems*. Naples: Istituto Universitario Orientale.

Godefroy, Frédéric (1961). *Dictionnaire de l'ancienne langue française*, vol. 4. New York: Kraus. Orig. pub. 1885.

Godelier, Maurice (1976). "Le sexe comme fondement ultime de l'ordre social et cosmique chez les Baruya de Nouvelle-Guinée." Pp. 268–306 in A. Verdiglione (ed.), *Sexualité et pouvoir*. Paris: Traces Payot.

—— (1982). *La production des Grandes Hommes: Pouvoir et domination masculine chez les Baruya de Nouvelle-Guinée*. Paris: Fayard.

Goedicke, Hans (1960). *Die Stellung der Königs im alten Reich*. Ägyptologische Abhandlungen 2. Wiesbaden: Otto Harrassowitz.

——— (1967). "Unrecognized Sportings." *Journal of the American Research Center in Egypt* 6:97–102.

Goff, Jacques Le (1968). "Apostolat mendiant et fait urbain dans la France médiévale: L'implantation des ordres mendiants." *Annales E.S.C.* 23:335–52.

——— (1970). "Ordres mendiants et urbanisation dans la France médiévale." *Annales E.S.C.* 25:924–46.

Goitein, S. D. (1979). "The Sexual Mores of the Common People." Pp. 43–62 in Afaf Lutfi Al-Sayyid-Marsot (ed.), *Society and the Sexes in Medieval Islam*. Malibu, Calif.: Undena.

Gold, Ronald (1982). "Gay Rights is a First Amendment Issue." *Civil Liberties* (Nov.):6–7.

Goldberg, David Theo (1988). "The Social Formation of Racist Discourse." In *Anatomy of Racism*. Minneapolis: University of Minnesota Press.

Golden, Mark (1981). *Aspects of Childhood in Classical Athens*. Ph.D. dissertation, University of Toronto.

——— (1984). "Slavery and Homosexuality at Athens." *Phoenix* 38:308–24.

Goldman, Irving (1963). *The Cubeo Indians of Northwest Amazon*. Urbana: University of Illinois Press.

Goldschmidt, Walter (1967). *Sebei Law*. Berkeley: University of California Press.

Goldstein, Richard (1984). "John O'Connor's Dark Victory." *Village Voice* (Sept. 25):23–24.

Gomme, George L. (1885). *The History of the Seven Wise Masters of Rome*. London: Villon Society.

Gonzalez, Gilbert G. (1977). "The Relationship between Monopoly Capitalism and Progressive Education." *Insurgent Sociologist* 7:25–42.

Goodich, Michael (1976). "Sodomy in Medieval Secular Law." *Journal of Homosexuality* 1:295–302.

——— (1979). *The Unmentionable Vice: Homosexuality in the Later Medieval Period*. Santa Barbara, Calif.: ABC-Clio.

——— (1982). *Vita Perfecta: The Ideal of Sainthood in the Thirteenth Century*. Monographien zur Geschichte des Mittelalters, vol. 25. Stuttgart: Anton Hiersemann.

Goodman, Raymond E. (1987). "Genetic and Hormonal Factors in Human Sexuality: Evolutionary and Developmental Perspectives." Pp. 21–48 in Glenn D. Wilson (ed.), *Variant Sexuality: Research and Theory*. Baltimore: Md.: Johns Hopkins University Press.

Goody, Jack (1983). *The Development of the Family and Marriage in Europe*. Cambridge: Cambridge University Press.

Gordon, Linda and Alan Hunt (1977). "Sex, the Family and the New Right." *Radical America* 11(6):9–25.

Gordon, Mary (1936). *Chase of the Wild Goose*. London: Hogarth.

Gordon, Michael (1971). "From an Unfortunate Necessity to a Cult of Mutual Orgasm: Sex in American Education Literature, 1830–1930." Pp. 53–77 in James Henslin (ed.), *Studies in the Sociology of Sex*. New York: Appleton-Century-Crofts.

Gorer, Geoffrey (1935). *Africa Dances: A Book about West African Negroes*. New York: A. A. Knopf.

—— (1938). *Himalayan Village: An Account of the Lepchas of Sikkim.* London: Michael Joseph.

—— (1966). *The Danger of Equality and Other Essays.* London: Cresset.

Gorham, Deborah (1982). *The Victorian Girl and the Feminine Ideal.* Bloomington: Indiana University Press.

Gossen, Gary H. (1974). *Chamulas in the World of the Sun: Time and Space in a Maya Oral Tradition.* Cambridge, Mass.: Harvard University Press.

Gottwald, Norman K. (1979). *The Tribes of Yahweh: A Sociology of the Religion of Liberated Israel, 1250–1050 B.C.E.* Maryknoll, N.Y.: Orbis.

Gough, E. Kathleen (1959). "The Nayars and the Definition of Marriage." *Journal of the Royal Anthropological Institute of Great Britain and Ireland* 89:23–34.

—— (1961). "Nayar: Central Kerala." Pp. 298–384 in David M. Schneider (eds.), *Matrilineal Kinship.* Berkeley: University of California Press.

Gouldner, Alvin W. (1966). *Enter Plato: Classical Greece and the Origins of Social Theory.* New York: Basic.

—— (1970). *The Coming Crisis of Western Sociology.* New York: Avon.

Graf, Fritz (1986). "Orpheus: A Poet among Men." Pp. 80–106 in Jan Bremmer (ed.), *Interpretations of Greek Mythology.* London: Croom Helm.

Granet, Marcel (1930). *Chinese civilization.* London: Kegan Paul.

—— (1975). *The Religion of the Chinese People.* Tr. Maurice Freedman. Oxford: Basil Blackwell.

Grant, Peter (1890). The Sauteaux Indians, About 1804. Pp. 303–66 in L.F.R. Masson, *The Bourgeois de la Compagnie du Nord-Ouest,* vol. 2. Quebec: A. Coté.

Grant, Robert M. (1970). *Augustine to Constantine: The Thrust of the Christian Movement into the Roman World.* New York: Harper and Row.

Graves, Robert (1955). *The Greek Myths.* Baltimore: Penguin.

Gray, G. B. and M. Cary (1926). "The Reign of Darius." Pp. 173–228 in J. B. Bury, S. A. Cook, and F. E. Adcock (eds.), *The Cambridge Ancient History.* New York: Macmillan.

Gray, J. Patrick (1985). "Growing Yams and Men: An Interpretation of Kimam Male Ritualized Homosexual Behavior." *Journal of Homosexuality* 11:55–68.

Gray, J. Patrick, and Jane E. Ellington (1984). "Institutionalized Male Transvestism, the Couvade, and Homosexual Behavior." *Ethos* 12:54–63.

Gray, John (1964). *The Canaanites.* New York: Frederick A. Praeger.

Gray-Fow, Michael (1986). "Pederasty, the Scantinian Law, and the Roman Army." *Journal of Psychohistory* 13:449–60.

Grayson, A. Kirk and Donald B. Redford (1973). *Papyrus and Tablet.* Englewood Cliffs, N.J.: Prentice-Hall.

Green, Richard (1974). *Sexual Identity Conflict in Children and Adults.* New York: Basic.

—— (1987). *The "Sissy Boy" Syndrome and the Development of Homosexuality.* New Haven: Yale University Press.

Greenberg, David F. (1977). "Delinquency and the Age Structure of Delinquency." *Contemporary Crises* 1:189–223.

—— (1985). "Why Was the Berdache Ridiculed?" *Journal of Homosexuality* 12:179–89.

————, and Marcia H. Bystryn (1982). "Christian Intolerance of Homosexuality." *American Journal of Sociology* 88:515–46.

———— (1984). "Capitalism, Bureaucracy and Male Homosexuality." *Contemporary Crises* 8:33–56.

Greenberg, Joseph H. (1941). "Some Aspects of Negro-Mohammedan Culture-Contact among the Hausa." *American Anthropologist* 43:51–61.

———— (1946). *The Influence of Islam on a Sudanese Religion.* New York: J. J. Augustin.

Greenhalgh, P.A.L. (1973). *Early Greek Warfare: Horsemen and Chariots in the Homeric and Archaic Ages.* London: Cambridge University Press.

Greenleaf, Richard E. (1961). *Zumárraga and the Mexican Inquisition, 1536–1543.* Washington, D.C.: Academy of American Franciscan History.

Greenson, Ralph (1968). "Dis-identifying from the Mother: Its Special Importance for the Boy." *International Journal of Psycho-analysis* 49:370–89.

Gregor, Thomas (1977). *Mehinaku: The Drama of Daily Life in a Brazilian Indian Village.* Chicago: University of Chicago Press.

Gregory of Nyssa, Saint (1967). *Ascetical Works.* Tr. Virginia Woods Callahan. Washington, D.C.: Catholic University of America Press.

Gregory of Tours (1927). *The History of the Franks,* vol. 2. Tr. O. M. Dalton. Oxford: Clarendon.

Greven, Philip J., Jr. (ed.) (1973). *Child-Rearing Concepts. 1628–1861: Historical Sources.* Itasca, Ill.: Peacock.

———— (1977). *The Protestant Temperament: Patterns of Child-Rearing, Religious Experience, and the Self in Early America.* New York: A. A. Knopf.

Griffin, Jasper (1976). "Augustan Poetry and the Life of Luxury." *Journal of Roman Studies* 66:87–105.

Griffiths, J. Gwyn (1969). *The Conflict of Horus and Seth.* Chicago: Argonaut.

———— (1980). *The Origins of Osiris and His Cult.* Leiden: E. J. Brill.

Grilier, Joseph (1957). *To the Source of the Orinoco.* London: Herbert Jenkins.

Grinnell, G. B. (1923). *The Cheyenne Indians,* vol. 2. Lincoln: University of Nebraska Press.

Gross, Jane (1987). "New York State's Curriculum on AIDS Criticized." *New York Times,* Nov. 3.

Grosskurth, Phyllis (1964). *John Addington Symonds.* London: Longmans, Green.

———— (1980). *Havelock Ellis.* New York: A. A. Knopf.

Grotzfeld, Heinz (1970). *Das Bad im Arabisch-Islamischen Mittelalter: Eine kulturgeschichtliche Studien.* Wiesbaden: Otto Harrassowitz.

Groube, Les M. (1971). "Tonga, Lapita Pottery and Polynesian Origins." *Journal of the Polynesian Society* 80:278–316.

Grumbach, Doris (1984). *The Ladies.* New York: E. P. Dutton.

Grumet, Robert Steven (1980). "Sunsquaws, Shamans, and Tradeswomen: Middle Atlantic Coastal Algonkian Women During the 17th and 18th Centuries." Pp. 43–62 in Mona Etienne and Eleanor Leacock (eds.), *Women and Colonization: Anthropological Perspectives.* New York: Praeger.

Grunebaum, G. E. von (1970). *Classical Islam: A History, 600–1258.* London: George Allen and Unwin.

Guerra, Francisco (1971). *The Pre-Columbian Mind.* New York: Seminar.

Guiart, J. (1952). "L'organisation sociale et politique du nord Malekula." *Journal de la Société des Oceanistes* 8:149–259.

———— (1953). "Native Society in the New Hebrides: The Big Nambas of Northern Malekula." *Mankind* 4:439–46.

Gulik, Robert H. van (1961). *Sexual Life in Ancient China.* Leiden: E. J. Brill.

Gummere, Francis B. (1892). *Germanic Origins: A Study in Primitive Culture.* New York: Charles Scribner's.

Gunther, John (1955). *Inside Africa.* New York: Harper.

Gusfield, Joseph R. (1963). *Symbolic Crusade: Status Politics and the American Temperance Movement.* Urbana: University of Illinois Press.

Gusinde, Martin (1937). *Die Yamana: Vom Leben und Denken der Wassernomaden am Kap Hoorn.* Mödling bei Wien: Anthropos Bibliothek.

Hass, Jonathan (1972). *The Evolution of the Prehistoric State.* New York: Columbia University Press.

Hadley-Garcia, George (1983). "The Greening of Gay Money." *Christopher Street* 7(4):30–36.

Hage, Per (1981). "On Male Initiation and Dual Organization in New Guinea." *Man* 16:268–75.

Hagenauer, M. C. (1929). "Sorciers et Sorcières de Corée." *Bulletin de la Maison Franco-Japonaise* (Tokyo) 2:47–65.

Hahn, Pierre (ed.) (1979). *Nos ancêtres les pervers: La vie des homosexuels sous le Second Empire.* Paris: Olivier Orban.

Hair, Paul (ed.) (1972). *Before the Bawdy Court: Selections from the Church Court and Other Records Relating to the Correction of Moral Offences in England, Scotland and New England, 1300–1800.* London: Paul Elek.

Hale, Nathan G. Jr. (1971). *Freud and the Americans: The Beginnings of Psychoanalysis in the United States, 1876–1917.* New York: Oxford University Press.

Hall, John Carey (1979). *Japanese Feudal Law.* Washington, D.C.: University Publications of America. Orig. pub. 1906.

Hall, Leslie A. (1986). "From *Self-Preservation* to *Love without Fear*: Medical and Lay Writers of Sex Advice from William Acton to Eustace Chester." *Society for the Social History of Medicine* 39:20–23.

Haller, John S., and Robin M. Haller (1974). *The Physician and Sexuality in Victorian America.* Urbana: University of Illinois Press.

Hallett, Judith P. (1979). "Sappho and Her Social Context: Sense and Sensuality." *Signs: Journal of Women in Culture and Society* 4:447–64.

Halliday, W. R. (1925). *The Pagan Background of Early Christianity.* Liverpool: University of Liverpool Press.

Hallowell, A. Irving (1955). *Culture and Experience.* Philadelphia: University of Pennsylvania Press.

Hallpike, C. R. (1972). *The Konso of Ethiopia: A Study of the Values of a Cushite People.* Oxford: Clarendon Press.

———— (1977). *Bloodshed and Vengeance in the Papuan Mountains: The Generation of Conflict in Tauade Society.* Oxford: Oxford University Press.

Halperin, David M. (1986a). "One Hundred Years of Homosexuality." *Diacritics* 16:34–45.

—— (1986b). "Plato and Erotic Reciprocity." *Classical Antiquity* 5:58–80.

Hamamsy, Laila Shukry (1957). "The Role of Women in a Changing Navaho Society." *American Anthropologist* 59:101–11.

Hambly, Wilfred D. (1934a). *The Ovimbundu of Angola*. Chicago: Field Museum of Natural History.

—— (1934b). "Occupational Ritual, Belief, and Custom among the Ovimbundu." *American Anthropologist* 36:157–67.

Hamilton, Allan McLane (1896). "The Civil Responsibility of Sexual Perverts." *American Journal of Insanity* 52:503–09.

Hamilton, Roberta (1978). *The Liberation of Women: A Study of Patriarchy and Capitalism*. New York: George Allen and Unwin.

Hammond, N.G.L., and H. H. Scullard (eds.) (1970). *The Oxford Classical Dictionary*. Oxford: Clarendon.

Hamowy, Ronald (1977). "Preventive Medicine and the Criminalization of Sexual Immorality in Nineteenth Century America." Pp. 35–97 in Randy E. Barnett and John Hagel III (eds.), *Assessing the Criminal: Restitution, Retribution and the Legal Process*. Cambridge, Mass.: Ballinger.

Hampson, J. (1965). "Determinants of Psychosexual Orientation." Pp. 108–32 in F. A. Beach (ed.), *Sex and Behavior*. New York: Wiley.

Handy, Craighill (1923). *The Native Culture in the Marquesas*. Bernice P. Bishop Museum Bulletin 9. Honolulu: Museum Press.

—— (1951/52). "The Polynesian Family System in Kau, Hawaii." *Journal of the Polynesian Society* 60:187–222.

Hannon, Gerald (1982). "Men Loving Boys Loving Men." In Ed Jackson and Stan Persky (eds.), *Flaunting It*. Vancouver: New Star.

Hanry, Pierre (1970). *Erotisme Africain: Le comportement sexuel des adolescents Guinéens*. Paris: Payot.

Hansen, Bert (1985). "American Physicians' First Confrontation with Homosexuality, 1870–1900." Paper presented to the Princeton University Program in the History of Science.

Hanson, F. Allan (1970). *Lifeways: Society and History on a Polynesian Island*. Boston: Little Brown.

Hanway, Jonas (1776). *Solitude in Imprisonment with Proper Profitable Labor and a Spare Diet*. London: J. Bow.

Harding, M. Esther (1971). *Women's Mysteries, Ancient and Modern*. New York: Harper Colophon.

Hardman, Edward T. (1889). "Habits and Customs of Natives of Kimberly, Western Australia." *Proceedings of the Royal Irish Academy*, 3d ser. 1:70–75.

Hare, E. H. (1962). "Masturbatory Insanity: The History of an Idea." *Journal of Mental Science* 108:1–25.

Harnack, Adolf (1908). *The Mission and Expansion of Christianity in the First Three Centuries*, vol. 2. Tr. James Moffat. New York: G. P. Putnam's Sons.

Harner, Michael (1977a). "The Ecological Basis for Aztec Sacrifice." *American Ethnologist* 4:117–35.

—— (1977b). "The Enigma of Aztec Sacrifice." *Natural History* 76:47–51.

Harris, Marvin (1977). *Cannibals and Kings: The Origins of Culture*. New York: Simon and Schuster.

——— (1981). *America Now: The Anthropology of a Changing Culture*. New York: Simon and Schuster.

Harris, R. (1961). "The Naditu Laws and the Code of Hammurapi in Praxis." *Orientalia* n.s. 30:163–69.

Harrison, Brian (1967). "Underneath the Victorians." *Victorian Studies* 10:239–62.

Harrison, Jane Ellen (1927). *Themis: A Study of the Social Origins of Greek Religion*. Cambridge: Cambridge University Press.

Harrisson, Tom (1937). *Savage Civilization*. London: Victor Gollancz.

Harry, Joseph, and William Devall (1978). *The Social Organization of Gay Males*. New York: Praeger.

Hart, C.W.M., and Arnold Pilling (1960). *The Tiwi of North Australia*. New York: Holt, Rinehart and Winston.

Hart, Mother Columba (ed.) (1980). *Hadewijch: The Complete Works*. New York: Paulist.

Hartland, E. Sidney (1907). "Concerning the Rite at the Temple of Mylitta." Pp. 189–202 in H. Balfour (ed.), *Anthropological Essays Presented to Edward Burnett Tylor*. Oxford: Clarendon.

Harvey, A. D. (1978). "Prosecutions for Sodomy in England at the Beginning of the Nineteenth Century." *Historical Journal* 21:939–48.

Hassrick, Royal (1964). *The Sioux: Life and Customs of a Warrior Society*. Norman: University of Oklahoma Press.

Hauser, Henri (1933). "The Characteristic Features of French Economic History." *Economic History Review* 4:257–72.

Hawkes, Jacquetta (1958). *Dawn of the Gods*. New York: Random.

Healy, P.W.J. (1978). "Uranisme et Unisexualité: A Late Victorian View of Homosexuality." *New Blackfriars* 59:58–65.

Heath, Stephen (1982). *The Sexual Fix*. New York: Schocken.

Heger, Heinz (1980). *The Men with the Pink Triangle*. Tr. David Fernbach. Boston: Alyson.

Heider, Karl G. (1976). "Dani Sexuality: A Low Energy System." *Man* 11:188–201.

——— (1979). *Grand Valley Dani: Peaceful Warriors*. New York: Holt, Rinehart and Winston.

Heiman, Elliot, and Cao Van Lê (1975). "Transsexualism in Vietnam." *Archives of Sexual Behavior* 4:89–95.

Heinsohn, Gunnar, and Otto Steiger (1982). "The Elimination of Medieval Birth Control and the Witch Trials of Modern Times." *International Journal of Women's Studies* 5:193–214.

Heissig, Walther (1966). *A Lost Civilization: The Mongols Rediscovered*. Tr. D.J.S. Thomson. New York: Basic.

Heizer, R. F., and M. A. Whipple (eds.) (1970). *The California Indians: A Source Book*. Berkeley: University of California Press.

Hell Upon Earth, or the Town in an Uproar (1729). London: J. Roberts and A. Dodd.

Heller, Peter (1981). "A Quarrel over Bisexuality." Pp. 87–115 in Gerald Chapple and Hans H. Schulte (eds.), *The Turn of the Century: German Literature and Art, 1890–1915*. Bonn: Bouvier Verlag Herbert Grundmann.

Helms, Mary W. (1979). *Ancient Panama.* Austin: University of Texas Press.

Hemming, John (1978). *Red Gold: The Conquest of the Brazilian Indians.* Cambridge, Mass.: Harvard University Press.

Hengel, Martin (1980). *Jews, Greeks and Barbarians: Aspects of the Hellenization of Judaism in the pre-Christian Period.* Philadelphia: Fortress.

Henke, Adolph Christian Heinrich (1832). *Lehrbuch der gerichtlichen Medizin.* Stuttgart: E. F. Wolters. Reprinted, pp. 225–38 in Joachim S. Hohmann (ed.), *Der unterdrückte Sexus.* Berlin: Andreas Achenback Lollar, 1977.

Henriques, Fernando (1961). *Stews and Strumpets: A Survey of Prostitution.* Vol. 1: *Primitive, Classical and Oriental.* London: MacGibbon and Kee.

Henry, Alexander, and David Thompson (1897). *New Light on the Early History of the Greater Northwest: The Manuscript Journals of Alexander Henry and David Thompson, 1799–1814,* vol. 1, (ed.) Elliot Coues. New York: Francis P. Harper.

Henthorn, William E. (1971). *A History of Korea.* New York: Free Press.

Herberstein, Sigmund, Freiherr von (1969). *Description of Moscow and Muscovy, 1557.* Tr. J.B.C. Grundy. New York: Barnes and Noble.

Herdt, Gilbert (1981). *Guardians of the Flutes: Idioms of Masculinity.* New York: McGraw-Hill.

—— (ed.) (1984). *Ritualized Homosexuality in Melanesia.* Berkeley: University of California Press.

—— (1987a). *The Sambia: Ritual and Gender in New Guinea.*

—— (1987b). "Semen Depletion and the Sense of Maleness." Pp. 339–451 in Stephen O. Murray (ed.), *Cultural Diversities and Homosexualities.* New York: Irvington.

Heriot, Angus (1956). *The Castrate in Opera.* London: Secker and Warbug.

Herlihy, David (1958). *Pisa in the Early Renaissance: A Study of Urban Growth.* New Haven: Yale University Press.

—— (1969). Vieiller à Florence au Quattrocento." *Annales E.S.C.* 24:1338–52.

—— (1970). *The History of Feudalism.* New York: Harper and Row.

—— (1974). "The Generation in Medieval History." *Viator* 5:346–64.

—— (1976). "Land, Family, and Women in Continental Europe, 701–1200." Pp. 13–45 in Susan Mosher Stuart (ed.), *Women in Medieval Society.* Philadelphia: University of Pennsylvania Press.

—— (1983). "The Making of the Medieval Family: Symmetry, Structure and Sentiment." *Journal of Family History* 8:116–30.

Herm, Gerhard (1977). *The Celts: The People Who Came Out of Darkness.* New York: St. Martin's Press.

Herman, Gerald (1976). "The 'Sin Against Nature' and its Echoes in Medieval French Literature." *Annuale Mediaevale* 17:70–87.

Hernandez, Ludovico (1920). *Les proces de bestialité aux XVIᵉ et XVIIᵉ siècles.* Paris: Bibliothèque des Curieux.

Hernández de Alba, Gregorio (1963). "The Tribes of North Central Venezuela." Pp. 475–93 in Julian H. Steward (ed.), *Handbook of South American Indians,* vol. 4. Washington, D.C.: Government Printing Office.

Hernsheim, Franz (1880). *Beitrag zur Sprache der Marshall-Inseln.* Leipzig: F. Theil.

Herodian of Antioch (1961). *History of the Roman Empire from the Death of Marcus Au-*

relius to the Accession of Gordion III. Tr. Edward C. Echols. Berkeley: University of California Press.

Herodotus (1954). *The Histories.* Tr. Aubrey de Selincourt. New York: Penguin.

Herskovits, Melville J. (1967). *Dahomey: An Ancient West African Kingdom,* vol. 1. Evanston, Ill.: Northwestern University Press.

Hervé, Guy, and Thierry Kerrest (1979). *Les enfants de Fez.* Paris: Editions Libres Hallier.

Herzer, Manfred (1985). "Kertbeny and the Nameless Love." *Journal of Homosexuality* 12:1–26.

Herzfeld, Ernst (1947). *Zoroaster and His World,* vol. 2. Princeton, N.J.: Princeton University Press.

Hetherington, E. M. (1966). "Effects of Paternal Absence on Sex Typed Behaviors in Negro and White Adolescent Males." *Journal of Personal and Social Psychology* 4:87–91.

Heurgon, Jacques (1964). *Daily Life of the Etruscans.* New York: Macmillan.

Heyd, Uriel (1973). *Studies in Old Ottoman Criminal Law.* London: Oxford University Press.

Hibbard, Howard (1983). *Caravaggio.* London: Thames and Hudson.

Hilger, Sister M. Inez (1957). *Araucanian Child Life and Its Cultural Background.* Washington, D.C.: Smithsonian Institution.

Hill, Christopher (1961). *The Century of Revolution, 1603–1714.* London: Nelson.

Hill, Polly (1967). *Rural Hausa: A Village and a Selling.* Cambridge: Cambridge University Press.

Hill, W. W. (1935). "The Status of the Hermaphrodite and Transvestite in Navaho Culture." *American Anthropologist* 37:273–79.

——— (1938). "Note on the Pima Berdache." *American Anthropologist* 40:338–40.

Hillers, Delbert (1973). "The Bow of Aqhat: The Meaning of a Mythical Theme." Pp. 71–80 in Harry A. Hoffner, Jr. (ed.), *Orient and Occident.* Neukirchner-Vluyn: Butzon and Bercker Kevelaer Neukirchener.

Hilliard, David (1982). "Unenglish and Unmanly: Anglo-Catholicism and Homosexuality." *Victorian Studies* 25:181–210.

Himmelstein, Jerome (1984). "The Social Basis of Antifeminism." Unpublished paper.

Hinde, R.S.E. (1951). *The British Penal System, 1773–1950.* London: Gerald Duckworth.

Hindess, Barry and Paul Q. Hirst (1975). *Pre-capitalist Modes of Production.* Boston: Routledge and Kegan Paul.

Hints to the Public and the Legislature, on the Prevalence of Vice, and on the Dangerous Effects of Seduction (1811). London: E. Wilson.

Hinz, Walther (1972). *The Lost World of Elam: Re-creation of a Vanished Civilization.* New York: New York University Press.

Hirayama, Hisashi and Kasumi K. Hirayama (1986). "The Sexuality of Japanese Americans." *Journal of Social Work and Human Sexuality* 4(3):81–98.

Hirschfeld, Magnus (1904). *Berlins Drittes Geschlecht.* Berlin: H. Seeman Nachfolger.

——— (1914). *Die Homosexualität des Mannes und des Weibes.* Berlin: Louis Marcus.

——— (1934). *The Sexual History of the World War.* New York: Panurge.

—— (1935a). *Women East and West: Impressions of a Sex Expert.* Tr. C. P. Green. London: William Heinemann.

—— (1935b). *Sex in Human Relationships.* London: John Lane.

Ho, Ping-Ti (1975). *The Cradle of the East.* Chicago: University of Chicago Press.

Hocquenghem, Guy (1978). *The Problem Is Not So Much Homosexual Desire as the Fear of Homosexuality.* Tr. Daniella Dangoor. London: Allison and Busby.

Hodgson, Marshall G. S. (1974). *The Venture of Islam.* 3 vols. Chicago: University of Chicago Press.

Hoebel, E. Adamson (1949). *Man in the Primitive World: An Introduction to Anthropology.* New York: McGraw-Hill.

—— (1978). *The Cheyenne: Indians of the Great Plains.* New York: Holt, Rinehart and Winston.

Hoffman, Martin (1968). *The Gay World: Male Homosexuality and the Social Creation of Evil.* New York: Basic.

Hoffman, Philip T. (1984). *Church and Community in the Diocese of Lyon, 1500–1789.* New Haven: Yale University Press.

Hoffman, Richard J. (1980). "Some Cultural Aspects of Greek Male Homosexuality." *Journal of Homosexuality* 5:217–26.

—— (1984). "Vices, Gods, and Virtues: Cosmology as a Mediating Factor in Attitudes toward Male Homosexuality." *Journal of Homosexuality* 10:27–44.

Hoffman, Walter James (1891). "The Midē'wiwin or 'Grand Medicine Society' of the Ojibwa." *U.S. Bureau of American Ethnology. 7th Annual Report, 1885–86.* Washington, D.C.: U.S. Government Printing Office.

Hoffner, Harry A., Jr. (1963). *The Laws of the Hittites.* Ph.D. dissertation, Brandeis University.

—— (1966). "Symbols for Masculinity and Femininity: Their Use in Ancient Near Eastern Sympathetic Magic Rituals." *Journal of Biblical Literature* 85:326–34.

—— (1973a). "Incest, Sodomy and Bestiality in the Ancient Near East." Pp. 81–90 in H. A. Hoffner, Jr. (ed.), *Orient and Occident.* Neukirchen-Vluyn: Verlag Butzen und Bercker Kevelaer.

—— (1973b). "The Hittites and Hurrians." Pp. 179–86 in D. J. Wiseman (ed.), *Peoples of Old Testament Times.* London: Oxford University Press.

Höfler, Otto (1934). *Kultische Geheimbünde der Germanen.* Frankfurt am Main: M. Diesterwey.

Hofstadter, Richard (1957). *The American Political Tradition and the Men Who Made It.* New York: A. A. Knopf.

—— (1968). *Social Darwinism in American Thought.* Boston: Beacon.

Hogarth, D. G. (1914). "Hierodouloi (Graeco-Roman)." Pp. 671–72 in James Hastings (ed.), *Encyclopedia of Religion and Ethics,* vol. 6. New York: Charles Scribner's Sons.

Hogbin, Herbert Ian (1963). *Kinship and Marriage in a New Guinea Village.* London: Athlone.

—— (1970). *The Island of Menstruating Men: Religion in Wogeo, New Guinea.* Scranton, Pa.: Chandler.

Hohenberg, Paul M., and Lynn Hollen Lees (1983). "Cities and Urban Industry in

Early Modern Europe." Unpublished paper presented to the Social Science History Association.

Hohmann, Joachim S. (ed.) (1977). *Der unterdrückte Sexus: Historische Texte und Kommentare zur Homosexualität.* Berlin: Andreas Achenbach Lollar.

Hollibaugh, Amber (1979). "Sexuality and the State: The Defeat of the Briggs Initiative and Beyond." *Socialist Review* 45:55–72.

Holloway, Robert (1813). *The Phoenix of Sodom, or the Vere Street Coterie. Being an Exhibition of the Gambols Practiced by the Ancient Lechers of Sodom and Gomorrah, Embellished and Improved with the Modern Refinements in Sodomitical Practices, by the Members of the Vere Street Coterie, of Detestable Memory.* London: J. Cook.

Holmberg, A. R. (1950). *Nomads of the Long Boy.* Washington, D.C.: Smithsonian Institution.

Homer (1951). *The Iliad of Homer.* Tr. Richard Lattimore. Chicago: University of Chicago Press.

Honigmann, John J. (1964). *The Kaska Indians: An Ethnographic Reconstruction.* Yale University Publications in Anthropology. New Haven: Yale University Press.

Hood, Sinclair (1971). *The Minoans: The Story of Bronze Age Crete.* New York: Praeger.

Hooker, Evelyn (1956). "A Preliminary Analysis of Group Behavior of Homosexuals." *Journal of Psychology* 42:217–25.

——— (1965). "Male Homosexuals and Their 'Worlds'." Pp. 83–107 in Judd Marmor (ed.), *Sexual Inversion: The Multiple Roots of Homosexuality.* New York: Basic.

——— (1967). "The Homosexual Community." Pp. 167–84 in John Gagnon and William S. Simon (eds), *Sexual Deviance.* New York: Harper and Row.

Hooker, J. T. (1980). *The Ancient Spartans.* London: J. M. Dent.

Hopkins, Charles Howard (1940). *The Rise of the Social Gospel in American Protestantism, 1865–1915.* New Haven: Yale University Press.

Hopkins, Keith (1978). *Conquerors and Slaves: Sociological Studies in Roman History,* vol. 1. Cambridge: Cambridge University Press.

Horn, Walter, and Ernest Born (1979). *The Plan of St. Gall,* 3 vols. Berkeley: University of California Press.

Horner, Tom (1978). *Jonathan Loved David: Homosexuality in Biblical Times.* Philadelphia: Westminster.

Hornung, E. (1982). *Conceptions of God in Ancient Egypt.* Tr. J. Baines. Ithaca, N.Y.: Cornell University Press.

Horst, P. W. van der (1978). *The Sentences of Pseudo-Phocylides.* Leiden: E. J. Brill.

Horwitz, Morton J. (1977). *The Transformation of American Law, 1780–1860.* Cambridge, Mass.: Harvard University Press.

Hosi-Wien Collective (1985). "Austria: The Gay Liberation Movement and the Law." Pp. 84–104 in *IGA Pink Book 1985.* Amsterdam: COC.

Hössli, Heinrich (1836). *Eros: Die Männerliebe des Griechen.* St. Gallen: P. Scheitlin.

Houel, Christian (1912). *Maroc: Marriage, adultère, prostitution: Anthologie.* Paris: H. Daragon.

Hounshell, David A. (1984). *From the American System to Mass Production, 1800–1932: The Development of Manufacturing Technology in the United States.* Baltimore: Johns Hopkins University Press.

Howard, John (1784). *The State of the Prisons in England and Wales.* 3d ed. Warrington: W. Eyres.

Howell, Martha C. (1986). *Women, Production, and Patriarchy in Late Medieval Cities.* Chicago: University of Chicago Press.

Howell, T. B. (1816). *A Complete Collection of State Trials and Proceedings for High Treason and Other Misdemeanors from the Earliest Period to the Year 1783,* vol. 1. London: Longman.

Howson, Gerald (1970). *Thief-Taker General: Jonathan Wild and the Emergence of Crime and Corruption as a Way of Life in Eighteenth Century England.* New Brunswick, N.J.: Rutgers University Press.

Hrdlička, Aleš (1944). *The Anthropology of Kodiak Island.* Philadelphia: Wistar Institute.

Hrozný, Frédéric (1922). *Code hittite provenant de l'Asie Mineure (vers 1350 av. J.-C.).* Paris: P. Geuthner.

Huart, Clement (1972). *Ancient Persia and Iranian Civilization.* London: Routledge and Kegan Paul.

Hudson, Charles (1976). *The Southeastern Indians.* Knoxville: University of Tennessee Press.

Hughes, Charles H. (1907). "Homo Sexual Complexion Perverts in St. Louis: Note on a Feature of Sexual Psychopathy." *Alienist and Neurologist* 28:487–88.

Hughes, Jonathan R. T. (1977). *The Governmental Habit: Economic Controls from Colonial Times to the Present.* New York: Basic.

Hugh-Jones, Stephen (1979). *The Palm and the Pleiades: Initiation and Cosmology in Northwest Amazonia.* Cambridge: Cambridge University Press.

Hull, Isabel V. (1982). *The Entourage of Kaiser Wilhelm II, 1888–1918.* Cambridge: Cambridge University Press.

Humphreys, Laud (1970). *Tearoom Trade: Impersonal Sex in Public Places.* Chicago: Aldine.

——— (1971). "New Styles in Homosexual Manliness." *Trans-Action* (March-April): 38–46, 64–65.

——— (1972). *Out of the Closets: The Sociology of Homosexual Liberation.* Englewood Cliffs, N.J.: Prentice-Hall.

Humphries, Drew (1977). "The Movement to Legalize Abortion: An Historical Account." Pp. 205–24 in David F. Greenberg (ed.), *Corrections and Punishment.* Beverly Hills, Calif.: Sage.

——— and David F. Greenberg (1981). "The Dialectics of Crime Control." Pp. 209–54 in David F. Greenberg (ed.), *Crime and Capitalism: Readings in Marxist Criminology.* Palo Alto, Calif.: Mayfield.

Hunter, James Davison (1983). *American Evangelism: Conservative Religion and the Quandary of Modernity.* New Brunswick, N.J.: Rutgers University Press.

Hunter, R. L. (1983). *A Study of Daphnis and Chloe.* Cambridge: Cambridge University Press.

Hutchinson, G. E. (1959). "A Speculative Consideration of Certain Possible Forms of Sexual Selection in Man." *American Naturalist* 93:81–91.

Hutchinson, Harry Wilson (1957). *Village and Plantation Life in Northeastern Brazil.* Seattle: University of Washington Press.

Hutstaert, R.P.G. (1938). *Le mariage des Nkundó*. Brussels: Georges van Campenhout.

Huusen, Arend H. Jr. (1985). "Sodomy in the Dutch Republic during the Eighteenth Century." *Eighteenth Century Life* n.s. 9:169–78.

Hyamson, Moses (1913). *Mosaicarum et Romanarum Legum Collatio*. London: Oxford University Press.

Hyde, J. K. (1966). *Padua in the Age of Dante*. New York: Barnes and Noble.

Hyde, H. Montgomery (1956). *The Three Trials of Oscar Wilde*. New York: University Books.

——— (1970). *The Other Love: An Historical and Contemporary Survey of Homosexuality in Britain*. London: Heinemann.

——— (1984). *Lord Alfred Douglas: A Biography*. London: Methuen.

Hyde, Louis (ed.) (1978). *Rat and the Devil: Journal Letters of F. O. Mathiessen and Russell Cheney*. Hamden, Conn.: Archon.

Hyman, Herbert H., and Charles R. Wright (1979). *Education's Lasting Influence on Values*. Chicago: University of Chicago Press.

Hynes, Samuel (1968). *The Edwardian Turn of Mind*. Princeton, N.J.: Princeton University Press.

Ibn Atiyah, Jarir (1974). *The Naqaith of Jarir and al Farazdaq*. Tr. Arthur Wormhoudt. Oskaloosa, Iowa: William Penn College.

Ibn Ḥazam, Ali ibn Aḥmad (1978). *The Ring of the Dove: A Treatise on the Art and Practice of Arab Love*. Tr. A. J. Arberry. New York: AMS.

Ibn Khaldûn, Abd-al-Rahman (1967). *The Muqaddimah: An Introduction to History*. Tr. Franz Rosenthal. Princeton, N.J.: Princeton University Press.

Ide, Arthur Frederick (1985). *The City of Sodom and Homosexuality in Western Religious Thought to 630 C.E.* Dallas: Monument.

Idell, Albert (1956). *The Bernal Diaz Chronicles*. New York: Doubleday.

Ignatieff, Michael (1978). *A Just Measure of Pain: The Penitentiary in the Industrial Revolution, 1750–1850*. New York: Pantheon.

Igra, Samuel (1945). *Germany's National Vice*. London: Quality.

Ihara, Saikaku (1972). *Comrade Loves of the Samurai*. Tr. E. Powys Mathers. Rutland, Vt.: Tuttle. Orig. pub. 1928.

Imparata, Fiorella (1964). *Le leggi Ittite*. Rome: Edizioni dell' Ateneo.

Inalcik, Halil (1973). *The Ottoman Empire: the Classical Age*. London: Weidenfeld and Nicolson.

Inge, William Ralph (1923). *The Philosophy of Plotinus*. London: Longmans, Green.

Ingram, Martin John (1976). *Ecclesiastical Justice in Wiltshire, 1600–1640, with Special Reference to Cases Concerning Sex and Marriage*. Ph.D. dissertation, Oxford University.

International Association of Lesbians, Gay Women and Gay Men (ed.) (1985). *IGA Pink Book 1985*. Amsterdam: COC.

d'Irsay, Stephen (1925). "The Life and Works of Gilles de Corbeil." *Annals of Medical History* 7:362–78.

Irwin, John (1977). *Scenes*. Beverly Hills, Calif.: Sage.

Isaacs, Tina (1982). "The Anglican Hierarchy and the Reformation of Manners, 1688–1738." *Journal of Ecclesiastical History* 33:391–411.

Isay, Richard A. (1986). "On the Analytic Therapy of Homosexual Men." *The Psychoanalytic Study of the Child* 40:235–54.

Issa, Ihsan al- and Britta al-Issa (1971). "Psychiatric Problems in a Developing Country." *Transcultural Psychiatric Review* 8:59–61.

Jackson, A. V. Williams (1965). *Zoroastrian Studies*. New York: AMS. Orig. pub. 1928.

Jackson, Gabriel (1972). *The Making of Medieval Spain*. New York: Harcourt Brace Jovanovich.

Jacobi, Hermann (ed.) (1968). *Jaina Sutras*. New York: Dover.

Jacobs, Eva (1979). "Diderot and the Education of Women." Pp. 83–95 in Eva Jacobs, W. H. Barber, Jean H. Bloch, F. W. Leakey, and Eileen Le Breton (eds.), *Woman and Society in Eighteenth-Century France*. London: Athlone.

Jacobs, Julius (1883). *Eenigen Tijd Onder de Baliers*. Batavia: G. Kolff.

Jacobs, Sue-Ellen (1968). "Berdache: A Brief Review of the Literature." *Colorado Anthropologist* 1:25–40.

Jacobsen, Thorkild (1930). "How Did Gilgamesh Oppress Uruk?" *Acta Orientalia* 8:62–74.

Jacobus X. (n.d.). *Untrodden Fields of Anthropology, by a French Army-Surgeon*. New York: American Anthropological Study Society.

Jacoby, Felix (1950). *Fragmente der Griechischen Historiker*, vol. 3. Leiden: E. J. Brill.

Jacoby, Henry (1973). *The Bureaucratization of the World*. Tr. by Eveline L. Kanes. Berkeley: University of California Press.

Jacquart, Danielle, and Claude Thomasset (1985). *Sexualité et savoir medical au Moyen Âge*. Paris: Presses Universitaires de France.

Jaeger, C. S. (1983). "Mark and Tristan: The Love and Gaiety of Medieval Kings and Their Courts." Unpublished paper presented to the Modern Language Association.

James, Edward (1982). *The Origins of France: From Clovis to the Capetians, 500–1100*. New York: St. Martin's Press.

James, E. O. (1958). *Myth and Ritual in the Ancient Near East: An Archaeological and Documentary Study*. London: Thames and Hudson.

James, Edwin (1822). *Account of an Expedition from Pittsburgh to the Rocky Mountains*. Philadelphia: H. C. Carey.

James, Montague Rhodes (ed.) (1945). *The Apocryphal New Testament*. Oxford: Clarendon.

Jay, Karla, and Allen Young (1977). *The Gay Report*. New York: Summit.

Jeanmaire, Henri (1939). *Couroi et courètes: Essai sur l'education spartiate et sur les rites d'adolescence dans l'antiquité hellenique*. Lille: Bibliothèque Universitaire.

Jeffreys, Sheila (1985). *The Spinster and Her Enemies: Feminism and Sexuality, 1880–1930*. London: Pandora.

Jenkins, Romilly J. H. (1967). *Byzantium: The Imperial Centuries, A.D. 610–1071*. New York: Random House.

Jennings, Hargrave (1891). *Phallic Miscellanies: Facts and Phases of Ancient and Modern Sex Worship*. Privately printed.

Jensen, Erik (1974). *The Iban and their Religion*. London: Oxford University Press.

Jewish Encyclopedia (1902). New York: Funk and Wagnall's.

Jochelson, Waldemar (1905). *The Koryak*. Leiden: E. J. Brill.

Jochens, Jenny M. (1980). "The Church and Sexuality in Medieval Iceland." *Journal of Medieval History* 6:377–92.

Jochim, Michael A. (1983). "Palaeolithic Cave Art in Ecological Perspective." Pp. 212–19 in Geoff Barley (ed.), *Hunter-Gatherer Economy in Prehistory: A European Perspective*. Cambridge: Cambridge University Press.

Johansson, Warren (1984a). "Whosoever Shall Say to His Brother, *Racha*." *Cabirion and Gay Books Bulletin* 10:2–4.

——— (1984b). "London's Medieval Sodomites." *Cabirion and Gay Books Bulletin* 10:6–7, 34.

——— (1985). "Ex Parte Themis: The Historical Guilt of the Christian Church." Pp. 1–7 in *Homosexuality, Intolerance, and Christianity: A Critical Examination of John Boswell's Work*. 2d ed. New York: Gay Academic Union.

John Chrysostom, Saint (1865). *Oeuvres complètes*, vol. 4. Tr. M. L. Abbé Joly. Paris: Bordes Frères.

Johnson, Paul (1986). "Assault on the Young." *Daily Telegraph*, Oct. 6.

Johnson, Wendell Stacy (1979). *Living in Sin: The Victorian Sexual Revolution*. Chicago: Nelson-Hall.

Johnston, Harry H. (1884). *The River Congo: From Its Mouth to Balōbó*. London: Sampson Low, Maiston, Searle, and Rivington.

Johnston, Jill (1973). *Lesbian Nation: The Feminist Solution*. New York: Simon and Schuster.

Johnston, William M. (1972). *The Austrian Mind: An Intellectual and Social History, 1848–1938*. Berkeley: University of California Press.

Jones, A.H.M. (1961). *The Later Roman Empire, 284–602*, vol. 2. London: Blackwell.

——— (1966). *The Decline of the Ancient World*. London: Longmans, Green.

——— (1967). *Sparta*. Oxford: Basil Blackwell.

Jones, Gareth Stedman (1971). *Outcast London*. Oxford: Oxford University Press.

Jones, George Fenwick (1963). *The Ethos of the Song of Roland*. Baltimore: Johns Hopkins University Press.

Jones, Michael (1986). "Preaching to the Infected." *Sunday Times*, Dec. 14.

Jones, Rex L. (1976). "Limbu Spirit Possession and Shamanism." Pp. 29–55 in John T. Hitchcock and Rex L. Jones (eds.), *Spirit Possession in the Nepal Himalayas*. Warminster, Eng.: Aris and Phillips.

Jones, William (1907). *Fox Texts*. Publications of the American Ethnological Society 1. Leiden: E. J. Brill.

Jong, Ben de (1985). "'An Intolerable Kind of Moral Degeneration': Homosexuality in the Soviet Union." Pp. 76–88 in *IGA Pink Book 1985*. Amsterdam: COC.

Jorstad, Erling (1981). *Evangelicals in the White House: The Cultural Maturation of Born Again Christianity, 1960–1981*. New York: Edwin Mellen.

Josephus (1880). *Complete Works*. Tr. William Whiston, Philadelphia: Henry T. Coates.

——— (1930). *Jewish Antiquities*. Tr. H. St. J. Thackeray. London: William Heinemann.

Jourard, S. (1974). "Some Lethal Aspects of the Male Role." Pp. 21–29 in Joseph Pleck and Jack Sawyer (eds.) *Men and Masculinity*. Englewood Cliffs, N.J.: Prentice-Hall.

J.S.H. (1921). "The Regulation of Sex." *Atheneum* 4733 (Jan. 14):47–48.

Julius Firmicus Maternus (1970). *The Error of the Pagan Religions.* Tr. Clarence Forbes. New York: Newman.

Junod, Henri A. (1962). *The Life of a South African Tribe,* vol. 1. New Hyde Park, N.Y.: University Books. Orig. pub. 1912.

Juviler, Peter H. (1976). *Revolutionary Law and Order: Politics and Social Change in the U.S.S.R.* New York: Free Press.

Jwaya, Suyewo (1902). "Nan sho k' (die Päderastie in Japan)." *Jahrbuch für sexuelle Zwischenstufen* 4:263–71.

Kaberry, Phyllis (1939). *Aboriginal Woman: Sacred and Profane.* London: Routledge.

Kamekau, S. (1961). *Ruling Chiefs of Hawaii.* Honolulu: Kamehameha Schools Press.

Kamen, Henry (1968). The Spanish Inquisition. New York: Mentor.

Kando, Thomas M. (1978). *Sexual Behavior and Family Life in Transition.* New York: Elsevier.

Kane, Joe (1985). "Officer Hicks, Gay Cop." *Esquire* 103(6):235–41.

Kaplow, Jeffrey (1972). *The Names of Kings: The Parisian Laboring Poor in the Eighteenth Century.* New York: Basic.

Kardiner, Abram (1939). *The Individual and His Society: The Psychodynamics of Primitive Social Organization.* New York: Columbia University Press.

—— (1945). *The Psychological Frontiers of Society.* New York: Columbia University Press.

Karlen, Arlo (1971a). *Sexuality and Homosexuality.* New York: W. W. Norton.

—— (1971b). "The Homosexual Heresy." *Chaucer Review* 6:44–63.

Karlinsky, Simon (1976). "Russia's Gay Literature and History (11th–20th Centuries)." *Gay Sunshine* 29–30:1–7.

Karol, K. S. (1970). *Guerrillas in Power: The Course of the Cuban Revolution.* New York: Hill and Wang.

Karsch-Haack, Ferdinand (1906). *Forschungen über gleichgeschlechtliche Liebe: Das gleichgeschlechtliche Leben der Ostasiaten: Chinesen, Japaner, Koreer.* Munich: Seiz und Schauer.

—— (1911). *Das gleichgeschlechtliche Leben der Naturvölker.* Munich: Ernst Reinhardt.

Käsemann, Ernst (1980). *Commentary on Romans.* Tr. Geoffrey W. Bromiley. Grand Rapids, Mich.: William B. Eerdmans.

Katz, Friedrich (1958). "The Evolution of Aztec Society." *Past and Present* 13:14–25.

Katz, Jonathan N. (1976). *Gay American History: Lesbians and Gay Men in the U.S.A.* New York: Thomas Y. Crowell.

—— (1983). *Gay American Almanac.* New York: Harper Colophon.

Kauffmann-Doig, Federico (1978). *Comportamiento sexual en el Antiguo Peru.* Lima: Kompaktos G.S.

Kay, Richard (1969). "The Sin of Brunetto Latini." *Medieval Studies* 31:262–86.

—— (1978). *Dante's Swift and Strong: Essays in Inferno XV.* Lawrence: Regent's Press of Kansas.

Keating, William Hypolitus (1924). *Narrative of an Expedition to the Source of St. Peter's River,* vol. 1. Philadelphia: Carey and Lea.

Kees, Hermann (1961). *Ancient Egypt: A Cultural Topography.* Chicago: University of Chicago Press.

Keesel, Dionysius Godefridus van der (1969–72). *Lectures on Books 47 and 48 of the Digest*. Capetown, So. Afr.: Juta.

Keesing, Roger M. (1982). "Introduction." Pp. 1–43 in Gilbert Herdt (ed.), *Rituals of Manhood: Male Initiation in Papua New Guinea*. Berkeley: University of California Press.

Kelly, Isabel T. (1934). "Ethnography of the Surprise Valley Paiute." Pp. 67–210 in *University of California Publications in American Archaeology and Ethnology 1931–1933*, vol. 31. Berkeley: University of California Press.

Kelly, Raymond C. (1974). *Etoro Social Structure: A Study in Structural Contradiction*. Ann Arbor: University of Michigan Press.

——— (1976). "Witchcraft and Sexual Relations: An Exploration in the Social and Semantic Implications of the Structure of Belief." Pp. 36–53 in Paula Brown and Georgeda Buchbinder (ed.), *Man and Woman in the New Guinea Highlands*. Washington, D.C.: American Anthropological Association.

Kennedy, Hubert C. (1980/81). "The 'Third Sex' Theory of Karl Heinrich Ulrichs." *Journal of Homosexuality* 6:103–11.

——— (1988). *The Life of Karl Heinrich Ulrichs: Pioneer of the Modern Gay Movement*. San Francisco: Alyson.

Kenyatta, Jomo (1953). *Facing Mount Kenya: The Tribal Life of the Kikuyu*. London: Secker and Warburg.

Keuls, Eva C. (1985). *The Reign of the Phallus: Sexual Politics in Ancient Athens*. New York: Harper and Row.

Kevles, Daniel J. (1984). "Annals of Eugenics: A Secular Faith-II." *New Yorker*, Oct. 15.

Khun de Prorok, Count Byron (1936). *In Quest of Lost Worlds*. New York: E. P. Dutton.

Kidd, Beresford James (1933). *The Counter-Reformation, 1550–1600*. London: Society for Promoting Christian Knowledge.

Kiefer, Monica (1948). *American Children through Their Books, 1700–1835*. Philadelphia: University of Pennsylvania Press.

Kiefer, Otto (1934). *Sexual Life in Ancient Rome*. London: Abbey Library.

Kiernan, James G. (1884). "Insanity. Lecture XXVI.—Perversion." *Detroit Lancet* 7:481–84.

Kilmer, Anne Draffkorn (1982). "A Note on an Overlooked Word-Play in the Akkadian Gilgamesh." Pp. 128–32 in G. Van Driel, Th. J. H. Krispijn, M. Stol, and K. R. Veenhof (eds.), *Zikir Šumim: Assyriological Studies Presented to F. R. Kraus on the Occasion of His Seventieth Birthday*. Leiden: E. J. Brill.

King, N. Q. (1960). *The Emperor Theodosius and the Establishment of Christianity*. Philadelphia: Westminster.

King, P. D. (1972). *Law and Society in the Visigothic Kingdom*. London: Cambridge University Press.

Kinsella, Thomas (1969). *The Táin [Táin Bó Cuailnge]*. Ireland: Dolmen.

Kinsey, Alfred C., Wardell B. Pomeroy, and Clyde E. Martin (1948). *Sexual Behavior in the Human Male*. Philadelphia: W. B. Saunders.

———, Wardell B. Pomeroy, Clyde E. Martin, and Paul H. Gebhard (1949). "Concepts of Normality and Abnormality in Sexual Behavior." Pp. 11–32 in Paul H.

Hoch and Joseph Zubin (eds.), *Psychosexual Development in Health and Disease.* New York: Grune and Stratton.

Kinsman, Gary (1987). *The Regulation of Desire: Sexuality in Canada.* Montreal: Black Rose.

Kirch, Patrick Vinton (1984). *The Evolution of the Polynesian Chiefdoms.* Cambridge: Cambridge University Press.

Kirchhoff, Paul (1963). "The Tribes North of the Orinoco River." Pp. 481–93 in Julian H. Steward (ed.), *Hanbook of South American Indians,* vol. 4. Washington, D.C.: Government Printing Office.

Kirkpatrick, John (1983). *The Marquesan Notion of a Person.* Ann Arbor: UMI Research Press.

Kirsch, John A. W., and James Eric Rodman (1977). "The Natural History of Homosexuality." *Yale Scientific Magazine* 51 (Winter):7–13.

——— (1982). "Selection and Sexuality: The Darwinian View of Homosexuality." Pp. 183–96 in William Paul, James D. Weinrich, John C. Gonsiorek, and Mary E. Hotvedt (eds.), *Homosexuality: Social, Psychological and Biological Issues.* Beverly Hills, Calif.: Sage.

Kleffens, E. N. Van (1968). *Hispanic Law Until the End of the Middle Ages.* Edinburgh: Edinburgh University Press.

Klein, Alan (1983). "The Political-Economy of Gender: A 19th Century Plains Indian Case Study." Pp. 143–73 in Patricia Albers and Beatrice Medicine (eds.), *The Hidden Half: Studies of Plains Indian Women.* Washington, D.C.: University Press of America.

Klein, Ethel (1984). *Gender Politics: From Consciousness to Mass Politics.* Cambridge, Mass.: Harvard University Press.

Klein, Richard G. (1980). "Review of *European Prehistory* by Sarunas Milisauskas." *American Antiquity* 45:209–10.

Klein, Stanley (eds.) (1974). "Towards an Anthropology of Sexual Inversion." Pp. 113–33 in Raymond Prince and Dorothy Barrier (eds.), *Configurations: Biological and Cultural Factors in Sexuality and Family Life.* Lexington: D.C. Heath.

Kleinberg, Seymour (1978). "Where Have all the Sissies Gone?" *Christopher Street* 2(9):4–12.

——— (1982). "It is 1699 and You Have Been Accused of Sodomy . . ." *Christopher Street* 6(3):46–53.

——— (1983). "*The Merchant of Venice:* The Homosexual as Anti-Semite in Nascent Capitalism." *Journal of Homosexuality* 8:113–70.

Kline, Paul (1972). *Fact and Fantasy in Freudian Theory.* London: Methuen.

Klunzinger, C. B. (1878). *Upper Egypt: Its People and Its Products.* New York: Scribner, Armstrong.

Knapp, Andrew and William Baldwin (1819). *The New Newgate Calendar,* vol. 3. London: J. J. Cundee.

Knauft, Bruce M. (1985). "Ritual Form and Permutation in New Guinea: Implications of Symbolic Process for Socio-Political Evolution." *American Ethnologist* 12:321–40.

——— (1986). *Good Company and Violence: Sorcery and Social Action in a Lowland New Guinea Society.* Berkeley: University of California Press.

——— (1987). "Homosexuality in Melanesia." *Journal of Psychoanalytic Anthropology* 10:155–91.

Knorr-Cetina, Karen (1982). "The Constructivist Programme in the Sociology of Science: Retreats or Advances?" *Social Studies of Science* 12:320–24.

Knowles, Dom David (1959). *The Religious Orders in England.* Vol. 3: *The Tudor Age.* London: Cambridge University Press.

——— (1969). *Christian Monasticism.* New York: McGraw-Hill.

Koehler, Lyle (1974). "The Case of the American Jezebels: Anne Hutchinson and Female Agitation during the Years of Antinomian Turmoil, 1636–1640." *William and Mary Quarterly* 30:55–78.

Koffler, Judith Schenk (1979). "Capitalism in Hell: Dante's Lesson on Usury." *Rutgers Law Review* 32:608–60.

Kohler, Joseph, and Willy Scheel (1968a). *Die Bambergische Halsgerichtsordnung in Niederdeutscher Übersetzung Hermann Barkhusens 1510.* Darmstadt: Scientia Verlag Aalen.

——— (1968b). *Die peinliche Gerichtsordnung Kaiser Karls V.* 4 vols. Scientia Verlag Aalen. Orig. pub. 1900–1915.

Kohn, Melvin L. (1977). *Class and Conformity: A Study in Values.* Chicago: University of Chicago Press.

———, Kazimierz M. Slomczynski, and Carrie Schoenback (1986). "Social Stratification and the Transmission of Values in the Family: A Cross-National Assessment." *Sociological Forum* 1:73–102.

Kolko, Gabriel (1963). *The Triumph of Conservatism: A Reinterpretation of American History, 1900–1916.* Chicago: Quadrangle.

——— (1965). *Railroads and Regulation, 1877–1916.* New York: W. W. Norton.

Koop, C. Everett (1986). *Surgeon General's Report on Acquired Immune Deficiency Syndrome.* Washington, D.C.: U.S. Dept. of Health and Human Services.

Kopp, Marie E. (1938). "Surgical Treatment as Sex Crime Prevention Measure." *Journal of Criminal Law and Criminology* 28:692–706.

Kors, Alan C., and Edward Peters (eds.) (1972). *Witchcraft in Europe, 1110–1700: A Documentary History.* Philadelphia: University of Pennsylvania Press.

Kosanbi, D. D. (1967). "Living Prehistory in India." *Scientific American* 216 (Feb.): 105–12.

Kracke, Ward H. (1978). *Force and Persuasion: Leadership in an Amazonian Society.* Chicago: University of Chicago Press.

Krader, Laurence (1968). *Formation of the State.* Englewood Cliffs, N.J.: Prentice-Hall.

Kraef, Justus van der (1954). "Transvestism and the Religious Hermaphrodite in Indonesia." *Journal of East Asiatic Studies* 3:257–66.

Krämer, Augustin, and Hans Nevermann (1938). *Ralk-Ratak (Marshall Inseln).* Hamburg: Friederichsen, De Gruyter.

Krafft-Ebing, Richard von (1877). "Über gewisse Anomalien des Geschlechtstriebes." *Archiv für Psychiatrie und Nervenkrankheiten* 7:291–312.

——— (1901). "Neue Studien auf dem Gebiete der Homosexualität." *Jahrbuch für sexuelle Zwischenstufen* 3:1–36.

——— (1965). *Psychopathia Sexualis: A Medico-Forensic Study.* Tr. Harry E. Wedeck. New York: G. P. Putnam's Sons. Orig. pub. 1886.

Kramer, Samuel Noah (1963). *The Sumerians*. Chicago: University of Chicago Press.
—— (1969). *The Sacred Marriage Rite*. Bloomington: University of Indiana Press.
Krenkel, Werner A. (1978). "Männliche Prostitution in der Antike." *Alterum* 24:49–54.
Krige, Eileen Jensen (1965). *The Social System of the Zulus*. Pietermaritzburg, So. Afr.: Shuter and Shooter.
——, and J. D. Krige (1943). *The Realm of a Rain-Queen: A Study of the Pattern of Lovedu Society*. London: Oxford University Press.
Kroeber, Alfred Louis (1925). *Hanbook of the Indians of California: U.S. Bureau of American Ethnology, Bulletin No. 78*. Washington, D.C.: Government Printing Office.
—— (1940). "Psychosis or Social Sanction." *Character and Personality* 8:204–15.
Kroll, W. (1963). *Die Kultur der Ciceronische Zeit*. Darmstadt: Wissenschaftliche Buchgesellschaft.
Kronemayer, Dr. Robert (1980). *Overcoming Homosexuality*. New York: Macmillan.
Kubary, J. (1888). *Die Religion der Pelauer*, vol. 1. Berlin: Bastian.
Kuhn, Anne L. (1947). *The Mother's Role in Childhood Education: New England Concepts, 1830–1860*. New Haven: Yale University Press.
Kuhn, Thomas S. (1962). *The Structure of Scientific Revolutions*. Chicago: University of Chicago Press.
Kumar, Pushpendra (1974). *Śakti Cult in Ancient India*. Varanasi: Bhartryà.
Kümmel, Werner G. (1975). *Introduction to the New Testament*. Tr. Howard C. Kee. London: S.C.M.
Kurtz, Donald V. (1978). "The Legitimation of the Aztec State." Pp. 169–89 in Henri V. M. Claessen and Peter Skalnik (eds.), *The Early State*. The Hague: Mouton.
Kuster, H. J. and R. J. Cormier (1984). "Old Views and New Trends: Observations on the Problem of Homosexuality in the Middle Ages." *Studi Medievali* 25:587–610.
Kyvig, David E. (1979). *Repealing National Prohibition*. Chicago: University of Chicago Press.
Labalme, P. H. (1984). "Sodomy and Venetian Justice in the Renaissance." *Legal History Review* 52:217–54.
La Barre, Weston (1948). *The Aymara Indians of the Lake Titicaca Plateau, Bolivia*. Washington, D.C.: American Anthropological Society.
—— (1970). *The Ghost Dance: Origins of Religion*. Garden City. N.Y.: Doubleday.
—— (1984). *Muelos: A Stone Age Superstition About Sexuality*. New York: Columbia University Press.
Lachèvre, Frédéric (1909). *Le procès du poète Théophile de Viau*. 2 vols. Paris: H. Champion.
—— (1911). *Disciples et successeurs de Théophile de Viau*. Paris: H. Champion.
Lacroix, Paul (1937). *History of Prostitution*, vol. 2. Tr. Samuel Putnam. New York: Covici, Friede.
Lactantius (1964). *The Divine Institutes*. Tr. Mary Francis McDonald. Washington, D.C.: Catholic University of America Press.
Laeuchli, Samuel (1972). *Power and Sexuality: The Emergence of Canon Law at the Synod of Elvira*. Philadelphia: Temple University Press.
Lafitau, Joseph Francis (1976). "Men Who Dress As Women." Pp. 288–89 in Jonathan

Katz (ed.), *Gay American History: Lesbians and Gay Men in the U.S.A.* New York: Thomas Y. Crowell. Orig. pub. 1724.

La Fontaine, J. S. (1959). *The Gisu of Uganda.* London: International African Institute.

Laing, R. D. (1965). *The Divided Self.* Baltimore: Penguin.

—— and Aaron Esterson (1964). *Sanity, Madness, and the Family.* Baltimore: Penguin.

Laistner, M.L.W. (1951). *Christianity and Pagan Culture in the Later Roman Empire.* Ithaca, N.Y.: Cornell University Press.

Lake, Kirsopp (ed.) (1925). *The Apostolic Fathers,* vol. 1. London: William Heinemann.

Lambert, Royston (1984). *Beloved and God: The Story of Hadrian and Antinous.* New York: Viking.

Lambert, W. G. (1960). *Babylonian Wisdom Literature.* London: Oxford University Press.

—— (1973). "The Babylonians." Pp. 179–96 in D. J. Wiseman (ed.), *Peoples of Old Testament Times.* London: Oxford University Press.

Lancaster, Roger N. (1986). "Comment on Arguelles and Rich." *Signs: Journal of Women in Culture and Society* 12:188–92.

Landale, Nancy S., and Avery M. Guest (1986). "Ideology and Sexuality among Victorian Women." *Social Science History* 10:147–70.

Landes, Ruth (1937). "The Ojibwa of Canada." Pp. 87–126 in Margaret Mead (ed.), *Cooperation and Competition among Primitive Peoples.* New York: McGraw-Hill.

—— (1940). *The City of Women.* New York: Macmillan.

—— (1947). "A Cult Matriarchate and Male Homosexuality." *Journal of Abnormal and Social Psychology* 35:386–97.

—— (1968). *The Mystic Lake Sioux: Sociology of the Mdewakantonwan Santee.* Madison: University of Wisconsin Press.

—— (1970). *The Prairie Potawatomi: Tradition and Ritual in the Twentieth Century.* Madison: University of Wisconsin Press.

Landtmann, G. (1927). *The Kiwai Papuans of British New Guinea.* London: Macmillan.

Lane, W. E. (1963). *Manners and Customs of the Modern Egyptians.* London: Everyman's Library. Orig. pub. 1860.

Laner, Mary Riege, and Roy H. Laner (1979). "Personal Style or Sexual Preference? Why Gay Men Are Disliked." *International Review of Modern Sociology* 9:215–28.

Langness, L. L. (1967). "Sexual Antagonism in the New Guinea Highlands: A Bena Bena Example." *Oceania* 37:161–77.

Lanteri-Laura, Georges (1979). *Lecture des perversions: Histoire de leur appropriation médicale.* Paris: Masson.

Lapidus, M. (1982). "The Arab Conquests and the Formation of Islamic Society." Pp. 49–72 in G.H.A. Juynboll (ed.), *Studies on the First Century of Islamic Society.* Carbondale: Southern Illinois University Press.

Larson, Magali Sarfatti (1977). *The Rise of Professionalism: A Sociological Analysis.* Berkeley: University of California Press.

Last, Hugh (1966). "The Social Policy of Augustus." Pp. 425–64 in S. A. Cook, F. E. Adcock, and M. P. Charlesworth (eds.), *Cambridge Ancient History,* vol. 10. *The Augustan Empire.* London: Cambridge University Press.

Latus, Margaret Ann (1983). "Ideological PACs and Political Action." Pp. 75–99 in Robert C. Liebman and Robert Wuthnow (eds.). *The New Christian Right: Mobilization and Legitimation.* New York: Aldine.

Laurance, J.C.D. (1957). *The Iteso: Fifty Years of Change in a Nilo-Hamitic Tribe of Uganda.* London: Oxford University Press.

Laurent, Emile (1893). *L'anthropologie criminelle et les nouvelles theories du crime.* Paris: Société d'Éditions Scientifiques.

Laurie, Alison (1985). "Homosexuality among the Maori of New Zealand." Paper presented to the Sex and the State Conference, Toronto.

Lauritsen, John (1974). *Religious Roots of the Taboo on Homosexuality: A Materialist View.* New York: Privately printed.

——— (1985), "Culpa Ecclesiae: Boswell's Dilemma." Pp. 16–22 in *Homosexuality, Intolerance and Christianity: A Critical Examination of John Boswell's Work.* 2d ed. New York: Scholarship Committee, Gay Academic Union.

———, and David Thorstad (1974). *The Early Homosexual Rights Movement (1864–1935).* New York: Times Change Press.

Lautmann, Rüdiger (1980/81). "The Pink Triangle: The Persecution of Homosexual Males in Concentration Camps in Nazi Germany." *Journal of Homosexuality* 6:141–60.

Lauvergne, H. (1841). *Les forçats: Considérés sous le rapport physiologiques, moral et intellectual.* Paris: J. B. Baillière.

Law, John, and Peter Lodge (1984). *Science for Social Scientists.* London: Macmillan.

Lawn, Brian (ed.) (1979). *The Prose Salernitan Questions.* London: Oxford University Press.

Layard, John (1942). *Stone Men of Malekula.* London: Chatto and Windus.

——— (1955). "Boar Sacrifice." *Journal of Analytical Psychology* 1:7–31.

——— (1959). "Homo-Eroticism in Primitive Society as a Function of the Self." *Journal of Analytical Psychology* 4:101–15.

Lea, Henry Charles (1884). *An Historical Sketch of Sacerdotal Celibacy in the Christian Church.* 2d ed. Boston: Houghton Mifflin.

——— (1896). *A History of Auricular Confession and Indulgences in the Latin Church,* vol. 2. Philadelphia: Lea Brothers.

——— (1907). *A History of the Inquisition of Spain.* New York: Macmillan.

Leach, Edmund R. (1958). "Magical Hair." *Journal of the Royal Anthropological Institutute* 88:147–64.

Leacock, Eleanor B. (1981). *Myths of Male Dominance.* New York: Monthly Review Press.

———, and June Nash (1977). "Ideologies of Sex: Archetypes and Stereotypes." *Annals of the New York Academy of Science* 285:618–45.

Leacock, Seth, and Ruth Leacock (1972). *Spirits of the Deep: A Study of an Afro-Brazilian Cult.* New York: Doubleday.

Leakey, L.S.B. (1977). *The Southern Kikuyu before 1903.* New York: Academic.

Leclant, Jean (1960). "Astarte a cheval d'après les représentations Égyptiennes." *Syria* 37:1–67.

——— (1977). "Les textes de la pyramide de Pépi Iᵉʳ (Saqqara): Reconstitution de la paroi et de l'antichambre." *Comptes Rendus de l'Académie des Inscriptions et Belles-Lettres* 269–88.

Lee, S. G. (1958). "Social Influences in Zulu Dreaming." *Journal of Social Psychology* 47:265–83.

Lee, Vera (1975). *The Reign of Women in Eighteenth Century France*. Cambridge, Mass.: Schenkman.

Leemans, W. J. (1952). *Ishtar of Lagoba and Her Dress*. Leiden: E. J. Brill.

Lefébure, Eugéne (1912). *Oeuvres diverses*, vol. 2. Paris: Ernest Leroux.

Lefort, Claude (1974/75). "What is Bureaucracy?" *Telos* 22:31–65.

Legman, Gershom (1966). *The Guilt of the Templars*. New York: Basic.

Legueval de Lacombe, B.-F. (1840). *Voyage à Madagascar et aux Iles Comores (1823 à 1830)*, vol. 1. Paris: Louis Desessart.

Lehne, Gregory K. (1976). "Homophobia among Men." Pp. 66–88 in D. S. David and R. Brannon (eds.), *The Forty-Nine Percent Majority*. Reading, Mass.: Addison-Wesley.

Leidy, Philip, and Charles K. Mills (1886). "Reports of Cases from the Insane Department of the Philadelphia Hospital: Case III.—Sexual Perversion." *Journal of Nervous and Mental Disease* 13:712–13.

Lemay, Helen Rodnite (1982). "Human Sexuality in Twelfth- through Fifteenth-Century Scientific Writings." Pp. 187–205 in Vern L. Bullough (eds.), *Sexual Practices and the Medieval Church*. Buffalo, N.Y.: Prometheus.

Lemberg, S. E. (1970). *The Reformation Parliament, 1529–1536*. Cambridge: Cambridge University Press.

Le Moyne de Morgues, Jacques (1875). *Narrative of Le Moyne, an Artist Who Accompanied the French Expedition to Floria under Laudonnière, 1564*. Tr. Frederick B. Perkins. Boston: James R. Osgood.

Leneman, Helen (1987). "Reclaiming Jewish History: Homo-erotic Poetry of the Middle Ages." *Changing Men* (Summer/Fall):22–23.

Lenman, Bruce (1984). "The Limits of Godly Discipline in the Early Modern Period with Particular Reference to England and Scotland." Pp. 124–45 in Kaspar von Greyerz (ed.), *Religion and Society in Early Modern Europe, 1500–1800*. London: George Allen and Unwin.

Leonardo, Micaela di (1983). "Warrior Virgins and Boston Marriages: Spinsterhood in History and Culture." Paper presented to the Social Science History Association.

Lerman, Hannah (1986). *A Mote in Freud's Eye: From Psychoanalysis to the Psychology of Women*. New York: Springer.

Lerner, Gerda (1969). "The Lady and the Mill Girl." *Mid-Continental American Studies Journal* 10:5–15.

——— (1986). "The Origin of Prostitution in Ancient Mesopotamia." *Signs: Journal of Women in Culture and Society* 11:236–54.

Lerner, Robert E. (1972). *The Heresy of the Free Spirit in the Later Middle Ages*. Berkeley: University of California Press.

Leroi-Gourhan, André (1968). *Treasures of Prehistoric Art*. London: Thames and Hudson.

Le Roy, Ladurie, Emmanuel (1975). *Montaillou, village occitan de 1294 à 1324*. Paris: Gallimard.

L'Esperance, Jean (1977). "Doctors and Women in Nineteenth-Century Society: Sexuality and Role." Pp. 105–27 in John Woodward and David Richards (eds.), *Health Care and Popular Medicine in Nineteenth-Century England: Essays in the Social History of Medicine.* London: Croom Helm.

L'Estoile, Pierre de (1943). *Journal du règne d'Henri III, 1574–1589.* Ed. by Louis-Raymond Lefèvre. Paris: Gallimard.

Leuchtenberg, William E. (1958). *The Perils of Prosperity, 1914–32.* Chicago: University of Chicago Press.

Levenson, Joseph R., and Franz Schurman (1969). *China: An Interpretive History, from the Beginnings to the Fall of Han.* Berkeley: University of Chicago Press.

Lever, Maurice (1985). *Les bûchers de Sodome: Histoire des "infâmes."* Paris: Fayard.

Levin, Jim (1982). "The Homosexual Rights Movement in the United States to 1959: Some Basic Questions." *Gay Books Bulletin* 7:19–22, 30.

Levin, Thomas Herbst (1870). *Wild Races of South-Eastern India.* London: W. H. Allen.

Levin, Yehuda (1986). "Defeat the Homosexual Rights Bill." *New York Times*, Feb. 3.

Levine, Daniel (1971). *Jane Addams and the Liberal Tradition.* Madison: State Historical Society of Wisconsin.

Levine, Harry G. (1979). "Temperance and Women in Nineteenth Century United States." In *Research Advances in Alcohol and Drug Problems*, vol. 5. New York: Plenum.

Levine, Martin P. (1988). *Gay Macho: Ethnography of the Homosexual Clone.* Ph.D. dissertation, New York University.

Lévi-Strauss, Claude (1943). "The Social Use of Kinship Terms among Brazilian Indians." *American Anthropologist* 45:398–409.

——— (1969). *The Elementary Structures of Kinship.* Tr. J. H. Bell and J. R. von Sturmer. Ed. Rodney Needham. Boston: Beacon.

Levitt, E., and A. Klassen (1974). "Public Attitudes Toward Homosexuality: Part of the 1970 National Survey by the Institute for Sex Research." *Journal of Homosexuality* 1:29–43.

Levy, Donald (1979). "The Definition of Love in Plato's *Symposium.*" *Journal of the History of Ideas* 40:285–91.

Levy, Gertrude Rachel (1963). *The Gate of Horn: A Study of the Religious Conceptions of the Stone Age, and Their Influence upon European Thought.* London: Faber and Faber.

Levy, R. (1948). "L'allusion à la sodomie dans Eneas." *Philological Quarterly* 27:372–76.

Levy, Reuben (1962). *The Social Structure of Islam.* London: Cambridge University Press.

Levy, Robert I. (1971). "The Community Function of Tahitian Male Transvestism." *Transcultural Psychiatric Research Review* 8:51–53.

——— (1973). *Tahitiians: Mind and Experience in the Society Islands.* Chicago: University of Chicago Press.

Lewin, Miriam (1984). *In the Shadow of the Past: Psychology Portrays the Sexes.* New York: Columbia University Press.

Lewin, T. H. (1870). *Wild Races of South-East India.* London.

Lewis, Bernard (1968). *The Assassins: A Radical Sect in Islam.* New York: Basic.

Lewis, Charlton T., and Charles A. Short (1955). *A Latin Dictionary*. New York: Oxford University Press.

Lewis, C. S. (1959). *The Allegory of Love: A Study in Medieval Tradition*. London: Oxford University Press.

Lewis, J. M. (1985). "Eros and the *Polis* in Theognis Book II." Pp. 197–222 in Thomas J. Figuera and Gregory Nagy (eds.), *Theognis of Megara: Poetry and the Polis*. Baltimore: Johns Hopkins University Press.

Lewis, Oscar (1941). "The Manly-Hearted Woman among the North Piegan." *American Anthropologist* 43:173–87.

Lewis, Robert A. (1978). "Emotional Intimacy among Men." *Journal of Social Issues* 34:108–21.

Lewis, Sasha Gregory (1979). *Sunday's Women: Lesbian Life Today*. Boston: Beacon.

Lewis, Thomas S. W. (1982/83). "Brothers of Ganymede." *Salmagundi* 58–59:147–65.

Leznoff, Maurice and William A. Westley (1956). "The Homosexual Community." *Social Problems* 3:257–63.

Lhote, Henri (1956). *The Hoggar Tuareg*. Paris: Payot. Tr. Mary-Alice Sipfle. New Haven: Human Relations Area Files.

Liberty, Margot (1983). "Comment on Callender and Kochems." *Current Anthropology* 24:461.

Licata, Salvatore J. (1980/81). "The Homosexual Rights Movement in the United States: A Traditionally Overlooked Area of American History." *Journal of Homosexuality* 6:161–90.

Licht, Hans (1963). *Sexual Life in Ancient Greece*. New York: Barnes and Noble.

Lieberman, Saul (1963). "How Much Greek in Jewish Palestine." Pp. 123–41 in Alexander Altmann (ed.), *Biblical and Other Studies*. Cambridge, Mass.: Harvard University Press.

Liebeschuetz, J.H.W.G. (1972). *Antioch: City and Imperial Administration in the Later Roman Empire*. London: Oxford University Press.

Liebman, Robert C. (1983). "Mobilizing the Moral Majority." Pp. 49–73 in Robert C. Liebman and Robert Wuthnow (eds.), *The New Christian Right: Mobilization and Legitimation*. New York: Aldine.

Liette, Pierre (1962). *The Western Country in the 17th Century: The Memoirs of Pierre Liette*. Ed. Milo Milton Quaife. New York: Citadel.

Lilja, Saara (1978). The *Roman Elegists' Attitude to Women*. New York: Garland. Orig. pub. 1965.

——— (1983). *Homosexuality in Republican and Augustan Rome*. Helsinki: Societas Scientiarum Fennica.

Lincoln, Bruce (1981). *Priests, Warriors and Cattle: A Study in the Ecology of Religions*. Berkeley: University of California Press.

Lindenbaum, Shirley (1987). "The Mystification of Female Labors." Pp. 221–43 in Jane Collier and Sylvia Yagisako (eds.), *Gender and Kinship*. Stanford, Calif.: Stanford University Press.

Lindholm, Charles (1982). *Generosity and Jealousy: The Swat Pukhtum of Northern Pakistan*. New York: Columbia University Press.

Linner, Birgitta (1968). *Sex and Society in Sweden*. London: Jonathan Cape.

Linnhoff, Ursula (1977). "Die zweifache Stigma: Zu einer Kulturgeschichte lesbische

Sexualverhaltens." Pp. 113–27 in Joachim S. Hohmann (ed.), *Der unterdrückte Sexus.* Berlin: Verlag Andreas Achenbach Lollar.

Linton, Ralph (1933). *The Tanala: A Hill Tribe of Madagascar.* Chicago: Field Museum of Natural History.

––––––– (1936). *The Study of Man.* New York: Appleton.

Lisiansky, Urey (1814). *A Voyage Round the World in the Years 1803, 4, 5, & 6.* London: J. Booth.

Lithgow, William (1906). *The Totall Discourse of the Rare Adventures and Painefull Peregrinations of Long Nineteene Years Travayles.* Glasgow: James Maclehose. Orig. pub. 1632.

Little, Lester (1978). *Religious Poverty and the Profit Economy in Medieval Europe.* Ithaca, N.Y.: Cornell University Press.

Livermore, H. V. (1971). *The Origins of Spain and Portugal.* London: George Allen and Unwin.

Loeb, E. M. (1934). "The Eastern Kuksu Cult." Pp. 139–232 in *University of California Publications in American Ethnology, 1932–1934*, vol. 33. Berkeley: University of California Press.

Lofland, Lyn H. (1973). *A World of Strangers: Order and Action in Urban Public Space.* New York: Basic.

Lombard, Maurice (1975). *The Golden Age of Islam.* Tr. Joan Spencer. Amsterdam: North-Holland.

Lombroso, Cesare (1912). *Crime: Its Causes and Remedies.* Tr. Henry P. Horton. Boston: Little Brown. Reprinted by Patterson Smith, Montclair, N.J., 1968.

Lommel, Andreas (1967). *Shamanism: The Beginnings of Art.* Tr. Michael Bullock. New York: McGraw-Hill.

Longabough, Richard (1973). "Mother Behavior as a Variable Modifying the Effects of Father Absence." *Ethos* 1:456–65.

Longus (1910). *Daphnis and Chloe.* Tr. George Thornley. London: Simpkin Marshall.

Lorence, Bolgna W. (1974). "Parents and Children in Eighteenth Century Europe." *History of Childhood Quarterly* 2:1–30.

Lorentzen, Louise (1980). "Evangelical Life Style Concerns Expressed in Political Action." *Sociological Analysis* 41:144–54.

Lorenzoni, Piero (1976). *Erotismo e Pornografia nella Letterutura Italiana: Storia e Antologia.* Milan: Formichiere.

Losev, Alexei (1985). "Ancient Culture: Historical and Theoretical Aspects." *Social Sciences* 16(2):182–90.

Loskiel, George Henry (1794). *History of the Mission of the United Brethren among the Indians in North America.* Tr. C. I. La Trobe. London: Brethren's Society.

Louis, Frederic (1972). *Daily Life in Japan at the Time of the Samurai, 1185–1603.* Tr. Eileen M. Lowe. New York: Praeger.

Lowie, Robert H. (1910). *The Assiniboine. Anthropological Papers of the American Museum of Natural History*, vol. 4, pt. 1. New York: The Trustees.

––––––– (1912). "Social Life of the Crow Indians." *Anthropological Papers of the American Museum of Natural History* 9:179–248.

––––––– (1935). *The Crow Indians.* New York: Farrar and Rinehart.

Lucas, Prosper (1847). *Traité physiologique.* Paris: J. B. Ballière.

Lucian (1919). "The Goddess of Surrye (De Syria Dea)." Pp. 337–411 in *Collected Works*, vol. 4. Loeb Classical Library. Tr. A. H. Harmon and M. D. McCleod. New York: G. P. Putnam's Sons.

——— (1959). "The Ship or the Wishes." Pp. 429–87 in *Collected Works*, vol. 6. Tr. K. Kilburn. Loeb Classical Library. Cambridge, Mass.: Harvard University Press.

——— (1961). *Collected Works*, vol. 3. Tr. M. D. MacLeod. Cambridge, Mass.: Harvard University Press.

——— (1967). "Lucius or the Ass." Pp. 47–148 in *Collected Works*, vol. 8. Loeb Classical Library. Tr. A. H. Harmon. New York: Macmillan.

Luker, Kristin (1984). *Abortion and the Politics of Motherhood*. Berkeley: University of Chicago Press.

Lurie, Nancy O. (1953). "The Winnebago Bardache." *American Anthropologist* 55: 708–12.

Lutz, Cora E. (1947). "Musonius Rufus, 'The Roman Socrates'." Pp. 3–147 in Alfred R. Bellinger (ed.), *Yale Classical Studies*, vol. 10. New Haven: Yale University Press.

Lyall, Charles James (1930). *Translations of Ancient Arabian Poetry, Chiefly Pre-Islamic*. New York: Columbia University Press.

Lybyer, Albert H. (1966). *The Government of the Ottoman Empire in the Time of Suleiman the Magnificent*. New York: Russell and Russell. Orig. pub. 1913.

Lydston, G. Frank (1889). "Sexual Perversion, Satyriasis and Nymphomania." *Medical and Surgical Reporter* 61:281–85.

Lynch, Michael (1985a). "The Age of Adhesiveness: Male-Male Intimacy in New York City, 1830–1880." Paper presented to the American Historical Association.

——— (1985b). "'Here is Adhesiveness': From Friendship to Homosexuality." *Victorian Studies* 29:67–96.

Lynn, D., and William Sawyer (1959). "The Effects of Father Absence on Norwegian Boys and Girls." *Journal of Abnormal and Social Psychology* 59:258–62.

McCaghy, Charles H., and James K. Skipper, Jr. (1969). "Lesbian Behavior as an Adaptation to the Occupation of Stripping." *Social Problems* 17:262–70.

McCone, Kim R. (1986). "Werewolves, Cyclopes, *Díberga* and Fianna: Juvenile Delinquency in Early Ireland." *Cambridge Medieval Celtic Studies* 12:1–22.

——— (forthcoming). "Hund, Wolf und Krieger bei den Indogermanen." *Studien zum indogermanischen Wortschatz*.

McCullough, W. Stewart (1975). *The History and Literature of the Palestinian Jews from Cyrus to Herod, 550 B.C. to 4 B.C.* Toronto: Toronto University Press.

MacDermot, Brian Hugh (1972). *Cult of the Sacred Spear: The Story of the Nuer Tribe in Ethiopia*. London: Robert Hale.

Macdonald, A. J. (1932). *Hildebrand: A Life of Gregory VII*. London: Methuen.

Macdonald, A. P., Jr., and R. G. Games (1974). "Some Characteristics of Those Who Hold Positive and Negative Attitudes toward Homosexuals." *Journal of Homosexuality* 1:9–27.

MacDonald, Michael (1981). *Mystical Bedlam: Madness, Anxiety, and Healing in Seventeenth-Century England*. Cambridge: Cambridge University Press.

MacDonald, Robert H. (1967). "The Frightful Consequences of Onanism: Notes on the History of a Delusion." *Journal of the History of Ideas* 28:423–31.

McGough, James (1981). "Deviant Marriage Patterns in Chinese Society." Pp. 171–202 in Arthur Kleinman and Tsung-Yi Lin (eds.), *Normal and Abnormal in Chinese Culture*. Boston: D. Reidel.

McGuire, Brian Patrick (1974). "Love, Friendship and Sex in the Eleventh Century: The Experience of Anselm." *Studia Theologica* 28:111–52.

McIntosh, Mary (1968). "The Homosexual Role." *Social Problems* 16:182–92.

Mackenzie, Compton (1928). *Extraordinary Women: Theme and Variations*. London: Martin Secker.

MacKenzie, Donald A. (1981). *Statistics in Britain, 1865–1930. The Social Construction of Scientific Knowledge*. Edinburgh: Edinburgh University Press.

MacKinnon, Donald W. (1938). "Violation and Prohibitions." Pp. 491–501 in H. A. Murray (ed.), *Explorations in Personality*. New York: Oxford University Press.

McLaren, Angus (1976). "Sex and Socialism: The Opposition of the French Left to Birth Control in the Nineteenth Century." *Journal of the History of Ideas* 37:475–92.

Maclean, Ian (1977). *Woman Triumphant: Feminism in French Literature, 1610–1652*. Oxford: Clarendon Press.

Macleod, David I. (1983). *Building Character in the American Boy: The Boy Scouts, YMCA, and Their Forerunners, 1870–1920*. Madison: University of Wisconsin Press.

MacMullen, Ramsey (1982). "Roman Attitudes to Greek Love." *Historia* 31:484–502.

McNeil, E. B. (1969). *Human Socialization*. Belmont, Calif.: Wadsworth.

McNeill, John J. (1976). *The Church and the Homosexual*. Kansas City, Kans.: Sheed Andrews and McMeel.

——, and Helena M. Gamer (1938). *Medieval Handbooks of Penance*. New York: Columbia University Press.

McNeill, William H. (1958). *History Handbook*. Chicago: University of Chicago Press.

McQuillan, Kevin (1984). "Modes of Production and Demographic Patterns in Nineteenth-Century France." *American Journal of Sociology* 89:1324–46.

Magnan, Valentin (1885). *Recherches sur les centres nerveux*. Paris: Masson.

—— (1895). *Des anomalies, des aberrations et des perversions sexuelles*. Paris: A. Delahaye et E. Lecrosnier.

——, and Paul Legrain (1895). *Les dégénérés*. Paris: Rueff.

Mahl, George F. (1971). *Psychological Conflict and Defense*. New York: Harcourt, Brace Jovanovich.

Main, John (1913). *Religious Chastity: An Ethnological Study*. New York: Privately printed.

Malamat, Abraham (1982). "How Inferior Israelite Forces Conquered Fortified Canaanite Cities." *Biblical Archaeology Review* 8:24–35.

Malcolmson, Robert W. (1973). *Popular Recreations in English Society, 1700–1850*. London: Cambridge University Press.

Malinowski, Bronislaw (1929). *The Sexual Life of Savages in North-Western Melanesia*. New York: Harcourt, Brace and World.

—— (1967). *A Diary in the Strict Sense of the Term*. New York: Harcourt, Brace and World.

Malo, David (1903). *Hawaiian Antiquities (Moolelo Hawaii)*. Tr. N. B. Emerson. Honolulu: Hawaiian Gazette.

Malone, Edward E. (1950). *The Monk and the Martyr.* Washington, D.C.: Catholic University Press.

Mandelbaum, David G. (1940). "The Plains Cree." *Anthropological Papers of the American Museum of Natural History* 37:155–316.

Mankoff, Milton (1971). "Societal Reaction and Career Deviance: A Critical Analysis." *Sociological Quarterly* 12:204–18.

Manniche, Lise (1977). "Some Aspects of Ancient Egyptian Sexual Life." *Acta Orientalia* 38:11–23.

——— (1987). *Sexual Life in Ancient Egypt.* New York: Routledge and Kegan Paul.

Manosewitz, M. (1972). "Development of Male Homosexuality." *Journal of Sex Research* 8:31–40.

Manselli, Raouel (1975). *La religion populaire au Moyen Âge—problems de method et d'histoire.* Paris: Librarie J. Vrin.

Mansson, Ulf (1985). "Finald: The Censorship Law of 1971." Pp. 109–13 in *IGA Pink Book 1985.* Amsterdam: COC.

Maquet, Jacques J. (1961). *The Premise of Inequality in Ruanda: A Study of Political Relations in a Central African Kingdom.* London: Oxford University Press.

Marchand, H. L. (1933). *Sex Life in France: Including a History of Its Erotic Literature.* New York: Panurge.

Marchello-Nizia, Christine (1981). "Amour courtois, societé masculine et figures du pouvoir." *Annales E.S.C.* 36:969–82.

Marcus, Steven (1964). *The Other Victorians: A Study of Sexuality and Pornography in Mid-Nineteenth Century England.* New York: Basic.

Marie de France (1911). *French Medieval Romances.* Tr. Eugene Mason. New York: E. P. Dutton.

Mark, Mary Ellen (1981). *Falkland Road: Prostitutes of Bombay.* New York: A. A. Knopf.

Markey, T. L. (1972). "Nordic Níðvísur: An Instance of Ritual Inversion." *Medieval Scandinavia* 5:7–18.

Markowitz, Gerald E., and David Rosner (1973). "Doctors in Crisis: Medical Education and Medical Reform during the Progressive Era, 1895–1915." Pp. 185–205 in Susan Reverby and David Rosner (eds.), *Health Care in America: Essays in Social History.* Philadelphia: Temple University Press.

Marmor, Judd (1965). *Sexual Inversion: The Multiple Roots of Homosexuality.* New York: Basic Books.

Marotta, Toby (1981). *The Politics of Homosexuality.* New York: Houghton Mifflin.

Marr, Andrew (1987). "Pink Politics that Bring a Blush to Labour Voters." *Independent* (April 9):17.

Marrou, H. I. (1956). *A History of Education in Antiquity.* Tr. George Lamb. London: Sheed and Ward.

Marschak, Alexander (1972). *The Roots of Civilization.* New York: McGraw-Hill.

Marsden, George (1980). *Fundamentalism and American Culture.* New York: Oxford University Press.

Marsden, William (1966). *The History of Sumatra.* Kuala Lumpur: Oxford University Press.

Marshall, Donald S. (1972). "Sexual Behavior on Mangaia." Pp. 103–62 in Donald S. Marshall and Robert C. Suggs (eds.), *Human Sexual Behavior: Variations in the Ethnographic Spectrum.* New York: Basic Books.

Marshall, John (1981). "Pansies, Perverts and Macho Men: Changing Conceptions of Male Homosexuality." Pp. 133–54 in Kenneth Plummer (ed.), *The Making of the Modern Homosexual*. Totowa, N.J.: Barnes and Noble.

Marti, Mario (1956). *Poeti giocosi del tempo di Dante*. Milan: Rizzoli.

Martin, Alfred von (1944). *Sociology of the Renaissance*. Tr. W. L. Luetkens. London: Kegan Paul, Trench, Trubner.

Martin, Del and Phyllis Lyon (1972). *Lesbian/Woman*. San Francisco: Glide.

Martin, Harold S. (n.d.). *Homosexuality: A Sinful Way of Life*. Hanover, Pa.: Bible Heps.

Martin, John Stanley (1972). *Ragnarok: An Investigation into Old Norse Concepts of the Fate of the Gods*. Assen: Van Gorcum.

Martin, M. Kay, and Barbara Voorhies (1975). *Female of the Species*. New York: Columbia University Press.

Martines, Lauro (1979). *Power and Imagination: City-States in Renaissance Italy*. New York: A. A. Knopf.

Martius, K.F.P. von (1844). *Das Naturell, die Krankheiten, das Arztthum und die Heilmittel der Urbewohner Brasiliens*. Munich: C. Wolf.

Marx, Karl, and Friedrich Engels (1959). *Basic Writings on Politics and Philosophy*. Ed. Lewis Feuer. Garden City, N.Y.: Anchor.

———, and ——— (1975). *The German Ideology. Collected Works*, vol. 5. New York: International Publishers. Orig. pub. 1846.

Maspero, Gaston C. C. (1884). *Receuil de travaux relatifs à la philologie et à l'archéologie Egyptiennes et Assyriennes*, vol. 5. Paris: Libr. a. Franck, etc.

Masters, William H., and Virginia E. Johnson (1966). *Human Sexual Response*. Boston: Little, Brown.

Masters, William M. (1953). *Rowanduz: A Kurdish Administrative and Mercantile Center*. Ph.D. dissertation, University of Michigan.

Mathews, R. H. (1900a). "Native Tribes of Western Australia." *Proceedings of the American Philosophical Society* 39:123–35.

——— (1900b). "Phallic Rites and Initiation Ceremonies of the South Australian Aborigines." *Proceedings of the American Philosophical Society* 39:622–38.

——— (1901). "Some Aboriginal Tribes of Western Australia." *Journal and Proceedings of the Royal Society of New South Wales* 35:217–22.

——— (1902a). "The Aboriginal Languages of Victoria." *Journal and Proceedings of the Royal Society of New South Wales* 36:71–106.

——— (1902b). "Languages of Some Native Tribes of Queensland, New South Wales and Victoria." *Journal and Proceedings of the Royal Society of New South Wales* 36:135–90.

Matignon, Jean-Jacques (1899). "Deux mots sur la pederastie en Chine." *Archives d'anthropologie criminelle* 14:38–53.

——— (1936). *La Chine hermétique, superstitions, crime et misère*. Paris: Librairie Orientaliste Paul Geuthner.

Matson, Floyd W. (1964). *The Broken Image: Man, Science and Society*. New York: George Braziller.

Matter, E. Ann (1986). "My Sister, My Spouse: Woman-Identified Women in Medieval Christianity." *Journal of Feminist Studies in Religion* 2:81–93.

Matza, David (1969). *Becoming Deviant*. Englewood Cliffs, N.J.: Prentice-Hall.

Maugham, Robin (1950). *Journal to Siwa*. London: Chapman and Hall.

Maurois, André (1960). *A History of England*. Tr. Hamish Miles. New York: Grove.

Mause, Lloyd de (1975). "The Evolution of Childhood." Pp. 1–73 in Lloyd deMause (ed.), *The History of Childhood*. New York: Harper.

Mavor, Elizabeth (1983). *The Ladies of Llangollen*. Middlesex. Eng.: Penguin.

Maxwell, Gavin (1966). *Lords of the Atlas: The Rise and Fall of the House of Glaoua, 1893–1956*. London: Longmans, Green.

Maybury-Lewis, David (1967). *Akwê-Shavante Society*. Oxford: Clarendon.

Mayne, Xavier (1908). *The Intersexes: A History of Similisexualism as a Problem in Social Life*. Rome: Privately printed. Reprinted, New York: Arno Press, 1975.

Mayo, Katherine (1927). *Mother India*. London: Jonathan Cape.

Maystre, Charles (1937). *Les déclarations d'innocence*. Cairo: Institut Français d'Archéologie Orientale.

Mazur, Allan (1985). "A Biosocial Model of Status in Face-to-Face Primate Groups." *Social Forces* 64:377–402.

Mead, Margaret (1928). *Coming of Age in Samoa*. New York: William Morrow.

——— (1930). *Growing Up in New Guinea*. New York: William Morrow.

——— (1955). *Male and Female: A Study of the Sexes in a Changing World*. New York: Mentor.

——— (1961). "Cultural Determinants of Sexual Behavior." Pp. 1433–79 in William C. Young (ed.), *Sex and Internal Secretions*, vol. 2. Baltimore: Williams and Wilkes.

——— (1978). "Needed: A New Sex Taboo." *Redbook* (Feb.):31, 33, 38.

Medicine, Beatrice (1983). "'Warrior Women'—Sex Role Alternatives for Plains Indian Women." Pp. 267–80 in Patricia Albers and Beatrice Medicine (eds.), *The Hidden Half: Studies of Plains Indian Women*. Washington, D.C.: University Press of America.

Meeks, Wayne A. (1983). *The First Urban Christians: The Social World of the Apostle Paul*. New Haven: Yale University Press.

Meer, Theo van der (1984). *De Wesentlijke Sonde van Sodomie en Andere Vuyligheeden: Sodomietenvervolgingen in Amsterdam, 1730–1811*. Amsterdam: Tabula.

——— (1985). "Legislation Against Sodomy and the Persecutions of Sodomites in the Eighteenth-Century Dutch Republic: The Acknowledgement of an Identity." Paper presented at the Sex and the State Conference, Toronto.

——— (1988). "The Persecutions of Sodomites in Eighteenth Century Amsterdam: Changing Perceptions of Sodomy." *Journal of Homosexuality* 15:245–85.

Megitt, M. J. (1964). "Male-Female Relationships in the Highlands of Australian New Guinea." *American Anthropologist* 66(2):204–24.

Mehler, Barry (1979). "In Neo-Nazi Germany." *Christopher Street* 3(11):60–67.

Meijer, Maaike (1983). "Pious and Learned Female Bosomfriends in Holland in the Eighteenth Century." Pp. 404–19 in *Among Men, Among Women*. Amsterdam: Conference papers.

Meleager (1975). *The Poems of Meleager*. Tr. Peter Whigham and Peter Jay. Berkeley: University of California Press.

Melikian, Levon H., and Edwin H. Prothro (1954). "Sexual Behavior of University Students in the Arab Near East." *Journal of Abnormal and Social Psychology* 49:63–64.

Melossi, Dario, and Massimo Pavarini (1977). *Carcere e Fabbrica: Alle Origini del Sistema Penitenziario.* Bologna: Il Mulino.

Mendelssohn, Kurt (1974). *The Riddle of the Pyramids.* New York: Praeger.

Mendenhall, George E. (1962). "The Hebrew Conquest of Palestine." *Biblical Archaeologist* 25:66–87.

Mendieta, D. Armand de (1955). "La virginité chez Eusèbe d'Emèse et l'asceticisme familial dans la première moitié du IVᵉ siècle." *Revue d'histoire ecclésiastique* 50:777–820.

Merriam, Alan P. (1972). "Aspects of Sexual Behavior among the Bala (Basonge)." Pp. 91–102 in Donald S. Marshall and Robert C. Suggs (eds.), *Human Sexual Behavior.* Englewood Cliffs, N.J.: Prentice-Hall.

Merton, Robert (1957). *Social Theory and Social Structure.* Glencoe, Ill.: Free Press.

Messing, Simon David (1957). *The Highland-Plateau Amhara of Ethiopia.* Ph.D. Dissertation, University of Pennsylvania.

Métraux, Alfred (1963). "Ethnography of the Chaco." Pp. 197–370 in Julian H. Steward (ed.), *Handbook of South American Indians,* vol. 1. Washington, D.C.: Government Printing Office.

—— (1967). *Religions et magies Indiennes d'Amerique du Sud.* Paris: Gallimard.

—— (1970). *The History of the Incas.* New York: Schocken.

—— (1971). *Ethnology of Easter Island.* Honolulu: Bishop Museum Reprints.

Meyer, Adele (ed.) (1981). *Lila Nächte: Die Damenklubs der Zwanziger Jahre.* Cologne: Zitronenpresse.

Meyer, Johann Jakob (1952). *Sexual Life in Ancient India: A Study in the Comparative History of Indian Culture.* London: Routledge. Orig. pub. 1930.

Meyerowitz, Eva L. R. (1955). *The Sacred State of the Akan.* London: Faber and Faber.

Meyerowitz, Joanne (1986). "Sexuality in the Furnished Room Districts: Working-Class Women, 1890–1930." Paper presented to the Organization of American Historians.

Michalowski, Raymond J., and Edward J. Bohlander (1976). "Repression and Criminal Justice in Capitalist America." *Sociological Inquiry* 46:95–106.

Michéa, Claude François (1849a). "Des déviations maladive de l'appétit vénérien." *L'union medicale* 3:338.

—— (1849b). "Lettres medico-psychologiques à M. le docteur Sichel." *L'union médicale* 3:354.

Michel, H. (1952). *Sparta.* Cambridge: Cambridge University Press.

Milgrom, Jacob (1978). "The Temple Scroll." *Biblical Archaeologist* 41:105–20.

Miller, Daniel R., and Guy E. Swanson (1958). *The Changing American Parent: A Study in the Detroit Area.* New York: Wiley.

Miller, George H. (1971). *Railroads and the Granger Laws.* Madison: University of Wisconsin Press.

Miller, Jay (1982). "People, Berdaches, and Left-Handed Bears: Human Variation in Native America." *Journal of Anthropological Research* 38:274–87.

Miller, Martin B. (1980). "Sinking Gradually into the Proletariat: The Emergence of the Penitentiary in the United States." *Crime and Social Justice* 14:37–43.

Miller, Patrick D. (1985). "Israelite Religion." Pp. 201–37 in Douglas A. Knight and Gene M. Tucker (eds.), *The Hebrew Bible and Its Modern Interpreters.* Philadelphia: Fortress.

Miller, Townsend (1972). *Henry IV of Castile, 1425–1474*. Philadelphia: J. B. Lippincott.

Millham, Jim, Christopher L. San Miguel, and Richard Kellog (1976). "A Factor-analytic Conceptualization of Attitudes Towards Male and Female Homosexuals." *Journal of Homosexuality* 2:3–10.

Milner, G. B. (1966). *Samoan Dictionary*. London: Oxford University Press.

Minto, William (1879). *Daniel Defoe*. New York: Harper.

Minturn, Leigh, Martin Grosse and Santoah Harder (1969). "Cultural Patterning of Sexual Beliefs and Behavior." *Ethnology* 8:301–18.

Mirsky, Jeannette (1937). "The Dakota." Pp. 382–427 in Margaret Mead (ed.), *Cooperation and Competition among Primitive Peoples*. New York: McGraw-Hill.

Mitamura, Taisuke (1970). *Chinese Eunuchs: The Structure of Intimate Politics*. Tr. Charles A. Pomeroy. Rutland, Vt.: Charles E. Tuttle.

Mitchell, B. R. (1983). *International Historical Statistics: The Americas and Australasia*. Detroit: Gale.

Mitchell, Stephen A. (1978). "Psychodynamics, Homosexuality, and the Question of Pathology." *Psychiatry* 41:254–63.

Mitzel, John (1980). *The Boston Sex Scandal*. Boston: Glad Day.

Mohr, James C. (1978). *Abortion in America. The Origins and Evolution of National Policy, 1800–1900*. New York: Oxford University Press.

Moll, Dr. Albert (1891). *Die konträre Sexualempfindung*. Berlin: Fischer.

—— (1893). *Les perversions de l'instinct génital*. Tr. Pactet et Romme. Paris: G. Carré.

—— (1897). *Untersuchungen über die Libido sexualis*. Berlin: Fischer.

Mollat, Michel, and Philippe Wolff (1973). *The Popular Revolutions of the Late Middle Ages*. Tr. A. L. Lytton-Sells. London: George Allen and Unwin.

Money, John, and Anke A. Ehrhardt (1972). *Man and Woman, Boy and Girl: The Differentiation and Dimorphism of Gender Identity from Conception to Maturity*. Baltimore: Johns Hopkins University Press.

Montaigne, Michel de (1948). *The Complete Works of Montaigne*. Tr. Donald M. Frame. Stanford, Calif.: Stanford University Press.

Monter, E. William (1974). "La sodomie a l'époque moderne en Suisse romande." *Annales E.S.C.* 29:1023–33.

—— (1976). *Witchcraft in France and Switzerland: The Borderlands during the Reformation*. Ithaca, N.Y.: Cornell University Press.

—— (1980/81). "Sodomy and Heresy in Early Modern Switzerland." *Journal of Homosexuality* 6:41–53.

——, and John Tedeschi (1986). "Toward a Statistical Profile of the Italian Inquisition, Sixteenth to Eighteenth Centuries." Pp. 130–57 in Gustav Henningsen and John Tedeschi (eds.), *The Inquisition in Early Modern Europe: Studies in Sources and Methods*. DeKalb: Northern Illinois University Press.

Montet, Pierre (1950). "Le fruit defendu." *Kêmi: Revue de Philologie et d'Archéologie Egyptiennes et Coptes* 11:85–116.

Moore, G. F. (1895). *Judges. International Critical Commentary*, 7th ed. Edinburgh: T. and T. Clark.

Moore, Katherine (1974). *Victorian Wives*. London: Allison and Busby.

Moore, R. I. (1977). *The Origins of European Dissent*. New York: St. Martin's.

Moore, Sally Falk (1958). *Power and Property in Inca Peru*. New York: Columbia University Press.

Moran, W. L. (1969). "New Evidence from Mari on the History of Prophecy." *Biblica* 50:15–56.

Morand, Paul (1977). "Venise, Sodome de l'Adriatique." *Arcadie* 288:629–35.

Moreau, Paul (1882). *De l'homicide commis par les enfants*. Paris: Asselin.

———— (1887). *Des aberrations du sens génétique*. Paris: Asselin.

Morel, Bénédict Auguste (1857). *Traité des dégénerescences physiques, intellectuels et morales de l'espèce humain*. Paris: Bailliere.

———— (1860). *Traité des maladiés mentales*. Paris: V. Masson.

Moret, Alexandre (1902a). *Le rituel du culte divine journalier en Egypte*. Annales du Musée Guimet, Bibliothèque d'Etudes, vol. 14. Paris: Ernest Leroux.

———— (1902b). *Du caractère religieux de la royauté pharaonique*. Annales du Musée Guimet, Bibliothèques d'Etudes, vol. 15. Paris: Ernest Leroux.

———— (1911). *Rois et dieux d'Égypte*. Paris: Librairie Armand Colin.

Morgan, Lewis H. (1966). *League of the Ho-dé-No-San-Nee or Iroquois*, vol. 1. New York: Burt Franklin.

Morgan, Thomas (1987). "Amid AIDS, Gay Movement Grows but Shifts." *New York Times*, Oct. 10.

Morin, Stephen F., and Ellen M. Garfinkle (1978). "Male Homophobia." *Journal of Social Issues* 34:29–43.

Morris, Philip A. (1973). "Doctors' Attitudes to Homosexuality." *British Journal of Psychiatry* 72:436.

Morris, Polly (1985). Sexual Reputation in Somerset, 1733–1850. Ph.D. dissertation, University of Warwick.

Mort, Frank (1980). "Sexuality: Regulation and Contestation." Pp. 38–51 in Gay Left Collective (eds.), *Homosexuality: Power and Politics*. London: Allison and Busby.

Morton, W. Scott (1973). *Japan: Its History and Culture*. Pomfret, Vt.: David and Charles.

Moses, Alice E. (1979). *Identity Management in Lesbian Women*. New York: Praeger.

Moses ben Maimon (1965). *The Code of Maimonides*. Book 5: *The Book of Holiness*. Tr. Louis I. Rabinowitz and Philip Grossman. New Haven: Yale University Press.

Mosse, George L. (1985). *Nationalism and Sexuality: Respectability and Abnormal Sexuality in Modern Europe*. New York: Howard Fertig.

Mott, Luiz (1984). "Report from Brazil." *Cabirion and Gay Books Bulletin* 11:14.

Moussa, Ahmed M., and Hartwig Altenmuller (1977). *Das Grab des Nianchchum und Chnumhotep*. Mainz am Rhein: P. v. Zabern.

Mukherjea, Charulal (1962). *The Santals*. Calcutta: A. Mukherjee.

Müller, C. O. (1839). *The History and Antiquities of the Dorian Race*. Tr. Henry Tifnell and George Cornewall Lewis. London: John Murry.

Müller, Johann Valentine (1796). *Entwurf der gerichtlichen Arzneywissenschaft*, vol. 1. Frankfurt am Main: Andreäischen Buchhandlung. Reprinted, pp. 211–24 in Joachim S. Hohmann (ed.), *Der unterdrückte Sexus*. Berlin: Verlag Andreas Achenbach Lollar.

Munro, Neil Gordon (1971). *Prehistoric Japan*. New York: Johnson.

Munroe, Robert L. (1980). "Male Transvestism and the Couvade: A Psycho-Cultural Analysis." *Ethos* 8:49–59.

———, Ruth H. Munroe and John W. M. Whiting (1973). "Institutionalized Male Transvestism." *American Anthropologist* 71:87–91.

———, John M. Whiting, and David Hally (1969). "Institutionalized Male Transvestism and Sex Distinctions." *American Anthropologist* 71:87–91.

Murphy, Lawrence R. (1985a). "Defining the Crime Against Nature: Sodomy in United States Appeals Courts, 1810–1940." Paper presented to the Sex and the State Conference, Toronto.

——— (1985b). "The House on Pacific Street: Homosexuality, Intrigue, and Politics during World War II." *Journal of Homosexuality* 12:27–47.

Murphy, Michael D. (1984). "Masculinity and Selective Homophobia: A Case from Spain." *ARGOH Newsletter* 5(3):6–12.

Murphy, Robert F. (1959). "Social Structure and Sexual Antagonism." *Southwestern Journal of Anthropology* 15:89–98.

Murphy, Timothy F. (1983/84). "Freud Reconsidered: Bisexuality, Homosexuality and Moral Judgement." *Journal of Homosexuality* 9:65–77.

——— (1987). "The Sinner from the Sin: Catholicism in the Age of AIDS." *Christopher Street* 10(5):25–33.

Murra, John (1963). "The Historic Tribes of Ecuador." Pp. 785–821 in Julian H. Steward (ed.), *Handbook of South American Indians*, vol. 2. Washington, D.C.: Government Printing Office.

Murra, Victor (1980). *The Economic Organization of the Inka State*. Greenwich, Conn.: JAI Press.

Murray, Alexander (1978). *Reason and Society in the Middle Ages*. Oxford: Clarendon Press.

Murray, Gilbert (1934). *The Rise of the Greek Epic*. London: Oxford University Press.

Murray, Stephen O. (1983). "Fuzzy Sets and Abominations." *Man* 18:396–99.

——— (1984). *Social Theory, Homosexual Realities*. Gai Saber Monograph 3. New York: GAU-NY.

——— (1987a). "Homosexual Acts and Selves in Early Modern Europe." *Journal of Homosexuality* 15:421–39.

——— (ed.) (1987b). *Cultural Diversity and Homosexualities*. New York: Irvington.

——— (1987c). "Dangers of Lexical Inference II: Some Aymara Terms." Pp. 165–67 in Stephen O. Murray (ed.), *Male Homosexuality in Latin America*. New York: GAU-NY.

——— (ed.) (1987d). *Male Homosexuality in Central and South America*. Gai Saber Monograph 5. New York: GAU-NY.

——— (1987e). "Sentimental Effusions of Genital Contact in Upper Amazonia." Pp. 351–63 in Stephen O. Murray (ed.), *Cultural Diversity and Homosexualities*. New York: Irvington.

——— (1987f). "A Note on Haitian Tolerance of Homosexuality." Pp. 92–100 in Stephen O. Murray (ed.), *Male Homosexuality in Central and South America*. New York: GAU-NY.

——— (1987g). "The Mamlukes." Pp. 213–19 in Stephen O. Murray (ed.), *Cultural Diversity and Homosexualities*. New York: Irvington.

—— (1987h). "The Hwarang of Korea." Pp. 511–13 in Stephen O. Murray (ed.), *Cultural Diversity and Homosexualities*. New York: Irvington.

——, and Kent Gerard (1987). "Renaissance Sodomite Subcultures?" Pp. 65–94 in Stephen O. Murray (ed.), *Cultural Diversity and Homosexualities*. New York: Irvington.

Musil, Alois (1928). *The Manners and Customs of the Rwala Bedouins*. New York: American Geographical Society.

Nabokoff, Vladimir (1903). Die Homosexualität im Russischen Strafgesetzbuch." *Jahrbuch für sexuelle Zwischenstufen* 5:1159–71.

Näcke, Paul (1904). "Die Homosexualität im Orient." *Archiv für Kriminal-Anthropologie und Kriminalstatistik* 16:353–55.

—— (1906). "Die Homosexualität in Konstantinopel." *Archiv für Kriminal-Anthropologie und Kriminalstatistik* 26:106–8.

—— (1908). "Über Homosexualität in Albanien." *Jahrbuch für sexuelle Zwischenstufen* 9:325–27.

—— (1966). "On Homosexuality in Albania." *International Journal of Greek Love* 1:39–47.

Nadel, S. F. (1955). "Two Nuba Religions: An Essay in Comparison." *American Anthropologist* 56:661–79.

Nafzawi, Shaykh (1975). *The Glory of the Perfumed Garden*. London: Neville Spearman.

Nanda, Serena (1984). "The Hinjras of India: A Preliminary Report." *Medicine and Law* 3:59–75.

—— (1985). "The Hijras of India: Cultural and Individual Dimensions of an Institutionalized Third Gender Role." *Journal of Homosexuality* 11:35–54.

—— (1987). "The Hijra of India." Pp. 488–509 in Stephen O. Murray (ed.), *Cultural Diversity and Homosexualities*. New York: Irvington.

Napheys, George H. (1871). *The Transmission of Life: Counsel on the Nature and Hygiene of the Masculine Function*. Philadelphia: Fergus.

Nash, Gerald D. (1957). "Origins of the Interstate Commerce Act of 1887." *Pennsylvania History* 24:181–90.

Nash, June (1978). "The Aztecs and the Ideology of Male Dominance." *Signs: Journal of Women in Culture and Society* 4:349–62.

Neale, R. S. (1972). *Class and Ideology in the Nineteenth Century*. London. Routledge and Kegan Paul.

Needham, Joseph (ed.) (1955). *Science, Religion and Reality*. New York: Braziller.

—— (1956). *Science and Civilization in China*, vol. 2. Cambridge, Mass.: Harvard University Press.

Needham, Rodney (1973). "The Left Hand of the Mugwe: An Analytical Note on the Structure of Meru Symbolism." Pp. 109–27 in Rodney Needham (ed.), *Right and Left: Essays on Dual Classifications*. Chicago: University of Chicago Press.

Nelson, Daniel (1975). *Managers and Workers: Origins of the New Factory System in the United States, 1880–1920*. Madison: University of Wisconsin Press.

Nelson, Ida (1977). *La sottie sans souci, essai d'interpretation homosexuelle*. Paris: Editions Honoré Champion.

Nelson, William E. (1975). *Americanization of the Common Law: The Impact of Legal Change on Massachusetts Society, 1760–1830*. Cambridge, Mass.: Harvard University Press.

—— (1982). *The Roots of American Bureaucracy, 1830–1900*. Cambridge, Mass.: Harvard University Press.

Neufeld, E. (1951). *The Hittite Laws*. London: Luzac.

Neumann, R. P. (1975). "Masturbation, Madness and the Modern Concepts of Childhood and Adolescence." *Journal of Social History* 8:1–27.

Neusner, Jacob (1966). *A History of the Jews in Babylonia*. Vol. 2: *The Early Sasanian Period*. Leiden: E. J. Brill.

—— (1976). *Talmudic Judaism in Sasanian Babylonia: Essays and Studies.* Leiden: E. J. Brill.

—— (1977). *A History of the Mishnaic Law of Purities*. Pt. 22: *The Mishnaic System of Uncleanness*. Leiden: E. J. Brill.

Newberry, Perce E. (1928). "Akhenaton's Eldest Son-in-Law 'Ankhkheprure'." *Journal of Egyptian Archaeology* 14:7–9.

Newman, L. E., and Robert J. Stoller (1974). "Nontranssexual Men Who Seek Reassignment." *American Journal of Psychiatry* 131:437–41.

Newton, Esther (1972). *Mother Camp: Female Impersonators in America*. Englewood Cliffs, N.J.: Prentice-Hall.

Ngubane, Harriet (1977). *Body and Mind in Zulu Medicine: An Ethnography of Health and Disease in Nywaswa-Zulu Thought and Practice*. New York: Academic.

Nibley, Hugh (1976). *The Message of the Joseph Smith Papyri: An Egyptian Endowment*. Salt Lake City, Utah: Deseret.

Nichols, Jack (1979). "Butcher Than Thou: Beyond Machismo." Pp. 328–42 in Martin P. Levine (ed.), *Gay Men: The Sociology of Male Homosexuality*. New York: Harper and Row.

Niditch, Susan (1982). "The 'Sodomite' Theme in *Judges* 19–20: Family, Community, and Social Disintegration." *Catholic Biblical Quarterly* 44:365–78.

Nilsson, Martin P. (1940). *Greek Popular Religion*. New York: Columbia University Press.

—— (1971). *The Minoan-Mycenaean Religion and Its Survival in Greek Religion*. New York: Biblo and Tannen.

Nimuendajú, Curt (1952). *The Tukuna*. Tr. William D. Hohenthal, ed. Robert H. Lowie. Berkeley: University of California Press.

Nisbet, Robert (1964). "Kinship and Political Power in First-Century Rome." Pp. 257–71 in Werner J. Cahnman and Alvin Boskoff (eds.), *Sociological History*. Glencoe, Ill.: Free Press.

Nock, Arthur Darby (1972). *Essays on Religion and the Ancient World*, vol. 1. Cambridge, Mass.: Harvard University Press.

Noonan, John T. (1966). *Contraception: A History of Its Treatment by the Catholic Theologians and Canonists*. Cambridge, Mass.: Harvard University Press.

Noordam, Dirk Jaap (1983). "Homosocial Relations in Leiden (1533–1811)." In *Among Men, Among Women*. Amsterdam: Conference Papers.

Nordenskiöld, Erland (1912). *Indianerleben: El Guan Chado (Südamerika)*. Leipzig: Albert Bonnier.

Norman, A. F. (1965). *Libanius' Autobiography*. Oxford: Oxford University Press.

Noss, John B. (1963). *Man's Religions*. 3d ed. New York: Macmillan.

North, Martin (1965). *Leviticus: A Commentary*. Tr. J. E. Anderson. Philadelphia: Westminster.

Numantius, Numa (1864). *Vindex: Social-juristische Studien über mannmännliche Geschlectsliebe*. Leipzig: Heinrich Matthes. Reprinted, pp. 271–308 in Joachim S. Hohmann (ed.), *Der unterdrückte Sexus*. Berlin: Andreas Achenbach Lollar, 1977.

Nungesser, Lon (1983). *Homosexual Acts, Actors, and Identies*. New York: Praeger.

Nussbaum, Martha C. (1986). *The Fragility of Goodness: Luck and Ethics in Greek Tragedy and Philosophy*. New York: Cambridge University Press.

Nye, Robert A. (1982). "Degeneration and the Medical Model of Cultural Crisis in the French *Belle Epoque*. Pp. 19–29 in Seymour Drescher, David Sabean, and Allan Sharlin (eds.), *Political Symbolism in Modern Europe: Essays in Honor of George L. Mosse*. New Brunswick, N.J.: Transaction.

—— (1984). *Crime, Madness, and Politics in Modern France: The Medical Concept of National Decline*. Princeton, N.J.: Princeton University Press.

Oakley, Thomas Pollack (1923). *English Penitential Discipline and Anglo-Saxon Law in Their Joint Influence*. New York: Columbia University Press.

—— (1932). "Commutations and Redemptions of Penance in the Penitentials." *Catholic Historical Review* 18:341–51.

—— (1937). "Alleviation of Penances in the Continental Penitentials." *Speculum* 12:488–502.

—— (1938). "Neglected Aspects in the History of Penance." *Catholic Historical Review* 24:293–309.

Oaks, Robert F. (1978). " 'Things Fearful to Name': Sodomy and Buggery in Seventeenth Century New England." *Journal of Social History* 12:268–81.

—— (1979/80). "Perceptions of Homosexuality by Justices of the Peace in Colonial Virginia." *Journal of Homosexuality* 5:5–42.

Oberschall, Anthony (1984). "The New Christian Right in North Carolina." Paper presented to the American Sociological Association.

Obeyesekere, Ganamath (1984). *The Cult of the Goddess Pattini*. Chicago: University of Chicago Press.

Obolensky, Dmitri (1948). *The Bogomils*. Cambridge: Cambridge University Press.

O'Brien, Patricia (1982). *The Promise of Punishment: Prisons in Nineteenth Century France*. Princeton, N.J.: Princeton University Press.

O'Callaghan, Sean (1961). *The Slave Trade Today*. New York: Crown.

O'Callahan, Edmund O. (ed.) (1968). *Calender of Dutch Historical Manuscripts*. Ridgewood, N.J.: Gregg Press. Orig. pub. 1865.

O'Carroll, Tom (1982). *Paedophilia: The Radical Case*. Boston: Alyson.

Ochshorn, Judith (1981). *The Female Experience and the Nature of the Divine*. Bloomington: Indiana University Press.

O'Connor, Daniel John (1968). *Aquinas and Natural Law*. New York: St. Martin's Press.

Oded, Bustenay (1977). "Judah and the Exile." Pp. 435–88 in John H. Hayes and J. Maxwell Miller (eds.), *Israelite and Judaean History*. Philadelphia: Westminster.

Oden, R. A., Jr. (1977). *Studies in Lucian's De Syria Dea*. Missoula, Mont.: Scholars.

O'Donnell, Mike (1985). *Age and Generation.* London: Tavistock.

O'Flaherty, Wendy Doniger (1969). "Asceticism and Sexuality in the Mythology of Śiva, Part I." *History of Religions* 8:300–337.

——— (1976). *The Origins of Evil in Hindu Mythology.* Berkeley: University of California Press.

——— (1980). *Women, Androgynes, and Other Mythical Beasts.* Chicago: University of Chicago Press.

Ogg, David (1925). *Ioannis Seldeni ad Fletam Dissertatio.* London: Cambridge University Press.

Ohlmarks, Åke (1939). *Studien zum Problem des Schamanismus.* Lund: C.W.K. Gleerup.

O'Keefe, Daniel Laurence (1982). *Stolen Lightning: The Social Theory of Magic.* New York: Continuum.

Oliver, Douglas L. (1955). *A Solomon Island Society.* Cambridge, Mass.: Harvard University Press.

——— (1974). *Ancient Tahitian Society.* Honolulu: University Press of Hawaii.

——— (1981). *Two Tahitian Villages: A Study in Comparisons.* Hawaii: Institute for Polynesian Studies.

Olmo, Rosa del (1979). "The Cuban Revolution and the Struggle Against Prostitution." *Crime and Social Justice* 12:34–43.

Olson, Ronald L. (1936). "The Quinault Indians." Pp. 1–190 in *University of Washington Publications in Anthropology* 6(1). Seattle: University of Washington Press.

Omlin, J. A. (1973). *Der Papyrus 55001 und seine satirisch-erotischen Zeichnungen und Inschriften.* Turin: Fratelli Pozzio.

O'Neill, John H. (1975). "Sexuality, Deviance, and Moral Character in the Personal Satire of the Restoration." *Eighteenth-Century Life* 2:16–17.

Onians, Richard Broxton (1951). *The Origins of European Thought about Body, the Mind, the Soul, the World, Time, and Fate.* Cambridge: Cambridge University Press.

Oost, Stewart Irwin (1968). *Galla Placida Augusta: A Biographical Essay.* Chicago: University of Chicago Press.

Oosterval, G. (1959). "The Position of the Bachelor in the Upper Tor Territory." *American Anthropologist* 51:829–38.

Opler, Marvin K. (1965). "Anthropological and Cross-Cultural Aspects of Homosexuality." Pp. 108–23 in Judd Marmor (ed.), *Sexual Inversion.* New York: Basic.

Opler, Morris E. (1941). *An Apache Life-Way.* Chicago: University of Chicago Press.

——— (1960). "The Hijara (Hermaphrodites) of India and Indian National Character: A Rejoinder." *American Anthropologist* 62:505–11.

——— (1969). *Apache Odyssey: A Journey Between Two Worlds.* New York: Holt, Rinehart and Winston.

Oppenheimer, Aharon (1977). *The 'Am Ha-Aretz: A Study in the Social History of the Jewish People in the Hellenistic-Roman Period.* Tr. I. H. Levine. Leiden: E. J. Brill.

Oraison, Marc (1975). *La questione homosexuelle.* Paris: Seuil.

Origo, Iris (1962). *The World of San Bernardino.* New York: Harcourt, Brace and World.

Orleans, Elisabeth-Charlotte, Duchess d' (1924). *Letters of Madame.* Tr. and ed. Gertrude Scott Stevenson. London: Chapman and Dodd.

Orr, Kenneth Gordon (1951). *Field Notes on the Burmese Standard of Living.* New Haven: Human Relations Area Files.

Ortiz de Montellano, Bernard R. (1978). "Aztec Cannibalism: An Ecological Necessity?" *Science* 200:611–17.

Osborn, Eric (1976). *Ethical Patterns in Early Christian Thought.* New York: Cambridge University Press.

Osgood, Cornelius (1951). *The Koreans and Their Culture.* New York: Ronald.

—— (1958). *Ingalik Social Structure.* Yale University Publications in Anthropology 53. New Haven: Yale University Press.

Otis, Leah Lydia (1985). *Prostitution in Medieval Society: The History of an Urban Institution in Languedoc.* Chicago: University of Chicago Press.

Pacion, Stanely J. (1970). "Sparta: An Experiment in State-Fostered Homosexuality." *Medical Aspects of Human Sexuality* 4 (Aug.):28–32.

Padgug, Robert A. (1979). "Sexual Matters: On Conceptualizing Sexuality in History." *Radical History Review* 20:3–33.

Page, Ann, and Donald A. Clelland (1978). "The Kanawha County Textbook Controversy: A Study of the Politics of Life Style Concern." *Social Forces* 57:265–81.

Paige, Karen Ericksen, and Jeffery M. Paige (1981). *The Politics of Reproductive Ritual.* Berkeley: University of California Press.

Panel on Youth of the President's Science Advisory Committee (1974). *Youth: Transition to Adulthood.* Chicago: University of Chicago Press.

Parent-Duchatelet, A.-J.-B. (1857). *De la prostitution dans la ville de Paris,* vol. 1. Paris: J.-B. Baillière.

Paribeni, R. (1908). "Il sarcofogo dipinto di Haghia Triada." *Monumenti antichi pubblicati per cura della Reale Accademia dei Lincei* 19:79.

Parin, P., F. Morgenthaler, and G. Parin-Matthey (1963). *Die Weissen Denken Zuviel: Psychoanalytische Untersuchungen in West Africa (Dogon).* Zurich: Atlantis.

Park, Willard Z. (1938). *Shamanism in Western North America.* Evanston, Ill.: Northwestern University Press.

Parker, Robert (1983). *Miasma: Pollution and Purification in Early Greek Religion.* Oxford: Clarendon.

Parsons, E. C. (1939). "The Last Zuñi Transvestite." *American Anthropologist* 41:338–40.

Partner, Peter (1982). *The Murdered Magicians: The Templars and Their Myth.* New York: Oxford University Press.

Patai, Raphael (1967). *The Hebrew Goddess.* New York: Ktav.

—— (1973). *The Arab Mind.* New York: Charles Scribner's Sons.

Patten, Simon (1912). *The New Basis of Civilization.* New York: Macmillan.

Patzer, Harald (1982). *Die Griechische Knabenliebe.* Wiesbaden: Franz Steiner Verlag.

Paul, William (1982). "Minority Status for Gay People: Majority Reaction and Social Context." Pp. 351–70 in William Paul, James D. Weinrich, John C. Gonsiorek, and Mary E. Hotvedt (eds.), *Homosexuality: Social, Psychological, and Biological Issues.* Beverly Hills: Sage.

Paulme, Denise (1940). *Organisation sociale des Dogon (Soudan Français).* Paris: Domat-Mont Chrestien.

Paulson, Ross Evans (1973). *Women's Suffrage and Prohibition: A Comparative Study of Equality and Social Control.* Glenview, Ill.: Scott, Foresman.

Pavan, Elisabeth (1980). "Police des moeurs, société et politique à Venise à la fin du Moyen Âge." *Revue historique* 536:241–88.

Payen, Jean Charles (1970). *Litterature Française*. Vol. 1: *Le Moyen Âge, des origines à 1300*. Paris: Arthaud.

Payer, Pierre (1984a). *Sex and the Penitentials: The Development of a Sexual Code, 550–1150*. Toronto: University of Toronto Press.

——— (1984b). "The Humanism of the Penitentials and the Continuity of the Penitential Tradition." *Mediaeval Studies* 46:340–54.

Peacock, James L. (1968). *Rites of Modernization: Symbolic and Social Aspects of Indonesian Proletarian Drama*. Chicago: University of Chicago Press.

Pearce, Frank (1973). "How to be Immoral and Ill, Pathetic and Dangerous All at the Same Time: Mass Media and the Homosexual." Pp. 284–301 in Stanley Cohen and Jock Young (eds.), *The Manufacture of News: Deviance, Social Problems and the Mass Media*. London: Constable.

———, and Andrew Roberts (1973). "The Social Regulation of Sexual Behavior and the Development of Industrial Capitalism in Britain." Pp. 51–72 in Roy Bailey and Jock Young (eds.), *Contemporary Social Problems in Britain*. Lexington, Mass.: Lexington.

Pearson, Birger A. (1975). *Religious Syncreticism in Antiquity: Essays in Conversation with George Widengren*. Missoula, Mont.: Scholars.

Pearson, Hesketh (1937). *Labby: The Life and Character of Henry Labouchere*. New York: Harper.

Pedersen, Lis (1985). "The Anti-Discrimination Law: The Experience So Far." Pp. 117–19 in *IGA Pink Book 1985*. Amsterdam: COC.

Pellat, Charles (1969). *The Life and Works of Jahiz*. Tr. D. M. Hawke. London: Routledge and Kegan Paul.

Pellicer, André (1966). *Natura: Etude sémantique et historique du mot Latin*. Paris: Presses Universitaires de France.

Pembroke, Simon (1965). "Last of the Matriarchs." *Journal of the Economic and Social History of the Orient* 8:219–47.

——— (1967). "Women in Charge: The Function of Alternatives in Early Greek Tradition and the Ancient Idea of Matriarchy." *Journal of the Warburg and Courtauld Institutes* 30:1–35.

Perelaer, M.T.H. (1870). *Ethnographische Beschrijving der Dajaks*. Zalt-Bommel: Joh. Noman and Zoon.

Perkins, James Breck (1886). *France under Richelieu and Mazarin*. New York: G. P. Putnam's and Sons.

Perry, Mary Elizabeth (1980). *Crime and Society in Early Modern Seville*. Hanover, N.H.: University Press of New England.

Person, E., and L. Ovesey (1974a). "The Transsexual Syndrome in Males I. Primary Transsexualism." *American Journal of Psychotherapy* 28:4–20.

——— (1974b). "The Transsexual Syndrome in Males II. Secondary Transsexualism." *American Journal of Psychotherapy* 28:174–93.

Perrens, Francois T. (1896). *Les libertins en France au XVIIᵉ siècle*. Paris: L. Chailley.

Pessen, Edward (1971). "The Egalitarian Myth of Jacksonian America." *American Historical Review* 76:989–1034.

Peters, Robert (1984). "Walt Whitman's Lost Homoerotic Poems." *Cabirion and Gay Books Bulletin* 10:10–11.

Petersen, W. L. (1986). "Can Arsenokoitai be Translated by Homosexuals (1 Cor. 6.9, 1 Tim. 1.10)?" *Vigilae Christianae* 40:187–91.

Peterson, M. Jeanne (1978). *The Medical Profession in Mid-Victorian London*. Berkeley: University of California Press.

Petersson, Stig-Ake (1985). "Parliamentary Commission Studies Homosexuality." Pp. 120–23 in *IGA Pink Book 1985*. Amsterdam: COC.

Petit-Dutaillis, Ch. (1936). *The Feudal Monarchy in France and England*. London: Kegan, Paul, Trench, Trubner.

Petrie, W. M. Flinders (1914). *A History of Egypt*, vol. 1. London: Methuen.

—— (1923). *Social Life in Ancient Egypt*. London: Constable.

Peyrefitte, Roger (1963). "La confession d'un Arcadien sous la Renaissance Italienne." *Arcadie* 111:125–36.

Pézard, André (1950). *Dante sous la pluie de feu*. Paris: Librairie Philosophique J. Vien.

Pharr, Klyde (1952). *The Theodosian Code*. Princeton, N.J.: Princeton University Press.

Phayer, J. Michael (1977). *Sexual Liberation and Religion in Nineteenth Century Europe*. London: Croom Helm.

Philippe de Remi, Sire de Beaumanoir (1842). *Les coutumes du Beauvoisis*. 2 vols. Paris: J. Renouard.

Philippson, Ernest Alfred (1953). "Die Genealogie der Götter in Germanischer Religion, Mythologie und Theologie." *Illinois Studies in Language and Literature* 37(3):1–94.

Phillips, Anthony (1970). *Ancient Israel's Criminal Law*. Oxford: Basil Blackwell.

Phillips, Kevin (1982). *Post-Conservative America*. New York: Random.

Phillips, William D., Jr. (1978). *Enrique IV and the Crisis of Fifteenth-Century Castile, 1425–1480*. Cambridge, Mass.: Mediaeval Academy of America.

Phillpotts, B. (1967). "German Heathenism." Pp. 480–95 in H. M. Gwatkin and J. P. Whitney (eds.), *Cambridge Medieval History*, vol. 2. Cambridge: Cambridge University Press.

Philo Judaeus (1935–37). *Collected Works*. Tr. F. H. Colson. Loeb Classical Library. Cambridge, Mass.: Harvard University Press.

Pietkiewicz, Barbara (1981). "Gorzki Fiolet." *Polityka* 3:1250–53.

Pigott, Stuart (1952). *Prehistoric India*. Harmondsworth, Eng.: Penguin.

Pike, E. Royston (1965). *Love in Ancient Rome*. London: Frederick Muller.

Pillard, R. C., J. Poumadere, and R. A. Carreta (1981). "Is Homosexuality Familial? A Review, Some Data, and a Suggestion." *Archives of Sexual Behavior* 10:465–75.

Pilling, Arnold R. (1983). "Tiwi: Omitted Features." Unpublished paper.

Pinkerton, John (1811). *A General Collection of the Best and Most Interesting Voyages and Travels in All Parts of the World*, vol. 7. London: Longman, Hurst, Rees, Orme.

Pirenne, Jacques (1965). *La religion et la morale l'Égypte antique*. Paris: Edition Albin Michel.

Pittin, Renée (1983). "Houses of Women: A Focus on Alternative Life-Styles in Katsina City." Pp. 291–302 in Christina Oppong (ed.), *Female and Male in West Africa*. London: George Allen and Unwin.

Pivar, David (1973). *Purity Crusade: Sexual Morality and Social Control, 1868–1900*. Westport, Ct.: Greenwood.

Pizzarro, Joaquin Martinez (1979). "On Nið Against Bishops." *Mediaeval Scandinavia* 12:149–53.

Plant, Richard (1986). *The Pink Triangle: The Nazi War Against Homosexuals*. New York: H. Holt.

Plato (1968). *Laws*. Tr. B. Jowett. Pp. 407–703 in *The Dialogues of Plato*, vol. 2. London: Oxford University Press.

———— (1975). *Dialogues*. Vol. 3; *Lysis, Symposium, Gorgias*. Loeb Classical Library. Tr. W.R.M. Lamb. Cambridge, Mass.: Harvard University Press.

Plessis, Joseph (1921). *Etude sur les textes concernant Iśtar-Astarté*. Paris: Librairie Paul Geuthner.

Ploss, Hermann H. (1917). *Das Kind in Brauch und Sitte der Völker*, vol. 2. Leipzig: Th. Grieben.

————, and M. Bartels (1899). *Das Weib in der Natur- und Völkerkunde*. Leipzig: T. Grieben.

Plucknett, Theodore F. T. (1922). *Statutes and Their Interpretation in the First Half of the Fourteenth Century*. London: Cambridge University Press.

———— (1956). *A Concise History of the Common Law*. Boston: Little Brown.

———— (1966). *Legislation of Edward I*. London: Oxford University Press.

Plumb, J. H. (1975). "The New World of Children in Eighteenth Century England." *Past and Present* 67:64–95.

Plummer, Kenneth (1975). *Sexual Stigma: An Interactionist Account*. Boston: Routledge and Kegan Paul.

———— (1981a). "'The Paedophile's' Progress: A View from Below." Pp. 113–32 in Brian Taylor (ed.), *Perspectives on Paedophilia*. London: Batsford.

———— (1981b). "Homosexual Categories: Some Research Problems in the Labelling Perspective of Homosexuality." Pp. 53–75 in Kenneth Plummer (ed.), *The Making of the Modern Homosexual*. London: Hutchinson.

Plutarch (1968–69). *Moralia*. 9 vols. Tr. W. C. Helmbold. Loeb Classics Library. Cambridge, Mass.: Harvard University Press.

Pogey-Castries, L. R. de (1930). *Histoire de l'amour grec dans l'antiquité*. Paris: Stendhal.

Polanyi, Michael (1957). *The Great Transformation*. Boston: Beacon.

Pollard, John (1965). *Seers, Shrines and Sirens: The Greek Religious Revolution in the Sixth Century B.C.* Cranbury, N.J.: A. S. Barnes.

Polomé, Edgar (1970). "The Indo-European Component in Germanic Religion." Pp. 55–82 in Jaan Puhvel (ed.), *Myth and Law among the Indo-Europeans*. Berkeley: University of California Press.

———— (1974). "Approaches to Germanic Mythology." Pp. 51–66 in Gerald James Larson (ed.), *Myth in Indo-European Antiquity*. Berkeley: University of California Press.

Pomeroy, Sarah B. (1975). *Goddesses, Whores, Wives, and Slaves: Women in Classical Antiquity*. New York: Schocken.

Ponse, Barbara (1979). *Identities in the Lesbian World*. Westport, Conn.: Greenwood.

Porta, Giovanni Baptista della (1652). *La Fisonomia dell'Huomo*. Venice: Sebastian Combi and Giovanni La Noù.

Porter, J. R. (1976). *Leviticus*. London: Cambridge University Press.

Porter, Roy (1982). "Mixed Feelings: The Enlightenment and Sexuality in Eighteenth Century Britain." Pp. 1–27 in Paul-Gabriel Boucé (ed.), *Sexuality in Eighteenth-Century Britain*. Manchester: Manchester University Press.

Portmann, Marie-Louise (1980). "Relations d'Auguste Tissot (1728–1797), médicin à Lausanne, avec le patriciat bernois." *Gesnerus* 37:21–27.

Posener, Georges (1957). "Le conte de Neferkharè et du General Siséné (Recherches Litteraires, 6)." *Revue d'Egyptologie* 11:119–37.

——— (1960). *De la divinité du Pharaon*. Cahiers de la Societé Asiatique 15. Paris: Imprimerie Nationale.

Posner, Donald (1971). "Caravaggio's Homo-Erotic Early Works." *Art Quarterly* 34:301–24.

Potter, David M. (1965). "American Individualism in the Twentieth Century." Pp. 92–112 in G. M. Mills (ed.), *Innocence and Power*. Austin: University of Texas Press.

Powdermaker, Hortense (1933). *Life in Lesu: The Study of a Melanesian Society in New Ireland*. New York: W. W. Norton.

Powers, William K. (1977). *Oglala Religion*. Lincoln: University of Nebraska Press.

——— (1983). "Comment on Callender and Kochems." *Current Anthropology* 24:461–62.

Price, Arnold (1969). "Differentiated Germanic Social Structures." *Vierteljahrschrift für Sozial- und Wirtschaftsgeschichte* 55:433–38.

——— (1974). "Die Nibelungen als kriegerischer Weihebund." *Vierteljahrschrift für Sozial- und Wirtschaftsgeschichte* 61:199–211.

——— (1980). "The Role of the Germanic Warrior Club in the Historical Process: A Methodological Exposition." *Miscellanea Mediaevalia* 12:558–65.

Price, J. L. (1974). *Culture and Society in the Dutch Republic during the 17th Century*. London: B. T. Batsford.

Prince Peter (1948). "Tibetan, Toda, and Tiya Polyandry: A Report on Field Investigations: Lecture to the Academy." Manuscript in HRAF Files.

——— (1963). *A Study in Polyandry*. The Hague: Mouton.

Pritchard, James B. (ed.) (1955). *Ancient Near Eastern Texts Relating to the Old Testament*. Princeton, N.J.: Princeton University Press.

——— (1958). *The Ancient Near East*. 2 vols. Princeton, N.J.: Princeton University Press.

Procopius of Caesarea (1914). *History of the Wars*. Tr. H. B. Dewey. New York: Macmillan.

Prothero, I. J. (1979). *Artisans and Politics in Early Nineteenth-Century London: John Gast and His Times*. Baton Rouge: Louisiana State University Press.

Prumières, Henri (1929). *La vie illustre et libertinage de Jean-Baptiste Lully*. Paris: Plon.

Przyluski, Jean (1940). "Les confréries de loups-garous dans les sociétés indo-européenes." *Revue de l'histoire des religions* 121:128–45.

Pugh, David F. (1983). *Sons of Liberty: the Masculine Mind in Nineteenth-Century America*. Westport, Conn.: Greenwood.

Puhvel, Jaan (1971). "Hittite ḫurkiš and ḫurkel." *Die Sprache: Zeitschrift für Sprachenwissenschaft* 17:42–45.

Purcell, B. H. (1893). "Rites and Customs of Australian Aborigines." *Zeitschrift für Ethnologie* 25:286–89.

Quaife, G. R. (1979). *Wanton Wenches and Wayward Wives: Peasants and Illegal Sex in Early Seventeenth Century England*. New Brunswick, N.J.: Rutgers University Press.

Quibell, J.-E. (1907). *Excavations at Saqqara, 1905–1906*. Cairo: Institut Français d'Archéologie Orientale.

Quinlan, Maurice (1941). *Victorian Prelude: A History of English Manners, 1700–1830*. New York: Columbia University Press.

Quinn, Robert E. (1977). "Coping with Cupid: The Formation, Impact and Management of Romantic Relationships in Organizations." *Administrative Science Quarterly* 22:30–45.

Quintilian (1887). *Institutes of Oratory*, vol. 1. Tr. John Selby Watson. London: George Bell and Sons.

Rabinbach, Anson (1982). "The Body Without Fatigue: A Nineteenth-Century Utopia." Pp. 42–59 in Seymour Drescher, David Sabean, and Allan Sharlin (eds.), *Political Symbolism in Modern Europe: Essays in Honor of George L. Mosse*. New Brunswick, N.J.: Transaction.

Rachewiltz, Boris de (1963). *Eros Nero: Costumi Sessuali in Africa dalla Preistoria ad Oggi*. Milano: Longanesi.

——— (1964). *Black Eros: Sexual Customs of Africa from Prehistory to the Present Day*. Tr. Peter Whigman. New York: Lyle Stuart.

Rad, Gerhard von (1962). *Old Testament Theology*, 2 vols. Tr. D.M.G. Stalker. Edinburgh: Oliver and Boyd.

Radcliffe-Brown, A. R. (1940). "On Joking Relationships." *Africa* 13:195–210.

Raditsa, Leo Ferrero (1980). "Augustus' Legislation Concerning Marriage, Procreation, Love Affairs and Adultery." Pp. 278–339 in Hildegard Temporini and Wolfgang Haase (eds.), *Aufstieg und Niedergang der Römischen Welt*. Vol. 2: *Principat*. Berlin: Walter de Gruyter.

Rado, Sandor (1949). "An Adaptational View of Sexual Behavior." Pp. 159–89 in P. Hoch and J. Zubin (eds.), *Psychosexual Development in Health and Disease*. New York: Grune and Stratton.

Raffalovitch, Marc André (1895). *L'uranisme, inversion sexuelle congénitale: Observations et conseils*. Lyon: A Storck.

——— (1896). *Uranisme et unisexualité: Etude sur differentes manifestations de l'instinct sexuel*. Lyon: A Storck.

Randall, John Herman, Jr. (1940). *The Making of the Modern Mind*. New York: Houghton Mifflin.

——— (1970). *Hellenistic Ways of Deliverance and the Making of the Christian Synthesis*. New York: Columbia University Press.

Randers-Pherson, Justine Davids (1983). *Barbarians and Romans: The Birth Struggle of Europe, A.D. 400–700*. Norman: University of Oklahoma Press.

Rappaport, Roy A. (1967). *Pigs for the Ancestors: Ritual in the Ecology of a New Guinea People*. New Haven: Yale University Press.

Rare Verities: The Cabinet of Venus Unlocked, and Her Secrets Laid Open (1657) (A Translation of Sinibaldus's *Geneanthropeia*). London: P. Briggs.

Rat, Maurice (1955). *Dames et bourgeoises amoureuses ou galantes du XVI siècle*. Paris: Plon.

Ravenscroft, A.-G. B. (1892). "Some Habits and Customs of the Chingalee Tribe, Northern Territory, S.A." *Transactions of the Royal Society of South Australia* 15:121–22.

Rawson, Philip (1973). *Primitive Erotic Art*. New York: G. P. Putnam's Sons.

Ray, Verne F. (1933). *The Sanpoil and Nespelem: Salishan Peoples of Northeastern Washington*. Seattle: University of Washington Press.

Read, Kenneth E. (1955). "Morality and the Concept of the Person among the Gahuku-Gama." *Oceania* 25:233–82.

——— (1978). *Other Voices*. Novato, Calif.: Chandler and Sharp.

——— (1980). *The High Valley*. New York: Columbia University Press.

Reade, Brian (ed.) (1970). *Sexual Heretics: Male Homosexuality in English Literature from 1850 to 1900*. London: Routledge and Kegan Paul.

Rechberg und Röthenlöwen, Karl von (1813). *Les peuples de la Russie: ou, Descriptions des moeurs, usages et costumes des divers nations de l'empire de Russie*. vol. 2. Paris: D. Colas.

Rector, Frank (1981). *The Nazi Extermination of Homosexuals*. New York: Stein and Day.

Reddy, D.V.S. (1973). "Glimpses of the Art of Medicine and Medical Aid in Ancient South India." *Bulletin of the History of Medicine* (Hyderabad) 3:135–39.

Reeder, Greg (1983). "Journey to the Past: Egypt and a Gay Tomb?" *Advocate* 367 (May 12):25–26.

Reichard, Gladys A. (1950). *Navajo Religion*. New York: Pantheon.

Reichel-Dolmatoff, Gerardo (1951). *Los Kogii: Una tribu de la Sierra Nevada de Santa Marta, Colombia*, vol. 2. Bogota: Iqueima.

——— (1971). *Amazonian Cosmos: The Sexual and Religious Symbolism of the Tukano Indians*. Chicago: University of Chicago Press.

———, and Alicia Reichel-Dolmatoff (1961). *The People of Aritama: The Cultural Personality of a Colombian Mestizo Village*. Chicago: University of Chicago Press.

Reicke, Bo (1964). *The New Testament Era: The World of the Bible from 500 B.C. to A.D. 100*. Tr. David E. Green. Philadelphia: Fortress.

Reina, Ruben E. (1966). *The Law of the Saints: A Pokomam Pueblo and Its Community Culture*. Indianapolis: Bobbs-Merrill.

Reinhard, J. R., and V. E. Hull (1936). "Bran and Sceolang." *Speculum* 11:42–58.

Reinhold, Robert (1987). "AIDS Issue at Fore as Pope Visits San Francisco Today." *New York Times*, Sept. 17.

Reischauer, Edwin O. (1956). "Japanese Feudalism." Pp. 26–48 in Rushton Coulborn (ed.), *Feudalism in History*. Princeton, N.J.: Princeton University Press.

Reiss, Albert J. (1961). "The Social Integration of Queers and Peers." *Social Problems* 9:102–19.

Reiss, Albert L. (1986). *Journey into Sexuality: An Exploratory Voyage*. Englewood Cliffs, N.J.: Prentice-Hall.

Renou, Louis (1968). *Religions of Ancient India*. New York: Schocken.

Reuilley, Jean de (1909). *La Raucourt et ses amies: Etude historiques des moeurs saphique au XVIIIᵉ siècle*. Paris: H. Daragon.

Rey, Michel (1982). "Police et sodomie à Paris au XVIIIᵉ siècle: du Peché au Desordre." *Revue d'histoire moderne et contemporaine* 29:113–24.

——— (1984/1985). "L'art de 'raccrochet' au XVIIIᵉ siècle." *Masques* 24:92–99.

——— (1985). "Parisian Homosexuals Create a Lifestyle, 1700–1750: The Police Archives." *Eighteenth-Century Life* n.s. 9:179–91.

Rhodius, H., and J. Darling (1980). *Walter Spies and Balinese Art.* Amsterdam: J. Stowell.

Riasanovsky, V. A. (1929). *Customary Law of the Mongol Tribes (Mongols, Buriats, Kalmucks).* Harbin: Artistic Printinghouse.

Richards, Cara B. (1957). "Matriarchy or Mistake: The Role of Iroquois Women Through Time." Pp. 36–45 in Verne F. Ray (ed.), *Cultural Stability and Change.* Proceedings of the 1957 Annual Spring Meeting of the American Ethnological Society. Seattle: University of Washington Press.

Richards, Jeffrey (1987). "'Passing the Love of Women': Manly Love and Victorian Society." Pp. 92–122 in J. A. Mangan and James Walvin (eds.), *Manliness and Morality: Middle-Class Masculinity in Britain and America, 1800–1940.* New York: St. Martin's Press.

Richardson, Frank (1972). *Napoleon, Bisexual Emperor.* London: William Kimber.

Richardson, James T. (1984). "The 'Old Right' in Action: Mormon and Catholic Involvement in an Equal Rights Amendment Referendum." Pp. 213–49 in David G. Bromley and Anson Shupe (eds.), *New Christian Politics.* Macon, Ga.: Mercer University Press.

Richlin, Amy (1983). *The Garden of Priapus: Sexuality and Aggression in Roman Humor.* New Haven: Yale University Press.

Richter, Jean Paul (1972). *The Notebooks of Leonardo da Vinci,* vol. 2. New York: Dover.

Ridgeway, James (1984). "'Fag Bashing': The Right's Secret Weapon." *Village Voice* (Sept. 25):32–33.

Riefstahl, Elizabeth (1972). "An Enigmatic Faience Figure." Pp. 137–43 in *Miscellanea Wilbouriana,* vol. 1. Brooklyn: Brooklyn Museum.

Rieff, Philip (1959). *Freud: The Mind of the Moralist.* Chicago: University of Chicago Press.

Riegel, Robert E. (1963). *American Feminists.* Westport: Conn.: Greenwood.

Riemenschneider, Margarete (1955). *Le monde des Hittites.* Paris: Corréa-Buchet-Chastel.

Riencourt, Amaury de (1974). *Sex and Power in History.* New York: David McKay.

Rist, John M. (1963). *Stoic Philosophy.* Berkeley: University of California Press.

——— (1978). "The Stoic Conception of Detachment." Pp. 259–72 in John M. Rist (ed.), *The Stoics.* Berkeley: University of California Press.

Ritchie, Jane, and James Ritchie (1979). *Growing Up in Polynesia.* Sydney: George Allen and Unwin.

Rivera, Rhonda R. (1979). "Our Straight-Laced Judges: The Legal Position of Homosexual Persons in the United States." *Hastings Law Journal* 30:799–955.

——— (1982). "Homosexuality and the Law." Pp. 323–36 in William Paul, James D. Weinrich, John C. Gonsiorek, and Mary E. Hotvedt (eds.), *Homosexuality: Social, Psychological, and Biological Issues.* Beverly Hills, Calif.: Sage.

Rivers, J. E. (1979). "The Myth and Science of Homosexuality in *A la recherche du temps perdu.*" Pp. 262–78 in George Stambolian and Elaine Marks (eds.), *Homosexualities and French Literature.* Ithaca, N.Y.: Cornell University Press.

Rivers, Theodore John (1977). *Laws of the Alamans and Bavarians*. Philadelphia: University of Pennsylvania Press.

Rivkin, Ellis (1966). "The Internal City: Judaism and Urbanisation." *Journal for the Scientific Study of Religion* 5:221–40.

——— (1970). "Pharisaism and the Crisis of the Individual in the Greco-Roman World." *Jewish Quarterly Review* 61:27–53.

Robbins, Jim (1985). "Anasazi Times in Old America." *New York Times*, Sept. 1.

Robbins, Miriam (1980). "The Assimilation of Pre-Indo-European Goddesses into Indo-European Society." *Journal of Indo-European Studies* 8:19–29.

Roberts, Alexander, and James Donaldson (eds.) (1926). *The Ante-Nicene Fathers*, vol. 1. New York: Charles Scribner's.

Robin, Gilbert (1963). "Les mignons de Henri III." *Arcadie* 117:395–446 and 118:437–46.

——— (1964a). "L'efféminé, étude psycho-sexuelle d'Henri III." *Arcadie* 129:395–400.

——— (1964b). "Le roi Henri III et le travesti." *Arcadie* 131:506–16.

——— (1964c). *L'enigma sexuelle d'Henri III*. Paris: Westmael-Charlier.

Robinson, Paul (1976). *The Modernization of Sex*. New York: Harper and Row.

Roby, Douglass (1977). "Early Medieval Attitudes toward Homosexuality." *Gai Saiber* 1:67–71.

Rocke, Michael (1987). "Il controllo dell'omosessualita a Firenze nel XV secolo: gli Ufficiale di Notte." *Quaderni storici* 66:701–23.

Rockhill, William W. (1900). *The Journey of William of Rubreck to the Eastern Parts of the World, 1253–55*. London: Hakluyt Society.

Rogers, Joseph W., and M. D. Buffalo (1974). "Fighting Back: Nine Modes of Adaptation to a Deviant Label." *Social Problems* 22:101–18.

Rogers, Robert William (1929). *A History of Ancient Persia*. New York: Charles Scribner's Sons.

Roheim, Geza (1926). *Social Anthropology: A Psycho-Analytic Study in Anthropology and a History of Australian Totemism*. New York: Boni and Liveright.

——— (1933). "Women and Their Life in Central Australia." *Journal of the Royal Anthropological Institute of Great Britain and Ireland* 63:207–65.

——— (1945). *The Eternal Ones of the Dream: A Psychoanalytic Interpretation of Australian Myth and Ritual*. New York: International Universities Press.

——— (1950). *Psychoanalysis and Anthropology*. New York: International Universities Press.

——— (1958). "The Western Tribes of Central Australia: Their Sexual Life." Pp. 221–45 in Warner Muestenberger and Sidney Axelrad (eds.), *Psychoanalysis and the Social Sciences*, vol. 5. New York: International Universities Press.

——— (1974). *Children of the Desert: The Western Tribes of Central Australia*, vol. 1. New York: Basic.

Rohrlich, Ruby (1980). "State Formation in Sumer and the Subjugation of Women." *Feminist Studies* 6:76–102.

Rollison, David (1981). "Property, Ideology and Popular Culture in a Gloucestershire Village, 1660–1740." *Past and Present* 93:70–97.

Roman, Bernard (1961). *A Concise Natural History of East and West Florida*. New Orleans: Pelican. Orig. pub. 1775.

Römer, L.S.A.M. von (1902). "Heinrich der Dritte, König von Frankreich und Polen." *Jahrbuch für sexuelle Zwischenstufen* 4:572–669.

—— (1903). "Über die androgynische Idee des Lebens." *Jahrbuch für sexuelle Zwischenstufen* 2:707–940.

—— (1978). *Uranism in the Netherlands Till the Nineteenth Century*. Tr. Michael A. Lombardi. Los Angeles: Urania Manuscripts.

Rorabaugh, W. J. (1979). *The Alcoholic Republic: An American Tradition*. New York: Oxford University Press.

Rosen, B. C. (1956). "The Achievement Syndrome: A Psychocultural Dimension of Social Stratification." *American Sociological Review* 21:203–11.

Rosen, George (1983). *The Structure of American Medical Practice, 1875–1941*. Ed. George Rosenberg. Philadelphia: University of Pennsylvania Press.

Rosenberg, Charles E. (1968). *The Trial of the Assassin Guiteau: Psychiatry and Law in the Gilded Age*. Chicago: University of Chicago Press.

—— (1973). "Sexuality, Class and Role in Nineteenth-Century America." *American Quarterly* 25:131–53.

—— (1974). "The Bitter Fruit: Heredity, Disease, and Social Thought in Nineteenth-Century America." *Perspectives in American History* 8:189–235.

Rosenberg, Rosalind (1982). *Beyond Separate Spheres: Intellectual Roots of Modern Feminism*. New Haven: Yale University Press.

Rosenkrantz, P., S. Vogel, H. Ber, and D. Braverman (1968). "Sex-Role Stereotypes and Self-Concepts in College Students." *Journal of Consulting and Clinical Psychology* 32:287–95.

Rosenthal, Franz (1971). *The Herb: Hashish versus Medieval Muslim Society*. Leiden: E. J. Brill.

—— (1978). "Ar-Râzî on the Hidden Illness." *Bulletin of the History of Medicine* 52:45–60.

Rosenthal, Michael (1985). *The Character Factory: Baden-Powell and the Origins of the Boy Scout Movement*. New York: Pantheon.

Ross, Allen V. (1968). *Vice in Bombay*. London: Tallis.

Ross, Anne (1973). "Celtic and Northern Art." Pp. 77–106 in Philip Rawson (ed.), *Primitive Erotic Art*. New York: G. P. Putnam's Sons.

Ross, Ellen (1984). "Response to Harold Benenson's 'Victorian Sexual Ideology'." *International Labor and Working Class History* 25:30–36.

Ross, H. Laurence (1976). "The Neutralization of Severe Penalties." *Law and Society Review* 10:403–13.

Rossman, Parker (1976). *Sexual Experience between Men and Boys: Exploring the Pederast Underground*. New York: Association.

Rotenberg, Mordechai (1974). "Self-Labeling: A Missing Link in the Societal Reaction Theory of Deviance." *Sociological Review* 22:335–54.

Roth, Henry Ling (1968). *The Natives of Sarawak and British North Borneo*, vol. 1. Kuala Lumpur and Singapore: University of Malaya Press. Orig. pub. 1896.

Roth, Norman (1982). "'Deal Gently with the Young Man': Love of Boys in Medieval Hebrew Poetry of Spain." *Speculum* 57:20–51.

Roth, W. E. (1908). "Notes on Government, Morals and Crime." *Northwest Queensland Ethnological Bulletin* 8:7.

Rothman, David B. (1971). *The Discovery of the Asylum: Social Order and Disorder in the New Republic*. Boston: Little Brown.

Rousseau, G. S. (1985). "The Pursuit of Homosexuality in the Eighteenth Century: 'Utterly Confused Category' and/or Rich Depository?" *Eighteenth-Century Life* 9:132–68.

Rousseau, P. (1978). *Ascetics, Authority, and the Church in the Age of Jerome and Cassian*. Oxford: Oxford University Press.

Rowbotham, Sheila (1977). "Edward Carpenter: Prophet of the New Life." Pp. 25–148 in Sheila Rowbotham and Jeffrey Weeks (eds.), *Socialism and the New Life; The Personal and Sexual Politics of Edward Carpenter and Havelock Ellis*. London: Pluto.

——— (1979). "The Women's Movement and Organizing for Socialism." *Radical America* 13:9–28.

———, and Jeffrey Weeks (eds.) (1977). *Socialism and the New Life: The Personal and Sexual Politics of Edward Carpenter and Havelock Ellis*. London: Pluto.

Rowley-Conwy, Peter (1983). "Sedentary Hunters: The Estebolle Example." Pp. 111–26 in Geoff Bailey (ed.), *Hunter-Gatherer Economy in Prehistory: A European Perspective*. Cambridge: Cambridge University Press.

Rowse, A. L. (1977). *Homosexuals in History: A Study of Ambivalence in Literature and the Arts*. New York: Macmillan.

Rubel, Paula G., and Abraham Rossman (1978). *Your Own Pigs You May Not Eat: A Comparative Study of New Guinea Societies*. Chicago: University of Chicago Press.

Rubin, Gabrielle (1977). *La source inconscient de misogynie*. Paris: R. Laffont.

Rubin, Nancy Felson, and William Merritt Sale (1983). "Meleager and Odysseus: A Structural and Cultural Study of the Greek Hunting-Maturation Myth." *Arethusa* 16:137–71.

Rudd, Niall (1986). *Themes in Roman Satire*. Norman: University of Oklahoma Press.

Rueda, Enrique T. (1982). *The Homosexual Network: Private Lives and Public Policy*. Old Greenwich, Conn.: Devin Adair.

Ruggiero, Guido (1975). "Sexual Criminality in the Early Renaissance: Venice 1338: 1358." *Journal of Social History* 8:18–37.

——— (1980). *Violence in Early Renaissance Venice*. New Brunswick, N.J.: Rutgers University Press.

——— (1985). *The Boundaries of Eros: Sex Crime and Sexuality in Renaissance Venice*. New York: Oxford University Press.

Rule, John (ed.) (1969). *Louis XIV and the Craft of Kingship*. Columbus: Ohio State University Press.

Ruse, M. (1981). "Are There Gay Genes? Sociobiology and Homosexuality." *Journal of Homosexuality* 6(4):5–34.

Russell, Bertrand (1959). *Wisdom of the West*. Garden City, N.Y.: Doubleday.

Russell, C. E. (1935). *General Rigby, Zanzibar and the Slave Trade*. London: George Allen and Unwin.

Russell, Jeffrey Burton (1965). *Dissent and Reform in the Early Middle Ages.* Berkeley: University of California Press.

—— (1972). *Witchcraft in the Middle Ages.* Ithaca, N.Y.: Cornell University Press.

Russell, Robert Vane (1916). *Tribes and Castes of the Central Provinces of India.* London: Macmillan.

Russo, Vito (1981). *The Celluloid Closet: Homosexuality in the Movies.* New York: Harper and Row.

Rutt, Richard (1961). "The Flower Boys of Silla (Hwarang): Notes on the Sources." *Transactions of the Korea Branch of the Royal Asiatic Society* 38:1–66.

Ryan, Mary P. (1979). *Womanhood in America: From Colonial Times to the Present.* 2d ed. New York: Franklin Watts.

—— (1981). *Cradle of the Middle Class: The Family in Oneida County, New York, 1790–1865.* New York: Cambridge University Press.

Ryan, Michael (1837). *The Philosophy of Marriage, in its Social, Moral and Physical Relations.* London: North London School of Medicine.

Ryckmans, Jacques (1986). "A Three Generations' Matrilineal Geneology in a Hassaean Inscription: Matrilineal Ancestry in Pre-Islamic Arabia." Pp. 407–17 in Shaikha Haya Ali al Khalifa and Michael Rice (eds.), *Bahrain Through the Ages: The Archaeology.* London: KPI.

Sabadino, Jean (1963). "Nouvelle XIII: Facéties Porretanes." *Arcadie* 111:128–30.

Sablatura, Bob (1985). "Gay Rights Bills Defeated in Houston." *In These Times* (Jan. 3–Feb. 5):7.

Sachs, Hannelore (1971). *The Renaissance Woman.* Tr. Marianne Herzfeld and D. Talbot Rice. New York: McGraw-Hill.

Sagan, Eli (1985). *At the Dawn of Tyranny: The Origins of Individualism, Political Oppression, and the State.* New York: A. A. Knopf.

Sagent, Philippe (1976). "Becoming a Limbu Priest: Ethnographic Notes." Pp. 56–99 in John T. Hitchcock and Rex L. Jones (eds.), *Spirit Possession in the Nepal Himalayas.* Warminster, Eng.: Aris and Phillips.

Saggs, H.W.F. (1962). *The Greatness that Was Babylon.* London: Sidgwick and Jackson.

—— (1965). *Everyday Life in Babylonia and Assyria.* New York: G. P. Putnam's Sons.

Saghir, Marcel T., and Eli Robins (1973). *Male and Female: A Comprehensive Investigation.* Baltimore: Williams and Wilkins.

Sahli, Nancy (1979). "Smashing: Women's Relationships Before the Fall." *Chrysalis* 8:17–27.

Sahlins, Marshall (1963). "Poor Man, Rich Man, Big-Man, Chief: Political Types in Melanesia and Polynesia." *Comparative Studies in Society and History* 5:285–303.

Sainte Croix, G.E.M. de (1963). "Why Were the Early Christians Persecuted?" *Past and Present* 26:6–38.

—— (1981). *The Class Struggle in the Ancient Greek World, from the Archaic Age to the Arab Conquests.* London: Duckworth.

Salas, Luis (1979). *Social Control and Deviance in Cuba.* New York: Praeger.

Saletore, R. N. (1974). *Sex Life under Indian Rulers.* Delhi: Hind.

Salisbury, Joyce E. (1985a). "The Latin Doctors of the Church on Sexuality." Paper presented to the American Historical Association.

———— (1985b). *Iberian Popular Religion 600 B.C. to 700 A.D.: Celts, Romans and Visigoths.* Texts and Studies in Religion, vol. 20. New York: Edwin Mellen Press.

Sallust (1960). *The War with Catiline.* Tr. J. C. Rolfe. Loeb Classical Library. Cambridge, Mass.: Harvard University Press.

Salmon, Thomas (1941). *A Collection of Proceedings and Trials against State Prisoners,* vol. 9. London: J. Wilcox.

Salmoral, Manuel Lucena (1966). "Bardaje en una tribu Guahibo del Tomo." *Revista Colombiana de Antropologia* 14:263–66.

Salvian (1930). *On the Government of God.* Tr. Eva M. Sanford. New York: Columbia University Press.

Sanday, Peggy Reeves (1981). *Female Power and Male Dominance: On the Origins of Sexual Inequality.* New York: Cambridge University Press.

Sanders, G. M. (1972). "Gallos." Pp. 984–1034 in Theodor Klausner (ed.), *Reallexikon für Antike und Christentum,* vol. 7. Stuttgart: Anton Hiersemann.

Sandin, Benedict (1957). "Salang Changed His Sex." *Sarawak Museum Journal* 8: 145–52.

Sanford, Nevitt (1951). *Self and Society.* New York: Atherton.

Sanger, William W. (1858). *The History of Prostitution: Its Extent, Causes, and Effects throughout the World.* New York: Medical.

Sankar, Andrea (1985). "Sisters and Brothers, Lovers and Enemies: Marriage Resistance in Southern Kwangtung." *Journal of Homosexuality* 11:69–82.

San Miguel, Christopher L., and Jim Millham (1976). "The Role of Cognitive and Situational Variables in Aggression toward Homosexuals." *Journal of Homosexuality* 2:11–27.

Sansom, G. B. (1962). *Japan: A Short Cultural History.* New York: Appleton-Century-Crofts.

Sartre, M. (1985). "Homosexuality in Ancient Greece." *Histoire* 76:10–17.

Sarup, Madho (1958). "Indus Valley Civilization." Pp. 110–28 in *The Cultural Heritage of India,* vol. 1. Calcutta: Ramakrishna Mission Institute of Culture.

Saslow, James M. (1985). "From Achilles to Antinous: The Classical World," *Advocate* 429–42.

———— (1986). *Ganymede in the Renaissance: Homosexuality in Art and Society.* New Haven: Yale University Press.

Satan's Harvest Home: Or the Present State of Whorecraft, Adultery, Fornication, Procuring, Pimping, Sodomy, and the Game at Flatts, and other SATANIC WORKS, Daily Propagated in this Good Protestant Kingdom (1749). London: Privately printed.

Sauer, Martin (1802). *An Account of a Geographical and Astronomical Expedition to the Northern Parts of Russia.* London: T. Cadell.

Sauneron, Serge (1961). "Remarques de philologie et d'étymologie (en marge des textes d'Esna)." *Bibliothèque d'Étude (Mélanges Mariettes)* 32:242–44.

Saussaye, P. D. Chantepie de la (1902). *The Religion of the Teutons.* Tr. Bert J. Vos. Boston: Ginn.

Sawyer, Jack (1970). "On Male Liberation." *Liberation* 15:32–33.

Saxo Grammaticus (1979). *The History of the Danes.* 2 vols. Tr. Peter Fisher. Totawa, N.J.: Rowman and Littlefield.

Sayers, Dorothy L. (1971). *The Song of Roland.* Baltimore, Md.: Penguin.

Scacco, Anthony M., Jr. (1982) *Male Rape: A Casebook of Sexual Aggression.* New York: AMS.

Scanzoni, Letha and Virginia Ramsey Mollenkott (1978). *Is the Homosexual My Neighbor?* New York: Harper and Row.

Schacht, J. (1970). "Law and Justice." Pp. 539–68 in P. M. Holt, Ann K. S. Lambton, and Bernard Lewis (eds.), *The Cambridge History of Islam.* London: Cambridge University Press.

Schactman, Max (1962). *The Bureaucratic Revolution: The Rise of the Stalinist State.* New York: Donald.

Schaeffer, Claude E. (1965). "The Kutenai Female Berdache: Courier, Guide, Prophetess, and Warrior." *Ethnohistory* 12:193–236.

Schärer, Hans (1963). *Ngaju Religion: The Concept of God among a South Borneo People.* Tr. Rodney Needham. The Hague: Martinus Nijhoff.

Schafer, Stephen (1969). *Theories in Criminology.* New York: Random House.

Schaff, P. et al. (1886). *A Select Library of Nicene and Post-Nicene Fathers.* Vol. 9: *Saint Chrysostom.* New York: Charles Scribner's Sons.

—— (1895). *A Select Library of Nicene and Post-Nicene Fathers.* Vol. 10: *Saint Ambrose.* New York: Charles Scribner's Sons.

Schapera, Isaac (1930). *The Khoisan Peoples of South Africa: Bushmen and Hottentots.* London: Routledge and Kegan Paul.

—— (1938). *A Handbook of Tswana Law and Custom.* London: Oxford University Press.

Schevill, Ferdinand (1961). *History of Florence.* New York: Frederick Unger. Orig. pub. 1936.

Schick, Alfred (1968/69). "The Cultural Background of Psychotherapy. *Psychoanalytic Review* 55:529–51.

Schieffelin, Edward (1976). *The Sorrow of the Lonely and the Burning of the Dancers.* New York: St. Martin's Press.

—— (1982). "The *Bau A* Ceremonial Lodge: An Alternative to Initiation." Pp. 155–200 in Gilbert Herdt (eds.), *Rituals of Manhood: Male Initiation in Papua New Guinea.* Berkeley: University of California Press.

Schilling, Heinz-Dieter (1983). *Schwule und Faschismus.* Berlin: Elephanten.

Schimmel, Annemarie (1975). *Mystical Dimensions of Islam.* Chapel Hill: University of North Carolina Press.

—— (1979). "Eros—Heavenly and Not so Heavenly—in Sufi Literature and Life." Pp. 119–42 in Afaf Lutfi al-Sayyid-Marsot (ed.), *Society and the Sexes in Medieval Islam.* Malibu, Cal.: Undena.

Schimmelpfennig, Bernhard (1979). "Ex Fornicatione Nati: Studies on the Portion of Priests' Sons from the Twelfth to the Fifteenth Century." Pp. 1–50 in J.A.S. Evans (eds.), *Studies in Medieval and Renaissance History,* vol. 2. Victoria: University of British Columbia.

Schirmacher, Käthe (1897). *Théophile de Viau, sein Leben und seine Werke.* Leipzig: H. Welter.

Schirmann, Jefim (1955). "The Ephebe in Medieval Hebrew Poetry." *Sefarad* 15:55–68.

Schlegel, Alice (1977). "Male and Female in Hopi Thought and Action." Pp. 245–69 in Alice Schlegel (ed.), *Sexual Stratification: A Cross-Cultural View*. New York: Columbia University Press.

——— (1983). "Comment on Callender and Kochems." *Current Anthropology* 24: 460–61.

Schmidt, Gunter (1984). "Allies and Persecutors: Science and Medicine in the Homosexuality Issue." *Journal of Homosexuality* 10:127–40.

Schmitt, Arno (1985). "Vorlesung zu mann-männlicher Sexualität: Erotik in der islamischen Gesellschaft." Pp. 1–22 in Gianni De Martino and Arno Schmitt (eds.), *Kleine Schriften zu zwischenmännlicher Sexualität und Erotik, in der muslimischen Gesellschaft*. Berlin: Privately printed.

Schnapp, Alain (1984). "Eros en chasse." Pp. 67–84 in *La cité des images: Religion et societé en Grèce Antique*. Paris: Fernand Nathan.

Schofield, J. N. (1967). "Megiddo." Pp. 309–27 in D. Winston Thomas (ed.), *Archaeology and Old Testament Study*. London: Oxford University Press.

Schofield, Michael G. (1965). *Sociological Aspects of Homosexuality: A Comparison Study of Three Types of Homosexuals*. Boston: Little Brown.

Scholes, France V., and Ralph L. Roys (1948). *The Maya Chontal Indians of Acalan-Tixchel: A Contribution to the History of Ethnography of the Yucatan Peninsula*. Washington, D.C.: Carnegie Institute of Washington.

Schoppmann, Chaudia (1985). *"Der Skorpion": Frauenliebe in der Weimarer Republik*. Berlin: Frühlings Erwachen.

Schorske, Carl (1980). *Fin-de-Siècle Vienna: Politics and Culture*. New York: A. A. Knopf.

Schucking, Levin (1929). *The Puritan Family: A Social Study from Literary Sources*. New York: Schocken.

Schuler, Einar von (1982). *Rechts- und Wirtschaftsurkunden: Historisch-Chronologische Texte (Texte aus der Umwelt des Alten Testaments)*, vol. 1. Gütersloh, Federal Republic of Germany: Gütersloher.

Schulthess, Friedrich (1922). "Zur Sprache der Evangelien. Anhang. A. *racha (raka)*, mōre." *Zeitschrift für die neutestamentliche Wissenschaft* 21:241–43.

Schur, Edwin M. (1965). *Crimes without Victims*. Englewood Cliffs, N.J.: Prentice-Hall.

——— (1971). *Labeling Deviant Behavior*. New York: Random.

——— (1979). *Interpreting Deviance: A Sociological Introduction*. New York: Harper and Row.

——— (1980). *The Politics of Deviance: Stigma Contests and the Uses of Power*. Englewood Cliffs, N.J.: Prentice-Hall.

Schutz, Alfred (1967). *The Phenomenology of the Social World*. Evanston, Ill.: Northwestern University Press.

Schutz, Herbert (1983). *The Prehistory of Germanic Europe*. New Haven: Yale University Press.

Schuvaloff, George (1976). "Gay Life in Russia." *Christopher Street* 1(3):14–22.

Schwartz, Barry Dov (1979). *The Jewish View of Homosexuality*. D.H.L. dissertation, Jewish Theological Seminary.

Schwarz, Gudrun (1983). "Women Supports Networks in Germany at the End of the Nineteenth and Beginning of the Twentieth Century." In *Among Men, Among Women*. Amsterdam: Conference Papers.

Schwendinger, Herman, and Julia Schwendinger (1974). *Sociologists of the Chair: A Radical Analysis of the Formative Years of North America Sociology, 1883–1922*. New York: Basic Books.

Schwimmer, Eric (1984). "Male Couples in New Guinea." Pp. 248–91 in Gilbert Herdt (ed.), *Ritualized Homosexuality in Melanesia*. Berkeley: University of California Press.

Scott, Colin (1896). "Sex and Art." *American Journal of Psychology* 7:153–226.

Scott, George Ryley (1954). *A History of Prostitution from Antiquity to the Present Day*. London: Torchstream. Orig. pub. 1936.

—— (1966). *Phallic Worship*. London: Luxor. Orig. pub. 1941.

Scott, Robert A., and Jack D. Douglas, eds. (1972). *Theoretical Perspectives on Deviance*. New York: Basic Books.

Scroggs, Robin (1983). *The New Testament and Homosexuality*. Philadelphia: Fortress.

Scullard, H. H. (1967). *The Etruscan Cities and Rome*. Ithaca, N.Y.: Cornell University Press.

Sears, R. R., E. E. Maccoby, and H. Levine (1957). *Patterns of Child-Rearing*. Evanston, Ill.: Row-Peterson.

Sedgwick, Peter (1982/1983). "Guerin: Out of Hiding." *Salmagundi* 58–59:197–200.

Séguin, Robert-Lionel (1972). *La vie libertine en Nouvelle-France au XVIIᵉ siècle*. Montreal: Leméac.

Seibert, Ilse (1974). *Woman in Ancient Near East*. Tr. Marianne Herzfeld and George A. Shepperson. London: George Preor.

Seligman, Charles G., and Brenda Z. Seligman (1932). *Pagan Tribes of the Nilotic Sudan*. London: George Rutledge and Sons.

Sellin, J. Thorsten (1976). *Slavery and the Penal System*. New York: Elsevier.

Seltman, Charles (1955). *Women in Antiquity*. New York: St. Martin's.

Semadini, Hekmut (1960). *Die Erbkrankheiten um 1850*. Unpublished dissertation, University of Zurich.

Semmel, Bernard (1960). *Imperialism and Social Reform: English Social-Imperialist Thought, 1895–1914*. Washington, D.C.: Howard University Press.

Semonov, A. (1911). "Zur Dorische Knabenliebe." *Philologus N. F.* 24:146–50.

Senate Subcommittee on Investigations (1950). *Employment of Homosexuals and Other Sex Perverts in Government*. Washington, D.C.: Government Printing Office.

Seneca, Marcus Annaeus (1974). *Controversiae*, vol. 1. Tr. M. Winterbottom. Cambridge, Mass.: Harvard University Press.

Sergent, Bernard (1984). *L'homosexualité dans la mythologie grecque*. Paris: Payot.

Serpenti, Laurent M. (1965). *Cultivators in the Swamps*. Assen: Van Gorcum.

—— (1984). "The Ritual Meaning of Homosexuality and Pedophilia Among the Kimam-Papuans of South Irian Jaya." Pp. 292–317 in Gilbert Herdt (ed.), *Ritualized Homosexuality in Melanesia*. Berkeley: University of California Press.

Service, Elman R. (1975). *Origins of the State and Civilization: The Process of Cultural Evolution*. New York: W. W. Norton.

Sextus Empiricus (1933). *Outlines of Pyrrhonism*. Tr. Rev. R. G. Bury. London: William Heinemann.

Shachtman, Max (1962). *The Bureaucratic Revolution: The Rise of the Stalinist State.* New York: Donald.

Shade, William G. (1978). "'A Mental Passion': Female Sexuality in Victorian America." *International Journal of Women's Studies* 1:13–29.

Shah, A. M. (1961). "A Note on the Hijadas of Gujerat." *American Anthropologist* 61:1325–30.

Shahar, Shulamith (1983). *The Fourth Estate: A History of Women in the Middle Ages.* Tr. Chaya Galai. London: Methuen.

Shapin, Steven (1975). "Phrenological Knowledge and the Social Structure of Early Nineteenth-Century Edinburgh." *Annals of Science* 32:219–43.

——— (1979). "The Politics of Observation: Cerebral Anatomy and Social Interests in the Edinburgh Phrenology Disputes." Pp. 139–78 in Roy Wallis (ed.), *On the Margins of Science: The Social Construction of Rejected Knowledge.* Sociological Review Monograph 27. Keele, Eng.: University of Keele.

Shapiro, H. A. (1981). "Courtship Scenes in Attic Vase Painting." *American Journal of Archaeology* 95:133–43.

Shapiro, Susan C. (1977). "Feminists in Elizabethan England." *History Today* 27:703–11.

Sharp, Harry Clay (1909). "The Sterilization of Degenerates." Pp. 143–44 in Jonathan N. Katz (ed.), *Gay American History.* New York: Thomas Y. Crowell, 1976.

Sharpe, J. A. (1983). *Crime in Seventeenth-Century England: A County Study.* London: Cambridge University Press.

Shaw, George Bernard (1914). "Common Sense About the War." *New Statesman* (Special War Supplement) 4(84) (Nov. 14):3–29.

Shaw, J. C., and G. N. Ferris (1883). "Perverted Sexual Instinct." *Journal of Nervous and Mental Diseases* 10:185–204.

Shell, Marc (1979). "The Wether and the Ewe: Verbal Usury in *The Merchant of Venice.*" *Kenyon Review* 1(4):65–92.

Shelley, Martha (1972). "Gay Is Good." Pp. 31–34 in Karla Jay and Allen Young (eds.), *Out of the Closets: Voices of Gay Liberation.* New York: Douglas.

Shepherd, Gill (1978). "Transsexualism in Oman?" *Man* 13:133–34.

——— (1987). "Rank, Gender and Homosexuality: Mombasa as a Key to Understanding Sexual Options." Pp. 240–70 in Pat Caplan (ed.), *The Cultural Construction of Sexuality.* London: Tavistock.

Shetter, W. Z. (1971). *The Pillars of Society: Six Centuries of Civilization in the Netherlands.* The Hague: Martinus Nijhoff.

Shipp, E. R. (1986). "Physical Suffering Is Not the Only Pain that AIDS Can Inflict." *New York Times,* Feb. 17.

Shiveley, Donald H. (1970). "Tokugawa Tsunayoshi, the Gewoku Shogun." Pp. 85–126 in Albert M. Craig and Donald H. Shiveley (eds.), *Personality in Japanese History.* Berkeley: University of California Press.

Shore, David A. (1981). *Sex-Related Issues in Correctional Facilities: A Classified Bibliography.* Chicago: The Playboy Foundation.

Shorter, Edward (1975). *The Making of the Modern Family.* New York: Basic Books.

——— (1977). "Female Emancipation, Birth Control, and Fertility in European History." *American Historical Review* 78:605–40.

Shoumatoff, Alex (1986). "Amazons." *New Yorker,* Mar. 24.

Shryock, Richard (1931). "Sylvester Graham and the Health Reform Movement, 1830–1870." *Mississippi Valley Historical Review* 18:172–83.

——— (1947). *The Development of Modern Medicine.* New York: A. A. Knopf.

Shupe, Anson, and William Stacey (1983). "The Moral Majority Constituency." Pp. 103–16 in Robert C. Liebman and Robert Wuthnow (eds.), *The New Christian Right: Mobilization and Legitimation.* New York: Aldine.

Sidney, Philip (1912). *The Countess of Pembroke's Arcadia.* Cambridge: Cambridge University Press.

Signorini, Italo (1983). "Comment on Callender and Kochems." *Current Anthropology* 24:463–64.

Silver, Catherine Bodard (1973). "Salon, Foyer, Bureau: Women and the Professions in France." *American Journal of Sociology* 78:836–51.

Simms, S. C. (1903). "Crow Indian Hermaphrodites." *American Anthropologist* 5:580–81.

Simpson, Antony (1984). *Masculinity and Control: The Prosecution of Sex Offences in Eighteenth-Century London.* Ph.D. dissertation, New York University.

Simpson, Colin, Lewis Chester, and David Leitch (1976). *The Cleveland Street Affair.* Boston: Little, Brown.

Simpson, John H. (1983). "Moral Issues and Status Politics." Pp. 187–205 in Robert C. Liebman and Robert Wuthnow (eds.), *The New Christian Right: Mobilization and Legitimation.* New York: Aldine.

Simpson, William Kelly (1972). *The Literature of Ancient Egypt.* New Haven: Yale University Press.

Singer, J. Milton, and Stephen J. Cutler (1984). "The Moral Majority Viewed Sociologically." Pp. 69–90 in David G. Bromley and Anson Shupe (eds.), *New Christian Politics.* Macon, Ga.: Mercer University Press.

Sinistrari, Friar Ludovico Maria (1958). *Peccatum Mutum.* Paris: Le Ballet de Muses.

The Sins of the Cities of the Plain or the Recollections of a Mary-Ann with Short Essays on Sodomy and Tribadism. 2 vols. (1881). London: Privately printed.

Siraisi, Nancy G. (1970). "The *Expositio Problematum Aristotelis* of Peter of Abano." *Isis* 61:321–39.

Skinner, Adamson (1911). "Notes on the Eastern Cree and Northern Sauteaux." *Anthropological Papers of the American Museum of Natural History* 9:1–77.

Skowronek, Stephen (1982). *Building a New American State: The Expansion of National Administrative Capacities, 1877–1920.* Cambridge: Cambridge University Press.

Slater, Philip E. (1968). *The Glory of Hera: Greek Mythology and the Greek Family.* Boston: Beacon.

Smallwood, E. Mary (1976). *The Jews under Roman Rule: From Pompey to Diocletian.* Leiden: E. J. Brill.

Smet, Pierre-Jean de (1905). *Life, Letters and Travels of Father Pierre-Jean de Smet,* vol. 3. Ed. Hiram M. Chittenden and Alfred T. Richardson. New York: Francis P. Harper.

Smith, Bonnie G. (1981). *Ladies of the Leisure Class: The Bourgeoisies of Northern France in the Nineteenth Century.* Princeton, N.J.: Princeton University Press.

Smith, Edmund Reul (1855). *The Araucanians, or Notes of a Tour among the Indian Tribes of Southern Chile.* New York: F. P. Harper.

Smith, Edwin M., and Andrew M. Dale (1920). *The Ila-Speaking Peoples of Northern Rhodesia*, vol. 1. London: Macmillan.

Smith, F. Barry (1976). "Labouchère's Amendment to the Criminal Law Amendment Bill." *Historical Studies* 17:165–75.

——— (1977). "Sexuality in Britain, 1800–1900: Some Suggested Revisions." Pp. 182–98 in Martha Vicinus (ed.), *A Widening Sphere: Changing Roles of Victorian Women*. Bloomington: Indiana University Press.

Smith, John Holland (1976). *The Death of Classical Paganism*. New York: Charles Scribner's Sons.

Smith, M. F. (1954). *Babo of Karo: A Woman of the Muslim Hausa*. London: Faber and Faber.

Smith, Morton (1956). "Palestinian Judaism in the First Century." Pp. 67–81 in Moshe Davis (ed.), *Israel, Its Role in Civilization*. New York: Jewish Theological Seminary.

——— (1973a). *The Secret Gospel: The Discovery and Interpretation of the Secret Gospel According to Mark*. New York: Harper and Row.

——— (1973b). *Clement of Alexandria and a Secret Gospel of Mark*. Cambridge, Mass.: Harvard University Press.

——— (1978). *Jesus the Magician*. New York: Harper and Row.

Smith, W. Robertson (1903). *Kinship and Marriage in Early Arabia*. London: A. and C. Black.

Smith-Rosenberg, Carroll (1972). "The Hysterical Woman: Sex Roles and Role Conflict in 19th-Century America." *Social Research* 39:652–78.

——— (1975). "The Female World of Love and Ritual: Relations between Women in Nineteenth Century America." *Signs: Journal of Women in Culture and Society* 1:1–29.

——— (1978). "Sex as Symbol in Victorian Purity: An Ethnohistorical Analysis of Jacksonian America." *American Journal of Sociology* 84 suppl.:S212–47.

——— (1983). "The Body Politic: Abortion, Deviance and the Sexualization of Language." In *Among Men, Among Women*. Amsterdam: Conference Papers.

Snortum, John R., John E. Marshall, James F. Gillespie, John P. McLaughlin, and Ludwig Mosberg (1969). "Family Dynamics and Homosexuality." *Psychological Reports* 24:763–70.

Socarides, Charles W. (1968). *The Overt Homosexual*. New York: Grune and Stratton.

——— (1978). *Homosexuality*. New York: Jason Aronson.

Soden, Wolfram von (1967). *Akkadisches Handwörterbuch*, Lieferung 8. Wiesbaden: Otto Harrasowitz.

Sofer, Yehuda (1985). "Israel: Gays Caught between Progressiveness and the Ideology of a State Religion." Pp. 64–75 in *IGA Pink Book 1985*. Amsterdam: COC.

Soggin, J. Alberto (1977). "The Davidic-Solomonic Kingdom." Pp. 332–80 in John H. Hayes and J. Maxwell Miller (eds.), *Israelite and Judaean History*. Philadelphia: Westminster.

Sokolow, Jayme A. (1983). *Eros and Modernization: Sylvester Graham, Health Reform, and the Origins of Victorian Sexuality in America*. Cranbury, N.J.: Associated University Presses.

Sole, Jacques (1976). *L'Amour en Occident a l'epoque moderne*. Paris: Albin Michel.

Soman, Alfred (1978). "The Parlement of Paris and the Great Witch-Hunt." *Sixteenth Century Journal* 9:30–44.

Sorenson, Arthur P. (1984). "Linguistic Exogamy and Personal Choice in the Northwest Amazon." Pp. 180–93 in Kenneth M. Kensinger (ed.), *Marriage Practices in Lowland South America*. Urbana: University of Illinois Press.

Sørensen, Preben Neulengracht (1983). *The Unmanly Man: Concepts of Sexual Defamation in Early Northern Society*. Tr. Joan Turville-Petre. Odense, Den.: Odense University Press.

Sørum, A. (1980). "In Search of the Lost Soul: Bedamini Spirit Seances and Curing Rights." *Oceania* 50:273–97.

—— (1984). "Growth and Decay: Bedamini Male Codification of Sexual Relations." Pp. 318–36 in Gilbert Herdt (ed.), *Ritualized Homosexuality in Melanesia*. Berkeley: University of California Press.

Sourdel, Dominique (1979). *Medieval Islam*. Tr. J. Montgomery Watt. Boston: Routledge and Kegan Paul.

Southern, R. W. (1953). *The Making of the Middle Ages*. New Haven: Yale University Press.

—— (1963). *Saint Anselm and His Biographer: A Study of Monastic Life and Thought, 1059–c. 1130*. London: Cambridge University Press.

Southgate, Minoo S. (1984). "Men, Women, and Boys: Love and Sex in the Works of Sa'di." *Iranian Studies* 17:413–52.

Spada, James (1979). *The Spada Report*. New York: Signet.

Spence, Jonathan D. (1984). *The Memory Palace of Matteo Ricci*. New York: Viking.

Spencer, Baldwin, and F. J. Gillin (1927). *The Arunta*. London: Macmillan.

—— (1938). *The Native Tribes of Central Australia*. London: Macmillan.

Spier, Leslie (1930). *Klamath Ethnography*. Berkeley: University of California Press.

—— (1933). *Yuman Tribes of the Gila River*. Chicago: University of Chicago Press.

Spierenberg, Pieter (1984). *The Spectacle of Suffering: Executions and the Evolution of Punishment*. Cambridge: Cambridge University Press.

Spiers, Herb, and Michael Lynch (1977). "The Gay Rights Freud." *Body Politic* (May):9.

Spijker, A.M.J.M. Herman van de (1968). *Die gleichgeschlechtliche Zuneigung*. Olten: Walter.

Spinden, Herbert J. (1928). *Ancient Civilizations of Mexico and Central America*. New York: American Museum of Natural History.

Spindler, George D., and Louise S. Spindler (1957). "American Indian Personality Types and Their Sociocultural Roots." *Annals of the American Academy of Political and Social Science* 311:147–57.

Spiro, Melford E. (1977). *Kinship and Marriage in Burma: A Cultural and Psychodynamic Analysis*. Berkeley: University of California Press.

Spitz, Lewis W. (1984). *The Protestant Reformation, 1517–1559*. New York: Harper and Row.

Spitz, René (1952). "Authority and Masturbation." *Psychoanalytic Quarterly* 21:490–577.

Spitze, Glenna, and Joan Huber (1983). *Sex Stratification: Children, Housework, and Jobs*. New York: Academic.

Spix, Dr. Johann Baptist von, and Carl F. Phil. von Martius (1824). *Travels in Brazil, in the Years 1817–1820*, vol. 2. London: Longman, Hurst, Rees, Orme, Brown and Green.

Sprague, Gregory (1985). "Discovering the Thriving Gay Subculture of Chicago in the 1920s and 1930s." Paper presented to the American Historical Association.

Spratt, P. (1966). *Hindu Culture and Personality*. Bombay: Manaktalas.

Stabiner, Karen (1982). "Tapping the Homosexual Market." *New York Times Magazine*, May 2.

Stanton, Theodore (ed.) (1910). *Reminiscences of Rosa Bonheur*. London: Melrose.

Staves, Susan (1982). "A Few Kind Words for the Fop." *Studies in English Literature* 22:413–28.

Stavorinus, Johan Splinter (1798). *Voyages to the East Indies*. Tr. S. H. Wilcocke. London: G. G. Robinson.

Steakley, James D. (1975). *The Homosexual Emancipation Movement in Germany*. New York: Arno.

—— (1983). "Iconography of a Scandal: Political Cartoons and the Eugglenberg Affair." *Studies in Visual Communication* 9(2):20–51.

Stehling, Thomas (1983). "To Love a Medieval Boy." *Journal of Homosexuality* 8: 151–70.

—— (1984). *Medieval Latin Poems of Male Love and Friendship*. New York: Garland.

Steinberg, Ronnie (1982). *Wages and Hours: Labor and Reform in Twentieth-Century America*. New Brunswick, N.J.: Rutgers University Press.

Steiner, Betty W. (ed.) (1985). *Gender Dysphoria: Development, Research, Management*. New York: Plenum.

Stenton, Doris May (1977). *The English Woman in History*. New York: Schocken. Orig. pub. 1957.

Stephan, G. Edward, and Douglas R. McMullin (1982). "Tolerance of Sexual Nonconformity." *American Sociological Review* 46:411–15.

Stephan, W. G. (1973). "Parental Relationships and Early Social Experiences of Activist Male Homosexuals and Heterosexuals." *Journal of Abnormal Psychology* 82:506–13.

Stephen, Leslie, and Sidney Lee (eds.) (1964). *Dictionary of National Biography*, vol. 10. Cambridge: Melrose.

Stephens, Leslie, and Sidney Lee (1964). *Dictionary of National Biography*, vol. 10. London: Oxford University Press.

Stephens, William N. (1962). *The Oedipus Complex: Cross-Cultural Evidence*. New York: Free Press.

Stern, Mikhail (1979). *Sex in the U.S.S.R.* Tr. Mark Howson and Cary Ryan. New York: Times Books.

Sternberg, Lev (1925). *Divine Election in Primitive Religion*. Göteborg: XXI Congrès International des Américanistes.

—— (1961). "The Sexual Life of the Gilyak." Tr. Chester S. Chard. *Anthropological Papers of the University of Alaska* 10:13–23.

Stevenson, Matilda Coxe (1904). "The Zuñi Indians: Their Mythology, Esoteric Societies, and Ceremonies." *U.S. Bureau of American Ethnology, Twenty-Third Annual Report, 1901–1902*. Washington, D.C.: Government Printing Office.

Steward, Julian H. (1963). "South American Cultures: An Interpretive Summary."
 Pp. 669–772 in Julian H. Steward (ed.), *Handbook of South American Indians*.
 Washington, D.C.: Government Printing Office.

——, and Louis C. Faron (1959). *Native Peoples of South America*. New York:
 McGraw-Hill.

Stewart, Larry (1976). "Freud Before Oedipus: Race and Heredity in the Origins of
 Psychoanalysis." *Journal of the History of Biology* 9:215–28.

Stewart, Omer C. (1942). "Culture Element Distribution: XVIII, Ute-Southern
 Paiute." *Anthropological Records* 6:231–354.

—— (1960). "Homosexuality among American Indians and Other Native Peoples."
 Mattachine Review 6(1):9–15, 6(2):13–19.

Stiefel, Tina (1985). *The Intellectual Revolution in Twelfth-Century Europe*. New York:
 St. Martin's Press.

Stoller, Robert J. (1968). *Sex and Gender*. Vol. 1: *On the Development of Masculinity and
 Femininity*. New York: Science House.

—— (1971). "The Term 'Transvestism'." *Archives of General Psychiatry* 24:230–37.

—— (1972). "Transsexualism and Transvestism." *Psychiatric Annals* 1:6–72.

—— (1976a). "Two Feminized Male American Indians." *Archives of Sexual Behavior*
 5:529–38.

—— (1976b). *Sex and Gender*. Vol. 2: *The Transsexual Experiment*. New York: Jason
 Aronson.

—— (1985). *Observing the Erotic Imagination*. New Haven: Yale University Press.

—— and Gilbert Herdt (1985). "Theories of Origins of Male Homosexuality: A
 Cross-Cultural Look." Pp. 104–34 in Robert Stoller, *Observing the Erotic Imagination*. New Haven: Yale University Press.

Stone, Katherine (1974). "The Origins of Job Structures in the Steel Industry." *Review of Radical Political Economics* 6:113–73.

Stone, Lawrence (1979). *The Family, Sex and Marriage in England, 1500–1800*. Abridged
 ed. New York: Harper and Row.

Stone, Merlin (1976). *When God Was a Woman*. New York: Dial.

Störk, Lothar (1977). "Erotike." Cols. 4–11 in Wolfgang Helck and Wolfhardt Westendorf (eds.), *Lexikon der Ägyptologie*, vol. 2. Wiesbaden: Otto Harrassowitz.

Storms, Michael D. (1978). "Attitudes toward Homosexuality and Femininity in
 Men." *Journal of Homosexuality* 3:257–63.

—— (1979). "Sex Role Identity and Its Relationships to Sex Role Attributes and
 Sex Role Stereotypes." *Journal of Personality and Social Psychology* 37:1779–89.

Strabo (1928). *Geography*, vol. 5. Tr. Howard Leonard Jones. New York: G. P. Putnam's Sons.

Straka, Gerald M., and Lois O. Straka (1973). *The Borzoi History of England*. Vol. 4:
 1640–1815: A Certainty in the Succession. New York: A. A. Knopf.

Strathern, Marilyn (1972). *Women In Between: Females in a Male World: Mount Hagen,
 New Guinea*. New York: Seminar.

Strehlow, Carl (1913). *Die Aranda und Loritja-stämme in Zentral-Australien*, vol. 4, pt.
 2: *Das soziale Leben der Arand- und Loritjastämme*. Frankfurt am Main: Joseph
 Baer.

Streiker, Lowell D., and Gerald S. Stroher (1972). *Religion and the New Majority: Billy Graham: Middle America, and the Politics of the 70s.* New York: Association.

Strömback, Dag (1935). *Sejd: Textsludier i nordisk religionshistoria.* Stockholm: H. Geber.

Strutynski, Udo (1974). "History and Structure in Germanic Mythology: Some Thoughts on Einar Haugen's Critique of Dumezil." Pp. 29–50 in Gerald James Larson (ed.), *Myth in Indo-European Antiquity.* Berkeley: University of California.

Stuard, Susan Mosher (1976). "Introduction." Pp. 1–12 in Susan M. Stuard (ed.), *Women in Medieval Society.* Philadelphia: University of Pennsylvania Press.

Stümke, Hans-Georg, and Rudi Winkler (1981). *Rosa Winkel, Rosa Listen: Homosexuelle und "gesunde Volksempfinden" von Auschwitz bis Heute.* Reinbeck bei Hamburg: Rowohlt.

Suggs, Robert (1966). *Marquesan Sexual Behavior.* New York: Harcourt, Brace and World.

Sulloway, Frank J. (1979). *Freud, Biologist of the Mind: Beyond the Psychoanalytic Legend.* New York: Basic.

Sumner, Colin (1979). *Reading Ideologies: An Investigation into the Marxist Theory of Ideology and Law.* New York: Academic.

Sumner, William Graham (1901). "The Yakuts." *Journal of the Anthropological Institute of Great Britain and Ireland* 31:103.

Surieu, Robert (1967). *Sarv é Naz: An Essay on Love and the Representation of Erotic Themes in Ancient Iran.* Geneva: Nagel.

Susman, Warren I. (1985). *Culture as History: The Transformation of American Society.* New York: Pantheon.

Sussman, George D. (1977). "The Glut of Doctors in Nineteenth-Century France." *Comparative Studies in Society and History* 19:287–304.

Sutherland, Edwin H. (1961). *White Collar Crime.* New York: Holt, Rinehart and Winston. Orig. pub. 1949.

Sutlive, Vinson H., Jr. (1976). "The Iban *Manang:* An Alternative Route to Abnormality." Pp. 64–71 in G. N. Appell (ed.), *Studies in Borneo Societies: Social Process and Anthropological Explanation.* De Kalb: Center for Southeast-Asian Studies, Northern Illinois University.

Swain, Joseph Ward (1916). *The Hellenic Origins of Christian Asceticism.* Ph.D. dissertation: Columbia University.

Swanton, John R. (1922). *Early History of the Creek Indians and Their Neighbors.* U.S. Bureau of American Ethnology Annual Report 43. Washington, D.C.: Government Printing Office.

——— (1929). *Social Organization and Social Usages of Indians of the Creek Confederacy.* U.S. Bureau of American Ethnology Annual Report 42. Washington, D.C.: Government Printing Office.

Sweet, Roxanna Thayer (1975). *Political and Social Action in Homophile Organizations.* New York: Arno.

Swindler, Mary Hamilton (1913). *Cretan Elements in the Cults and Ritual of Apollo.* Bryn Mawr, Pa.: Bryn Mawr College.

Sylvestre, Paul-François (1983). *Bougerie en Nouvelle France.* Montreal: Editions Asticou.

Syme, Ronald (1968). *Ammianus and the Historiae Augusta.* London: Oxford University Press.

Symonds, John Addington (1975). *A Problem in Greek Ethics.* New York: Arno. Orig. pub. 1883.

Szasz, Thomas (1961). *The Myth of Mental Illness.* New York: Delta.

—— (1970). *The Manufacture of Madness.* New York: Delta.

Szemerényi, Oswald (1977). "Studies in the Kinship Terminology of the Indo-European Languages, with Special Reference to Indian, Iranian, Greek, and Latin." *Acta Iranica* 7:1–240. Leiden: E. J. Brill.

Takagi, Paul (1975). "The Walnut Street Jail: A Penal Reform to Centralize the Powers of the State." *Federal Probation* (Dec.):18–26.

Talbot, Eugene S. (1899). *Degeneracy—Its Causes, Signs and Results.* London: Walter Scott.

Talbot, P. Amaury (1926). *The Peoples of Southern Nigeria,* vol. 3. London: Oxford University Press.

—— (1927). *Some Nigerian Fertility Cults.* Loda: Oxford University Press.

Talbot, Serge (1963). "Les tabous sexuels d l'Islam." *Arcadie* 118:451–59.

Talley, Jeannine E. (1974). "Runes, Mandrakes, and Gallows." Pp. 157–68 in Gerald James Larson (ed.), *Myth in Indo-European Antiquity.* Berkeley: University of California Press.

Talmon, Shenaryahu (1970). "The Old Testament Text." Pp. 159–99 in *Cambridge History of the Bible,* vol. 1. Cambridge: Cambridge University Press.

Tamari, Meir (1987). *"With All Your Possessions": Jewish Ethics and Economic Life.* New York: Free Press.

Tannahill, Reay (1980). *Sex in History.* New York: Stein and Day.

Tanner, John (1956). *A Narrative of the Captivity and Adventures of John Tanner.* Ed. Edwin James. Minneapolis: Ross and Haines.

Tarachow, Sidney (1955). "St. Paul and Early Christianity: A Psychoanalytic and Historical Study." Pp. 223–81 in Warner Muensterberger (ed.), *Psychoanalysis and the Social Sciences,* vol. 4. New York: International Universities Press.

Tardieu, Dr. Ambroise (1857). *Etude médico-légale sur les attentats aux moeurs.* Paris: J.-B. Baillière.

Tarnowsky, Benjamin (1886). *Die krankhaften Erscheinungen des Geschlechtsinnes: Eine forensisch-psychiatrische Studien.* Berlin: Hirschwald.

Tatian (1982). *Discourse to the Greeks.* Tr. Molly Whittaker. Oxford: Clarendon.

Tatlock, J.S.P. (1950). *The Legendary History of Britain.* Berkeley: University of California Press.

Tauxier, Louis (1912). *Le Noirs du Soudan: Pays Mossi et Gourounni.* Paris: Emile LaRose.

Taylor, Barbara (1979). "'The Men Are as Bald as Their Masters . . .': Socialism, Feminism, and Sexual Antagonism in the London Tailoring Trade in the Early 1830s." *Feminist Studies* 5:7–40.

Taylor, Clark (1987). "Precolumbian and Colonial Mexican Syncretism and Homosexuality." Pp. 4–21 in Stephen O. Murray (ed.), *Male Homosexuality in Central and South America*. Gai Saber Monograph 5. New York: GAU-NY.

Taylor, G. Rattray (1954). *Sex in History*. New York: Vanguard.

——— (1965). "Historical and Mythological Aspects of Homosexuality." Pp. 140–65 in Judd Marmor (ed.), *Sexual Inversion: The Multiple Roots of Homosexuality*. New York: Basic.

——— (1974). *The Angel-Makers: A Study in the Psychological Origins of Historical Change*. New York: E. P. Dutton.

Taylor, William, and Christopher Lasch (1963). "Two 'Kindred Spirits': Sorority and Family in New England, 1839–1846." *New England Quarterly* 36:23–41.

Tcherikover, Victor (1959). *Hellenistic Civilization and the Jews*. Tr. S. Applebaum. Philadelphia: Jewish Publication Society of America.

Teal, Donn (1971). *The Gay Militants*. New York: Stein and Day.

Teit, James A. (1930). *The Salishan Tribes of the Western Plateau*. U.S. Bureau of American Ethnology, Annual Report No. 45. Washington, D.C.: Government Printing Office.

Teixidor, J. (1977). *The Pagan God: Popular Religion in the Greco-Roman Near East*. Princeton, N.J.: Princeton University Press.

Tentler, Thomas N. (1977). *Sin and Confession on the Eve of the Reformation*. Princeton, N.J.: Princeton University Press.

Terrell, John (1986). *Prehistory in the Pacific Islands: A Study of Variation in Language, Customs, and Human Biology*. Cambridge: Cambridge University Press.

Terrien, Samuel (1970). "The Omphalos Myth and Hebrew Religion." *Vetus Testamentum* 20:326–27.

Tertullian (1954). *Opera*. Turnholt: Brepols.

Tessman, Günter (1930). *Die Indianer Nordost-Perús*. Hamburg: Friederichsen, de Gruyter.

——— (1959). *The Fang Peoples: An Ethnographic Monograph on a West African Group*. Tr. Richard Neuse. New Haven, Conn.: HRAF.

Testart, A. (1982). "The Significance of Food Storage among Hunter-Gatherers." *Current Anthropology* 23:523–38.

Te Velde, H. (1967). *Seth, God of Confusion*. Leiden: E. J. Brill.

Thaussig, Gertrud, and Tradl Kerszt-Kratschman (1969). *Das grosse Ägyptische Totenbuch (Papyrus Reinisch)*. Cairo: El-Masry.

Theocritus (1950). *Theocritus*, vol. 1. Tr. A.S.F. Gow. Cambridge: Cambridge University Press.

Thesiger, Wilfred (1959). *Arabian Sands*. New York: E. P. Dutton.

Thieuloy, J. (1974). *L'Inde des grand chemins*. Paris: Gallimard.

Thomas, D. Winston (1960). "Kelebh 'Dog': Its Origin and Some Usages of it in the Old Testament." *Vetus Testamentum* 10:426.

Thomas, Elizabeth M. (1959). *The Harmless People*. New York: A. A. Knopf.

Thomas, Keith (1971). *Religion and the Decline of Magic: Studies in Popular Beliefs in Sixteenth and Seventeenth Century England*. London: Weidenfeld and Nicolson.

Thompson, E. A. (1969). *The Goths in Spain*. London: Oxford University Press.

Thompson, E. P. (1963). *The Making of the English Working Class*. New York: Vintage.

—— (1972). " 'Rough Music': Le charivari anglais." *Annales E.S.C.* 27:285–312.

—— (1978). *The Poverty of Theory and Other Essays.* New York: Monthly Review Press.

Thompson, J.E.S. (1966). *The Rise and Fall of Maya Civilization.* Norman: University of Oklahoma Press.

Thompson, Norman L., Jr., David M. Schwartz, Boyd R. McCandless, and David A. Edwards (1973). "Parent-Child Relationships and Sexual Identity in Male and Female Homosexuals and Heterosexuals." *Journal of Consulting and Clinical Psychology* 41:120–27.

Thompson, Roger (1974). *Women in Stuart England and America: A Comparative Study.* Boston: Routledge and Kegan Paul.

—— (1979). *Unfit for Modest Ears: A Study of Pornographic, Obscene and Bawdy Works Written or Published in England in the Second Half of the Seventeenth Century.* London: Macmillan.

Thomson, George (1955). *Studies in Ancient Greek Society.* Vol. 2: *The First Philosophers.* London: Lawrence and Wishart.

—— (1965). *Studies in Ancient Greek Society.* Vol. 1: *The Prehistoric Aegean.* New York: Citadel.

Thoreau, Henry David (1961). *A Week on the Concord and Merrimack Rivers.* Cambridge, Mass.: Riverside.

Thwaites, Reuben Gold (1900). *The Jesuit Relations and Allied Documents.* Vol. 59: *Travels and Explorations of the Jesuit Missionaries in New France, 1610–1791, Lower Canada, Illinois, Ottowa, 1673–1677.* Cleveland: Burrows Brothers.

Tielman, Rob (1982). *Homoseksualiteit in Nederland.* Amsterdam: Boom, Meppel.

Tigar, Jeffrey H. (1982). *The Evolution of Gilgamesh.* Philadelphia: University of Pennsylvania Press.

Titiev, Mischa (1951). *Araucanian Culture in Transition.* Ann Arbor: University of Michigan Press.

Tixier, Victor (1940). *Travels on the Osage Prairies.* Tr. Albert J. Salvan. Norman: University of Oklahoma Press.

Tomasic, Dinko (1945). "Personality Development of Dinaric Warriors." *Psychiatry* 8:449–93.

—— (1948). *Personality and Culture in Eastern European Politics.* New York: George W. Stewart.

Tompkins, Peter (1962). *The Eunuch and the Virgin: A Study of Curious Customs.* New York: Clarkson N. Potter.

Toorn, K. van der (1985). *Sin and Sanction in Israel and Mesopotamia: A Comparative Study.* Assen: Van Gorcum.

Topley, M. (1954). "Chinese Women's Vegetarian Houses in Singapore." *Journal of the Malayan Branch of the Royal Asiatic Society* 27(1).

Torday, E., and T. A. Joyce (1905). "Notes on the Ethnography of the Ba-Mbala." *Journal of the Anthropological Institute of Great Britain and Ireland* 35:398–426.

Trautmann, Thomas R. (1981). *Dravidian Kinship.* Cambridge: Cambridge University Press.

Treasure, G. R. (1972). *Cardinal Richelieu and the Development of Absolutism.* London: Adam and Charles Black.

Tregear, Edward (1969). *The Maori-Polynesian Comparative Dictionary.* Oosterhout, N.B.: Anthropological Publications.

Trevisan, João (1986). *Perverts in Paradise.* Tr. Martin Foreman. London: G.M.P.

Trexler, Richard D. (1981). "La prostitution florentine au XVᵉ siècle: patronages et clienteles." *Annales E.S.C.* 36:983–1015.

Trezenem, Edouard (1936). "Notes ethnographiques sur les tribus Fan du Moyen Ogooné (Gabon)." *Journal de la Société des Africanistes* 6:65–93.

Trimberger, Ellen Kay (1983). "Feminism, Men, and Modern Love." Pp. 131–52 in Ann Snitow, Christine Stansell, and Sharon Thompson (eds.), *Powers of Desire: The Politics of Sexuality.* New York: Monthly Review Press.

Trimingham, J. Spencer (1979). *Christianity among the Arabs in Pre-Islamic Times.* London: Longman.

Tripp, C. A. (1975). *The Homosexual Matrix.* New York: Signet.

Trowbridge, Charles C. (1938). *Meearmeear Traditions.* University of Michigan Museum of Anthropology Occasional Contributions, vol. 7. Ann Arbor: University of Michigan Press.

Trudgill, Eric (1976). *Madonnas and Magdalens: the Origins and Development of Victorian Sexual Attitudes.* New York: Holmes and Meier.

Trumbach, Randolph (1977). "London's Sodomites: Homosexual Behavior and Western Culture in the Eighteenth Century." *Journal of Social History* 11:1–33.

——— (1978). *The Rise of The Egalitarian Family: Aristocratic Kinship and Domestic Relations in Eighteenth-Century England.* New York: Academic.

——— (1984). "Sodomitical Subcultures, Sodomitical Roles, and the Gender Revolution of the Eighteenth Century: The Recent Historiography." *Eighteenth-Century Life* 9:109–21.

——— (1987). "The Birth of the Queen: Sodomy and the Emergence of Gender Inequality in Modern Culture, 1660–1750." Unpublished paper.

Tsai, Yung-mei, Peter L. Heller, and H. Paul Chalfont (n.d.). "Protestant Fundamentalism and Support for the Moral Majority Political Platform: Effects of Anomia." Unpublished paper, Texas Tech University.

Tsang, Daniel (ed.) (1981). *The Age Taboo: Gay Male Sexuality, Power and Consent.* London: Gay Men's Press.

Tschopik, Harry, Jr. (1946). "The Aymara." Pp. 501–73 in Julian H. Steward (ed.), *Handbook of South American Indians*, vol. 2. Washington, D.C.: Government Printing Office.

Tüllman, Adolf (1961). *Das Liebesleben der Natürvolker.* Stuttgart: Hans Güntherverlag.

Turkle, Sherry (1978). *Psycho-Analytic Politics: The French Reception of Freud.* New York: Basic.

Turnbull, Colin M. (1965). *Wayward Servants: The Two Worlds of the African Pygmies.* Garden City, N.Y.: Natural History Press.

Turnbull, John (1813). *A Voyage Round the World, in the Years 1800, 1801, 1802, 1803 and 1804.* 2d ed. London: A. Maxwell.

Turner, Bryan (1974). *Weber and Islam: A Critical Study.* London: Routledge and Kegan Paul.

Turner, Frank M. (1974). *Between Science and Religion: The Reaction to Scientific Naturalism in Late Victorian England.* New Haven: Yale University Press.

Turville-Petre, Edward O. G. (1964). *Myth and Religion of the North: The Religion of Ancient Scandinavia.* New York: Holt, Rinehart and Winston.

Tyler, Parker (1977). *A Pictorial History of Sex in Films.* Secaucus, N.J.: Citadel.

Tyrrell, Ian R. (1979). *Sobering Up: From Temperance to Prohibition in Antebellum America, 1800–1860.* Westport, Conn.: Greenwood.

Ullman, Walter (1962). *The Growth of Papal Government in the Middle Ages.* 2d ed. London: Methuen.

——— (1969). *The Carolingian Renaissance and the Idea of Kingship.* London: Methuen.

Ulrich, Laurel Thater (1979). "Vertuous Women Found: New England Ministerial Literature, 1668–1735." Pp. 58–80 in Nancy F. Cott and Elizabeth H. Pleck (ed.), *A Heritage of Her Own: Toward a New Social History of American Women.* New York: Simon and Schuster.

Underhill, Ruth M. (1939). *Papago Women.* New York: Holt, Rinehart and Winston.

Ungaretti, John R. (1978). "Pederasty, Heroism, and the Family in Classical Greece." *Journal of Homosexuality* 3:291–300.

——— (1982). "De-Moralizing Morality: Where Dover's *Greek Homosexuality* Leaves Us." *Journal of Homosexuality* 8:1–17.

Ure, P. N. (1951). *Justinian and His Age.* Baltimore: Penguin.

U.S. Bureau of the Census (1909). *A Century of Growth.* Washington, D.C.: Government Printing Office.

Ussel, Jos van (1977). *Sexualunterdrückung: Geschichte der Sexualfeindschaft.* Gressen: Focus.

Vaerting, Mathilde and Mathias Vaerting (1923). *The Dominant Sex: A Study in the Sociology of Sex Differentiation.* Tr. Eden and Cedar Paul. New York: George H. Doran.

Valmiki (1978). *The Ramayana.* Tr. Makhan Lal Sen. New Delhi: Munshiram Manoharlal.

Van Baal, Jan (1966). *Dema: Description and Analysis of Merindanim Culture (New Guinea).* The Hague: Martinus Nijhoff.

——— (1984). "The Dialects of Sex in Marind-Anim Culture." Pp. 167–210 in Gilbert Herdt (ed.), *Ritualized Homosexuality in Melanesia.* Berkeley: University of California Press.

Van Gennep, Arnold (1960). *The Rites of Passage.* Tr. Monika B. Vizedom and Gabrielle L. Caffee. Chicago: University of Chicago Press. Orig. pub. 1909.

Vanggaard, Thorkil (1972). *Phallos: A Symbol and Its History in the Male World.* New York: International Universities Press.

Van Straten, N. H. (1983). *Concepts of Health, Disease and Vitality in Traditional Chinese Society: A Psychological Interpretation.* Wiesbaden: Franz Steiner.

Varley, H. Paul, with Ivan and Nobuko Morris (1970). *The Samurai.* London: Widenfeld and Nicolson.

Vasiliev, A. A. (1950). *Justin the First: An Introduction to the Epoch of Justinian the Great.* Cambridge, Mass.: Harvard University Press.

Vellois, H. V. (1961). "The Social Life of Early Man: The Evidence of Skeletons." Pp. 214–35 in S. L. Washburne (ed.), *Social Life of Early Man.* Chicago: Aldine.

Venette, Nicolas (1688). *Tableau d'amour considéré dans l'estat du mariage.* Parma: Chez Franc d'Amour.

—— (1696). *De la generation de l'homme*. Cologne: Claude Jolly.

Verbruggen, J. F. (1977). *The Art of Warfare in Western Europe during the Middle Ages*. Amsterdam: North-Holland.

Vercoutter, Jean (1954). *Essai sur les relations entre Egyptiens et Prehéllenes*. Paris: A. Maisonneuve.

Vermaseren, Maarten Jesef (1977). *Cybele and Attis: The Myth and the Cult*. London: Thames and Hudson.

Vernadsky, George (1938). "The Scope and Contents of Chingis Khan's Yassa." *Harvard Journal of Asiatic Studies* 3:337–60.

Verstraete, Beert C. (1979). "Homosexuality in Ancient Greek and Roman Civilization: A Critical Bibliography." *Journal of Homosexuality* 3:79–89.

—— (1980). "Slavery and the Social Dynamics of Male Homosexual Relations in Ancient Rome." *Journal of Homosexuality* 5:227–36.

—— (1982). *Homosexuality in Ancient Greek and Roman Civilization: A Critical Bibliography with Supplement*. Toronto: Canadian Gay Archives.

Veyne, Paul (1982). "L'homosexualité à Rome." *Communications* 35:26–33.

—— (1985). "Homosexuality in Ancient Rome." Pp. 26–35 in Philippe Ariès and André Bejin (eds.), *Western Sexuality: Practice and Precept in Past and Present Times*. Tr. Anthony Béjin. New York: Basil Blackwell.

Veze, Raoul (1921). *Baisers d'Orient*. Paris: Bibliothèque des Curieuses.

Vice Commission of Chicago (1911). *The Social Evil in Chicago: A Study of Existing Conditions, with Recommendations*. Chicago: Gunthrop-Warren.

Vicinus, Martha (1983). "Distance and Desire: English School-Girl Friendships. 1870–1920." Pp. 389–403 in *Among Men, Among Women*. Amsterdam: Conference papers.

—— (1985). *Independent Women: Work and Community for Single Women, 1850–1920*. Chicago: University of Chicago Press.

Villermé, Louis-René (1824). *Rapport sur l'état actuel des prisons*. Paris.

Vink, J. G. (1969). "The Date and Origin of the Priestly Code in the Old Testament." Pp. 1–144 in J. G. Vink et al. (eds.), *The Priestly Code and Seven Other Studies*. Leiden: E. J. Brill.

Vööbus, Arthur (1951). *Celibacy, a Requirement for Admission to Baptism in the Early Christian Church*. Stockholm: Estonian Theological Society in Exile.

—— (1960a). *History of Asceticism in the Syrian Orient*, vol. 2. Louvain: Secretariat du Corpus SCO.

—— (1960b). *Syriac and Arabic Documents Regarding Legislation Relation to Asceticism*. Stockholm: Papers of the Estonian Theological Society in Exile No. 11.

Voss, Jerome A. (1980). *Tribal Emergence during the Neolithic of Northwestern Europe*. Ph.D. dissertation, University of Michigan.

Vries, J. de (1981). "Patterns of Urbanization in Preindustrial Europe, 1500–1800." Pp. 77–109 in H. Schmal (ed.), *Patterns of European Urbanization since 1500*. London: Croom Helm.

Vries, Jan de (1933). *The Problem of Loki*. FF Communications No. 110. Helsinki: Societas Scientiarum Fennica.

Wagley, Charles (1977). *Welcome of Tears: The Tapirapé Indians of Central Brazil*. New York: Oxford University Press.

Wagner, Günter (1949). *The Bantu of North Kavirondo.* vol. 1. London: Oxford University Press.

Wagner, Peter (1985). *Eros Revisited: A Study of Eighteenth-Century Erotica.* London: Secker and Warburg.

—— (1987). "The Discourse on Sex—or Sex as Discourse: Eighteenth Century Medical and Paramedical Erotica." In George S. Rousseau and Roy Porter (eds.), *Liberty's a Glorious Feast: Sexual Underworlds of the Enlightenment.* Manchester, University of Manchester Press.

Wagner, Thomas (1977). "Missverstandis und Vurorteil: Homosexualität in theologischen Werken des 19. Jahrhunderts." Pp. 73–95 in Joachim S. Hohmann (ed.), *Der unterdrückte Sexus: Historische Texte und Kommentäre zur Homosexualität.* Berlin: Verlag Andreas Achenbach Lollar.

Waitz, Theodore (1864). *Anthropologie der Naturvölker,* vol. 4. Leipzig: F. Fleischer.

Wakefield, Walter (1974). *Heresy, Crusade and Inquisition in Southern France.* Berkeley: University of California Press.

Wales, H. G. Quaritch (1957). *Prehistory and Religion in South-East Asia.* London: Bernard Quaritch.

Waley, Daniel (1969). *The Italian City-Republics.* New York: McGraw-Hill.

Walker, Benjamin (1968). *The Hindu World: An Encyclopedic Survey of Hinduism.* 2 vols. New York: Praeger.

Wallace, Anthony F. C. (1971). "Handsome Lake and the Decline of the Iroquois Matriarchate." Pp. 367–76 in Francis L. K. Hsu (ed.), *Kinship and Culture Change.* Chicago: Aldine.

Wallace-Hadrill, Andrew (1982). "The Golden Age and Sin in Augustan Ideology." *Past and Present* 95:19–36.

Wallace-Hadrill, J. M. (1967). *The Barbarian West, 400–1000.* London: Hutchison University Library.

Wallis, R., and R. Bland (1979). "Purity in Danger: A Survey of Participants in a Moral Crusade Rally." *British Journal of Sociology* 30:188–205.

Walmsley, Roy (1978). "Indecency between Males and the Sexual Act Offences Act 1967." *Criminal Law Review* 1978:400–407.

Walter, Fritz H. (1921). *Etruskische Malerei.* Halle (Saale): Max Niemeyer.

Walter, Richard D. (1956). "What Became of the Degenerate? A Brief History of the Concept." *Journal of the History of Medicine* 11:422–49.

Walters, Ronald (1974). *Primers for Prudery? Sexual Advice for Victorian America.* Englewood Cliffs, N.J.: Prentice-Hall.

Walzer, Michael (1974). *The Revolution of the Saints: A Study in the Origins of Radical Politics.* New York: Atheneum.

Ward, Donald J. (1970a). "The Threefold Death: An Indo-European Trifunctional Sacrifice." Pp. 123–42 in Jaan Puhvel (ed.), *Myth and Law among the Indo-Europeans.* Berkeley: University of California Press.

—— (1970b). "The Separate Functions of the Indo-European Divine Twins." Pp. 193–200 in Jaan Puhvel (ed.), *Myth and Law among the Indo-Europeans.* Berkeley: University of California Press.

Ward, Edward (1709). *The Secret History of Clubs; Particularly the Kit-Cat, Beef-Stake,*

Vertuosos, Quacks, Knights of the Golden-Fleece, Florists, Beaux, Etc. With their Original; And the Characters of the Most Noted Members Thereof. London: Privately printed.

Warren, Carol A. B. (1974). *Identity and Community in the Gay World.* New York: Wiley.

Watkins, Oscar D. (1920). *A History of Penance.* New York: Longmans, Green.

Watson-Franke, Maria-Barbara (1974). "A Woman's Profession in Guajire Culture: Weaving." *Antropologica* 37:24–40.

Watt, Ian (1957). *The Rise of the Novel: Studies in Defoe, Richardson and Fielding.* Berkeley: University of California Press.

Weber, Max (1946). *From Max Weber: Essays in Sociology.* Tr. H. H. Gerth and C. Wright Mills. New York: Oxford University Press.

——— (1958). *The Religion of India: The Sociology of Hinduism and Buddhism.* Tr. Hans H. Gerth and Don Martindale. New York: Free Press.

——— (1968). *Economy and Society.* Ed. by Guenther Roth and Claus Wittich. New York: Bedminster.

Webster, Hutton (1948). *Magic: A Sociological Study.* Stanford: Stanford University Press.

Wedgewood, Camilla H. (1943). "Notes on the Marshall Islands." *Oceania* 13:1–23.

Weeks, Jeffrey (1977a). *Coming Out: Homosexual Politics in Britain from the Nineteenth Century to the Present.* Totowa, N.J.: Barnes and Noble.

——— (1977b). "Havelock Ellis and the Politics of Sex Reform." Pp. 139–85 in Sheila Rowbotham and Jeffrey Weeks (eds.), *Socialism and the New Life: The Personal and Sexual Politics of Edward Carpenter and Havelock Ellis.* London: Pluto.

——— (1980). "Capitalism and the Organization of Sex." Pp. 11–20 in Gay Left Collective (ed.), *Homosexuality: Power and Politics.* London: Allison and Busby.

——— (1981a). *Sex, Politics and Society: The Regulation of Sexuality since 1800.* London: Longman.

——— (1981b). "Discourse, Desire, and Sexual Deviance: Some Problems in a History of Homosexuality." In Ken Plummer (ed.), *The Making of the Modern Homosexual.* London: Hutchinson.

——— (1985). *Sexuality and Its Discontents: Meanings, Myths and Modern Sexualities.* London: Routledge and Kegan Paul.

Weeks, John (1909). "Anthropological Notes on the Bangala of the Upper Congo River (Part 2)." *Journal of the Royal Anthropological Institute of Great Britain and Ireland* 39:416–59.

Weigert-Vowinkel, Edith (1938). "The Cult and Mythology of the Magna Mater from the Standpoint of Psychoanalysis." *Psychiatry* 1:347–78.

Weinberg, George (1973). *Society and the Healthy Homosexual.* Garden City, N.Y.: Anchor.

Weinberg, Martin S., and Colin J. Williams (1974). *Male Homosexuals: Their Problems and Adaptation.* Oxford: Oxford University Press.

——— (1975). "Gay Baths and the Social Organization of Impersonal Sex." *Social Problems* 23:124–36.

Weinberg, Thomas (1983). *Gay Men, Gay Selves.* New York: Irvington.

Weinberger, Linda E., and Jim Millham (1979). "Attitudinal Homophobia and Support of Traditional Sex Roles." *Journal of Homosexuality* 4:237–46.

Weininger, Otto (1903). *Geschlecht und Charakter: Eine prinzipielle Untersuchung.* Vienna: Wilhelm Braumueller.

—— (1906). *Sex and Character.* New York: G. P. Putnam's Sons.

Weinrich, James (1976). *Human Reproductive Strategy.* Ph.D. dissertation, Harvard University.

—— (1987). *Sexual Landscapes: Why We Are What We Are, Why We Love Whom We Love.* New York: Charles Scribner's Sons.

Weinstein, Donald (1970). *Savonarola and Florence: Prophecy and Patriotism in the Renaissance.* Princeton, N.J.: Princeton University Press.

Weinstein, James (1968). *The Corporate Ideal in the Liberal State, 1900–1918.* Boston: Beacon.

Weir, Anthony, and James Jerman (1986). *Images of Lust: Sexual Carvings on Medieval Churches.* London: B. T. Batsford.

Weiser-Aall, Lily (1927). *Altgermanische Jünglingsweihen und Männerbünde.* Bühl (Baden): Konkordia.

Weisweiler, Josef (1933). "Beiträge zur Bedeutungsentwicklung germanischer Wörter für sittliche Begriffen." *Indogermanische Forschungen* 41:16–79.

Weisz, George (1978). "The Politics of Medical Professionalization in France, 1845–1848." *Journal of Social History* 12:1–30.

Welch, Stuart Cary (1979). *Wonders of the Age: Masterpieces of Early Safavid Paintings, 1501–1576.* Cambridge, Mass.: Fogg Art Museum.

Wellhausen, Julius (1885). *Prolegomena to the History of Israel.* Edinburgh: A. and C. Black.

Wells, Anna Mary (1978). *Miss Marks and Miss Woolley.* Boston: Houghton Mifflin.

Welter, Barbara (1966). "The Cult of True Womanhood, 1820–1860." *American Quarterly* 18:157–74.

—— (1976). *Dimity Convictions: The American Woman in the Nineteenth Century.* Athens: Ohio University Press.

Weltfish, Gene (1971). "The Plains Indians: Their Continuity in History and Their Indian Identity." Pp. 200–227 in Eleanor Burke Leacock and Nancy O. Lurie (eds.), *North American Indians in Historical Perspective.* New York: Random House.

Wemple, Suzanne Fonay (1981). *Women in Frankish Society: Marriage and the Cloister, 500–900.* Philadelphia: University of Pennsylvania Press.

Wenley, R. M. (1963). *Stoicism and Its Influence.* New York: Cooper Square.

Werner, B. (n.d.). *Indisches Liebesleben.* Berlin: Peter J. Oestergaard.

Werner, Dennis (1979). "A Cross-Cultural Perspective on Theory and Research on Male Homosexuality." *Journal of Homosexuality* 4:345–62.

Westendorf, Wolfhardt (1977a). "Homosexualität." Cols. 1272–74 in Wolfgang Helck and Wolfhardt Westendorf (eds.), *Lexikon der Ägyptologie,* vol. 2. Wiesbaden: Otto Harrassowitz.

—— (1977b). "Erotik." Cols. 4–11 in Wolfgang Helck and Wolfhardt Westendorf (eds.), *Lexikon der Ägyptologie,* vol. 2. Wiesbaden: Otto Harrassowitz.

—— (1977c). "Götter, androgyne." Cols. 633–35 in Wolfgang Helck and Wolfhardt Westendorf (eds.), *Lexikon der Ägyptologie*, vol. 2. Wiesbaden: Otto Harrassowitz.

Westermarck, Edward (1917). *The Origin and Development of the Moral Ideas*, vol. 2. Rev. ed. London: Macmillan.

—— (1921). *The History of Human Marriage*, vol. 1. London: Macmillan.

—— (1926). *Ritual and Belief in Morocco*, vol. 1. London: Macmillan.

Westphal, Karl Friedrich Otto (1869). "Die konträre Sexualempfindung: Symptom eines neuropathologischen (psychopathischen) Zustandes." *Archiv für Psychiatrie und Nervenkrankheiten* 2:73–108.

Wettley, Annemarie (1953). *August Forel, ein Arztleben im Zwiespalt seiner Zeit*. Salzburg: O. Müller.

—— and W. Leibbrand. (1959). *Von der "Psychopathia Sexualis" zur Sexualwissenschaft*. Stuttgart: Enke.

Weyer, Edward, Jr. (1961). *Primitive Peoples Today*. Garden City, N.Y.: Doubleday.

Whisman, Vera (1986). "The Social Construction of Homosexual Identity." Paper presented to the American Sociological Association.

Whitam, Frederick L. (1987). "Bayot and Callboy in the Philippines." Pp. 452–79 in Stephen O. Murray (ed.), *Cultural Diversities and Homosexualities*. New York: Irvington.

——, and Robin M. Mathy (1985). *Male Homosexuality in Four Societies: Brazil, Guatemala, the Philippines and the United States*. New York: Praeger.

White, J. E. Manchip (1953). *Ancient Egypt*. New York: Thomas Y. Crowell.

Whitehead, Harriet (1981). "The Bow and the Burden Strap: A New Look at Institutionalized Homosexuality in Native North America." Pp. 80–115 in Sherry B. Ortner and Harriet Whitehead (eds.), *Sexual Meanings: The Cultural Construction of Gender and Sexuality*. Cambridge: Cambridge University Press.

Whiting, John M. (1941). *Becoming a Kwoma*. New Haven: Yale University Press.

——, Richard Kluckhohn and Albert Anthony (1958). "The Function of Male Initiation Ceremonies at Puberty." Pp. 359–70 in Eleanor Maccoby, T. M. Newcomb, and E. L. Hartley (eds.), *Readings in Social Psychology*, 3d ed. New York: Henry Holt.

Whyte, Martin King (1978). *The Status of Women in Preindustrial Societies*. Princeton, N.J.: Princeton University Press.

Wickler, Wolfgang (1972). *The Sexual Code: The Social Behavior of Animals and Men*. Garden City, N.Y.: Doubleday.

Wickliffe, Ron (1981). "Queerbashers Meet Resistance in the Streets of San Francisco." *WIN* (Aug. 31):15–20.

Widengren, Geo (1969). *Der Feudalismus in alten Iran: Männerbund, Gefolgswesen, Feudalismus in der iranischen Gesselschaft im Hinblick auf die indogermanischen Verhältnisse*. Cologne: Westdeutscher Verlag.

—— (1977). "The Persian Period." Pp. 489–538 in John H. Hayes and J. Maxwell Miller (eds.), *Israelite and Judaean History*. Philadelphia: Westminster.

Wiebe, Robert H. (1962). *Businessmen and Reform: A Study of the Progressive Movement*. Cambridge, Mass.: Harvard University Press.

—— (1967). *The Search for Order, 1877–1920*. New York: Hill and Wang.

Wied, Prinz Maximilien zu (1839). *Reise in das innere Nord Amerika in den Jahren 1832 bis 1834.* Coblenz: Hoelscher.

Wiedeman, G. H. (1962). "Survey of Psychoanalytic Literature on Overt Male Homosexuality." *Journal of the American Psychoanalytic Association* 10:386–409.

Wiedemann, Thomas (1981). *Greek and Roman Slavery.* Baltimore: Johns Hopkins University Press.

Wiener, Leo (1915). *Commentary to the Germanic Laws and Medieval Documents.* Cambridge, Mass.: Harvard University Press.

Wikan, Unni (1977). "Man Becomes Woman: Transsexualism in Oman as a Key to Gender Roles." *Man* 12:304–19.

Wikander, Stig (1938). *Der arische Männerbund: Studien zur indoiranische Sprach- und Religionsgeschichte.* Lund: H. Olson.

——— (1946). *Feuer priester in Kleinasien und Iran.* Lund: C.W.K. Gleerup.

Wilbert, Johannes (1972). *Survivors of Eldorado: Four Indian Cultures of South America.* New York: Praeger.

Wilken, G. A. (1884). *Das Matriarchat (Das Mutterrecht) bei den Alten Arabern.* Leipzig: Otto Schulze.

Wilkenson, L. P. (1978). "Classical Approaches IV: Homosexuality." *Encounter* 51:20–31.

Willens, Michele (1986). "Lesbian at War." *New York Life* (July 10):37.

Willetts, R. F. (1962). *Cretan Cults and Festivals.* New York: Barnes and Noble.

Williams, Bruce (1982). "Homosexuality and Christianity: A Review Discussion." *Thomist* 46:609–25.

Williams, Colin J., and Martin S. Weinberg (1971). *Homosexuals and the Military: A Study of Less than Honorable Discharge.* New York: Harper and Row.

Williams, E. N. (1962). *Life in Georgian England.* London: B. T. Batsford.

Williams, F. E. (1936). *Papuans of the Trans-Fly.* Oxford: Clarendon.

Williams, Gordon (1968). *Tradition and Originality in Roman Poetry.* London: Oxford University Press.

Williams, J. H. (1977). *Psychology of Women: Behavior in a Biosocial Context.* New York: W. W. Norton.

Williams, Walter L. (1985). "Sex and Shamanism: The Making of a Hawaiian Mahu." *Advocate,* Apr. 2.

——— (1986). *The Spirit and the Flesh: Sexual Diversity in American Indian Culture.* Boston: Beacon.

Williamson, Robert Wood (1924). *The Social and Political Systems of Central Polynesia,* vol. 2. Cambridge: Cambridge University Press.

Wilson, Andrew (1876). *The Abode of Snow: Observations on a Journey from Chinese Tibet to the Indian Caucuses, Through the Upper Valleys of the Himalaya.* Edinburgh: William Blackwood and Sons.

Wilson, Edward O. (1978). *On Human Nature.* Cambridge, Mass.: Harvard University Press.

Wilson, Glenn D. (1987). "An Ethological Approach to Sexual Deviation." Pp. 84–115 in Glenn D. Wilson (ed.), *Variant Sexuality: Research and Theory.* Baltimore: Johns Hopkins University Press.

Wilson, James (1799). *A Missionary Voyage to the Southern Pacific Ocean 1796–98 in the Ship "Duff."* London: T. Chapman.

Wilson, John A. (1958). "The Instruction of Amen-em-Opet." Pp. 237–43 in James B. Pritchard (ed.), *The Ancient Near East.* vol. 1. Princeton, N.J.: Princeton University Press.

Wilson, Monica (1951). *Good Company: A Study of Nyakyusa Age-Villages.* Boston: Beacon.

——— (1959). *Communal Rituals of the Nyakyusa.* New York: Oxford University Press.

Wilson, Samuel Graham (1896). *Persian Life and Customs, with Scenes and Incidents of Residence and Travel in the Land of the Lion and the Sun.* 2d ed. Edinburgh: Oliphant Anderson and Ferrier.

Wilson, Thomas C. (1985). "Urbanism and Tolerance." *American Sociological Review* 50:117–23.

Winkler, John J. (1988). "Unnatural Acts." In David Halperin, John J. Winkler, and Froma I. Zeitlin (eds.), *Before Sexuality: The Construction of Erotic Experience in the Ancient Greek World* Princeton, N.J.: Princeton University Press.

Winter, T. N. (1973). "Catullus Purified: A Brief History of Carmen 16." *Arethusa* 6:257–60.

Wirz, P. (1922). *Die Marind-Anim von Hollandisch-Sud-New Guinea.* Hamburg: L. Friederichsen.

Wishart, Alfred Wesley (1900). *A Short History of Monks and Monasteries.* Trenton, N.J.: Brandt.

Wishy, Bernard (1968). *The Child and the Republic: The Dawn of Modern American Child Nurture.* Philadelphia: University of Pennsylvania Press.

Wittels, Fritz (1944). "Collective Defense Mechanisms against Homosexuality." *Psychoanalytic Review* 31:19–33.

Wittfogel, Karl A. (1957). *Oriental Despotism: A Comparative Study of Total Power.* New Haven: Yale University Press.

Wittkower, Rudolf, and Margot Wittkower (1963). *Born Under Saturn: The Character and Conduct of Artists.* London: Weidenfeld and Nicolson.

Witzel, Klaus-Dieter (1985). "The Ebbinghause Case: The Death Sentence in Installments." Pp. 105–8 in *IGA Pink Book 1985.* Amsterdam: COC.

Wobst, H. M. (1976). "Locational Relationships in Paleolithic Society." *Journal of Human Evolution* 5:49–58.

Wolf, Deborah G. (1979). *The Lesbian Community.* Berkeley: University of California Press.

Wolfe, Alan (1977). *The Limits of Legitimacy: Political Contradictions of Contemporary Capitalism.* New York: Free.

Wolfenstein, Martha (1951). "The Emergence of Fun Morality." *Journal of Social Issues* 7:15–25.

Wolff, Charlotte (1971). *Love Between Women.* New York: St. Martin's Press.

——— (1980). *Hindsight.* London: Quartet.

——— (1986). *Magnus Hirschfeld: A Portrait of a Pioneer in Sexology.* London: Quartet.

Wood, Charles T. (1981). "The Doctor's Dilemma: Sin, Salvation, and the Menstrual Cycle in Medieval Thought." *Speculum* 56:710–27.

Wood, Michael, and Michael Hughes (1984). "The Moral Basis of Moral Reform: Status Discontent vs. Culture and Socialization as Explanations of Anti-Pornography Social Movement Adherence." *American Sociological Review* 49:86–99.

Wooden, Wayne S., and Jay Parker (1982). *Men Behind Bars: Sexual Exploitation in Prison*. New York: Plenum.

Wormhoudt, Arthur (1980). "Classical Arabic Poetry." *Gay Book Bulletin* 4–23–25.

Worsley, T. C. (1967). *Flanneled Fool: A Slice of a Life in the Thirties*. London: Alan Ross.

Wright, A. D. (1982). *The Counter-Reformation: Catholic Europe and the Non-Christian World*. London: Weidenfeld and Nicolson.

Wright, David F. (1984). "Homosexuals or Prostitutes? The Meaning of Arsenokoitai (1 *Cor.* 6:9, 1 *Tim.* 1:10)." *Vigilae Christianae* 38:125–53.

Wright, Gordon (1983). *Between the Guillotine and Liberty: Two Centuries of the Crime Problem*. New York: Oxford University Press.

Wrigley, E. A. (1967). "A Simple Model of London's Importance in Changing English Society and Economy, 1650–1750." *Past and Present* 37:44–70.

Wulff, Inger (1960). "The So-Called Priests of the Ngadju Dyaks." *Folk* 2:121–32.

Xenophon (1870). *The Cryopaedia*. Tr. J. S. Watson and Henry Dale. London: Bell and Daldy.

———— (1890–97). *The Works of Xenophon*. Tr. H. G. Dakyms. London: Macmillan.

X.X.X. (1962). "Les Incas condamnaient-ils l'homophilie?" *Arcadie* 108:636–39.

Yadin, Yigael (1963). *The Art of Warfare in Biblical Lands*, vol. 1. Tr. M. Pearlman. New York: McGraw-Hill.

———— (1982). "Is the Biblical Account of the Israelite Conquest of Canaan Historically Reliable?" *Biblical Archaeological Review* 8:16–23.

Yamauchi, Edwin M. (1973). "Cultic Prostitution: A Case in Cultural Diffusion." Pp. 213–22 in Harry A. Hoffner (ed.), *Orient and Occident*. Neukirchen-Vluyn: Verlag Butzon and Bereher Keveker.

Yankelovitch, Daniel (1981). *New Rules: Searching for Self-Fulfillment in a World Turned Upside Down*. New York: Random.

Yasin, Mohammed (1958). *A Social History of Islamic India, 1605–1748*. Lucknow: Upper India.

Yglesias, Jose (1968). *In the First of the Revolution: Life in a Cuban Country Town*. New York: Pantheon.

Yoffee, Norman (n.d.). "Aspects of Political Authority in Early Mesopotamian Legal Systems." Unpublished paper.

Yokel's Precepter: or More Sprees in London! Being a Regular and Curious Show-Up of All the Rigs and Doings of the Flash Cribs in this Great Metropolis (1850). London: H. Smith.

Yoshihashi, Pauline (1985). "170 Homosexual Officials Confer on Tactics and National Platform." *New York Times*, Nov. 25.

Young, Alan (1973). "Gay Gringo in Brazil," Pp. 60–67 in L. Richmond and G. Noguera (eds.), *The Gay Liberation Handbook*. San Francisco: Ramparts.

———— (1982). *Gays under the Cuban Revolution*. New York: Grey Fox.

Zacchia, Paulus (1688). *Questionum Medico-Legalium*, vol. 3. Frankfurt: Johannis

Melchioris Bencard. Reprinted in part in J. S. Hohmann (ed.), *Der unterdrückte Sexus*. Berlin: Andreas Achenbach Lollar, 1977.

Zaehner, R. C. (1961). *The Dawn and Twilight of Zoroastrianism*. London: Weidenfeld and Nicolson.

Zeitlin, Irving M. (1984). *Ancient Judaism: Biblical Criticism from Max Weber to the Present*. Cambridge, Mass.: Polity.

Zeitlin, Solomon (ed.) (1954). *The Second Book of the Maccabees*. Tr. Sidney Tedesche. New York: Harper.

———— (1962). *The Rise and Fall of the Judaean State*, vol. 1. Philadelphia: Jewish Publication Society of America.

Zeldin, Theodore (1979). *France, 1848–1945*. Vol. 1: *Ambition and Love*. New York: Oxford University Press.

Zeller, E. (1962). *The Stoics, Epicureans and Sceptics*. Tr. Oswald J. Reichel. New York: Russell and Russell. Orig. pub. 1879.

Zimmerman, Carle C. (1947). *Family and Civilization*. New York: Harper.

Zimmern, Heinrich (1922). *Hethitische Gesetze aus dem Staatsarchiv von Boghazköi (um 1300 v. Christ)*. Leipzig: J. C. Hinrichs.

Zoglin, Richard (1979). "The Homosexual Executive." Pp. 68–77 in Martin P. Levine (ed.), *Gay Men: The Sociology of Male Homosexuality*. New York: Harper and Row.

Zweig, Stefan (1943). *The World of Yesterday*. Lincoln: University of Nebraska Press.

Index